LEARNING TO PERFORM

LEARNING TO

Perform

An Introduction

CAROL SIMPSON STERN

and

BRUCE HENDERSON

NORTHWESTERN UNIVERSITY PRESS

EVANSTON, ILLINOIS

Northwestern University Press
www.nupress.northwestern.edu

The Northwestern University Research Grants Committee has provided partial support for the publication of this book. The authors gratefully acknowledge this assistance.

Printed in the United States of America

10   9   8   7   6   5   4   3   2   1

The authors and the publisher have made every reasonable effort to contact the copyright holders for material reprinted in this book and to obtain permission to use the material presented here for educational purposes. Credits are printed starting on page 547.

Library of Congress Cataloging-in-Publication Data

Stern, Carol Simpson.
  Learning to perform : an introduction / Carol Simpson Stern and Bruce Henderson.
    p. cm.
  Includes bibliographical references and index.
  ISBN 978-0-8101-2667-1 (pbk. : alk. paper)
  1. Performing arts. I. Henderson, Bruce, 1957– II. Title.
  PN1584.S745 2010
  791—dc22

                  2010005625

For J. Allyson Stern and Daryl Bem

CONTENTS

Learning to Perform, as its title suggests, is a text that introduces its readers to performance as an ongoing process—one that develops from the moment the performer considers creating a performance of some kind and that extends far beyond the time the performer finishes speaking. Indeed, while both of the writers of this textbook have been teachers of performance for more than thirty years, we consider ourselves very much still in the process of *learning to perform*—and we invite you to join us, wherever you are in your own journey as a performer.

Both of us began our study of and creation of performance in a field known as interpretation (sometimes oral interpretation), which focused on the performance of literary texts. As the design of this book indicates, the literary text still remains a primary focus for us and for our students, particularly the solo performance of such genres as poetry, prose fiction, drama, and nonfiction. But the field of performance studies has, over the past few decades, expanded its scope in exciting and innovative ways, drawing upon traditions in and explorations of such fields as folklore, personal narrative, ethnography, popular culture, cultural studies, and media and technology studies, and the possibilities performance holds are richer for it. Where performance once resided—at least in the academy—in the domain of aesthetics, the study of fine arts, today it is also considered crucial to our everyday actions and studied as part of cultural belonging and participation. So while the study and performance of literary texts remains the core of our book, we also integrate other disciplines and forms into our text. For some, the point of entry into performance is a brief poem heard or read; for others, it may be a song lyric internalized almost unconsciously or a story told or heard (perhaps even overheard on a bus or train); and for still others, it is a moment when something that seemed as matter-of-fact as an announcement in a newspaper takes on a resonance and emotional meaning beyond its documentary value.

We encourage you to begin your study wherever you find inspiration (and teachers using this book will no doubt have their own preferences—whether it be a story of family remembrance, a contemporary piece of music, a gesture, or a clip from a reality show). Students, trust your instincts and discover your passions as performers. Teachers, lead your students in the ways that make sense for them and for you. While we have devised a textbook that conceivably could be taught over the course of a semester, we have also kept in mind that different instructors and different programs will choose to emphasize different parts of the book more than others. The first chapters lay a common foundation for thinking about and embarking upon performance as an art, as a cultural activity, and as a way of knowing. After that, some classes may choose to emphasize either the traditional genres of "imaginative" literature (poetry, prose fiction, and drama); others may focus on a central activity, such as narrative and story, across such categories as personal narrative, oral history, and literary fiction; still others may organize the introductory course around particular performance techniques and challenges—such as vocal development, the body as performing material and social text, or the juxtaposition of consciousness and dramatized encounter. Similarly, we have provided sample texts within the chapters and in the appendix suitable for class study and performance, but we also encourage teachers and students to develop their own set of texts (or to draw on the many fine anthologies now in print) for material. While we have emphasized the perspective of the solo performer, we hope there is also much here that would be relevant for classes wishing to work in duos or groups as well.

There is no wrong way, there are many paths. Now, begin your journey of *learning to perform.*

ACKNOWLEDGMENTS

We want to thank the many people who have made this book possible. Alex Kotlowitz, Joyce Carol Oates, Lesley Francis, Jane Hamilton, and Robert Olen Butler generously granted us permission to quote from their works or the works of their relatives and waived their permission fees, making it possible for us to include materials that we would have been unable to include otherwise. For this generosity of spirit and purse, we are particularly grateful. Similarly, the University of Pittsburgh Press kindly allowed us to reprint a poem by Cathy Song without fee. Many other authors and their estates or publishers substantially reduced their permission charges. They are too numerous to mention by name, but they are recognized in the credits at the end of the book, and we thank them. In addition, we are particularly indebted to Donna Shear, David Bishop, Anne Gendler, Jenny Gavacs, and Mike Levine of Northwestern University Press: they urged us to write this book and offered invaluable assistance in bringing it to publication. To our wise and persevering editor, Siobhan Drummond, we are forever grateful; her insights, editorial suggestions, and good-natured, patient support were invaluable. In addition, we want to thank John Anderson for his close reading of our manuscript and his substantive suggestions that helped shape the book. We are greatly indebted to Joe Gerdeman of the University of Chicago Library and the libraries of Northwestern University and Ithaca College.

Books are never completed alone and this one owes a very special debt to Alan Shefsky for his meticulous handling of the preparation of the manuscript and the seeking of permissions and also for his personal inspiration and belief in this project. His example, literary taste, humor, and patience made a task manageable that at times seemed to be overwhelming. We also want to thank two work-study students, Kalee Danussi and Rachel Pologe, and an intern, Hillary Sowatsky, for their help and persistence in tracking down texts.

Carol Simpson Stern has been privileged to receive support from Barbara O'Keefe, dean of the School of Communication at Northwestern University, and from her colleagues in the Department of Performance Studies at Northwestern University—Frank Galati, Paul Edwards, E. Patrick Johnson, D. Soyini Madison, Margaret Thompson Drewal, Mary Zimmerman—and from David Zarefsky, former dean of the School of Communication, as well as from graduate and undergraduate students whose friendship, support, and suggestions contributed significantly to this book. Peter Amster deserves special mention—his performance of Whitman's poem inspired both of us many years ago and remains a deep and inspiriting touchstone for us.

Bruce Henderson would like to thank the many teachers who provided him with such fine examples of pedagogy. In addition to Carol Simpson Stern, he would like to name two in particular: Leslie A. Wiberg, retired from Oak Park and River Forest High School, who from the first day of high school taught him the possibilities inherent in studying the stories people have told of themselves and each other across time and to read with care, imagination, and, always, joy; and Leland H. Roloff, professor emeritus, Northwestern University, who more than three decades ago led him into the world of performance with brilliance, compassion, wonder, and a sense of respect for all beings. In addition, he would like to thank colleagues who have offered support, insight, and friendship along the way, reminding him that teaching and scholarship are two names for the same performance: Sarah Trenholm, Robert Sullivan, Katharine Kittredge, Lee-Ellen Marvin, and Scott Thomson, all at Ithaca College; Noam Ostrander, DePaul University; Gary Balfantz, Lake Superior State University; Scott Dillard, Georgia College and State University; Timothy Gura, Brooklyn College, City University of New York; Jennifer Shamrock, Monmouth University. He also wishes to thank his chair, Laurie Arliss, for helping to make some of the procedural hurdles around permissions so much easier than they otherwise might have been. His students from the past two decades and then some at Ithaca College have been a source of inspiration, wisdom, and knowledge. He would also like to remember his friend Gary Zanke, who saw and shared in the excitement of his first book with Carol Simpson Stern, and whose wit, thoughtfulness, and sensitivity remain constant companions even seventeen years after he left us, far too soon.

We save our deepest debts of gratitude and affection for last. To her husband, J. Allyson Stern, Carol dedicates the book and thanks him for his belief in this project, his prodding, his infectious storytelling and good humor, and for his love and companionship. To his partner, Daryl J. Bem, Bruce dedicates the book and thanks him for his generosity of spirit, unconditional enthusiasm for the work, and seemingly endless patience and love. Without them, there would be no book.

LEARNING TO PERFORM

Chapter 1

GETTING STARTED

Let us go then, you and I . . .
—T. S. ELIOT, "THE LOVE SONG OF J. ALFRED PRUFROCK"

Try to remember the first time you saw a theatrical performance, or your earliest recollections of being read to aloud when you were a child, or the first time you performed and people watched you and reacted. These memories and the performances they call forth are very special. We, the authors of this book (hereafter referred to as Bruce and Carol), find them magical. Analyzing and understanding them and creating your own performances are the central subjects of this textbook.

As children, both of us were forever calling on our parents to "read us a story" or "show us a picture book." We were constantly asking our friends and siblings to play make-believe with us. Carol recalls her mother reciting the words of the poem "The Owl and the Pussy-cat," by Edward Lear, the mischievously witty nineteenth-century writer of limericks and nonsense verse. Mother and daughter would repeat Lear's words together: "The Owl and the Pussy-cat went to sea / In a beautiful pea-green boat; / They took some honey, and plenty of money / Wrapped up in a five-pound note." She can still visualize the illustrated book of Lear's verse and the pictures of the Owl and the Pussy-cat, with the Pussy-cat, wooing the Owl, twanging on his guitar and the pair "dancing by the light of the moon." The poem has its origins in children's rhymes and dates back many, many centuries. It is no wonder it has lasted so long, taking courtship and romance as its subject and situating the lovers in exotic lands. Scholars from the Darwinian school of literary criticism (also referred to as evolutionary psychological criticism) might point to the courtship themes, mating rituals, and the like present in the poem. From their perspective, we are human animals, descended from primates, and "hardwired" to reproduce (Gottschall), and this, in part, contributes to the longevity of the rhyme. She can also vividly recall her British father, in his marvelous voice, rich, textured, with an Oxford accent, reading aloud Samuel Taylor Coleridge's poem "Kubla Khan," about Xanadu, the idyllically beautiful city, and its emperor, Kubla Khan. The vision in the poem of the "stately pleasure dome" and the Abyssinian "damsel with a dulcimer" is unforget-table, as is the excitement of listening to Coleridge's phantasmagorical poem evoking enchanted kingdoms, romantic visions, and passionate emotions. Later she learned that the poem was thought to have taken its origin in one of Coleridge's opium-induced dreams. Many years later, she performed this poem during a performance hour at the university where she taught. You will find that you will want to tap into your past and your recollections of poems and stories that moved you when you go about the business of choosing selections for performances.

Bruce remembers that while other mothers were reading fairy tales to their children, his mother preferred to recite from memory long sections from Alfred Noyes's romantic ballad "The Highwayman." She had learned the poem as a student four decades earlier, when she was growing up in a small mining town in the Upper Peninsula of Michigan. He can still hear his mother's voice setting the scene with the words "The moon was a ghostly galleon," and painting the picture vocally of "riding . . . riding . . . riding." Even in old age, when other parts of her memory started to fade, his mother still held the words of this poem deeply inside her. When she had a stroke, he sat by her bedside and read the poem to her, hoping that the rhythms, images, and story would give her the pleasure she had given him and his sister in her performance. When he mentioned the poem at her memorial service, his sister and his mother's friends and relatives nodded in assent, recalling the power and enjoyment the poem—and his mother's impromptu performances of it—had given them all.

He also recalls his first sacrifice in the name of performance. One Christmas season, the television series *The Wonderful World of Disney* was broadcasting the Hayley Mills film of the children's classic *Pollyanna* over the course of three Sundays. He was invited to be the one child performer in the Christmas play at his church but was told it would mean missing the last episode of *Pollyanna* (this was long before VCRs and DVDs!). As much as he wanted to know what happened to the heroine (would she get to go to the church fair?), he chose to perform in the play instead. The next year, he was chosen for the title role in the elementary school class play, "Nobody Listens to Andrew," about a little boy who tries, unsuccessfully, to get the attention of the adults (also played by elementary school students), finally shouting, in exasperation, "THERE'S A BEAR IN MY BED!!!" He's understood the power of performing ever since.

We both can remember playing dress-up and putting on plays. Carol vividly recalls a childhood game she played, "Death in the Streets." She and her sister were living across the Midway from the University of Chicago, a neighborhood that was pretty rough at the time, where faculty members from the university lived alongside blue-collar workers—rudely described as "slum-dwellers"—in an area that always seemed grubby, the grass near the street thoroughly scuffed, mothers standing with switches in their hands, gabbing with each other while idly threatening their kids to behave or get a "lickin'." In the game, played in the street, one child, demanding to be the victim, was the character who got to fall to the ground repeatedly, while another leaned over her and began screaming "Death in the street," and a third played the self-important doctor, who would come quickly to make a huge fuss over the fallen body. The whole game had been scripted and was played over and over again, reversing the roles. Later, there were school plays, the business of memorizing a text, assembling props, and putting on costumes. Dance classes, singing, playing the piano, wanting to see a play and go to a real live performance opened up worlds that have held her captive ever since. These worlds, with their sense of wonderment, lush language, rich imagery, characters, and their all too obvious melodramatic qualities, as well as their secret places, have served both of us all our lives. They awaken passionate emotions and they offer deep comfort, even during some of the loneliest and darkest times we have experienced. They actively involve us as agents and as performers who can call forth, at will, performances that can be relived, re-created, shared, and made the stuff of performance for others.

We also loved that special kind of excitement that is aroused when the lights in a theater house or movie theater are dimmed and the hall becomes dark, and we are held, enthralled, by actors on a stage or pictures on a screen. There is always a sense of risk, of being a little afraid, of needing to pay attention, and of knowing that we'll see live performers or media images that can inspire us, or frighten us, or make us laugh, or weep, or both together at the same time. There is also the excitement of a prospective role that we can play. Very often, it is we who are the heroes or heroines of our imagined and real plays.

This textbook asks you to reenter the world of imagination, language, and performance and learn how to use your talents as a performer and reader to bring numinous performances to the classroom throughout your course and to experience for yourself the thrill of creating, rehearsing, and sharing them. We also want to equip you with a performance method- ology that offers you the tools you need to refine your skills and enhance your performance, analyze texts, understand the materials you use in performance, talk about performances, and write about them.

The textbook will introduce you to the art and craft of performing literary and cultural texts. It will teach you how to read closely and criti- cally and how to learn to use your voice and body to perform texts for an audience. The immediate audience we have in mind is your classmates, but later, it could be extended to a much larger and more diverse audi- ence, depending on the directions life takes you and the way you shape your performing self in everyday life. In addition, some of you may plan to make performance your career, either as a theatrical performer or as an eloquent public speaker, an intellectual, a politician, lawyer, or leader of business or industry. Others may have little or no performance experi- ence and want to use this textbook and the college course it accompanies to acquire skills in communicating with and performing for an audience in any number of everyday ways. In short, our designs in this book are ambitious: we want to introduce you to a performance experience that is supple and can be shaped to enhance the quality of your life and sharpen your powers of attention. To see keenly, to imagine vividly, to use your body and voice expressively, and to communicate passionately and wisely are some of the qualities and skills that you will acquire as you practice this art of performance and employ a performance methodology.

We have deliberately drawn on our own personal experiences of reading and performing in this introduction in order to encourage you to trust yourself and share your performances with others. Your own voice and body are inextricably involved in your performances, and we encourage you to be introspective and reflect on your life and how it informs your performing self. We also want you to recognize the ways in which the personal figures in performance.

Performance is such a popular term these days that it threatens to encompass almost any and all human behaviors, at the risk of losing any intelligible meaning. Consequently, we will spend a little time considering what the term means in the context of this book and in a discipline that once called itself "oral interpretation" and is now named "performance studies." Some programs in performance studies take their origins in theater and alternative theater in the 1960s. The program at New York University is one such program, mounted by Richard Schechner and others. The other tradition, much older, grew out of the elocution movement in the late nineteenth century in America. In the academy, it was a discipline known by a number of different names, culminating originally in oral interpretation and then, during the mid-1980s, renaming itself performance studies.

The term *performance* incorporates a whole field of human activity. It includes verbal acts derived from everyday life, such as rapping, which may occur on urban streets or in neighborhood or Broadway theaters, and can be seen in the movies and other media. Some rapping is featured in "slamming" or "headlining" and can be experienced in poetry jams and slams and the coffeehouses where they are shared. Performance, especially performance of poems, stories, nonfiction, and drama, can be found in classrooms and onstage, whether at colleges and universities or in public auditoriums or outside venues, such as parks. And, of course, a whole host of performances can be found in digital forms and on the Internet.

We are particularly interested in student performances that feature either a solo performer or a group of performers and occur in classrooms and, on occasion, are taken to larger theatrical stages or open public spaces. The classroom performances typically take advantage of an open playing space and desks, stools, music stands, scripts, props, and costumes. In these cases, the performer or performers create their performances to be shared with classmates and the teacher. Students enjoy performing with lecterns and music stands or performing in open stage space, or classroom space, where they can use simple props and create a minimalist set using desks, chairs, lamps, and media, all objects that are readily available in college and university classrooms and in the home. They can easily create costumes, or the suggestion of a costume, drawing from their closets and using items such as hats, scarves, suit jackets, peacoats, or sweat clothes to convey the sense of a character or speaker in the work they are performing. Sometimes students take their performances outside and make use of special places on campuses to perform.

Lectern is the term used to refer to a reading stand of the kind you see in church pulpits or on ceremonial occasions, such as graduations, public lectures, or presidential inaugural addresses. Performers often use music stands or reading desks to substitute for the lectern. The advantage of a lectern is that it anchors the performer, freeing him or her to use gesture and the art of suggestion to evoke characters and scenes. The surface of the lectern provides the performer a place to rest a script, a book, or a prop, and it also serves as an object that can be used during performance; in fact, the entire lectern can be tilted, lifted, or rested on its side on the floor, becoming an elaborate prop or piece of stage furniture, allowing the performer to work from the space around it. The lectern performance can also make use of props or a costume piece that is easily adaptable to assist in creating a character or characters and scene to bring a text to life. Performers can also choose to stand or sit in front of their audience with no props and speak the words of the literary or cultural text from memory. Memorization, which we will speak more about later, is often required for classroom performances. However, it is also important to know how to perform a text that is not memorized and for which one must rely on the written text, using it as a script. A well-rehearsed performance where the text is not memorized can be astonishingly effective. Scripts can be cunningly concealed, and they can also be decked out with a book-like cover and very visibly displayed. And, of course, they can be read in performance. What should be avoided is the reliance on a messy-looking text or bunch of papers, unless the messy or sloppy appearance is part of the performance.

The beauty of these classroom performances is that they can easily be made portable and carried to other settings. They can be shared in a dorm room, and they can also be designed for bigger audiences, such as those who attend performance hours, festivals, or public readings. Many performances that originated in a class become stock pieces in a student's repertoire and are performed in more professional settings, emerging finally on theatrical stages or other environmental or public places where larger audiences can participate. Performances are also developed to serve political ends, to produce change in our society. Many student activists find performance a powerful tool for change. When we discuss later the use of nonfiction materials and cultural texts, we will show you how performances can serve an activist political agenda. And of course, literary texts, such as poems and short stories, can also be put to political purpose.

Let us turn now to consider the nature of this "performance" that you will be creating and sharing and discuss its purpose. In an earlier textbook, *Performance: Texts and Contexts*, we defined performance, stating, "a *performance act, interactional* in nature and involving *symbolic forms* and *live bodies,* provides a way to constitute meaning and to affirm individual and cultural values" (p. 3). The italicized terms in this definition are used in a technical sense. To increase your comfort with the definition and to show you what it means and what it does not mean, we will offer an exegesis of it.

Some Defining Terms

A Performance Act

A *performance act* is a technical term used by people in the disciplines of performance studies, theater, communication, and anthropology. Schechner, a performance theorist and avant-garde theater director in New York during the 1960s, refers to these types of acts as "restored behavior" or "twice-behaved behavior" in his book *Between Theater and Anthropology* (p. 36). By these terms, he refers to behavior that can be worked on, rehearsed, and repeated; it is a behavior that is never done for the first time. He goes on to say that it "means: for the second to the *n*th time"(ibid.). In his textbook *Performance Studies: An Introduction,* he stresses that these kinds of behavior are ones that performers are trained to do, often requiring repetition, practice, and rehearsal (p. 22). He uses these terms to capture the idea of acts that are enacted, self-conscious, repeatable, and reflexive. Some scholars have questioned whether the "repeatability" of a behavior is, in fact, an essential quality to differentiate what we might call "theatrical" performance from ordinary, first order, or real-life behaviors occurring in everyday life. They point to the fact that it is never possible to "repeat" a behavior exactly, however simple the behavior. Actors who perform the same role in a theater night after night try to "repeat" a standardized performance, but the actual event always shows differences, even when the same words, stage blocking, movements, and gestures are used. As humans, we are incapable of making our bodies exactly repeat what they have just done. But for now, we need not belabor this point. Later we will discuss performance more fully and expand on the fact that it cannot be held stable and repeated exactly, that it is ephemeral.

Schechner uses the terms *enacted, self-conscious, repeatable,* and *reflexive* to define the action we execute when we do what is called "performance" and, in effect, play a role. When he writes about role-playing and performance and speaks of the performance act as "twice-performed behavior" or "restored performance," he is indebted to the work of a leading sociologist, Erving Goffman. Goffman, in his classic text, *The Presentation of Self in Everyday Life*, examines human interaction in social situations, and he defines performance as "all activity of a given participant on a given occasion which serves to influence in any way any of the other participants" (p. 15). As you can see, when we talk of the "performance act," we must, of necessity, discuss not only the agent of the action, the social actor, but also the person or persons for whom the action is performed. In short, we need to think about both the performer and the people who constitute the audience.

It is also important to recognize the way that reflexivity, or self-conscious awareness of the self simultaneously as performer and witness of the performance, is an essential defining characteristic of what is called "twice-performed behavior." This aspect of performance will be one we discuss at length when we begin to help you think about role-playing and identity and how you construct a performance.

Interactional

In the course of this textbook, we will continually be examining the ways in which you, as students, can embody and enact a "performance act." In chapter 2, we will discuss performing a personal narrative, a poem, a haiku, an obituary, a short story, or a work of fiction. Later, as we explore more fully how narrative functions, we will discuss the performance of other nonfictional materials, such as memoirs, biographies, histories, and newspaper accounts, as well as other nonfictional texts. The act of performance is part of a communicative process—its end is to convey or communicate a message to another, referred to as the audience, and its means involve the body, the body's expressive qualities, and the aesthetic or artistic intentions as they exist in a text and as they are realized in a performance. Insofar as the performance communicates its meaning to another, and its meaning depends on the interplay between the agent of the action and the physical body of those that receive or observe the act, it is understood to be *interactional* in nature.

While we have just alluded to the ways in which performers communicate with each other, it is also important to recognize that performers also perform to an audience of themselves. In other words, were I to speak the words of T. S. Eliot's poem "The Love Song of J. Alfred Prufrock" aloud to myself, the audience of my performance is myself. Some people might even say that as I read the Eliot poem to myself silently, I am engaged in a performance of it, since I bring to that reading my own sense of the voice and character of the poem's speaker and the rhythms of Eliot's verse and see in my mind's eye the complex and vivid images evoked by the language. Performance, for many, may most simply be defined as active and engaged reading, when we understand reading to involve a kind of embodiment. Scholars have found that many of the same throat muscles that are used in speaking are also used when reading silently.

Dyadic communication is also known as interpersonal communication. You may have heard either phrase, or taken a course in the subject. It refers to the communication that occurs between two individuals, although the context may vary, for example, the intimacy of a romantic date or a more formal employer-employee exchange. Intrapersonal communication is that which occurs within the self. It might seem that intrapersonal communication should logically be the primary form of communication, as we are always in the presence of ourselves, but many scholars argue that the dyadic is primary, that the sense of dialogic encounter between self and other, whatever the context, is the fundamental building block on which all other communication contexts are based. Even when speaking to oneself, or within oneself (that silent speech of thinking), they argue, we create an audience of speaker and listener.

Clearly, there are significant differences, technically and otherwise, between those inner dialogues and performances we have with ourselves and the performances we externalize for a listening and viewing audience of other people. We know that the addition of just one other person to a setting changes the dynamic of communication radically. Think about the differences you would experience if you performed a text in these different contexts: 1) you read it silently; 2) you rehearsed it out loud in an empty room; 3) you rehearsed it for a friend or roommate; 4) you performed it for your teacher in the privacy of the studio or office; 5) you performed it for a set of fellow students who have seen your work in a classroom, and 6) you performed it for an audience in a performance space filled with people, some familiar, some strangers. How does Eliot's "you and I" change each time for you?

Bearing in mind the distinction between the intrapersonal communication and the interpersonal communication that is taking place in these hypothetical performances of T. S. Eliot's poem, we know that there is an important difference between performing for an audience that is another physical presence, a person, someone outside of the margins of one's body, and performing for an audience that is, in fact, me, the speaker of the poem to be heard only by me as I speak it.

When we refer to the *performance act as interactional,* we mean that it involves interplay between two real and distinct physical bodies: the performer's and the participant's. Together they construct meaning through the performance act. These *interactions* include observers and coparticipants, and they also include a kind of interaction that goes on within the self, between two parts of your own self. Throughout this textbook, the interactional nature of performance will be examined closely in order to assist you with performing and relating to others, known usually as your audience, and to inner aspects of your self, your deeper self, your public and your personal self. You call on these parts of yourself, your inner experiences, recollections, and desires, as you perform. Often your audience may not directly know what you are drawing upon to fuel your performance. We will help you to understand better what is involved and how it can be harnessed, channeled, and communicated through performance.

Consider two poems and how the performance of them is an *interactional act.* The first poem is from a collection by the American poet John Berryman.

Dream Song 4

Filling her compact & delicious body
with chicken páprika, she glanced at me
twice.
Fainting with interest, I hungered back
and only the fact of her husband & four other people
kept me from springing on her

or falling at her little feet and crying
'You are the hottest one for years of night
Henry's dazed eyes
have enjoyed, Brilliance.' I advanced upon
(despairing) my spumoni. — Sir Bones: is stuffed,
de world, wif feeding girls.

— Black hair, complexion Latin, jewelled eyes
downcast . . . The slob beside her   feasts . . . What wonders is

she sitting on, over there?
The restaurant buzzes. She might as well be on Mars.
Where did it all go wrong? There ought to be a law against Henry.
—Mr. Bones: There is.

Can you see that in this poem there is an interaction going on between the speaker, Henry, and an imaginary speaker who talks in blackface and refers to Henry as Mr. Bones? The convention of blackface comes from minstrelsy traditions, where whites blackened their faces and played white representations of black people. Amos and Andy made these conventions popular to radio audiences in the 1950s, who grew up hearing their voices and, later, seeing them on television. The poem seems to invoke a real situation which takes place in a restaurant, involves a table with people eating and another table, or chair, where Henry sits, feasting on his food and lusting after a woman. In addition, there are other interactions internal to Henry, part of his fictive world. The question of whether the names Henry and Mr. Bones refer to the same person is one that initially causes problems of interpretation for the reader. We have to figure out what is going on here and how much, if any, of it is real. By real, we mean assumed, within the fiction of the poem, to be an event that is actually taking place, not simply imagined by one of the characters.

See if you can describe the scene in the restaurant, who seems to be there, and what each of the characters is doing. You can also see that there are lines quoted within the poem, suggesting that someone is speaking them directly to someone else. Look, too, at these clues and see what they show you about the interactional aspect of the performance situation within the world of the poem. When you first read and study a poem, don't be overly concerned if you find that your interpretation, or understanding, of the poem is different from that of your classmates or teacher. Part of the richness of poetry is that it is able to carry so many different meanings.

There is also another level on which we can consider the interactional aspects of this poem. If it were read aloud, or enacted by a solo performer, then we would have a situation where a performer takes on several roles, speaks the poem's words faithfully, saying them all, and doing this in front of a class. In this hypothetical performance, we also can examine the interactional nature of the relationship between performer and audience. You might want to experiment with the poem in performance. Initially, don't be afraid to follow your instincts, speak the words, even if you don't actually think you understand them. Over time, and often with the help of a friend and audience, you will find a clue, a rhythm, or a way of speaking the poem's words that seems to begin to make sense. Keep rehearsing and playing with the poem in performance and see what emerges. Classroom discussion or your own private exploration of the poem will help you gain greater clarity about what the poem is saying and doing and how it achieves its effects.

The second poem, "The Boy Died in My Alley," by the poet Gwendolyn Brooks, is also used to demonstrate the interactional nature of performance. We chose it not only because we admire and love it, but because it provides a more conventional presentation of the speaker and a story. Readers generally find it easier to understand literary works when they can recognize who is speaking and what they are speaking about. In this poem, the action involves a speaker, characters, and a scene. We are more likely to believe that this poem is based on real events that have happened or can happen, whereas in Berryman's "Dream Songs," we are less certain about whether or not these poems express dreams, daydreams, longings, or something that is make-believe, something that happens in the fictive world of the poem. In Gwendolyn Brooks's poem, we see that the story unfolds as though someone is recounting a traumatic incident that has occurred, or keeps on occurring. Also, and most important, it uses dialogue, capturing directly the speech of some of its characters, such as the policeman and the boy. According to Brooks, an African American poet, she fused two separate real-life incidents in this poem, one involving a death of an honor student who was killed when fleeing a policeman; the second involving a boy Brooks saw running in Ghana, Africa.

The Boy Died in My Alley

to Running Boy

The Boy died in my alley
Without my Having Known.
Policeman said, next morning,
"Apparently died Alone."

"You heard a shot?" Policeman said.
Shots I hear and Shots I hear.
I never see the Dead.

The Shot that killed him yes I heard
as I heard the Thousand shots before;
careening tinnily down the nights
across my years and arteries.

Policeman pounded on my door.
"Who is it?" "POLICE!" Policeman yelled.
"A Boy was dying in your alley.
A Boy is dead, and in your alley.
And have you known this Boy before?"

I have known this Boy before.
I have known this Boy before, who
ornaments my alley.
I never saw his face at all.
I never saw his futurefall.
But I have known this Boy.

I have always heard him deal with death.
I have always heard the shout, the volley.
I have closed my heart-ears late and early.
And I have killed him ever.

I joined the Wild and killed him
with knowledgeable unknowing.
I saw where he was going.
I saw him Crossed. And seeing,
I did not take him down.

He cried not only "Father!"
but "Mother!
Sister!
Brother."
The cry climbed up the alley.
It went up to the wind.
It hung upon the heaven
for a long
stretch-strain of Moment.

The red floor of my alley
is a special speech to me.

Earlier in this chapter, when we discussed the performance act, we mentioned that some of these acts are not only communications, but acts with an aesthetic intent and purpose. The term *aesthetics* refers to the beautiful, or to the art and the means used to make something perceived as satisfying, pleasurable, and belonging to the world of the "beautiful." When we describe those qualities that are perceived as beautiful or pleasing, even if ugliness is being used in a work that elicits artistic feelings, we are talking about the aesthetic nature of the experience. The matter of the author's intent, or intentionality, is a complex one. At this stage, we won't say more about it, but in later chapters we will discuss it further.

As you can see in the poem by Brooks, the subject is painful and terrible; the imagery is of blood; the poem is taut with violence and conveys a sense of dread and doom. All these elements may be deeply disturbing and certainly ugly, but through the symbolic form as a whole, the poem is beautiful. In other words, in its aesthetic elements, it is deeply satisfying. Much of its effect is due to the way Brooks handles symbols and symbolic forms.

Symbols

Symbols are devices that can be used to convey meanings that go beyond the literal, denotative meanings of words. In a literary performance, based on a poem or a short story, biography, or other works of nonfiction, symbols are used and symbolic forms are created and used to communicate a meaning. Words at their denotative level of meaning convey a message, or a meaning, that can be translated into ordinary language. We can determine the denotative meaning of a word by consulting a dictionary and selecting the definition appropriate to the context in which the word functions. But the word or words also function in a more complex manner, evoking feelings and emotions and streams of so-called unconscious or subconscious associations that are more aptly understood by reference to the *symbolic functions* of the words in the work as a whole. In addition, in performance or in texts, the whole work can be treated as an example of a symbolic form, and a performance, taken in its entirety, can be seen as a symbolic form.

Therefore, let us examine the next important key term necessary to an understanding of performance, namely *symbolic forms*.

Symbolic Forms

A symbol, when verbal, refers to a figure of speech in which one thing stands in for another but also has a value in itself. When visual, it takes the form of an image that calls forth meanings beyond its representational aspect. I could speak of eggs, and the egg can function literally as a hen's egg that I am about to eat, poached. Or, it can function symbolically, calling forth other eggs, not just those that are produced by hens and cooked and eaten, but eggs such as Christopher Columbus's egg, which symbolically refers to the New World and, according to legend, was used to demonstrate that the world was round. In F. Scott Fitzgerald's novel *The Great Gatsby*, Fitzgerald uses eggs symbolically. The novel is about the American dream and its corruption. The suburbs of New York and the slender island that extends due east of New York City are referred to as West Egg and East Egg to make us aware that this novel is about the loss of innocence. If a performer holds up an ordinary egg for us to look at, we will recognize that it is likely to be functioning not simply as an egg to be eaten, but as something more. How we understand this performer's performance will depend on how we come to see this egg and its symbolic form.

Symbols can be used conventionally in a manner that is readily understandable to an educated audience. The symbol of a cross in Christian iconography will be readily associated with Christ's crucifixion. In other cases, the set of meanings that the symbol calls forth, or evokes, is unconventional and must be established by the writer or speaker so that, through an accretive process, the reader becomes aware of a multiplicity of meanings that are evoked by the symbol. In Herman Melville's *Moby Dick*, Ahab fanatically pursues a great white whale. Over the course of many hundreds of pages, this white whale becomes more than a whale, seemingly indomitable and elusive, and although white, it becomes a symbol of absolute evil, absolute nihilism. Whiteness, and not the conventional blackness, becomes the color to dread. In creating this effect, Melville demonstrates his genius through his symbolic handling of the whale, investing it with an elaborate set of meanings that finally makes this beast akin to Iago, the villain in Shakespeare's play *Othello*, who also is finally unfathomable in the depths of his wickedness. With both the whale and the man, their evil is so disproportionate to any explanation of motive we can glean that we feel it is the ultimate negative act of free will and beyond understanding.

Think back now to Berryman's "Dream Song 4" and to Brooks's "The Boy Died in My Alley" and consider how each uses symbols. In Berryman's poem, Henry's "hunger" functions symbolically as well as literally. As he satisfies his bodily hunger by eating food in the restaurant, such as spumoni, he also hungers figuratively for the Latin woman, eyeing her lasciviously and wanting her sexually, and we are told that the world is "stuffed . . . wif feeding girls." We are told that the "slob" at the other table "feasts." Think about these references and how they function symbolically. In the case of the poem by Gwendolyn Brooks, "the red floor of my alley" is symbolic. Can you figure out some of the many ways in which this line resonates with symbolic meanings?

Look now at another poem, again chosen because it will help you understand some of these concepts, and it can help you develop your skills as a close reader of literary texts, something that is very useful to a performer of literature. Consider how it uses intrapersonal and interpersonal communication. Consider the interactional elements in the communication act that occur when this poem is performed. Think about how symbolic forms are handled. This poem was written by Cathy Song, an Asian American poet born in Honolulu, Hawaii.

Book of Hours

What led you to the book
and kept you there
was pleasure, a simple
stirring—unconditional.

The function of spelling,
the mechanics of handwriting
fed an orderly compulsion, repetitive
acts as tight as stitches—
a balm for inner disruption.

Pure to the task of setting
letters in a row, filigreed nonsense
curved extravagant and slow.
Intent on making O just so,
sound connected on air's blue note.
Meaning broke, lifted: sky poured in.
The hand's enactment of the mind's enchantment.
The letters illuminated—glowed.

Hours spent in odd posture,
girl with head bent, her hair a scrawl.
Who knows where she went,
hanging letters on pale blue lines—
hook of star,
tiny magnificent clothes,
adornments to an original country.

Live Bodies

One of the most exciting aspects of performance studies and the opportunity to perform in class for each other is that the nature of this engagement between a student, a text, and an audience is realized through the embodiment of texts, and this embodiment involves the live bodies of you, the performers, and your audience, their physical selves.

We are all very vulnerable. Even those most seemingly exhibitionistic of us usually also experience tremendous insecurity or fragility when confronted with the challenge of performing in a mode where it is your own body that is the instrument of the performance. In one respect, there seems to be nowhere to hide. It is your body that is on display; it receives the gaze, as we say, of others. We are sure you can all recall your own moments of stage fright. We may well feel heady, secure, and nearly ecstatic while we perform, but most of us would also admit that as we do this, we channel our fear and, in fact, are fueled by the adrenaline rush that in part derives from the fight-or-flight complex of animals and humans. As we introduce you to performance and help you develop further your performing self and explore your full potential, we need to help you grow comfortable with the recognition that it is your own, and other, live bodies that are engaged in this task of performance.

It is useful to consider the *kinesics* of the performer's body. *Kinesics* is the science of bodily motion in relation to speech. We will be examining the way the interplay of gesture with speech in performance functions in order to help you understand character and motive as they unfold in performance.

Later in our textbook, we discuss a number of technical issues related to bodily performance. For now, suffice it to say that in the kind of performance acts we will be studying and creating, the live body of the performer is inextricably involved in the performance. We need to acquire a vocabulary to help us talk about the live bodies, describe them, and write and speak critically about them in performance. We will be discussing ideas about somatic thinking, bodily thinking, and considering the ways in which we as performers inhabit our bodies and use them as expressive instruments while we also feel ourselves being shaped by them in ways that are not always well understood or intended.

To summarize the definition of performance, recall that we defined it as "a *performance act, interactional* in nature and involving *symbolic forms* and *live bodies.*" The purpose of the performance is "to constitute meaning and to affirm individual and cultural values." The performance serves aesthetic ends and purposes and, in effect, is created to give pleasure and instruction. It remains for us to consider how performance constitutes meaning and affirms individual and cultural values.

Scholars of poetry and poetics, the study of poetry, taking their impetus from Aristotle's *Poetics,* have argued that poetry, through mimesis, the act of imitation, gives pleasure. Horace, the classical Latin scholar, argued that the end of poetry is to delight and instruct. One of the ways this delight and instruction occurs results from the way in which art and performance employ acts of imitation of human actions and in so doing affirm the human experience. In our definition of performance acts, we draw a distinction between how the meaning communicated by the performance involves individual and cultural values to alert you to two important dimensions of meaning-making and sense-making in performance: the personal and individual and the cultural and collective.

Individual or Cultural Values

Performances express individual and cultural values and an understanding of each is necessary to an understanding of performance and its worth.

By individual values, we refer to those values that are expressed by the individual in society and that take their origin in personal experiences and function to express identity of the self. Psychologists writing about individual identity posit that one is both a self with the freedom to create itself and a self shaped in relation to collective identities. These two ways of conceptualizing the self are inseparable. I am who I am not only because throughout my life I am constantly involved in the task of becoming a person, but also because I involve myself with and am shaped by groups of people, collectivities, with whom I identify. Therefore, it follows that the performances that I construct and share will speak both to elements of my individuality and uniqueness and also to elements of my identity that depend on my involvement in collectivities, or cultures, in order to be understood.

By culture, we refer to the totality of socially transmitted behavior patterns, institutions, arts, beliefs, religions, and other products of human work and thought characteristic of a community or population. When we reflect on culture, we need to be mindful of the contributions that neuroscience, cognitive psychology, evolutionary biology, and anthropology have made to our understanding of culture, human nature, and the human mind. As E. O. Wilson writes in his "Foreword from the Scientific Side": "The evidence from the biological and behavioral sciences converged to establish that the brain is, in fact, intricately wired from birth. Human behavior is determined by neither genes nor culture but instead by a complex interaction of these two prescribing forces, with biology guiding and environment specifying" (Gottschall and Wilson, p. viii). He goes on to clarify that it is not just genes, nor universal traits of culture, "such as the creation myths, incest taboos, and rites of passage, possessed by all societies. Rather, it is the inherited regularities of sensory and mental development that animate and channel the acquisition of culture" (ibid.). In his theory, "the mind is a narrative machine, guided unconsciously by the epigenetic rules in creating scenarios and options" (p. ix). Recent developments with the genome project and new discoveries about the mind in the fields of neuroscience and human cognition are both fascinating and helpful to an understanding of culture and the human animal. We will be making further references to this exciting line of research as we talk about narration and art-making.

In our definition of the performance act, we wrote that the act is designed "to constitute meaning and to affirm individual and cultural values." To paraphrase this, we are asserting that your individual self, in all its aspects, as well as your social self, or cultural self, is involved and the meaning that you impart through the performance act is one that expresses values, including ethical values, that are both individual and cultural. You are constituting meaning and affirming values, and you, as a performer and also as an audience for other performers, will want to think closely about what, exactly, are the meanings and the values that the performance expresses and conveys.

Critical Understanding

The task of determining the meaning of a performance and the meaning of the texts on which the performance is based is one of the most difficult tasks confronting the critic of performances. It requires that you develop and hone the perceptual and cognitive skills necessary to make sense of the performance—and the literary and cultural texts on which it is based—as a unified whole and as a whole that communicates meaning and has significance. Your performances need to be whole. They need to have a shape, with a beginning, middle, and end. This textbook will teach you about understanding texts and performances as aesthetic objects with formal structures. We will show you how to think about the elements in your performance and how they cohere to make a whole. One of the exciting challenges of being an astute observer and describer of performances based on literary or cultural texts is to try to put into words an explanation of how you think a performance conveys meaning. Often this task requires multiple acts of understanding on your part. It also calls for different critical tools and vocabularies to assist you in both understanding and communicating your understanding to others.

Let us consider some examples of what is involved in making sense of the meaning of a performance act and naming and describing the meaning of the work and the values it imparts, both individual and cultural. Assume you want to perform Brooks's poem "The Boy Died in My Alley," quoted earlier in this chapter. You will need to understand the poem in its own right and also as it is handled when it is interpreted by you the performer, or by another performer, in the act of performance. The performer and the text become intertwined in performance. The very nature of this process of taking a text into your body is central to the discipline of performance studies or interpretation and vital to an understanding of how a performance of a text conveys meaning.

Scholars often speak of this process of taking a poem, or any kind of text, into your body as a process of "matching." Wallace Bacon, a leader in the discipline of interpretation, in his book *The Art of Interpretation*, wrote:

> What the interpreter does, through the arduous discipline that constitutes the art of interpretation, is to establish some congruence between the inner form of the poem and his own inner sense (working backward and forward between the poem and himself), and

then to embody the poem—literally giving body to experience—so that through his own outer form (his voice, his countenance, his body) he in a sense becomes the poem. The poem now becomes audible and visible—and if the interpreter succeeds in establishing congruence between the inner form of the poem and his own inner form, if he achieves a coalescence of the two things, the poem will be alive, will have presence, will be an organism. (p. 33)

Bacon imbues this process of matching with a spirit that at times seems almost mystical. Using language drawn from anthropology and philosophy, particularly phenomenology, Bacon idealizes the encounter between a performer and a text as an encounter between self and the other. To be able, through empathy, defined as the power of feeling into and with an other, Bacon believes that performers (he called them oral interpreters) can achieve consummate intellectual and bodily knowledge of imaginary worlds or real worlds, created in literary texts, or oral texts, by others.

Other scholars, such as Schechner, speak of the way in which an actor is both an "I" and a "not-I." When, as a performer, you take on this I/not I, you understand that the "I" is the socially and biologically determined sense of identity that a person has, while the "not-I" refers to those aspects of the actor that seem to owe their origins to something outside of and other than the self of the actor. This helps you understand some of the components of the performer who enters into a relationship with the text being performed in this process of matching. Important as it is in this example to think about who the performer is as he or she performs Brooks's poem, it is also essential to remember that the performer is performing a poem written by another person, its author, and the performer's relationship to this text and his or her fidelity to it are elements that need to be understood critically when we analyze such performances. Later in this textbook, we will discuss the process of matching much more extensively. We will also give much closer attention to the intentions of performers and address the question of the extent to which performers of a text are obliged to remain faithful to the text. If they depart from an author's intent, how much latitude do they have in appropriating the text and redeploying its author's meaning to their own ends while still claiming to be performing the work of the author? For now, assume that the first obligation of the performer of the poem by Brooks is to try to understand the poem in its own terms and perform it. Later, we can give more thought to the other end of the spectrum of performance possibilities for this poem, where the performer takes over the poem and uses it to an end of his or her own, which could be entirely different from the meaning expressed in the poem.

First, to understand Brooks's poem, you need to wrestle with the tasks of close reading and understanding the words in the poem, their symbolism, the speaker in the poem, the other characters, and a rash of other elements that Brooks uses to shape meaning. You will also notice that the performer's performance colors the text or, put differently, offers a specific interpretation of the text that may or may not closely adhere to the consensual meaning that an ordinary audience would ascribe to the poem. In fact, once you watch many performances of the same poem by many different performers, you begin to see how varied the interpretations of a poem can be. The poem lends itself to multiple understandings, some more valid than others. Although some of the interpretations may strike you as simply insufficiently understanding of meanings that are clearly expressed in the poem to be considered valid interpretations of the poem, you will also note how many different inflections of the meanings of the same poem can appear to be "right" and true to the poem's meaning. In order to be able to speak critically and cogently about such performances, your task as a critic of performance is twofold. You need to describe the performance as accurately as you can and analyze how it achieves meaning in relationship to both the Brooks poem and to the performer's interpretation of the poem. In some cases, the performer's interpretation may seem very close to the meaning of the poem as Brooks intended it; in others, the interpretation of the poem may seem radically different. Audiences seeing multiple renderings of the same text will come to a consensus regarding a range of meanings that seem legitimately to rest in the poem itself, in contrast, for example, to meanings that seem to be exported from other sources and imposed on the text. We quoted several poems earlier in this chapter and initiated the discussion of their meaning. Look back now at those poems and ask yourself what values were imparted in them. If you performed the poems, can you see how your interaction with the poem can affect the values that the poem will affirm in the audience? At the opening of the chapter, we talked about performance and performance methodology. A dictionary definition of *methodology* emphasizes that the word refers to a manner of procedure, a regular and systematic way, an orderly way, to accomplish anything or to proceed. Within the discipline of performance studies, the term is used to describe the particular approach taken by performance scholars and performers to the act of performance itself, and to criticism of performance. Throughout this textbook, we will be applying this methodology to various kinds of performance. So far, we have discussed the performance of poetry and emphasized that both the performance and the poems are part of the methodology of performance and criticism. Let us turn now to another literary genre, the short story, and consider methodologically how performers go about analyzing the short story and understanding performance conventions useful to translating a literary text in this genre into a performance text for the purposes of a performance.

Finding the Narrative Voice

Poems offered one entry point into an examination of how to read a literary text closely and how to adapt it so that it can be featured in a performance. Another entry point could be a performance of a selection of narrative fiction, drawn from a short story or novel. Once we have given you a taste of what it feels like to think about performing a segment of a short story, we will move to a discussion of the kinds of critical approaches that can assist you in understanding literary and nonfictional texts and understanding performance. Our emphasis will be placed equally on matters addressing how you understand the texts you are performing—and this involves critical reading and interpreting of the texts—and how you understand the conventions used to explore your performing self. We want to teach you how to speak and write about performances knowledgeably and with grace.

Look at the opening paragraph of "Act of Solitude" by Joyce Carol Oates and consider how you would describe the speaker who narrates these sentences. We are trying to prepare you to imagine how you will go about performing the opening passage of this story for a solo performance. When considering the performance of narrative, whether it is in poetry, fiction, nonfiction, or drama, you always have to consider who is speaking. Narration is a telling; it refers to telling a story, whether orally or in written form. The narrator is a character with human will and is always narrating about something, be it people, or events, or actions. Narration always involves a narrator and the characters the narrator is telling about. One of the first tasks for a performer of narrative is to figure out who the narrator is, since you will be assuming the voice and the character of the narrator.

For example, in Brooks's poem, the speaker is the person in the alley where the boy died. The speaker seems to be a woman, although some might argue that the gender is not specified in the poem itself. The speaker also seems to be African American, an extension of the author, Gwendolyn Brooks. Some performers of the poem, especially if the performers are women, might make the speaker a woman, and if the performer is not black, the performer again will have to make a choice: is it better for the white performer to transpose the poem's setting and speaker so that the speaker can plausibly be white, or should the white performer try to suggest a black speaker? To achieve this latter goal, should the white performer take on stereotypical black gestures and dialect, or would this seem gross, or presumptuous, or too risky? Should the white performer imagine herself as a black woman and speak from conviction but without attempting impersonation? These are the kinds of matters that require attention when performers take on a speaker that is different from themselves in respect to gender, race, or ethnicity, and in other regards. Now consider what we know about the speaker in Oates's story.

The narrator holds the greatest knowledge and, consequently, power in narrative. To understand how to conceive and perform the character of the narrator, it is very useful to employ the dramatistic questions presented by Kenneth Burke in his book *A Grammar of Motives*. Burke understands literature as "equipment for living." He is primarily concerned with the examination of human motives in acts, and he considers language, thoughts, feelings, and deeds as modes of action. He invites the performer to think of literature as a symbolic act by its author, deriving from a situation in life experienced by the author. Burke's system brings rhetoric and ethics, as well as an examination of motives, into the analysis of literature. Questions about the verbal act encountered in literature led him to a consideration of terms, the grammar, that are necessary to describe an action. Burke's pentad provides the five principles for the discovery of motive: *act, scene, agent, agency,* and *purpose.* Later he added the sixth term, *attitude.* To explain fully the motive behind an act, one must know what the act that took place is, be it a deed, a thought, or a feeling. One must identify the scene, the situation in which the act occurred, or its background. One must know who performed the act, its agent, and what kind of person this is. In addition, one must know what kind of means or instruments were used to perform the act, what its agency is. One must know for what purpose or reason the act is performed. Finally, one must know not only the instruments or agency used to execute an act, but also in what manner or attitude it was carried out. Burke believed that the relationship between life and theater is literal, not merely figurative. Students of performance have found his approach useful to probe the motive of the narrative or character voice in literature and oral texts.

The narrator is the character who tells the story and, as the teller, the narrator has the greatest position of power in relationship to all that unfolds in the fictive world. Consequently, when performers approach fiction in order to perform it, they need to learn all they can about this narrator, right down to how the narrator looks, speaks, moves, thinks, imagines, conceals or reveals, and oh so many other aspects of this teller.

Look at the opening paragraphs of Oates's short story "Act of Solitude," from the collection *Will You Always Love Me?*

> It had been an accident, of that he was convinced.
>
> If he hadn't driven himself. If he'd gone in a company car.
>
> If, driving, he'd taken another route through the city, avoiding that stretch of lower Decatur Avenue. If he'd left his home in suburban Willow Lake five minutes earlier, or later—nothing would have happened.
>
> Or, assuming something *must* happen, it would not have been what had happened. It would have been . . . another story.
>
> Another ending, another set of consequences.
>
> And his truest self unaltered. Undefiled. (p. 3)

Assume for the purposes of this exercise that this is all you know of the story. This is the passage that you must use for your performance and you need to answer the dramatistic questions cited above. Using Burke's system, what is the act described in this passage? Is it composed of deed, thoughts, or feelings? What is the scene? Who is the agent of the action? Obviously, someone is the speaker of these lines in the story. What do we know about the speaker? Who is he? Or, is it a she? We know little more than that the speaker is someone who, at this stage in the story, has no name. We can conjecture about the speaker's age based on the fact that he appears to be an experienced driver and someone who works for a company, lives in a suburb, and is accustomed to being driven in company cars. Consider also the agency in this scene, in Burke's sense of the term. What is the purpose behind the narrator's actions, thoughts, and feelings? It appears that the speaker may not be speaking aloud, but rather may be involved in a mental dialogue with himself/herself. The character being spoken about seems to be guilty, confused, and afraid. Think about the other questions cited above and look for clues in the text that help you answer them. Could it be that this is spoken by a narrator who is talking about or re-creating what one of the characters, the person who thinks there might have been an accident, is thinking? Or is this language the silent reverie of the character who lives in a suburban home in Willow Lake? Also, imagine that you are going to take on the voice and character of this speaker. Are there further clues in the story to help you find a speaking voice for this speaker? Obviously, given only these opening lines, many aspects of the character have been withheld. Some are purposely made ambiguous, and consequently the author has not specified certain details about the character. For example, we are told very little about how exactly the character looks. Even in texts where we might be given information telling us a character has a pretty face, or a certain kind of smile, or look, or height, et cetera, many other features remain unspecified, leaving performers a broad range of choices as to how to use their own bodies, voices, movements, et cetera, to portray the character.

Look also at the verb forms in the passage. They all are in the subjunc-tive mood—they are conjectures, constructions starting with "if . . ." What effect does this create? How might your understanding of this mood affect how you perform the passage? What would happen if you thought of it as a dream rather than the thoughts of someone awake? Performers have an interesting range of choices before them when they try to decide how to approach and realize this text in performance.

Consider another opening passage from the novel *The House of Breath*, by William Goyen:

> . . . and then I walked and walked in the rain that turned half into snow and I was drenched and frozen; and walked upon a park that seemed like the very pasture of Hell where there were couples whis-pering in the shadows, all in some plot to warm the world tonight, and I went into a public place and saw annunciations drawn and written on the walls. I came out and felt alone and lost in the world with no home to go home to and felt robbed of everything I never had but dreamt of and hoped to have; and mocked by others' midnight victory and my own eternal failure, un-named by name-less agony and stripped of all my history, I was betrayed again. (p. 3)

Here you have the first person pronoun, I, used repeatedly. The technical term to describe this point of view is *first person narration,* where the speaker speaks directly to the reader/audience, using the first person pronoun and restricting what he or she can say to knowledge only available to the fictive speaker, not permitting any knowledge to reside in this speaker that does not lie in the speaker's ken. The reader learns to infer things about first person speakers that the character does not know, by noting discrepancies between things the person says and things that are said by other characters or things that are omitted. In later chapters on prose fiction, we will consider narrators and their reliability or unreliability at much greater length. For now, we are just getting you started in learning how to think about the choices that face you as a performer when you approach short fiction or personal experience performances.

Imagine you have been asked to perform this passage for your class. As a performer, how do you want to go about this? Do you want to develop a lectern performance? If so, will you memorize the text or will you bring it with you to the lectern and feature it during your performance? Will you want to introduce your selection? Do you need to find out a little bit of background about the author and the book? In an ideal situation, you would read the entire novel before performing its opening so that you could be wholly confident about where the novel is going, what it is about, who is speaking, and why it is opening with this description. If you decide to introduce the segment, you should prepare your remarks, even if you plan to ad-lib them during the performance. Nothing is worse for a performer than to get up to introduce a performance and draw a blank, forgetting what you had planned to say or where you were going to start. It is better to reduce the likelihood of this happening by making deliberate plans for how you will begin. Many performers memorize their opening line, if no more, to ensure against performer nerves.

You need to decide on the identity of the speaker. Who is he? Or she? Does gender matter? You would want to look closely at the language of the segment to give you clues about who is speaking and what he or she feels about the things described or the moods within the speaker.

Now consider another opening paragraph, this time from the novel *Bright Lights, Big City,* by Jay McInerney. This novel is written entirely in the second person point of view. In other words, the "you . . ." construction is used throughout. Although this is a difficult mode to sustain, it does occur in writing, and it poses interesting issues for performers. We discuss this mode more fully later in our chapters on performing prose fiction.

It's Six A.M. Do You Know Where You Are?

You are not the kind of guy who would be at a place like this at this time of the morning. But here you are, and you cannot say that the terrain is entirely unfamiliar, although the details are fuzzy. You are at a nightclub talking to a girl with a shaved head. The club is either Heartbreak or the Lizard Lounge. All might come clear if you could just slip into the bathroom and do a little more Bolivian Marching Powder. Then again, it might not. A small voice inside you insists that this epidemic lack of clarity is a result of too much of that already. The night has already turned on that imperceptible pivot where two A.M. changes to six A.M. You know this moment has come and gone, but you are not yet willing to concede that you have crossed the line beyond which all is gratuitous damage and the palsy of unraveled nerve endings. Somewhere back there you could have cut your losses, but you rode past that moment on a comet trail of white powder and now you are trying to hang on to the rush. Your brain at this moment is composed of brigades of tiny Bolivian soldiers. They are tired and muddy from their long march through the night. There are holes in their boots and they are hungry. They need to be fed. They need the Bolivian Marching Powder. (pp. 1–2)

Think about the way the speaker treats himself in this passage. Ask yourself Burke's dramatistic questions. Think about the language, how formal or colloquial it is. In each of the different passages quoted in this chapter, you were also given details that allowed you to picture the scene, the setting, where the story is situated, and you are given details to help you determine the period in which the story is set. Again, these details give you as a performer a wealth of information on which to base your choices regarding performance.

Showing Versus Telling

Percy Lubbock, in *The Craft of Fiction*, draws distinctions between showing and telling in expository writing. When a narrator shows the reader something, we are able to visualize the scene, or event, or people. In narration that shows, we become concerned about the manner in which showing reveals its subject. Prose that shows will include direct discourse, passages where characters speak in their own voices. Direct discourse is generally represented by quotation marks set around the spoken words, or dashes that precede the quoted speech. Indirect discourse, when we are told what a character says and not shown it by direct quoting of it, is another kind of exposition. Performers learn to become sensitive to these different kinds of discourse, making it possible to capture the very subtle nuances of prose. There is also free indirect discourse, a subject we will explore more fully in later chapters.

Performing Warm-ups and Tips About Performance

Students find it useful to engage in improvisational exercises and workshops in class and at home in order to play with texts they plan to perform. These exercises take all sorts of forms. Sometimes a class will use a large rubber ball, like those used in fitness classes, or a basketball or a smaller bouncing ball. They will establish different rhythms with the ball, dribbling and passing it to each other to a beat, then introducing language and using the ball to inflect a rhythm undergirding the speech. Try this with the language in Brooks's poem or with another poem of your own choosing.

Other exercises involve vocal warm-ups. The class can speak, first with performers speaking separately, and at a fixed tempo, then at varying rhythms and utilizing solo and group speaking, the latter sometimes referred to as choral reading or speaking. Sometimes tongue twisters, such as "rubber baby buggy bumpers," or lines from a poem such as Edgar Allan Poe's "The Bells" will be intoned together, at different rates of delivery and with rising pitch.

Students also use physical warm-ups, stretching exercises, and mime to free their bodies, become more physically expressive, and develop a richer sense of play and creativity. Throughout the book, we will suggest various exercises, theater games, verbal trysts, and the like, all to the end of broadening the range of the performer's physical instrument—voice and body.

Improvisational exercises or theater games provide rich sources of creativity. Viola Spolin's *Improvisation for the Theater* and, more recently, *The Second City: Almanac of Improvisation*, edited by Anne Libera, are invaluable sources for guidelines to inform improvisation and descriptions of games and exercises that involve the performer in physical and intellectual actitivities. Key for us in this text is their idea that improvisation is used to "expand and heighten the discoveries in the moment" and that it avoids preconceived ideas, relies on active choices, follows dictates such as " 'Yes, and' is always better than 'no, but' or 'No, and' or 'Yes, but,' " urges you to trust your instincts and intuition, follow your characters, and remember that "everything is important, everything matters" (Libera, p. 23).

Feel free to experiment with space and equipment in your performances. In addition to mastering the fundamentals of a basic lectern performance, try performing utilizing the entire available space, be it a room or an outdoor environment. In the confines of a classroom, you can use just a few props or media (PowerPoint, visual projection, DVDs, BlackBerrys, and the like) or, if space allows, a fuller set, with costumes, furniture, paint, water, sandboxes, black-box cubes, and items such as mirrors or musical instruments, to amplify your performances. More will be said about ways to create your performances throughout this text.

Memorization

There is much to be said for the virtues of memorization. It is an excellent mental exercise, and materials committed to memory can serve you throughout your life. We urge you to memorize as much as you can within the constraints of time. Some instructors require all performances to be memorized; others offer students the choice of memorizing the material or using a physical text. In any event, students must rehearse, and rehearse often, in order to become thoroughly familiar with the text. Many suggest trying to memorize material immediately before bedtime. Sleeping on it seems to make the text easier to recall. There are many other ways to memorize. Drill yourself and get your friends to listen and rehearse with you. As you are memorizing a text, speak it in conventional ways but also just play with it, almost without regard for its meaning. Often, if you give in to the sounds of the words, the rhythms, and the expressivity, suddenly the meaning of a work that had seemed obscure becomes clear. Or you might get an inspiration about how you want to perform the text.

If you plan to read the text, be sure to think about it as a physical prop. Think about how the book or script will look from the audience's perspective. If you are performing a formal Shakespeare sonnet and trying to suggest Elizabethan England, you won't want to be holding a bedraggled looking piece of paper or a huge tome that is difficult to maneuver and hard to see during your performance. Make these kinds of choices consciously, thinking about them from an aesthetic and also a practical standpoint. Don't leave this aspect of your performance to chance.

Finding Source Materials

In this chapter, we have concentrated on literary texts, poems, short stories, and novels, and said little about nonfictional materials or found texts. By found texts we mean texts that you have gathered yourself from materials in your world. Often found texts are the stuff of performance art, a subject that this book does not discuss but that you may want to explore on your own. We will be discussing the performance of nonfiction, including autobiography, letters, obituaries, newspaper stories, and materials found on the Internet, blogs, Facebook, and other electronic technologies.

When you put together your own performances, and when you do research in order to explore the texts you are performing, you will be drawing on the resources of libraries, museums, and the Internet. Later we will talk more about the conventions to be followed when you cite source materials in your papers and during performances, and we will talk about critical performance papers employing performance methodology.

Ethics of the Performer

This chapter has challenged you to think about yourself as a performer and interpreter of texts, employing a performance methodology in your work and learning by doing. Here we want to speak briefly about your ethical obligations as a performer and a critic. Performance involves students in acting and taking on the roles of others; it involves you with audiences; it places you in an active stance as a maker of meaning and sense, and it puts you in a powerful rhetorical position. With this power comes responsibilities, chief among them the responsibility to respect yourself and others and be accountable in ethical ways.

The subject of ethics is complex. Aristotle's *Nichomachean Ethics* and Plato's writings have provided a basis in Western civilization for understanding and practicing ethics, detailing the obligations people have to be honest, truthful, of high moral quality, and judicious. You want to be fair in the way you handle others' work; in discussing performances, you want to be honest intellectually; you want to be searching in your criticism, while at the same time expressing it in a manner that enables others to hear you and to learn. Free and lively debate is the lifeblood of institutions of learning, so you must always be willing to answer speech, no matter how loathsome, with more speech. To suppress your thoughts in the interests of civility can be dangerous, as you most likely will end by simply pushing distasteful or destructive ideas underground where they feed on themselves, often leading to violence.

In scholarship, you have a responsibility to the authors whose works you discuss and analyze; when you are performing literary or cultural texts, you have the obligation to understand the material you are addressing, acknowledge your sources (there are conventions of academic writing and research you will want to consult), and be mindful of the academic freedom and the freedom of speech of your classmates, peers, teachers, and publics. Most universities have honor codes or statements regarding academic integrity and plagiarism that you will want to consult. Fine-tune these statements so that they are helpful to you in performance arenas where some of the etiquette of citation, handling of sources, and the like are tailored to speak to issues such as fair use and copyright as they apply to the performance of materials authored by others and shared with the public. Be sure you are conversant with these concepts and that you adhere to good practices in your writing, performing, and discussion of performances.

Go Forth

We think you are now ready to begin the active business of making performances and making sense of them. We opened with lines from T. S. Eliot in which a speaker invites another to make a journey. We now ask you to read on, journey with us, make this visit, and then do not take the Prufrockian course of submerging yourself in sea kingdoms but rather follow the course of another poet, Archibald MacLeish, who said of poetry that it must not mean, but be. Let performance be!

KEY TERMS

aesthetic

dramatistic pentad

dyadic communication

kinesics

lectern

oral interpretation

performance act

performance studies

restored behavior, or "twice-behaved behaviors"

showing and telling

symbolic forms

Chapter 2

YOUR FIRST PERFORMANCES

You Begin

You begin this way:
this is your hand,
this is your eye,
that is a fish, blue and flat
on the paper, almost
the shape of an eye.
This is your mouth, this is an O
or a moon, whichever you like. This is yellow.

Outside the window
is the rain, green
because it is summer, and beyond that
the trees and then the world,
which is round and has only
the colors of these nine crayons.

This is the world, which is fuller
and more difficult to learn than I have said.
You are right to smudge it that way
with the red and then
the orange: the world burns.

Once you have learned these words
you will learn that there are more
words than you can ever learn.
The word *hand* floats above your hand
like a small cloud over a lake.

The word *hand* anchors
your hand to this table,
your hand is a warm stone
I hold between two words.

This is your hand, these are my hands, this is the world,
which is round but not flat and has more colors
than we can see.

It begins, it has an end,
this is what you will
come back to, this is your hand.

Margaret Atwood's poem speaks from the point of view of an adult (a parent? a teacher?) guiding a child through her first experiences in the world. The use of the second-person voice ("you") suggests that it may either be an adult's description of a child who is observed closely or an adult's set of directions to a child. Notice that it begins with the child's recognition of a self, a "you" who will become an "I" (as well as an "eye" — the poem is filled with visual imagery). The child quickly connects to the act of drawing a fish in crayon and also begins to perceive the world in terms of similarities and differences, between self and other: the fish's oval shape is like the eye's shape, the mouth both a natural body (the moon) and a facial gesture (the "Oh!" shape of surprise and sound play) and the written alphabet (the letter O). In the world of Atwood's child, the experiencing self does not take long to become the performing and the symbol-making and symbol-using self.

The poem shifts its locus, stanza by stanza, to a world outside the immediacy of the home or the classroom, to a perceptual field beyond that of the limited selection of colors offered by the smallest box of crayons — as when the speaker tells the child "you are right to smudge it that way . . . the world burns." In the fifth stanza, the child learns — even if at an unconscious level — some complex linguistic facts, that "there are more / words than you can ever learn" and that the word *hand* is something somewhat different from the body part, that it "floats above your hand" and that it "anchors / your hand to this table." The speaker completes the connection between herself and the child in the gestural phrase "your hand is a warm stone / I hold between two words." As the poem ends, the speaker calls the child back to the primacy of experience, to the sense of embodied being of the opening phrase "this is your hand."

Atwood's poem is a deceptively simple celebration of development, of knowledge through embodiment, through awareness and consciousness of what philosophers might call "being in the world." In this sense, it also suggests a kind of symbolic journey into performance, as well. Performance, like all other human endeavors, is a process—it doesn't happen "all at once" (though some aspects of it may seem to emerge out of nowhere at times!) but through a combination of first attempts, intermediate discoveries, development of skills, insights, and methods, movements forward—and sometimes backward—and ever-changing and ever-evolving repetitions or what might be called "iterations" and "reiterations" of actions and behaviors. As anyone who has ever performed knows—whether it be in a play, in a musical group, on the athletic field, or anywhere else—no two performances are ever quite the same even if the exact words are repeated, the same movements and gestures enacted. In a sense, we are always "coming back to the hand," as Atwood says, but never in the same way. Every beginning has an end and, as Atwood suggests, every ending takes us back—and forward—to a new beginning.

In chapter 1, we introduced you to some of the principal concepts and ideas that will guide your work throughout the course in performance you are taking. In this chapter, we will suggest some ways to begin the actual journey into the world of performance. Your teacher may have specific beginning performance assignments, as well, but our goal here is to identify some short and contained performances you might start with, in a spirit of exploration and in order to become accustomed to taking on the roles of both performer and audience member and to start practicing some of the processes you will use for longer performances. Remember: just because a text is brief does not mean that it is necessarily any less challenging, nor does it mean that your preparation should be approached with any less seriousness than if you were working on an full-length production. Each performance should be "complete" in its sense and also as open-ended as any performance leaves its performer, text, and audience.

We will describe and take you through the processes for a number of different kinds of performance assignments, which will, in many respects, preview the more developed and sustained chapters on analysis and performance to come later in this textbook. You might think of each of these assignments as the equivalents of études in the study of musical performance: they have their own intrinsic value as aesthetic and

Qty Title   Locator

1 Learning to Perform: An Introduc....   L01-1-18-006-001-1758

Marketplace: AmazonMarketplaceUS
Order Number: 4295293
Ship Method: Standard
Customer Name: Amy Miller
Order Date: 2/9/2020 8:42:20 PM
Marketplace Order #   112-5810953-8383411
Email: h3blxzm1ywb0255@marketplace.amazon.com

If you have any questions or concerns regarding this order, please contact us at serviceohio@hpb.com performative experiences, but they also function as building blocks. You will find that, in some cases, the line between that which is familiarly "literary" and that which intersects with other kinds of performances, such as popular music, conversational dialogues, gossip, genealogy, and so on, may be more blurred than you think. The act of performance constantly reminds us of what the sociologist Erving Goffman called the theatricality of everyday life. The earliest poems we may remember are embedded in the lullabies caregivers sang to us as they rocked us to sleep; in turn, such lullabies may themselves be attempts to externalize our own inner rhythms as human beings, ways of both stimulating and calming ourselves and each other from as early as the womb. They may be nursery rhymes, in which teachers, parents, or siblings use the rhythms to help us develop verbal and motor skills, to appreciate the pleasures of patterns, to stretch our imagination to begin to see places, creatures, and people who might be possible only in our dreams or fantasies. Our first stories may be ones in which the teller, trying to build on the natural self-interest of the child, makes the child-listener the hero of a story, or tells about the day the child was born. The line from such stories to contemporary memoir or to self-conscious works of fiction in which the author becomes a character, such as Laurence Sterne's *Tristram Shandy*, is more direct than we might think.

We will begin with the performance of a poem written in one of the oldest and most prescriptive of forms—a form that has yielded texts that are often anything but simple or singular in their potential for analysis and performance.

Performing the Haiku

The haiku is a verse form that began in Japan and was developed during the tenth through thirteenth centuries. It is derived from a longer form called the tanka, but the haiku is the form best known today; despite its brevity and its appearance of delicacy, it has proven to be a sturdy and powerful form of verbal expression whose almost childlike form belies subtle and complex passions and insights. Its form is based on a prescribed number of syllables per line, following the pattern of 5-7-5. Because translation often alters form, in Japanese haiku translated into English you may find translations that do not follow the line form and syllable count. However, most haiku, even in translation, tend to follow the form fairly strictly.

The content of the haiku varies considerably in contemporary verse, but in its original tradition, a haiku usually centered on a single image, usually drawn from nature, often commenting on some aspect of the seasons and capturing a brief, singular moment of insight, reflection, or experience. The compression of the form is well suited to the experience of the image and sentiment, as in the following example:

No sky and no earth
At all. Only the snowflakes
Fall incessantly.
— HASHIN

A total of seventeen syllables, but let's consider the various possibilities for meaning and performance inherent in both the specific images created and the setting of the syllables and the lines (realizing that in the original Japanese, the line breaks might come at slightly different spots, we can nonetheless analyze this English translation on its own terms).

Where might we begin with this poem? Perhaps the first thing we notice is that it consists of two sentences, each of which spills over the length of a single line. The first sentence, the shorter of the two, is not, by some grammatical standards, even a complete sentence, but a fragment—its verb is only implied: the reader supplies the "There is" that might precede the actual text and which the poet has omitted, perhaps for the sake of form, perhaps to make even more stark the sense of isolation. Thus, what we encounter first is simply the statement of an absence: "No sky and no earth / At all." Almost immediately, we might ask ourselves, who is saying (or thinking) these words? Is it the poet himself? Is it a specific person the poet imagines? Is it a kind of universalized perception that we as readers are asked to share? The starkness and spareness of the description, enforced by the mathematical discipline of the syllable count, allows—indeed requires—each one of us to fill in our own specific skyscape and landscape. For Bruce, reading it in his office in upstate New York, it may evoke a scene of masked and slippery hills and mountains, the treacherous darkness he will face as he drives home; for Carol, sitting in a library facing Lake Michigan, just outside Chicago, the absence of sky and earth may evoke memories in which everything she could see on the horizon seemed to be water or fog, stretching across a flat plain.

There is an interesting tension between the first line and the first sentence of this poem, one that the eye, the ear, and the mouth must consider in reading the poem. The balanced phrase "No sky and no earth" is a reminder of the lack of distinction between these two spaces for the speaker but also, ironically, that there is the possibility of a division between these two elemental ideas (recall that, for the ancients, creation consisted of four elements, earth, air, water, and fire). As both of these entities, sky and earth, are negated, there is a sense in which naming them is, on a surface level, impossible and irrelevant. For the observer, neither exist or are perceptible, so how can they be distinguished from each other? Yet, the fact that we have words for each—as the child learned the word for hand in the Atwood poem—suggests that even in the absence of these two entities, we maintain memories of the possibilities of such distinctions between the ground and the air.

But the poem doesn't put a period to its first sentence at the end of its first line, which would have created a kind of absolute symmetry. Rather, the sentence ends with the two additional syllables that begin the second line: "At all." In the strictest of logical senses, these words are unnecessary, superfluous: they serve to intensify the experience of absence, rather than to delineate it in any kind of geographical or scientific way. "At all" extends the felt sense of emptiness, of the void, suggesting that, even in the imagination, this lack of sky and earth goes on indefinitely, like the words of which there is no end in the Atwood poem. These two words function both as an afterthought to the initial presentation of scene and as an absolutely necessary emotional punctuation to the internal experience the speaker has of this scene.

Think about how the division of this sentence between the two lines affects your reading of the sentence. Our eyes become trained, as we learn to read, both to be aware of and to ignore the ends of lines: certainly, as we read prose, where the line breaks only because a margin requires it to, we often move so quickly from one line to the other that we could not tell someone just precisely which word ended which line. It is true, too, that we are told to read not just for individual words, but for larger units, such as phrases, clauses, and entire sentences. At the same time, we also learn, fairly quickly, thanks to such childhood verse forms as nursery rhymes, limericks, and other poems, that the ends of lines often lead the way to such pleasures as rhymes, puns, and other kinds of wordplay. We know, at some level, that line breaks matter to what the poem is trying to do. They do not matter in the same way in every poem, and we learn that in some poems, we are encouraged to read on, more or less ignoring the line breaks in how we speak or hear the line in terms of breath, pauses, intonation, and pace. But sometimes these line breaks have a great effect on the atmosphere or the feelings a sentence or phrase may have.

Let's return to the first sentence of the haiku. One option, certainly, is to read the sentence solely in terms of its grammatical coherence and flow (what we might call its syntax, the ways in which words relate to other words from beginning to end of a sentence): "No sky and no earth at all." Certainly the fact that the sentence consists of only seven syllables, no word longer than a single syllable, suggests that there is no physical reason why we could not read the sentence through without any kind of a pause. But is "No sky and no earth at all" the same as "No sky and no earth / At all"? Why or why not? Does that slight moment where the line breaks mean something different from the sentence without a break? Try saying it both ways a few times — even if you can't entirely explain what is different, can you feel a difference?

Let's move on to the second sentence of the haiku: "Only the snow-flakes / Fall incessantly." This sentence specifies the time of year during which the poem takes place and also makes concrete the reason why there is "no sky and no earth": the visual field is filled with the white-ness of snow in motion. The poem describes the snowflakes in a way that places them in action ("falling") and in a particular kind of action ("incessantly"). While, on a literal level, we know that the statement is false — the blizzard will end eventually — on the level of immediate experience, the statement is emotionally and psychologically true. Have you had the experience, while a snowstorm is going on, that it will never end? So, the words take on more than what is called denotative meaning — an objective report — and imply a state of emotion through such words and phrases as "at all" and "incessantly."

As with the first sentence, this second sentence spans two lines. The segment in line two, "Only the snowflakes," introduces specific aspects of the physical environment and heightens the sense of isolation and loneliness with the opening word "only." The third line begins with the only verb in the poem, "fall," and the word's position at the beginning of the line draws it into especial focus. As with the first sentence, we must consider how to weigh the importance of maintaining the integrity of the sentence with some attention to the integrity of the line break. Again, try saying the sentence and the lines in different ways, with and without some kind of pause. What different effects can you achieve? And what do we do about the fact that the second line contains parts of two sentences? Is there a way to communicate that?

Notice that even as we have begun to examine the poem from critical and analytic perspectives, we have inevitably begun to talk about it in terms of various kinds of performance choices we might make. Thus far, we have been focusing on what we call a microcosmic level, looking at individual words and phrases. We also need to think about the poem as a kind of *gestalt*, a term used in psychology to refer to the sense of an entire perceptual field of experience in which the whole is greater than the sum of its parts. In addition to describing a scene, in a glimpse that begins and ends more quickly than the time it takes a snowflake to reach the ground, this haiku also may point to larger, macrocosmic concerns. Does this moment in time point to more eternal philosophical, even spiritual concerns? One reading might be that, in the midst of all of the world of time, space, and experience, we are still most aware of the present moment, a moment dominated by what is right in front of us and what may seem unending. Is the speaker aware of the larger metaphorical implications of his or her observation? How might you as a performer give us this sense—either of a speaker who is living only in this moment of watching the blizzard (or immersed in it physically—where does the speaker stand, how does his or her body respond to the snowflakes?) or a speaker who knows on some overt or sensed level that such a moment in time is only one of an infinite number, in which he or she is only a single snowflake, "falling incessantly"? One of the beauties of the haiku as a textual form is that, while usually grounded in some very specific image or moment, it nonetheless usually allows for any number of readings and performances.

Suppose you have been assigned this haiku for your first performance. We have talked through some of the issues you might have to address as a performer. For some of you, it might be the individual words that first pull you to it, and you may find that you spend hours trying out different ways of saying specific words—giving shape and tone to "only" or "incessantly": it may be that you begin with the smallest parts possible and then build toward the whole. Others of you might spend your initial preparation time memorizing the two sentences so that you can speak the entire poem in its two largest linguistic units, and only then do you move on to break it down into smaller units, testing out different inflections for words, different ways of vocalizing the tensions between the two sentences and the three lines.

Other performers might find other ways to enter into the process of turning this poem from words on a page into an embodied experience. Some performers may prefer to start with a more physical approach.

Here is a challenge: can you find a way of expressing the images, the emotions, the overall sense of the poem using only your body, not the words or your voice? Experiment with how the poem might live within your body, or what environment you might move through in the poem's created world. Are there specific gestures that emerge as you try to live with the poem through your body? Postures? Movements and actions? We're not suggesting charades, where the object is to get an audience to guess the words. Rather, we are imagining a performance in which your audience might be able to describe the kind of place, the mood, the climate, the emotion the performer is expressing—something that may feel prelinguistic, or before language articulates (some would say the language cocreates) the experience.

Yet another approach might be to begin with imagining a kind of dramatic setting or moment in which the haiku is uttered. What specific things give rise to the speaker thinking or speaking these words? Here we encourage you to allow your imagination to interact with and beyond the specificity of the words of the haiku. Invent a concrete character for the poem's speaker. You may come up with your own scenario—is this a speaker who has just finished his day at work and is contemplating the drive home (as we suggested Bruce might, living in a terrain where a sudden snowstorm makes travel dangerous), thinking the words to himself? Or could the speaker be a person, male or female, who is saying farewell to a loved one, using the words not to describe a literal snow-scape, but as a way of expressing sadness that is enveloping the speaker at parting? If so, is this a temporary farewell or a permanent one? If this is the ending of a relationship, who has ended it, and why? Is there anger mixed in with the sense of loss? Where does the speaker stand physically with regard to the beloved? A foot away, after the last embrace? Halfway out the door? Having left, only to return, because the snowflakes have made it impossible to leave? There are as many possibilities as you can justify by the words of the poem itself; we have imagined one centered on a love affair—we are certain you can up with many other, equally interesting and defensible scenarios. Again, we want to stress that here you are creating something that could be the dramatic scene, something the words can justify, but not arguing for something that is necessarily the only case. Such dramatic invention may be a way into the poem but not the final choice you make when you present the poem to an audience.

Try reading, analyzing, and performing one or more of the haiku below. Some of them come from classical Japanese tradition; others are more recent. Some are sad, some funny—several are a mix of the tragic and comic.

Haiku for Performance

Far from the busy town
This Buddha stands, and from his nose
An icicle drips down.
—Issa

Asleep within the grave
The soldiers dream, and overhead
The summer grasses wave.
—Basho

I dwell here all alone
For no one passes by this road
Now that autumn's gone.
—Basho

The romance is gone,
But we're staying together
For the apartment.
—Joel Derfner

How can we fix us?
The fights, the silence . . . I know!
Let's get a puppy!
—Joel Derfner

The wire fence is tall
The lights in the prison barracks
Flick off, one by one.
—Etheridge Knight

Eastern guard tower
Glints in sunset; convicts rest
Like lizards on rocks.
—Etheridge Knight

I take off my glove
to show my daughter
the Pleiades
      — TEMPLE CONE

midsummer
a truck rusting in a field
of sunflowers
      — LAURA GARRISON

chipped nail polish
the red
of a leaf falling
      — SANDRA MOONEY-ELLERBECK

One more possibility: compose and perform your own haiku!

Performing Song Lyrics

If you wish to do a slightly longer performance than haiku allows, but still work with some of the elements of poetry you may find song lyrics accessible yet challenging in intriguing ways. While the song lyric may at first strike you as a curious choice for a spoken performance, it (or some variation of it) has been an important part of popular and artistic performance traditions dating back as far as the ancient Greeks in Western civilization and in many other world cultures. The epics of Homer, for example, *The Iliad* and *The Odyssey*, began not as book-length narratives but as oral compositions that scholars believe involved a combination of fixed phrases (formulas) and free improvisation in which new sentences and phrases were generated each time the work was performed, restricted primarily by the performer's ability to make the phrases fit the set rhythm of the poem. The static versions of these epics were standardized in later centuries. Scholars still argue about the exact nature of the performances, most believing that some kind of instrument accompanied the performer and that the performer delivered the words in a mode that to our ears would sound like some combination of speaking, singing, and chanting. Similarly, there are many popular ballads we know today primarily as narrative poems ("Edward, Edward," "The Daemon Lover," and others) that began, as the genre suggests, as songs. While some of them continue to be sung, many find a separate, equally satisfying existence as spoken and silently read poems.

Thus song lyrics often have dual and sometimes intersecting lives as musical texts and literary texts, depending on the context through which they are transmitted and the nature of the performance situation. Since the advent of printing, the texts of songs have tended to become fixed and unchanging, but it is still not unusual for song lyrics to be changed and adapted by different performers in different situations. A singer may decide that the context in which she is performing a song demands the omission or editing of a lyric; slips in memory under the pressure of live performance may produce some changes. Whether we call these different versions "variants" or "errors" depends on how important we deem fidelity to the text and on whether the song has a specific author. Changes made in the performance of the folk song "John Henry," which has been passed down through generations and is not viewed as having a single author, are likely to seem different to us than the liberties an individual singer takes with a song written by a known composer. For example, a number of years ago Barbra Streisand recorded some songs by the esteemed theater composer Stephen Sondheim, and she requested that he change some lyrics in his famous song "Send in the Clowns" in order to accommodate her preferences regarding how to perform the song. Sondheim obliged (and we might wonder for how many other performers he would have been willing to change his lyrics), but more importantly, Streisand asked. While some changes in lyrics are viewed as conventions in adapting to different performers (most notably, altering pronouns to match the gender of the singer), as a rule one is moving into dangerous ethical territory when changes are made to lyrics written by an individual composer—if the performer is doing it for rhetorical or political reasons, at the very least he or she is obliged to acknowledge the changes.

What are the particular challenges song lyrics pose for the performer of literature? Timothy Gura has written wisely and insightfully about such issues. He suggests that the performer must first decide whether to use music as part of the performance approach: will you actually sing the lyrics? If not, will you still attempt to maintain the rhythm, phrasing, and tempo of the song as given in the musical score? This approach may at first sound like a pale substitute, but for certain songs it can retain the powers such musical features provide while allowing the performer to focus more intensely on the content and nuances of the words. Songs sung often require emphasizing the sonic qualities of notes—over the grammatical and semantic flow of words, while a spoken performance can reveal less often noticed aspects of the lyrics. As Gura points out, in such a performance, the words become central, and the performer must decide from the start whether the song is one whose words can be separated from its melody and retain their interest. If not, it may not be the best choice for such a performance.

Let's look at a specific song to consider some of these initial issues. It is one you may have been taught to sing in school or at camp, in church or temple, or at political rallies. It is by Pete Seeger, a twentieth-century singer, composer, and folklorist, and it was written in 1961.

Where Have All the Flowers Gone?

Where have all the flowers gone, long time passing?
Where have all the flowers gone, long time ago?
Where have all the flowers gone?
Young girls have picked them every one.
Oh, when will they ever learn?
Oh, when will they ever learn?

Where have all the young girls gone, — long time passing?
Where have all the young girls gone, — long time ago?
Where have all the young girls gone? —
Gone for husbands every one.
Oh, when will they ever learn?
Oh, when will they ever learn?

Where have all the young men gone, — long time passing?
Where have all the young men gone, — long time ago?
Where have all the young men gone? —
Gone for soldiers every one.
Oh, when will they ever learn?
Oh, when will they ever learn?

Where have all the soldiers gone, — long time passing?
Where have all the soldiers gone, — long time ago?
Where have all the soldiers gone? —
Gone to graveyards every one.
Oh, when will they ever learn?
Oh, when will they ever learn?

Where have all the graveyards gone,—long time passing?
Where have all the graveyards gone,—long time ago?
Where have all the graveyards gone?—
Gone to flowers every one.
Oh, when will they ever learn?
Oh, when will they ever learn?

One of the first things you no doubt notice when you read these lyrics is the amount of repetition they contain. Indeed, in some respects, they are not dissimilar in form to a nursery rhyme, in which only one or two nouns or verbs change in each succeeding stanza. Like certain nursery rhymes (which are also often sung), the repetitions create an interlocking progression, in which one element is retained from one stanza to the next and there is a cumulative force to the chain of associations. Think of such rhymes from your childhood as "The Farmer in the Dell," in which a series of relationships is mapped out as the song progresses, leading to the inevitable "cheese stands alone."

Seeger is clearly playing off such traditions in this song, and if you have ever heard it sung, you may have noted that its melody is also fairly simple, repetitive, and insistent: it is easy to learn, and its surface cheeriness is countered by subtle chord modulations that reveal a mournfulness and even an anger underneath the childlike series of questions and answers. Let's look at the basic structure of each stanza: it begins with a question of location and change, "Where have all the _____ gone," followed by a phrase that is repeated in each case, "long time passing," suggesting the eternal span of human cycles of life, particularly Amy Lowell's "a pattern called war." The question and the phrase are repeated with the single alteration of "ago" for "passing"? How does the word *ago* shift the emotional and intellectual meaning of "long time"? The question is repeated a third time, and this time, the question is answered in a more specific way involving an action, "Young girls have picked them every one" in the first stanza. The final line concludes with a ruminating, remonstrating question, "Oh, when will they ever learn?" In ordinary conversation, this question likely would not be repeated. Here it is repeated to fill out the measure of the line, but is there something else gained by repeating it?

The first stanza seems innocent enough, asking about the disappearance of flowers, easily explained by the action of girls (not women, note) picking them "every one," possibly suggesting a kind of careless stripping of the landscape; we can assume that flowers grow again each year, so we don't worry too much about their removal—at most it seems to suggest the inevitable changing of seasons, for the flowers would wither and die if the girls didn't pick them. The second stanza takes singer and audience to a broader social context in which the young girls take husbands "every one." But with the repetition, "Oh, when will they ever learn," the lyric begins to take on a more searching meaning. What is it that such young girls (and their husbands, presumably) must learn that the the cycle of marriage does not seem to teach each generation to pass down to the next? There is some sense of foreboding here. Stanzas three through five, while following the same formal and syntactic structure as the first two, move away from the pastoral scene of flowers and marriage into a landscape of war—with the young men "gone to soldiers," then, in the next stanza, "gone to graveyards," and, finally, "gone to flowers," thus beginning the song again. In a sense, this is like the song you may have grown up hearing Lamb Chop and her friends sing, "the song that never ends"—the song of war. Its specific details change from generation to generation and from war to war; in recent years, the gendered division of labor (women to marriage, men to war) is not nearly as polarized as it was when Seeger composed the song, but the pattern of birth (symbolized by flowers) to death (graveyards) remains present. The very nature of the song's form underscores the ceaselessness of war as a lesson we never seem to learn to avoid.

At first, this song may seem like one we might identify as being less than appropriate for spoken performance: its childlike form and its degree of repetition seem to work against the spoken medium, in which such repetition can seem simply unnecessary. But, we would argue, the form actually becomes another fascinating challenge. How can the speaking performer retain the sense of childlikeness that the repetitive form and the simple word choice suggest, while communicating a subtext of the many different emotions at work in this song?

In preparing your performance, you might want to listen to a number of different renditions of the song to hear just how many different "texts" the song yields, depending on the performer, the context, and the moment in history when the song is performed. Search the Internet for different versions. Try to find a version sung by Seeger himself to begin with—they range from fully sung folk-traditional versions to angry, abbreviated versions, sung live at protests against the Vietnam War. It makes a difference whether Seeger chooses to accompany himself on the guitar, which often has the effect of softening the message into something shared and rueful, or to sing a capella, without accompaniment, which often leads him to shorter, more bitten off lines. (You may also be surprised by how many variants of the lyrics there are, including several in which Seeger himself alters or edits the lyrics for a particular situation.)

What about other performers? One fascinating one we have heard is a recording done by Marlene Dietrich, the famous German actress and performer. Dietrich became famous not only as an exotic, European sex symbol in such films as *The Blue Angel* and *Morocco* in the 1930s but as an outspoken anti-Nazi American citizen and patriot during World War II and, in later life, as a symbol of the German expatriate who wanted the world to avoid more senseless conflicts and loss of young lives. While never known as a virtuoso singer, she nonetheless was a popular entertainer in nightclubs until the end of her life and recorded everything from the popular German love songs of her youth to contemporary music of the 1960s. One song she performed frequently in her later years was Seeger's "Where Have All the Flowers Gone?"

To listen to Dietrich sing the song next to a recording of Seeger singing it is to hear the extraordinary range of possibilities inherent in a single, deceptively simple lyric and melody. By the time Dietrich recorded the song, her voice, never terribly true to pitch to begin with, must struggle to reach the notes and sustain them for any length of time. What is simply a function of age becomes meaningful in creating a sense of the singer — and it is important that, despite its huskiness, it is still recognizably a woman's voice — trying to make her antiwar message heard. Dietrich, it is not too hyperbolic to say, becomes not unlike Hecuba, the Trojan queen, in defeat, mourning for the loss of the young men, who in one war may have been her suitors, in another her sons, and if she lives long enough, her grandsons. Her phrasing is just idiosyncratic enough to draw attention to itself and to different ways of emphasizing particular words. Whereas Seeger tends to sing his questioning phrases in a single breath, connecting "where" and "when" to the words that immediately follow (thus throwing the emphasis on "have" and "will"), Dietrich tends to elongate the interrogative word and take a slight pause before singing the rest of the question; the effect is to make the act of questioning that much more forceful, almost despairing, as though she knows the answer is probably "Never."

Still other performers have recorded this song, including the soul ensemble Earth, Wind, and Fire, bringing a kind of gospel quality to it and a sense of choral voice that speaks to the collective experience of war and its losses, not to mention a subtext of the racial imbalance in the losses of the Vietnam War, which was fought by more minority soldiers than white, middle class ones. Look, too, for more recent versions. How are they similar to and different from the ones we have described? What remains constant in all versions? What changes?

How would you perform this song, if you were assigned to do it as a spoken piece? What different words or phrases might you emphasize and why? How would you use pauses? Inflections? Timing? Can you think of different tensions you might create between the surface form and your own thoughts and feelings about war? You might seek other kinds of texts and countertexts to use in performing this poem. Are there visual images you might project? Instrumental versions of songs to play softly in the background (war songs from the past, such as "The Battle Hymn of the Republic" or "Over There"—which might or might not seem less complicated).

You no doubt have song lyrics that you admire and that carry important meaning for you. Some may be drawn from popular music of the day, by such writers as Bob Dylan, Ani di Franco, Janis Ian, Tracy Chapman, Michael Stipe, John Lennon, Paul McCartney, and others. Others may come from the virtuoso hip-hop and rap traditions, such as those by Queen Latifah, Eminem, and Three 6 Mafia, to name just a few. Still others may come from the vast storehouse of songs in musical theater, ranging from the art song lyrics of Stephen Sondheim to the character-filled solos by Stephen Schwartz (composer and lyricist of such musicals as *Pippin* and *Wicked*). Some of you may turn to classical music, where composers often turned to poetry for lyrics to set to music, such as Schubert's famous rendition of Goethe's frightening ballad "The Erl-King." Performing song lyrics can take you from very internal, meditative memories to fully dramatized moments of encounter between characters and audiences.

Performing the Work Story

The first two types of beginning performances we discussed are drawn from existing texts: the haiku and the song lyric. In both cases, performance nonetheless functions transformatively, in a sense creating new texts from the printed poem or the sung lyrics. There are a number of other brief texts you can draw on for an initial performance, such as Aesop's fables, children's picture books, and so on. However, your teacher might instead assign you to do a performance that involves creating an original text, perhaps drawn from your own life experience. When told in the form of a story, these are called personal narratives, and we will have more to say about them in a later chapter. While some have the appearance of being completely informal and spontaneous, emerging in the impromptu flow of conversation, they can be more sophisticated and crafted in their artistry. A personal narrative might fall somewhere in between these two poles of the conversational and the completely staged and scripted, much as public speeches are often presented in what is called extemporaneous style, planned and rehearsed but allowing room for change and adaptation in the delivery.

What are the essential characteristics of a personal narrative? Like any story, a personal narrative must have what Aristotle called a plot—a shaped and articulated action, involving the ordering of events. For Aristotle, the idea of a plot was even more necessary than the development of character: that a person is born, lives a certain kind of life, and then dies forms the kernel of everyone's life story—though Aristotle and later critics would probably argue that this set of events, told in chronological order, does not yet function as a plot. The novelist and critic E. M. Forster made a useful distinction in his book *Aspects of the Novel* when he said that "the king died and then the queen died" is an example of story; "the king died and then the queen died of grief" is an example of plot, because it adds the dimension of causality, motivation, of a perspective on the simple enunciation of two events—it connects them.

Similarly, character is more than the mere existence of people (or other creatures) who experience events or perform actions. For Aristotle, who used the word *ethos* for his concept of character, character involves moral attributes, psychological disposition, social action, and other elements that both bind people together and allow us to see them as individuals. Can you see why narratives with plot but without any but the sketchiest sense of character are not satisfactory?

So, plot and character are necessary for a narrative, and, many critics would argue, so are elements such as time and place—a when and where for the story. Again, we will return to more detailed discussions of time and place in later chapters, but an important distinction to keep in mind is that there is almost always at least a double sense of time and place in even the simplest of narratives: narrative time and place—the time and the location of the telling of the story—and narrated time and place—the time and place in which the events of the story occur. The gap between

narrative and narrated time and place may be quite large or quite small—
from a story told in a classroom about "a galaxy far, far away and long,
long ago" to the story told at the lunch table about what happened in the
cafeteria line.

The final requirements of a narrative, already indirectly alluded
to, are the storyteller, or the narrator, and some sense of audience. In a
personal narrative, the assumption is that, unless otherwise indicated, the
narrator is identical with the "I," that the embodied individual performing
the story lived it. While theories of the self complicate the direct identification of the narrating self with the narrative self, even in the example of
the lunch table story, in ways that will become more apparent when we
examine longer examples of personal narrative in later chapters, for now it
is reasonable to assume that when you tell a brief personal narrative, even
though you may be reshaping and revising the events and your perspective on them, you are usually striving to represent yourself in a way that
you believe is true to the reality of your experience. While many tellers of
personal narrative violate this seemingly self-evident convention—often
quite deliberately—for the purposes of this exercise, you are trying to
report your perceptions of reality in a way that you believe is accurate.

Similarly, audiences may range from the intrapersonal (stories we tell
ourselves privately or in such externalized private forms as diaries and
journals) to the mass or mediated, telling our stories to people whose
bodies do not share our space. The growth of digital/electronic forms
such as blogs and websites have made the narrative performance one of
increasing complexity. But for the moment, we will assume your audience for this assignment is a small, live audience composed of your
classmates.

It is not simply the reporting of events you experienced or witnessed
that qualifies a personal narrative as an artistic performance. Rather, it is
the conscious and deliberate shaping, selecting, and articulating of the
experience through language, image, voice, and body with some kind of
reflection, no matter how brief, indirect, or implicit, that gives the personal
narrative a sense of meaning and value. Scholars of human development,
such as the sociologist and anthropologist Brian Sutton-Smith, have
observed that narrative ability, like other kinds of cognitive abilities, is
acquired over the course of time at predictable ages. Very young children,
under two years of age, typically do not have the linguistic knowledge
and competence to generate a real sentence. A year later, the child may
be able to string words together into sentences, often held together by

"and," which suggests the child is beginning to understand connections. A little later, around school age, the child learns how to establish either causality or subordination as cognitive, linguistic, and narrative markers and categories of importance.

With this brief survey of the essentials of narrative, you now have a way of thinking about what you need to begin creating a personal narrative performance. Your next question might be—what should I tell a story about? There is no single correct answer to this question, and your instructor might specify the subject matter, but if not, think about what the possible functions of performing a brief personal narrative might be in the context of the first few weeks of a course in performance. Certainly the assignment can serve to get you up on your feet and help you overcome some of the nervousness associated with performing for a new audience in what we hope is an unthreatening environment. But, in addition, a personal narrative assignment can serve to introduce you to the class and to tell your classmates something about you; this is accomplished both in the content of the story you tell and in the manner in which you tell the story. In this sense, such a performance becomes a powerful aspect of what Goffman called "the presentation of self in everyday life" and one of your first acts in the process of what he called "impression management."

Keeping this in mind, consider the types of stories you might choose to tell and which ones you might be better off not telling. You may be tempted to tell a story that is centered on some very intense and dramatic event in your life (such as a life-or-death situation or a story involving trauma), but consider what you put at stake, for you and your audience, in making such a selection: you may be asking too much, on such short acquaintance, of yourself and your audience. Stories about a car crash the night of your school prom can be moving and powerful, but you might find that, when you are actually standing in front of an audience, the emotional vulnerability involved could be counterproductive. You may find yourself disclosing more about yourself than you intended or asking your audience to share too quickly in an experience with a relative stranger with whom they will be sharing a common space for ten or fifteen weeks.

Family stories of various kinds are popular choices, and they can be an excellent source of personal narrative as a form of introduction, particularly if they focus on an aspect of family life common to most families, such as holiday celebrations, special foods, the family vacation, and so forth. This is not to say that you should avoid serious stories; rather, the thoughtful and imaginative narrative based on both special and everyday aspects of family life is among the most serious kinds of stories, because they suggest ways in which families define and know themselves as a family. Similarly, school stories, such as your first week at college or your first trip home, can serve the double purpose of building a bridge of common experience and letting your audience know what is special and unique about you and about your point of view.

One kind of personal narrative we recommend is the work story. Even if your work history has consisted of something as mundane as scooping ice cream or shelving books at the local library, people always seem to be interested in what people do "all day and how they feel about what they do," as Studs Terkel subtitled his oral history collection, *Working*. Sigmund Freud, founder of modern psychoanalysis, theorized that two things make human experience satisfying and bearable: love and work. Think about this: most of us would probably agree that love is as important a form of nourishment as food itself. But what is there about work that also makes it critical? To what degree do we define ourselves—for better or for worse—by our occupations, by how society views our "usefulness," by job titles and ranks and by our salaries? Some might argue that Americans place far too much emphasis on jobs, which nonetheless attests to their centrality in our lives. Is there a difference between "work," "job," and "occupation" for you? Do we sometimes think of our "work" as something we enjoy, something that we are called to, as opposed to our "jobs," the things we do in order to pay bills and support the things we wish to do? Studs Terkel's book is an excellent source of examples of the work story, told by people ranging from a newsboy to presidents of corporations and professional entertainers. A more recent book, *Gig: Americans Talk About Their Jobs*, edited by Bowe, Bowe, and Streeter, continues Terkel's tradition with a contemporary edge. Excerpts from these books are good source material for performance assignments in nonfiction and oral history, but most of them are too long for this particular assignment; you may find it more useful to seek out stories within the interviews and oral histories, those self-contained narratives that serve as examples of larger points speakers wish to make about their jobs.

There are many Internet sites devoted to the collection of personal narratives, some of which allow you to listen to the original storytellers performing their own stories. The format of these performances may range from impromptu tellings, in which you can hear the performer making discoveries as he or she tries to articulate his or her experience aloud for the first time, the presence of a live or mediated audience perhaps drawing different and unexpected elements from the experience than might have existed in the purely internal reflection on the events, to others such as National Public Radio's *This American Life*, written for performance but also with the knowledge of potential publication and as polished and finished as the most stylized literary novel.

One site we have found particularly useful for inspiration is StoryCorps (www.storycorps.net). StoryCorps began encouraging people to record their own stories in 2003, when it opened its first booth in Grand Central Terminal in New York City. Its staff helps customers tell their stories by taking them through an interviewing process that elicits interesting stories; the organization takes care of the technical elements of recording and, for a modest fee, provides the storyteller with a recording of the stories. StoryCorps has opened another booth in New York City and is in the process of setting up booths in other cities and sending mobile units on the road. If you go to their site, you can hear examples of brief personal narratives, including one of the most powerful work stories we have ever heard. We reproduce it below, from Dave Isay's *Listening Is an Act of Love*; we encourage you to go to the StoryCorps website and listen to its teller's performance of it.

Bus driver Ronald Ruiz, 57, interviewed by facilitator
Brett Myers, 27
Recorded in New York City

I love my passengers. I remember one woman in particular—a senior who had gotten on my bus. She seemed completely lost. She said she was going to a restaurant on City Island Avenue. I could see she was confused. There was just something about her. She looked so elegant, but with a fur coat on a hot summer day, so I said, "Are you okay?" She said, "I'm fine, but I don't know what restaurant I'm meeting my friends at." I said, "Get on. Sit in the front." I asked a gentleman to get up so she could sit near me, and I said, "I'll run in, and I'll check each restaurant for you."

So I checked the restaurants, and no luck, but this was at the very, very last restaurant on the left, I said, "It's got to be this one. Let me swing the bus around," and I swung it around. I said, "Don't move. Let me make sure this is the place before you get out." It was a hot day, and she's got a fur on. She could pass out. So I said,

"Stay here, sweetie. It's nice and cool in here." I went in and I said, "There's a lady in the bus, and she's not sure of the restaurant," and I saw a whole bunch of seniors there, and they said, "Oh, that's her."

I ran back to the bus and I said, "Sweetie, your restaurant is right here." I said, "Let me kneel the bus." Kneeling the bus means I bring it closer to the ground so she gets off easier. And I said, "Don't move." I remember my right hand grabbed her right hand. I wanted to make her feel special, like it was a limousine. It was a bus, but I wanted to make her feel like it was a limousine. And she said, "I've been diagnosed with cancer—but today is the best day of my life."

And I never forgot that woman. (*Weeping.*) She's diagnosed with cancer, and just because I helped her off the bus, she said she felt like Cinderella. Can't get better than that. And doing your job and getting paid to do a job where you can do something special like that? It's pretty awesome.

July 28, 2004

Let's look in more detail at this story. It is a model of brevity—indeed, if you listen to it, it takes scarcely a minute or so for Ruiz to tell. Yet, in that minute of narrative time, the storyteller demonstrates how fundamental Aristotle's notions of plot and character remain today, even in a performance such as Ruiz's, derived from conversation. What is the plot of the story? In its simplest terms, it is the story of an odyssey, a journey, literally and figuratively, across a seemingly anonymous cityscape. It is located in a very specific place (in the Bronx) and season (summer). Note that the performer does not specify how long ago the events of the story took place—though the final line suggests the passage of time. But the very ambiguity of the distance between the event and its retelling places the story in a kind of timeless, even mythic dimension.

The story tells of a worker (a bus driver) performing a "random act of kindness," putting aside his orderly, almost mechnical routine of scheduled stops in order to help a confused, distressed elderly woman find her destination, a luncheon with some friends. Because the woman cannot remember the name or location of the restaurant, the driver stops at every restaurant until he finds the right one. He offers her his hand to help her disembark, she thanks him, and goes to meet her friends.

But that it is not all. This is where Aristotle's notion of ethos, or character, complicates the plot. It is not simply the act of going beyond the usual job requirements of driving the route that gives the story meaning and value for teller and listener, but the sense of a moral self that emerges for the storyteller in his action and his encounter with this elderly woman.

It is all in the details of telling. The storyteller begins, as the ancients put it, in medias res, "in the middle of things." He does not provide us with any real background or exposition but allows his occupation to emerge in the first sentence, where he presents himself on an ordinary, hot summer day, driving his bus route. While hundreds, if not thousands, of passengers must pass by his fare box each day, something draws his attention to this woman: he "could see she was confused" and that "she looked so elegant, but with a fur coat on" (the phrase's fragmentation adds to the vernacular sense of the moment of encounter). Something is very different about this elderly woman; by the time he tells us the story, he knows what is different about her, but he presents his first sense of her as though it were occurring as he tells it: "I don't know if it was an illness" that made her confused, lost, he says.

He moves, almost effortlessly, from his initial description to their dialogue, in which the woman declares that she's "fine . . . but I don't know what restaurant I'm meeting my friends at." The storyteller repeats her words as though verbatim, and we note the grammar is a little off, which suggests how its spontaneity gives it a sense of authenticity.

Whether he is consciously aware of it or not, Ruiz begins to insert narrative elements that place his work story in realms of other narrative traditions. In describing his quest to find her restaurant, there is something of the chivalric romance of the gallant knight and his fair lady—a chastity that is pure but devoted. Also, his description of the restaurant as "the very, very last restaurant on the left" takes the discovery of the restaurant beyond the commonplace. From a purely logical standpoint, of course, the right restaurant is the "very, very last one"—for why would he continue looking once he has found her friends? But stating it this way points out the borders of the adventure. (It also may be that he is speaking professionally—"the very, very last restaurant on the left" may refer to the end of his route, but this is not specified in his telling). He also puts himself in the role of the rescuer willing to place himself at risk for this damsel, telling her, "Stay here, sweetie. It's nice and cool in here," acknowledging that he must face the sweltering concrete of a New York City summer afternoon. Even his colloquial address of her as "sweetie," which might sound condescending or even sexist in other contexts, here has the flavor of the urban worker and of the man who sees this rare passenger as particularly lovable and precious.

In addition, he moves his story into the realm of the fairy tale, indeed, into what folklorists consider the favorite and most ubiquitous of all such tales, "Cinderella." In describing his own desires, he admits that he wants the woman to think of the bus "like it was a limousine," paralleling the transformation of the pumpkin into a coach in the familiar tale. The woman herself remarks on the fairy-tale sense of the plot, saying she felt like Cinderella.

At the end of the plot, when our heroic bus driver–knight has safely delivered his Cinderella to her ball, the plot reverses itself, returning to the mundane, all too real world of bodies and mortality, when the woman tells him, "I've been diagnosed with cancer—but today is the best day of my life." Her one sentence permits us to imagine an entirely different story: her story rather than the driver's. Imagine an equally compelling tale of the courage it probably took her to dress herself in as fancy an outfit as she can muster—including the unseasonal fur, perhaps for her a symbol of her life at its most vibrant, of parties and dances attended in days when she felt healthier, and then finding herself on the bus (can she no longer afford a taxi or does she get on the bus, aware that she has no idea where she is going, but hoping she will recognize it once she sees it?), unable to figure out when and where to get off—just as the cancer inside her probably seems to be driving the bus without her permission. Something in her own phrasing suggests that the diagnosis is a recent one—or at least is powerful enough that it is foregrounded in all of her own actions. Think of the many different ways you might speak her line. Is it tearful? Brave? Cynical and bitter? (We don't think there is anger here, but if you do, consider how that impacts the entire arc of the story.) Is it an acknowledgment of the ironies of life—here she is, facing a death possibly sooner than she had hoped, and yet she can say that, at this moment, she feels "better" than she has ever felt. So many possibilities. And then there's the question of whether she tells her own version of the encounter to her friends in the restaurant, or does she simply move on, shifting her attention to the gossip, conversation, and meal ahead of her?

The driver appropriately allows his leading lady her exit and then takes the story back into his own worldview. He comments, almost in wonder, after the woman has revealed her cancer and her feeling that this is "the best day of her life," that she says this "just because I helped her off the bus." He is beginning to return to his ordinary self, the occupational self, if you will, in which helping someone off a bus is part of his duties (although stopping the bus every time he sees a restaurant and disembarking is not part of the job and may have irritated some of the other passengers). Of course, we know that he has done much more than just help an old lady step down from a bus.

He has done much more for her and for himself, as his final sentence tells us: "And I never forgot that woman." The use of the conjunction to open this sentence indicates that he has incorporated the story as part of his own self-concept. While being a bus driver may not be a particularly high-status job in American culture, this encounter has restored his pride and meaning—that he does more than earn a paycheck, he helps people get where they need to go, may, in some cases, help them find their way when they are lost. It is, in the terminology of Dan McAdams, a tale of the "redemptive self"—the selves redeemed being both the driver and his passenger, and perhaps by extension, we the listeners. The redemptive element comes through more powerfully in his oral performance of the story; we can hear him choke up as he repeats her words revealing her medical condition and his own sense of humility and awe at what his seemingly simple act meant to her (and, by inference, to him).

Storyteller and teacher Doug Lipman writes about a concept he uses in his own performances and as a very successful storytelling coach: the Most Important Thing (MIT). Looking for the MIT in a story helps the storyteller structure the plot—to find a shape for relating events, to find a rationale for which moments to emphasize and elaborate, for how to think about what Aristotle called the *telos*, or "end point" of the story. It also helps the storyteller move beyond the merely objective crafting of plot and character, the matter-of-fact statement of what and who, the "just the facts, ma'am" approach to narration we associate with police procedures in which witnesses are discouraged from imposing their own interpretations on events they have witnessed or experienced. Lipman is saying all storytellers *must* get beyond "just the facts," or there is no reason to share in the communal acts of storytelling and story listening, both of which are creative and active processes.

Lipman is careful and emphatic in making it clear that there is no one single Most Important Thing that will be true for every telling of the same events, not even when the story is told on multiple occasions in multiple contexts by the same performer. Just as people change, so do stories and their telling. What can be fascinating is to take a personal narrative you have told over many years and try to determine what the MIT has been in each telling (we will explore this in more detail in our later chapter on the personal narrative performance). In the meantime,

Lipman suggests brainstorming a list of possible Most Important Things for any given set of events or actions which the storyteller is contemplating turning into a story. Try this with Ruiz's story; here are a few we have come up with:

In the Bronx, One Passenger in a Thousand: Possible MITs

1. In the middle of an ordinary day, an extraordinary encounter can happen.
2. A bus driver's work is more important than he and we might think.
3. The people we help may end up helping us.
4. In the process of dying, we may be most alive.
5. The simplest gestures often produce the most magical results.
6. Everyone can be a hero.
7. All who wander are not lost (thanks to J. R. R. Tolkien for this one).

Can you think of others? In reading or listening to Ruiz's version of the story, which of the above do you think is the Most Important Thing, and why? Lipman goes on to explain that a story can have many "important things," that even the briefest of stories is rarely reducible to a single layer of possibilities, so we would argue that everything on our list is present in the story. But Lipman requires that we choose among them—and that, in the choosing, we will find the reason we need to tell this particular version of the story at this particular moment. One can imagine any of the MITs on the list being the center for a telling of this story and that each MIT will lead us to tell the story in a somewhat different way. We would include all of the necessary plot and character items (bus, summer day, driver, woman, need to find restaurant, fur coat, cancer revelation), but how we describe them, what we say about each, and how much time we give to each will change the story in very significant ways.

We have not said much about the actual vocal and physical techniques of telling this (or any story), and we will devote a separate chapter to some of the conventions for using voice, body, and space in performing literature. One reason we have not emphasized these elements in analyzing Ruiz's story is that we have been only an audience to it through the audio recording and our transcription. While we have described a few aspects of Ruiz's vocal delivery, we have not seen him tell the story nor heard him tell it in a face-to-face situation. Were you to tell this story to a live audience, where your bodily presence becomes an element of the situation, you would want to consider how to relate spatially to your audience, how to use gestures, visualization, pauses, and inflection of the voice to draw attention to the MIT you have chosen.

We have taken you through a fairly detailed analysis of the work story of another person. Ruiz's story falls somewhere between what we might think of as purely impromptu conversational storytelling, in which the storyteller begins telling a story without even perhaps an awareness that he or she is actually going to tell a story, and more theatrical or oratorical storytelling as a conscious art form (as found in the work of such performers as Garrison Keillor and David Sedaris, for example). Ruiz's performance is a result of working with StoryCorps, so we can imagine that the interviewer(s) may have helped him move beyond the "just the facts" or stream of consciousness reportage, perhaps asking him questions about his life or his work to trigger his memories and to heighten the level of detail and meaning. Now it is your turn to do the same.

There are a number of ways to approach this assignment (and your instructor may also give you specific directions). Allowing yourself to brainstorm, even to daydream, is a legitimate point of entry. Simply plant the word *work* in your mind and write or say whatever comes into your mind. Let your imagination take you where it wants to, at least initially, and trust that eventually a particular event or set of events asks to be given shape into a story. Another approach might be to serve as interviewers and interviewees with your classmates (perhaps best done with groups of no more than three people to allow ample time for each group member to receive careful and focused attention). You might come up with a simple, open-ended set of questions to help your group start talking about their work experiences. You are looking for those seemingly mundane but often transformative moments when the self as public and private being starts to emerge—when we move from one way of knowing who we are to another. For some people, such processes may be more comfortable alone in the intrapersonal domain of their private memories; for others, having a concrete, external, and supportive audience of one or two may provide just the stimulus or the object that will inspire them to begin turning experience into story. As interviewer, focus on not directing the interviewee or selecting and evaluating material; suspend judgment—your role is to serve as a medium through which the interviewee's thoughts, images, and experiences can emerge.

We recommend beginning this kind of adventure into storytelling by fashioning and performing a story from your own experience, but some of you may find it more accessible or less intimidating to tell a story based on someone else's experience. For some performers, the self-consciousness of focusing on their own life experiences can block the flow of creativity. If this is the case, you might find the group provides a transitional process. Agree to tell each other's stories, basing them initially on the same kind of interviewing process. One benefit of this approach is its potential for helping you become more empathic with regard to the experiences and perspectives of other people. In this kind of performance assignment, you will have to decide whether to tell the story as though you *are* the person you have interviewed (using the first person and essentially trying to become the person as a character) or whether to tell the story the way an omniscient narrator does, with the grammatical distance of the third person, but maintaining the rich details and sense of the inner experience of the character or characters, filtered through your own consciousness.

Also, be aware that, while it is true that any act of storytelling carries with it serious and important issues of ethical responsibility toward the characters, toward the actions, and toward the audience (think of the ways in which Ruiz respected the older passenger, honoring the meaning of her words and experiences), such ethical issues may become even more complex and crucial when we take on the responsibility and privilege of being allowed to tell the stories of other people.

Performing Found Texts: The Obituary

The last of our introductory performance approaches is perhaps the most unusual: the found text. The idea of found texts (originally poetry, although we are expanding the boundaries to include other genres) originates in the work of the surrealists in the early twentieth century, artists such as Marcel Duchamp and Pablo Picasso, who sought art in less familiar places and whose methods often involved less conventional "crafting" of the artwork—pushing the boundaries as far as possible from the classic haiku, with its highly specific mode of composition. In the composition of found texts, the "author" (if such a term is appropriate) literally "finds" a new text within a preexisting one, typically within a text not intentionally written to be artistic, such as technical and scientific materials or political testimony (for example, Tom Simon's *Poetry Under*

Oath, taken from the testimony of former president Bill Clinton in the Monica Lewinsky hearings). There can be a satiric edge in such "new" texts, in the juxtaposition of the original context of the words and the new meanings that can be derived when the words are stripped of their original purpose. There can also be a powerful sense of the ability of language to renew itself, over and over, each time it is uttered or read by a different person in a different place, and time.

One example from Bruce's classroom will suffice to demonstrate how poetry may be "found" and read by a new community. One day, leaving his apartment and walking to the front door of the building, he saw a sign that had been hastily made from a page of lined notebook paper:

DANGER!

The bees are angry
today, they are
dying.
Tomorrow they will
be gone.

Be careful.

He was struck by the ways in which this functional, cautionary sign seemed very much like the short poems he had been teaching in his classes. The shortness of the lines, not necessarily dictated by the beginnings and endings of sentences, but whose line breaks made certain words prominent ("today," "dying," "be gone"), the use of typographical and spatial appearance for emphasis (the use of capital letters for the first line, making it almost seem like a title; the skipping of a line before the final warning), and the content itself, focusing on death, mortality, anger, and temporality, made this seem as much a poem to him in some respects as the following text, which is by a well-known poet and frequently included in anthologies of poetry:

This Is Just to Say

I have eaten
the plums
that were in
the icebox

and which
you were probably
saving
for breakfast

Forgive me
they were delicious
so sweet
and so cold

This poem is by the twentieth-century American poet William Carlos Williams and was first published in 1934. Williams was well known for the crisp directness of his language and for his desire to use poetry to help readers apprehend the concreteness—the "thinginess," if you will—of the world; in this way, he was sometimes aligned with a group of people who called themselves Imagists and whose motto was "the thing itself."

As an experiment, Bruce brought both texts into his classes, stripping the Williams poem of the author's name, and offered them to his students as two poems by twentieth-century writers. He gave the students the Williams poem first and asked them whether it was a poem or not, and why. A lively discussion ensued, in which a fair number of students insisted that it was not a poem, as it wasn't "about" anything (by which they meant that there was, for them as readers, no apparent theme or major idea that gave meaning to the poem) and that its plain language kept it from the realm of poetry. Some of them said that they thought the writer had simply jotted this down as an apology to a housemate for stealing food that didn't belong to him.

When presented with the other poem (the "bee" poem), most of the class readily agreed that this was indeed clearly a poem. Not only did the eccentric placement of line breaks signal that the language was intended to be viewed in a special, non-everyday way, but this poem was clearly grappling with large questions of life and death and the struggle between the two through the traditional imagery and metaphors of nature and the brevity of insect life. One student likened this poem to one he had read by the Welsh poet Dylan Thomas, "Do Not Go Gentle into That Good Night," in which the speaker-poet addresses his dying father and admonishes him to live life fully and pugnaciously until the "dying of the light." For these students, the bee poem succeeded as a poem because it deployed language in a way that drew attention to its potentially submerged layers of meaning, its deployment of metaphor and figure of speech, its attention to form, and its serious theme. Some of them were outraged when Bruce revealed the source of this poem, feeling betrayed, as though Bruce had set them up; others were amused by the revelation and used this opportunity to express their suspicions about poetry in general; still others insisted that the revelation of the source of the bee poem did not contradict their evaluation of it as a poem. Into which camp do you think you fall, and why?

Bruce's point was not to make fun of his students but to get them to consider what made something a poem and how one might go about making/finding poetry in everyday circumstances. This is what the surrealists and their followers were also striving to do in their found poetry and other approaches, such as chance poetry, in which words were drawn at random out of a container. Try your own hand at "finding" a poem—think of all the different places you might look. Where on the Internet are likely sources for such poems? In mass and popular culture in general? How much tinkering (that is, editing, rearranging) of the original text can you do before you feel you are no longer "finding" poetry, but writing new material?

One source, which may seem morbid or eerie, is the obituary page, particularly obituaries that are not simply a recitation of the dead person's dates. Particularly in small-town newspapers, friends and family write the obituary for a loved one; many newspapers distinguish such writing by nonstaff members as "death notices," as opposed to obituaries written by professional journalists. While new texts—or what we might call submerged or emerging texts—can be found in both types, death notices can be particularly fascinating because the writers have a sense of the standard format but also a personal stake in expressing themselves.

Indeed, as Marilyn Johnson discusses in her lively and surprisingly entertaining book, *The Dead Beat: Lost Souls, Lucky Stiffs, and the Perverse Pleasures of Obituaries*, there are enough conventions in such writing to permit her to devise names for the formulaic elements. In this sense, the obituary combines both the formal elements of poetry with the plot- and character-driven elements of the narrative. Johnson sees the standard obituary as following this format and sequence:

1. the tombstone: the phrase, often following the person's name and comma, which serves as the primary identifier for the dead person;
2. the bad news: the announcement of death and its cause;

3. the song and dance: an elaboration of the person's life, prefer-
ably in a way that evokes the personality;

4. the stinging telegram: optional, a sentence at the end of the song
and dance that sums the person up and reminds us of his or her
demise;

5. the lifeboat: the list of survivors, often with an expression of
sentiment that summarizes their sense of loss.

Within obituaries, we can find multiple voices and perspectives, perhaps
even that of the deceased person (indeed, some people, knowing that
their death is coming, write their own obituaries, usually maintaining the
fiction of the third-person voice). Read the following obituary, found in
the local newspaper one morning. What aspects of it seem to you to take
it near or into the realm of the literary or the artistic, and why? How many
different voices can you hear competing for time and space in telling the
life of this man who has died? What is left unspoken? If the language
sounds like that written by one person, what can you infer about the character of this person, and how?

GERALD N. "JERRY" PROTTS

ITHACA—Went to celebrate his 57th birthday with his father,
Roger; his uncle, Maurice; aunt, Geraldine; and sister, Ruth Ann.
Jerry was born on February 17, 1949, in Ithaca, NY. Graduated in
1968 from Newfield Central School. He joined the U.S. Marine
Corps in June 1968 and was promoted to Lance Corporal. He
served in Vietnam where he was awarded the following medals,
Combat Action Ribbon, Vietnam Service Medal, Vietnamese Cross
of Gallantry and Vietnamese Campaign Medal. Jerry chose to live
in seclusion from his family for the past 25 years, but never left the
hearts of his mother, Gertrude (Ithaca); brothers, Ronald (Karen)
and Jim (Deborah) Protts of Ithaca, NY; sisters, Claudia Protts of
Newfield, NY, and Barbara Hall and friend Joe of Brookfield, CT,
plus many nieces and nephews. He was lost, then he was found.
Now at last he is home. Services to be held in the spring and will
be announced by Bangs Funeral Home. Interment will be in
Woodlawn Cemetery, Newfield, NY.
(*Ithaca Journal*, March 14, 2006, p. 4A)

There is much to note in this brief narrative of Mr. Protts's life (we have not changed any of the names or details, as the obituary was published in a public newspaper), much that goes beyond a mere listing of dates and places. Let's look at it the way we might look at a poem or narrative.

It begins with a very peculiar way of announcing death: "went to celebrate his 57th birthday with his father . . ." and three other relatives. In another context, such a sentence might lead off an item about a local celebration on the society page, but because of its placement in the paper, we know that the language is euphemistic, a more pleasant phrase substituted for what Johnson calls "the bad news." This reminds us of young readers of Louisa May Alcott's *Little Women* who think that the narrator's declaration that Beth "was well at last" meant that she had recovered from her illness, rather than understanding it as a Victorian convention meaning that she had died and, hence, had been restored to health in the afterlife. Indeed, the sentence in the Protts obituary initiates the reader into a Christian narrative of continuous life, wherein the death of the body is but a momentary interruption in the flow of the spirit through eternity. That he is described as having "gone" to meet the three relatives who preceded him in death creates a comforting narrative image of whom he will find on the "other side."

The second paragraph is a somewhat formal version of the "song and dance" (closer to what newspaper editor James Ferguson calls the "desperate chronology," a recitation of events rather than a full evocation of life). It begins by referring to Protts by his first name, "Jerry" (and note that this nickname has been announced previously in the headline), gives us his date and place of birth, his schooling and, in greater detail, his military service, including a list of honors he received for his time spent in the Vietnam War. It is clear that whoever wrote this obituary was proud of Protts's wartime service: there is a patriotic narrative present here.

But then the obituary takes a sudden turn; the next sentence might be a kind of elaboration of what Johnson calls the "stinging telegram": "Jerry chose to live in seclusion from his family for the past 25 years, but never left the hearts of [his family]." One can imagine an entire novel based on this one sentence, and myriad questions leap to mind: Why did he choose to live in seclusion? Was there a single, dramatic incident that precipitated this break? Is there some connection between the wartime service, so proudly announced in the previous sentence and this break from family? (If we assume the "25 years" is a round number, there may have been a period after the end of the war when he had not secluded himself from his family.) What is the tone of the sentence? Is it defensive (his family declaring that, even though he rejected them, they never rejected him)? Heartbroken (was there never a resolution while he was alive)? Hopeful (even though he placed himself at a distance from his family, was there still a sense in which he remained part of them)? Can you imagine the time and thought, perhaps even arguing among family members, it might have taken to agree on this sentence? And why was it important to them to announce it in the obituary? Can you write and perform a set of countertexts or intertexts, spoken by family members who have their own version of the break to tell or from Jerry's own point of view? Could different family members speak this sentence in different ways to suggest the sense of dialogue between them? Notice, too, that this "stinging telegram" is followed immediately by the "lifeboat," the list of his immediate survivors.

The obituary deviates from Johnson's conventional format in that it provides a kind of redemptive statement (not unlike the redemptive narrative we found in the work story of Ronald Ruiz, the bus driver). "He was lost, then he was found. Now at last he is home." There is the simple parallelism of short phrases, all using the verb "to be" and predicates of location ("lost," "found," "home"). The first sentence is a variation on a line from the Protestant hymn "Amazing Grace": "I once was lost, but now am found / Was blind, but now can see." It is likely that the choice of these words is not accidental; the cadence of these phrases is ingrained in the traditional Protestant imagination, and most readers of the age and upbringing of Jerry and his family would instantly recognize them. Their use in this context places Jerry's own narrative journey in the long traditions of the pilgrim's progress (the allegorical narrative written by the seventeenth-century author John Bunyan) in which the path toward salvation is seen as having twists and turns. That it ends with the phrase "Now at last he is home" completes the traditional Christian narrative of redemption in the house of God, that is, heaven. It also echoes poet Robert Louis Stevenson's famous epigraph for himself, "Here he lies where he longed to be; / Here is the sailor, home from the sea, / And the hunter, home from the hill." Whether this expresses Jerry's thoughts and feelings or simply those projected onto him by whoever wrote the obituary remains for us ambiguous.

There are a number of performance-based approaches one might take with this found text. One we have already imagined is to perform it as a complex narrative, with opportunities for suggestion of different voices and perspectives within it. If you decide on the voice of a single third-person narrator, someone who stands outside the story being told, how do you speak the lines that go beyond the "objective"? If you decide to take on the role of a family member, someone you imagine wrote the obituary for the family, who among the survivors might it be, and can you create a character for them, based on the writing? If you decide it is Jerry himself, looking back from the distance of the afterlife, how would you embody this perspective?

Other possibilities might involve fragmenting the text in different ways. Can you script it in a way that divides the lines between different perspectives? Can you imagine the different ways the same words might be said by different people involved in the plot of the story? Might repetition of some words, phrases, or sentences, spoken in different ways, suggest just how complicated Jerry's life was? Can you write a dialogue in which Jerry interjects his own thoughts and his own version at various points? Or a monologue spoken by him in response to this public depiction of his life (similar to the voices Edgar Lee Masters gave the dead in his well-known poetry collection, *Spoon River Anthology*, or the frequent dialogues between David Fisher, the funeral director, and the corpses he is embalming on the HBO series *Six Feet Under*).

The found text in this example is a very traditional form, found in every kind of newspaper, no matter how small the community, but it shows how the formal conventions can be re-viewed and reimagined in ways that reveal a number of embedded or hidden texts. In a sense, all obituaries may be seen as a way of trying to "find" someone who has, at least in a biomedical sense, been "lost." While the obituary may seem like an uncanny place to look for a text, it is one in which many participate — along with birth announcements and those involving such milestones as graduation, and marriage/commitment ceremonies. Any of them (as well as many other kinds of publicly available texts) can provide you the basis for a fascinating performance experience. These are the stories of our lives.

Conclusion

These four brief performance exercises — haiku, song lyric, work story, and found text/obituary — are only a handful of possible ways for you to begin your journey into the world of performance. Each offers a different emphasis, from the set texts of haiku, to the transformation of popular culture in song lyrics, to the everyday conversational impulse to talk about work, to the exploration of the artistic in the documentary domain of the obituary. Within the seventeen syllables of the haiku, we see the possibilities of a wide range of performances, just as in the end-of-life words of an obituary, we find the hope of making and telling of stories beyond the last breath. Whichever of these assignments pulls your interest, commit yourself, within the brevity of the text, to an authentic and vital performance!

KEY TERMS

haiku

impression management (theatricality)

Most Important Thing (Doug Lipman's concept)

narrator: first person (I, we), second person (you),
and third person (he, she, it, they)

prelinguistic

theatricality

telos

Chapter 3

PERFORMANCE CRITICISM: TALKING AND WRITING ABOUT PERFORMANCE

Performance criticism provides a methodological approach to spoken and written evaluation of live performances experienced in class and beyond. Students often want to know how to talk about and criticize each other's performances. What sort of things can be said, especially to a classmate, and often, a friend? It is natural to worry about the feelings of the performer, but it is also necessary to learn how to offer specific judgments of performances that are helpful. Many of the same considerations that affect how students go about the art of oral criticism of live performance obtain when writing critical essays about performances, whether your own or those of others. Most of us find it easy to utter words of praise, but to demonstrate how the praise was earned and to show why a performance is excellent, or good, or average, or poor is more difficult. The ability to offer negative criticism orally in a manner that benefits the performer requires real skill—you need to gauge how much criticism is appropriate at the time, whether the performer, in the moments immediately following a performance, is able to digest substantive criticism. How much negative criticism can be absorbed? Criticism directed to the political, social, and ethical issues involved in a performance require us to think not only about the performer and the critic, but also about the context of the performance, including race, gender, ethnicity, and political ideologies of the performer and the audience. Performance criticism at its best discusses or writes not only about individual aspects of performance but also about its social and political implications, and sometimes these issues can generate very controversial opinions and judgments. This chapter explores the role of the audience member as performance critic and the art of talking and writing analytically and in a socially responsible way about performance.

Student performers generally treasure the opportunity to receive constructive criticism from their classmates and teachers. Most of us hunger for praise and want to succeed and grow. If the classroom is only a lovefest, where everything said is positive, full of expressions such as "I loved your performance" or "Wow, that was amazing!" the students are likely to complain that although they love adulation, the criticism isn't helping them learn how to do better or to understand what made their intentions successful. There are not too many opportunities in live performance for performers to engage in frank discussion of what works and what doesn't, what is emerging and full of possibility, and what is hampering their effectiveness. Clearly, there are good reasons for performers to feel some apprehension about criticism. The performer wants candor but also wants to be respected. It is best if the critic can step into the performer's shoes, recognizing that this is a vulnerable moment and that the manner in which criticism, especially negative criticism, is offered can make all the difference.

Criticism done well can spark a lively dialogue between performers and audience as they grapple with questions about what a performance does and what it means. At its highest level, it offers performers insight into how they and the works they embody or construct are perceived by an audience, and it helps them discover what they might do to ensure that the performance conveys what they intended. It gives them ideas about what they can add, change, or delete from their performance so that it achieves its ends and communicates its meaning clearly to the audience. Discussion can make explicit the underlying assumptions on which the performance rests. For example, some performances are designed to feature issues of gender, queerness, transsexuality, race, nationality, or religion, and if these dimensions remain unexplored, the performer feels a loss. Students may not feel confident that the elements the audience is praising are worthy of the praise; in fact, the group may be praising something that had troubled them in the performance. For example, a student might perform a nonfictional text about his or her struggle with homophobia on campus or the discovery that a beloved uncle is gay, treating the account as though it were someone else's experience without revealing that he or she was the subject of the performance. Can you see how it would make a difference if the audience recognizes that the performances are autobiographical rather than biographical? If the class thinks they are discussing a phenomenon that they know well but that is not understood to have been experienced by the performer, they will talk quite differently than if they know that the story performed is the performer's own. Often, the deeper issues in a student's performance don't get talked about because it is so much easier to keep the discussion on a superficial level.

Performance criticism involves empathy as well as cognitive understanding on the part of the critic. Empathy is defined as the ability to stand in for and share the feelings of the performer and the characters. For example, consider the final lines of Dylan Thomas's elegy "Do Not Go Gentle into That Good Night": "And you, my father, on that sad height / Rage, rage against the dying of the light / do not go gentle into that good night." If you share the feelings of the speaker, who is poet and son, Dylan Thomas, as he begs his father not to die quietly but to rage against his end, you are empathizing with the speaker and with his condition as a son who has lost his father and as a man who is a poet struggling to find words on such a momentous occasion. Gender is not very important in this poem, at least not in its most universal aspect. Whether this is a son or a daughter mourning the loss of the father is not of much moment, at least not insofar as we are talking about the audience member's capacity to empathize with the speaker's loss. Cognitive understanding equips the student to analyze the performance and explain the ways in which it communicates meaning and the devices used to achieve the effects. A cognitive understanding of Thomas's poem involves your coming to terms with the progression of the imagery in the poem, the poem's themes, its poetic form, the villanelle, among other things. It also requires the audience to address the feelings aroused by the poem, both within the terms of the world of the poem and in the relationship created by the performer with the audience.

The student critic not only plays an empathic role, but can reaffirm a performance and empower its maker, take issue with aspects of a performance, or be brutal, taking power away from the performer or performance. Many students open their responses in class with a phrase like: "I loved your performance! It was awesome! You were so believable." This is a good opener but say more, add description and judgment. Describe what you saw and understood and why you "loved" the performance. We can learn from brutal performance criticism, but if we have a choice, we would rather learn in a nurturing and constructive environment. Think of examples outside of the classroom where you have seen a performer heckled or where you have seen the opposite, in a church, for example, where the congregation actively interacts with the preacher, affirming the words and performance of the preacher. You can probably think of many examples where an audience member is angered by a performance and writes a sharply negative review or sends letters to the editor or to the church board, expressing his or her outrage at the speaker or performer. Or think about a rock concert where members of the audience rise to extreme heights of emotion, expressing themselves physically as well as vocally as they convey their enthusiasm or disgust. Often the audience members in public amphitheaters or rock concerts scream with enthusiasm or trash the event verbally, and sometimes physically. In festivals devoted to Irish music, Celtic rock performers enthrall audiences, who pick each other up and over their heads, passing each other's bodies over the bodies of others—surfing, it is called—in their excitement. In a church where call and response takes place, can you see how an exclamation such as "amen, brother!" and a crescendo of affirming expressions from the audience can influence the preacher, making him or her press harder and rise to a feverish pitch while the congregation is energized and rises, often chanting and almost dancing, to affirm the power of the word? The audience/critic partially shapes the performance through the act of reviewing, by speaking and writing of meanings that may have been only latent in the performance. In these cases, an audience member's response to a performance begins to shape the response of others, solidifying some responses and silencing others.

Think about the dynamics of the audience in the classroom or imagine how an audience might have responded to performances of poems or narratives described in chapters 1 and 2. You may recall times when the audience was completely thrilled by a performance. And undoubtedly you can remember times when some of the audience members were inattentive, distracted, whispering to each other, or conveying by some bodily gesture—nervous tapping of the foot or fussing with a book bag or a purse—that they did not like the performance or were bored by it. Of course, this affects others in the audience and can take its toll on the performer. We will talk more later about the ways the performative act of criticism and audience behaviors during performance collaborate with or against the performance itself in the act of making multiple meanings.

For now, note that a written evaluation of a performance and an oral one have some distinctive differences. In an oral discussion, the process is dynamic and evaluators often revise and change their responses to a performance on the basis of comments of other audience members. The criticism can be quite fluid, suggestive, and evolving. Often performers enter into the discussion, shedding light on their performance, sharing with the audience the reasons behind some of their choices or asking the audience whether alternatives they had considered might have been more effective. Of course, sometimes performers simply disagree with the responses from the audience. A written evaluation of a performance by other class members can offer a range of possible interpretations, but it is less fluid and does not have the immediacy of exchange that occurs in oral reviews. A very useful assignment is one that asks the performers themselves to write about their performance process, from rehearsal through performance to postperformance discussions, commenting on how they approached their performance, what they felt worked and did not work, and how they responded to the criticisms from the class.

Written evaluations or reviews can take different forms. Your instructor may indicate the kind of response, written or oral, that is wanted. Student writers can elect to use a narrative mode of expression to tell about their experience of the performance and the way they reacted to it. Such a piece of performative criticism places emphasis on the critic's role as a co-witness or co-collaborator in the construction of the meaning of the performance. Or the written response might take the form of a probe, a review, or a report. The probe generally isolates one aspect of the performance or the response it elicited and examines it; it may be written as a series of impressions, or it may take the form of a note to the performer; it might be highly idiosyncratic. A review usually offers both a description of the overall event and a judgmental assessment of the performance. A report about a performance may focus on a theme or contain the backstory of the performance, tracing how it developed from the time the performer first decided to perform the selection, through early rehearsal and memorization of it, to the point when the performance became set and refined for the public presentation. It may concern itself less with the evaluative aspect of the performance's content and focus more on a historical account of the performance, its evolution, rendition, and impact.

Often students ask us whether it is permissible to write in the first person. We heartily encourage you to do so. You are writing about your own performances as well as those of your classmates, and you are describing your processes and talking about yourself. There is no reason to go to great lengths to avoid using the personal pronoun. Avoid writing in the passive voice; use strong verbs and nouns, words that are forceful and direct. In addition, take time to develop and support your ideas with lively examples to illustrate the points in your argument, showing what you mean and what you do not mean. For class, you may be writing lengthier essays than the typical review.

Whether the evaluation is written or oral, it should reflect the seriousness of the student critic's attention to the performance. A good critic learns to watch with rapt attention and to write in "excited reverie," to borrow a phrase from poet W. B. Yeats. Memory—the power to recall, albeit often imperfectly, selectively, and incompletely—and desire—the yearning of libido so keenly excited by sensory stimuli—are integral to criticism. Empathy, too, is as essential to good criticism as the capacity to be disinterested and objective. You may want to write a fiercely polemical kind of criticism: you may be committed to an agenda for social change and wish to use the platform of your writing to press your case. Many scholars of performance studies have explicitly committed themselves to being active agents of social change. By all means, use your voice to fight for what you believe, but always remember to anticipate your most intelligent, most forceful opponents, confront their best arguments against your position, and drive your argument home. Finally, a good critic has an ethical responsibility to be fair.

Being an Audience Member Responding to a Performance

Witnessing performance and participating in the act of criticism actively involves the class in what performance scholars sometimes refer to as "audiencing." Performance scholar Linda Park-Fuller writes about audiencing, using the term to define the active process audience members engage in when they experience a performance and, later, become involved in talkbacks or write reviews of the performance. She describes a trend in recent performance scholarship that prefers *audiencing* to other words, such as *spectator* or *viewer*, to describe an audience's act of perceiving or witnessing a performance. She argues that the term is a more supple descriptive term than the other two in that it gives agency to the audience member. The term is part of a conceptual view of audience members as part of a process of performance in which performer and audience members act as collaborators to make meaning. The term perceives audience members as doing something active in contrast to merely watching as though they do not actually alter or affect the thing they are watching as they watch it. Audience members contribute actively to performances even when they adhere to the etiquette of conventional Western theatergoers.

If you have experienced an audience member who is not conversant with the conventions and standards or who does not share them, coming from a different culture and participating in different practices as an audience member, you can quickly see the extent to which our theater assumes conformity with its Western audience's expectations. We recall a performance attended by an audience including a number of disabled individuals that took place on a black-box stage configured with the audience seated on raked bleachers on three sides of the space on the same plane as the stage. Several audience members were so excited by the stimulus of the event that when a clothesline was stretched across part of the stage, they stood up and started reaching out to play with it. The chaperone of the group became rattled and started shuffling around, speaking loudly to some of the group, trying to gain their attention. The program onstage continued, but some audience members lost their bearings, torn between watching the disruption and keeping their attention on the stage. The stage performers struggled valiantly to keep their focus and disregard the interference, but at times throughout the show the boundaries between stage and audience threatened to collapse as the audience members' behaviors challenged the twice-performed behaviors being enacted on the stage.

In cases such as this, we are reminded of how powerfully the social etiquette of being an audience member governs the behavior of audiences at staged theatrical events in Western countries. In a conventional performance situation, the audience is expected to watch the performance, to do so silently, with only occasional noises such as laughs, coughs, gasps, and whispers allowed. Audiences are routinely and ritualistically asked by stage managers to turn off cell phones and other electronic devices that can be disruptive. Sometimes they are warned that a performance contains controversial, sexually explicit material that may be offensive to viewers. If the performance is participatory or experimental and designed to involve the audience members, the conventions governing the way in which the audience is asked to participate are explicit and normally the audience will respect them. Even where the audience has a fuller, more participatory role, conventions constrain the range of responses expressed by an audience. Some of these same injunctions obtain in classrooms, but here we need to be mindful of the need to preserve academic freedom as a privileged value when trying to judge what can and cannot be shared in performances in institutional and classroom settings.

Presentational Versus Representational Modes of Performance

When writing about performances, it is important to take into account the conventions the performer relies on in their presentational and representational styles and also to take note of the way the performer uses the audience, employs spaces, and manipulates the environment through other means such as live or electronic sound, music, videotapes, computer-driven projected images, pictures, blackboards, video screens, and so forth. The term *presentational* refers to the conventions and devices the performer uses to utter or figure forth the performance to an audience, to present or make visible the performative act. *Representational* refers to the manner in which the world or objects are re-presented, imitated, shown anew or again, to an audience.

To understand the distinction between these two modes, consider a performance of Robert Browning's poem "My Last Duchess," where a performer chooses to use the lectern and speak the first lines of the poem: "That's My Last Duchess painted on the wall, / looking as if she were alive . . ." If the poem is rendered in the presentational mode, the performer suggests rather than enacts the character of the duke. In this mode, the lectern performer conveys the illusion of the scene between the duke and the emissary. He or she speaks the duke's lines out toward the audience while establishing the scene of the poem as if it were taking place, not onstage, but out in front of the stage, in a central position in the room, about two thirds of the way toward the back of the hall and slightly above the heads of the audience. Two technical terms, *placement* and *locus*, are used to refer to conventions that assist the performer in firmly establishing the illusion of these imagined characters and the audience in understanding who is speaking to whom.

If the poem is performed as a dramatic monologue, the performer takes on or acts the role of the duke and speaks his lines, addressing them to the emissary. In this case, the performer places the action on the stage or in the front of the room in which the performance takes place. In the presentational mode alluded to above, the performer will "suggest," not "embody," the duke, allowing the audience to imagine him rather than see a representation or imitation of him physically present. In other words, the performer suggests, or evokes, or "presents" the character, rather than representing the character.

In a representational performance of this work, the performer acts out the role of the duke, playing him there on the stage or in front of the class, using conventions of verisimilitude to make us see in his or her imitation of the character an actual representation of the duke. In this mode, the actor might actually dress as the duke, using period costumes, and use pieces of stage furniture to create the sense of a room, placing the portrait of the duchess on the back wall of the stage space, with a chair in front of it in which he might place the emissary who is addressed by the duke. At the end of the poem, when the duke asks the emissary to rise and shows him a sculpture that he has commissioned, cast in bronze, the actor might usher the emissary through a staged gallery.

This distinction between modes of performance becomes important to consider when discussing and evaluating a performance or writing about it. Bert O. States, in *Great Reckonings in Little Rooms: On the Phenomenology of Theater*, offers excellent examples of presentational versus representational modes, drawing important distinctions between the narrative mode and the dramatic mode. You will also want to think about examples that allow you to contrast the lyrical mode and narrative mode in performance with the dramatic mode.

Another way we can think about the distinction between presentation (sometimes called suggestion) and representation is to recall the discussion in chapter 1 of dramatic analysis and Burke's pentad and the distinctions we made when we discussed the lyrical, narrative, and dramatic modes. In chapter 2, we used haiku, obituaries, and song lyrics to show the ways in which the lyrical, dramatic, and epic modes function. Performers often choose to use conventions of suggestion (presentation) when they do solo lectern performances of poems written in the lyric mode and want to capture the delicacy and uniqueness of the speaking voice. The representational mode of performance places the speaker-as-character on the stage, in front of the audience, rather than being invoked and placed in an imaginary position in the space above the heads of the audience and only suggested, not represented by the actor on the stage. We are dwelling on this distinction in order to show you why description is a crucial component of good criticism. When writing about performance or discussing it, it is important to be as precise as possible in describing the performance act you have witnessed. The purpose of description is to evolve, in common with your audience, an understanding of what has been seen and what has not been seen in the performance. Performances will always give rise to multiple understandings, but part of the richness of these understandings derives from the subsequent description of the ephemeral live performance event.

The role of the audience often begins considerably in advance of actually witnessing the performance and it continues after the performance, taking into account the immediate postperformance situation when students talk about a performance and later, write about it. Through memory, playback, further discussions, or reading reviews and criticism, the act of being an active audience member, or audiencing, to use Park-Fuller's term, continues to give new shape and meaning to the event recalled.

An audience has expectations regarding what they are going to see. How does this process work in your class? What do you know about a performance before you experience it in your role as a classroom audience member? What factors contribute to your expectations about the performance? Most of you will recognize that if you have seen the work of the performer before, or if you know the performer, if he or she is your friend, it will affect what you expect and the degree to which you look forward to or resist the performance. Similarly, you may be influenced by the work that is being performed if you have read or studied it before or if you have seen other performances of it, or you may have performed it in a different setting yourself. It may be based on a text you like, or dislike.

There are personal, private factors specific to you that affect how you feel when you go to a performance. Sometimes a performance strikes such a raw chord in audience members that they find it difficult to separate their own emotional circumstances from the performance they are witnessing. A poem exploring death, for example, is likely to affect an audience member who has just experienced the death of someone very close. In such cases, students watching the performance begin to lose themselves in their own private feelings of loss and can move quite far from the performance. This phenomenon of confusing one's own emotions for the emotions in the performance piece or text is referred to as the "affective fallacy," a term W. K. Wimsatt and Monroe Beardsley define and discuss in *The Verbal Icon: Studies in the Meaning of Poetry*. Nowadays, we are less inclined to refer to this attribution of our own personal emotions to the performance as a philosophical fallacy. Rather, we ask that students distinguish between the feelings the performance is likely to call up in a community audience and the very private feelings that are awakened within the individual audience members by virtue of their having imposed their own private feelings, their own affects, on the performance to the exclusion of the work's emotional field.

Politically engaged, activist performances—whether they are challenging hegemonic ideologies, patriarchal power structures, heterosexual normative attitudes toward sexuality, or interrogating ideas about hypermasculinity, sexuality, and race—require their audiences to involve themselves in their political and ideological assumptions with the intent to bring about social change. Many of these performances, taking their impetus from performance studies and fields such as cultural studies, challenge the status quo. The critic describing and analyzing these performances must be conversant with their underlying assumptions and the set of conventions they employ to advance an agenda, which gained increasing attention by theorists such as Augusto Boal, Henry Louis Gates Jr., and performance studies scholars Dwight Conquergood, E. Patrick Johnson, Mindy Fenske, and D. Soyini Madison. In addition, performances that take as their subject other people, especially from different cultures, need to be particularly attentive to still another constituency, namely the subjects themselves. Madison, who has done considerable research and performance in Ghana, Africa, writes movingly about the "performance of possibilities" and the ways in which performances can become an integral part of a process to produce political and social change on national and global stages.

In addition, there are external realities—the performance environment, among others—that influence how you feel. Also, your private memories triggered by the production and your personal desires play an active role in fueling or shaping your perceptions. They, too, can figure importantly in your criticism of a performance and are part of the performance environment. Sometimes the room in which the performance takes place, or the acoustics of the room, or its lighting or lack thereof hinder or enhance the performance. You might want to take note of such elements in your response. Sometimes, your own mood at the time you see a performance or emotions evoked by the performance but too private to mention figure in your response. Of the utterly private feelings, you may simply want to state that personal issues that you do not want to divulge were excited by the production and affected how you responded. Obviously, if you are willing to elaborate on these kinds of responses, it would be valuable to the performer and other audience members. Sometimes a performance calls forth frightening or happy but again very private emotions which have deep significance to you, based on your own personal history, but which may not be all that useful to others. You must judge whether it is useful to the performer and audience to discuss these kinds of highly personal, sometimes idiosyncratic responses.

Performers quickly come to recognize some of the ways in which an audience actively contributes to the shape of a performance. A performer can feel the audience's energy level, its degree of interest in the performance. Sometimes the performer knows this because the audience makes little or loud noises, laughs or gasps, during the performance itself; or the room becomes exceptionally still, with the audience held taut, nearly breathless and fully attentive to every word, the smallest gesture, and every sound. A performer, looking out at the audience, may search for a face that is animated and play to it. If an audience is restless or bored, the performer generally knows it and tries to grab the audience's attention. Sometimes this leads to a forced performance; the audience sees the performer straining for a laugh or milking an emotional moment for all it is worth, sensing that the audience's attention is lost. Can you recall times when you have seen this happen? At other times, the audience members may be fans or friends of the performers, and it is common then to hear cheers, whistles, and stamping of feet when a performer comes onstage. Such enthusiasm palpably raises the spirits of both the performers and, usually, the other audience members, making us more likely to mold ourselves into an audience community, highly receptive to the event offered.

But the opposite can also happen. From the perspective of an audience member, you can probably recall situations when you felt you were fighting or struggling to retain your own response to a performance because the reactions of other audience members to the event threatened to overwhelm your own and affect your feelings, sometimes in ways you didn't like. A friend sitting beside you and visibly, if not audibly, disliking the performance or withdrawing from it can give you a feeling of oppression, especially if you are inclined to like what you are seeing. Most audience members don't want to be distracted or taken away from their own emotional or intellectual response because they are being unduly influenced during the performance by the reactions of others, often quite proximate to them in the audience. An overly enthusiastic audience, an audience that seems to have cliques of people who evince groupie behavior toward the performer, can leave other audience members feeling quite cold toward the performance, feeling left out, as though their lack of membership in the clique leaves little room for their response to the performance. Usually they know all too well what they feel about the imposition of the others on them.

All these aspects of audience behavior contribute to the dynamics of an audience and partly account for the reasons why most performers find themselves alternately loving and hating the audience, which is so difficult to know, understand, and control and yet so vital to the magic of performance. Audiences also pose a challenge to the critic. The critic often struggles to interpret the audience's reactions to a performance. Sometimes, when the critic's response to a performance is markedly different from the response of others in the audience, critics report that they are fearful that their response will be contaminated by other people's reactions. It is often difficult to trust one's own reaction or response, especially when other audience members in spoken and unspoken ways are threatening to influence it.

All the elements discussed above are legitimately included in the experience of an audience at a performance event. Your performance criticism will want to recognize some, if not all, of these elements.

The Goals of Performance Criticism

How, then, should you, as classmates and students engaged in being an active audience, go about performing your role and offering performance criticism? The goal of performance criticism in a classroom or in written evaluations is threefold: 1) to describe for the performer in minute detail what you as an audience member saw, heard, understood, and felt during the performance, and if touch and smell were important to your response, they, too, should be included; 2) to evaluate, or judge, the performance by saying what succeeds and what fails; and 3) to create a synergistic, open-ended dialogue between performer and audience to constitute as a community multiple understandings of the emergent meanings in a performance. Of course, the criticism may also attempt to describe and discuss what the class as a whole or as a set of separate communities felt during the performance and afterward.

We deliberately use the words *succeeds* and *fails* because we think it is disingenuous and not very helpful to use less incisive language. Over many years, in many contexts, our students and colleagues have told us, and we believe ourselves, that critics of performance should be forthright and honest. Performance, being a public and very visible act, occasions strong emotions and beliefs. Most performers know all too well what it feels like to fail at what they hoped to create, just as they know the thrill of accomplishment. Rather than speaking in euphemisms or describing a performance as "interesting" to avoid saying something more negative but accurate, we have decided to use the words *fail* and *succeed*, trusting that they will be understood as constructive, not destructive, in their intent. While saying this, we know full well that in the thrill of a performance, often the audience describes the performance as "wonderful," "inspired," or "awesome." And often the words are just, but to demonstrate what one means and how these words are just and not merely hyperbolic, it is helpful to always follow them with an example of what it was that the performer did to warrant such words of praise.

Performance criticism recognizes the collaborative role of an audience in the performance situation and examines the performer's process or the group's processes. The performer's process includes the preperformance, performance, and postperformance stages. The criticism should reveal whether the performance seemed to realize its ends, its intentions, or whether some things fell short or exceeded expectations. It can comment on the nature of performance as a process, how some of the things that happened seemed unplanned or unfocused while other moments exhibited powerful command on the part of the performer. The performance criticism takes as its object the actual performance in class, but it often makes reference to things that happened during rehearsal or discoveries made during the postperformance discussion. It can also comment on how the audience seemed to experience the performance. When performers tackle a difficult subject or issues that polarize the audience, it is particularly useful to try to capture the range of responses in the audience. In addition to describing the different responses of the audience, try to explore them, attempting to account for some of the differences and examining the values and beliefs that underlie them. Take advantage of the educational opportunities these kinds of performances create; don't shy away from controversial material or unpopular ideas; discuss them, even at the risk of offending some.

Trust in the Classroom

Before discussing the nature of performance criticism, we want to say a few words about the optimal environment for it. Often performers will quickly tell audiences and classes that they want criticism, but they also fear it. Few students or faculty have egos strong enough to easily absorb a barrage of negative criticisms in response to their work. On the other hand, as we mentioned earlier, students frequently complain that class discussions of their work are too bland, or too generous, too congratulatory, and lacking in criticism. Students are eager to know more about what each and every audience member felt, possibly resenting the way in which a critical response to a performance is often prematurely "locked in." It is as though the audience begins to cohere around a certain set of responses, and some starkly different attitudes toward a performance go unuttered. The performer is often left wondering whether the views expressed actually do represent what the bulk of the audience felt or whether there is a broader range of responses, some of which were not expressed. Sometimes an audience just does not seem to "get it." The performer needs to understand why not, but also wants to have a chance to direct the audience to the performer's meaning, explaining part of it, encouraging the audience to trust other, latent responses they may have had. Outside the classroom, audiences do not often have the opportunity to know what the performer wanted, except insofar as it is realized in performance, so it is worth trying to glean the multiple understandings audiences have of a performance absent any overt commentary by the performer trying to shape their response. However, even as we write this, we want to welcome the addition of the performer's commentary. Both are needed to do justice to an artistic work, but they mean different things, and in some instances, the performer may take the position that the work speaks for itself and wish to remain silent about their own views or motives while they wait to see how they were understood. One of the beauties of the instructional technologies offered through the Internet, with its blogs and websites like Blackboard, is that student performers can quickly elicit responses from audience members and are likely to receive a much fuller range of views than in the past, when we often encouraged students to write comments for each other during class as they watched a performance, to be given to the performer at the end of class.

In the ideal classroom, the class over time develops a sense of trust, and performers become more adept at telling each other what worked and did not work in a performance. Students learn to offer to each other the kind of criticism they privately hope the others will offer them. Here we are not talking about the student loving to be praised and wanting to hear only about what worked. Of course, we all love this and want to be reinforced and praised, but we also want to be respected and given the truth about what audience members felt or thought. In live performance events, it is quite rare to have an audience that can speak candidly with the performer about their work. The beauty of the classroom situation or written criticism is that both afford an opportunity to take risks and take advantage of frank criticism, both positive and negative.

Ask yourself what would help you the most in perfecting your performance persona and urge your classmates to provide you with the kind of criticism that can help you achieve your goals. Think about one of your recent performances. Did you accomplish what you set out to do? If so, how and in what ways? If not, why, and what could you have done to improve it?

A good discussion of your performance will be a discussion that provides you with feedback that helps you judge your own work. Consequently, in talking about performance or writing about it, you need to learn to describe a performance carefully, explaining what you saw. If you encounter difficulties as you try to describe the performance accurately, you need to name these difficulties, pursue them, reveal what you are thinking, what evidence you rally to support your contentions, what factors trouble your argument, leading you to think that maybe there is something more at work than you recognize. It is far more important to capture the complexity of the experience than to write a neat explanation that has actually masked, if not omitted, references to parts of the performance that were difficult to describe, explain, or judge.

Be mindful that performance is transitory and its meaning is fluid, although most would agree that there are limits to the meanings that can be attributed to a performance. It is possible to talk about what a performance means in a general sense, capturing the meaning of the piece that the audience as a whole is likely to agree has achieved a sort of consensus, while acknowledging that, of course, many private meanings will also obtain among the individuals that may well not be shared by many others because their very nature is unique to the individual's personal experience. Clearly, as individuals, many of the members that make up the communal audience may have quite different reactions to a performance. Some members will "love" a performance that others remained indifferent to or even "hated" or disliked. Good performance criticism should try to capture these different reactions while at the same time seeking a consensus of sorts in the audience's responses. Performers faced with varied responses to their work should try to understand the sources of the differences and judge for themselves how to handle them.

Teachers and students employ different approaches to facilitate the criticism of performances and create a climate conducive to caring and constructive criticism "with an edge." By "edge" we mean "bite," but in a good sense. Often it is the keen observations about what works and doesn't work or the emotionally strong reactions of a class member that, in fact, spark a critical discussion and bring insight into the work under discussion. Some of the performances that seem at first to fail thoroughly offer the most instructive moments of a class and contribute the most to a performer's growth. A daring disaster is preferable to a bland, timid, or conventional performance. Students should also take advantage of opportunities to re-perform. Through re-performance, a student gets another chance to make the performance work. Sometimes in class, memorization fails or a student, underrehearsed, loses focus in the middle of the performance or becomes so concerned about the ending that he or she muffs it. These are the kinds of occasions when the chance to re-perform has great benefit. Nothing is more frustrating to a performer than to have a performance that had worked well in rehearsal misfire and go very badly in front of the real audience. You may want to ask your instructor to consider permitting re-performances if time allows.

The Role of the Buddy or Performance Group

Because criticism of something as personal to performers as their own embodied performance can be very sensitive, teachers often establish a buddy system or performance groups, where each performer is assigned a buddy or a group, sometimes for just a single performance or for the duration of the term, if logistics and schedules permit. The buddy is expected to observe at least one rehearsal of the piece, and the buddy or group leads the postperformance class discussion of the performance. Class time is scarce and students often get no more than three to five minutes of discussion of their work, so it can be helpful to have the buddy frame a leading question that will focus the class's responses, showing the performer what they did or did not understand about the performance. Or the buddy might simply lead class discussion, only offering their own view if the class is slow to respond or if their view was not voiced by anyone else in the class. Usually, the buddies are discouraged from offering their own views in class at the expense of hearing from other audience members, but they may point the class to fruitful areas of discussion about the performance based on their more extensive experience of the performance, since they saw it during rehearsal. In addition, buddies are frequently assigned to write a brief, one-page response to the performance that can be shared with the other members of the class through an exchange of e-mails or online. Others can then chime in, sharing their views.

This approach to class discussion of performance is highly interactive, and it gives the buddy the opportunity to see the performance at least twice before being asked to describe and evaluate it. When the buddy relationship works best, the buddy acts as a director for the student performer, giving feedback during the rehearsal which enables the student performer to refine the performance, trying different approaches in rehearsal before "locking in" the performance that they intend to present to the class.

The instructor, too, plays a role in evaluating the performances seen in class. Some instructors choose to share their commentary and grades with the student, often outside of class, either in the form of a written evaluation or oral feedback. Other teachers may join the class in discussing and evaluating the performance. The nature of this sharing varies: some teachers wait until the other students have given their responses before offering their own; others join in the discussion right from the start. Often teachers find it is useful to distinguish between descriptive and evaluative commentary, first offering the performer a description of what he or she did and then following it with more evaluative judgments. This approach allows the student performer to compare how the teacher describes the performance with the way in which the performer intended it to be perceived and received.

In other cases, the class is encouraged to work in small groups or as a whole in offering oral, and sometimes written, feedback to the performer. Sometimes criticism takes the form of a playback, where another group of students stand in for the performer and re-perform the performance for the performer, opening up other avenues of discussion.

What should be included in a rich, analytic performance criticism? For the purpose of this discussion, we are considering the kind of performance criticism useful to an introductory class where performances will be based on literary and cultural texts. The performances may be solo or group, they may be minimalist or more elaborate, involving props, media, lights, sound, and costume. They are offered to a class in an ordinary classroom or possibly an outdoor space. Whether the performances are subsequently taken to larger, more public arenas is a matter for the performers, teachers, and audience to decide. Earlier we stated that the criticism should involve three components: descriptive, evaluative, and speculative, and be dialogic and open-ended. Let us now consider these.

Descriptive Criticism

How the Performance Looked

In descriptive criticism, the students try to tell the performer how the performer looked and sounded and what the audience saw and heard. They talk about how the performance appeared in its physical, external dimensions — how it was staged, whether it employed a lectern or whether the performance was produced in a performance space, complete with props, costumes, and stage furniture. The description will state whether there was a single character or narrator or multiple characters; it will describe how the performer(s) looked, what they were doing with their bodies, what the lighting was like, and how they used their voice, video, and sound. If the performance involved the use of visual media, this element would also be included in a description of the physical appearance of the performance.

The description of the performance can also address textual matters and describe the way in which the performer presented the fictive, poetic, or cultural world of their performance. How was the text used in the stage space? What mode of performance did the performer employ — lyric, epic, or dramatic? Within the world of the text, describe the time of the story and the time of the discourse as the performer handled it.

Gender   The criticism will also want to consider issues of gender. Gender refers to culturally and socially conditioned views of what is considered feminine or masculine. Individuals who behave in a way that seems contrary to the gender ascribed to them are described as gender nonconforming. Gender, unlike sex, is a construction; it is not a result of one's sex, although the concepts are often thought of as being coterminous. It involves a complex set of psychological and political situations that result from or are created by such constructions. Think about the assumptions you make regarding behaviors attributed to gender. Can you describe some behaviors that are typically considered feminine or masculine? Can you think of individuals, including perhaps yourself, who behave in ways that are gender nonconforming? What is happening when a woman teacher is described as being "tough as nails" or "castrating"? Many letters of recommendation for male students who aspire to be scientists describe the student as "aggressive," "forceful," "tough-minded," and as someone who "goes for the jugular." These attributes are considered complimentary. Can the same terms be used to describe a woman scientist's behavior? And, if they are, are they likewise complimentary? Is it more likely that a different vocabulary will be employed, one that is "softer," less focused on aggression and leadership? What, for example, are the assumptions implied when a man is described as "sensitive and artistic"? Think of examples that you find in your own culture, in newspapers, and in the media. What do the terms *masculine* and *feminine* mean to you?

Judith Butler, in *Gender Trouble: Feminism and the Subversion of Identity*, writes that "gender ought not to be construed as a stable identity or locus of agency from which various acts follow: rather, gender is an identity tenuously constituted in time, instituted in an exterior space through a *stylized repetition of acts*" (p. 140). She also writes that gender is "a set of repeated acts within a highly regulatory frame that congeal over time to produce the appearance of substance, or a natural source of being" (p. 33). To understand this concept, it is useful to contrast the idea of gender with that of sex. Sex refers to purely biological differences, such as genitalia and the ability to bear children. We typically divide people into two categories—male and female—but some biologists and psychologists would argue that this division is too restrictive. Biologist Anne Fausto-Sterling proposes that there may be as many as six sexes. In past times, people who possessed the physical features of both males and females were referred to as hermaphrodites. Today, scientists prefer the term *intersex* to refer to individuals who have either sexual characteristics of both males and females or ambiguous sexual characteristics. Some individuals believe that they were born into a body that is physically different from their own sense of sexual identity; they often refer to themselves as transsexual.

When a female performer plays a male character, such as Sarah Bernhardt when she played Hamlet, it is clear that she performed across sex. It can also be said that she performed across gender. If a female student plays the role of a very masculine woman, the discussion of the masculine traits is part of a discussion of gender; similarly, feminine characteristics performed by a man are also expressions of gender. The same character, or person, may enact different genders. It is also important to recognize that gender behaviors are historically and geographically defined.

There are critics such as Judith Butler who resist the categorization implied by terms such as *gender* or *sexuality*, arguing that the categories are themselves artificial and simply perpetuate socially constructed dualisms. For our purposes, the terminology is useful for referring to the way characters are represented or presented in performance. It is worth noting, as Butler does, that gender, which is constituted in social and temporal space, has the appearance of substance but is in fact constructed and reveals a performative accomplishment which the ordinary audience and performers come to believe in, acting as though it were real while actually it is not. Gender as a critical term is also useful in performance since very often ideas about how gender expresses itself inform the way a performer plays a part, or shifts gendered behaviors within a single body and performance.

Sexuality The term *sexuality* refers to one's sense of erotic being, one's attitude toward sexual behavior, and one's attraction to others, whether the same or other sex. Terms of sexuality are useful when describing performances and performers' behaviors and attitudes. It is important to keep in mind that these categories have also been historically constructed and named. For example, the word *homosexual* did not exist until the late nineteenth century. Similarly, some individuals today would eschew any such labeling to describe their own sexuality. For some, the sex of the individual to whom they are attracted may be less important than other characteristics, such as hair color, body type, and personality.

Race Race, too, is something worthy of discussion in performances. The term *race* is also socially constructed, and since it lacks a basis in biology, it is often treated as a suspect term. It is a problematic word that refers to human beings in physical and cultural terms, and it frequently occurs in anthropological, sociological, and medical contexts. The term carries a great deal of negative, painful, and oppressive baggage, since race in the history of the United States was often used unjustly to distinguish between peoples who are so-called fully human from those said to be less than human. We refer here to the term as it is used in the Constitution of the United States or as it has often been invoked in the context of affirmative action.

A leading black feminist scholar, bell hooks, argues persuasively that any consideration of race needs to be positioned in the context of class and sex. She takes great pains to differentiate between the issues of black feminist women and white feminist women, and she is quick to point out that feminism is not something that is exclusive to women but also includes males; and to understand and speak of blackness in the United States, she insists, also requires us to understand whiteness; the two terms are interdependent. In her compelling book *Ain't I a Woman*, she discusses issues of the black female and black woman in the context of sexism, racism, and feminism in America and Western hegemonic cultures. You may find her writings useful to a deeper exploration of the social and political significance of the discussion of racism, sexism, and feminism in contemporary American society.

The term *race* is useful to us as performance scholars because it permits us to explore what is meant and not meant when stereotypical behaviors that are said to be racial characteristics are attributed to speakers and characters in performance. Think about how performances you have seen convey whiteness or blackness and how these constructions have informed your understanding of the performance. You may also want to experiment with playing these racial stereotypes. You may also decide, as have many other performers, that to draw a distinction in performance behaviors based on a character's race is itself a racist move and, therefore, refuse to allow your performance choices to be assessed with regard to these kinds of considerations.

Ethnicity Another term that denotes people or behaviors based on cultural similarities or differences is the term *ethnicity*, which describes the national heritage and immigration patterns of groups of people sharing a culture and living in close proximity. When we refer to Latino culture or Asian American culture or Anglo-American culture, we are drawing distinctions based on ethnicity. You might want to think also about nationalities, such as Irish, Arab, French, Polish, or others, and consider how they demonstrate ethnicity.

Race in a Poem by Langston Hughes

Let us look at a poem by Langston Hughes, a poet of the Harlem Renaissance who drew liberally on blues and spirituals and whose poems were often set to music. Consider that you are a performer who has chosen to perform Hughes's "The Weary Blues," written in 1926 and set on Lenox Avenue, a major street in Harlem in New York.

The Weary Blues

Droning a drowsy syncopated tune,
Rocking back and forth to a mellow croon,
 I heard a Negro play.
Down on Lenox Avenue the other night
By the pale dull pallor of an old gas light
 He did a lazy sway. . . .
 He did a lazy sway. . . .
To the tune o' those Weary Blues.
With his ebony hands on each ivory key
He made that poor piano moan with melody.
 O Blues!
Swaying to and fro on his rickety stool
He played that sad raggy tune like a musical fool.
 Sweet Blues!
Coming from a black man's soul.
 O Blues!
In a deep song voice with a melancholy tone
I heard that Negro sing, that old piano moan—
 "Ain't got nobody in all this world,
  Ain't got nobody but ma self.
  I's gwine to quit ma frownin'
  And put ma troubles on the shelf."

Thump, thump, thump went his foot on the floor.
He played a few chords then he sang some more—
 "I got the Weary Blues
  And I can't be satisfied.
  Got the Weary Blues
  And can't be satisfied—
  I ain't happy no mo'
  And I wish that I had died."
And far into the night he crooned that tune.
The stars went out and so did the moon.
The singer stopped playing and went to bed
While the Weary Blues echoed through his head.
He slept like a rock or a man that's dead.

Think about the speaker in this poem. Is it a man speaking, or a woman, or does it matter? Does race matter? Or ethnicity? Hughes is a black poet, born in Joplin, Missouri; he went to high school in Cleveland, Ohio, and eventually left the Midwest for New York and Harlem. His biographers call him either homosexual or bisexual. Can you think about how his race and sexuality and thoughts you might have about his gender and ethnicity could figure in your performance of this poem or in a critical response you might write on a performance of this poem?

The blues are being sung, and we suspect that most of you would agree that given that this poem is by Langston Hughes, who is black, and given that it alludes to a blues song, it is likely that you would want, as a performer, to preserve the blues music and suggest the blues traditions. You might well raise your speech to the level of song, singing the words of the blues lyrics rather than speaking them, or speaking them at first until the music takes over and they become sung. But how would you treat the speaker of the poem? You might recognize the lyrics, the song, and the poet and, in performance, feature the racial legacy of the poem and its traditions. But what if you are a white performer who is a woman wanting to perform this poem? What choices would you make about the way you handle the music, the speaker, and the piano player? What rationale would you offer for your choices? If you were an audience member of a white student's performance, would you agree that the audience should discuss the issue of race in the poem and the choices that the student made regarding how to handle race? If the white student performer argued that she loved the poem, its music, its language, and its hauntingly lonely setting, and that it did not matter whether the speaker was black or white, would you agree with her and support her performance? If she said she simply chose to be herself, a white woman recalling the song and the player, what would you think and say? How would an understanding of gender and race issues, as well as issues of ethnicity and sexuality, help you in formulating a written response to her performance?

Do you agree that the evaluation of this hypothetical performance ought to address the performer's choices in regard to the race, gender, ethnicity, and perhaps sexuality of the speaker in the poem and the crooning piano player? We would argue that one of the most exciting aspects of performance is its capacity to let a performer experience the other. In some cases, performers may enter into the poem's world completely, trying to transcend their own particularity and enter into another's race and gender. In other cases, performers may choose to play down the importance of race or convert the speaker to their own race while trying to preserve the inflections and themes and voice of the poem. These are all matters worthy of exploration in performance criticism and discussion. One of the beauties of this kind of performance is that it brings to the surface and makes explicit some of the most vexing social issues, enabling performers and their audience to grow.

How the Performance Sounded

The criticism also describes what was heard—how did the performance sound? Was it spoken? Did it involve multiple voices? Were dialects used? What was the vocal range of the speaker's voice? Did the performer modulate pitch, play with the rate of speech, and alter the volume of the spoken word? Were there other sound affects, created by the use of other media, amplified sound, or tapes, or was music used? Was the language clearly articulated? As you think about these questions, you might try to develop your own performance of the Langston Hughes poem above and consider the different ways you made the poem sound. How do its rhythms and sounds, denotative and connotative meanings, produce the world of sound in your performance of the poem?

How the Performance Felt

The descriptive component also describes how the audience felt, in so far as those feelings made themselves manifest in external reactions from the audience. The criticism should attempt to name the emotions elicited, noting whether the audience listened and watched with rapt attention, or whether their involvement was more varied, and perhaps uneven. Were there peak moments during the performance? Where did it climax? What did the audience feel? These details about the look, the sound, and the feeling of a performance are key components of descriptive criticism.

How It Was Understood

The descriptive component of how a performance was understood and what it communicated can easily become an evaluation of what was understood, unless we are very careful. Try to keep the classifications distinct. Start by describing the way in which the performer appears to have represented the text on which it is based. If the performer is performing a poem, a selection of short fiction, a novel, an autobiographical text, an obituary, a snippet from the press, or some other nonfiction or cultural text created by someone other than the performer, the criticism should describe how the text was made manifest in the performance. What elements do you think you should include?

We would suggest that you describe the characters in the text or the landscape evoked by the text and represented in the performance. Be careful to describe what the performer did with the text, how the performer appeared to have understood its meaning, and try not to enter into argument at this stage. In other words, be descriptive, not evalua-tive. Don't address whether or not you agree with the interpretation the performer presented until you have described it.

Return to Langston Hughes's poem and ask yourself how the poem will be understood differently depending on whether the performer chose to make the speaker part of the black community in 1926, or whether the performer chose to make the speaker white or some other race, ethnicity, and gender. Can you also see how you will have different understandings of the poem if you stress the difference between the soul-singing Negro piano player and the speaker, whether black or white? If the performer chose to make a distinction between the social class of the piano player and of the one walking through the Harlem streets, again, the poem's meaning will alter.

We are not arguing that there is only one way of understanding the poem. Quite the contrary: there are many ways. Part of the richness of performance and texts is that they can assume many, many meanings while remaining faithful to the text and performance. Yes, there are limits that should be set on how far a performer departs from the meaning of a poem and the intention of the writer. Some meanings cannot easily be traced to the text or the performance; rather, they come from something unique in the viewer, which when tested against a group of responses don't seem to owe much to the performance that ostensibly inspired them. They seem to derive from something in the viewer that is apart from the performance. We are sure you can think of many examples when you thought that the interpretation offered for a line or a whole performance did not really reside in the line or in the performance but rather was imposed on it. For the purposes of descriptive criticism, if you are making this point, you need to be able to argue and rally evidence to defend your description. You should be able to point to features in the performance or aspects of the text that support your contention.

Evaluative Criticism

The evaluative component of the criticism tells the performer how the audience has weighed the strengths and weaknesses of the performance in the four areas discussed above. The same elements that were carefully described when students talked or wrote about what they saw, heard, felt, or understood now become the subject of a judgmental evaluation. In essence, the student critics now ask themselves and the others in the class whether, overall, the performance succeeded in realizing the intentions of its creator and equally, if not more important, in the terms as defined by the audience.

Let us imagine a couple different performances of a passage from a short story by Margaret Atwood, "Gertrude Talks Back," in which Hamlet's mother, Gertrude, lazes on her bed, talking to her son as she puts on makeup, etc. The segment concludes with Gertrude fully acknowledging and justifying her part in the murder of Hamlet's father. In one performance, Gertrude is a loud, brassy, New York Jewish mama, berating her dead husband and praising her current husband, Claudius, to her son. When she concludes by pronouncing to Hamlet that it was she, SHE, not Claudius, who killed Hamlet and that she is glad she did, this performer deliberately chose a flamboyant, exaggerated style, forcing the audience to see the parodic elements in the story and experience it as a lampooning of the psychologist, Sigmund Freud, and the host of followers who have offered their own analyses of the troubled Hamlet and his Oedipal complex. When this performer's Gertrude gloats about her act to her son, she also creates a seductive atmosphere that makes the audience think that Gertrude also wishes to have an incestuous relationship with her son. In another performance, the performer was timid in her rendition of Gertrude. Although she said all the words in the story, she did not have a consistent interpretation of Gertrude nor had she figured out the ways in which this piece offered a feminist reading of the famous Shakespeare play, and the audience could not tell what they should feel.

Think about how you would evaluate the two performances we have described. What kind of observations would you include? What kind of evidence would you rally to justify your assessment of the strengths and weaknesses of the performance? Obviously, it is rather difficult to answer these questions without the benefit of seeing a performance or reading the selection, but we have chosen this example and sketched the different performance approaches with broad brushstrokes in order to encourage you to enter fully into this example or seek out your own example of a work you have seen performed in different ways so that you can see what kinds of things you would discuss in your evaluation.

Did you consider whether the performance realized its creator's and its audience's intentions? Did you consider in what ways the performance could be considered "faithful" to the poem, short story, or cultural text performed, and the ways in which it departed from the text? Did you consider whether the performance moved the audience and made them feel, think, and understand? How effective was the performer in communicating a meaning to the audience? These are the kinds of questions you should address in performance criticism.

Open-Ended Dialogue Between Performer and Audience

We alluded earlier to the collaborative relationship in performance criticism between audience and performer. Let us provide some examples. Often, in live performance, the audience members grapple for a word or phrase to describe something they feel. As student audiences start finding words for their experiences, there is often some trepidation. The students are not sure they understood what they saw, or what was meant. Let us take two provocative examples. A student has performed Audre Lorde's poem "Hanging Fire," written in 1978.

> I am fourteen
> and my skin has betrayed me
> the boy I cannot live without
> still sucks his thumb
> in secret
> how come my knees are
> always so ashy
> what if I die
> before morning
> and momma's in the bedroom
> with the door closed.
>
> I have to learn how to dance
> in time for the next party
> my room is too small for me
> suppose I die before graduation

they will sing sad melodies
but finally
tell the truth about me
There is nothing I want to do
and too much
that has to be done
and momma's in the bedroom
with the door closed.

Nobody even stops to think
about my side of it
I should have been on Math Team
my marks were better than his
why do I have to be
the one
wearing braces
I have nothing to wear tomorrow
will I live long enough
to grow up
and momma's in the bedroom
with the door closed.

In this poem, different student performers chose to handle the bedroom door and what is going on behind it in quite different ways. One performance uses a doorframe, with the wood of the closed door lit with a light; the rest of the performance space is in darkness. The performer, who is white, plays a young, nubile girl, pretty, with bright lips and a bright dress. At the end of the poem, the young girl is kneeling on the floor, pressing her cheek and the weight of her shoulder against the door; the skin on her legs is exposed; the short, colorful miniskirt is askew, showing the flesh of her thighs. She is quietly whimpering. She seems afraid. Pent up inside her are emotions she can hardly contain. You feel she might explode and shatter the door, and yet she does nothing like this.

In another performance, the performer is a young, pretty black girl. Her skin looks blemished; she appears to have acne. She is awkward. She wears a little tank top, loose fitting, over very small but accentuated breasts. She is in her bedroom, a room with lots of clutter and memorabilia spread around it. A table is covered with a bedspread, and there is a teddy bear on it. The girl speaks her lines from a chair beside the bed. She looks out across the audience to a spot slightly above their heads where she has placed the imaginary bedroom door. She talks in a pouty voice when she calls up her mother, behind the bedroom door. It is as if the girl's mother is there to spite her, as if she has no use for the girl, is a busy, working mom who wants to be left alone. The girl's tone is crybabyish.

The audience for these performances struggles to say what they were made to feel by the girl, searching for words to capture the feel of the pieces. In the first performance, it is the image of the closed door of the bedroom, its hard surface, its texture, the way it is lit, and how the girl appears at the end that commands the attention of the class. They are uneasy about what they feel. One student mentions the door—what a powerful image it is. Another asks what it seems to mean. Another responds that the girl appears so helpless, so locked out. The reference to feeling locked out makes another want to guess at why the girl is kneeling there. What is she afraid of? The class begins conjecturing about what or who is behind the bedroom door. Slowly the group collectively begins to hazard guesses, confessing what they thought was going on. Something feels wrong. The inklings of meaning that begin to emerge as the class works to define the space behind the door are what we call residues, or traces of meaning. Ultimately, the group settles on an interpretation where the girl has only a single parent. The mother has a lover, or many lovers, suggests another student. The door is always closed to the growing girl. Now you can go on and explore this poem, its imagery, and its situation on your own. Some of the students began to talk about the poet, her race, her sexual orientation. Some mused about what the title means, wondering what, exactly, is "hanging fire" in this poem. Try an Internet search and see what meanings you can find for the phrase "hanging fire." How do they assist you in interpreting the meaning of the poem?

When you contrast the first performance with the second, you get a very different scene and a different set of issues. In the second performance described above, the poem has a more middle-class setting to it. The girl protagonist is angered by her mother's selfishness but there is no suggestion that the closed door conceals a lover, or many lovers. Rather, it closes the mother off in her own space, one that does not include her daughter and her daughter's growing pains. By comparing the two different performances, the audience begins to concoct other hypothetical renderings, each seeking to strike a slightly different meaning.

Now let us turn to another poem. In this case, imagine that a student has performed a poem by Theodore Roethke, called "My Papa's Waltz."

You may want to work on it yourself if you have not seen a performance of it, to get it into your bones and give you some performance material for this exercise.

My Papa's Waltz

The whiskey on your breath
Could make a small boy dizzy;
But I hung on like death:
Such waltzing was not easy.

We romped until the pans
Slid from the kitchen shelf;
My mother's countenance
Could not unfrown itself.

The hand that held my wrist
Was battered on one knuckle;
At every step you missed
My right ear scraped a buckle.

You beat time on my head
With a palm caked hard by dirt,
Then waltzed me off to bed
Still clinging to your shirt.

In this poem, the class concentrates on two images: the one of the boy's right ear that "scraped a buckle" and the image of the battered knuckled hand that "beat time on my head." Is this a poem about abuse? Is the boy's drunken father hurting the boy, beating him even? Is there love on the father's part? What does the boy feel about the nightly ritual and the waltz? These moments and lines in performance are likely to evoke conflicting reactions from the audience. Depending on the performer's experiences, he or she may not have thought of some of the reactions or may be trying to do something entirely different. Some students have performed this using three performers, one boy playing the drunken father and dancing dizzily with the other boy, while a third plays the mother standing by. Another performer chose to recite the poem from the lectern, beating on the surface to suggest the rhythm of the dance and also to let the audience hear sounds of beating and see knuckles bruised. You might try using a belt with a buckle, manipulating it in different ways to show the different aspects of the boy's dance with his father. You might want to put the sound of music, a waltz, on a tape recorder, with the pace of the music quickening and timed to correspond to the way in which you rhythmically pace the speaking of the poem. Can you see the rich possibilities you have in creating your performance?

It is the classroom audience in collaboration with the performance and performer that affix meaning to the event. Often it is the dynamic of class discussion that begins to bring something into being that was only latently in the performance, if there at all. Again, as in the Lorde poem discussed earlier, there is a residue of meaning in the audience and it gives rise to a whole series of provocative responses, increasing the student performer's understanding of complex issues and leading to new meanings to be inferred from the work and new discoveries on the part of some, if not all of the students.

As you can see from these examples, discussion that grows out of them involves the class in collaborative meaning making. This chapter is concerned with considering how audiences function and offer criticism to performances that are developed for and enacted in a classroom. You may want to investigate and think about the ways in which larger, public performances interact with their audiences and how such performances can be used as social criticism or how an activist agenda can exploit the talkback forum in order to increase an audience's understanding of social and political problems and prompt an engaged activist response from the audience.

Before concluding this chapter, we thought it would be useful to describe a typical short checklist of rubrics for performance that are often used to judge the effectiveness of a performance and to suggest areas for improvement. Typically, the rubrics include the following: familiarity with or memorization of the text; clarity of the vocal delivery; control of gestures, body, and movement; control of the performance space, the props used, and the costumes worn; understanding of the meaning of the text; depth of character development in performance; clarity in communicating who is speaking, to whom, where, when, with what motive, and why; and aesthetic dimensions of the performance—its beauty.

Others find it useful to pose the following questions regarding a performance and incorporate the answers to these questions in a written performance evaluation. What are the intentions of the performance? Did the performance succeed in communicating its intentions? Did it move the audience? Did the performance do justice to the material of its text?

In almost all cases, as a critic/evaluator, you want to tell a performer what worked and why, and what did not work and why not. It is always helpful to accompany criticisms with suggestions for improvement. And when the performance excels, let the performer know that but, again, try to tell the performer why it was so successful. Even with the strongest performances, there are always possibilities for further improvement. To help each other grow, keep pressing yourselves to show each other how to become still better performers. As you grow accustomed to each other's work as performers, you come to recognize each performer's style, or signature trademarks. Some students have stunning voices and always speak with great passion and feeling. Others veer toward flamboyant material, designed to bring out the dramatic. Some performers are great comedians or masters of satire—they often seek comic material and handle it with flair. Musicians, dancers, composers, and film students bring the tools or instruments of their art to bear on their performances. You will come to look forward to how your classmates stretch themselves as performers. You'll learn each other's tricks and shortcomings. Again, relying on trust and candor, try to make explicit the nature of the style, the kinds of tricks or technique that work, the kinds that don't. Be humble and true and you will help each other become seasoned performance critics.

KEY TERMS

audience and audiencing

communally based, process-oriented performance criticism

descriptive criticism

dialogic

empathy

ethnicity

evaluative criticism

gender

race

sexuality

Chapter 4

CRAFTING YOUR PERFORMANCE: TECHNIQUES AND CONVENTIONS

Consider the following performance situations:

Situation 1: It is Saturday morning, around 9:00 A.M. You are dressed in nice clothes, unusual for you on a weekend—a coat, tie, and khaki pants or a suit if you are male, a formal but not too fancy skirt and blouse or dress or pants suit if you are female. You have been assigned to a classroom on a campus not your own, and you have been given a code number which will be yours for the entire weekend; it is intentionally designed so that you cannot be identified by name or by your home institution. Your code number is printed in a list that has been distributed among all performers and is also posted on a wall. At the appointed time, you go to the classroom, where you see a blackboard on which other people have written their code numbers. One or two of these code numbers is followed by the letters "DE" or "TE" written in parentheses. A minute after the appointed time, an adult who looks old enough to be a faculty member, but who is not one of your own teachers, walks in. She sits down, takes a few sheets out of an envelope, writes some things on them, and then looks up. She calls out the code numbers to see who is present; when a few numbers are called, other students in the room say, "That person is double entered and said he'll be back as soon as he finishes his other event." The teacher says, "Does anybody here need to go first?" Hearing no reply, she says, "All right then, we will begin with"—and she calls your number.

You go to the front of the room, carrying a small black binder in which you have carefully placed the text you will be performing. As part of your preparation for the performance, you have heeded seriously your own teacher's and fellow students' admonitions to make sure that it is a *black* binder and that it is a small one. You wait until the teacher looks up and says, "You may begin." You speak a brief introduction to your text, being careful to keep it under a minute in length and stating very clearly and emphatically the name and author of the selection. Then you open your binder and begin to perform.

As you perform, you are aware of time passing, in part because the teacher has started a stopwatch, but also by looking occasionally, almost imperceptibly, at the clock on the wall. You may have even written time markers in the margins of your text in order to keep yourself "on time." Of course, depending on when in the year you are giving this performance, you may have performed it so many times that the element of time has become almost irrelevant—the performance always clocks in at the same time, give or take a few seconds. You remember to look down at the script from time to time, although, truth be told, you could probably recite it from memory if necessary. You remind yourself not to look down when you are turning a page, as this may signal a gap in your performance.

Because of all the DEs and TEs on the board, your audience consists primarily of the teacher and a few students scattered around the room. Nonetheless, you try to sustain the illusion that you have a full house, and you make sure to direct your eyes across the room when the text suggests you are speaking to the listening audience. When the text moves into dialogue between characters, you angle your head and shoulders slightly, to the left when you are speaking as one character, to the right when you are speaking as another, centering yourself when the narrator speaks. While you may shift your body position slightly to help underscore character differences, you depend primarily on your voice to make meaning. You make sure to slow down as you complete your performance, in order to signal to your audience that you are ending. After you say your last sentence, you hold for a moment, then decisively shut the binder, wait for a brief, polite smattering of applause, and sit down. If you also are DE or TE, you ask permission to leave the room and thank the teacher. If you are only entered in this one "event," you know you are expected to sit and listen to other performers, though you wonder if this extends to the DEs and TEs who enter between performances and who go up to the blackboard and cross off the DE or TE (sometimes changing the TE to DE). After everyone has finished performing, the teacher thanks the audience, and you leave the room. You repeat this process two more times, possibly a third. You receive feedback the next day, through written critiques, with numerical evaluations—and in some cases, a trophy or certificate.

Situation 2: You have just left a performance classroom in which an argument has broken out over whether texts written by members of certain groups (racial, ethnic, gender, sexual orientation, nationality, ability) should only be performed by performers who share the identity of that group. The discussion grew so heated that one student burst into tears and another student stood up and stalked out of the room slamming the door. The teacher, who has tried to manage the many voices clamoring to be heard, was clearly shaken and suggests that it might be a good idea for class to end early and for members to think about what happened in the discussion and what is at stake—whether the classroom discussion in any way mirrors the complexities of making decisions about who has the right to perform what.

You are not certain what you think, but you feel stirred up inside—in part relieved because the class ended early, in part frustrated because you feel as if the shortened class was a way for the teacher to avoid escalation of the argument, which you found upsetting but intriguing. You are not ready to go back to your room to study between classes, so you go to the student center and pick up a snack from the cafeteria and see a table where a friend of yours is sitting, another student from your department but not someone who was in the previous class.

Your friend waves to you and beckons to you to come sit. You do so. Your friend looks at you and says, "You look upset. Did something happen? Do you feel like talking?" All of a sudden, words start pouring out of you, fragmented, disconnected sentences. Your friend says, "Slow down. Why don't you start at the beginning?" You say, "Well, you know 230 [the number of the class]? The most amazing thing just happened. Johnson Wu did a performance from Alice Walker's *The Color Purple*, and all hell broke loose." You proceed to tell your friend, as sequentially and with as much fidelity as possible, what happened in the classroom discussion. At times you simply summarize the points being made, at other times, particularly when you are describing and quoting a student known by both of you, you try to re-create that student's vocal patterns and qualities, maybe even suggesting their habitual body position. When you get to the point when the student stood and walked out, you don't actually reproduce these actions but your voice gets louder, and you find yourself almost rising from your seat and your body stiffening. You end by saying, "Anyway, I don't know if I even feel like going to class next time."

Throughout this "performance," your friend nods from time to time, especially when you pause to take a breath or when a sentence ends on an upward inflection, suggesting that you are unsure about what an action or statement meant or that you are asking a question. At various moments, your friend interjects phrases like, "You're kidding," or "Yeah, I know what you mean," or simply "Uh-huh," to let you know she is still listening carefully to the story. She keeps her eyes focused on you throughout your narrative, though you find yourself looking away or off into space at times, as if trying to reenvision the scene for yourself. At the end of the story, there is a moment of silence, in which you both seem to be acknowledging that you have finished performing this classroom incident. Then, you turn to your friend and say, "Well, I feel better now. So, what's up with you? It seems like I haven't seen you all semester." And your friend begins to talk about her recent experiences.

If we can agree, based on the previous chapters, that both of these situations constitute performance events, a follow-up set of questions we could ask might be: Which of the two is "more" of a performance? Does one seem more "formal" than the other? Does one seem more driven by specific techniques than the other? Do both make use of implied or mutually understood conventions of performance? Does one seem more responsive to prescriptions than the other? Is it possible to evaluate each performance—what standards would one apply to each (this will take you back to the issues discussed in chapter 3)?

Our ability to answer these questions will rest at least in part on how we choose to define such terms as *technique* and *conventions*. *Technique* is a word that has produced many different definitions and, perhaps equally important, many different reactions, positive and negative, over the centuries of its usage. It is derived etymologically from the Greek word *techne*, which the *Stanford Encyclopedia of Philosophy* translates as "either craft or art." Its meaning in classical philosophy is a complex one, changing from thinker to thinker in many cases. For some, it is placed in contrast to *episteme*, traditionally translated as knowledge, often quite specifically theoretical or abstract knowledge, using *techne* to map out the realm of practical knowledge or the world of actual experience. Aristotle, however, was careful to acknowledge *techne* as way of knowing in itself—"because it is a practice grounded in . . . something involving theoretical understanding" (*Stanford*). So, as we can already see, the line between theory and practice is by no means clear or distinct. Indeed, many performance studies scholars and artists would argue that *techne* is not only grounded in a kind of *episteme*, but indeed produces *episteme*. Can you see how practice can produce knowledge and not simply be seen as following from an a priori theoretical knowledge?

Technique is related to other words, such as *technical* and *technology*, all having their root in the sense of a realm of practice, of "how to do things," to borrow from J. L. Austin's words. For some, the word *technique* carries with it negative connotations, as it may be associated with a kind of superficial way of doing—a set of mechanical actions that can be dissociated from thinking deeply about a specific action or from reflecting on *why* one is doing something in a particular way. Thus, one may hear a performer being described as "technically brilliant," meaning he excels at simply carrying out some of the building blocks of performance— voice, movement, gesture, audience placement, even specific things such as accents and dialects—without using them in particular service of the text he is performing or for their own impressive, often entertaining effects. Undergirding such a negative use of the term is the conviction, which we share, that technique is most successfully used when it illuminates either a particular text or achieves a particular rhetorical effect (such as a social or political statement). In this sense, performance technique may be akin to learning handwriting skills (an art that indeed may be disappearing as the digital revolution makes handwriting less and less essential): unless one is a calligrapher (that is, an artist whose medium is handwriting taken to the level of aesthetic beauty), what is most important is to learn how to write in cursive or to print in a way that allows the message to be legible. To be sure, such technique need not be purely utilitarian or commonplace: you will need to adapt your handwriting depending on the potential reader and the potential context—think about how different your handwriting would be if you were writing a note to a six-year-old or to a close friend who has known you for years.

Can you think of performers, either well-known public ones or fellow students, whose technique you particularly admire? What do you admire about their technique? Is it the sense of confidence it suggests? Is it the ease with which it allows you to be an audience member? Is it because the technique is so subtle that you are unaware of it and you find yourself believing the performer has become a character? Or conversely, is it because the technique draws attention to itself *as* technique and you take pleasure in the awareness of artifice for its own sake? Can you think of instances in which a performer's technique (or what you experienced as deficiencies in it) intruded on the success of the performance? Can you think of examples in which you highly valued a performance, despite what you deemed problems in its technique?

Later in the chapter we will expand on some specific areas of performance technique and offer you some suggestions about them and some exercises and activities for working on your own repertoire of techniques (we prefer the plural, as it suggests flexibility and adaptability, rather than a single, unchanging approach to performance). These will include: voice, body and gesture, movement and space, focus and location. This chapter can only offer you some rudimentary thoughts and approaches to technique, as entire books have been written on each of these areas; the bibliography at the end of the book will help guide you to other sources, and you may find it useful to take specific courses in speech and voice, movement, and so forth.

Conventions: Implicit "Rules" of Performance

If *technique* refers to the building blocks by which a performer makes a performance visible and audible for an audience—the tools for "publishing," so to speak, a performance, we might then think about identifying which specific techniques are deployed in specific contexts of performance: this second area is referred to as *conventions*, explicit or implicit rules that govern the use of techniques in performance situations. We can then extend our discussion to thinking about how individual performers or groups of performers mark these techniques in their own ways, describing different performance *styles*—styles may be determined by myriad elements, including historical setting, cultural context, individual preferences and goals, and textual characteristics.

For the moment, let's focus on conventions and return to the two situations described at the beginning of the chapter. First, we need to consider what it means to say that there are *rules* for performance. Do we mean that there are prescribed rules and that disobeying them or ignoring them may in a sense "disqualify" a performance from "counting" as a performance? Yes and no. In some contexts, there are indeed specific rules that govern what may or may not be presented as a performance, or at least as a particular kind of performance. For example, there has been an increase in one-person shows in the last few decades, often based on the life and writings of a figure from history, such as Julie Harris's performance of the play *The Belle of Amherst*, based on the poetry, letters, and biographies of the American poet Emily Dickinson. Harris was awarded the Tony Award for Best Actress for her performance that year. A more recent one was Doug Wright's play *I Am My Own Wife*, which won the Pulitzer Prize in Drama and the Tony Award for Best Play and was about the historical figure Charlotte von Mahlsdorf, a German transvestite who survived Nazism and the Stasi in Germany in the twentieth century; its performer on Broadway, Jefferson Mays, won the Tony Award for Best Actor.

Other forms of the one-person show have also developed, such as the autobiographical performance; recent examples of these on Broadway include such shows as *Elaine Stritch: At Liberty,* in which the performer, a longtime diva of the musical theater, told her life story, punctuated by performances of many musical numbers she performed in her prime. That show also won a Tony Award, but in a category called "Special Theatrical Event," suggesting that when a performer performs as herself and not as a dramatic or fictional character, she is no longer acting. Yet, just a year or so later, another musical legend, Chita Rivera, performed the title role in a show called *Chita Rivera: The Dancer's Life.* Rivera performed a narrative similar to Stritch's, but a young girl was cast as her younger self and an ensemble of dancers provided support for the re-creation of dance numbers from such shows as *West Side Story, Bye Bye Birdie,* and *Chicago,* all of which Rivera originally starred in. When the time came for Tony nominations, Rivera was nominated in the category of Best Actress in a Musical, even though she played herself. Is there a consistent rule at work here—does the presence of other performers distinguish Rivera's performance from Stritch's? If so, then how to explain other productions nominated as Special Theatrical Events which feature multiple performers? The simplest explanation here is probably that the Broadway theater is undergoing a period of transition in which traditional forms and genres are being rethought and pushed beyond easily discernible boundaries, and there is no formal set of rules that can produce a grammar for making such distinctions consistently.

We use the word *grammar* intentionally here, as we see the conventions of performance as being similar to the rules of language (indeed, Joanna Hawkins Maclay wrote a book on performance called *Readers Theatre: Toward a Grammar of Practice*). Linguists often draw a distinction between what they call "descriptive grammars" and "prescriptive grammars" for a language. The former *describes* how people actually use language; the latter *prescribes* how the grammarians think people ought to use language. Of course, there tends to be a lot of overlap between these two kinds of grammar. But descriptive grammars tend to be more interested in the changing, unstable nature of language and are less concerned with ensuring that people speak in a "proper" way. Such grammars are interested in rules insofar as linguists look for implicit (or sometimes explicit) rules people tend to follow but also the ways in which usage changes over time to the point where some rules are no longer followed by the majority of speakers of a language. Descriptive grammars are not simply interested in what we traditionally think of as grammar (such as subject-verb agreement) but extend to what linguists call pragmatics—how rules operate at the level of conversations and other forms of communication. Prescriptive grammarians are more interested in standardizing language usage, believing that standards ensure clearer communication or that the standardized rules follow the inherent logic of the language and deviation from them marks an intellectual decline for a culture.

Let's consider one or two examples. We were both raised to make a clear distinction between how we use *from* and *than* when speaking of difference. We were taught that *than* is correct when a speaker is making a quantitative comparison, as in "His voice is louder than mine," where "louder" indicates a difference in degree. However, a sentence such as "Your choice for dinner is different than mine" would be considered ungrammatical; it violates this rule because the difference is one of quality or category rather than of quantity or degree. Yet, what is undeniably true, if one pays attention to English as it is spoken both publicly in the media and privately in conversation, is that this is a distinction that seems to be disappearing, to the point that we are aware of what seems like our own fussiness in maintaining this distinction or in taking note when others do not.

Prescriptive grammarians, however, might make the counterargument that to allow this distinction to disappear is to lose a conceptual way of thinking in language: we conflate all kinds of comparisons rather than being able to make subtle or obvious grammatical distinctions between differences of kind and differences of degree. This strikes us as a reasonable observation to make; at the same time, despite the efforts of teachers to enforce such rules in formal situations (such as essays for courses or classroom discussions), language, because it is a living, changing thing, is likely to drop the distinction—it may be that for many intelligent readers, this is a distinction of which you yourselves are not aware.

Given the distinction between descriptive and prescriptive rules in grammar, let's turn back to the realm of performance. Reread situations 1 and 2 above and try to derive the rules that are implicit in each performance situation. As many of you have no doubt discerned, situation 1

presents the general outline of a solo performance presented at a competitive speech contest, typically known in the United States as a forensics
tournament (the term *forensic* is derived from its classical meaning, originally referring to legal speech, now expanded to refer to any competitive
speech or performance activity, usually interscholastic or intercollegiate).
We initially described it without identifying the specific name for it to try
to defamiliarize it, to get you to see its rituals and activities as an outsider
might. For example, if you have participated in forensics, you probably
recognized the abbreviations DE and TE as standing for double-entered
and triple-entered, meaning that the performer is entered in two or three
events that are taking place simultaneously in different rooms. The abbreviations communicate to the judge that the performer will arrive late to
the round because they are off performing in another event. Situation
2 is what might be called an everyday life performance, a spontaneous
personal narrative that is typically situated in a conversational setting.
What are the various rules at work in each?

We'll identify one or two for you and allow you to try to find others.
In situation 1, much consideration is given to the presence and format of
the physical text or script that the performer uses in competition, down to
the color of the binder and its size. Those of you who have participated in
forensics activities are probably familiar with the requirement that such
performers must have physical copies of their selections present in their
performances (such requirements may vary from event to event and from
one league to the next, but in general the presence of the physical text
remains a constant in events involving the performance of literature —
there are different rules for public speaking events). In some leagues, if
one were to perform without a physical script, one would be immediately
disqualified from competition. This is clearly an example of a prescriptive
rule, and there is no room for "interpretation" or choice about whether to
follow it. But what about the actual binder used, its size and color? You
may remember seeing performers in competition who used a nonblack
binder or one that was 8 x 10, not 5 x 7. If you look at the rule books for
various forensics associations, it is less common to see anything that specifies color or size. We have had students, however, who received ballots
from judges that upbraided them for having a white binder or one larger
than the ubiquitous 5 x 7, although it was not clear from the judge's written
comments to what degree the performer's nonstandard binder color or
size played a role in how the judge ranked the performer. The judge in
this case might be applying a rather idiosyncratic standard, one that those

who participate in the activity might agree should not play a role in evaluation. Others might argue that what the judge is doing is articulating
an implicit rule, essentially turning what might be a descriptive rule of
typical practice (such contests are a sea of nearly identical binders) into a
prescriptive criterion for lowering a performer's rating in the competition.
The judge may be either assuming that such a rule is actually prescriptive or simply using his position to normalize performance practice in
that setting. It would be interesting to hear such a judge explain why it
is important that all performers use the same size and color binder for
the script. He might suggest that such a rule helps create a level playing
field, where differences in color or size might distract the judge visually
or lead to differences in the challenge of how to use the script physically
in performance, and thus make for a fair arena in which to compete—
after all, he might argue, softballs and basketballs have regulations about
size, why not binders?

How would you respond to such an argument? Is it logical to you?
To what degree do you think the presence of such a rule is appropriate
or not in the context of performance wherein competition is involved
and people must be ranked and rated on the basis of some criteria? Do
you think a judge should have the right to draw distinctions between
performers on the basis of such a criterion? Are there some prescriptive
rules whose conventions do make sense within the world of performance
competition? Which ones and why?

Now let's consider situation 2. On the face of it, fewer rules seem
to be operative here—the performer ("you") simply finds an audience
("your friend") spontaneously and "performs" the story of the class argument as a way of letting off steam, working through emotions, and trying
to make sense of the issues raised. No rules here, right? Just blurt out the
story as it occurs to you.

Perhaps not. It may be more difficult to discern rules operating in
this performance situation (and some people might be reluctant even to
call this event a performance, though we hope that later chapters will
convince you that such speech acts are every bit as performative as more
clearly marked theatrical experiences), but they are there nonetheless.
Some of them intersect with the kinds of rules you may have learned if you
have studied interpersonal communication. Some of them may be more
explicitly interactional than those at work in situation 1. For example,
notice that your friend, who serves here as your audience (in addition to
yourself, as this is also probably an instance, if primarily unconscious, of

intrapersonal communication), interrupts the initial flow of language and instructs you to "slow down . . . start at the beginning." What your friend has done is to remind you of two implicit rules of conversational narrative performance: first, you must speak at a speed that allows your audience to understand what you are saying and to follow the story, and second, audiences tend to make sense of stories more easily when they follow a chronological sequence. The second rule is particularly sensitive to the context and medium in which the story is being performed. There are many fascinating narratives that intentionally disrupt chronology (think of such films as *Memento*, which moves backward in time, or novels in which a longer narrative may interweave stories from different generations, leading eventually to a meeting point somewhere in the middle), but in an oral, conversational setting, when the audience does not have the luxury of lingering over a page or shifting from chapter to chapter on a DVD (which has altered how many of us view and think of film narrative), the listener needs the context and coherence that starting at the beginning provides. This rule also challenges the performer to think about when (and where) the story does indeed begin. Does it begin with the moment you walked into class? Does it begin with a performance given in the last round of assignments when someone else performed outside their own gender or ethnic identity? Does it begin with the post-performance discussion, which perhaps went differently from what you had anticipated on an ordinary class day? Can you see how rules operate just as significantly here as in situation 1? The rules may be more implicit and they may stem more clearly from a descriptive notion of performance conventions: your friend is prompting you with rules not because you must follow them or be viewed as having broken a code of what is acceptable behavior, but because she is responding to the way people typically do tell stories to friends—and that, by the way, may include beginning, as classical writers put it, in medias res, in the middle of things, and then backtracking to the "real" beginning of the story. What other kinds of conventions are present in this performance situation?

We have used the language of rules so much in our discussion of conventions that we may have given the impression we advocate a very strict adherence to standards of acceptability and conformity in performance. Actually, what is truer is that we recommend a very inductive approach to creating performances, including the use of conventions. Similarly, we believe that such conventional rules are there to be questioned, tested, pressed, reinvented, crossed, and, at times, honored for how they may help a performer and her audience experience together. No performance rule is of any use if it cannot be defended for aesthetic or social reasons, true in life as much as in art, we would suggest. Transgressing certain rules can be very invigorating, revelatory, and productive, but again, only if the performer has sound reasons for disregarding or moving beyond particular conventions and can somehow engage her audience in the meaning of the conventions and the departure from them. It may be worthwhile, for some performers, to test the question of the presence of a physical script at a forensics contest—and it may be worth the chance of being disqualified if the violation of that rule produces a conversation about the assumed necessity of such an element in the conventions of the performance situation (although the performer may have to have a complex conversation with her coach before or after!). Indeed, as Aristotle suggested, we encourage you to approach the *techne* of each performance as an opportunity to engage in *episteme*, and vice versa: performance conventions should be informed by theoretical discourse and convictions—and, in turn, may create additional theoretical work to be done.

Either as a class or in small groups, compile a list of performance situations, such as athletic contests, homecoming parades, wedding toasts, musical theater productions, and see if you can come up with conventions, prescriptive and descriptive rules, explicit or implicit, that are present in each. At what point, for each category, does a rule define the performance (what theorists call "constitutive")? Are some conventions optional or do some provide choices, leading to different outcomes? At what point does the failure to adhere to a convention so violate the nature and spirit of the performance as to disqualify it from belonging to that category? Can there be a musical comedy that does not end happily? One in which there is no speaking or singing, but only instrumental music and movement or dance? One in which there is no plot or story line?

In the remainder of the chapter, we outline areas of technique and conventions you are likely to need to consider in performances involving spoken language. Our primary goal here is not to dictate prescriptively but to describe the kinds of tools you will want to have as you continue to learn to perform.

Performance Techniques and Conventions: A Brief Guide

Before we begin outlining some of the major areas of performance technique to consider, whatever text you choose to perform, read the following passage, which will serve as our case study throughout this guide. Read it silently first, just to get a sense of its content and its overall style of language, then try reading it aloud. After you have read it aloud a few times, try standing up and reading it aloud; try to feel the language in your body as well as in your voice.

The passage is the opening paragraphs of "In Chancery," the first chapter of Charles Dickens's great novel *Bleak House,* published in 1853 after its initial serialization; the title refers both to a location (a chancery court, where cases involving equity and financial and property disputes were heard and determined) and a state of being, in this case, the interminable legal case of *Jarndyce v. Jarndyce* that forms much of the plot of the novel. There are a few other references that may be unfamiliar to you. "Michaelmas Term" is a phrase used in academic and legal calendars in England, referring to the period from October to December. "Lincoln's Inn Hall" is the name of one of the four associations to which lawyers belonged in London; it served as a kind of all-inclusive campus, with libraries, dining halls, and offices. Other geographical references, such as Essex marshes, Kentish heights, and Greenwich pensioners (retired sailors) would be worth investigating in more detail should you choose to work more extensively on a formal performance of this passage.

London. Michaelmas Term lately over, and the Lord Chancellor sitting in Lincoln's Inn Hall. Implacable November weather. As much mud in the streets as if the waters had but newly retired from the face of the earth, and it would not be wonderful to meet a Megalosaurus, forty feet long or so, waddling like an elephantine lizard up Holborn Hill. Smoke lowering down from chimney-pots, making a soft black drizzle, with flakes of soot in it as big as full-grown snow-flakes—gone into mourning, one might imagine, for the death of the sun. Dogs, undistinguishable in mire. Horses, scarcely better; splashed to their very blinkers. Foot passengers, jostling one another's umbrellas in a general infection of ill-temper, and losing their foot-hold at street-corners, where tens of thousands of other foot passengers have been slipping and sliding since the day broke (if this day ever broke), adding new deposits to the crust upon crust of mud, sticking at those points tenaciously to the pavement, and accumulating at compound interest.

Fog everywhere. Fog up the river, where it flows among green aits and meadows; fog down the river, where it rolls defiled among the tiers of shipping and the waterside pollutions of a great (and dirty) city. Fog on the Essex marshes, fog on the Kentish heights. Fog creeping into the cabooses of collier-brigs; fog lying out on the yards and hovering in the rigging of great ships; fog drooping on the gunwales of barges and small boats. Fog in the eyes and throats of ancient Greenwich pensioners, wheezing by the firesides of their wards; fog in the stem and bowl of the afternoon pipe of the wrathful skipper, down in his close cabin; fog cruelly pinching the toes and fingers of his shivering little 'prentice boy on deck. Chance people on the bridges peeping over the parapets into a nether sky of fog, with fog all round them, as if they were up in a balloon and hanging in the misty clouds.

Before we present some general definitions, concepts, and thoughts about particular areas of performance technique, we'd like to work inductively for a few minutes with this text. As you read it, what struck you as the primary vocal challenges it presents? Were you struck with unusual aspects of phrasing? With the kinds of words that dominated the passage? With the simple (or perhaps not so simple) act of maintaining the breath required to keep the performance moving?

What about bodily or physical techniques? As you stood and read the passage aloud, how did you find your body responding to the language? Did you consider whether particular gestures would make sense or heighten the language of the text? How was your sense of space involved in this preliminary performance? To what extent did you find yourself remaining stationary throughout your reading, or did you have an impulse to move? If the latter was the case, what made you wish to move and when? How did the space in which you tried this experiment affect your decisions? Did you do this in a small private room or in a larger classroom or even outside?

Notice that, with each of the questions we posed, we asked you to consider them with respect to this particular text; we believe that all technique is only effective within the specific contexts of a particular text and a particular performance. Thus, while we will try to clarify what technical issues typically face all performers across texts and contexts, it is always also with a mind to specific performances. We cannot stress this enough, for we wish to avoid suggesting that there is a technique or set of techniques that can be applied uniformly to all texts and situations. Indeed, some critics may describe a performer as too "technique-y" (to use a slang word) because their use of technique seems too mechanical or unchanging, placing the performer's style in the foreground, rather than the specific qualities of the text and performance setting.

Vocal Technique

We begin with issues surrounding the use of the voice because the kinds of performances we are focusing on in this textbook are those involving the speaking of verbal texts (those composed of words). The name of the course in which you are enrolled may identify this emphasis: "oral inter-pretation" takes the centrality of voice and speech as a given. Some of these courses, though by no means all, go one prescriptive step further, holding as a "rule" that the performances given should restrict themselves primarily to the domain of the voice and engage the rest of the body as an extension of the voice. Thus, in some philosophies of forensics (the performance setting described in situation 1 above), performances that use too much of the body beyond the domain of the vocal may be seen as violating aesthetic principles. We do not hold with this as a general prin-ciple, but we remind you that, as a performer, you must always take into account the conventions of the performance setting in which you find yourself. The best performers, we maintain, are the most adaptable ones.

It is outside the scope of this book to detail all the possible issues involved in the use of the voice in performance. At the end of the book, we list a number of the most popular and well-regarded books on vocal technique for the performer. Indeed, the study of vocal technique can be complex and lengthy enough to warrant multiyear courses, particularly for those performers seeking professional careers in theater and other related professions. Our goal is to identify the general areas of vocal production and then apply them to the text above as an example of how you might combine technical and analytic work together—how, as Aristotle put it, *techne* and *episteme* might interact.

Breathing: The Core of Life and Performance

If there is one thing virtually all teachers and performers agree upon, it is the primacy of useful breath work as the foundation for all effective performance. Without it, of course, performers not only cannot make themselves heard, but they cannot continue to live! One thing that can make breath work initially challenging for a performer is the very fact that we all engage in it unconsciously as a reflexive response to our living, functioning state. You might find that during early stages of your work on breathing, you may feel a bit panicky, as if you no longer remember *how* to breathe: this is the price of conscious study.

While we will try to minimize the amount of technical language and discussion, it is necessary to introduce a few terms and concepts along the way. Breathing consists fundamentally of two processes, rarely totally distinct from each other: inspiration and expiration. It is no accident that you are probably more familiar with these terms in ordinary language, the former describing a process of creativity, the latter the running out of time (or life). For the ancient Greeks, *inspiration* meant the breathing into the human being by the gods—hence, the sense of divine intervention in inspiration. We may more often use the synonyms *inhale* and *exhale* for the processes of taking in and expelling air. We breathe through two cavities located in the head: the nose (nasal) and the mouth (oral). Most of the time, we are more likely to inhale and exhale through our noses, unless a head cold has blocked that passage and we are then more consciously aware of breathing through our mouths. In speaking (and singing), we tend to shift our breathing to our mouths, which allows us to draw air in more quickly and in greater volume, thus giving us more power for speech. There can be dramatic differences in the amount of time we take to exhale during speech and during quiet breathing; speech specialist Hilda Fisher has estimated that there is a 5:1 exhale/inhale ratio while speaking against a 1:1 ratio in silence (p. 50).

There are three areas where we focus the air we inhale: chest, thorax (rib cage), and diaphragm (the muscle right above the abdomen; see figure 4.1). While stereotypical representations of speech often show a soldier being told to stick out his (or her) chest and take in a deep breath, the opposite is actually the most effective: breathing from the diaphragm allows the greatest intake and the greatest control for speaking. Such effective breathing is inextricably tied to posture (the relative straightness of the spine), which may be where the military stereotype comes from. We optimize breathing when our spine is as close to straight as possible; however, as acting teacher Kristin Linklater reminds us, while the spine is "the support of breath," it is most effectively used when it is accompanied by relaxation and when we "observe" what we are doing "without controlling" it (p. 19). While we cannot help but be overly conscious initially, our ultimate goal is to become aware of the natural processes that allow us to speak. Voice and acting teacher Arthur Lessac draws on research that indicates that a straighter spine actually increases height by half an inch and chest circumference by up to three inches. Lessac is careful to remind us that the increased height and chest is actually the body at its most effective and that we tend to sit or stand in postures that do not optimize our bodily abilities (p. 26).

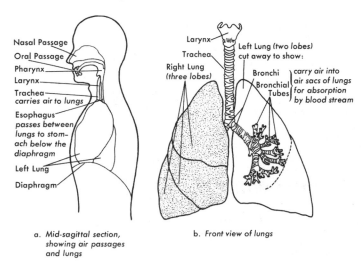

a. Mid-sagittal section,
   showing air passages
   and lungs

b. Front view of lungs

FIGURE 4.1: THE MECHANICS OF BREATHING

From Hilda B. Fisher, *Improving Voice and Articulation* (Boston: Houghton Mifflin Company, 1966). Copyright © 1966 by Hilda B. Fisher.

Learning to control your breath intake and output can be accomplished through fairly simple exercises. Begin by doing some silent counting as you inhale, then hold your breath (although never to the point where you feel as though you might pass out), and then exhale. Try starting with a count of 5-5-5, which should be comfortable for those without any respiratory difficulties, and then build up. As you increase the length of time, remember that inhaling usually takes less time than exhaling in speech. Once you have reached a level that feels both more expansive and more comfortable (and this may take weeks or even months), begin experimenting with testing your breath control using the text by Dickens above.

To start with, choose a fairly short sentence or phrase to speak on the exhale (in English, speech only occurs during exhalation, unless the purpose is to create a sense of distress or discomfort for a character)— any of the short ones will do, such as "Fog everywhere" or "Implacable

November weather." Experiment with rate, as well. Since both of these phrases are brief enough to be spoken even on a 5-count exhalation (the counting should be internal and silent, of course), see what happens when you vary the speed with which you say them—do you have extra breath left over? Can you extend certain words for effect, such as "everywhere," to create a sense of an enveloping fog, or "November," to heighten the autumnal mood? Then, as you build up more breath control, start taking on the challenge of longer sentences.

Resonance: Foundation for Projection, Rate, and Quality

While breathing is the core of speech and life, *resonance*, the frequency of vibration of the vocal folds, is the foundation for what makes speech audible and flexible. Look again at figure 4.1, which shows the vocal apparatus. Notice the *pharynx*, the tube at the back of the mouth leading to the throat and lungs. Directly below the *pharynx* lies the *larynx*, which you may know better by its nontechnical name, the voice box, in which two vocal folds (or vocal cords) are housed. It is the vibration of these folds during exhalation that produces sound, a process technically known as *phonation*. More or less resonance in the voice accounts for both greater and lesser control by a performer of certain aspects of speech and for habitual vocal qualities, which can be viewed as positive or negative and employed by performers to create desired effects (you may, for example, want a harsh vocal quality for some of the descriptive sentences in the Dickens). Performers need to be careful whenever they work against their natural resonance to ensure that they are not actually harming their vocal apparatus by doing things that will form vocal nodes or growths than can damage their voices permanently; if you are cast in a production that calls for unnatural manipulation of your voice, always consult with a vocal coach, your director, or, if necessary, a speech therapist to find out how to achieve the effect you wish without risking the health of your vocal organs.

Resonance affects virtually every aspect of vocal control and technique and, of course, cannot be separated from breathing. The ability to control your breath in and of itself will increase your flexibility in terms of producing vocal resonance. It is useful to think about resonance in terms of the laws of physics; as Fisher says, "resonance does not add energy; it increases the rate of energy output in reduced time" (p. 90). So it is not a matter of "ramping up" more physical energy but of deploying what is there in ways that produce vocal variations. For example, loudness is not effectively increased by shouting and straining the vocal folds, but by gaining more breath and controlling the rate at which it is exhaled and the forcefulness (not tension) of the muscles used to project it. The vocal folds open more slowly and close more quickly (and remain closed longer) the louder one's voice gets, but it is not this alone that creates the sense of loudness in a voice.

Loudness (and volume in general) may thus be thought of as a matter of projection and of focusing energy vocally, rather than as a mechanical process. Where do you want your voice to reach (and why) and how is such a shift in volume related to the changing mood or meaning of the text you are performing? Return to the Dickens passage and study it carefully. Can you identify sentences that you would want to speak more loudly than others? In the first paragraph, after the narrator has set the time and place, what follows is a series of sentence fragments that serve as vivid descriptions—everything from images of prehistoric dinosaurs to the ubiquity of dogs and the actions of horses splashing through the mud. In order to paint these pictures, you may wish to increase the volume of your voice.

Similarly, you will need to modulate volume depending on where and to whom you are performing this text. If you are sitting at a desk reading it to a classroom of students, your volume will be quite different from what you would use in a theater seating a thousand or more (as Dickens himself did when he performed selections from his novels to packed audiences all over England and America in the nineteenth century).

We began with loudness, but it is clear that a number of other aspects of vocal technique, which grow out of breathing and resonance, are involved: rate, phrasing, and intonation, to name a few. So in order to control volume, you may find that you also have to decrease the rate at which you speak these sentences (which is not synonymous with slowing down the movement of the vocal folds, as described above); if you speak too quickly, you may not have enough breath to increase the resonance of the speech. So, volume is intimately related to rate (or speed) of speech, as well. Beginning performers often have a tendency to read texts too quickly, perhaps for fear of boring their audiences. It is true that the rate of speech for texts read aloud tends to be slightly faster than the rate of extemporaneous speech (although there is not as much a difference as one might expect—it can be 160 words per minute for reading and 159 words per minute in speaking, according to Fisher), but this will always depend on text, space, audience, and occasion. Nonetheless, volume and rate depend much on each other.

This, in turn, leads to questions of phrasing and voice, and thus closer to the analysis of specific texts. While various writers develop recogniz-able styles, almost like voice prints (no one would mistake the sentences of Dickens for those of Ernest Hemingway, who could fit a dozen of his terse sentences into one of Dickens's more elaborate ones), within a single writer's work—indeed, within a paragraph—the writer will vary sentence length, sentence structure, and so forth. Looking at the example from *Bleak House*, specifically at the second paragraph, notice that the vast majority of its sentences begin with the word *fog*, as do some of the compound and complex clauses within longer sentences. At the same time, no two sentences are phrased in quite the same way, nor do they make quite the same demands on the performer in terms of phrasing, volume, and rate. The first sentence—"Fog everywhere"—is as stark as imaginable, two words, four syllables. Indeed, it is a kind of title for the paragraph, and hence, part of the decision in phrasing might be not only to decide how long to take saying these two words, but how long a pause to take between the two words and after the sentence. Do you want the words to run together, as if they are a single clustered image? Or do you want to hold the first word, with its lower vowel that makes you almost yawn when you say it, then pause to build suspense as your audience wonders what the next word will be and then say "everywhere" with greater speed? Or perhaps you decide to take extra time saying "everywhere," drawing the syllables out, making us aware of the compound structure of the word (*every* plus *where*) to make the fog fill the room? You will need to wed technical choices to the artistic effects you wish to achieve.

As you proceed from this two-word sentence, you will find questions of volume, rate, and phrasing become more complicated as the sentences become more complicated. Take the next sentence, for example: "Fog up the river, where it flows among green aits and meadows; fog down the river, where it rolls defiled among the tiers of shipping and the waterside pollutions of a great (and dirty) city." Let's break this sentence down for the purposes of vocal analysis. It is composed of two parallel sentences, tied together by a semicolon. The parallel structure of each half may clue us in to how we might maintain phrasing in some respects (both halves map out a direction for the fog—"up the river" and "down the river"). In terms of intonation (the movement of pitch up or down), the sentence directs us by its very use of "up" and down"; at the same time, each directional word is followed by the exact same phrase, "the river," which might suggest a return to a neutral intonational phrasing, so that the listener hears the echoing repetition of "the river," so important to Dickens's landscape.

If we keep going, we notice that the phrasing becomes more varied, with the first half ("up the river") ending fairly quickly with a compound noun phrase "aits and meadows," two images drawn from nature, whereas the second half of the sentence ("down the river") becomes complex in both its structure and in its reference to man-made forms of industry and pollution, culminating in that ironic phrase simultaneously praising and critical, marked by its use of parentheses, "a great (and dirty) city." This second half clearly takes longer to say and has more of a sense of building. Its intonational contours may also be more complex, with the insertion of "(and dirty)" perhaps a cue to the performer to take a slight pause, perhaps to lower volume and pitch, as if sneaking in the criticism, and so forth.

Yet another set of variables to consider in order to examine this passage from a technical vocal standpoint is what speech scholars tend to call "vocal quality." Vocal quality is often described in negative terms, identifying what some consider to be deficits in the way a voice sounds, usually based on problems related to resonance. While we do not question the genuine issues of people who, either because of organic, psychological, or habitual reasons, find themselves using their voice in ways that make them unhappy, we also acknowledge that there can be difficulties in establishing what constitutes a "normal" or "ideal" vocal quality, that such norms are often culturally and historically constructed and can be grounded in power-based assumptions about gender, race and ethnicity, class, and ability. What we advocate is encouraging performers (and all people, for that matter) to develop as wide a range of vocal possibilities as they find useful. It is, however, helpful for performers to have ways of thinking about particular qualities, if primarily to know how to reproduce them for texts and performances where they might be appropriate. Here are some of the most common:

1. Hypernasality: when the voice is projected primarily through the nasal cavity, producing a sometimes harsh sound.
2. Denasality: when the voice is projected exclusively through the mouth (often because of a cold or allergies) making particular consonant sounds indistinct.

3. Harshness: when the pharynx is hypertense (too tense) and there is insufficient resonance.
4. Throatiness: when the tongue is positioned too far back in the mouth; the voice seems held back in the throat rather than projected forward.
5. Thinness: when the tongue is positioned too far forward; the voice sounds airy or as if resonance is restricted.
6. Vocal fry or raspiness: not enough air meets the vocal folds and the sound breaks up.

Can you think of performers whose voices are distinguished by one or more of these qualities? Looking at the Dickens passage, can you identify words, phrases, or sentences in which the use of one or another of these particular vocal qualities might be artistically effective?

Articulation: Making Individual Sounds Distinct

The last aspect of vocal technique we will address is articulation, which refers to the process by which the organs of the vocal apparatus make sounds that are meaningfully distinct from each other. People often use the words *articulation, enunciation,* and *pronunciation* synonymously. It is useful to understand the differences between these terms, as they map out different, if related, areas of emphasis. *Articulation* is a technical term, referring to the mechanics of how a sound such as *s* or *th* is made by the contact between and positioning of sounds in the mouth; it also may refer to how sounds combine into words. *Enunciation* is an evaluative term, referring to clarity and audibility of sounds. *Pronunciation* is a more sociolinguistic or sometimes geographical term, referring to how a word is actually said (combining how particular letters are spoken in a given word, such as the *gh* pronounced as *f* in *enough,* and where the stress falls in any word of more than one syllable). Pronunciation can vary depending on such factors as the meaning of a word (some words are stressed differently depending on whether they are being used as a noun or a verb in a given sentence), geography (*greasy* may be pronounced with either the *s* sound or a *z* sound depending on where in the United States the speaker lives or comes from), and historical period (the word *knife* was originally pronounced with a spoken *k*). All of these aspects of speech and voice are, of course, important. *Enunciation* is a complex concept because, depending on the text, what constitutes an appropriate "clarity" may vary (and this can be true of regional dialects, as well). *Pronunciation* is equally important, because a performance can be completely undermined if the performer consistently mispronounces a word; appropriate pronunciation speaks to the knowledge of the performer and to the sense of authenticity a performance projects.

However, here we are most concerned with helping you think about articulation as a building block of vocal technique. An entire subarea of linguistics, articulatory phonetics, has been developed to try to describe how specific sounds within and across languages are made. Figure 4.2 shows the principal articulators of the human vocal apparatus. While most of the articulators (the parts of the mouth) will be familiar, there may be some new terms, such as *alveolar ridge* (the part of the roof of the mouth that meets the teeth), the *hard* and *soft palates* (the latter is also called the *velum*), and the *vocal folds* (also called the *vocal cords* or *glottis*).

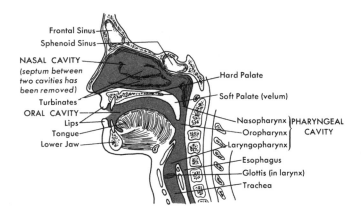

(Midsagittal section of head and neck, looking into
right side from central plane)

FIGURE 4.2: THE VOCAL APPARATUS

From Hilda B. Fisher, *Improving Voice and Articulation* (Boston: Houghton Mifflin Company, 1966). Copyright © 1966 by Hilda B. Fisher.

Sounds are divided into two major categories (and arguably a third): consonants and vowels; diphthongs, which involve the quick, sometimes imperceptible combining of vowels in rapid succession are sometimes regarded as a third area. The principal difference between consonants and vowels is that consonants are produced by some kind of contact between the articulators, whereas vowels involve a free flow of air and are distinguished from each other by tongue position and the relative tenseness or laxness of the mouth. Consonantal contact consists of either a stopping of airflow followed by a release of the air (such sounds are called "stop-plosives"); a rubbing together (fricatives), or a combination, called "affricates." In addition, they are described as either "voiced" or "unvoiced" (sometimes "voiceless"), depending on the degree to which the vocal folds resonate in the production of the sound. Vowels are usually described as either high, middle, or low and front, central, or back, depending on the height and position of the tongue. Articulatory phoneticians actually have even more detailed ways of describing sounds, but this basic set of attributes will suffice for our purposes.

Figure 4.3 is a list of the consonants of American English. The symbols used are drawn from the International Phonetic Alphabet (IPA), in which each symbol describes a unique sound. The IPA is useful in trying to describe the actual sounds produced in speaking a word, rather than the often confusing spelling of English in which one symbol may be pronounced in multiple ways (such as the letter *c*, which can be sounded as either *s* or *k*, and in some languages may be pronounced as "ch"). You will notice that the list also groups certain sounds together; one of the fascinating aspects of English phonetics is that some sounds are distinguished from each other exclusively on the basis of whether they are voiced or unvoiced: an example would be *b* and *p*. Virtually all babies who grow up in an English-speaking family learn to make this distinction without being taught it and so know that *bat* and *pat* mean different things, but some languages don't make this distinction and it can be confusing for speakers of these languages to hear the differences and articulate them. This is also true for English speakers learning second languages.

Figure 4.4 is a vowel chart for English, roughly representing where the tongue sits in the mouth when each vowel is produced. Vowels are much harder to specify than consonants precisely because there is not the same articulatory contact found in consonants; this also explains why vowels tend to vary more from individual to individual and from region to region. For example, while both of us grew up in the Chicago area and speak a fairly standard dialect of that region, Bruce has a sister who has always pronounced the word *milk* as if it were spelled "melk." Try saying the word both ways—can you hear and feel how close the two vowel sounds are and why it would be easy for someone to slip into the "melk" pronunciation. Similarly, we have a friend who grew up in Denver, Colorado, with parents who were originally from Texas, who pronounces

IPA Symbol	Articulators	Manner	Voiced/Voiceless	Example
b	bilabial	stop-plosive	voiced	bad
p	bilabial	stop-plosive	voiceless	pad
d	alveolar	stop-plosive	voiced	done
t	alveolar	stop-plosive	voiceless	ton
g	velar	stop-plosive	voiced	goat
k	velar	stop-plosive	voiceless	coat
v	labiodental	fricative	voiced	van
f	labiodental	fricative	voiceless	fan
ð	dental	fricative	voiced	those
θ	dental	fricative	voiceless	thin
z	alveolar	fricative	voiced	zip
s	alveolar	fricative	voiceless	sip
ȝ	palatal	fricative	voiced	azure
ʃ	palatal	fricative	voiceless	sugar
h	glottal	fricative	voiceless	had
dȝ	palatal	affricate	voiced	joke
tʃ	palatal	affricate	voiceless	choke
m	bilabial	nasal	voiced	mope
n	alveolar	nasal	voiced	nope
ŋ	velar	nasal	voiced	bang
l	alveolar	lateral	voiced	lap

The following sounds are often classified as "semi-vowels," combining some characteristics of consonants and some of the vowels

r		fricative	may be either	run/rhetoric
w	bilabial	glide	voiceless	witch
ʍ	bilabial	glide	voiced	which

Note: in many dialects and for many individual speakers, the distinction between ʍ and w no longer exists.

FIGURE 4.3: CONSONANTS IN AMERICAN ENGLISH

the words *pin* and *pen* in almost identical ways, with a vowel that sounds to us as though it fits somewhere between the way we make those two sounds ourselves—context is the only way we can determine which word our friend means. Diphthongs (which we list after the vowel chart) also can sound more or less like a single sound or two distinct sounds, depending on upbringing and regional dialect. Think of many southern speakers who tend to draw out the sounds of the diphthong to the point where they sound like two syllables rather than one sound. It is important to realize that one or another way of making such sounds is not right or wrong; what matters is the ability to be understood and to understand each other—reminding us to be sensitive to where we are, to whom we are speaking, and to strive to become more careful and flexible listeners.

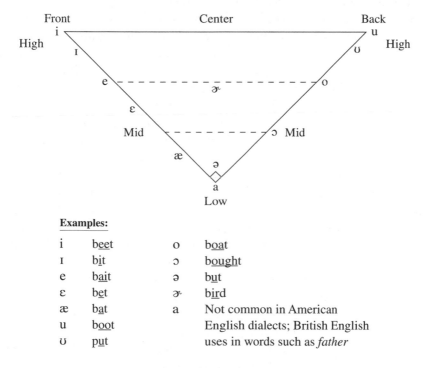

Examples:

i	b**ee**t	o	b**oa**t
ɪ	b**i**t	ɔ	b**ough**t
e	b**ai**t	ə	b**u**t
ɛ	b**e**t	ɚ	b**ir**d
æ	b**a**t	a	Not common in American
u	b**oo**t		English dialects; British English
ʊ	p**u**t		uses in words such as *father*

FIGURE 4.4: VOWEL TRIANGLE

From Wallace A. Bacon, *The Art of Interpretation* (New York: Holt, Rinehart, Winston, 1972).

Studying articulation is obviously useful and important to a performer who wishes to have the greatest flexibility and range possible. Should you wish to study the IPA further, it would be a useful challenge to try transcribing the Dickens passage (or a portion of it) into IPA to get a sense of how to listen to specific sounds. Another useful exercise is ask someone to listen to you read the passage aloud, marking sounds that were indistinct or unclear, particularly places where sounds became indistinct in succession; sometimes we speak too quickly to articulate each sound as fully as it warrants (although it is also possible to overarticulate). For example, take the phrase "Kentish heights." It is easy to say these two words so quickly that what emerges is "Kentisheights" and the important second word, *heights*, which contrasts to the previous "Essex marshes," gets lost. Another example, in our experience, is the problematic vowel in *fog*. Carol's family is half English and many of her relatives speak with a British accent (she also spent much time in that country as a child); Bruce's mother came from the Upper Peninsula of Michigan and his father grew up in one of the western suburbs of Chicago. While decades of living in Chicago have made our dialects more alike than not, if we both read the sentence "Fog everywhere," there are differences in how we say the vowel in *fog*. Is the difference sufficient to make the word difficult for a listener to understand? Probably not, but that might depend on the listener. Also, we would both make a point of working on that vowel as a result of analyzing the sounds of the passage, as it is critical to the effectiveness of the selection. Indeed, one might decide to perform this passage with a British accent in order to capture the sounds Dickens originally had in his own phonetic inventory (the sounds individual people habitually make), and then the *o* in *fog*. would sound even more different from the sound either of us would normally make.

A reasonable question you might have at this point is to what degree you should "prepare" a performance technically in the ways we have mentioned. For example, should you go through and mark all words that require special emphasis? Should you use a system to indicate on the page where intonation goes up or down? Should you write relative rate of speech in the margins of a script (if you are using a script)? The answer will vary from performer to performer (and from instructor to instructor). The history of the performance of literature suggests that different eras have produced different answers to such questions (the same questions can be posed for issues surrounding body, movement, gesture, and location); even within historical periods, different performers and theorists have taken different approaches to preparation. During the period spanning the late eighteenth and early nineteenth centuries, known as the Elocutionary Period, there existed two distinct schools of thought on performance as an art, schools based on fundamentally different ways of understanding the relationship of art to nature. One school, known today as the Mechanical School, held that one of the functions of art is essentially to "tame" nature, to impose on it formal structures; the Natural School argued that art grows out of nature. Teachers and writers who adhered to the philosophy of the Mechanical School often devised very intricate notational systems, almost like musical scores in many cases, instructing the performer on how to speak a particular text; they often tried to generalize about such things as which intonational patterns should be used for which kinds of sentences, and so forth. Their goal, in one sense, was to create performances that could be repeated down to the last nuance. Those associated with the Natural School emphasized what they viewed as a process more centered on the relationship between the specific performer, text, and occasion of performance. While they hardly advocated a free-for-all approach and believed that a careful and close analysis of a text would lead to a level of understanding and feeling that would produce reasonably consistent performances, they acknowledged that nature always allows for change, spontaneity, and discovery. If they used technical notation, it was to guide and remind the performer of what to think and feel, rather than to dictate a very specific vocal pattern.

We are more in sympathy with the Natural School, as we believe the relationship between performer, text, and context is more complex and mutable than the approach the Mechanical School suggests. Our advice would be to work on the performance for a while in a way that encourages discovery and experimentation before considering placing performance notations on your script (or encoding them in a fixed way in your mind, if you are working from memory); then do so if you think it will help you to have a technical reminder (say, a note to slow down at a point where rehearsal has proven you tend to speed up or the IPA notation for a word you consistently find difficult to pronounce). We can imagine some performance texts and situations in which a more technically notated script might be of use, such as one involving choric speech or in which ritual or rhythm is critical to the effects desired. A general principle might be to provide technical notation only to the extent that you need it to produce a performance that is true to your intentions with regard to the text and the situation and that still allows the performance and text to remain in a dynamic relationship throughout the processes of rehearsal, presentation, and repeated performances.

We hope the preceding sections have given you at least an introductory glance at how complex and how interesting the combining of work on vocal technique and textual analysis can be. It brings together everything from anatomical science, to physics, to geography, history, and linguistics. While it is possible to do so much work on technique that the rich emotional, social, and psychological life of a text can get lost in the "science," it is preferable to find a way of integrating the inner and outer lives of the texts we choose to perform. Beginning with the voices of the performer(s) and of the text is a useful starting point. We now move to questions of the body—again, questions that are never separable from language and voice but which may be seen as extending and integrating them.

Physical Techniques

The Body: Instrument, Medium, and Site

The term *body*, which sounds so simple and obvious to most of us, today holds a complex and, some might even say, contested position in theory and practice. On the one hand, what could be more self-evident than the existence of the body—after all, we all spend our days living in one, sometimes with pleasure, sometimes not, but while we may not be constantly mindful of it, any more than we think about breathing every time we take a breath, it is always there. Yet critical theorists argue that the body, for all of its seeming "naturalness," is also as much a social construction—or, to put it another way, experienced through social codes and scripts—as anything that exists naturally. The body, such theorists argue, is not simply *there* but is something that we experience through a complex web of interpretive strategies, some which we internalize (such as our psychological experiences beginning in infancy) and some which are imposed upon us (such as legal control of our bodies through laws governing everything from reproductive freedom to sexual actions to prison systems). Our bodies are not ourselves—at least not in a way that is unmediated by social forces and conventions.

Having said that, we turn to ways of thinking about how we use our bodies in the making of performances; three of these may be articulated as: an instrument, a medium, and a site. We will explain what we mean by each of these terms and then offer some more concrete examples of how to think about and explore the use of the body in technical terms.

When we say that the performer's body is an *instrument*, we draw upon two different ways of understanding that word. First, we may think of the body as analogous to a musical instrument, such as a violin, a trumpet, or a guitar; singers frequently speak of their voices and, by extension, their bodies as their "instrument"—the thing that allows them to produce music. So it is for the performer of literature and other verbal texts. While other elements may become part of the performance (such as the performance space, costumes, properties, electronic media), first and foremost, the performer uses her body as the "instrument" on which a text is "played." Thinking about the body as an instrument reminds us that to learn to play musical instruments, we must practice with them, work on specific skills, learn particular techniques, usually at the same time we are also learning to play specific pieces—and that we tend to begin with pieces at whatever level of technical skill we have acquired: a beginning violinist starts with "Twinkle, Twinkle, Little Star," not a Beethoven sonata or the Barber Concerto for Violin and Orchestra. What a violinist learns first are such techniques as how to hold the instrument, how to bow, and where the fingers are placed for first position; vibrato, eighth position, double stops, and spiccato come later. Nonetheless, simple melodies are played from the start, as technique divorced from any content quickly becomes tedious. So it is with verbal performance technique, which is why we suggested working with a short form such as haiku in chapter 2.

Another use of the word *instrument* is allied with the notion of professional or technological work: we speak of medical instruments and the tools of an auto mechanic, for example—and we hope that, while there may be some shared functions between the two, a surgeon doesn't use the mechanic's instruments to operate on us! What this use of the term suggests is that there can be particular ways of doing certain actions that are expected and sometimes required in order to accomplish the work of the specific profession. So it is with oral performance: the solo performer is likely to use space and directionality in ways that are different from an actor performing in an ensemble of ten in a realistic staging of a play by Anton Chekhov or Eugene O'Neill. At the same time, with the exception of very specialized work, it is also often the case that there is more than one way of accomplishing a physical task—and more than one instrument or tool that can be successfully employed.

Another way to think about how we use our bodies in performance is to think of the body as a medium. Perhaps the most common use of this word is as a synonym for "middle," which is its meaning in Latin. To be "medium" means, in a sense, to be in the "middle" of things. A related definition of *medium* is as a form through which information is conveyed (television is an electronic medium) or a specific art form (oil paint and modern dance are mediums) or even a person who acts as a conduit between the spirit world and the living world. What is common to all of these definitions is the idea that the performer serves a link through which a text is transmitted to an audience. The performer's body, then, can also be seen as a medium in the sense of being the materials of an artistic form—just as a painter uses oil paint and canvas, so the performer uses his body (including voice) as the material, which is handled in both conventional and unconventional ways, and through which a text is "painted" and made visible (and audible—sensible, in the largest meaning of that word) to an audience.

Some theorists may object to the notion of the performer and the performer's body as a medium because, they argue, it suggests a kind of mindlessness—that the performer and his body as materials are merely passive receptacles for performance. We would suggest that thinking of the body as medium is one of a number of ways of understanding how the body functions and does not preclude a mindful, conscious performing presence. In this sense, the performer is both artist and material at the same time.

Stop for a moment and think about your experiences as a performer in an ensemble—whether it be theater, music, or dance. Are there times the conductor has asked you to function simply as a medium in the sense of allowing music to emerge without you giving considerable thought to how it is produced, what it means, or where the piece is headed? Or, as a dancer, to simply perform a particular step or to hold your body in a specific position without an explanation about how it will fit into a larger vision of the work? Or, as an actor, to try a line reading without much explanation about why that particular intonation, rate, or use of pause is one desired? Has that ever been valuable? If so, why? If not, why not? Would you be satisfied as an artist if the process never moved beyond that—if you remained only the material and never a creative part of the process?

The last way we have suggested for thinking about the body is as a site. We use this word to suggest a place where something (a battle, a dialogue, a performance) is to be built or staged—a location for activity. While we may be used to thinking of site as a geological place, think about one of the most ubiquitous terms in current usage: website. While there is a material element to a website, most people think of it as a process or as being essentially nonmaterial, a series of electronic impulses that converge in cyberspace. The word *site* also carries more specific connotations in that it suggests a location identified for particular use: it is not simply a place, but a place designated for a structure or an event—a school, a hospital, a theater, a war. Each of these sites carries with it many possible meanings, open to multiple interpretations and manipulations. A school can indeed be used as a kind of hospital—or, if you are a critic of systems of education, as a site for war. If we believe that performance can teach, then a theater can be a school. And so forth.

Therefore, we encourage you to think of your performing body as a site—a site whose meaning is open to a number of interpretations and uses, some under your control, some imposed upon it by society, by various audiences. Think about the opening passage of *Bleak House*, for example: how many different ways might you use your performing body as a site? As a place where the fog lives and breathes? As a seat of judgment on the industrialization of Victorian England? As a place where mysteries are created through occluded vision? Can you think of others?

Physical Memory, Responsiveness, and Gesture

If we think of the performer's body as instrument, medium, and site, we might then consider how we can best train (or "discipline") this body for effectiveness in performance. As with vocal technique, many performers training for a professional life in theater will spend several years working on such techniques as movement, dance, posture, periods and styles (historical differences in bodily use), and so forth, and, just as with the voice, there are a number of systems various people adhere to, such as the Alexander technique, Feldenkrais Method, and, in the twentieth century, Rudolf Steiner's total system of education, eurythmics, based on a blend of mystical philosophy, physical education, and dance. The scope of this book does not permit investigation of these specific methods, and we also respect similar systems for the voice, such as those developed by Linklater, Lessac, and Berry, which have a consistency, method, and process (see the selected bibliography). Our goal is more modest and limited, but, we hope, useful: to encourage you to think and feel *with* and *through* your body in ways that will allow you to develop more strategies for and confidence in using your body.

As with other aspects of performance technique, historically there has been disagreement about approaches and limits to physical engagement. For some teachers and artists, the solo performer of literature was expected to locate her performance primarily in what could be accomplished through the use of voice, facial expression, and, to a limited extent, gesture (the expressive use of arms and hands). Performers who engaged their entire bodies in overt movement were often deemed to have stepped over the line from "(oral) interpretation" into "acting." Those who maintained such distinctions argued for differences in aesthetics, intention, audience, and the nature of specific kinds of texts as their reasoning. Some, such as Charlotte Lee, a pioneer in the field, argued in favor of "suggestion," a limited use of body that would allow the audience to "complete," in their imagination, certain physical actions, just as the audience would typically be called on to imagine the physical setting in which a text might be set. This aesthetic of limited physical expression remains present today for a number of teachers and is seen in many of the regulations enforced in certain competitive speaking arenas.

Our position respects much of this philosophy for its value of being *selective* about physical expressiveness, but we see ourselves as taking a more open-ended approach. Occam's razor, a philosophic rule attributed to a fourteenth-century monk, argues that the best explanation is usually the most direct and uncomplicated one that can successfully explain a phenomenon. In other words, don't add unnecessary complications that may only muddy the waters. This approach argues for a kind of economy, and here the notion of suggestion is valuable: it may indeed provide the audience with a clearer performance and one that makes stronger the important elements. In the same way that the primary subject of a painting might get lost if surrounded by too much detail, so it may be with performance.

Another useful set of terms in thinking about physicality are drawn from the Canadian media theorist Marshall McLuhan, who distinguished between "hot" and "cool" media. Hot media were those in which the audience was given much detail and sensory input and left with little to do beyond taking it in (up to the point of becoming overloaded!); cool media were those that provided a minimum of sensory detail and input and gave the audience much work to do intellectually, emotionally, and imaginatively. Different media tend to produce different effects and are more useful for some kinds of material and audiences than for others. Can you think of performances that you have seen that you can definitely place as either hot or cool? Do you have a preference for one over the other? Does it vary? When and why?

At the same time, it is important to be careful that one doesn't shave a performance down to the point where it is left to bleed its life away! One can oversimplify a performance to a point where it does an equal disservice to the text and to the audience. Think back to some of the brief performances you did of haiku or other short texts. The balance between the simplicity of the form of seventeen syllables and the multiple possible meanings inherent in each haiku required careful thought and experimentation. Think back in particular to the exercise of performing the haiku without speaking the language—which performances you gave or saw felt most exciting or interesting to you? The ones that simply illustrated in a literal way the surface content of the poem? Or those that somehow managed both to show the concrete images and to hint at other more symbolic or unconscious or emotional levels?

Similarly, there are some texts and contexts in which more *is* more! Think about such spectacles as big musical theater productions (*Les Miserables* or *Cats*, for example) or ballets based on *The Nutcracker* or circuses. What we usually want as audiences of spectacle is as much stimulation and sensory delight as possible—to strip them down would be to miss the point of such performances.

Whether a performer chooses to show as much as possible physically or to withhold physical actions, he or she should learn to be physically *responsive* to the language and content of the text, as well as to the audience, to other performers, and to the physical space. There are many ways to work on such skills, a number of which can be traced back to the work of the Russian actor-director Konstantin Stanislavsky, whose teachings were developed in the middle of the twentieth century in America into something called the Method by American actor-director-teacher Lee Strasberg, who helped form the Actor's Studio, an institution that continues to exist today, although in a somewhat different form. Other teachers felt that Strasberg misunderstood Stanislavsky and developed their own versions of acting method; these include Stella Adler, Sanford Meisner, and Uta Hagen (see the list of resources).

At the root of Stanislavsky's approach was the development of what might be called "sensory memory" (it goes under various names, depending on the writer). What Stanislavsky encouraged his actors to do was to become very much in touch with their inner emotional histories and current lives, particularly in terms of how particular past events made them feel in a physical and emotional way, so that they could call on these memories when a script required them to portray parallel experiences onstage as a character. Those who criticize this approach argue that it puts emphasis incorrectly on the lives of the actors, rather than on the imagined lives of the characters—for example, that an actor's feelings of loss at the death of his father is not the same as Hamlet's experience—and that all too often such actors play themselves rather than the character.

This is a justifiable concern, but not one without remedy, it seems to us. Just as training on a musical instrument calls into play both the techniques and resources of the musician (the way she holds the instrument, the feelings she has about the music, the associations lyrics may evoke from her own experience) and then extends them beyond the solipsism of the performer's own ego experience, so it is with the performer of verbal texts. We begin with what is familiar and then, we hope, move to what is shared, but also to what is unfamiliar, different, and new.

Turning once again to our Dickens selection, we may think of how to develop responsiveness, using sense memory as a basis. Let's look at one phrase from the first paragraph: "gone into mourning, one might imagine, for the death of the sun" (a description of the smoke from the chimneys, responsible for producing some of the fog). Clearly, Dickens is using personification here—giving human qualities to a nonhuman phenomenon. To do so, he chooses a very human activity, one he complicates through a double metaphor—mourning for the death of a loved one and depression or other negative feelings resulting from the coming of winter (as days grow shorter and the sun is more often behind the clouds).

The performer of this phrase has a number of challenges—not only to express the concept of mourning but also the sense of seasonal change. It would probably not be our choice, in an actual classroom or public performance, to try to mimic the various rituals of mourning in order to express the physical feelings of this phrase: after all, it is a fairly brief phrase and too much "acting out" of it will be disproportionate to its relative place in the dense set of descriptions in this passage. At the same time, we will want to embed fully in ourselves what this vivid, evocative phrase means, so in rehearsal we might indeed act out some of the physical memories we have of mourning. These might include a posture of pulling inward, as we try to keep the feelings of sadness inside, or conversely, a display of physical loss of control that some people feel when they hear of the death of a loved one. Does the phrase point us in one direction more than another? We might think back to any experiences we have had of mourning—have we expressed them differently in different situations, for example, when an elderly relative died in his sleep after a long life or a young friend died suddenly as a result of a car accident? Dickens's phrase seems to us to point to a kind of mourning that is inevitable, that we expect, that we learn to prepare for—though we also acknowledge that the preparation for a loss is not the same as the actual experience of it. Similarly, we would want to recall our experiences as fall turns into winter (easier to do if you grew up in northern climes). What does our body remember about those days each year when we first felt the chill that let us know our light sweaters would not keep us warm, that we would be walking home from school in the dark?

Our remedy for the dangers of narcissism in the use of sense memory is to recognize that we must always endeavor to translate our own sense memory into the world of the text being performed. Thus, it is not enough for us simply to recall an instance of mourning in our own lives and use it to produce a physical response as we speak the words; we must be careful to consider the personal memory in light of the individual speaking it in the Dickens passage (we can presume a third-person narrator here). Our physical responsiveness will ultimately have to be integrated with the larger discourse of the entire passage. Is the narrator as mournful as one of the "pensioners" described in the second paragraph?

How much to show of our sense memory and physical responsiveness will always be dependent on what we think a text asks us to do (and we may think it offers us many options and choices) and what we want our audience to experience. It may be that what we want most is for our audience to feel the chill and the sadness that go together in the phrase. If so, we may decide to minimize our own vocal sorrow and physical chattering and shaking. Or, we may want the audience to see the narrator in this state, in which case we will embody the literal actions more. Neither approach is by definition right or wrong, but each produces different effects.

Connected in important ways to sense memory and physical responsiveness is the question of gestures—the use of hands and arms to express ideas and emotions. If you have studied interpersonal communication or public speaking, you have no doubt considered the use of such actions before. Gestures have been of interest to teachers and practitioners of speech and performance for centuries and, as with vocal technique, during the Elocutionary Period in particular, some writers tried to codify and label particular kinds of gestures and prescribe which ones were most useful to express particular moods, emotions, or attitudes. (You may find the work of such historical figures as Gilbert Austin, whose *Chironomia* was a manual for hand gestures, and the French acting teacher François Delsarte fascinating in this regard). Such theorists believed in universals of hand and arm gestures that could be employed in the performance of virtually any text to express an emotion.

More recent work in nonverbal communication suggests that gestures are typically more historically and culturally specific and contextual. (What counts as an obscene gesture in one culture may be quite inno-cent in another, so one must learn the local signs!) Similarly, we would argue that gestures are even more individualized and need to be consid-ered within the setting of a particular text. Students will often ask, how do I know when to gesture? Or, what gesture can I put here? Our answer, as with voice, is to experiment but also, as Linklater suggests about breathing, "observe without controlling." In other words, some texts do indicate particular gestures—such as "he shook his finger at the dog" or "she grabbed the handle of the hot tea pot and then dropped it." These situations are relatively easy: the performer will either decide to enact the gesture (particularly if she is trying to be the character, rather than describe the scene from a distance) or will allow the language to help the audi-ence imagine the gesture—or the performer may seek a middle ground in which some of the action is gestured, leaving the audience to complete it.

A more difficult realm to consider is nonindexical gestures, that is, gestures that are not described in words but are part of a more abstract level of emotion, mood, or general self-presentation. We use such gestures all the time in ordinary conversation, to underscore a point we are trying to make or to intensify a psychological response we have had. But similar to the problems performers face when they first start learning techniques for improving breathing, when placed in a performance situation, our first impulse may be that we have to invent gestures to accompany every-thing we say. We have all seen such performers—for example, people making sales pitches on late-night infomercials!—and the gestures seem artificial to the point of being ridiculous. They carry no meaning, conscious or unconscious, and only draw attention to the phoniness of the person saying the words. While sometimes very invented and planned gestures are useful (and, in some historical and cultural traditions, may be appropriate, such as if one is performing in a Victorian melodrama), we think it more effective to allow gestures to emerge in rehearsal. The more comfortable you become with the language, the deeper you place yourself in both the interior and exterior life of the text and of its characters, the more likely your body (and the text) will tell you how and when to gesture. One thing we do not recommend is rehearsing in front of a mirror in order to work on such aspects of physical technique as facial expressions and gestures; it can create a false sense of audience, as well as making the performer even more self-conscious about his appearance.

Questions of Location: Focus, Placement, and Space

The final area of physical technique we will consider is that of location. By this we don't mean venue (such as a theater as opposed to a classroom as opposed to an outdoor rally), although clearly different venues do present different opportunities and challenges. Rather, we are referring to how the solo performer uses his body and the performing space to create a sense of scene and of interaction between characters and between performer and audience. As with all the other elements we have been discussing, there are few hard-and-fast rules, but there are some accepted conventions that may be useful to you.

The words *locus* and *focus* are used quite frequently in discussions of techniques of solo performance. Wallace Bacon defined the term *locus* as: "'Place,' the location of a thing. In literature and the performance of literature, it involves the relationship between reader and poem and between reader and audience . . . The situation may be open, closed, or mixed" (p. 480). What Bacon was describing was whether the speaker of a literary text (he uses "poem" to refer to all literature) addressed the audience directly (open locus) or whether the speaker (or speakers) was speaking without direct acknowledgment of the audience (closed—either to each other, in the case of multiple speakers, or within or to oneself, if only one speaker is present) or whether there was some combination or alternation (such as when a narrator speaks directly to an audience, but characters speak to each other).

Let's turn back to our Dickens passage for an example. Is the locus of this selection open, closed, or mixed? In its broadest sense, it seems obvious that it is open in that we assume that its narrator is speaking to us, the readers (transformed into listeners in the context of performance). There are no other characters, so in that sense there is no possibility of it being closed locus unless we assume the narrator is observing and describing the scene for his own benefit. Is there any sense in which an argument could be made for a mixed locus? Most would probably say not, but one possibility might be to imagine that the narrator moves back and forth between describing the scene directly to us and gazing at the scene and going into a kind of spoken reverie to himself. Perhaps such short declarative sentences as "London. Michaelmas Term lately over, and the Lord Chancellor sitting in Lincoln's Inn Hall" and "Fog everywhere" are straightforward enough to be clearly open locus. But as the sentences become more complex and compound, it is possible to imagine a narrator who is fixed on watching the scene and describing what he sees—simultaneously locating his speech inwardly and toward the audience. Go through the two paragraphs and identify how you might move back and forth between open and mixed locus.

A closely related word is *focus*. Once again, Bacon provides a straightforward and useful definition: "Sharpness of definition; central point of attention. One may speak of the focus of the reader, of the poem, or of the reader's placement and location of the poem" (p. 481). So, if *locus* refers primarily to the sense of place—and the speaker's relationship to it—we may see *focus* as specifying the direction of the speaker's (or speakers') gaze, speech, and action. You may be familiar with some of the terminology of focus from cinematic theory and criticism, ideas like "deep focus," in which the camera looks beyond what is in the foreground to what is in the background. So we may, in some respects, think of focus in these terms.

In the solo performance of literature, a distinction is typically drawn between *onstage* and *offstage* focus. Simply put, onstage focus places the "action" of the performance literally onstage, as in a traditional realistic play that takes place in a room and in which an audience is asked to assume that they are viewing what is happening through a fourth wall, and the characters interacting with each other are not aware of the audience's presence. While it is not impossible for a solo performance to use onstage focus in a performance, can you imagine the ways in which it might present difficulties for both the performer and the audience? If a solo performer wishes to speak as multiple characters and use onstage focus, she will have to move around in ways that may interfere visually with the audience, cutting off sight lines and creating extremely artificial movements that violate audience conventions of the impression of realistic interaction. In some cases, the performance might profit from the comic effects produced by a solo performer trying to embody multiple characters in this way—such effects can highlight incongruity (and also, for a more serious effect, a character in the grip of a psychotic episode), but it would be difficult to imagine a solo performer managing to keep an audience attentive to serious interaction between characters if they must also attend to a body trying literally to occupy too many different spaces in succession.

Instead, most solo performers use offstage focus, sometimes referred to as presentational focus, and performances with multiple performers use offstage focus more often than we might initially imagine. Think, for example, of moments in musical plays when characters break into song. While sometimes they maintain onstage focus (as in a love duet), they just as often turn out and project their voices and focus toward the audience (which also enables them to follow the conductor). Similarly, if a character is meant to address an audience directly (as does the stage manager in Thornton Wilder's *Our Town*) or to speak to a character who is offstage, then offstage focus is used.

In solo performance of literature, offstage focus is used more often for one of the following purposes: direct address to the audience, visualization of a setting or scene, or interaction between characters. The first of these is easily and fairly unambiguously achieved: the performer simply addresses the audience as would a public speaker and talks to them. Sometimes the directness may be an illusion, if stage lighting or distance between performer or audience makes actual direct address impractical or impossible. Also, the performer has to decide whether to choose one person (or one spot) to address consistently, as a kind of representative of the audience as a whole, or whether to try to include as much of the audience as possible, through a kind of "panning" of the space, like a camera.

For the second use of offstage focus, to visualize a scene, performers have a number of options. Some performers choose a single spot, usually over the heads of the audience, upon which to focus their eyes and toward which to project their voice and performance energy. If this is the option you choose, you must be careful not to expect the choice of spot to do all the imaginative work for you. Audiences are often able to tell when a performer is simply staring at a spot and when the single focus becomes a site where the performer is actually imaginatively "seeing" what she is describing. Other performers prefer to vary the focus in such situations, shifting their heads (and torsos) slightly when there is a shift in the location of what is being described. Thus, in our example from *Bleak House*, one can imagine the performer shifting at various times throughout the paragraphs to indicate to the audience where each thing being described is located. The recommendation here is again to be selective—too much, too wide, and too varied shifting can result in both performer and audience becoming confused about what is being described and where it is supposed to be.

Connected to this, whether the performer chooses a single spot or multiple spots for focus, is the question of depth and distance. If the performer chooses to focus above the heads of the audience, it is still necessary for her to make decisions about where in relation to the speaker and to other places in the scene each focal point is located. In *Bleak House*, how close is the narrator to Lincoln's Inn Hall? Is the narrator actually seeing the hall or simply using it as an informational guidepost? How close is he to the dogs, to the horses? Does he move closer to the river and travel up and down it? If so, will his focus change for each and which is closer? Experiment with this in your room or in a classroom—try describing some object in the room, first standing as far away as possible, then gradually moving right next to it. How does your language change? How does your visual focus change? Does your body relate to it in space differently? Then take a few sentences from *Bleak House* and try the same experiment—here, of course, you have the added challenge of imagining what is described, rather than having it as a tangible object in your line of vision.

The final use of offstage focus is that which occurs when multiple characters interact. In a sense, the techniques used for this situation may be seen as extensions of the others we have been discussing. Because the excerpt from *Bleak House* that we have been using throughout this chapter has only one speaker, we will use a very brief excerpt from later in the chapter as an example. It is set in the High Court in Chancery.

> Thus, in the midst of the mud and at the heart of the fog, sits the Lord High Chancellor in his High Court of Chancery.
>
> "Mr. Tangle," says the Lord High Chancellor, latterly something restless under the eloquence of that learned gentleman.
>
> "Mlud," says Mr. Tangle. Mr. Tangle knows more of Jarndyce and Jarndyce than anybody. He is famous for it—supposed never to have read anything else since he left school.
>
> "Have you nearly concluded your argument?"
>
> "Mlud, no—variety of points—feel it my duty tsubmit—ludship," is the reply that slides out of Mr. Tangle.

This is the beginning of a conversation between the Lord High Chancellor and Mr. Tangle, a lawyer; Dickens is poking fun at Tangle's verbosity and at his speech style—"Mlud" substitutes for "Milord," "tsubmit" for "to submit."

How to express the shifts in speaker in a passage this brief? To begin with, of course, the text helps initially by providing dialogue tags ("says the Lord High Chancellor," and so forth) that cue the reader or listener as to the identity of the speaker. This is insufficient in performance, as all the lines of dialogue begin with the characters' words; besides, part of the pleasure of performing and listening to a performance of a writer like Dickens is creating and hearing the rich panoply of characters he creates for us. So, the performer must also draw on vocal technique to distinguish between the narrator, the Lord High Chancellor, and Mr. Tangle. It is, of course, more than vocal technique in its mechanical sense; the vocal technique works in the service of the performer's ability to make the minds, emotions, and intellects of these speakers come alive.

Some would argue that vocal distinction and the use of bodily posture would be sufficient to keep the characters separate. Indeed, one of our teachers, Leland H. Roloff, often suggested that maintaining a single line of focus while performing multiple characters can lead to an intriguing and enjoyable rendition of multiple personality disorder! We have seen performers successfully use a single line of focus to do such performances, and they can be impressive.

But they can also become confusing, both for performer and for audience. It takes a very practiced and skilled performer to convince us of the shift from speaker to speaker using voice and characterization alone. The human eye values variety to help us make such distinctions in our minds. So what is more customary is for the performer to create focal lines or lines of placement that aid both performer and audience in keeping characters distinct from each other; they serve the purpose of illuminating elements of locus—where characters might be in relation to each other. The performer chooses a particular angle from which to speak as each character (and it can be a slight angle—it should never put the performer even remotely close to profile, as that cuts off half of the performer's facial expression).

Figure 4.5 provides you with an example of focal lines for this passage. We have placed the narrator in the middle, which highlights his centrality to the entire scene; he is the one who describes and, in a sense, gives voice to the two characters (or at least allows us to hear them). We have arbitrarily assigned the right focal line to the Lord High Chancellor

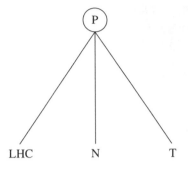

Key: P = Performer
      N = Narrator
      LHC = Lord High Chancellor
      T = Mr. Tangle

FIGURE 4.5: FOCAL LINES FOR DICKENS'S *BLEAK HOUSE*

and the left to Mr. Tangle. In this case, there is no reason to assign one or the other, but in a scene specifying location in more directional terms, the choice of which focal line to assign to each character can be more complicated.

As with the use of offstage focus to visualize a scene, so here the performer must endeavor to actually imagine and to project to the character with whom he is interacting. The narrator may switch his focus between open and closed here, depending on whether the performer wishes to show him sharing his description of the characters and the scene with us, taking us into his confidence as fellow satirists of the judicial system, or whether he wishes to show the narrator actually watching the interaction. Again, the performer may opt for a mixture of the two, if he can defend it on textual grounds.

What happens when there are more characters in a scene and a single character may speak to more than one character at different times? Different performers have proposed different solutions. Some performers choose to maintain the same general angle of focus but to vary it slightly (although within the same general area) to indicate that the character has shifted the person to whom he is speaking. In addition, of course, we use different tones of voice or attitudes when speaking to different people, and characters may be of different height or on different levels, so simply shifting angles slightly will not be enough. Other performers find the addition of more focal lines confusing for themselves and for the audience, which they claim is not likely to note such subtle or minute distinctions enough to warrant them; these performers maintain a constant focal line and draw upon other aspects of characterization, projection, and attitude to make the shift from one addressee to another clear and convincing.

Begin with scenes that involve no more than two characters or two characters and a central narrator and build up skill in shifting from one speaker to another; transitions are particularly critical and there needs to be as little gap between shifts as possible in order to make the sense of interaction believable. It can be useful to devote rehearsal time to working on transitions in and of themselves, and even those performers who prefer to work with a physical script often endeavor to memorize transitions. After you feel somewhat confident with scenes involving a few characters, you can begin to expand your repertoire and decide which approach to focus with multiple characters being addressed works best for you and for your selection.

Finally, a few words about *where* you perform and *where* you perform *from*. Again, during different historical periods, performances of the kind we have described in this chapter have taken place in different kinds of spaces and have been framed in different ways. During the nineteenth century, for example, it was not uncommon for the American Shakespearean actress Charlotte Cushman, when she was not acting as Romeo or some other great character, to give readings of entire Shakespearean plays. Such performances, by all accounts, were as dramatically thrilling as fully staged plays, but Cushman simply sat behind a desk or small table with an edition of Shakespeare, and that sufficed as the locus of the performance event. It was her vocal and dramatic skills, rather than visual interaction with other performers, that made her readings a success: audiences understood this convention—and were perhaps better prepared to listen and imagine—in an era less saturated with visual images presented by the electronic media of today. It would not be accurate to say that there was no visual component to such performances; the visual presence of Cushman as reader was what audiences knew to expect and responded to. Some writers of that era developed their performance skills in ways similar to that of an actor: Charles Dickens was well known for his dramatic solo readings of his novels and there are many accounts of the effects on audiences of his performance of the murder of Nancy by Bill Sykes in *Oliver Twist*.

In our own time, author-monologuist Spalding Gray often adopted a similar visual and physical aesthetic of staging and space in his personal narrative performance art, such as *Swimming to Cambodia* and *Monster in a Box*. We see this approach to staging more frequently today when authors give readings from their own works; since most writers are not trained as performers and are doing such performances primarily to sell their books, they emphasize the opportunity for audiences to hear the writer speak her words in her own voice, rather than what most of us would recognize as a more fully developed performance for its own sake.

In the twentieth century (and continuing into the twenty-first), a number of approaches to staging and use of space have developed, sometimes with one more dominant than another, at other times with multiple approaches coexisting side by side. Up until the late 1960s and mid-1970s, the dominant approach was a variation of the performance aesthetic described in situation 1 at the beginning of the chapter, although typically less rule-bound than the forensics competition. Performers were generally expected to use physical scripts, either the actual book from which the performer had selected material or a typescript contained in some kind of a binder. In classrooms and in public venues, such as reading hours, performers typically used lecterns, usually made of wood or metal, which freed the performer from the confinement of holding the script. The presence of the script was viewed as serving a number of purposes: some insisted on its presence to help maintain distinctions between acting and what was called interpretation (or oral interpretation). For others, it was a visual and symbolic reminder of the performer's role as medium between text (or author) and audience. The script was also a useful aid to memory, particularly if the performer (authors especially) only intended to present the text once or a few times and thus felt the time spent on memorization could be better used for analysis and close attention to exploring the possibilities in a text through performance. Yet another function of this approach to staging was as a way of framing the performance; in this sense, a lectern, with or without the presence of a physical script, became the equivalent of the proscenium arch. In larger spaces in particular, the lectern could focus both performer and audience attention.

In more recent decades, there has been a movement to disband with the physical presence of the text and the use of the lectern, although many performers still use both; it is probably accurate to say that as many performers of literature choose to memorize their texts as choose to use scripts, and it may be that the memorized performance is itself dominant or becoming more dominant. The reasons for this are many. One is that fewer and fewer performers are invested in drawing distinctions between acting and other kinds of performance (in the early part of the twentieth century, there were very serious debates about the relative value of impersonation versus interpretation). Many performers and theorists have come to believe that there is just "performance," and that no single set of aesthetic conventions will serve each text or context. Also, as more and more performers choose to work with nonliterary texts or from texts that do not originate in the fictional or poetic writings of others, the need to have a physical text present seems less and less a requirement. For example, a performance based in the performer's own life and composed by the performer (either as a fixed script or in a kind of continually extemporaneous form) may be better served by staging that configures space and performer-audience relationships in a semblance of the conversational, the interpersonal, rather than the classroom or public lecture. Such performances may even extend into actual interaction with an audience, breaking down accepted or assumed barriers that have traditionally been the hallmark of conventional performance, whether theatrical or literary.

It is also the case that more and more performers, even if they remain grounded in the performance of literary texts, are expanding and mixing the media they use in performing such texts. Bruce collaborated with choreographer Gary Schaaf on a performance of Gertrude Stein's poetry in which the speaking voice coexisted onstage with tap dancers, to create a performance that emphasized the percussive, rhythmic nature of Stein's language. We have also seen performances, such as those directed by Beverly Whitaker Long, in which the many powerful relationships between literary texts, particularly poems, and the visual arts were brought to the fore. While physical texts could certainly have been present, Long's choice was to have performers function in ways analogous to docents and guides, and so it was more useful to have the performers not use scripts and to have the freedom to use their bodies, eyes, and gestures to point to and establish complex relationships with paintings. The more the lines between acting and other kinds of performances of literary texts are questioned, blurred, and dismantled, the more some performers will wish to be free of the physical text and to treat the text as something very much like a play script or monologue. Particularly with poems and narrative written in the dramatic mode, such as poetry by Robert Browning, Richard Howard, and Ai, to name just a few, and novels by writers such as William Faulkner, Jean Rhys, Louise Erdrich, and many others, the performer may wish to use a greater degree of theatrical embodiment and to move through space for various effects (such as changes in time and location, to suggest the shifting of mood, to signal the beginning and ending of episodes).

To all of these developments, we give full support. The most useful and creative performer is one who has learned to utilize a variety of performance approaches, from the highly text-centered ones conventionally using a lectern and script to approaches that center more on personal experience, social encounter and intervention, and producing dialogues between various forms of artistic and performance media. One approach is not categorically "better" than the other, although it is possible to argue that some texts and some settings are better served by some approaches than others. But part of what makes performance dynamic, personal, and exciting is the freedom and the ability of the performer to experiment, try different things, discover what kinds of techniques produce what kinds of effects, and make decisions accordingly.

Conclusion

Our survey of techniques and conventions has been just that: an introductory overview of some of the challenges faced and tools used by solo performers, some of which also apply to performers working in ensembles, which we will discuss in later chapters. One can only read so much about technique before one needs to leap in and start developing it and applying it to specific texts. We encourage you to continue to work on technique as you begin to explore various kinds of texts in performances, to which we turn now.

KEY TERMS

articulation

conventions

enunciation

episteme

focus

gesture

hot and cool media

inspiration and expiration (breathing)

instrument, medium, and site (body)

physical memory

placement

projection, rate, and volume

pronunciation

resonance

responsiveness

techne

technique

vocal quality

Chapter 5

PERFORMING PERSONAL NARRATIVE, FAMILY HISTORIES, AND MEMOIRS

This chapter offers you the opportunity to explore the performance of nonfiction, looking closely at personal narrative, family histories, and memoirs. In chapter 12, we consider more nonfictional source materials and performances—historical, ethnographic, and cultural works.

Nonfiction texts, such as personal narratives, family histories, memoirs, and autobiographies, differ from imaginative texts—poems, short stories, novels, or plays—in that the events they recount are drawn from real life and are expected to be true. The accounts in these texts are narrated by the person who has lived and experienced them or by others who are reporting on them. The question of whether the events in nonfiction texts are actually true can be problematic: there are personal narratives, memoirs, and autobiographies that are almost entirely fabricated and others where the mix of truth and make-believe is considerable. However, for now, we will treat personal narratives, family histories, and memoirs as works in which narrators try to be honest and true to the people and lives reported. Having said this, we acknowledge that narrators, of necessity, reflect their own subjectivity and the vagaries of memory and desire. At the end of the chapter, we will discuss fabricated works where the narrators compromise or forfeit any regard for truth.

There is actually no sharp division between nonfiction and fiction: these genres should not be treated as if they are a pair of opposites, one true and the other false. Rather, nonfiction texts, filtered as they are through a narrator who recounts the events, reflect gradations of truth as measured by objective reality. It is useful to think of these nonfictional works as lying along a continuum: on one end, works in which the narrator's account adheres closely to facts and people in the material world, clearly deserving to be labeled nonfiction, and on the other end, works in which the narrator's account is not reliable and the events recounted hold only a tenuous relationship to real events and people. In the middle are works that are clearly about events taken from real life and recounted by a narrator who is more or less reliable.

A staple of many introductory courses in the analysis and performance of literary and cultural texts is the creation of a performance drawn from personal experience. Sometimes the performances are required to be as short as one minute and used to break the ice and let students and teachers get to know each other; often, these personal experiences are later elaborated and developed into a performance text or the script for a one-person show or a recital. Leland H. Roloff, author of *The Perception and Evocation of Literature*, used to encourage students to think about the "me search" in their research. In short, he wanted them to understand their own personal story in their academic efforts, and especially in their performances. In the personal experience performance, students are urged to exploit their understanding of themselves, their lives, and the me-in-the-performance that they experience, corporeally, in their bodies and know intimately, intellectually, emotionally, and psychologically.

The Me in the Personal Experience Performance

Let us start by considering two examples of nonfiction personal experience stories recounted and performed by Carol. The Haiti story is fairly dramatic, situated in another country, and has certain characteristics that might mark it as a tourist's story. We wrote about one of its renditions in our earlier textbook, *Performance: Texts and Contexts*. The other example is highly personal, involving her brother's death. In both cases, these stories have been shared, in various forms, over many years. Her brother's death occurred in 1995; the Haiti story has its origins in a trip in 1970. The people with whom she shared these stories, her audiences, have changed significantly over the years and responded to them in markedly different ways, of which we will say more later.

The personal story of her brother's death was kept private at first and then, as time passed, she told it to more people. It has its origins in a lived experience, beginning when she spoke to him as he lay near death in an intensive care unit at Mount Sinai Hospital in New York City. After the brutal and devastating days of his dying, she went with her sister to their family farm to speak of the death to her parents—they had been too weak to travel to the hospital and her brother had not wanted them to have to witness his dying of leukemia. He was a relatively young man of forty-three at the time. Over the years, haunted by the death and somehow able to hold on to her brother by recalling him, she came to talk of his death frequently, making it into a nonfiction narrative. For the past four or five years, she has shared the account more publicly, starting with students in the intimacy of the classroom. As the story has taken on a more public life, she has come to recognize the ways in which it serves to exemplify how nonfictional storytelling (a narrative), drawn from lived experience, can commemorate and heal. She also uses the nonfiction personal experience story to show how deeply traumatic personal events can serve as the basis for a personal experience performance.

As we discuss personal experience performance in this chapter, think about your own life and what analogous types of personal experiences you have had that might be developed into performance for your class or for others. Also think about the pitfalls of these kinds of performances and the risks and challenges they pose for the performer.

When first-person, personal experience performances are required in a classroom context, the teacher often accompanies the assignment with cautionary words, telling students that they should probably not draw on personal experiences involving family members—parents or siblings—or boyfriends, girlfriends, or other people who are very close to them. The concern is that the student may be too close to the person to judge accurately whether that person would be of sufficient interest to people outside the immediate circle of family and friends. In short, loved ones may be very dear to us, but they can, in some instances, make lousy subjects for performance. We are mindful of this cautionary advice, but we do not want to discourage you from undertaking this kind of performance. Ask yourself whether you think you can sustain your audience's interest in your family member. Clearly, since we discuss the death of Carol's brother at length, treating it as a family story, you can see that we think that performances based on family members and people very close to you can be very valuable, both to the performer and to audiences who do not know the person.

Let us turn first to the Haiti story. Its exotic and dramatic features make it in some ways easier to perform, we suspect, than the kind of personal experience performance in which you are drawing on deeply felt, private feelings and experiences and are very vulnerable psychologically. Yet, it too carries emotional and intellectual baggage that can weigh it down. You need to be aware that this kind of story, with its so-called exotic features, can be received very differently by different audience members, with some feeling great discomfort, pain, or anger. In this story of Carol's, which she transforms into a kind of adventure story, she stands as an outsider to the culture, history, and people of Haiti. Furthermore, she is white, the product of a private education, with a keen interest in anthropology and the study of culture. Audience members might take issue with her story, saying it reflects the perspective of a privileged European American, steeped in the traditions of the Western world. They might consider her account ignorant and careless of the lives of the people she describes: in short, they could accuse her of elitism and cultural insensitivity.

At this point in our discussion, we'll summarize the story in its kernel form and then move on to a discussion of it as it evolved. The rendition set forth below is only the second written version of the story, the first appearing in our earlier textbook. The story itself was oral, always evolving. Carol cannot capture the story as it was originally told. What we have here is another version in which she has tried to remember and retell it as faithfully as she can, more than thirty-five years after the event took place. The story would be very different if she wrote it for the first time now as a part of an autobiographical, nonfictional memoir, but more about that later. Bear in mind that a performance of this kind of personal experience story requires a script, either fully written out in advance or taking the form of notes to cue the performer, and rehearsed a number of times preparatory to presenting it. These different approaches pose different performance challenges to the solo performer. Originally this tale was performed in an improvisational manner and was not taped in order to be transcribed later as a script—an approach a number of students use in circumstances such as these. This version has been written to provide illustrative material in our textbook; it would have to be adapted for different performance situations and to fit certain time requirements—this version would take much longer than the usual classroom performance.

The Haiti Story

It began back in 1970. My husband, J., and I had decided to travel to Haiti during my semester break (I was teaching at Roosevelt University at the time) and we had about three weeks in January and February, just enough time to take in Haiti and three or four other Caribbean islands—Martinique, St. Martin and Sint Maarten,

Guadeloupe, and Grenada, if I remember correctly—before returning to the United States. I had studied anthropology for a time in college, in fact, I had wanted to be a physical or cultural anthropologist, and I was fascinated by ritual. Haiti seemed just the place to go.

Haiti has a fascinating history, with its share of troubles and violence, making it much like so many countries in our world. At its finest moments, the history is heroic—it was the first black republic to gain its independence in the Western world and to free its slaves; however, the price colonialism exacted on this country is very high. It was once the wealthiest French colony in the Caribbean; today, after so much civil and political strife and warfare, it is the poorest nation in the Western world.

When Christopher Columbus landed on the island in 1492, it was populated by people called the Arawaks; when the Spaniards invaded and settled the country in the fifteenth century, the native Taíno or Amerindian population was nearly decimated, leading to the importation of slaves, and with them voodoo (also referred to as Haitian Vodou) from Africa. It is a multiracial country and highly stratified by race: there were indigenous people, the Spanish and French invaders, the multiracial generations of children born of these peoples and born of mixed marriages between white masters and black slaves, between European men and African women. Several of the first founders of the republic embarked upon programs to kill all whites in the country.

Haitian voodoo had its roots in the religions of several tribes from Africa's West Coast. In the seventeenth century French colonizers settled in the western third of the country, establishing a plantation society based on forestry and sugar-related industries and relying heavily on the importation of African slaves. They used agricultural practices that over time led to considerable environmental degradation. In 1791 the black slaves revolted, led by Jean-Jacques Dessalines and Toussaint-Louverture (or Toussaint L'Ouverture). The French harshly repressed the first uprising. Later the generals Henri Christophe, Dessalines, and Alexandre Pétion revived the war. Ultimately in 1804 Haitians triumphed and the country gained independence and its name—Haiti—and became the first black republic in the Western world.

Its history since the 1820s and through the 1950s was bloody and brutal, marked with military assassinations and wars with the Dominican Republic, a country that is part of the same island, but with much richer natural resources. In the second decade of the twentieth century, the United States Marines occupied the island. In 1957, François Duvalier was elected president. Duvalier was an American-educated physician turned politician, a man of color but of mixed lineage. Initially, he was a leader concerned about social justice, but ultimately, he was corrupted and ruled Haiti as a despot, with a brutality excessive by any standard. During this latter period, the powerful, wealthy, educated elite (largely light-skinned blacks) kept the black masses in abject poverty and control through a presidential private militia that paralleled the army and was peopled with criminal, corrupt hoodlums. These bogeymen, the terrorist death squads known as the Tonton Macoutes, drove many Haitians to flee in exile. Later, Duvalier altered his title to president for life, a title that was passed on to his son, Jean-Claude, who ruled until he was driven into exile in 1986. The practice of ruling for life was not an uncommon one, and it could be argued that the country was better served with a president with a lifetime term, there had been so much turmoil in the earlier part of the last century, and this model, one followed by Haiti's founders, held some promise. However, in this case, greed, ambition, and corruption ultimately held sway.

To return now to Carol's story of her trip to Haiti, let us add a few words about the context. The innkeeper of the hotel she stayed in feared for her safety. She referred to Duvalier, known as "Papa Doc" (he was a physician), as "the parrot." This nickname held local currency in the area at the time of her visit. The innkeeper used coded language to refer to Papa Doc in order to safeguard against being heard and reported to Papa Doc's henchmen.

We have omitted references to more recent history of Haiti since it is not relevant to this story. Suffice it to say that in 1990 a former priest, Jean-Bertrand Aristide, won an election. His mandate began on February 7, 1991, and within six months his government faced a no-confidence vote, which he lost. On September 29, 1991, he resigned and went into exile. Elections for his successor were blocked and the country fell into chaos. In 1994, during the Clinton administration, a Haitian general asked former U.S. president Jimmy Carter to help avoid an invasion of Haiti and assist in the restoration of Jean-Bertrand Aristide. Clinton asked Carter to undertake a mission to Haiti, and the way was paved for Aristide's restoration as president. He served until 1995. There was more turmoil. He was reelected in 2000, but the international community would not recognize the election; charges of election fraud were levied, and by 2004 the populace rose up against him, claiming corruption and poverty, and he again went into exile in February 2004. After another period during which Haiti was governed by an interim authority, a protégé of Aristide's, René Préval, was elected, and there has been a United Nations Stabilization Mission in Haiti since then. For those of you interested in learning more about Haitian history, read *Toussaint Louverture: A Biography*, by Madison Smartt Bell.

In spite of the country's desperate poverty and repressive political regimes, it has remained an attraction to the tourist industry for many years. Its tropical climate, natural beauty, beaches, and artistic creativity all contribute to its success as a tourist site. In the late 1940s, there was a renaissance in Haitian painting that featured the so-called primitive style of the people. Their paintings and hand-carved wooden objects, bowls, statues, and drums, all circulated widely, both within the country and abroad. At the time of Carol's trip, there was an affluent Creole community living in Pétionville; there were Haitian children, many very poor, reading Latin grammar books, leaning against benches or sitting in the streets of the public square in Port-au-Prince. It was a country of extremes, richness and abject poverty, lush bananas hanging from trees, and riverbeds filled with water in winter but utterly parched in summer, with teeming numbers of people suffering from rickets and sleeping in the riverbeds, sometimes in hastily made lean-tos. If you wish to read more about Haiti and the ecological disasters that have devastated it, read the section about it in Jared Diamond's fascinating book *Collapse*.

For the rest of this segment on Haiti, we have decided to narrate it in Carol's voice, since this story is serving as an example of a personal experience performance. Hence, it is she who opens, writing:

> We were staying in a lovely inn, set in the mountains above Port-au-Prince, in Pétionville. The large, colonial house had a wraparound verandah, with slatted bamboo jalousies (large louvered shades) that were drawn down in late afternoon or at night. The house and garden and the outside patio were bedecked in bougainvillea that cascaded down the balustrades in a profusion of colorful purple and red floral bracts. On the patio, in a recessed area, was an open-air bar, with high bar stools and a tall ornately carved cabinet of mahogany, the shelves lined with assorted liqueurs, wines, gin, rum, whiskey, and other hard liquor. The place was colorful. The first afternoon there, some young artists offered to hand-paint with colorful dyes the soft,

white, pima cotton shifts purchased and worn by people staying in the hotel. I had several made for me.

Early in our stay, I decided I wanted to see voodoo. Transplanted by the slaves from West Africa, voodoo coexists with Catholicism. Since the mid-1990s, it has been recognized as an official religion in Haiti. When we had been driving about Port-au-Prince, viewing the landscaped plazas, wide avenues, and fountains and making a visit to the Iron Market, we had learned that you could see voodoo ceremonies. I didn't want to see the commercial voodoo that was performed by Haitians catering to tourists. I wanted the real religious rite. I got this bright idea that we should try to meet people in the Christian missionary nearby, and I would try to get to know the missionary's wife and learn more about how to get to one of the actual sites where voodoo was practiced in the mountains. One afternoon, my husband and I had managed to do just this. When we returned to our inn from the lovely and information-laden tea we had had with the missionary's wife, I announced that I was going to go up into the hills that night, sometime after 11 P.M. and leave the car and walk toward the voodoo ceremony. We had been told that if we approached the ceremony once it was underway, it could not, for reasons of religion and ritual, be interrupted or stopped. J. wasn't keen on my making the trek by myself, and I did not want our newly acquired friends to join us. We were with a distinguished woman in her early sixties—an anthropologist from Columbia University in New York—and her younger acquaintances, a New York doctor completing his residency, his hippie girlfriend, and their Haitian tour guide, all of whom we had met at our hotel where they, too, were staying. We needed to go by ourselves. In order to placate them, I promised them we would give them a full report on our return and then we could all traipse down to Port-au-Prince to gamble in one of the hotels. In recalling this, it all seems youthful, foolhardy, and ignorant about much of Haiti's history. At the same time, the events were and remain etched on my memory, and partly because of the power of the events, my husband and I transformed them into stories, maybe to try to make them more manageable and also, in part, because they lent themselves to storytelling.

I went with J. into the mountains and we saw the voodoo (much of that story I will leave for another time). Suffice it to say, it was quite an experience. We wandered in the dark in the hills, following the lights from candles and fires and drawn by the sounds of the drums, and we came upon the voodoo dancers. We witnessed extraordinary performances by the voodoo participants. Young Haitian men, half-naked with bare feet, mimed their elders, and young women likewise took on the mannerisms of the aged. Seemingly effortlessly, the dancers transformed themselves and as they reached their frenzied pitch, appearing to be in a trancelike state, they walked or danced on the coals of fire beneath their feet. Their feet and skin were covered with some sort of oil or balm, and I believe the oil somehow protected the flesh from burning. We drank some dreadful tasting brew that was passed around in goatskin canteens. It was bitter, and frankly, I think it had something in it that left me giddy or probably a bit high (my husband didn't swallow any of it). Finally, we stumbled away from the ceremony as it closed, trying to find where we had left our white, rented Volkswagen automobile. When we arrived back at the hotel, we were full of our tale. Afterward, we urged everyone into our car to head down to town. I couldn't persuade the young doctor to leave his tour guide behind—he insisted he must come—so there we were: the anthropologist (I'll call her Selma) in the back seat and the young doctor (Brad) in the front seat, next to J., who was driving, and the guide in the middle. I was in the back seat next to Selma. I believe we had left the girlfriend behind—she was complaining of some stomach disorder. It was about 2 A.M.

When we reached Port-au-Prince, the city was mostly dark. The guide directed us to the casino, but it was closed. I felt the need to provide some entertainment for our friends, so I said something like, "No matter, let's go see the presidential palace." I had spotted it from the window and saw a narrow dirt-covered alley leading toward some barracks, which seemed to open onto the grassy, manicured lawns of the presidential palace. I urged J. to turn quickly down the road. He did so, but moments later he abruptly stopped, and I saw search-lights sweeping down on our car. Before I knew it, J. was ordered out of the car, and he was opening the door, slowly, raising his arms. In the next moment, I saw that he was getting out of the car, and soon we were all led from the car, the guide was taken away from us rudely, and the rest of us submissively followed J. and members of the Haitian army into the barracks. There, for what seemed like hours, we were held. J. tried to pacify the army guards. They wanted his papers, and he indicated he wanted to speak to people at the American Embassy. J. could not speak the Haitian patois; in fact, neither of us could understand what the Haitians were saying, except in the most limited way. Our French and Spanish were of little use. Selma and I huddled together, at first paralyzed with fear. Two soldiers were standing very close to us with their rifles. In fact, at one point I think they were nodding their heads and almost sleeping, with their chins on the tips of their rifles. When I sensed this, I whispered to Selma and indicated with my eyes and slight gestures that I thought they were asleep. We relaxed momentarily, but of course they were not asleep, and they abruptly gave a signal to us to stand still.

J. kept haggling with an army major in the presidential guard, being alternately obliging and submissive, but then firm, almost loudly insistent that he would not sign anything they were asking him to sign. J. is a large man, aggressive in manner, often impatient, with very keen, almost always sparkling hazel eyes. Physically, he had the shape of Orson Welles or Burl Ives. Saul Bellow had been one of J.'s professors at the University of Chicago and later became a close friend. He used J. as the basis for his physical description of Lionel Feffer, a character in his novel *Mr. Sammler's Planet*. I have always thought Saul's description of J. was quite brilliant, so I will share it with you here. He describes Feffer (read J.) as "an ingenuous operator, less student than promoter. With his florid color, brown beaver beard, long black eyes, big belly, smooth hair, pink awkward large hands, loud interrupting voice, [and] hasty energy, he was charming . . ." (p. 38). To my mind, it was very much this J. who was trying to maneuver his way out of an arrest.

J., faced with nonstop demands that he sign papers that the army major was forcing on him, announced that he "didn't understand the political significance" of the papers and would not sign them until he talked to a diplomat. Neither of us to this day is really sure why, but finally, the major seemed less interested in J.'s confessing to something—we never knew quite what but it had to do with the charge of trespassing on the grounds of the presidential palace— and he and his men agreed that we could return to our inn, and they would pursue the issue further in the morning. By this point, J. was unwilling to try to drive anywhere, let alone to our hotel, on his own. He asked them to escort us so that we could find the inn and not get lost again. They agreed and led us to the hotel; they were in front in their huge open-air jeep, with their rifles, and we followed behind in our car. J. attempted to inquire about our guide, but they wouldn't hear any of it. When we arrived at the inn, to our horror, the army major and his men smashed all the bamboo shades that were covering the verandah with their rifle butts, and after destroying them and forcing in the front door, they left us. J. and Brad said they were going upstairs to bed and taking sleeping pills, which Brad had announced he had. Neither wished to be awakened in the morning. I limply said that I would try to stay awake and get up in the morning to tell the innkeeper what had happened and offer to make reparations for the damage. And, of course, tell her we were very worried about the safety of Brad's guide.

By morning, when I awakened and walked downstairs and through the gardened terrace, I saw two members of the Tonton Macoutes sitting on the bar stools, looking ominous, wearing their mirrored shades in full daylight and 45 automatics tucked in their waistbands (if you ever saw *The Comedians*, a movie based on Graham Greene's novel of the same title, you will know what they look like). Tonton Macoutes means "bogeyman" and was the name given the members of the terrorist private army that Duvalier used as part of his system of violent repression and terror. It was J. who recognized the type of gun. I managed to tell the innkeeper what had happened. She led me down the hall and snuck me into a hidey-hole beneath the staircase, and we whispered to each other about what had happened. She told me that we must stay put; that, in effect, we were under house arrest, and that we must do nothing unless we were accompanied by the members of the Tonton Macoutes assigned to keep us under surveillance. She said she would try to get me in touch with the American Embassy, but when I reached them, they told me that the Haitians would not allow us to leave the country for another ten days, and then, if we were lucky, our visas would be returned to us. In short, they didn't want to hear anything more from us until they, the officials at the embassy, contacted us some ten days hence. Our friends all departed the country without difficulty, but we were stuck there, not daring to disobey orders. We were later told that the guide had been released and that he had been held because his brother had been part of an assassination attempt on Duvalier's life just two weeks earlier. We never knew whether we had been told the truth and whether he had, in fact, been released.

The next eight or ten days were unforgettable and involve too much to recount here. But one highlight occurred several days later when we persuaded the two Tonton Macoutes to drive us some twenty-odd miles to a beach where we wanted to swim. We were guarded so closely that when I tried to descend a ladder on the raft to swim, one member of the Tonton Macoutes, in his skimpy, body-revealing swimsuit with a pistol stuck under the waistband and his shades on, pursued me, passing his gun over to his comrade only as he and I actually descended into the water. Toward the end of the trip, J. and I wanted to eat at the Grand Oloffson Hotel in the center of Port-au-Prince. As we drove to the hotel, two cars bearing the Tonton Macoutes followed us: the first bore the guards originally assigned to us and the second carried two more Tonton Macoutes who had been assigned to follow and keep tabs on the first set of guards. Apparently, the authorities believed we had suborned the first set of guards when we went swimming, and consequently they assigned another set. When we arrived at the hotel's restaurant, the maître d' cleared the entire open-air porch where we were to be served of about two thirds of its guests and placed us at three tables that were set apart from all the others. It was chilling. J. and I dined, watched by the two sets of Tonton Macoutes from each of the two separate tables where they sat. We did, indeed, get our visas back ten days later, and to my amazement, as the visas were given back to us at the airport, there were several Haitian customs officials telling us "Welcome back to Haiti." I might have gone back, but J., never!

Now, consider this segment of nonfiction writing in Carol's voice as if it were your script for a performance based on personal experience. You obviously are not actually the person who experienced the snippet of autobiography. Rather, you are a performer taking on the character of the narrator and trying to preserve a sense of nonfiction. One of the first important matters to consider is what makes this nonfiction and how can you preserve the features of the genre in performance in such a way that it differs from fiction.

It is essential that you respect the teller of the tale as someone who has actually experienced what is recounted. You need to capture the teller's self as it emerges from the text. Let us rule out the possibility that you will attempt to impersonate Carol (the actual author) in your telling of this tale. We want you to focus on the relationship of the teller to the told.

For a nonfiction performance, you generally treat the narrator as representing a real person who lived through the events recounted. In short, this Haiti tale is a story about real events.

Audiences to whom Carol has told this story have responded in different ways. Some audiences have been captivated by the story and listened to it in a manner that was uncritical of the story, except in ways intended by the teller. Others have been offended, insulted, or angered by it. When Carol spoke with some of these people, she learned that they felt the story reflected the privilege of a white outsider who fails to recognize the implications of her words and fails to respect the people of Haiti. They believe the story is deeply prejudiced, reflecting the biases of Western powers, deeply implicated in the colonial enterprise that has wreaked such havoc in Haiti; or, if they do not feel this way themselves, they think that others might share these negative reactions. They think the story does its teller no good, finding it unworthy. Obviously, it is difficult to hear this kind of criticism, but it is also educational. You need to be mindful that your politics, identity, nationality, gender, race, and ethnicity are all reflected in your performances, in your choices about what to tell and not tell, whether you are conscious of the fact or not. These factors are important to think about when you decide what to share in your personal experience narratives and in other performances that you may do. How did you respond to Carol's narrative? Can you say why?

Would you perform the character of this narrator differently than you would the narrator in a selection of fiction? In chapter 8, we analyze a story by Jane Hamilton, "Rehearsing 'The Firebird.'" It is written with a first-person narrator telling the story. In Hamilton's story, she draws on people and events from her past but disguises their identities, making fiction, not nonfiction. When you finish reading that chapter, you will be in a better position to consider what is different about performing a nonfiction narrative and a fictional account. It matters whether the person you perform is real or fictional and you will more fully understand these differences.

In a performance of nonfiction, it is important that you believe in the truth of the events and people you are depicting, remembering that they are based on reality. The authors actually experienced the things they are writing about; the events are not made up. Remembered experiences by necessity are not the experience itself, but a remembered experience as opposed to an invented experience is different. How do you as a performer feel these differences? As the performer, you are trying to capture the narrator of the Haiti story as she is constructed by her text.

One approach to this kind of text involves researching the story, its author, and the reliability of the account of Haiti during Duvalier's regime. An invaluable source for students interested in reading other accounts of Haiti and voodoo (also known as Vodou) is Zora Neale Hurston's *Tell My Horse* (1938). Hurston began her career in anthropology, studying under Franz Boas, and was a pioneer in the field of Afro-American folklore. In *Tell My Horse*, she treats Vodou as a major world religion, brought to Haiti and the Americas by the peoples of Africa; she argued that it was a serious religion, to be considered alongside other great religions of the West. In the ritual call and response and the shouts of the southern black church (rituals she had participated in growing up in the South), she experienced the power of the church and its roots in voodoo. At the time she wrote *Tell My Horse*, she knew all too well the sensational and fanciful tales that were associated with voodoo. Her travels took her to Jamaica and Haiti, where she immersed herself in the study of and participation in rituals and beliefs of voodoo practitioners. Her book about voodoo takes its title from a phrase spoken by initiates after they have become "possessed" by the boisterous Loa, or spirit, Guedé. One approach to performing the Haiti story would be to create a dialogue between Hurston's account of Haiti and Carol's, or use Hurston's account to frame Carol's.

Another invaluable resource about Haiti and its famed liberator is *Toussaint Louverture*, by Madison Smartt Bell. Toussaint's reputation is controversial. On the one hand, he is praised as the liberator of Haiti and credited for leading the first successful slave revolution in history. On the other hand, he is considered a betrayer, a man who himself owned slaves and who instigated some of the most violent events that plague Haiti's history. His reputation and role in history are still undergoing serious scholarly reassessment; many parts of his story are only now resurfacing and gaining attention. Students of communication often perform his speeches, as they are noted for their oration.

Returning to Carol's account and how you might perform it, you need to decide how to render the teller, how to handle her voice. As the teller of the account, is her biography relevant to your performance? Are you going to treat her sympathetically or perform her in a manner that highlights the shortcomings and politics of her story? What other approaches might you choose between in order to anchor the narrator in your performance?

Let us assume for the purpose of this discussion of personal experience performance that you accept her story as told and decide to perform her in that spirit. This Carol needs to be inferred from and supported by the text. Thus, in this hypothetical performance, you are not trying to present biographical information about Carol, nor are you trying to mimic her mannerisms or give a representational performance of her, nor are you trying to undermine her authority or the worldview of her story. Rather, you will be treating her as a narrator and investing this character with a level of belief wherein you keep the audience mindful that this person that you are performing is someone who lived through the experience.

In your attempt to be true to the nonfiction elements of the performance and the truth of the personal experience on which it is based, you might prepare by learning still more about the time when the event was set, the regime of Duvalier. Alternatively or in addition, you might decide to learn more about Carol; if you had access to her or people who knew her or heard her story, you could draw on what you learn about her. How much time you have to prepare your performance will obviously influence the degree to which you will research your subject. Regardless, for this performance assignment, as the performer trying to do justice to a nonfictional figure you will be constantly reminding yourself that your subject is a real person, who lived at a certain time, in a certain place, with a host of characteristics having to do with self, identity, nationality, ethnicity, and gender, all of which command your attention as you prepare for your performance of nonfiction.

We will not attempt to direct your performance of the Haiti story nor exhaust the many ways you might approach it, but we want to encourage you to look at certain features in this text that are present in most nonfiction you might want to perform. You need to get a sense of the narrator's self. Are there any clues to help you understand her as a person? Ask yourself the dramatistic questions regarding the narrator—who, what, why, when, where, and how? Decide how you want to stage your performance, how you want to present her and the information in the text. You might choose to use a prop or two, for example, a carved Haitian mask, a statue, or a tourist poster of Haiti. The prop would suggest the exotic elements of the tale. Or you could use video clips of Haiti, its landscapes, and its people. Consider how the text treats historical and political elements, such as the time when the story occurred, the place or places that form its setting, and historical people to whom it refers.

Consider the contrasting ways in which some parts are described using exposition and telling rather than showing the action, while at other times the narrator is preoccupied with showing, through careful description (for example, the hotel, its verandah, the flowers, and the bar area). Direct discourse is employed, albeit it rarely (for example, when Carol quotes the customs official saying, "Welcome back to Haiti!"), and throughout there is a fair amount of indirect discourse. The passage she quotes from Bellow's novel, describing Feffer, gives you the opportunity to take on another voice that is not Carol's and use this not only to show what J. looks like but to comment obliquely on Carol and her motives for quoting it. Look for clues in the text that enable you to theatricalize it, embody it, and use your performance techniques to highlight its nonfictional features. Think about how you will handle yourself in the performance. Will you be offering your own commentary on the narration through nonverbal gestures or spliced-in verbal commentary of your own making? If you have dance experience, you might render the voodoo dancing, maybe even adding a sound track with native drumming. In chapter 12, we will look at how other historical documents give you a keener understanding of how to handle place, time, and historical figures as well as ethnographic and cultural materials in a manner that is consonant with nonfiction. For now, concentrate on the nonfictional elements within the text that stand out for you and that you want to honor in your performance.

We have offered this story to help you understand how to craft your personal experience performance. Take some time now to think about experiences you have had in life that are comparable to the Haiti story and consider how you might use them in a performance featuring auto-biographical elements from your life, thinking analytically about the assumptions that underlie your account. Think about the problems you might encounter in performing yourself as the subject of an autobio-graphical tale.

Rupert's Death

Now let us consider the more personal first-person autobiographical story of the death of Carol's brother, Rupert. Even as Carol sets this account down on paper as an example of how one might handle a similar personal experience in performance, she feels discomfort, almost a sort of viola-tion. She both does and does not want to share the story. Part of this discomfort is endemic to this kind of performance. Its material is raw and deeply felt, and its subject, her brother, is someone you are unlikely to know. What he means to her is quite different from what he will mean to you. However, we are considering the genre of nonfiction and even a cursory survey of memoirs, biographies, and autobiographies will reveal that they are filled with accounts of terrible losses experienced by human beings. An excellent book by performance scholar Jodi Kanter, *Performing Loss: Rebuilding Community Through Theater and Writing*, explores this subject more fully to discover how, for Western communities, "a greater ability to respond to loss is a matter of political, cultural, and social survival" (p. 3). We believe that the act of writing about loss, or performing it, is one way of affirming our humanity; it is also a means of perpetuating the life of the dead.

The Death of My Brother

My brother, Rupert Alan Simpson, died of leukemia when he was forty-three. The cancer had been first diagnosed three years earlier. With him in the intensive care unit of Mount Sinai Hospital in Manhattan was his love of more than seven years, Laura, a beautiful, tall, elegant model who had stood by him heroically as they tried to manage the difficult knowledge of his almost certain death. They had tried to defy it. They were even buying a penthouse condominium in Manhattan, with the closing date of the purchase corresponding with the exact month and day of his death, so powerful was their wish to deny what seemed inevitable. My brother would constantly announce that he was going to "live for Laura" up until the very end. He was a Wall Street lawyer who had been working in the United States and London when he was first diagnosed with the fatal illness. Also gathered there were me, my sister, our husbands, and my niece who lived in Manhattan. In addition, there were attending nurses and other patients close by in their beds.

The part of this story that I cannot forget was near the very end, when we were all gathered by his bedside. His doctors had told us that they would withdraw the life support when we were ready. They had sustained his life long enough for my sister and me and our husbands to arrive from Chicago. They were also waiting for Laura to be ready. Laura was lying on the bed with Rupert, her head on his chest. He was attached to monitors and feeding tubes and a ventilator. Laura had been with him for several days and was near exhaustion. We were ready to have them withdraw the life support. I heard myself leaning over my brother and saw myself dropping to my knees by the cast-iron bed rails (which were down) as I said I would tell him a story. He loved stories, and I would simply talk and keep talking until the monitor stopped. I cannot for the life of me remember much of the story. I know I found a structure. He loved stories from the Greeks, he loved epics, he had been a reader, he was funny and irreverent, his language sprinkled with the *F* word. And he was bawdy. I began calling up these aspects, regaling him with racy stories, images of Hector, Achilles, and Odysseus, and other things fantastical. I kept talking, but suddenly I felt I could not keep on in this vein. I thought I must pray, must speak the version of the twenty-third psalm from the King James Bible. I am not sure I had any religious beliefs at the time, but we had been confirmed in the Anglican church, and I had sung with my sister in the choir and had memorized many of the psalms.

Psalm 23: A Psalm of David

The LORD is my shepherd; I shall not want.
He maketh me to lie down in green pastures: he leadeth me beside the
    still waters.
He restoreth my soul: he leadeth me in the paths of righteousness for
    his name's sake.
Yea, though I walk through the valley of the shadow of death, I will fear
    no evil: for thou art with me; thy rod and thy staff they comfort me.
Thou preparest a table before me in the presence of mine enemies:
    thou anointest my head with oil; my cup runneth over.
Surely goodness and mercy shall follow me all the days of my life: and I
    will dwell in the house of the LORD for ever.

The words came, but when I got to "Yea, though I walk through the valley of the shadow of death, I will fear no evil," I couldn't keep going. There was a kind of fierce urgency in my voice when I started declaring that *yea*, even in the valley of death, "I will fear no . . ." Those were the words I needed to tell myself; I felt defiant, almost as though I were daring some god, letting him know that not here, no, nothing now could give me fear. To say this allowed me try to hold on to him; to deny that he could be taken or slip into death. When I reached the words "I will fear no . . . ," something changed and I could not summon up from memory the rest of the words from the prayer. I heard myself trying to gather my words, and I looked up first toward my husband, then back to my sister, who was just behind me, mumbling that I did not think I knew the words. Then I realized he had died. The monitor had a straight line. I remember pressing my forehead on the hard, hard iron bed rail. It had no give; it was cold; I felt it was implacable; it somehow forced me to know, as I slipped down toward the floor with my head against it, that he had died. I still cannot accept this death; the loss, contrary to what they say, has not lessened. Oh, yes, it is less anguishing, but at unexpected times, the feelings of the loss engulf me, and I find myself almost crying out or trying to talk to Rupert. Later, as my family regrouped on our farm in Rhode Island, and we tried to comfort each other and my parents, those who were at the bedside kept telling the rest of my family about my story, my talking, and how it had carried us all. I believe it had; language, frankly, had saved me, language and my love of stories and hearing old, very familiar words.

This is enough to give you an idea about the content of an autobiographical nonfiction story to immortalize the dead and keep some part of the person for the living. Think about ways in which you could use a nonfiction performance assignment to teach about death, or loss, and to learn yourself. In our classes over many years, we have witnessed students performing a personal experience story of this kind. The performances generally have not been maudlin or sentimental; they have been powerful, often more so when the style is very understated. The real people evoked in these nonfiction narratives have been etched indelibly on my mind by the performances of my students, as these students—their children or siblings—knew them. The power of this kind of real-life performance about real people is unequalled.

In highly personal performances such as this one, we have a word of cautionary advice. Consider whether the event and the emotions it contains, which mean so much to you, will also be relevant to others. In short, why might this story matter to others? Clearly there are many universal elements in the story. We all have or will experience the death of someone very dear to us. The loss of a sibling or parent is something we can all identify with or relate to. Hospitals and deathbed scenes are easily found on television, in books, and on the Internet. In addition, you are someone your classmates know, and it is likely that they will be interested in your account, provided it reveals something that is true to you and part of your individuality. But the danger of this kind of performance is that you risk losing control of your emotions or that the story becomes maudlin, melodramatic, sentimental, soppy, or just too stagy. Does Carol's story contain any of these flaws? What do you think?

How Stories Connect

Of course, one of the reasons we tell personal stories is to make connections with the lives of other people, both publicly and privately. There is a sense, then, in which all such stories live in what may be called *intertexual* relationships with the stories of others. Carol's story of the death of her brother Rupert is one such story. Bruce relates the following story, which shows how Carol's story was not only healing for her to tell but also for Bruce to hear and to use to begin a period of healing of his own.

Bruce's Story

Winter is the dying time in my family: I have already decided that when it is my turn I, too, will pass out of this life on a gray day, in one of the early months of the new year. This comes not out of any morbid obsession with death, nor any suicidal plans, nor even a kind of New Age mysticism or variation on the pathetic fallacy (snow = death), but simply because my father, my best friend Gary, my mother, and my brother all died in the months of January and February—in different years, but at that time of year "thou mayest in me behold," seated in "bare ruined choirs" of mourning and loss.

The only death I have witnessed firsthand (other than that of a pet) was my mother's. I had always felt guilty about not being there when my father died, as I was the only member of my family who was not present at his bedside. I was teaching four hours away at my first job, my first production opened that weekend, and it wasn't clear when my father would actually die, so I waited. He died between opening night and the Saturday evening performance and I headed back to Chicago the next day.

So when my mother had a stroke and was, in the medical terms my sister quoted to me over the phone, "nonresponsive" (a term I did not at first understand to be synonymous with a stroke and a coma), I waited the weekend to see if she would improve and then flew back to Chicago on a Monday morning. My brother and his wife picked me up at O'Hare. I had somehow managed to maintain a state of numbness until I saw them. Neither were people I felt close to, but seeing them in person, I blurted out, "She's really going to die this time, isn't she?" and burst into tears in the middle of the baggage area. Lynn, my sister-in-law, said, almost as if out of a bad movie, "We need to talk."

Well, we didn't actually talk. We drove straight to the hospital in Winfield, a suburb I'd been to only a few times, once a happier time when I helped my sister go through labor with her first child while her husband, Dean, drove back from Champaign-Urbana at eighty miles per hour and a few other times as my mother grew older and had to be hospitalized for emphysema and diverticulitis. As we drove into the quiet parking lot, I did not know what the week held in store. Would my mother regain consciousness? Would she continue to breathe on life support beyond the week or so I could stay (we were on winter break, but classes were to begin in another week)? What would happen to her cat Chloe, whom she had adopted just a year before at my urging? What would happen to me, possibly an orphan at age thirty-eight?

My mother looked peaceful, somewhat herself but hooked up to so many machines (an image that would return to me when I had surgery myself twelve years later) that I had a hard time finding *her*—the woman with whom I had bonded, quarreled, laughed for so many years. We stayed for a while, I met her nurses in the ICU, and then Scott and Lynn drove me back to my mother's house in Glen Ellyn, where Chloe yowled nonstop until I fed and held her—she had always been territorial and possessive, but she was a source of nurture in an emergency, I guess.

I drove back to the hospital that night in my mother's fourteen-year-old Chevy—the car she and my father bought when he retired from the bank, two years before he died at age fifty-nine from lung cancer, two months after his diagnosis which he received on the day after Christmas. It smelled of the decades of Kent cigarettes that had dominated her life and which had always been a source of tension between us. The week before, when she was in the hospital but had not yet had the stroke, she told me her doctor had told her, "Leave the cigarettes at home . . . you won't be able to smoke them here."

Before I got to the hospital, I stopped at the public library and, using her card, checked out a copy of the collected poetry of Alfred Noyes. I'd heard that it was important to keep in communication with people in coma, as we didn't know what they could or couldn't hear. I had begun to speak to her even that afternoon but wanted some way to break through that silence where the other person does not, cannot answer. Scott and Lynn tacitly decided to leave the two of us alone that night. So at some point, I found the poem "The Highwayman" ("And the highwayman came riding—/Riding—riding— . . . Bess, the landlord's daughter") and began to read it to her. A nurse came in at some point to check vitals, and I stopped, but I then returned to reading it. I'm not sure if I finished it or not—I know I felt determined to, but the "performance" having been interrupted, I wondered if it was doing any good, was there any point to it? Whom was I reading it for? Her? Or me—the child who thrilled to hear her recite this poem, which she had been required to memorize seven decades earlier as a schoolgirl in Negaunee, Michigan, a small mining town in the Upper Peninsula.

I went home about 11 P.M. (visiting hours apparently didn't apply to the families of those in the ICU) and slept restlessly—it did not help that Chloe insisted on sleeping with me on a twin bed that was already too small for me. The next day I drove back to the hospital. The day was spent in small talk with my brother and sister-in-law, who came in the afternoon, with my mother's brusque, hurried doctor, and with the sympathetic, thoughtful nurses who seemed to me to keep the unit human. I made sure they knew my mother had been an RN—and when two of them came in to turn my mother (was that an actual grimace of pain I saw on her face when they lifted her or just some autonomic response of the nervous system—*autonomic* a term I had lately learned from Daryl, my new boyfriend, about whom my mother knew nothing as I had never shared my sexual identity with her), one of them turned to the other and said, "Hey, did you know she was an RN?" The sisterhood looks after itself.

It was never clear, from hour to hour, how long my mother would continue in this condition and what it would mean for that condition to change. Would my mother have brain damage if she lived? Would she be one of those metaphorical vegetables? Or would she recover her already declining mental abilities? She had become frailer and frailer as she passed through her seventies, a widow depressed thirteen years after the death of my father. What did she want? What would I want?

I did not go home that night—so vigilant was I about being there at the moment should she die that I did not trust my ability to get back to the hospital quickly enough, and I did not go home until after she died three days later. It would only be one night, I said to myself—the doctor had come in on Tuesday and said, "Your mother will probably die today or tomorrow." We all agreed—my brother, my sister-in-law, and my sister, who lived two hours away in Freeport—that we would have my mother taken off life support on Wednesday, after which, my mother's doctor said, "it would only be a matter of hours." We decided to wait until my sister got into town to have the life support removed—of course, there was an ice storm Tuesday night, but my sister persevered and made it to the hospital by about noon. Before the tubes were removed, we each took our turn being alone with my mother—I asked to be last, as I had been the only one not there while she was still conscious and, in my self-theatricality, wanted to be the "last"—I was the youngest. We all kissed her good-bye, either said or didn't say what we wanted to, and then the medical team came into her room to remove the machinery. We then went back into her room to wait. At times, my mother's eyes opened and seemed to roam the room, even seemed to gaze into our eyes, a smile on her face—we wondered if this meant she was conscious. Nurses told us this probably just meant her nervous system was still functioning at some level, but didn't really mean "consciousness"—I remembered this years later when people interpreted the movements of Terri Schiavo's eyes and body with Talmudic precision.

And we waited. And we waited. So much for the doctor's prognosis. Eventually, my sister had to start the drive back home—she had three children, all high school age and younger, and she did not want to risk dark ice on the state highways. My brother and sister-in-law left for dinner. I ran down to the cafeteria, had a very quick dinner of something, bought a thick John Grisham novel in the gift shop, and went back. I watched television, but the more compelling, if less labile drama, was the monitor of respiration, pulse, and blood pressure on the bedside monitor. Scott and Lynn came back for a few hours of small talk, Scott as always saying the things that would irritate me the most, Lynn being silent and, when she did speak, practical. They went home. I sat up late into the night, not even willing to go down the hall to the men's room but using the in-room toilet, separated from my mother only by a curtain, watching anxiously to make sure she did not die while I emptied my bladder. Finally, a nurse pointed me down the hall to a lounge— "You can sleep there," she said, "there's a couch." "You will come and get me if anything happens?" I asked anxiously. "Yes. I promise," she said, clearly used to the anxieties of family members.

Thursday dawned. Mom remained stable—meaning she was dying but had not died yet. She was, unexpectedly, breathing on her own. We had agreed that we would only have life support removed if we were assured that she would be given as much pain medication as she needed. "You realize," Lynn said, daughter of a doctor, "that the more morphine she gets, the longer it will take her to die." It was true, but I couldn't have hated her more at that moment than if she had simply said we should smother her. She said, "My father always said, 'You'd be surprised how hard it is to die.'" Nonetheless, we continued to have her float on the morphine.

"Your mother will die today," the doctor said on Thursday. How the hell do you know, I wanted to scream at this officious presence. You were wrong yesterday—just a matter of hours, my ass. And I was right. Thursday passed without any real change. One of the nurses who was there most frequently came in Thursday night and said, "There's a problem. The insurance is insisting that she be moved out of the ICU to a regular cardiac unit tomorrow. We hope that it won't come to that, but we wanted you to know." "You mean, they'd wheel my mother through the halls in her state?" I asked, astonished and angry. "We hope it won't come to that," she repeated, with feeling and genuine sympathy.

It didn't. Friday morning, her breathing became more and more labored. I had heard of the "death rattle," and now I knew what it actually sounded like. There began to be more time between breaths. As I listened to her measured breathing and started counting seconds between breaths, I thought of Scott Dillard and his description of "breathing Darrell," his piece about his bedside vigil for his partner— I understood in a physical and even performative way what that piece meant. About 10 A.M., a nurse came in and said, "I think she's gone." "No," I shouted, with a combination of melodrama (isn't that what Shirley MacLaine did?) and an almost atavistic bodily response, throwing my body down on the guardrails—I felt genuine pain in my guts. The nurse checked. "No, she's started breathing again."

I felt even more confused than ever. This death was taking what seemed like forever, but I knew that once it was over I would wonder forever what the rush was. I had spoken with Daryl briefly each day from the pay phone, calling collect, but as loving as he was, we had only been together for three months—he could not know yet what all this was meaning to me. I deflected my real feelings by obsessing about what to do if I weren't back by Monday when classes started. The nurse asked if we wanted a clergyman—my mother, raised a Methodist, hadn't been to church since my brother's wedding. No thanks. "Do you want me to call your brother?" she asked. The last thing I wanted was him here—if I were to get through this, it had to be (selfishly) alone with my mother, not with him making me want to throw him out a window or Lynn saying things that I would inevitably read as judgmental and unfeeling and, well, overly opinionated.

As the breathing once again grew more and more labored, I spoke aloud to my mother, saying, "You know I don't want you to go, but if you need to, it's all right." This, too, was cribbed from a movie, *Longtime Companion*, when Bruce Davison gives his lover Mark Lamos permission to die from AIDS. And, strange as it sounds, fewer than five minutes later, she stopped breathing. I don't attribute agency to my words—for all my artistic proclivities, I tend to be hardheaded about these things. She stopped. For whatever reason. Even if she somehow "heard" me, I didn't assume she would follow my instructions. I think it was my way of saying to myself, it's all right if she goes now, you've been here.

When it was clear that my mother had indeed died, the hospital staff began their process—moving quickly almost like a movie sped up, calling in a doctor to declare time of death, getting paperwork moving. I called Scott and Lynn—Lynn answered and said, "We'll be right there." And they were. I called my sister, and she said she would be there the next day—after all, there was no real need for her to come right away. I tried calling Daryl but only got his machine. I called my chair to tell her I would not be back by Monday, but that I had left instructions on my desk.

After all arrangements had been made, all the papers signed, Scott and Lynn asked "if I would be all right," meaning did I want to be with them. I assured them I would be fine (meaning, I do not want to be with you now). I went back to my mother's house, seeing

Chloe for the first time in three days (Lynn and Scott had stopped in to feed her each day). The house seemed more than empty—it seemed as if it contained all the years of my relationship with my mother, fewer of them in this actual house, which had been my parents' retirement home and in which my father lived for only a year and a half. The odors of cigarette smoke lingered with my mother's clothing and half-empty coffee cups. I could stay there all afternoon. I called Carol and, as usual, got her Cerberus, J., who always answered first. Carol came on almost immediately, and I told them what had just happened. J. immediately broke in and said, "Come to us!"

And so I did. It seemed to take forever to drive from Glen Ellyn to Wilmette, even though it should be less than an hour by tollway. I stopped at a Borders Books five minutes from their house, putting off the moment of contact with people who knew me deeply and whose feelings for me would no doubt force me to come to terms with my own feelings. When I did arrive, it was almost dark, and I sat in their den, in the chair I had sat in many times over the years I had known them, and told them about my mother's illness and death—I had not spoken with them since our last professional conference a month or so earlier. When I mentioned that my mother had been suffering from a particular form of leukemia that had apparently progressed in the past few months, Carol told me that that was what her brother had died from (her brother's leukemia had progressed farther than my mother's—my mother officially died from the stroke). Her brother was forty-three; my mother was seventy-eight.

She told me the story included above. It is interesting that I do not remember the recitation of Psalm 23, but I do remember another incident that Carol has not included. She said that at some point during her brother's final stay in the hospital, she was standing out at the nurses' station and a woman, clearly a local, was on the phone, talking to someone. "It's so faaaaar," she said, Carol mimicking the woman's authentic New York accent and explaining that the woman was referring to the distance between the hospital and wherever she and her listener were supposed to meet. Carol told me she wanted to turn to the woman and say, "Lady, I'll tell you about 'far,'" thinking about how far her brother was moving from the world of the living, from the irreverent childhood she shared with him and her sister Barbara, her baby brother, who had become a dashing man, partying with Richard Gere and the social circle of fashion models. How all such journeys take us on far paths — and how insignificant the problems of taxicabs or subways seem compared to devouring illness. This is the detail of the story that remains with me twelve years later, the "farness" of life, as I turn the other side of fifty, two years from the age my brother was when he died, nine years from my father's age when he died. And this story is part of the bond between me and Carol and J.

We now step outside the story again, awkward as it can be to try to examine it as if someone else were telling it. We suggested that Carol's story and Bruce's story stand in intertextual relationship with each other, by which we mean that they intersect, they "read" each other. In what ways does this seem to you to be true? Carol makes no reference to Bruce's story — does it still, in any way, seem to be in a kind of dialogue with it? How does Bruce's story seem influenced by Carol's? How is his telling of it informed by his reading of Carol's version? Can you imagine retelling Carol's story in ways that would make more overt its relationship to Bruce's? Add to this that we are not only coauthors, but also former teacher and student (that defines how we were first related to each other). What other stories — personal, literary, media, or cultural — does Bruce's story invoke? If Carol and Bruce were to perform their stories cooperatively (perhaps rewriting them) in a way that did not view them as separate entities but as collaborative, interwoven narratives, what techniques might they use?

Family Stories in Performance

Another kind of nonfiction that lends itself, often brilliantly, to performance is the story of a family member. E. Patrick Johnson, a professor at Northwestern University and a performer par excellence, has written about his grandmother, Mary Rhyne, in a book entitled *Appropriating Blackness*. Johnson first wrote about his grandmother as a part of his ethnographic dissertation in partial fulfillment of his master's degree. His grandmother raised him in the Deep South. For the purposes of his dissertation and subsequent writings, he visited her, observed her, recorded her on tape, and transcribed her words, capturing her speech patterns, intonations, and inflections during an interview in 1993. The full transcript of this remarkable interview, "Nevah Had uh Cross Word," is in the appendix of his book. He learned to mimic her speech, capturing its vernacular elements exactly. He paid astute attention to her pitch and tempo and other phonetic features, including how she pronounced words, when she paused, how she prolonged certain sounds, and how her voice would rise and fall in pitch as she spoke. He also later developed a script from her life story and wrote a play about her, in which he acted the role of the grandson, the ethnographic interviewer who gathered her story, casting Njoki McElroy as his grandmother. McElroy was a professor who pioneered courses in black poetry, drama, and short stories at Northwestern University in the Department of Interpretation, beginning in the 1960s.

Carol attended the inaugural production of "Nevah Had uh Cross Word" at Northwestern University in the Struble Theatre, a black-box theater set up like a proscenium stage. As I watched my colleague, Patrick, play the grandson and her interviewer and another colleague, Njoki, embody his grandmother, I realized that Patrick's mother was behind me in the audience. In fact, I heard his mother say that Njoki was just like her mother, Patrick's grandmother. The performance was a remarkable achievement and a testament to the power of nonfiction performances. Much more recently, I invited Patrick to perform his grandmother's story for my class in the performance of family stories and memoirs. It was a fascinating and disarming performance. One moment, Patrick is himself, in the next he slips into the voice of his grandmother, her rising and falling, high-pitched, somewhat whiney voice, talking about her days in the South when she was the maid for Mrs. Smith, a white woman, taking care of Mrs. Smith's household and children while Mr. and Mrs. Smith were running a hotel in another town.

This example is offered to inspire you to think about collecting material about a family member or relative and compiling a performance script for a nonfiction performance. When we give this assignment in a class, we realize that students have little time to gather the actual biographical and archival materials they need to do full justice to the performance. They can, however, make a start, and often, we have found, the students later flesh out these texts, developing them into full stage performances onstage or in documentary films. Sometimes, students go home over the Thanksgiving or winter holidays, just for a few short days or weeks, but during this time, they closely observe one of their family members, or the whole family, with the aim to perform a family ritual or a family member for the class on their return. In some cases, students have used a tape recorder, sometimes covertly, and taped their relatives for the purpose of the performance. They then transcribe the tape and memorize it in order to embody their human subject fully in their performance.

The ethics of this situation require some attention, and we will speak a little here and elsewhere in the book about whether or not it is appropriate to tape someone unbeknownst to the person for the purposes of a performance shared in class or in a larger venue. In most cases, when we are dealing with family narrative to be staged in public spaces or theaters in the university, we insist—to be safe—that the student get permission from their relatives to use the material. But in the classroom, we have been less insistent about this, asking the student performers and their peers to reflect on the ethics of the performance and make their own judgments. The responses have run the gamut, from a defense of performing material acquired without permission to a condemnation of it. You will want to reflect on these issues and seek advice from your teachers and classmates if you decide to perform a narrative of a family member based on actual transcription of their words. You should also be aware that many universities adhere to strict protocols regarding federally funded research on human subjects. In cases where human subjects are used for instructional purposes and confined to a classroom, not being a federally funded project, you have more latitude to make your own ethical judgments, but we caution you to be aware of protocols for securing permission from your human subjects to use them in this manner, particularly if you are thinking of taking your performance to a public audience beyond the classroom. Some students fear that they are violating the privacy of people dear to them, yet they sorely want to perform their relative or friend. We have occasionally told our classes that if the students have serious reservations about letting their classmates know the real identity of their performance subjects, then they should take appropriate liberties and conceal the identities. For example, the students might give their nonfiction subjects a "cover" name, a pseudonym, for the purpose of preserving privacy. Or, they might misidentify the nature of the relationship—sister, father, loved one—in an effort to preserve confidentiality. In chapter 12, where we address ethnographic research and matters of ethics, we will expand on this topic.

To prepare your performance, you need to learn as much as you can about your subject—be it grandmother, uncle, sibling, or a more distant person of interest to you. To be faithful to the genre of nonfiction, the student must observe their subjects as closely as possible. Be an actor and study the person whose role you will be playing. Observe how they dress, move, speak, looking as closely as you can. See if you can isolate aspects of their speech, movement, or manners that epitomize them and capture these in your solo performance.

Think also about how you, as a performer performing in a classroom with only the props and lighting that you can assemble with a little lead time, are going to stage your narration. Students often use simply a table, or desk, perhaps some objects they have assembled, such as photographs of the relative, diaries or journals, books, or a favorite stuffed toy, to suggest the world of their subject. You want to think economically about your choice of props and costume. Whether you use different stage spaces for different moments in time that are being captured in your performance, or whether you want to move around a desk and then cross to a chair, and maybe later to the lectern, in each case determine exactly what motivates the action and what is being accomplished by it. You will want to choose the lines at which you make a move, looking at them to see whether they reinforce the drama of the movement. In performance, even the slightest gesture or movement is important and is marked, so to speak. Your audience needs to know why the action is necessary. You want to make sure that you clearly convey with movement what you intend and take care that your performance does not become too cluttered. You don't want to be upstaged by your stage furniture. You want to maintain tight control of the arc, the shape, of your performance, giving it a clear beginning, middle, and end in Aristotelian fashion.

Gray Matters: Memoir, Memory, and Invention

Thus far, we have been discussing personal narratives in which the tellers endeavor to perform with fidelity to the actual events that constitute their stories; at the same time, we have acknowledged that, even in retelling our own personal narratives for this book, time and memory have an impact on how we tell such stories and on what we remember as "reality." In addition, we have identified desire as central to the telling of personal narratives: from the conscious desire of our aims and goals in telling personal stories to what we might see as unconscious desires that impel us to tell particular stories, including certain details and omitting others. We may omit a detail or event, not out of a conscious desire to deceive, but either to focus a story in a specific way or because our memories have blocked out some details or have caused us to remember them in ways that are not accurate. Some would distinguish between documentable reality and narrative truth, to use historian Hayden White's terms.

The memoir as a literary form takes us to a middle ground that can easily blur with autobiography; it is customary to view autobiography as a more historical record of a life and memoir as something that is a representation of a subject's memories, often a way of making sense of a particular phase or ongoing theme in one's life. For example, poet Mark Doty, in his memoir *Dog Years*, acknowledges that he had not only dogs but also two cats but is choosing not to write about the cats in his book, as he wishes to focus on how two particular dogs functioned in his life as he was going through his lover's death from AIDS and rebuilding a life with a new partner. As such, the memoir often plays more with what Philippe Lejeune calls the "autobiographical pact," itself a fairly minimal set of mutually assumed conventions, such as an identity between the "vital statistics" of the author and the narrator (quoted in Couser, *Vulnerable Subjects*, p. 143). The memoir may push this even farther—though to different levels of comfort and discomfort for writer and reader. We will examine texts that are outright attempts to commit fraud in terms of fact and truth later in the chapter. For the moment, we would like to consider a few brief examples of the gray areas of the memoir and the ethical and artistic issues they raise for the performer.

A very popular memoir of the past few decades is Lucy Grealy's *Autobiography of a Face*, first published in 1995. It falls into a category critic G. Thomas Couser calls "autopathography," the narrative of one's own illness or disability. In this memoir (although, notice Grealy uses the word *autobiography* in her title), Grealy writes the story of her childhood and adolescence, providing some family and personal background, but focusing closely on her own experience from the age of nine, when she was diagnosed with Ewing's sarcoma, a rare form of cancer that affected her jaw and lower face, disfiguring her and resulting in a large number of surgeries. Grealy eventually graduated from Sarah Lawrence College and the famed writing program at the University of Iowa and died at age thirty-nine from an apparently accidental overdose of heroin.

Most readers of Grealy's memoir assume that her memoir is a faithful representation of the facts of the life she lived, understanding that it could not be an inclusive record of every day of her life. The memoir, in its powerful and eloquent evocation of the common joys and sorrows of childhood and of the unique elements specific to Grealy's experience has connected with many readers. After Grealy's death, which shocked her friends and family as well as her reading public, a new edition of her memoir was published with an afterword by her friend and former graduate school roommate, novelist Ann Patchett. Patchett, who wrote a feature story about Grealy's last years for *New York* magazine, which she then expanded into a book-length memoir called *Truth and Beauty: A Friendship* (the title is drawn from Keats's poem "Ode on a Grecian Urn," in which truth and beauty are equated), writes with candor about Grealy's struggles with depression, pain, and substance abuse.

In the afterword to Grealy's book, Patchett portrays a memorable exchange at a reading Grealy gave at Rizzoli's, an upscale bookstore:

> "It's amazing how you remember everything so clearly," a woman said, her head wrapped in a bright scarf. "All those conversations, details. Were you ever worried that you might get something wrong?"
>
> "I didn't remember it," Lucy said pointedly. "I wrote it. I'm a writer."
>
> This shocked the audience more than her dismissal of illness, but she made her point: she was making art, not documenting an event. That she chose to tell her own extraordinary story was of secondary importance. Her cancer and subsequent suffering had not made this book. She had made it. Her intellect and ability were in every sense larger than the disease.
>
> By telling us that the sentences spoken in the book were not necessarily verbatim, Lucy claimed complete ownership of her history. It was her world and she would present it the way she wanted to. Her memory and desire were indeed the facts. (p. 231)

Think about this passage. Patchett is, of course, herself "interpreting" the exchange between Grealy and the audience member. Is her final paragraph, in which she explains what Lucy meant by her response to the questioner, any more factual than the disputed or disputable events in Grealy's memoir? If you think it is, why? Is Patchett's degree of truthfulness the same as the truthfulness of Grealy's account? Can you explain in what way?

Patchett's own memoir, her narrative of the friendship that gives the book its subtitle, has been a source of controversy. Many readers have objected to Patchett's revelations about Grealy's less saintly qualities when the person about whom she is writing can no longer present her own side.

Would we raise the same objections if this were a biography, perhaps written by someone who did not have a personal relationship with her subject? Others find Patchett's self-representation somewhat one-sided and self-serving; some even suggest that she comes across as a kind of martyr, a "perfect" friend who never wavered in her support of a difficult friend. Grealy does not write about Patchett; she ends her memoir at a point in her life before the two met. You may wish to read both books and make up your own mind.

Grealy's family members have had complicated responses to Patchett's (and Grealy's) memoirs. Suellen Grealy, an elder sister, wrote a column for the British newspaper *The Guardian*, in which she questions Patchett's motivations for writing the magazine article, the afterword, and the memoir, suggesting there was haste to get her word in and a kind of opportunism. Most painful for her [and, she suggests, for Grealy's nonidentical twin, who barely registers in Grealy's memoir] was the fact that, from her perspective, Patchett "stole" the process of mourning from the family, moving Grealy's tragic death into too public a sphere too soon after the actual event. She calls Patchett a "grief thief." A brother, Nicholas Grealy, offers another perspective, on a blog:

> Where was her family? Always there for her, but Lucy did neglect to mention us a lot! But that was fine, we're always proud of her, and were thankful for the success she did have . . . Realize that Lucy's interpretation of her life naturally had parts missing. It's an interesting story, but should perhaps be also included in the fiction category as well! (retrieved from cheesedip.com on July 1, 2003)

Indeed, some critics and writers have coined a rather cumbersome term, *autobiofictionography*, to name the blend of factual reality and imaginative truth that a book like Grealy's may convey.

Other writers navigate the tension between fact and imagination in other ways. Lauren Slater, a psychologist who has written four memoirs, titled one about her childhood experience of what she thinks was epilepsy (never formally diagnosed) *Lying: A Metaphorical Memoir*, in which she uses categories once associated with an epileptic seizure as the structuring device for her narrative (critics, such as Couser, have taken her to task not so much regarding the factuality of her representation of her own life, but for what they see as her misrepresentation of people with epilepsy — finding fault with her ethics in how she places personal experience in a larger cultural and stigmatized experience). The Nobel laureate Doris Lessing has written a book titled *Alfred and Emily,* in which, as she explains in the foreword, she tries to reclaim possible lives for her parents, whose lives, she believed, were destroyed by World War I; her father emerged as an amputee after serving as a soldier and her mother lost the great love of her life, "a doctor, drowned in the Channel" (p. vii). Lessing divides her book into two sections, the first a deliberately fictionalized novella in which she imagines different lives for her parents, no longer haunted by the war, the second a memoir of their lives as she experienced them as their daughter. Lessing clearly asks the reader to engage with each section in a different way but also to experience the book as a whole in which fiction and memoir speak to each other.

Think about the different ways you might deploy the techniques of performance to different ends in creating your own memoirs. How might you use space, voice, body, and media to signal the complex relationship between memory and fact in your performance? To what degree do you want such distinctions to be clear and legible to your audience? If you wish to blur the lines, consider why you wish to do so and the aesthetic and ethical implications of such a choice.

To conclude this chapter and its consideration of different kinds of nonfictional texts in performance, we will discuss texts that intentionally blur the line between fiction and truth, personal or other kinds of texts that set out to deceive their audiences, texts that claim the status of nonfiction but are, in fact, frauds.

This matter of the authenticity or truth regarding the events described in a work that claims to be nonfiction, as well as autobiographical, is important to a student planning to perform it as nonfiction. If the work is invented and therefore not based on real life, it is not nonfiction even if it purports to be. However, the fact that it purports to be nonfiction requires us to analyze it in those terms, even if we later conclude it does not belong in the category. For students assigned to do a nonfiction performance, clearly, the first task is to ascertain that the work by definition is nonfictional. If it is a work that claims the status of nonfiction but actually fails the first criterion, namely, that the events and people be real, then it can be admitted into this category, but only as a work that is bending the genre and faking a status it does not hold.

Let us briefly consider some noteworthy frauds, such as the book *Love and Consequences,* penned under the name Margaret B. Jones. Jones claimed she was raised in a foster home in South Central Los Angeles and was a child of mixed race, half Native American and half black. Actually, the book was written by Margaret Seltzer, of Eugene, Oregon, and she was neither the product of urban gang culture nor of the race and ethnicity that she claimed. You can imagine the furor that broke out when the truth was learned.

Another kind of fraud is written about in a book called *The Sokal Hoax: The Sham That Shook the Academy* and explored further in a subsequent volume, *Beyond the Sokal Hoax: Science, Philosophy, and Culture.* Alan Sokal, a physicist teaching at New York University, had submitted an article, "Transgressing the Boundaries—Toward a Transformative Hermeneutics of Quantum Gravity," to the cultural studies journal *Social Text*, which published it in its Spring/Summer 1996 special topics issue on the "Science Wars." The editors were pleased to have an article appear in their journal written by an author they assumed was interested in their disciplinary concerns. In fact, Sokal's intention was to satirize their breed of postmodernist, relativistic criticism and its careless, and to his mind, ignorant understanding of physics. The editors had not questioned the scientific assertions made in the article or the good faith of the author. When Sokal later revealed the truth, many cultural scholars and others were furious, attacking and condemning him for his lack of ethics. They argued that the ethics of scholarship and publication required him to offer science, not falsehoods; they found his defense of his parodic intentions unimpressive in this context. What do you think?

Both these examples point to potential sources of deep embarrassment, not to mention misguided readings and interpretations, all occurring because an all too trusting readership assumed the authors were the persons they said they were and accepted the works as nonfiction, in short, as true. By "true" we mean that the work objectively captured the facts it represented and that the facts were based on the real world, real objects, real events, and real people.

Another infamous example of a fraudulent autobiography is the book *The Education of Little Tree*, by Forrest Carter. He claimed to be an orphan boy of Cherokee origins who had grown up on a Cherokee reservation in Oklahoma. He wrote at length about his boyhood rites of passage and education on the Cherokee reservation. Later it was discovered that the author's actual name is Asa Carter and that he was a member of the Ku Klux Klan and a speechwriter for the right-wing governor of Alabama, George Wallace, widely regarded as a racist. Wallace was the governor who, in 1963, tried to deter racial integration by preventing two African-

American students, James Hood and Vivian Malone, from registering at the University of Alabama. Attorney General Robert Kennedy had to mobilize the National Guard in order to assure them safe admission to the university. As you can see, Carter was not a Cherokee; he was a white, virulent racist for a considerable part of his life. He later recants, but for the purposes of this discussion, we are focusing on the initial publication of the book by Forrest Carter and the author's claims at the time. Carter, in the same book, alluded to another figure, a Jewish peddler whom he referred to as Mr. Wine. In his depiction of Mr. Wine, he drew on all the negative stereotypes about Jews to flesh out this character, for example, claiming that he was free in giving advice about money. Carter made it appear that real Jews acted completely in accord with behavior attributed to them by anti-Semites. An accurate understanding of the events described in this work of nonfiction requires us to know who wrote it and to assess the biases of the writer based on our knowledge of the writer's real identity and intentions, insofar as we can know them.

Still another egregious example of these so-called nonfiction works that are actually works of invention and fiction is Clifford Irving's biography of the life of Howard Hughes, the great industrialist of the early part of the twentieth century, widely known for his eccentricities and obsessive desire in later life to live as a recluse and keep his once very public life extraordinarily private. Irving claimed that the very private Howard Hughes, who refused to give any potential biographers access, had in fact opened his life to him. Irving promoted his biography aggressively based on this false claim. A great scandal occurred when it was revealed that Irving had absolutely no access to Hughes, and the book was withdrawn just before publication, when it was exposed as a fraud.

Fraudulent memoirists abound, some causing acute humiliation to gullible readers. These frauds are particularly embarrassing when the audience to whom they have been addressed are people who pride themselves on their broad-mindedness, their tolerance, their liberal values — on what is often referred to as their political correctness. Teachers trying to be inclusive in their curriculum planning had adopted Carter's book in courses featuring Native American literature. The discovery that the book is not an authentic account undercuts the authority of the course and the teacher and betrays the intentions of students.

If you have chosen to perform from one of the fraudulent nonfictional works of the sort we have just described, you will need to decide how you are going to portray the narrator of the account. Are you going to signal in your performance that the account is not nonfictional or are you going to conceal this? You might well ask at this point, "Why would we want to perform a fraudulent work as a nonfiction personal experience performance?" One answer is that you might know the work is a hoax but be intrigued by the deception. Or you might have unwittingly chosen a fraudulent account and not known it. Regardless, are you going to handle the narrator with a sort of wink, to let your audience know from the start that the depiction you are offering is fake and that the narrator is unreliable? Maybe not, since you might want to let the illusion of truth prevail until you determine when, and if, you want to expose it. In this case, you would be offering a "straight" performance of the narrator's text, remaining faithful to the hoax, or misrepresentation, that the writer is practicing. If you are a student fulfilling an assignment to perform nonfiction, do you think you should consider these nonfictional frauds? If so, why? If not, why not? Think, too, about the ethical implications of your choice and how the audience will respond. And, most important, how will your choice inform your decisions in your performance?

Imagine that you are undertaking an assignment to offer a solo performance of a fraudulent work of nonfiction. Will you employ two narrators, one the "frame narrator," a version of yourself who offers the context for the first-person nonfictional text, and the other a solo rendering of the first-person narrator who is the subject of the nonfiction? Or will you take the stage and confront your audience directly with your solo embodiment of the nonfiction subject, without providing any context? For example, imagine you have decided to draw on a passage from Jones's account of her days as a gang member in South Central Los Angeles or from Carter's boyhood as a member of the Cherokee tribe. Will you treat the details regarding the experiences the writers describe as if you believe they had been experienced just as told? If you decide not to frame your performance, you might launch directly into the lines actually spoken by the narrator, taking on that character. The fact that the character in the case of Jones's or Carter's autobiographical work is not nonfictional would be something you would need to deal with in some way or other in order to have your performance ultimately understood as a work of nonfiction. How are you going to accomplish this?

You might choose to stage your event and use the blackboard, prompt cards, or video or slide images to show your audience information about your performance necessary to understanding it as nonfictional. Students frequently provide printed programs for their nonfiction performances in which they offer a biographical program note, identifying the source of their performance in order to enable the audience to know that the character they are performing onstage is a real person. When a student chooses to use a frame narrator, he or she employs performance conventions that allow us to recognize that the framing narrator is an extension of the performer, who has compiled and is presenting the nonfictional performance. Often, the students speak in their own voices, giving a brief (but rehearsed, even if it is improvised) introduction to their nonfiction performance. This technique enables them to declare explicitly that the topic of their performance is a representation of a real, as opposed to invented, character. Or, they might go directly into the character of the author of the nonfiction work. You will want to experiment with both these approaches.

This chapter has shown you ways in which you can draw on personal narratives, family history, and memoirs for your nonfiction performances. We have discussed the genre of nonfiction and explored inauthentic or fraudulent works of nonfiction. We have left the discussion of other kinds of nonfictional works for performance for chapter 12, where we will explore historical documents, writings about real places, and ethnographic materials and the method of inquiry that underlies them, as well as other kinds of nonfiction performances that permit the performer to assume an activist, political stance.

KEY TERMS

autobiofictionography

autopathography

documentable reality

family narratives

intertextual

memoir

narrative truth

Chapter 6

PERFORMING POETRY I:
THE SELF AND THE SPEAKER IN THE
LYRIC, DRAMATIC, AND EPIC MODES

Whose woods these are I think I know.
—ROBERT FROST, "STOPPING BY WOODS ON A SNOWY EVENING"

That's my last duchess painted on the wall, . . .
—ROBERT BROWNING, "MY LAST DUCHESS"

Poetry is "a way of remembering what it would imperil us to forget," the poet Robert Frost writes. In *A Prosody Handbook*, Karl Shapiro and Robert Beum compare poetry to music: "Sound, its movement and pattern, is at the very heart of the poem; it is part of the poet's technique, and as important in determining our imaginative and emotional responses to a poem as are the meanings of the words themselves" (p. 2). Because poetry is so rich in its language, sounds, and patterns, it is relatively easy to memorize. It offers many mnemonic devices that assist the performer, as well as the reader, in memorization. Poetry appeals not only to the ear but to the eye, both in its form and also in its images—verbal pictures. It offers spoken pictures, uses language metaphorically and symbolically, and expresses a language of feeling. The poem's appearance on the printed page, its typography or iconography, also informs the poem's meaning. Because poetry is grounded in rhythm, rich in sound, and visually provocative, it has an immediate sensory and kinesthetic impact when performed, both for the performer and for the audience. It also features a speaker and, in some cases, dramatic characters.

Your most important task as a performer of poetry is to decide how to embody the speaker's voice and character in your performance. Don't be disturbed if you feel a bit fearful or self-conscious when handling poetic language, especially if you have not had prior experience performing poems. Language in poetry is often used with great economy, and figures of speech can be highly allusive, making pointed reference to meanings that lie outside the body of the poem, that is, extrinsic to the text, as opposed to intrinsic, or internal to it. You may find it difficult to understand the allusions and a struggle at first to figure out the attributes of the speaker and the nuances of his or her character as you prepare your performance of the poem. Sometimes the persona seems to most closely resemble the poet or an extension of the poet's voice rather than a character from a play, as in the Frost poem at the beginning of the chapter. In other cases, such as Robert Browning's poem above, the speaker seems almost to be a character from a play, so particularly is he or she delineated. In this chapter, we will use the concepts of lyric, dramatic, and epic modes in poetry to help you understand the choices you will be making as you decide how to perform the speaker's character in the poem. When you read a poem silently, there are many different ways in which you can conceive and understand the poem's speaker, but when you perform the poem, you must make specific choices about the speaker, narrowing the range of meanings that you ascribe to the voice and persona of the character in your silent reading. Typically, we refer to the speaker of the poem as the poem's persona; if the speaker is a dramatic character, we can refer to that speaker by the name or title. In the Frost poem, we speak of the persona of the man journeying through the woods; in the Browning poem, we identify the duke as the speaker.

You also need to understand the poem's prosody because the language and form of a poem are inextricably intertwined and integral to an understanding of the speaker and the meaning of the poem. The term *prosody* evolved in Europe and describes systems and forms of versification in poetry. It provides concepts and a vocabulary to understand the craft of poetry. This understanding is important when you consider how to capture and translate the form of poetry into your performance.

The Speaker in the Poem

The performer must embody the voice and character of the speaker in a poem. In a silent reading of a poem, the reader, even a careful one, does not have to focus primarily on the matter of embodying the speaker and, as a consequence, may not be accustomed to thinking about the speaker as a particular, individual self. Other features of the poem may dominate the reader's attention, but in performing poetry, you ignore or underestimate the character of the speaker at your own risk. Your performing self must embody the speaker even if you believe the speaker's self is not highly individuated. To do this well, you need to understand both the relationship of your performing self to the speaker and poem and the form of poetry with which your performing self is matching. *Matching* is a term that Wallace Bacon uses to describe the process whereby a performer uses empathy to feel the way into the character of the poem's speaker and to match the character's being with his or her own in the performance of the poem. The performer matches not only the inner form of the poem, the emotions and ideas it evokes, but also the outer form, or what we call the prosodic features of the poem. We will talk more of this later. For now, remember that you need to enter fully into the world of the poem and its speaker in a nearly mystical and figurative way, matching with it as you perform it.

Thus it is essential to answer the question: Who is the speaker in the poem? Sometimes you can easily decide whether the speaker is understood to be the implied poet or a dramatic character identified by name or role, not to be confused with the poet who wrote the poem; in other cases it is more difficult. We find it useful in thinking about how to perform the speaker to refer to the modes of poetry—lyric, dramatic, or epic. We have spoken about these modes in earlier chapters; now let us look at them more closely in the context of performing poetry.

The concept of modes derives from Aristotle's *Poetics*, and it was adapted and amplified by scholars in the field of interpretation/performance studies, two of the most well known being Wallace Bacon in *The Art of Interpretation* and Leland Roloff in *The Perception and Evocation of Literature*. In the lyrical mode, the speaker is assumed to be an extension of the poet expressing himself or herself in a manner that does not draw marked attention to character, per se, but to the speaking voice. In this mode, the speaker often appears to be a person not importantly distinct from the poet who wrote the poem. Consider, for example, the speaker in Robert Frost's poem "Stopping by Woods on a Snowy Evening" (the poem is readily available on the Internet). Frost opens with the line: "Whose woods these are I think I know," and the speaker goes on to describe a New England landscape of woods and frozen lake, a house in the village, and his little horse before he concludes with the haunting, hypnotic quatrain: "The woods are lovely, dark and deep, / But I have promises to keep, / And miles to go before I sleep, / And miles to go before I sleep." When you first encounter the poem, you may visualize the scene almost as though it were a picture on a Christmas card. The poem is lovely, lyrical, and nostalgic, evoking a wintry landscape that we may wish to imagine ourselves inhabiting. However, as the poem continues, it reveals a more unsettling world and different associations and meanings. The speaker, a poet and traveler, is tempted to forsake his journey and succumb to the seductive lull of the snowy woods before he remembers his responsibilities, promises made that call him back to the business of life and draw him onward, away from the woods.

In this poem, the nameless speaker appears to be a man very close in spirit and experience to the poet who writes about him. In short, the speaker can be interpreted as someone similar to the poet. There is extensive scholarship about the relationship of an implied author, namely the author that the reader infers from the text, to the actual author, in this case Robert Frost. The author and the implied author can both be further differentiated from one or more characters created by the poet to function as the speaker(s) of the poem. In scholarship on authorship and the rhetoric of fiction, the *author* is defined as the person who actually writes the poem; the *implied author* refers to the author you infer from reading and understanding all the particulars of the poem. The author and the implied author may not be at all similar. The *speaker* in the poem, who seems to be the all powerful shaping voice of the poem, may be conceived and presented as someone quite similar to the author or, at the other extreme, a dramatic character created by the author but significantly different.

Let us apply these abstract concepts to the speaker in Frost's poem. Does the poem's speaker seem to be a different kind of person than Robert Frost himself? What are some of the choices a performer might make about the character of the speaker? You will probably agree that a performer is likely to keep the speaker's character consonant with the character described in the poem, but also a speaker who may inhabit the landscape that the actual author, Frost, knew. Insofar as you are thinking about the author, Frost, when you read the poem, you are probably adhering to ideas about who this poet—a poet laureate—is in the American public imagination. From this perspective, the speaker in the

poem appears to be similar to the implied poet/author, the reader's imagined persona for Robert Frost as a man who is a New Englander, familiar
with the winters in Maine, Vermont, and New Hampshire. You might
be imagining a speaker who shares some aspects of Frost, the real man.
However, if you choose to interpret the speaker in the poem as quite
individualized, and not necessarily similar to the poet Frost, you will
be employing the dramatic mode and casting the speaker as a dramatic
character importantly distinct from the poet Frost. You may envision the
speaker as an eccentric New England character, or a suicidal depressive,
or a cranky curmudgeon, or a reserved New Englander, a kind of rustic.
As you move from the more general sense of the speaker as the poet to
your more particularized imaginings of the speaker's character emphasizing individual traits that draw attention to themselves, you are moving
away from the lyrical voice of Frost as poet and toward a sense of the
speaker as a dramatic character. To the extent that you invest the speaker
with strong dramatic character traits, you downplay or subordinate other
more lyrical aspects of the poem as you press its meaning toward a more
dramatistic interpretation.

We have been speaking so far as though the poem's speaker must be a
man, whether performed by a man or woman. However, you may choose
to change the poem's speaker to a woman, perhaps because you are a
woman and you want to draw on your gender in your embodiment of the
poem's speaker. If you imagine the speaker of the poem as a woman, can
you point to evidence in the poem to support the interpretation? Or do
you think it is more a question of a certain coloration that you must give
to certain feelings in the poem if you are to transpose the poem's speaker
to a woman successfully? One could argue that if you keep the performance of the poem in the lyric mode, it doesn't matter which gender you
ascribe to the speaker; however, if you dramatize the speaker's character,
the character is likely to take on gender. Could you keep the speaker
androgynous in the dramatic mode?

In the Frost poem, the sense is that we are overhearing the musings of
the speaker; there is no reason to believe he actually speaks these words,
nor do we have to have a keener sense of him than the one he provides
by revealing his reflections. If you favor an interpretation of the poem's
meaning that views the speaker as someone musing aloud, reflecting on
the snow-covered woods and a wintry landscape in contrast to the world
of the village and the call to travel on, you will be treating the speaker in
the lyric mode.

The dramatic mode, in contrast to the lyric, features a speaker who is a character inferred from what he or she says and does not say, and the character is distinctly different from that of the implied author/poet. The speaker need not actually be identified by name in the poem, but the character of the speaker is revealed in considerable particularity. In the dramatic mode, the speaker functions in a manner similar to a character in a play. For example, in "My Last Duchess," by Robert Browning, the poem opens with the words of the duke, who is addressing an emissary and making arrangements to acquire another wife: "That's my last duchess painted on the wall, / Looking as if she were alive" (this poem, too, is available on the Internet). In this dramatic monologue, the duke sets the scene and, with a pride born of his nine-hundred-year-old name, negotiates the dowry he expects as he arranges to acquire another wife. He is understood to be a character distinct from and not to be confused with the implied author of the poem (who controls the poem's irony) nor with the actual poet, Robert Browning.

In a poem in the epic mode, the lyric and dramatic modes are combined and the speaker functions as narrator and unfolds the poem by employing both his or her own voice, often using third-person narration, and the voices of characters in the poem's story. In the epic poems by Homer, the *Iliad* and the *Odyssey*, the poet opens by invoking the muse and then telling the tale of Achilles and the war between the Greeks and the Spartans (in the *Iliad*) and the journey home of Odysseus (in the *Odyssey*). In epic poems, whether lengthy or short, the dialogue of the characters is set off in quotation marks or with dashes to indicate direct discourse and a narrator acts as storyteller.

These modes—lyric, dramatic, and epic (narrative)—help you decide how to perform the speaker in poetry. They provide a useful vocabulary to describe the choices you see embodied in a performance of poetry. They also enable you to speak about the relationship between your performing self and the speakers and characters in poems that you are performing.

When considering your performing self, you will want to consider the characters and speakers you are performing, but you also need to reflect on your own life experiences and inner emotions and how you are channeling and transforming them in the service of the poem. In other words, you need to consider the "me" in your performance and how your experiences are a part of your performance. For example, you may have actually experienced a wintry New England landscape at some point in your life, and you may have a number of very personal associations that you can readily call up from memory when you think about these experiences. You may also have rich sensory associations that accompany your memories, some so powerful they threaten to overwhelm you. These are emotions and recollections that you will draw on as you shape your performances and delve deeply into the poem. After we have shown you more about the three modes and how they shape the speaker's relationship to the world of the poem and the audience, we will elaborate further on narrative poetry—a kind of epic poetry that includes ballads and tales. Narrative poems have special prosodic features and also interesting features of storytelling that are worth a separate discussion.

A Poem in the Lyric Mode

Consider the following work by E. E. Cummings as an example of a poem written in the lyric mode (we have numbered the lines for ease of reference). Take time to read it carefully before you read our extensive analysis of it. It is always valuable to simply play with a poem's language, speaking it aloud again and again, to prepare yourself for a performance.

> since feeling is first
> who pays any attention
> to the syntax of things
> will never wholly kiss you;
>
> wholly to be a fool
> while Spring is in the world
>
> my blood approves,
> and kisses are a better fate
> than wisdom
> lady i swear by all flowers.   Don't cry
> —the best gesture of my brain is less than
> your eyelids' flutter which says
>
> we are for each other:then
> laugh,leaning back in my arms
> for life's not a paragraph
>
> And death i think is no parenthesis

Who is the speaker? Why do you think the speaker refers to himself with a little "i," and uses inverted syntax—a term that refers to the order of the words—and no terminal punctuation? Is the poem written to be performed in the lyric mode? If you elect to construct a performance that adheres to the lyric mode, you will recognize the personality traits of the character of the speaker, but you will subordinate them to other ends in the poem in order to keep the speaker in the lyric rather than the dramatic mode. If you were to translate the performance into the dramatic mode, you would give the speaker a very distinctive personality, and you would have to make various decisions about placement and locus, deciding where to situate the loved one and the person addressed by the poem as well as how to handle the audience. We will first consider the poem as an example of the lyric mode in performance, but even at this stage, it is worth thinking about arguments for the dramatic mode. This will deepen your understanding of the implications of casting the poem in the lyric mode.

It is important to understand that when we use this modal approach to the performance of poetry, we take on the voice of the speaker in a poem; the performer is dramatizing that speaker, translating the speaker into a person with particular traits. In so doing, the performer's self is very much involved. Try as you may to embody or, as Bacon put it, "match" the speaker, you cannot escape your own particularity—the way you look, your size, your gender, your nationality, ethnicity, and a host of other aspects of your personality and body. However, in performing poetry written by someone other than yourself, you are initially expected to try to focus on what is often called the other, the speaker in the poem, and adjust your self and identity to the expression of this other. When you consider which mode of performance is most suited to the poem, the lyric or the dramatic, you are judging whether the performing self you select should be interpreted more as an extension of the voice of the poem and the implied poet, or whether it seems to be a dramatic character, conceived by the poet but given a separate identity, marked by very particular characteristics and set forth in a manner that answers questions about who this character is.

You also derive information about the speaker that your performing self will embody by considering the form of the poem, beyond its overt content and the clues it provides to the speaker's identity. In poetry, it is an oft-stated truth that form and content are one and cannot be disentangled if we are to be faithful to the poem's meanings. However, it is possible to analyze form and content separately for the purpose of gaining clarity of understanding about how the poem operates and what it means.

Prosody is the term used to describe the study of versification, including rhythmic devices and other patterns in poetry. It addresses sound, tempo, pause and flow, duration of sounds, line lengths, stanzas, typographical and iconographical elements, pictograms, meter, rhyme and the lack of rhyme, and syllable counting. A poem's prosody offers rich clues to a performer, helping you to make informed choices about how to speak the poem and understand its meaning, making form and substance complement each other.

The poem "since feeling is first" is unconventional in its handling of grammar and punctuation. It comprises one complete sentence, concluding with the word "flowers" in line 10, and a fragment consisting of a series of utterances without terminal punctuation in line 16. We will consider the prosodic elements of the poem further, but first let us return to a discussion of the poem's speaker.

Look at how an aspect of the poem's prosody, the speaker's use of the uncapitalized personal pronoun "i" to refer to himself, contributes to the poem's meaning. The poem celebrates feeling and emotion rather than reason and logic. The speaker sets up an opposition between order, which he equates with syntax, or the order of words, and feeling, emotion, which he declares supreme. It is a love poem in which the speaker addresses his lover as "lady" and offers his argument for love, an age-old theme. In the traditions of love poetry, this kind of poem expresses the theme of carpe diem, gather ye rosebuds while you may. This lover asks his loved one to laugh, lean back in his arms, and revel in their love. The speaker does not explicitly invite the lover to bed down with him in a nakedly sexual invitation, but we can infer that the poet's plea is to give in to him, assumedly in a sexual fashion although the poet is discreet in his expression, and it could be argued that his plea is not for sex, but for coy and sensuous exploration of each other. He tells her, and by extension, the reader/performer, that it is springtime, a time of budding and birthing, and a time for laughter and love. He is speaking of feeling; his language invites her to laugh and lean into his arms. He wants to "wholly" kiss her, and he alludes to the flutter of her eyelids.

In this paradigmatic interpretation of Cummings's love poem, a male "I" speaks to a male "us" (the audience) about a beloved "she." Of course, we can challenge the poem's construction of gender, but we read (interpret) this gendered cluster of meanings—the male love of a female beloved presented to a male audience—as an expression of the typical gender assumptions of the lyric poem in Western poetry. Even if we shift the gender of the lovers in the poem, we still have the same love triangle and the themes of possession, exclusivity, and jealousy that are typical of love sonnets and lyrics.

You may be initially a little surprised at his conceit, that is, his extended figure of speech, in this case his plea for love. He uses terms such as "syntax," "paragraph," and "parenthesis," terms that describe principles of order by which one arranges parts of speech and sentences according to rules of grammar. But he has disdain for such terms and argues that it is "feeling," not syntax, that governs and that she should yield to its laws. Of course, the words "grammar," "govern," and "laws," in the context of the poem, are used ironically, since the meaning of each word is negated in the poem. A chief indicator of this negation is the speaker's studied choice to flatter his loved one, praising the flutter of her eyelids and deprecating his stature by referring to himself with the uncapitalized "i." Do you think this is disingenuous of him? As he takes his oath on flowers and urges her to lean back, laugh, and flutter her eyelashes in his arms, we might think that he is a disarming lover, full of flattery and exerting a powerful pull, with his argument about feeling, not reason. What do you think? Are you concerned about the gender assumptions embedded in the poem? He speaks of his brain and her eyelids; she is aligned with feeling, he with sense, and yet he wants to give sense over to feeling and the play of love. The poem is firmly grounded in traditions of love sonnets with their gender-based conventions about courtly love, male lovers and their dominant behavior, and female loved ones, the object of the love and more submissive. Of course, these conventions can be inverted, but if they are, you should invert them knowingly.

Many students find the final line of the poem the most difficult to understand. At a literal level, throughout the poem, from its first line to its last, the speaker is using a metaphor, a figure of speech that is an implied comparison of two seemingly unlike objects, in this case comparing life and death with "paragraph" and "parenthesis" that refer to the way ideas are ordered in grammatically correct writing. If the comparison had been explicit, using the words "like" or "as" to compare life to a paragraph, the figure of speech, or trope, would be a simile. Cummings's metaphor requires us to understand that a well-written paragraph has a beginning, middle, and end and the sentences that constitute it develop a sustained idea. A parenthesis is often composed of a sentence fragment, usually contained within parentheses, and its ideas are subordinate to those expressed in the main clause that lies outside. The lover in this poem argues that life is not an ordered part of a greater whole, with a neat beginning, middle, and end; in short, he says life defies the rules of syntax, and to bring this argument home, he insists that death, too, needs to be rethought—it is not an aside, a parenthesis, something that can be thought of as subordinate to life; rather, he implies, it is the whole. Death can take all away; to defy it, lovers must live for the day and to the full, or so he argues as he woos her.

When you are making choices about how to embody this speaker, you might choose to interpret the poem as an innovation on the traditions of love poetry and the sonnet. You could also choose to keep the speaker, the lover, in your performance very close to the implied author, an extension of Cummings. In your performance, certain aspects of this lover—his decision to talk about love in a didactic way as well as his preoccupation with the rules of grammar, his clever verbal wordplay, and his interest in the typographical aspects of how the poem appears on the printed page—would all be featured. In such a performance, you would be creating a character for your speaker that would make him appear to be an embodiment of the implied author, the poet Cummings, concentrating as much on the speaker as poet as on the qualities of the lover. Or, you might research Cummings's biography and photos of him and decide to make your interpretation of the poem feature the man, Cummings, more than anything else within the poem. Can you see how very different this interpretation of the poem would be from considering the speaker in the lyric mode? If you had chosen to delineate the speaker as the actual biographical man, Cummings, you would be performing this poem's speaker in the dramatic, not the lyric mode.

Earlier, we alluded to the ways the performer could adapt the poem in performance so that it offered a gender-based political commentary on the poem's speaker. Such a performance, offered by a female performer, could be shaped to punctuate all the sexism in the poem's construction of the male speaker with his logic and the female beloved with her fluttering eyelids. It might show the speaker to be highly manipulative, controlling, not subscribing to feeling at all but exploiting feeling in order to use the woman in the poem. The poem could be depicted as a poem to silence all opposition, not giving the woman, the so-called loved one, any room to speak in her own voice or resist. Such a performance deliberately deconstructs the poem's meaning, offering its own subversive reading.

A male performer, too, could play with the poem's gender assumptions. Think about how such a performance might work. If you were witnessing either of these two hypothetical gender-bending performances in a class, you might want to take note of the ways in which the performer redeploys the language and images in the poem, and the speaker's self. The modal approach can help you do this.

On Scansion and Other Prosodic Matters

Let us now consider how to handle and describe rhythm in a poem with the ultimate goal of understanding how the poem's structure and form serve its meaning, often making it clearer. There are many different systems of scansion used to describe syllable-stressed or traditional meter in poetry. The system of scansion of English traditional verse derives from Latin prosody modified to conform to the English language. We will focus on syllable-stressed or traditional meter in English poetry, but there are other systems of prosody, such as stress-based rhythm that describes the oldest form of rhythm in English poetry; in the twentieth century it was revived in an altered form by writers such as T. S. Eliot in "The Love Song of J. Alfred Prufrock" and "The Waste Land." There is also syllabic prosody, a form of prosody based on syllable counting: the number of syllables that compose each line determines line length. The number of syllables that constitute different lines of each stanza may vary in a recurring pattern. Marianne Moore's poems are often in syllabic prosody. There is also free verse, where features other than meter are used to organize and structure the poem.

To ground your understanding of scansion, we will start with an experimental poem and then will move to more traditional poems, using the system of scansion most commonly used in metered poetry in the English language. You may have read more unmetered verse, or free verse, and you may be accustomed to the poet taking liberties with conventional metered verse. The Cummings poem, which is experimental and departs from the conventions of metered poetry, also contains one line of pure metered poetry. Most prosodists would describe the poem as written in free verse, in contrast to metered, or syllable-stressed verse, but it relies heavily on the iambic and anapestic foot, and it has a regular last line.

Our scansion is diagrammed in figure 5.1. To consider form in poetry and to write about it in technical terms, we look at the poem's form, the line lengths, number of syllables per line, rhyme scheme (if it has one), and the rhythmic ground of the poem. You should always consider these elements when you approach a poem for performance. The technical features of a poem include a scansion: a description of the number of syllables per line, the number of strongly and weakly stressed syllables or words per line, the kind of feet that predominate if the poem is written in foot prosody, and the rhyme scheme. The word *accent* is used to describe the amount of effort given to articulate one syllable in comparison to the effort given to the adjacent syllable. When we speak of accent without reference to context, we call it *lexical* accent. If a word is given emphasis because of its meaning in context, we say it is given *rhetorical* accent. *Stress* refers to the intensity of utterance given to a phoneme, syllable, or word in relation to metrical feet in verse. In addition, in the scansion for the Cummings poem we have indicated feet divisions while reminding you that the poem is written in free verse. One of the clues for discovering whether a poem is in metered verse or free verse is to look at line length. When it varies widely and in a manner that is not patterned, it is likely that the poem is free verse. In Cummings's poem, you can see that the line lengths vary, but can you also see how there are shades of iambic pentameter in the lines of the poem? Note the marked regularity of the five iambic feet in the final line of the poem.

since feeling is first	1
who pays any attention	2
to the syntax of things	3
will never wholly kiss you;	4
wholly to be a fool	5
while Spring is in the world	6
my blood approves,	7
and kisses are a better fate	8
than wisdom	9
lady i swear by all flowers. Don't cry	10
—the best gesture of my brain is less than	11
your eyelids' flutter which says	12
we are for each other:then	13
laugh,leaning back in my arms	14
for life's not a paragraph	15
And death ˘i think ́ is no ́ paren thesis ́	16

KEY
˘ = unstressed syllable
́ = stressed syllable

FIGURE 5.1: SINCE FEELING IS FIRST

An iambic pentameter line is made up of five feet and the predominant foot is an *iamb*, namely, a foot of two syllables (two monosyllabic words, a two-syllable word, or a combination of adjacent syllables from longer words), the first unstressed and the second stressed. The concept of the foot in poetry involves a metrical unit made up of the relative emphasis, intonation, and length or time taken to express each syllable that is then repeated. We are going to use a two-level system of feet in which we differentiate stressed and weakly stressed syllables. Prosodists use the terms "unstressed" or "weakly stressed" to refer to the syllable that receives less emphasis in a foot of poetry; for example, in the word *feeling*, the second syllable is weakly stressed and the first syllable carries the strong stress. We prefer "weak" to "unstressed"; rhythm and sound patterns are so keenly important in speech acts that it seems misleading to speak of a word as being unstressed or without stress. There are more complicated systems of foot prosody that rely on three or four levels of stress, but for our purposes, we do not need a system more complicated than the one that recognizes stressed and weakly stressed.

A foot in prosody is a group of syllables constituting a metrical unit. In the most common form of foot prosody, there are four kinds of feet: *iambic* (a weakly stressed syllable followed by a stressed syllable), *trochaic* (the opposite of an iamb, or a stressed syllable followed by a weakly stressed syllable), *anapest* (two weakly stressed syllables followed by a stressed syllable), and a *dactyl* (two stressed syllables followed by a weakly stressed syllable). Edgar Allen Poe's poem "Annabel Lee" includes many lines with anapestic feet, such as "it was many, and many, a year ago." Many nursery rhymes, such as "Hickory Dickory Dock," employ the dactyl; "hickory" is scanned with a stress mark on "hick," followed by two weakly stressed syllables. There are also two other frequently used feet: the *spondee*, a foot comprised of two stressed syllables, and the *pyrrhic* foot, comprised of two weakly stressed syllables. In scansions of poetry, we use an accent mark above the syllable that receives the stress and a breve above unstressed syllables; vertical lines are inserted between feet.

Try scanning the last line of Cummings's poem: "and death i think is no parenthesis." Count the number of syllables in this line. You will see that there are ten, with the stress on every second syllable, thus there are five feet. This last line in Cummings's poem is of great importance in terms of the poem's meaning: it is written in iambic pentameter and is a completely regular line of metered poetry appearing in a poem where the other lines are quite unconventional and not metered.

You will find it helpful to consult a dictionary when you are scanning poetry. The dictionary provides a description of how a word is inflected, showing where the strong and weak, and sometimes intermediary, stresses are placed. Sometimes poets invert the customary stress in a word for poetic effect, but this kind of inversion is easily recognized. An etymological dictionary (such as the *Oxford English Dictionary*) is also very useful for providing the denotative meaning of a word—its literal meaning—and tracing the meaning of a word over time, to show other words from which it is derived. The connotative meanings of a word—meanings that are suggested by or associated with it—are also necessary. For this, a dictionary of poetic terms can be very helpful. Poets often also use double entendres, words that convey two, often opposite, meanings at the same time. For example, in the Elizabethan period, the word *die* not only referred to mortality but was a term for sexual intercourse. John Donne played with these double meanings in a number of his metaphysical poems; an expression such as "come let us die together" is understood much more richly when you are aware of the double meaning. We encourage you to use the dictionary to divide words into syllables and place the appropriate strong and weak stress marks on the syllables of the words that make up a line, or lines, of verse.

You may find it useful to refer to the beat in a line of poetry. The beat (the Latin term is *ictus*), refers to metrical stress and is used to find the rhythm or meter in a line of verse. *Caesura* refers to a pause, however slight, within a line of metrical verse. It is indicated by two slanted parallel lines. If the caesura comes at the end of the line, but the syntactic meaning of the line or the sentence structure extends over into the next line, the line is said to be *enjambed*, or run on. When speaking such a line, you will usually use a slight, but noticeable pause, slowing down your speech while keeping the pitch of your voice up, therefore signaling not closure but moving forward toward the conclusion of the thought that comes in the next line or later. Delivered properly, we feel the caesura as the end of the line but not the end of the sentence. If a line concludes with terminal punctuation, such as a semicolon or period, the line is described as *end-stopped.* Sometimes, in order to preserve the meter, the poet uses *elision* and omits a syllable or runs two syllables together. For an excellent, sophisticated account of prosody written for writers of poetry, *A Poet's Guide to Poetry*, by Mary Kinzie, is unrivaled.

If you look at the earlier lines in Cummings's poem and attempt to scan them using a conventional system of foot prosody, you will see that they defy your efforts. They are too irregular, a clue to you that the system of prosody in the poem is unconventional and that, in all likelihood, this is an example of a poem written in free verse, a term used to describe poetry without any set meter. The poem is a hybrid of sorts, since it concludes with a regular, metered line.

Free verse relies on other forms and techniques of patterning, many of which are also present in metered verse. Alliteration, the repetition of a sound, includes consonance, repeated consonant sounds, and assonance, repeated vowel sounds. The smallest unit of meaningful sound is referred to as a phoneme (*phone* is a linguistic term describing an individual speech sound). For example, in the Cummings poem, the "f" sound is repeated and carried throughout the poem in "feeling," "first," "fool," and "fate," illustrating alliteration, specifically, consonance. The long "a" vowel sound repeated in "pays," "fate," "lady," and "brain" is an example of assonance. Cummings varies the play on sounds in the letter *f* by using the "fl" sound in "flowers" and "flutter." Look for other sound patterns that he employs to structure his free verse.

Another way poets use sound is to employ onomatopoeia, wherein a word or phrase describing a sound actually sounds like the sound being described. For example, "buzzing" sounds like the noise made by a bumblebee. Sound and sense participate in an even more complex way in synesthesia, where a word used to describe one of the five senses stimulates a different sensory reaction, for example, colors experienced as sounds. Fascinating recent research in the areas of psychoneurobiology and genetics has begun to identify the parts of the brain that process synesthesia.

In considering the poem's rhythm, in addition to paying attention to how the stressed and weakly stressed syllables are distributed throughout the poem, look at the techniques Cummings uses to influence the tempo, the rate at which you speak the words. Here you may want to play some improvisational games with the poem's language. Try speaking the words and the lines at different rates or bouncing a ball on each stressed word as you recite the poem. Can you see how pause functions in the poem? Look at line breaks and stanza breaks, as well as the typographical conventions that affect the way the poem looks on the page. Experiment with using pauses of different durations. Can you describe how the character of the speaker or the evocative meanings of certain words alters when you change the lengths of the pauses? Bodily, do you find yourself experiencing different muscular tension or different movements or impulses to move as you speak the poem in different ways?

Poetry lives in its words. Relish them for themselves. You may feel that you can almost taste them as you speak them. Try exaggerating some of the sounds, varying pitch or protracting the duration of a word or sound. Are some of the sounds in the poem more suitable to this kind of wordplay than others? Can you say why?

Sensory imagery abounds in this poem. Poetic language appeals to the five senses: sight (visual), sound (hearing or acoustical), touch (tactile), smell (olfactory), and taste. Look again at the Cummings poem and identify the different kinds of sensory images he uses. How can you exploit the sensory imagery in a performance? Also think about how you might use movement to enhance your performance and inflect the poem's prosody. Are there particular images that stand out? How might you construct a performance to feature a visual element in the poem? How could you economically use a prop in your performance? If you were to choose an environment for this poem's performance, what would it be? Would you like to be able to perform the poem outside on a spring day, with grass and flowers nearby? What prop or object, natural or man-made, might you use? If you were to stage your performance, employing different props to suggest the two different worlds, one of feeling, the other of syntax, what props might you use?

Since the poem is explicitly commenting on the act of writing and the typographical layout of the poem is designed to invite response, capturing or playing with these elements is something to consider for a performance. How could you emphasize the poem's unusual layout on the page, its typography? Would you want to use media to represent some of the formal features of the poem, such as the parenthesis? You could project an image of the poem on a screen at the front of your classroom and perform the poem in front of it, playing with the way the image of the poem's typography plays across your face and body, breaking up the display of the words as well as marking your body and face with letters and punctuation. Would you make cutouts of letters or bring toy letters to capture the playful feel of the poet's wooing? You could use a partner to manipulate paper cutouts of the words and letters in a puppetlike manner on or around your body as you enact dramatically the wooing of the lover and his loved one (or do it solo). Think about the different ways such a performance can unfold. You will want to anticipate your audience's reactions and shape your performance choices very clearly so that you can control the audience's response to some extent, or at least so that you can clearly signal that you know the liberties you are taking with the poem's text and that you are doing so for a reason.

Having discussed Cummings's poem from the perspective of both the lyric mode and the dramatic, let us turn now to consider Michael Drayton's sonnet no. 61, "Since There's No Help," written in 1619 in the dramatic mode. Bear in mind that a performer can subvert the author's mode, but here we will examine this poem as an example of the dramatic mode. Also note that this poem is written in conventional metered verse.

Sĭnce thére's | nŏ hélp, | cóme lĕt | ŭs kíss | ănd párt;   1

Náy, Í | hăve dóne, | yŏu gét | nŏ móre | ŏf mé,   2

Ănd Í | ăm glád, | yĕa glád | wĭth aĺl | mў héart   3

Thăt thús | sŏ cléan|lў Í | mўsélf | căn frée;   4

Sháke hánds | fŏr é|vĕr, cán|cĕl aĺl | oŭr vóws,   5

Ănd whén | wĕ méet | ăt á|nў tíme | ăgáin,   6

Bĕ ít | nŏt séen | ĭn éi|thĕr óf | oŭr bróws   7

Thăt wé | ŏne jót | ŏf fór|mĕr lóve | rĕtáin.   8

Nŏw át | thĕ lást | găsp óf | lóve's lá|tĕst bréath,   9

Whĕn, hĭs | pŭlse fáil|ĭng, Pás|sĭon spéech|lĕss líes,   10

Whĕn Fáith | ĭs knéel|ĭng bý | hĭs béd | ŏf déath,   11

Ănd Ín|nŏcénce | ĭs clŏ|sĭng úp | hĭs éyes,   12

   Nŏw ĭf | thŏu wóuldst, | whĕn aĺl | hăve gíven | hĭm óvĕr,   13

   Frŏm déath | tŏ lífe | thŏu míghtst | hĭm yét | rĕcóvĕr.   14

FIGURE 5.2: MICHAEL DRAYTON'S SONNET #61

Remember that your central question when considering your performing self and the poem is: who is the speaker? At the time this poem was written, in the early 1600s in England, the speaker, in conformity with conventions of the sonnet—a fourteen-line poem written in iambic pentameter with a set rhyme scheme—would likely be interpreted as a male lover, pleading with his female beloved to rekindle their love. He begins by declaring in hyperbolic terms that their love is over, all vows are to be cancelled, and she will get no more of him, but at the end of the sonnet, he uses the last couplet to urge her not to let love die, but to recover him. Notice that the lover is making characters out of love and faith, employing personification, in which human attributes are given to inanimate objects. Love is "gasping" and faith is "kneeling." Drayton's lover uses an elaborate extended metaphor to make his plea.

In Cummings's poem, a switch of gender in the poem's speaker would be likely to produce a very different effect because Cummings uses a stereotypical, gender-based rendering of the woman in the poem. Is Drayton's poem similarly laden with gender-based assumptions about the lover and the loved one? What happens to this poem if you transpose the gender of the speaker in performance, transforming the speaker into a woman? What if you were to defy the conventions of heteronormativity (the assumption that the normal love relationship is between male and female) and make the poem between lovers of the same sex, either male or female?

Look at this poem in light of the questions we asked about the Cummings example and consider its form, and particularly its dramatic mode, as well as its prosody. This interpretation of the poem assumes that the speaker, whether male or female, is directly addressing his (or her) lover. There is no intermediary interpreting the words of this speaker; rather the character speaks directly and, therefore, the poem is in the dramatic mode.

The Sonnet

You may recall the structure of a sonnet from studying poetry. There are two kinds of sonnets: the Shakespearean (English) sonnet, which has a rhyme scheme of *abab cdcd efef gg* with its characteristic concluding couplet, and the Petrarchan (Italian) sonnet, which is divided into two stanzas—an octave with a rhyme scheme of *abba abba* and sestet with a varying rhyme that can involve two or three words, such as *cdc dcd* or *cde cde* or *cdc dee*. Most commonly, the sestet uses one of the first of the two schemes, but there are instances where a rhymed couplet ends a sonnet that is otherwise Petrarchan in form. In addition, in the Petrarchan sonnet there is usually a sharp division between the ideas expressed in the octave and those in the sestet.

There are all sorts of variations over the centuries on the sonnet form, including experimental thirteen-line sonnets and shifts in the placement of the stanza divisions to novel effect. By convention, the English sonnet is written in iambic pentameter. Scan the poem in the manner we described above, including marking the rhyme scheme, line lengths, feet, and syllable counts. Once you have done this, think about how the argument in the poem progresses and what occurs in each of the three quatrains and the concluding couplet. Watch the progression of the imagery throughout the poem, noticing how the couplet gains part of its strength by summing up all the ideas that come before it but turning them to a very different purpose. The speaker begins by insisting that all is over between himself and his lover, but in the concluding couplet, he offers a twist and suggests a way by which all can be recovered; the loved one can breathe life back into their love, recovering all they had before their love was seemingly cancelled at the onset of the poem. You might want to write a paraphrase of the poem, restating the meaning of each line. This exercise is a useful way to recognize which lines you understand and which ones are leaving you uncertain about their meaning.

Returning to the Drayton poem's structure, you will notice that the twelfth line is enjambed, a run-on line where the meaning is carried over from the end of one line to the beginning of the next. The poem concludes with a couplet that does not have perfect rhyme, but rather a half rhyme, ending as it does with the words "over" and "recover," which differ slightly in their pronunciation of the o sound in the penultimate syllable.

In Cummings's poem, we suspect that you will have the greatest difficulty interpreting the last line. In the Drayton poem, you will probably find the extended metaphor in the third quatrain and concluding couplet the most difficult to understand. We find that it is best when confused about what a poem means to simply give into the language and the sound of the poem and play with it. Speak it again and again, and then start playing around with movement and staging and see where the poem takes you. Usually, after many recitations and rehearsals, something suddenly becomes clear—you have what we call an "aha!" experience—and you gain an entry point into the poem that helps you make concrete decisions about how to embody the speaker and how to evoke an image: the performance takes life.

What do you visualize when you start invoking the deathbed scene of Love? When the poet speaks of Faith and Innocence kneeling and closing up the lover's eyes, respectively, what does he conjure up? These lines offer an example of personification, operative in both Cummings's poem and in Drayton's sonnet. What kind of scene do you envision?

Finally, before we move to another poem, think about the ways in which this poem by Drayton, like the one by Cummings, is also about poetry itself. In Cummings's poem, the lover spoke explicitly about matters of grammar and played with the typographical aspects of the printed poem, drawing attention to the way the poem's form reinforced its content and also talking about poetry. Is Drayton's poem talking about poetry? If so, how and why? What lines provide evidence to support your interpretation? What aspects of the speaker and what aspects of the form could you draw on to make your case that this poem, too, speaks about poetry and practices the poetry that it describes? When we discussed the performance of Cummings's poem, we offered several different ways in which it could be performed, along with several examples of ways in which the poem's meaning could be subverted or deconstructed to serve ends different than those intended by the poet. Can you think of different ways to represent Drayton's poem in performance? If you were to stage the poem, how would you do it? What furniture, if any, would you use? Would you play with lighting? Are there different settings you envision for the poem?

If you were to bring in music to amplify parts of the poem, at what point in the performance would you introduce it, or would you use it throughout? What kind of music would you select? Different kinds of music would provide different tones and would likely create very different moods. If you were to experiment with using music to inform this poem, you would probably find that you need to make the poem's rhythms work with the music you select. Think about this interplay between words and music. In the next chapter, we are going to discuss imagery in poetry in greater depth and explore more fully the ways in which performance can enhance poetic language, but for now, begin thinking about how poetry and music work together.

A Poem in the Dramatic Mode

We will turn now to a longer poem, called "The Laboratory," by Robert Browning, a nineteenth-century English poet mentioned earlier. It offers an opportunity to discuss other ways in which a dramatic monologue functions and challenges performers, and it provides us with a female speaker, albeit conceived by a male writer.

The Laboratory

Ancien Régime

I
Now that I, tying thy glass mask tightly,
May gaze thro' these faint smokes curling whitely,
As thou pliest thy trade in this devil's-smithy—
Which is the poison to poison her, prithee?

II
He is with her, and they know that I know
Where they are, what they do: they believe my tears flow
While they laugh, laugh at me, at me fled to the drear
Empty church, to pray God in, for them!—I am here.

III
Grind away, moisten and mash up thy paste,
Pound at thy powder,—I am not in haste!
Better sit thus, and observe thy strange things,
Than go where men wait me and dance at the King's.

IV
That in the mortar—you call it a gum?
Ah, the brave tree whence such gold oozings come!
And yonder soft phial, the exquisite blue,
Sure to taste sweetly,—is that poison too?

V
Had I but all of them, thee and thy treasures,
What a wild crowd of invisible pleasures!
To carry pure death in an earring, a casket,
A signet, a fan-mount, a filigree basket!

VI
Soon, at the King's, a mere lozenge to give,
And Pauline should have just thirty minutes to live!
But to light a pastille, and Elise, with her head
And her breast and her arms and her hands, should drop dead!

VII
Quick—is it finished? The colour's too grim!
Why not soft like the phial's, enticing and dim?

Let it brighten her drink, let her turn it and stir,
And try it and taste, ere she fix and prefer!

VIII
What a drop! She's not little, no minion like me—
That's why she ensnared him: this never will free
The soul from those masculine eyes,—say, "no!"
To that pulse's magnificent come-and-go.

IX
For only last night, as they whispered, I brought
My own eyes to bear on her so, that I thought
Could I keep them one half minute fixed, she would fall
Shrivelled; she fell not; yet this does it all!

X
Not that I bid you spare her the pain!
Let death be felt and the proof remain;
Brand, burn up, and bite into its grace—
He is sure to remember her dying face!

XI
Is it done? Take my mask off! Nay, be not morose;
It kills her, and this prevents seeing it close:
The delicate droplet, my whole fortune's fee—
If it hurts her, beside, can it ever hurt me?

XII
Now, take all my jewels, gorge gold to your fill,
You may kiss me, old man, on my mouth if you will!
But brush this dust off me, lest horror it brings
Ere I know it—next moment I dance at the King's!

Who is the speaker in this poem? To whom is the speaker in the poem speaking? What is the setting? When does the action in the poem take place, in what historical time period? These are some of the dramatistic questions we discussed in chapter 1 when we first spoke about Burke's pentad. This poem is a dramatic monologue. As you will recall, in the dramatic monologue you have a character within the poem speaking directly to the audience. The character of the speaker is unmediated, in other words, there is no expository commentary about the speaker's character within the body of the poem. Another characteristic of the monologue is that there is, in addition to the single speaker, a setting and an auditor, or addressee, to whom the words are spoken. The poem's language also gives us information about other theatrical matters, such as costume or lighting. The spectacle of the poem is elaborated; the dramatic scene established within the world of the poem functions almost as if it were a set in a play.

In this poem, each of the twelve stanzas is a quatrain, four lines rhyming *aabb*. The first quatrain, written in slightly irregular iambic pentameter, finds the speaker tying on the glass mask of the chemist in order to watch him closely as he practices his trade, mixing a poisonous droplet for her to use. The setting is the Ancien Régime in France, specifically the reign of Louis XIV from 1643 to 1715. The dramatic character is that of a minion, a court favorite, a little darling, which emerges vividly in the poem. She is given a striking individuality. With a performance in mind, we hear and somatically experience her speech, watch her hatred and jealously feeding her wicked plot to poison her rivals and return to dance at the king's court. This woman is impetuous and full of contradictions. Convinced that her rivals are with the king and believing, or rather wanting desperately to believe that they are consumed by her every move, she actually reveals a diametrically different character and situation. We discover that it is she who is consumed by jealousy and ultimately undone by her own treachery. She maliciously revels in the fact that she is "here," in the chemist's laboratory, the "devil's-smithy," getting her poison rather than weeping in desolation in the "drear / Empty church, to pray God in, for them!" as she has feigned and her rivals imagine.

We gain a vivid sense of the setting in which the action takes place in this poem: the white smoke curling in the laboratory; the potions, poisons, and powders all around her, along with exquisite glass phials; the chemist placidly preparing the poisonous droplet; and the dust that enshrouds the place, ultimately threatening her life.

Tactile and other sensory images abound in the poem. Greed and lust and all the other deadly sins cross the stage. The poem's diction—a term that refers to word choice—captures the full range of pleasures and vices that govern the speaker and the world in this poem.

We also know the addressee or auditor. He is the old man, the chemist, on whom she presses the urgency of her need, offering him her jewels and gold, even a kiss on her mouth, if he will but give her the poison she needs. Can you see how he evolves as the poem unfolds, even though he never speaks a word and only emerges as a character through the words of the speaker? In both this poem and in Browning's "My Last Duchess," the addressee or auditor is given considerable individuality, such that you can read between the lines, discerning how the auditor would be responding to the line, and how his response prompts the next utterance of the speaker's. Try performing this dramatic monologue with another person, cast as the auditor in the poem, the chemist. What clues do you find in different lines of the poem that tell you about how the auditor responds to the speaker?

Returning to the speaker of the poem, notice how her moods vary wildly. At one moment, she insists that she is "not in haste" and is sitting patiently to observe his strange doings; at another moment, she is imperious, angrily urging him to "Grind away, moisten and mash up thy paste, / Pound at thy powder" and becoming caught up in the world of the laboratory with its dangerous toxins. Later she urges him to quicken his work, finish the brew. She is fitful, at one moment caught up in the minutiae of the place, at the next moment envisioning carrying "pure death in an earring, a casket, / A signet, a fan-mount, a filigree basket!" How do you think the chemist is responding to these lines? What would you have him do if you had another actor playing his role in your performance?

The speaker/protagonist of this poem brings other characters to life in her utterances, making us see her rivals, Pauline and Elise, as well as the chemist. You could experiment with different spaces in your performance to capture the different places described in the poem and the different scenes taking place within them. You would have to consider how to stage the multiple sets in order to give the performance a sense of focus and wholeness.

Even more intriguing is the psychological development of the protagonist/speaker of this poem. Overtaken by her own fury, alternately coquettish and fiendish, a minion, a conniver, she is ultimately a woman who undoes herself. Look at the final stanza of the poem. She had longed to have her rivals dead, not just dead, but in pain, burned, branded, and disfigured. She longs for the vengeful pleasure and satisfaction of having her lover see the beautiful face of her elegant rival become disfigured; she wished that her rival would fall to the floor, dead, with her face completely disfigured from the poison. She envies her rival's height and stature. She sees herself as little and tries to give herself more importance by thinking of herself as a minion, meaning one who is highly favored. At the poem's end, she is pressing all her jewels and gold and even her kisses on the "old man," before she recoils in horror, terrified that the dust from his coat contains its own poison and will kill her before she can return victorious to dance at the king's court. Her hatred has surpassed all bounds. She knows she will die but is careless of the fact, so caught up is she in her own diabolical plot.

There are other fascinating psychological elements displayed in this poem. The dramatic portrait of the speaker, so rich in its variety, is a delight to perform for an actress or actor. But, equally fascinating is the fact that this is a woman character conceived by a male writer. Robert Browning has taken on the dramatic persona of a woman and found a rich language to express her jealousy, rage, and coquetry, combined with her beauty, diminutiveness, vivacity, and impetuousness. Notice, also, that her wild, passionate jealousy is directed against her female rival and her male lover is only secondarily wounded by her plans. You may want to fashion a performance that can probe this dimension of the poem's speaker and addressee. What kind of performances can you create based on this dramatic monologue?

The dramatic monologue, which came into fashion with Browning's poems, continues to intrigue poets today. He influenced T. S. Eliot, Edgar Lee Masters, and Sylvia Plath, to name just a few. You may want to look at some of their dramatic monologues when you search for performance material. The English Pre-Raphaelite painter Dante Gabriel Rossetti took the subject of "The Laboratory" for the subject of his first watercolor. You might use an image from Rossetti's painting in your performance of this poem.

A Poem in the Epic or Narrative Mode

As you will recall from our earlier discussion, the epic, or narrative mode, is a hybrid, combining features of the lyric and dramatic mode. In an epic or narrative poem, there is a storyteller and there are characters: the teller tells the tale or story and the characters within the story speak their own lines directly to the audience. Homer's epics from classical antiquity and ballads from England dating back to the medieval period provide useful examples of epic or narrative poetry for performance.

Ballads were originally intended to be sung, and they often feature a refrain and depend heavily on repetition. The ballad stanza is usually made up of four lines of alternating iambic tetrameter and iambic trimeter, with a rhyme scheme of *abcb*. Ballads stem from oral traditions and later were set down in writing. The story tends to have a universal theme with a powerful effect. "Barbara Allen," "When Johnny Comes Marching Home," or "Where Have All the Flowers Gone" are ballads which have been sung and which you probably all know. "Frankie and Johnny," the story of two sweethearts and their demise, is a ballad. Another popular ballad, "Lord Randall," illustrates the kind of strongly affective tale that is typical in a ballad. In "Lord Randall," the mother laments that her son is dying, having eaten poison berries. Often the speaker in a ballad is impersonal and universal—the speaker boldly sets forth the story of the tale, focusing on the characters central to the action, and giving less attention to his or her own character.

Consider John Betjeman's ballad, written in 1932. It uses the familiar rhyme scheme of the ballad and, as is often the case, is composed of four-line stanzas with the *abcb* rhyme scheme. Betjeman was a British poet. When he uses the word *chintz*, he is referring to a florid patterned fabric used for upholstery and wall hangings. Do you think Betjeman also wants to suggest that the curtains are "chintzy" as in cheap when you interpret the poem? The Leamington Spa is a health resort in Warwickshire, England, complete with medicinal facilities.

Death in Leamington

She died in the upstairs bedroom
    By the light of the ev'ning star
That shone through the plate glass window
    From over Leamington Spa.

Beside her the lonely crochet
    Lay patiently and unstirred,
But the fingers that would have work'd it
    Were dead as the spoken word.

And Nurse came in with the tea-things
    Breast high 'mid the stands and chairs—
But Nurse was alone with her own little soul,
    And the things were alone with theirs.

She bolted the big round window,
    She let the blinds unroll,
She set a match to the mantle,
    She covered the fire with coal.

And "Tea!" she said in a tiny voice
    "Wake up! It's nearly *five*."
Oh! Chintzy, chintzy cheeriness,
    Half dead and half alive!

Do you know that the stucco is peeling?
    Do you know that the heart will stop?
From those yellow Italianate arches
    Do you hear the plaster drop?

Nurse looked at the silent bedstead,
    At the gray, decaying face,
As the calm of a Leamington ev'ning
    Drifted into the place.

She moved the table of bottles
    Away from the bed to the wall;
And tiptoeing gently over the stairs
    Turned down the gas in the hall.

Can you see why we have chosen this poem as an example of the epic mode in poetry? It has both a speaker—and notice the speaker is impersonal, not given any individual character traits beyond being a teller of a tale—and it has characters who are given lines of dialogue, set apart by quotation marks. The nurse speaks as a character within the frame of the poem. Play with the poem's language as you speak it. Pay particular attention to the moments when you feel you are offering lines of indirect discourse, where the nurse is being described but the language sounds as though it is she who is experiencing them and giving expression to them. For example, lines 11 and 12 could be assigned to the poem's narrator, or you could choose to slip into the character and voice of the nurse and speak them as if she were priding herself on being alone with her soul and with the objects in the room. Depending on which way you choose to interpret these lines, you create quite different feelings about the nurse, her world, and how she treats the patients in the spa.

Notice that, as is typically the case with ballads, there is strong action, the death of the old woman in the Leamington Spa, and the story is told in a fatalistic mood. The action of the poem darkens quickly. The tight form of the quatrains and the cadences and rhyme contribute to the poem's haunting lilt. The simplicity of the tale makes it more frightening, and there is a very keen sense of the place, its furnishings as well as its inhabitants.

Conclusion

This chapter has shown you a number of different ways to handle the character of the speaker in poetry, encouraging you to engage the speaker dramatically as a character when performing poems in the dramatic mode and showing you how to employ the lyric voice to construct the speaker in poems in the lyric mode. We also dwelt on matters of prosody and the language in poetry because they are integral to your understanding of the poem's speaker, meaning, and tone. The concluding example of a ballad showed you how the epic mode functions in poetry, combining as it does the lyric and dramatic modes while it tells a story.

KEY TERMS

beat and ictus

matching

modes: lyric, epic, and dramatic

onomatopoeia

prosody

sensory imagery

synesthesia

tropes: simile and metaphor

Chapter 7

PERFORMING POETRY II: IMAGES, PAINTING, MUSIC, AND DANCE IN POETRY

> O body swayed to music, O brightening glance,
> How can we know the dancer from the dance?
> —W. B. YEATS, "AMONG SCHOOL CHILDREN"

In the previous chapter, we discussed the ways in which a performer might handle the speaker in a performance of poetry, drawing on the concepts of lyric, dramatic, and epic modes. We also introduced a technical vocabulary to help you describe poetry and its prosody. In this chapter, we will consider other features of a poem's language and imagery, including its cadences. In addition, we will discuss how poets use visual imagery, painting, and music and suggest how you might construct performances featuring these related arts. We will conclude with an examination of poetry slams and spoken-word poetry, showing how they draw on movement, rhythm, music, dance, and a flamboyant articulation of words, producing poems that flourish in live venues, on the page, and in digital and Internet forms.

We will begin with the final section of Walt Whitman's "I Sing the Body Electric" to explore ways in which visual imagery in poetry can be captured in performance, and at the same time, we will use this example to build on the discussion of free verse, also known as vers libre, set forth in the previous chapter. Whitman's poem presents an image of the human body; think about the performance implications of its visual images. We will offer several other examples of how images in poetry can inspire your performances, and then explore other poems that draw on the arts of painting, music, and dance, in their subject matter, but equally important, in their form. If you have training in other art forms, whether painting, sculpture, drawing, dance, or music, or are practitioners of rap, hip-hop, slams, and spoken-word poetry, you will have an opportunity here to use these talents in your performances.

Free verse is not easy to define. In fact, the term has been used to describe a broad range of practices. Basically, it refers to nonmetered prosody, and it takes its impetus from the poetry of Walt Whitman. In free verse, features other than meter, such as internal rhyme and repetition, parallel syntax running across many lines of the poem, syntactical cadences, and certain kinds of rhythm, such as the "sprung rhythm" of Gerard Manley Hopkins, as well as some other forms of quasi-metrical poetry, give shape and form to the verse. Free verse is not prose, although even this statement must be qualified since in recent years the genre of the prose poem has emerged. Free verse is verse that has been liberated from the traditions of meter that dominated the three centuries of British poetry and two centuries of American poetry. There is also a point where free verse is so free, is so lacking in pattern, that it does not make sense to consider it verse at all.

Let us consider two examples of a poem in free verse: Walt Whitman's "I Sing the Body Electric" and "A Supermarket in California," written in 1956 by Allen Ginsberg, an American poet of the Beat generation, in tribute to Whitman. Whitman's poem is quite long, written in nine parts, and you will want to read it in its entirety, but for the purposes of this discussion, we will look at the final part.

I Sing the Body Electric

O my body! I dare not desert the likes of you in other men
     and women, nor the likes of the parts of you,
I believe the likes of you are to stand or fall with the likes of
     the soul, (and that they are the soul,)
I believe the likes of you shall stand or fall with my poems,
     and that they are my poems,
Man's, woman's, child's, youth's, wife's, husband's, mother's,
     father's, young man's, young woman's poems,
Head, neck, hair, ears, drop and tympan of the ears,
Eyes, eye-fringes, iris of the eye, eyebrows, and the waking
     or sleeping of the lids,

Mouth, tongue, lips, teeth, roof of the mouth, jaws, and the
    jaw-hinges,
Nose, nostrils of the nose, and the partition,
Cheeks, temples, forehead, chin, throat, back of the neck,
    neck-slue,
Strong shoulders, manly beard, scapula, hind-shoulders, and
    the ample side-round of the chest,
Upper-arm, armpit, elbow-socket, lower-arm, arm-sinews,
    arm-bones,
Wrist and wrist-joints, hand, palm, knuckles, thumb,
    forefinger, finger-joints, finger-nails,
Broad breast-front, curling hair of the breast, breast-bone,
    breast-side,
Ribs, belly, backbone, joints of the backbone,
Hips, hip-sockets, hip-strength, inward and outward round,
    man-balls, man-root,
Strong set of thighs, well carrying the trunk above,
Leg-fibres, knee, knee-pan, upper-leg, under-leg,
Ankles, instep, foot-ball, toes, toe-joints, the heel;
All attitudes, all the shapeliness, all the belongings of my or
    your body or of any one's body, male or female,
The lung-sponges, the stomach-sac, the bowels sweet and
    clean,
The brain in its folds inside the skull-frame,
Sympathies, heart-valves, palate-valves, sexuality, maternity,
Womanhood, and all that is a woman, and the man that
    comes from woman,
The womb, the teats, nipples, breast-milk, tears, laughter,
    weeping, love-look, love-perturbations and risings,
The voice, articulation, language, whispering, shouting
    aloud,
Food, drink, pulse, digestion, sweat, sleep, walking,
    swimming,
Poise on the hips, leaping, reclining, embracing, arm-curving
    and tightening,
The continual changes of the flex of the mouth, and around
    the eyes,
The skin, the sunburnt shade, freckles, hair,
The curious sympathy one feels when feeling with the hand
    the naked meat of the body,

The circling rivers, the breath, and breathing it in and out,
The beauty of the waist, and thence of the hips, and thence
    downward toward the knees,
The thin red jellies within you or within me, the bones and
    the marrow in the bones,
The exquisite realization of health;
O I say these are not the parts and poems of the body only,
    but of the soul,
O I say now these are the soul!

This poem of thirty-six lines opens with an exclamatory, bardic cry, "O my body!" followed by thirty-five enjambed lines of poetry, with only two semicolons interrupting the flow of language. It is a quintessential example of free verse. Try speaking this poem, listening carefully for the cadences and the pauses and how you handle breath control as you speak this astonishing catalog of the anatomical parts of the body. The poem consists of one extremely long sentence, marked often with parallel syntax and preceded by the opening exclamatory utterance. This kind of lengthy sentence is often referred to as a left-branching sentence, so named because the main subject and verb that govern the sentence, "I say," come at the very end, while to the left of them are two long clauses, separated by semicolons. Look at the two semicolons in the poem, and notice that at the end of all the other lines, with a couple of exceptions, there is a comma. The exceptions occur at the opening and closing lines, where there are exclamation points. Because of the extraordinarily long delay before we arrive at the main subject and verb, you will discover a sense of relief combined with a kind of exaltation when you finally reach the lines asserting the subject. Play around with reading the poem aloud and performing it using your complete body and see how you experience this special kind of punch we are describing.

The poet also uses other devices to structure his free verse. Notice how pairs of lines begin with a parallel structure, such as "I believe the likes of you" and "Oh I say," the first followed by a catalog of body parts, and the numerous lines opening with the article "the" followed by more listing of body parts. Can you see how this use of parallel syntax contributes to the structure of the verse? The repetition of a word, expression, or phrase at the beginning of successive phrases, clauses, lines, or verses, when it is done for rhetorical or poetic effect, is referred to as anaphora, used here in many lines. You will also notice that Whitman relies heavily on alliteration, repeating vowel and consonant sounds and whole words to tighten the free verse. The poem's language builds and builds, gaining momentum, as he evokes image after image, uttering his litany of anatomy and celebrating the body and the soul. The effect is thrilling!

You may have found the images, made up largely of evocations of the parts of the body, lavish in their language and often explicit in their sexuality. The voice of the poem is bardic—the voice of the world's poet. It is primal, expressing a poetic impulse that transcends the ordinary, amplifying the effects of all it touches. The images are sensuous; made up of the stuff of the body, they are visceral and immediate, but the effect of having so many piled one on another gives the poetic line a freedom and a hugeness appropriate to its content. Throughout the poem, he draws a comparison between the parts of his body and the parts of his soul. The figure of speech that he employs to effect this comparison can be referred to as an elaborate metaphor, but another term for this is metonymy, a figure of contiguity. In metonymy, the name of one thing is used to express another logically related to it. In this case, the contiguity involves the relationship of the parts of the body to the parts of the soul, or the parts of the soul to the parts of the poet, the bard.

We have chosen this poem not only because it exemplifies free verse, but also because its images, rhythms, and subject matter cry out to be performed in an incantatory manner, inviting the performer to utilize the body in movement and dance to capture its full effect. In one student performance, Peter Amster dressed in a black leotard danced the poem, displaying all the parts of his body as he named them, using many different planes with the students surrounding him in a circle, which enhanced the ritualistic aspects of the poem. At times, he lay on the floor; at other points, he rose, extended his arms outward, and stood with legs apart, his head lifted upward as he spoke or almost chanted the words celebrating his body. Think about how you would choreograph a performance of this poem as a dance. How do you handle the poem's buildup, the cascading effect of its images? In what ways has Whitman given you clues to suggest how you should speak a phrase, invoke a part of the body, or address your audience? To whom is this bard speaking? These are but a few of the questions you will want to consider as you perform this poem.

One hundred years after this poem was written, Allen Ginsberg wrote "A Supermarket in California." In interpreting this poem, it is useful to have some biographical information about Ginsberg and Whitman; both poets were homosexual, and each, in his way, makes this explicit in a manner appropriate to the time when the poems were written.

A Supermarket in California

What thoughts I have of you tonight, Walt Whitman, for I walked down the sidestreets under the trees with a headache self-conscious looking at the full moon.

In my hungry fatigue, and shopping for images, I went into the neon fruit supermarket, dreaming of your enumerations!

What peaches and what penumbras! Whole families shopping at night! Aisles full of husbands! Wives in the avocados, babies in the tomatoes!—and you, García Lorca, what were you doing down by the watermelons?

I saw you, Walt Whitman, childless, lonely old grubber, poking among the meats in the refrigerator, and eyeing the grocery boys.

I heard you asking questions of each: Who killed the pork chops? What price bananas? Are you my Angel?

I wandered in and out of the brilliant stacks of cans following you, and followed in my imagination by the store detective.

We strode down the open corridors together in our solitary fancy tasting artichokes, possessing every frozen delicacy, and never passing the cashier.

Where are we going, Walt Whitman? The doors close in an hour. Which way does your beard point tonight?

(I touch your book and dream of our odyssey in the supermarket and feel absurd.)

Will we walk all night through solitary streets? The trees add shade to shade, lights out in the houses, we'll both be lonely.

Will we stroll dreaming of the lost America of love past blue auto-mobiles in driveways, home to our silent cottage?

Ah, dear father, graybeard, lonely old courage-teacher, what America did you have when Charon quit poling his ferry and you got out on a smoking bank and stood watching the boat disappear on the black waters of Lethe?

Ginsberg's poem employs a language from everyday life, using colloquialisms. He sets his poem in a supermarket, rich with commercial images, reflecting the capitalistic venture in the United States. But he also makes allusion to Charon, a figure from Greek mythology who ferries people across the river Lethe to the kingdom of death, Hades. Can you understand why Ginsberg uses such allusions? How does he position himself as a poet in relation to Whitman, whom he celebrates?

If you were to feature the political implications of both poems in a contemporary context, what performance choices might you make? If you wanted to use the poem to advance gay and lesbian rights, how might you perform the poems? Try imagining how you might stage the two poems. Could you use movement, dance, and visual images? Would you have props?

Both poems use images that appeal to the eye, that are essentially pictorial, and we discussed one example of a performance of the Whitman poem that utilized movement, dance, and an incantatory vocal style to achieve certain of the poem's effects. The visual image created by the performer's body in the space was intended to depict a Promethean man, or an image of man from a William Blake engraving or a Leonardo da Vinci painting.

Ekphrastic poetry is poetry that writes about and is occasioned by a painting. Such poems use visual imagery to summon the images in the paintings. A well-known example is W. H. Auden's "Musée des Beaux Arts," which refers to Brueghel's painting *Icarus* (the actual painting is entitled *Landscape with the Fall of Icarus*). In the poem, Auden describes how well the Old Masters knew the place of suffering, "Its human position," and alludes to Brueghel's depiction of Icarus, the mythical son of Daedalus, as a tiny figure falling into the sea. In his poem he describes the other characters in the painting as seeming to almost turn away "quite leisurely from the disaster" as the ship sails "calmly on." Students interested in ekphrastic poetry should consult "Contemporary American Ekphrastic Poetry: A Selected Bibliography," by Beverly Whitaker Long and Timothy Scott Cage. The article will lead you to many rich sources of material for developing a performance of ekphrastic poetry.

Consider another short poem, "Proletarian Portrait," by William Carlos Williams.

Proletarian Portrait

A big young bareheaded woman
in an apron

Her hair slicked back standing
on the street

One stockinged foot toeing
the sidewalk

Her shoe in her hand. Looking
intently into it

She pulls out the paper insole
to find the nail

That has been hurting her

This poem is typical of a movement in poetry in the early twentieth century called Imagism. Note that the image is very precise and the poem, lacking any terminal punctuation, is made up of short, two-line, unrhymed stanzas that are nonmetrical. These features are trademarks of Imagistic poetry. Notice how the poet distills the language, stripping it of embellishments and compressing its meaning into a single, albeit complex, image of a working woman. The poem self-consciously reflects on its use of painting. The title, "Proletarian Portrait," is an unlikely combination of words; typically we associate portraiture with high social status, with class connotations, but in this case, it is used to describe a working-class woman. "Proletarian" signals to us that this is a poem about class structure, alluding to the Marxist or socialist revolution and the American worker. By using the word *portrait* in its title and sketching, almost as if it were a drawing, a picture of the woman, the poet places the poem in the ekphrastic tradition, where poetry takes its impetus from a painting or offers a verbal picture that draws attention to traditions of visual art. The poem appeals to the eye.

There are also some of the same conventions that we observed in Whitman's poem, but in this case, you can see that they are employed with startling concision. The poem is written in free verse using parallel syntax, repeatedly using gerunds—"standing," "toeing," "looking," "hurting"—and separating the main action, "she pulls out the paper insole" a considerable distance from the main noun clause that opens the poem. The description of the woman and her action, and finally her pain, is almost clinical. We see her vividly, and her movements are crisply depicted.

What ideas do you have about performing this poem? How can you preserve the point of view of the speaker and also capture the woman with great economy? The costume in the poem can be easily exploited, the shoe serving as a physical prop: put on an apron, slick your hair back, position your body so that it suggests weight, bigness, a certain toughness, remove your shoe so that you can look at it, use your stockinged foot to toe the floor/sidewalk, and pull out a paper insole to reveal a nail in your shoe. Think about the last line and how it gains power; in all the other lines of the poem the woman has been described from the vantage point of the observer, the portrait maker, but in the last line the observer describes what the woman is feeling, her pain, rather than her actions. The pain is far more than physical; we sense how she experiences the burdens of a lower class, working woman.

William Carlos Williams's poem provides an example of how image, movement, and portraiture, a visual art, combine to enrich the poem's meaning. Let us now consider a poem where the poet has combined language and music. "Victor," by W. H. Auden, is denoted as a song by the poet; he calls it a musical piece, set to the tune of "Frankie and Johnny," a familiar ballad.

Victor

Victor was a little baby,
  Into this world he came;
His father took him on his knee and said:
  "Don't dishonour the family name."

Victor looked up at his father
  Looked up with big round eyes:
His father said: "Victor, my only son,
  Don't you ever ever tell lies."

Victor and his father went riding
  Out in a little dog-cart;
His father took a Bible from his pocket and read,
  "Blessed are the pure in heart."

It was a frosty December,
 It wasn't the season for fruits;
His father fell dead of heart disease
 While lacing up his boots.

It was a frosty December
 When into his grave he sank;
His uncle found Victor a post as cashier
 In the Midland Counties Bank.

It was a frosty December
 Victor was only eighteen,
But his figures were neat and his margins straight
 And his cuffs were always clean.

He took a room at the Peveril,
 A respectable boarding-house;
And Time watched Victor day after day
 As a cat will watch a mouse.

The clerks slapped Victor on the shoulder;
 "Have you ever had a woman?" they said,
"Come down town with us on Saturday night."
 Victor smiled and shook his head.

The manager sat in his office,
 Smoked a Corona cigar;
Said: "Victor's a decent fellow but
 He's too mousey to go far."

Victor went up to his bedroom,
 Set the alarum bell;
Climbed into bed, took his Bible and read
 Of what happened to Jezebel.

It was the First of April,
 Anna to the Peveril came;
Her eyes, her lips, her breasts, her hips
 And her smile set men aflame.

She looked as pure as a schoolgirl
 On her First Communion day,

But her kisses were like the best champagne
    When she gave herself away.

It was the Second of April,
    She was wearing a coat of fur;
Victor met her upon the stairs
    And he fell in love with her.

The first time he made his proposal,
    She laughed, said: "I'll never wed";
The second time there was a pause;
    Then she smiled and shook her head.

Anna looked into her mirror,
    Pouted and gave a frown;
Said: "Victor's as dull as a wet afternoon
    But I've got to settle down."

The third time he made his proposal,
    As they walked by the Reservoir;
She gave him a kiss like a blow on the head,
    Said: "You are my heart's desire."

They were married early in August,
    She said: "Kiss me, you funny boy";
Victor took her in his arms and said:
    "O my Helen of Troy."

It was the middle of September,
    Victor came to the office one day;
He was wearing a flower in his buttonhole,
    He was late but he was gay.

The clerks were talking of Anna,
    The door was just ajar;
One said: "Poor old Victor, but where ignorance
    Is bliss, et cetera."

Victor stood still as a statue,
    The door was just ajar;
One said: "God, what fun I had with her
    In that Baby Austin car."

Victor walked out into the High Street,
  He walked to the edge of the town;
He came to the allotments and the rubbish heap;
  And his tears came tumbling down.

Victor looked up at the sunset
  As he stood there all alone;
Cried: "Are you in Heaven, Father?"
  But the sky said "Address not known."

Victor looked up at the mountains,
  The mountains all covered with snow;
Cried: "Are you pleased with me, Father?"
  And the answer came back, "No."

Victor came to the forest,
  Cried: "Father, will she ever be true?"
And the oaks and the beeches shook their heads
  And they answered: "Not to you."

Victor came to the meadow
  Where the wind went sweeping by;
Cried: "O Father, I love her so,"
  But the wind said: "She must die."

Victor came to the river
  Running so deep and so still;
Cried: "O Father, what shall I do?"
  And the river answered: "Kill."

Anna was sitting at a table,
  Drawing cards from a pack;
Anna was sitting at table
  Waiting for her husband to come back.

It wasn't the Jack of Diamonds
  Nor the Joker she drew at first;
It wasn't the King or the Queen of Hearts
  But the Ace of Spades reversed.

Victor stood in the doorway,
  He didn't utter a word;

She said: "What's the matter, darling?"
    He behaved as if he hadn't heard.

There was a voice in his left ear,
    There was a voice in his right,
There was a voice at the base of his skull
    Saying: "She must die to-night."

Victor picked up a carving-knife,
    His features were set and drawn,
Said: "Anna, it would have been better for you
    If you had not been born."

Anna jumped up from the table,
    Anna started to scream,
But Victor came slowly after her
    Like a horror in a dream.

She dodged behind the sofa,
    She tore down a curtain rod,
But Victor came slowly after her;
    Said: "Prepare to meet thy God."

She managed to wrench the door open,
    She ran and she didn't stop.
But Victor followed her up the stairs
    And he caught her at the top.

He stood there above the body,
    He stood there holding the knife;
And the blood ran down the stairs and sang:
    "I'm the Resurrection and the Life."

They tapped Victor on the shoulder,
    They took him away in a van;
He sat as quiet as a lump of moss
    Saying, "I am the Son of Man."

Victor sat in a corner
    Making a woman of clay;
Saying: "I am Alpha and Omega, I shall come
    To judge the earth one day."

This poem is written as a ballad, with four-line stanzas using the *abcb* rhyme structure. It tells a tale, thus it is written in the epic mode. We have a stark line of action, including a love story and a death—typical elements in ballads—and we have a number of different speakers, speaking in dialogue, including Anna, the clerk, the manager, Victor's father, and, of course, Victor himself.

We have included this poem to invite you to think about how to perform a poem that uses music. The poem offers rich performance choices. Auden has indicated that the poem can be set to the tune of "Frankie and Johnny." You could actually record the melody and have it play softly in the background as you speak the words of the poem. Or, you could listen to the song until you are very familiar with its tune and give a performance where you are only speaking, not singing, but where your phrasing and diction is colored by your knowledge of the song that lies behind the poem.

You might choose not to feature live music or the referenced song in your performance. Instead, you decide to speak the poem as an oral ballad that tells a tale with the intention of holding the audience spellbound as you unfold the frightening story, tinged with pathos as well as horror. The poem makes reference to many voices, the most frightening being the voices the mad Victor hears in his head. The wind, the river, the sky, the oaks and beeches, and many other images from nature speak to Victor, or so he believes. The poet almost orchestrates the voices that haunt Victor, posing interesting challenges to performers. Think about playing with vocal color to try to capture the different sounds of the voices. A powerful lectern performance of this poem might use the lectern to suggest a pulpit where God's judgment is offered or a podium in a courtroom where an accused faces his accusers. You could also simply deliver the poem from a chair or from the stage or center of the room, dispensing with a lectern and holding your audience with the story. A lectern performance would probably use out-front focus and placement, where you imagine the scene you describe enfolding in space somewhere toward the back of the room and slightly above the heads of your audience. You could also elect to perform the poem with onstage conventions, in which case you would employ the convention of the fourth wall and represent the action of the poem on the stage itself, even if you are the only performer. In these types of performance, you need to project powerfully and control your placement of the characters so that you do not confuse the audience (review chapter 4 for focus and placement).

You could also present a choral reading of this poem, using multiple voices to speak in chorus in some places. When various voices in the poem speak to Victor, you could magnify their effect on his mind and ear by having a chorus whisper or shout some of the lines. Reread the poem and see how you might develop a reading for multiple performers.

We have offered you these examples of how to use images from painting, sound from music or song, or movement and dance to enrich your performance and staging of poetry. At the beginning of the chapter, we quoted a line from Yeats's "Among School Children" that captures the idea that dancer and dance cannot be separated. By extension, form and meaning ultimately cannot be disentangled: they are inextricably one. We urge you to look at poems in which dance and movement are evoked. In "Susie Asado," by Gertrude Stein, she evokes the movement of a flamenco dancer, opening with a line that repeats "sweet" five times before ending on "tea." Consider how to adapt William Carlos Williams's "Danse Russe," a poem he wrote after seeing a performance by the Ballets Russes of Sergei Pavlovich Diaghilev, or "The Dance" for a staged perfor- mance. Another poem that could inspire a dance-oriented performance is Edith Sitwell's "Country Dance." These are but a few examples of poems written about dance. Our challenge to you is to search for such poems and translate them into a performance that features the related art.

In the last chapter, we wrote about poems based on old English ballads and suggested that you might develop a poetry performance in which you sing the poem. You might want to think about how you could sing Auden's poem "Victor," placing it more explicitly in the ballad tradition, or even in such theatrical traditions as Stephen Sondheim employs in the musical *Sweeney Todd*. Many poems derive from song; and composers often set poems to music. Allen Ginsberg toured the country singing William Blake's poems from *Songs of Innocence and of Experience*, accompanying himself on a harmonium. Kurt Elling has scored Theodore Roethke's poem "The Waking"; the sung version varies the lyrics, adding lines and actually changing the ending of the poem so it ends with a different last line. In the song version, the final line is far more affirmative than in Roethke's poem. In addition, the villanelle form that Roethke employs is substantially altered, again because the music and the sentiment it expresses are more peaceful, comforting, and uplifting than in Roethke's original.

Poems that have been set to music, and there are many, present you with the option of performing the poem in either media, singing it or speaking its language. The emotional mood evoked by the spoken poem usually differs significantly from the mood of the song version, leading to lively class discussions comparing performances of the same poem both ways. Some of you may write music or may have written poems for musical accompaniment. Think about a poetry performance that makes use of these talents. If you like early music, you will find a rich source of material in many poems, dirges, and songs in Shakespeare as well as other Elizabethan and Jacobean poets' writings. Many poems have also been scored for different musical instruments, and these, too, lend themselves to class performances.

We will now turn to a contemporary movement in poetry that offers other performance possibilities drawing on movement, voice, music, and song: spoken-word and slam poetry.

Spoken-Word and Slam Poetry

The spoken poetry revolution dates roughly to the mid-1980s in America. It emerged in public and commercial spaces and also in underground venues, such as the Nuyorican Poets Café and the Brooklyn Moon Café in New York; the Green Mill Jazz Club and the Heartland Café in Chicago; and Beyond Baroque in Venice Beach, California. It came to bookstores, community centers, and churches as well; it thrived in huge cities and in many small college and university towns. The poets strutted their stuff in these often cramped performance spaces, the audience and performers jammed against one another and the poets making their words "pop," while the audience shouted out acclaim or scorn or snapped their fingers to the rhythms. The spoken-word poets—Tracie Morris, Saul Stacey Williams, Tish Benson, Jessica Care Moore, willie perdomo, and mariahadessa ekere taillie, to name but a few—revel in the power and authority of their own body and the "aura" that surrounds it. The works of spoken-word poets ultimately were reproduced in print, audiotape, or video recording, but before they were documented, they existed as a part of a live, vital performance act—raw, powerful, and immediate. Scholar Kathleen Crown observed and celebrated the demand for a return to "voice" and "presence" to which these poets and their poetry responded. "Poetic voice in these locations is public, exoteric, material, explosive, confrontational, human, and fully embodied," she declared in her article "'Sonic Revolutionaries': Voice and Experiment in the Spoken Word Poetry of Tracie Morris" (p. 216).

The emphasis in this poetry is on the poet's live body, the performance of the poetry, and the "authentic self." The medium exploits the sonic qualities of the spoken voice. Often, it is through the oral sounds, some guttural, some verging on music, that words are augmented and infused with the memories that seem to inhabit the medium. For example, words taken from the languages of the Yoruba, a people of West Africa, evoke the experiences and legacy of the slave trade with all its horrors, pain, and suffering. In other ways, also, the medium is manipulated to enable it to carry collective pasts of trauma, suffering, loss, and grief.

The practitioners of spoken-word poetry resisted being co-opted by the American mainstream culture, but ultimately they failed, in part as a consequence of their decision to preserve their live performances in print or audiovisual texts and products. Practitioners who experienced success in small public spaces discovered they wanted to reach broader audiences and capitalize on their endeavors. Performances that had come into being as improvisations suited to the conditions of local settings and moments were transformed. The poets wanted their work to be more than a memory: they wanted lasting material forms that would be around long after their makers were no longer performing their poems aloud. We now have a spate of books by slam and rap poets, but one of the consequences of converting this primarily oral performance mode to text is that the voices of the practitioners can be co-opted by others who take the once rather subversive material into the mainstream culture. You may have seen the film *Slam*, made in 1998 and directed by Marc Levin, or *Slam Nation: A Documentary*, made in the same year and directed by Reg E. Gaines, or *Words in Your Face*, directed by Mark Pellington. These films might give you ideas for your performances, and they will provide you with an opportunity to experience this kind of poetry. You might also read Yusef Komunyakaa's poem "Facing It," about a veteran's return to the Vietnam War Memorial in Washington, D.C. (it is widely anthologized). On *Love Notes from the Madhouse* (1998), he performs live with jazz musicians John Tchicai and his ensemble. These movies and recordings are all in the tradition of slam, rap, hip-hop, and spoken-word poetry.

Our print culture has made celebrities of such talents as Eminem and hip-hop artists such as Dr. Dre, Big Daddy Kane, Z Live Crew, Snoop Dog, and others. Rudy Ray Moore, a precursor of rap, took some of the most outlandish insults he could recall or invent and rendered them in a form that combined black rhymed storytelling over a beat. The poets in this genre were originally offering a critique of our commodity-based, postcapitalist American and global culture. They wanted to use natural speech; many did not have recourse to writing their poetry down and getting it published. Later, many realized that only if they converted their work to a more permanent medium — print or audiovisual recording — would they be able to assure that their voices would be widely known and remembered.

Scholars of this kind of poetry trace its origins in the 1950s when the Beat poets reacted against the formalism of Yeats and Eliot and burst onto the scene with wild and zany free-verse poems, many celebrating while also criticizing America. It was the America of the open road, to use Jack Kerouac's term. Examples include Allen Ginsberg's "America" and "A Supermarket in California"; Lawrence Ferlinghetti's "Dog" and "The World Is a Beautiful Place . . . ," both about the America of the 1950s, the House Committee on Un-American Activities (HUAC) and Joseph McCarthy, Red-baiting and the witch hunt for communists; and Gregory Corso, with his collection of poems, *The Vestal Lady on Brattle*. Poets of the Black Arts Movement, many of whom adopted African names, such as Haki Madhubuti (originally writing under the name of Don Lee) or Amiri Baraka (originally writing under the name of Leroi Jones), and Mari Evans are also precursors of rap, hip-hop, slam, and spoken-word poetry. Free love, LSD and other mind-bending drugs, love-ins, and Vietnam War protests were all part of our popular culture at that time. Poets read aloud in cafés, public parks, and on the streets. They often collaborated with musicians, who put a beat behind or under their words; blues musicians such as Muddy Waters and jazz artists such as Dizzy Gillespie and others inspired many of these poets. A public audience for poetry congealed, and the poets used television and film as well as radio to share and promote their works.

In the late 1990s, American poet laureate Robert Pinsky promoted a poetry project to develop community involvement in poetry writings, readings, and performances, reminding all of us that poetry thrives when spoken, that its sound and its words are thrilling. He understood the ways that a poem can transform its audience from a group of individual attendees at a public event to a pulsing body of feeling and receptive people who form a supportive community. Scott Dillard, a performance scholar, in his article "The Art of Performing Poetry: Festivals, Slams, and Americans' Favorite Poem Project Events" described how Robert Pinsky, a winner of the Nobel Prize, urged the public to read poetry aloud, telling them not to "worry about interpreting it, or what it means, inhabit it, speak it, and relish its consonants and vowels." Pinsky read his favorite poems following the nightly news on television, bringing them to the mass culture. Dillard called upon performance scholars to write more about spoken-word and slam poets, and you may want to take up his challenge.

Much of the strength of this poetry depends on its performative power, how it is played, how its practitioners thrive in competitive forums where performers are required to compete with each other in a truly physical as well as spoken way. Slam poetry events were often competitive, rule-based, and fiercely populist. The poetry often had an activist agenda, usually political, and practiced a communitarian poetics. Best understood in terms of orality and performance, it begs for community involvement and a political response.

Spoken-word and slam poetry rely heavily on musical components. Often it is technophilic, adopting new technologies for manipulating sound and voice. Or it may be textually based but highly experimental in the ways in which it is written and reproduced typographically.

The first collection of Harryette Mullen's poetry, *Tree Tall Woman*, published in 1981, includes the poem "Playing the Invisible Saxophone on el Combo de las Estrellas." She enjoined poets to write: "words turning into dance" and "body moving music / a get-down poem so kinetically energetic / it sure put disco to shame. / Make it a snazzy jazzy poem with extravaganza, with pizzazz" (p. 54). Her poem was multivocal, practicing a code-switching lingo that spoke to black and white people. Writers who practice code-switching move effortlessly from the language they speak within their own culture, in their own vernacular, such as Black English or Yiddish, to standard English as practiced by dominant, mainstream culture. Putting into practice the performance ideals that drove the language of her poem, she calls out for poems to "go solo" and asks that they be "flying high on improbable improvisational innovation." The poem ends with the line "Poem be blowing hard." This poem epitomizes the features of slam and spoken-word poetry. It is multivocal, reflects the spoken voice of a black speaker, and is pronounced in its orality. She plays with the repetition of sounds within words, for example, "improbable" and "improvisational," both words starting with the same syllable and ending with rhyming syllables that are spelled differently but sound the same. This practice of using words that sound alike but are spelled differently is also frequently employed in spoken-word poetry. This line of hers cries out to be performed and practically scores its music and movement.

Her poems speak to a female black audience, expressing her ideas on race and speaking directly to the black, female, feminist community, openly celebrating matriarchy and the idea of birthing a poetry to be passed on from woman to woman. To perform it, you would want to get into and under its skin.

Spoken-word and slam poems are snazzy, sassy, bold, full of puns (double entendres) and jazzy rhythms. Many of the poets in this movement look back to the 1950s jazz masters and soulful singers. The singer Nat "King" Cole figures large in the poetry of the movement generally, and before him, Sam Cooke. One poem by Tracie Morris, "Chain Gang," works with a line of a song sung by Sam Cooke: "that is the sound of the man working on the chain gang." Crown writes about it in *We Who Love to Be Astonished* (pp. 213–14). The poem draws on rhythms heard in the language of the Yoruba in West Africa and calls on the Yoruba deities. The listener cannot escape the hard "g" sounds, slashing the air, pounding rhythmically, accentuating the movements of the chain gang. When you hear the poem in performance, listen for Cooke's song; if you are performing the poem, you might even put his song in the background or precede the performance of the poem with a recording of Cooke's singing. Crown tells us that the poem's themes are violence, protest, and healing. Very often a powerful trauma (in this case, a deep cultural wounding—the slave trade and its dreadful consequences) are the stuff of the poetry. When Morris performs the poem, Crown says she breaks apart the sounds in the lines (the phonemes) and renders them sometimes as a sigh, sometimes as a stutter, a whisper, or a strained, prolonged set of sounds, letters, and words. She beats time as she performs, striking her upper torso or her throat, making us almost writhe as we hear her. As performers, you will want to feel physically, as well as emotionally, how these poets handle breath and pause; when performing this kind of poetry, be conscious of the ways you experience the musculature of the poems and your own kinesthetic and muscular involvement. Their message is often equally powerful spoken with a bold, declarative, possibly angry spirit and a relentless beat behind the words.

Tracie Morris, a powerful practitioner of spoken-word poetry, speaks of lyrics as "words accompanied by music but *not* sung" (italics added). In *Aloud: Voices from the Nuyorican Poets Café*, edited by Miguel Algarín and Bob Holman, the two founders of the café, and in *The United States of Poetry*, a book, film, and compact disc produced by Bob Holman, you can sample an excellent cross-section of slam and spoken-word poems and read Morris's poems. In her poems on jazz, in which she pays tribute to its greats as well as to black orators and musicians, you can see and hear how this poetry moves to music and invites performers to employ movement and display themselves, their bodies and their vocal instruments, in rendering the verse. Black poets in the slam movement often draw on the history of servitude and slavery, the traditions of the black church and liberation theology, and speaking in tongues, drawing richly on the traditions of "testifyin'" and "getting the spirit." Zora Neale Hurston, with her anthropological writings on voodoo and the Yoruba, has strongly influenced this movement in poetry. Tracie Morris, in *Intermission*, offers a debate of her "live style." Her poem "Project Princess" is an epic catalog and ode to the young black women in a Brooklyn housing project. Morris has become a diva of spoken-word poetry and widely recognized in the world of hip-hop and slam. Her work has influenced many others, for example, singer Tracy Chapman, whose voice and lyrics are reminiscent of Tracie Morris.

The language in these poems is usually in the vernacular, and the poems are shamelessly formulaic, offering clichés with gusto and pride in a manner that refers back to the traditions of Homeric epic and the *guslars*, a Serbo-Croatian oral tradition in which the storyteller is accompanied by a single-stringed musical instrument (see Albert Lord, *Epic Singers and Oral Tradition*). The poems are "in your face," chiming and clanging with their obvious rhymes, full of very sophisticated use of alliteration, using both assonance and consonance, and by virtue of the way the words are delivered, reveling in their sheer sound and theatricality. "Anthony Baez," by Morris, in memory of Anthony Baez, a young man killed by a member of the New York police force which resulted in charges of police brutality, consists entirely of "z" words, and his name is repeated over and over, with Morris's voice shifting pitch, tempo, tone, and volume, ultimately transforming "Baez" into "bias," the parallel subject of the poem.

We have included this section about slam and spoken-word poetry cognizant that the words in the poetry, and many of the poems themselves, may not endure. Some of the poems are embarrassingly bad; you may think that some of them are pure trash. A number of eminent poets have denounced this genre, blaming it for debasing the English language and dulling and hardening our sensibilities. We believe the poetry is uneven, some of it lousy, but some of it quite wonderful. In any case, the movement is important and offers rich performance opportunities.

Many students in our classes have drawn on *The Spoken Word Revolution (Slam, Hip Hop and the Poetry of a New Generation)* and *The Spoken Word Revolution Redux,* both edited by Mark Eleveld. These collections also feature compact discs, and *Redux* includes a valuable essay, "The New Oral Poetry: An Excerpt from the Essay 'Disappearing Ink: Poetry at the End of Print Culture,'" by Dana Gioia.

An Outing to the Heartland Café: An Evening of Spoken-Word Performance

Carol recalls a number of outings with her students to the Heartland Café in Rogers Park, a north side Chicago neighborhood. They would meet there on a Wednesday night, at about 10 P.M., and stay until the wee hours. The students had to be eighteen years of age or older. Crowded into a large room with a two-tiered wooden platform, the audience watched poets perform. Throughout the evening, sipping their drinks, Carol and her students would comment on the various performers and debate whether they had the courage to throw themselves and their poems into the ring. There were regulars, people from the neighborhood and farther away, who came to read their poems; there were headliners— spoken-word or slam poetry performers who made the circuit locally and nationally and often produced recordings of their poems. On entering, or later in the evening, the host would encourage the audience members to sign up to perform.

One night, one of the students decided to sign up for the open mike and perform one of her poems from class. They waited until the very end and then she claimed the mike and performed. She met with wildly enthusiastic responses. At these kinds of performances, the audience weighs in, either calling out for a performer to give them more or ignoring and booing performances they don't like, but the poets and their community also have great tolerance for the poets' work—in fact, it is more than tolerance, they are keen on sharing poems in performance and enjoy the freedom of the mode. One of Carol's students invited a guest performer, a Northwestern alum who at the time was performing on the national circuit. He performed in class that day and then in the evening, they all watched him "strut his stuff" at the Heartland. He had written a long poem about riding on Chicago's famed "El," the mass transit train that connects the metropolitan region with the Loop. The poem described a homophobic encounter on the train and the reactions of the passengers and the poet, the spoken-word performer whose story it was.

Conclusion

In chapter 4, we described the etiquette and rules that surround debate competitions. Slam competitions have an analogous set of rules, but in the slam situation, the crowd, the audience, hold the power in their feet and voices. The goal of the performer is to get a physical, bodily response from the audience. Audiences can clamor for more or they can shut the slammer down. The themes of the poems are often topical and current; they can be confrontational, taking up subjects of police violence, riots, homophobia, racism, and woman bashing; they are frequently political. They offer social commentary and appeal to public issues, not private, personal, or introspective reveries. Crown writes:

> Despite the sonic flux and intensity of these spoken word poems [referring specifically to those of Tracie Morris], which are deeply inflected by the language-expanding influences of hip-hop and rap, the poetic voice develops mostly through the natural rhythms of speech and popular culture and through rhyming riffs on outworn phrases ("smoking gun" and "you can't touch this").

Morris is a performer who revels in her own outlandishness; as Crown reports, she uses her poems as vehicles for displays of excess and pyrotechnics. In her poem "Project Princess," she exploits the princess's costume, her "multidimensional shrimp earrings," "clinking rings," and "dragon fingers" (p. 219).

We have included this segment on slam and spoken-word poetry to encourage you to go to these public events, write poems and perform them, and become part of these active communities. Some of you may have already entered these arenas, but to those of you who haven't, we suggest you give it a try. There is much to learn from performing in these public performance spaces; you will see how unpredictable they can be. The mike can malfunction, you don't know how few or how many people will be there to experience your poem. You will discover the limitations of your body, which can be more and less limber, and your voice, which can obtain greater or lesser range. All these variables function prominently in spoken-word performances and poems. The experienced performer learns how to mobilize them to their own benefit. They often report that they don't know what to expect, cannot anticipate how the audience will respond, nor can they know how their own bodies and voices will serve them.

These features contribute to the vitality of the genre. In the aesthetics of the genre, they function, according to Crown, to make the act of performance an act of "critical memory" and "history making" (p. 222). Our discussion in chapter 12 of critical ethnography will help you understand this kind of project. These performers pull against the grain, against the dominant culture, and place the performer at the service of remaking, reinventing, or augmenting our culture. They utter things not said before, recover memories too long repressed, and speak in a way that presses back against more conventional understandings and often takes them to regions they had not anticipated and to levels of knowledge that they had not known were within their reach. In the case of Morris, these forces are used to recover and participate in African diasporic traditions; they help her heal. Scholars who write about this process often compare the state achieved by the poet practitioner as being akin to the state of ecstasy or the heightened, out-of-body possession experienced in a Vodou trance. They have the possibility of building communal, spiritual energies and so transcending ordinary states. The technology of sound, the enhanced and amplified voice, the powerful physicality of the performers' articulation of words, half words, and sounds all converge to achieve this effect.

In this chapter, we have briefly presented many different kinds of poems and discussed how they lend themselves to performances that draw richly on the arts of painting, music, and dance. Our challenge to you is to seek out more poems like these and develop them into rich performances that use the body, movement, painting, visual arts, music, and dance.

KEY TERMS

anaphora

ballad stanza

critical memory

ekphrasis

free verse (vers libre)

history making

metonymy

slam poetry

spoken word

Chapter 8

PERFORMING PROSE FICTION I:
NARRATIVE, POINT OF VIEW,
AND CONSCIOUSNESS

The story of *The Firebird* was not clear to me at first.
— JANE HAMILTON, "REHEARSING *THE FIREBIRD*"

Prose fiction is a category that may best be described as encompassing imaginative texts written in prose rather than verse, spanning in length from the single page of the short-short story to the multivolume novel; there is a tacit assumption between writer and reader that the story told is either wholly invented or has, at best, a tenuous and nondocumentary relationship to the kind of actual worlds and people discussed in chapters 2 and 5 on nonfiction. While many works of prose fiction are set in a world that is rooted in real geographical and historical times and places and may recount events drawn from the life of the writer, there is no expectation that the text will faithfully reproduce what actually happened.

Let's look at the epigraph for this chapter, the opening sentence from Jane Hamilton's short story "Rehearsing *The Firebird*," which we will return to in more detail below. It establishes the point of view, the voice in which the sentence is spoken and the perspective it represents. The narrator (to be kept distinct from the author) makes reference to herself indirectly through the phrase "to me." What is implied in this sentence is that there is an "I" who will be telling the story and that this "I" is someone who is engaged as an actor within the story. The narrator signals to us from the very beginning that she is personally involved in the events of the story, not a distanced observer or a godlike fabulist or a kind of supreme psychoanalyst who has access to the inner lives of the characters.

The sentence places us in a temporal and epistemic relationship to both the narrator and *The Firebird*: "[It] was not clear . . . at first." That the story was not clear is a statement of the narrator's own relationship to the work cited in the title; we do not yet know in what ways the story was not clear to the narrator. Is it a dense, complex story with many characters, winding paths of events and actions? Or is it the meaning of the story that is unclear to the narrator—in the sense that we may read or hear a story and not understand its significance? We do not know because the narrator has not yet elaborated on this phrase. The words "at first" point to a later time when the narrator has gained more knowledge, although the nature of that knowledge is yet unspecified. There is an implication that the narrator will gain some understanding, though no assurance that the narrator will ever find the story completely clear. Indeed, is it ever possible for a story to be completely clear to anyone, including the teller, the writer, the inventor?

The second sentence in Jane Hamilton's story introduces more characters, including the narrator's grandmother (a minor figure) and Mr. Smedley, who will become a central character. Following a tradition that stretches back at least as far as the great Homeric epics, the narrator begins her story in medias res—in the middle of things. This is frequently how we tell and how we hear stories in our own lives—we begin by saying something that is drawn from somewhere within the chronology of a story and then go back to some starting point before which we don't need to go in order to make sense of the story, which then frames our story. Stories can begin "at the beginning"—the traditional opening gambit of the European fairy tale, "once upon a time"—but Hamilton's narrator begins in medias res. She draws attention to herself as an everyday person, who lives both in the present of the telling of the story, what narrative theorist Seymour Chatman calls the "scene of discourse," that is, the lived performance of narrating the story, and in the remembered action recounted, what theorists call the "scene of story," the events that provide what we might think of as the content of the story itself.

Now consider how you might perform this sentence. It is a declarative sentence in most respects, straightforward, a statement of the narrator's mental position, her consciousness regarding a particular text. However, pay attention to the very deliberate syntactic choices: the narrator does not begin with an "I" statement, such as "I found the story of *The Firebird* unclear at first," which would place the emphasis on the person viewing the ballet, listening to the music, or reading the folktale; rather, the word order centers on the work of art itself. Similarly, she puts off the temporal shift until the end of the sentence. Think about phrasing as you speak the sentence: do you speak it all in one breath, continuously, or do you make a brief pause before "at first," signaling that the story you are about to read or hear will somehow clarify the meaning of *The Firebird* (both the folktale and the story of the narrator's experience of its performance)?

We will return to a more detailed discussion of "Rehearsing *The Firebird*" below. Let us now move on to an overview of some central ideas and terms we will be using in our exploration of prose fiction.

Elements of Prose Fiction

The study of stories, their elements, their functions and conventions is called narratology. While some of the terms we will be using are drawn from this field, which looks at everyday stories and visual and other media as well as the written and spoken word, we will focus on those most relevant to literary traditions of prose fiction and apply them to specific examples. The study of narrative is wide-ranging and complex; we encourage you to delve more deeply into some of the theoretical and critical texts included in the reference list.

Story and Plot

The first two terms we need to explore in our analysis of prose fiction are *story* and *plot*. Recall that in chapter 2 we introduced these terms, drawing on the work of novelist and critic E. M. Forster, who based his distinction on the simple recitation of events (story) and the structuring of them based on causal relationships (plot).

As a performer, it is important to understand the distinction between the story and the plot at hand. One must begin with the straightforward "what happens," which Forster refers to as story, but this is seldom sufficient to enable a performer to enter the world and the lives of the characters of the narrative. In some contemporary fiction, the very absence of causality and explanation is itself a crucial element of plot—it suggests a view of the world as a place without logic, without connections, without causality, psychological or otherwise. As you read the various selections in this chapter and the next, consider to what degree the stories yield discernible plots, in the sense Forster used the terms.

Character: Round and Flat

Forster was also concerned with the people who inhabit novels and other works of prose fiction. To keep fictive inventions separate from actual, historical people, he used the term *character* to designate invented people that we encounter and come to know (or not know) in prose fiction. The term *character*, as used by Aristotle in his *Poetics*, not only denotes the presence of fictive people in a story, but their moral, psychological, social, political, spiritual, and other dimensions. Aristotle used the word *ethos* to refer both to dramatic characters and to the sense of moral agency of orators and rhetors in the public arena.

Forster distinguished between two major categories or kinds of characters, which he called flat characters and round characters. Flat characters are one-dimensional, usually defined by a single characteristic or a small set of predictable traits, and their function is to move the plot along in a necessary way, to reflect round characters, or to help set a scene or establish an atmosphere. They are rarely capable of any kind of change or growth in personality, and when such changes do occur, it is usually through melodramatic means, such as a sudden revelation or unmasking. Round characters, on the other hand, are usually capable of change, development, and growth—as Forster himself put it, they can "surprise" us, though in ways that ultimately make sense once we have the entire story in our grasp.

Think about how distinctions between flat and round characters are determined: while the critical distinction is a useful one for literary study, in real life, individuals are unlikely to view themselves as flat characters— we are all round characters in the narratives of our own lives. So while we may find the either/or categories useful, the line between flat and round characters is often permeable. A character who seems flat to one reader may reveal multiple dimensions to another. Similarly, simply because a character may be flatly described does not necessarily mean he or she is devoid of interest, color, or vitality—one only need look at the multitude of secondary or minor characters who populate the novels of Dickens or the many fantastic figures from Lewis Carroll's *Alice* books or J. K. Rowling's *Harry Potter* series to understand that flat characters offer for performance wonderful, rewarding pleasures of their own.

Narrators and Point of View   The use of the term *narrator* to refer to the storyteller of a work of prose fiction suggests a person, a human embodiment of the storyteller, and this is its most common meaning in critical analysis. These narrators are also and at the same time characters, actors within the plots of their respective prose, and the text does not draw a distinction between them as narrator and as actor—though in each case, the text indicates that some amount of time has passed between the events and the telling of them, the scene of story and the scene of discourse. Theorists remind us that, even so, such narrators remain fictive inventions of the writer, as are all the characters and events, so the sense of an imagined reality—what poet Samuel Taylor Coleridge called the "willing suspension of disbelief"—remains consistent for these particular narrators.

Other kinds of narrators pose thornier problems, both for the reader and for the performer. Brian Richardson, in his book *Unnatural Voices: Extreme Narration in Modern and Contemporary Fiction*, suggests that the seemingly commonsense notion that all fiction must have a narrator is actually in considerable dispute. He argues that there are some works of prose fiction that, while they present narration, do not seem to have a stable or embodied, corporeal sense of a storyteller—including texts written in the second person and certain kinds of third-person perspective.

Closely aligned to the idea of the narrator is that of point of view. *Point of view* refers to the perspective from which a narrative is told and is one of the fundamental questions that must be explored by the performer. Conventionally, point of view is distinguished by grammatical and rhetorical categories of speech and language:

1. first person singular or plural: "I" and "we"
2. second person: "you"
3. third person singular or plural: "he, she, it, they"

First person singular and third person, either singular or plural, are the most common points of view in prose fiction, particularly those written in English. In English, we do not make a linguistic distinction in second person between singular and plural except in some dialects, such as the southern "y'all" (for "you all"). There are some interesting examples of fiction written in second person and in first person plural, which we will look at briefly below.

A writer's selection of point of view is every bit as important as decisions about what story to tell and how to shape the plot: indeed, the choice of point of view may be critical to determining what the story is and what it means. Think about this in your own social storytelling—have you and a friend ever tried to tell the same story and found yourselves either contradicting each other or emphasizing different aspects of the story? Have you ever tried to tell a story about yourself and found yourself using the third person as a strategy either for gaining a control over events that may not have been in your control when they happened or to gain distance from what might seem too emotional to speak of in the first person?

Audience/Listener   Just as we begin from a commonsense assumption that all stories have tellers or narrators—and then contest that assumption—so we might begin with the assumption that stories have audiences, listeners (or readers) to whom a story is being told. The question of audience may be even more open-ended from a critical standpoint: from childhood, we are so used to being readers of prose fiction that we don't often reflect on the roles we are performing as we read or listen. In a sense, we assume a universal transparency—a generalized audience role as readers—and do not think about how our individual subjectivity, our sense of how we experience the world, plays an important role in the narrative experience. When two readers disagree about the merits of a book they have both read, for example, they may be disagreeing along aesthetic lines (that is, whether they think the novel has convincing characters, an interesting plot, good use of language), but whether they acknowledge it or not, other factors, often intangible, from their lives and literary experiences may come into play. This does not mean that, as readers, we are captives of our own life experiences, but that such parts of our experiential horizons are never wholly absent. To the extent that we can become conscious of them, we may be able to resist their effects on our reading, such that we put aside our prejudices or limited experiences and allow the story to fill us as much as we fill the story.

Stories may have what theorists call *narratees*, audiences implied by the narrative, by the telling of the story, as much as they have narrators. Narratees are often less explicit, more generalized, than narrators. Nonetheless, especially for the performer, it is useful, in reading and rehearsing a story, to look for cues and clues as to what kind of audience the story seems to be addressing. Think about the opening sentence of "Rehearsing *The Firebird*": "The story of *The Firebird* was not clear to me at first." Can we determine things the teller assumes about the listener or narratee from this sentence? Of course, we need to have the entire story in our mind before we can answer this question with any informed intelligence, but one thing does stand out: the narrator includes the italicized words *The Firebird* in the sentence. The italics indicate that *The Firebird* is the title of something—this narrator is not going to be talking about an actual creature called a firebird. She does not, in this sentence, feel the need to provide a qualifying description. We will discover soon enough that Hamilton's text is about the birth of artistic consciousness, thus this sentence invites an audience of those involved in the arts who have sufficient knowledge to know that this is a ballet, even if they are unclear about the specifics of the plot of the folktale on which it is based. It places us in an identifying stance with the narrator and, by extension, with the younger self of the narrator, who will become one of the primary actors within the story.

How does a performer perform the narratee? This may seem like a peculiar question, as we might assume that only readers, listeners, audiences can actually "perform" the narratee and in the most important sense, of course, this is true. But the performer needs to consider how to construct a performance that allows, encourages, perhaps even demands that the audience play the role they are supposed to. Aspects of performance such as open and closed locus, space, and proxemics—even the use of media, such as a recording of Stravinsky's music for the ballet—will help the audience assume its role as narratees.

Writers and Implied Authors   We have tried to draw distinct lines between narrators, authors, and writers, as well as between readers and audiences or narratees, reminding ourselves and you to avoid the fallacy of assuming that such identities are interchangeable. We would like to draw one more distinction, building on the work of Wayne C. Booth, whose *The Rhetoric of Fiction* was a landmark in theorizing about point of view and narrators. Booth differentiated, on the one hand, between real authors, implied authors, and narrators and, on the other hand, between real readers, implied readers, and narratees. Booth's main point was to stress that there may be a difference between the actual author and the actual reader and the implied ones suggested by the text—and that both are distinctly different from the narrator and the narratee within the fictive world of the text. For example, a beloved children's classic may imply an author who loves children, but the actual author may be someone who is ambivalent about children, spends as little time as possible around them, and prefers the children he or she imagines or conjures up from memory.

Rhythm of Action:
Scene, Summary, and Description

We move from the what and who of prose fiction to the how, when, and where (see chapter 9 for more detail about the when and where). Phyllis Bentley first made the distinction between scene, summary, and description, which are sometimes collectively called the "rhythm of action," pointing to the sense of timing and emphasis found in narration that is analogous to rhythm in other art forms, such as music and dance. They refer to the three principal ways in which narration handles details of space, place, and time. Scene is the form of narration that occurs in the time of immediate dialogue and interaction—in this sense, it is the same as scene in dramatic literature, a kind of transcript of the ongoing action. Summary speeds up time, often omitting details beyond what is absolutely necessary to clarify an action, place, or person. Description is the equivalent of slow motion or a close-up in film, in which time stretches to allow greater observation, often in extreme detail, of a static phenomenon or an event.

It is rare for a work of narrative to exist solely in any one of these forms of narration; rather, it is the intermingling or juxtaposition of them that creates a text's own rhythm of action. Certainly there are stories that exist almost exclusively in dialogue; these stories sometimes seem to be little plays, encounters in almost dramatic form, where what narration there is exists primarily to identify speakers, the same way plays include the name of a character to indicate the speaker. Even so, "he said" and "she said," known as dialogue tags, however brief and parsimonious, alter the rhythm from how the dialogue would be spoken in a staged play. At the other extreme, there are works of prose fiction that eschew scene in the sense in which we are using the term: dialogue may be absent from the narrative, the story existing almost entirely in description, whether of an exterior landscape or an interior subjective state of being. Stories composed entirely of interior description may contain passages that feel like monologue, in which a character's inner thoughts are represented, either directly as if in speech or indirectly, in which case it is called free indirect speech.

Let us examine some prose fiction texts to see in particular how different ways of handling narrators, point of view, and consciousness pose specific challenges and opportunities for performers. To begin, read Jane Hamilton's story, "Rehearsing *The Firebird*," (pages 420–32).

First Person Character Narration:
Reliability and the Performance of Memory

All narrators are, in some sense, unreliable in that all narrators, in whatever voice they speak, if we grant them fictional status as people or at least as sensibilities guiding a story, have some degree of subjectivity to them — even the most reportorial, seemingly observational narrator — often viewed as "objective" — selects some details to include in a narrative and others to omit. Nonetheless, within the range of possible kinds of narrators, it is safe to say that those who most frequently cause questions of reliability are first-person character narrators, narrators who live not only within the scene of discourse, but within the scene of story as well, narrators who are also actors. Within that subset, we find considerable variation in terms of the general trustworthiness: some we trust as reliable reporters and evenhanded describers and interpreters of events, with the tacit assumption that all narrators may be prone to lapses in memory, which may lead to a story's details varying from telling to telling and to changes in consciousness and perspective occurring over time. Other narrators we find ourselves reluctant to trust, either because their accounts explicitly signal that their relationship to reality is suspect, or because their motives seem ambiguous (and sometimes clearer to the narratee than to themselves), or because they have limited perspectives and abilities. Each kind of first-person character narrator provides different challenges and opportunities for the performer — from the experience of recalling, interpreting, and reinterpreting, of gaining new knowledge about one's past, as more reliable narrators provide us, to the sometimes humorous, sometimes frightening experience of being in the presence of a storyteller who seems unstable, either unwilling or unable to share a "truthful" or "complete" version of what has happened and what it means.

GeorgeAnne Mealy is an example of a reliable narrator. Nothing in the way Hamilton has portrayed GeorgeAnne gives us any reason to doubt the overall accuracy of this narrator's depiction of the events of the story, although we may choose to question her interpretations of various characters. One of the reasons we trust GeorgeAnne as a narrator is because she seems willing to look at herself with the same interpretive framework of affection, criticism, and, at times, ironic humor that she uses on Tiffany, Mr. Smedley, Mrs. Vogel, and her parents: in art, as in life, we often trust those who seem as candid about their own shortcomings and foibles as those of other people.

Earlier we distinguished between the scene of discourse and the scene of story. The scene of story is what we have summarized above, but even here the plot is not reducible to the recitation of events we have provided in the above paragraph. Look closely again at the story—how have Hamilton as author and GeorgeAnne as narrator made choices about which episodes and details to include and which not? Are we privy to all the letters between Brucie and Patricia of the Poplars? If not, why these letters? Similarly, why does GeorgeAnne emphasize *The Firebird*, almost to the exclusion of the other pieces played by the All-Village Orchestra (Handel's *Messiah* and a medley from *The Sound of Music*). Clearly, this piece of music and Mary Clare Rankin's French horn solo in it, as well as the reactions of Mr. Smedley and GeorgeAnne, become central to the plot, to the shape and meaning narrator and author want the events of the story to carry.

As you analyze the story with performance in mind, identify which sections are dominated by each kind of narrative strategy—scene, summary, and description—which creates the rhythm of action referred to above. For example, GeorgeAnne's description of Mary Clare's playing is detailed, impressionistic in some respects, almost outside of ordinary time—a moment of aesthetic arrest, as some critics would call it, when GeorgeAnne (and Mr. Smedley, perhaps) are transformed. In performing this section, you would want to make sure you take the necessary time to feel what GeorgeAnne feels and to express this through body and voice. GeorgeAnne also uses summary in efficient, yet evocative, ways: when she describes the rituals she and Tiffany go through in preparation for the orchestra rehearsal, GeorgeAnne speeds up the action (in the sense that the summary takes less time than the action) but shows her ability to recall these actions with fidelity through the detail of the specific brand of gum (Teaberry's), its taste, appearance, and smell. Because the story and its author seem more interested in the meaning of the events for the narrator than the fact of the events themselves, scene is vivid but restricted—even in the scenes dominated by exterior action, such as Mrs. Vogel grabbing the note or the dressing-down of the girls by the principal, where dialogue does occur, it is limited to what is necessary for the narrator to remember the scene and for us to relive it with her.

This leads to the other dimension of narrative, the scene of discourse. Just as the plot cannot be reduced simply to what happens between these two girls and the adults around them, so we need to think about what dimensions of plot are being represented in the actual telling of the story—the narrating, as opposed to the narrated, as some might distinguish the two. Again, at its simplest level, the scene of discourse is someone telling a story, but can we push our description and analysis farther? Why is GeorgeAnne telling the story? To whom? When? There are no specific, single answers to these questions.

Return to the title and the first sentence—both involve statements of process, partial knowing, lack of closure—of someone (and something) in the process of becoming. The title is not "Performing *The Firebird*" or "Understanding *The Firebird*," but "Rehearsing" it. Similarly, the lack of clarity about the story of the ballet in the first sentence reminds us that, within the world of the story, the teenaged GeorgeAnne is on a journey into adolescence and puberty (look for the number of references to bodies in the story, particularly references to hygiene, hair, sweat, and other things that make young people uncomfortable about the changes they are experiencing and becoming aware of in other people). She is also on a journey into vocation: at the end of the ultimately minor incident around the purloined letters comes a kind of challenge and blessing by Mr. Smedley, who, in response to her questions about the meaning of Mary Clare's solo, says, "I leave it to you to describe it sometime, GeorgeAnne," in a sense sending her off to become the kind of artist she can be (a writer, as opposed to the musician she knows she will never be). The plot of the scene of discourse, then, might be interpreted as following in the tradition of the *Künstlerroman*, the story of the artist's initiation, told after the events that lead to the girl taking on her identity as an artist. As you make choices about how to speak the language, how to pace it, what emotions to feel as the narrator, think about how she has shaped her own autobiography. Are there other motives for telling this story that you can infer or imagine?

The questions of when and to whom GeorgeAnne is telling the story are equally compelling and open-ended. As part of your development of the character of GeorgeAnne, you will need to think not only about her motivations, but about the passage of time within the events of the story and beyond the story to its transformation into the discourse of a narration of it. How much time has passed between the actions on which the story focuses (the narrated) and the telling of it (the narration)? No specific amount of time is indicated within the text of the story. Could GeorgeAnne have told this story a week after her conversation with Mr. Smedley about *The Firebird*? Why or why not? What allows you to make such determinations? We would point you to the language the narrator uses to describe various people and actions. For example, when GeorgeAnne, in the first paragraphs, introduces Mr. Smedley, she says, "I learned a lot from Mr. Smedley, but personal hygiene and comeliness were not among the gifts he bestowed." The word choices ("comeliness," "bestowed") and the irony of the phrasing, loving and slightly censorious, seem to emerge from an older consciousness, someone who has had sufficient time to live and hence reflect on what Mr. Smedley has indeed taught her.

The narrator seems older than when the events happened, yet she does not seem to be in a mood to sum up the meaning of this experience in her own life story. Look at the last sentences again: that final image—"For Mr. Bruce Smedley there was maybe even me"—suggests a narrator still tied emotionally and psychologically to her younger self and still seeing herself as a "work in progress." There is a wonderful kind of double consciousness in this sentence. On the one hand, it may be the voice of the younger GeorgeAnne thinking of herself for the first time as a romantic companion (is she developing a crush on Mr. Smedley, imagining him as someone who might have an erotic life?) or, more important, we think, she might be, for Mr. Smedley, the one who can tell the story, who can make him live eternally in her version of their relationship—she can be the "girl-bird" of *The Firebird*, "both the lover and the beloved . . . the storyteller," and storytellers, as she notes, have power, they are the ones who make "the story take its course."

Even more open-ended is the question of her audience for this story. We can infer from the story that GeorgeAnne has probably become a writer, and one might argue that she has written this story as a memoir and her intended audience is anyone who picks it up to read. Or we can imagine her telling it to friends or to a loved one or to a class of students or to an audience who has come to hear her speak or be interviewed. The amount of detail and the highly polished language of the story removes it from the spontaneous and the conversational—the language, while never ornate or pretentious, is crafted and polished, careful and artistic; it does not replicate the kinds of linguistic maneuvers and stumbling we make in our daily speech. This is not to suggest that Hamilton's language is not performative—indeed, we think its grace and strength have considerable power when spoken (as anyone who has heard Hamilton read from her own works will attest to)—but that it might suggest a performance style that captures the written quality of the style.

So far we have not said much about characterization in the story. Try to apply Forster's distinction between flat and round characters, bearing in mind that these terms are not evaluative, but descriptive and analytic, and grouping the characters into the two categories. How do we classify GeorgeAnne in her role as narrator? It is important to avoid disconnecting her entirely from her younger self: the older GeorgeAnne can only grow out of the complex qualities found in her younger version. In this sense, she cannot help but be round, particularly the more we think about the myriad meanings the story might have for her and what prompts her to tell the story, and why the story became a turning point for her.

Similarly, the ways in which she describes the other characters suggests a way of understanding human beings that does not reduce them to stereotypes or cardboard figures. At some level, most of the other char-acters in the story do get defined by one or two salient characteristics or functions—Tiffany as future cheerleader, Mrs. Vogel as grieving widow, the parents as exasperated and stern, and so forth. Part of the narrator's (and the writer's) artistry is that even within this limited scope (they have their own stories to tell, but this is GeorgeAnne's—and Mr. Smedley's), we can tell that they each have complex inner lives that the younger GeorgeAnne may not yet intuit and that the older GeorgeAnne can only speculate upon. Tiffany, for example, is not simply a cheerleader, but a girl who must choose—and may actually choose unconsciously or even be seen as having had chosen for her by the peer pressures of the often terri-fying culture of adolescent American life—between maintaining a kind of outsider status with GeorgeAnne—the role of the artist—or blending in, accepting the safety of not taking the risks of making art, being caught, and punished for it.

Mr. Smedley is one character who is as round as GeorgeAnne, although his roundedness is implied rather than fully embodied. He remains a supporting character within the scene of story and the scene of discourse but narrator and author consistently suggest the ways in which his life is complex and, yes, capable of surprising us. While GeorgeAnne's fantasies of him at home, on the wrong side of the tracks, slugging whiskey and playing his violin, are quite funny in their imaginative projection of clichés drawn from Hollywood films about tortured artists, the real Mr. Smedley, in the occasional glimpses we get of him, is even more intriguing. Reread the various sections of the story in which GeorgeAnne describes him, both physically and performatively—her images of his clothes and his chickenlike arms proffer a vivid personage, but her descrip-tions of his unstated but powerful responses and moments of reaching for articulateness are what make him most memorable as a human being.

His ability to be amused when confronted with the correspondence the girls have invented between him and Mrs. Vogel suggests something of the artist who can take pleasure in invention and creativity, even when they would seem to be at his own expense: he has the knowledge and appreciation of what an artist must do and the ability to understand that he, like *The Firebird*, is, at some level, a perfectly acceptable "text" for their "performance."

Even in a straightforward, unambiguous story such as "Rehearsing *The Firebird*," there remains much left for you to explore. If you are considering performing it, see if you can break the story down into its major units of action and description—does it work like a play, like a piece of music? Find a section that will give you a satisfying sense of beginning, middle, and end if the time constraints of your performance venue do not permit performance of the entire story. GeorgeAnne clearly needs just this amount of space and time to tell her story, so we advise against cutting within it—better to seek a section that speaks deeply to you.

First-Person Character Narration:
Unreliability and the Limitations of Subjectivity

Just as our designation of the narrator of Hamilton's story as "reliable" does not exclude the fact of her subjectivity—she has feelings, attitudes, and opinions that color the way she re-creates the past—so the fact that we designate a narrator as "unreliable" does not necessarily mean that we view that narrator as deceptive, negative, or lacking in any credibility. All such categories are best viewed as points on a continuum, rather than as either/or categories. Part of the pleasure of reading first-person character fiction and constructing performances of it is in the process of discovering the shifts and nuances in such characters.

Unreliability can be made more complicated by the source and meaning of its lack of accuracy: is the narrator unreliable by his or her own design or motive—that is, intentionally misleading the narratee or audience—or is the narrator unreliable because of either cognitive or psychological limitations? Such narrators may be seen as part of what Wayne Booth called a "rhetoric of irony," in which writers put distance between what is said and what is meant. While Hamilton may not have embarked on the same fantasy compositional exercise as GeorgeAnne, many of us assume that she found similar outlets for her artistic yearnings (in point of fact, Hamilton has disclosed that she was an indifferent violinist in an All-Village Orchestra in her hometown of Oak Park, Illinois, and that Mr. Smedley, Mrs. Vogel, and even her postnasal-dripping stand partner have their origins in people she knew in her youth—though they have been transformed into new beings).

It is important not to confuse irony with satire or cynicism. Irony is, in some ways, a larger, more ambitious strategy, with myriad possible effects in artistic and rhetorical terms, ranging from the horrible, tragic dramatic irony of Sophocles' *Oedipus the King,* in which the audience understands that Oedipus's call for the punishment of the bringer of plague to Thebes is a call for his own destruction long before Oedipus knows the truth, to the irony of Jonathan Swift's famous essay "A Modest Proposal," in which he excoriates the British for their neglect of the Irish by suggesting that a solution to famine would be to sell, cook, and eat Irish babies. Not all unreliable narrators are themselves consciously ironic, but their unreliability implies a kind of instability of meaning and truth that usually produces ironic effects within the story and for the readers and audiences.

Robert Olen Butler's "The Ironworkers' Hayride," drawn from his collection *Had a Good Time: Stories from American Postcards,* provides an example of a story in which the narrator's unreliability comes from his own cognitive and emotional limitations and in which much of the pleasure we as audiences derive from the story is our own understanding of social dimensions of the events that at least initially escape Milton, the narrator. Butler's narrator gains insight and knowledge by the end of the story—in a very complicated sense, which we will need to unpack, he becomes a bit more "reliable" by the end. The story is found on pp. 433–44.

Notice how from the very beginning there are marked differences between this story and the Hamilton story. The heading to Butler's story is the text of an antique postcard, which he collects, and in the book from which the story is taken it is reproduced showing both sides, a couple kissing on a bench with the caption "Performance now going on" and, on the reverse, the date, place, addresses, stamp, and text. The basic premise of Butler's story is a given, from which he weaves his own imaginings of what actually did transpire on the hayride (which he has the narrator consenting to go on, despite his message to Mathilda that he isn't going to). It is set in a particular place (Sunnyvale, California) and time (the postcard was written on July 14, 1911, and the actual hayride was presumably sometime soon after), thus making the fictional distance between writer and narrator much more distinct than in Hamilton's story. There is no way to conflate the real writer, the implied writer, and the narrator in this story in any literal sense and, by the end of the story, most readers will infer a sizable distance between the writer and the narrator psychologically as well.

What of the narratee and the audience? As with the story by Hamilton, there is no narratee named specifically within the story. We may be tempted to decide that the story is told to (or written to) the Mathilda of the postcard. What arguments can you make either in favor of or against this possibility? Does it seem likely, on the basis of your reading of the whole story, that Milton would share all this with Mathilda? (And who is Mathilda—a sister, a sweetheart, a friend? The postcard does not tell us.) But the story does have the feeling of being told: the language has the conversational style of talk, from the sometimes awkward syntax of sentences that mark spontaneous speech to the alternation between present and past tense that is also characteristic of unedited oral language. Butler may have taken a cue from the postcard, in which Milton, while following some of the formal writing conventions of correspondence ("Regards to all," as a closing), also demonstrates some errors, such as the run-on grammar in his final sentence and the misspelling of a common word ("I am awfull tired that is the main reason"). This suggests a narrator who is somewhat unused to expressing himself in writing and, we discover in the course of the story, unused to speaking—someone who is generally silent and, hence, within the culture of the factory and working class, not a "regular fellow."

The opening sentence in Butler's story starts us memorably on its narrator's journey: "So this fellow at the new ironworks in Sunnyvale where I am a cost-sheet man and he is a furnace man, he comes over to me at the Ironman Saloon." Butler begins in medias res, but Milton has a very different way of speaking from Hamilton's GeorgeAnne Mealy. The word "so" places the narration within the familiar genre of barroom anecdotes ("So, two men walk into a bar")—colloquial and everyday—as does the ongoing present tense, "comes over to me," which actually expresses a completed action but does so in a way meant to create the sense of the events as they unfolded. The phrase "at the new ironworks in Sunnyvale where I am a cost-sheet man and he is a furnace man" suggests that the narratee not be as familiar with Milton or his immediate surroundings as Mathilda of the postcard—here we may feel the author poking through to provide some exposition for the reader. At the same time, the way in which the phrase becomes unnecessarily convoluted in specifying the different jobs of Milton and the "fellow" marks a kind of educational and social level for Milton that places him in relation to the everyday factory laborer; in the terms of the day, Milton no doubt had at least a junior high or high school education, while the laborer—the "regular fellow"—may have had less education. The appositional use of "he," as in "this fellow . . . , he comes over," again marks the orality of the narration—the speaker needing to go back and begin the active part of the sentence again, once he has clarified the two different jobs. The sentence ends by locating this interaction at the Ironman Saloon, suggesting a communal, masculine place of interaction.

What follows, the exchange in which the fellow convinced Milton to take his sister-in-law on the factory hayride, is an encounter between men in a traditional male space, but one in which Milton feels at odds with his fellow workers. Indeed, Minnie's brother-in-law (and notice that Butler foreshadows the coupling by the alliteration of Milton and Minnie's names) finally persuades Milton by saying, "The others will think you're a regular fellow." This wording is interesting in that it implies that they currently do not think Milton is "regular," and that Milton may be able to perform "regularness" by going on a date, even if he isn't actually regular.

Milton's reflection on this encounter reveals him to be a complex character and, hence, a complex narrator of his own story and his own transformation. On the one hand, Milton reveals that he knows he is not "regular," in part because he has never gone on a date but also because of the way he does or does not interact with the men with whom he works. He does not completely lack self-consciousness or self-awareness, but he *is* aware that he does not experience the world and other people the way those around him do. He reports his perceptions as he experiences them (this makes him ethically reliable), but he clearly knows that his interpretation of them marks him as very different from others (in this sense, he is cognitively or interpretively unreliable). This is, in a sense, what makes him truly fascinating—he is aware of his own differentness, as opposed to a narrator who would only demonstrate differentness. This is part of what makes him round rather than flat.

One might go further and suggest that Milton, if he lived today, would be likely to be diagnosed as having a condition on the autistic spectrum, perhaps Asperger's syndrome, in which the individual is high-functioning, able to communicate and interact with others in society, but lacks the social knowledge and skills that most people acquire without formal instruction. Some theorists of the autistic spectrum have defined people living along it as lacking a "theory of mind"—an abstract ability to understand how other people think and respond to the world. More recently, researchers, particularly cognitive psychologists, have called this blanket statement into question, suggesting that many people who live with forms of autism do indeed have "theory of mind," but it may be underdeveloped or differently developed compared to those people considered, in the scientific language of the day, "neurotypical."

There are many instances throughout the story in which Milton reveals how aware he is of his differentness from other people and thus cues us to keep some kind of ironic distance between his description of events and, most important, his interpretation of them—he alerts us to his own unreliability. One of the important things the story does is create a narrator many people might dismiss as odd, peculiar, or even pathological, incapable of normal human feelings and, through his point of view, prevents us from homogenizing Milton into being a "regular fellow." Instead, the story helps us understand his way of making sense of and in the world and to value what he brings to the world. His support of Minnie's suffragist position, for example, and his acceptance of her prosthetic leg as part of her are not simply the politically correct attitudes of a liberal man of his time; rather, they emerge from his way of being open to the world, not bringing the same set of judgments and expectations to it that those who have been, in the word of Louis Althusser, "interpellated" or initiated as typical men of his time might do.

Butler uses this limited point of view (limited both in terms of the subjectivity of a first-person character narrator and also the stereotypical views of people on the autistic spectrum) for poignant and gently comic effect again in the scene of the date between Milton and Minnie. Thus, Milton's lengthy description of his attempts to engage Minnie in conversation, to "spoon" with her, to explore her body, including his explanation of why touching her prosthetic leg is not "fresh," and his transformation, in her presence, into someone who understands the value of companionship and the promise of love gain power because the narrator appears limited at the start—we go on a journey with him as we witness his discoveries and as we overcome our assumptions. It is a credit to Butler's artistry and to his implied respect for people with disabilities that he does not conclude the story by curing Milton's autism, but by having deepened

our understanding, and Milton's, of how he might profitably live with it
in the world.

Imagine telling the story from the point of view of Minnie, who does
seem to fit the neurotypical way of perceiving the world, but who is in
other ways quite atypical, both in her political attitudes and in her corporeal experience. While she seems quite comfortable living with her "cork
leg" (actually made of willow, as Milton informs us), she lives in an era
when maintaining a sense of herself *as* a woman with these attitudes and
impairments would have been a challenge. Many such women would
have been resigned to a spinsterhood not of their choosing and probably
unwanted, but not Minnie. The ending of the story makes it clear that
she and Milton will continue to build this relationship—not because
each must settle for someone less than whole as a mate, but because,
perhaps as a result of their experience of disability, each sees in the other
a different kind of wholeness. We, as readers and listeners, get glimpses
into Minnie's point of view in the occasional moments of her dialogue—
sentences such as "I was frightened for a while," "Sometimes you have to
face a difficult thing," and "Sometimes we are compelled to embrace the
thing we fear the most, don't you think," all said in immediate reference
to the appearance of Halley's Comet the previous year, but also carrying
subtextual reference to the loss of her leg and to the encounter she and
Milton are having (and her understanding of how much of a challenge
an ordinary first date might be to someone like Milton). Butler restricts
Minnie's overt expression to such remarks, perhaps because she is an
attractive and admirable character, but not someone we cannot understand or with whom we would have difficulty identifying. She clearly
has reserves of strength and depth, but it is Milton who can change and
surprise us.

What do you think choosing Minnie as the narrator might gain for
the telling of the story? What might get lost? Experiment with a retelling
of the hayride. How might the use of a third-person narrator shift the
story's plot and meaning in even different ways?

Try working in pairs or small groups with this story, asking each
person to perform Milton and either Minnie or Minnie's brother-in-law.
We suggest working dyadically because so much of the story is about the
difficulties Milton has interacting with others. In particular, experiment
with the hayride scene, especially the part where Milton feels Minnie's
cork leg; while initially uncomfortable and potentially risky (it must be
done in ways that honor the action's place in the story), it might yield

fascinating results and powerful knowledge about the limits, boundaries, and possibilities of bodies in contact, particularly if each performer must be both Milton and Minnie—the one who touches and the touched. This approach can help test Milton's complex, profound statement: "The leg is part of Minnie, but it really isn't." The philosopher Maurice Merleau-Ponty has written about how the white cane becomes an extension of the blind person's body; to what degree is Minnie's leg similar to or different from this in the world of Butler's story? In one sense, Minnie answers this question, in what we come to understand as her common-sense way, in the story's final sentence: "'Just for future reference, Milton. It's the other leg.'" But is it? Does Milton understand something about the body—perhaps because his own relationship to thinking and embodiment has been a text all his life—that remains different from Minnie's understanding? How might Milton address his audience? Is he comfortable speaking directly to them? (Much will depend, of course, on who you decide his audience is.) Go through the story again and see if you can explain specifically how Milton makes the interpretations he makes, chooses the actions he chooses, comes to the conclusions he does—how much are they like your own cognitive processes? How unalike?

Returning to the question of the narrator's reliability, we have used Butler's story to explore the issue of unreliability because Milton provides us an example of a narrator whose cognitive difference makes him seem unreliable to us in terms of what most readers would probably describe as their way of understanding people and the world. It would seem that we cannot generalize from Milton's thoughts and experience to our own (and, even though we all have individual minds, bodies, and experiences, part of living in the world does require us to make such connections, what we might call intersubjectivities). But, in the final analysis, the question is not whether Milton is different from us, but what that difference means and how we understand and value it, how such understanding helps us to understand ourselves and our own Minnies.

Third-Person Narration, Reportorial: Reading/Writing/Performing "Cases"

Predating your ability to read on your own, parents, teachers, librarians, and other caregivers probably read you picture books or told you fairy tales. The most familiar way to begin a story are the four words "Once upon a time." We learn early to accept and understand the conventions of the third-person voice—that narrative voice in which the narrator telling the story is not an active character. Such narrators have active parts but typically remain outside the actual drama unfolding within the story. There are numerous exceptions, of course, but here we are generalizing about a difference between first- and third-person narrative technique.

Critics distinguish between what they term *objective* and *omniscient* third-person narrators, between those who remain outside the inner lives of the characters of the story and those who have access to and display knowledge of the characters' feelings, thoughts, and unconscious responses, often having more insight into the characters than the characters themselves. Because of the complex connotations of the word *objective*, we will use the word *reportorial*, which carries with it an acknowledgment that the narrator's principal function in such stories is to attempt to report the actions of one or more characters and to make inferences about the characters based on their actions. As contemporary journalistic literature suggests, the idea that such reports have any truly pure status as indifferent and unbiased accounts is indeed problematic: even the journalist who aspires to write "just the facts" must be involved in processes of selection and arrangement that belie a kind of implicit subjectivity. Indeed, much of what has been called new journalism blends the quasi-objective style of traditional journalism with the subjectivity long associated with fiction.

A second point we would make about this category of third-person narration is that it is comparatively rare for writers of fiction to maintain a strictly exterior perspective throughout a text, particularly in longer works such as novels. Think about this in our everyday lives: how difficult is it to resist the temptation to make imaginative leaps into what we suppose is going on in the minds of others around us, even when trying to give a merely physical description of a person, place, or event? We are almost incapable of accomplishing this. It seems to be something close to hard-wired in us to be inferential in our contact with people. We imagine—sometimes inventing—motives for people's actions (sometimes at our own peril), we spin entire narratives based on overheard conversations on trains and buses. For writers of fiction, the impulse to enter the inner lives of their characters seems almost inevitable, although different writers handle this in different ways. Some make the exploration and expression of the consciousness and inner life of a character the central theme of their narrative; we will look at one such example in the last section of this chapter. Some fiction writers impose restrictions on themselves, allowing entry into a character's inner life only at critical, revelatory moments but staying outside the rest of the time. Keeping the distinction between author (real or implied) and narrator in mind, we also acknowledge that there is dispute among critics as to whether third-person narrators can be limited by definition (that is, the author limits the narrator's ability to enter the inner lives of characters) or whether such narrators are omniscient and simply make strategic choices of what to reveal to the narratee or whom to focus on. It is likely that different authors and different readers will experience third-person narrators in different ways. Whatever critical approach we take as readers of fiction written in the third person, it is useful to begin by thinking of such narrators as created people who have their own sense of being and reality, different from but equivalent to the more clearly defined characters within a story or novel. As we have indicated earlier, some critics argue against the "personhood" of third-person narrators, stating that, in at least some instances, the narration does not appear to be emanating from anyone with a tangible reality— that the language is not spoken by a speaker (or written by a writer) in the everyday sense but simply exists, floating in a kind of nonhuman, maybe noncorporeal plane. While we are sympathetic to the validity of this as a description of the effects of some narration, we will start from the premise that, for the performer, it can be helpful to begin by trying to imagine and construct an actual person who might embody the narration—its style, its attitude, its language.

Whether the narration is primarily reportorial, omniscient, or some blend of both, we also encourage you to consider the ways in which the third-person narrator may indeed be the most critical character in many fictional texts. Without such a narrator, for example, we would have no way of knowing Gustave Flaubert's *Madame Bovary* or Henry Fielding's *Tom Jones.* Using the terms we introduced earlier, one might see the third-person narrator in *Tom Jones* as the protagonist of the scene of discourse and Emma and Tom as the protagonists of the scenes of story, both being simultaneously and equally crucial to the experience of their respective texts. Do not look at the third-person narration as language to "race through" in order to get to what may seem like the more character-revealing dialogue or inner monologues—do as much analysis of the narration as necessary to build a sense of the narrator as a character. Consider the kind of language the narrator uses and what attitudes, opinions, biases, and emotions the narrator expresses. Even if the narrator is seemingly objective, are there ways in which he or she demonstrates both consciousness and unconsciousness, awareness and self-awareness? If you were to stage the relationship between the narrator and the characters, how would you use space and proximity, and how might this narrator relate to the narratee/audience?

We turn now to sample text—a "case," if you will, looking ahead to the specific story. It is Willa Cather's classic American story "Paul's Case," published in her 1905 collection *The Troll Garden*, based in some way on her experience as a high school English teacher in Pittsburgh, after she left her native Nebraska and before she settled in New York City. Although the story was written over a hundred years ago, its sense of yearning and inevitable tragedy are still powerfully relevant to the lives of young people trying to find their way in life: details may have changed, but the identity crises remain. The story can be found on pp. 445–460.

The title, as always, helps us understand the story and the narrative techniques used to tell it: "Paul's Case: A Study in Temperament." The word *case* has multiple meanings: lawyers argue a case, defending or prosecuting someone accused of a crime; doctors and psychiatrists may view their patients as cases, pathologies to be named and either cured or determined to be terminal or chronic. Cather's title suggests that Paul, whose last name we never learn, remains in the childish realm of first names, not the adult world of surnames. He is a mystery to be solved or a transgression or crime to be proven and, presumably, disciplined or punished (to use terms made notable by the French theorist Michel Foucault). The subtitle, which is sometimes omitted in published versions, suggests the psychiatric domain of this case: "temperament" carries with it the emerging culture of Freudian psychoanalysis and the "case study" as a narrative that purported to use observation and interpretation as a way of creating a credible solution to an ongoing problem (such as Dora's famous hysteria, made symptomatic by a chronic cough; notice how many times Paul is described as "hysterical," suggesting a kind of feminizing of him by the narrator and by Paul's teachers, family, and employers).

For the moment let us focus specifically on the interrogation of Paul on the afternoon during which the story begins. Look in particular at how the narrator presents this event. She (the story does not specify a sex for the narrator so we will, for convenience, adopt the convention of associating the narrator's sex with that of the author, given no reason to do otherwise) begins with a summary of what has led to this moment, and then describes Paul's appearance in the faculty room almost as a court reporter might: "Paul entered the faculty room suave and smiling." Notice that the narrator describes how he looks, not necessarily how he feels—"suave" suggests a kind of performance, a pose or posture that has been artificially learned (perhaps from the plays and operas Paul devours). The narrator then proceeds to provide the reader with a sketch of Paul's clothing:

> His clothes were a trifle outgrown, and the tan velvet on the collar of his open overcoat was frayed and worn; but for all that there was something of the dandy about him, and he wore an opal pin in his neatly knotted black four-in-hand, and a red carnation in his buttonhole. The latter adornment the faculty somehow felt was not properly significant of the contrite spirit befitting a boy under the ban of suspension.

In a first, silent reading, this may seem simply a recitation of physical detail, but try reading it aloud, working to visualize the boy's appearance. Don't proceed until you can see in your imagination each item described. Do you find the language leading you to certain attitudes, judgments, emotions? What is the tone underlying the word "trifle," which modifies "outgrown" in the first sentence? Is it forgiving, suggesting that Paul has just begun his growth spurt, moving from boyhood to adolescence? Is it slightly mocking, perhaps a kind of understatement? The attitude of the narrator shifts even within the sentence as she describes, perhaps more sympathetically, the velvet on the collar as "frayed and worn," as if there is something touchingly pathetic in Paul's efforts to be stylish, even in dated clothes, clothes he has perhaps worn too many times. She says "there was something of the dandy about him." The word "dandy," one we don't use often today, can carry both positive and negative associations—on the one hand, it suggests a joyfulness and optimism, but it can also suggest a hollowness, a spiritual and intellectual emptiness. In Cather's time, it also could be read as code for a kind of nontraditional masculinity, with the red carnation perhaps an homage to the green carnation that signaled homosexuality in the England of Oscar Wilde and his circle. The sentence also reveals that the narrator is very attentive to the details of Paul's appearance—and she recognizes the degree to which people will infer moral and psychological characteristics about Paul based on his appearance.

The last sentence of the paragraph shifts the narrator's focus from Paul to the faculty assembled to judge his case. She connects the red carnation in Paul's buttonhole to a kind of collective condemnation of him by his teachers, provoked by this detail. The narrator attributes a censorious tone to the faculty here. Has she been privy to their discussions of Paul? If so, has she stepped over the reportorial line into something more blatantly subjective? Notice that even at this point there is a kind of slippage of third-person technique. Just as the teachers draw inferences about Paul, so the narrator seems to be able to generalize about them, based on their behavior, biases, attitudes. The wording of this sentence is portentous, formal—a kind of verdict, finding Paul guilty of lack of contriteness.

The second paragraph continues the physical description, but also moves into more openly evaluative language, as well: the narrator says, "His eyes were remarkable for a certain hysterical brilliancy, and he continually used them in a conscious, theatrical sort of way, peculiarly offensive in a boy." Here is where the question of the boundaries of narrative distance becomes more complex. The phrase "certain hysterical brilliancy" is layered in its diagnostic potential: as we mentioned, the word *hysterical*, borrowed from classical myth and Freudian psychology, is etymologically and culturally connected with the feminine (*hysteria* is Latin for "womb"); the word *brilliancy* today would probably be viewed positively, suggesting attractiveness and brightness, but in the time of the story it might simply have been descriptive of a shininess—and one that is unnatural, womanly. Some recent critics have argued that what is unspoken in the story is Paul's homosexuality—and that perhaps even he was unaware of it. They suggest that the conventions of the historical period in which Cather's story was written required a set of indirect details and inferences about the meaning of Paul's unmanliness—and they build on Cather's own sexuality, which biographers today generally assume to have been same-sex in its orientation.

The narrator attributes agency to Paul's eyes, saying that he "continually used them in a conscious, theatrical sort of way"—in other words, he is aware that he is performing—and, most damning, that such behavior is "peculiarly offensive in a boy." Thus, not only is Paul impudent and poorly behaved, his performance is unmanly, violating expected gender norms of his time and class. Is this the narrator's interpretation of him, or is it her filtered report of the opinion of the teachers about him? Try performing this sentence first as though the narrator shares the teachers' distaste for Paul and then as though she is simply describing their attitudes, and finally as though she mocks them, siding with Paul rather than with the adults. Which do you think most accurately matches the narrator as you see her in the story as a whole, and why?

In the third paragraph, the narrator briefly allows us entry into Paul's mind—"This was a lie, but Paul was quite accustomed to lying; found it, indeed, indispensable for overcoming friction." Just as with the insight into the teachers' collective reading of the meaning of the red carnation, the narrator interprets Paul's mind in what seems to be her language, not his; given that Paul only speaks aloud once within the story, words like "indispensable" and "overcoming friction" feel more like the reporting narrator than the actual words of the character. Again, there is a kind of blurring going on—the narrator and Paul are both engaged in this moment of consciousness, but the narrator's own language dominates, as well as the attitude she has toward Paul based on his perspective.

Go through the ensuing paragraphs, looking closely at the language and attitudes expressed in the language and consider how the narrator's perspective on the scene, on its characters, and on the moral and social values shows itself. They lead up to the one moment of overt speech from Paul, when he says, in response to being asked whether he has meant to be discourteous to a female teacher, "I don't know . . . I didn't mean to be polite or impolite, either. I guess it's a sort of way I have of saying things regardless." The narrator has built up to this moment over the course of a few pages, so we (and his teachers, no doubt) may have expected something more dramatic, articulate, definitive, but what he says, however truthful, is more symptomatic about his lack of control and of selfhood; although, ironically, he diagnoses his social malady accurately, he does not have any internal self-monitor. There is something simultaneously frustrating and poignant in this statement—and in the fact that it is the only time the narrator gives Paul the opportunity to speak directly in reproduced dialogue.

While the narrator remains consistent in voice and style throughout the story, readers have noted that her management of point of view shifts into different modalities as the story progresses toward its fatal ending. For example, once Paul moves outside the constricting, hypersurveillant realm of the school, the narrator frees up access to his inner life. She allows us more understanding of Paul's attitudes, his ways of experiencing the world, but, at least through the middle of the story, reins in the degree to which we actually get his unmediated consciousness: she remains the filter, putting into her own language Paul's perspective. Then, when he leaves Pittsburgh for his eight-day whirlwind trip to New York City, there is a palpable shift even deeper into Paul's point of view. Again, the narrator never cedes complete control over our access to Paul's mind or to his voice, but her interpretation of him becomes more solidly based in his subjectivity rather than her own and more empathic of his dilemma than judgmental about his failings.

Think about this in spatial terms: theorists have sometimes described narrators, particularly third-person narrators, in terms drawn from film technique; you might also consider the nonverbal study of proxemics. If the narrator serves as a kind of camera, what kind of shots dominate the scene in the faculty room? How does the narrator move with Paul in the middle part of the story, as we see him visit Charley Edwards and watch the opera singer and the conductor? Does the narrator stand across the room from him, next to him, behind the narratee, facing him? Is there any moment when the narrator and Paul overlap, superimposed images on top of each other? How might you draw storyboards for each major shot in the story?

Turn to the end of the story and consider the end of Paul's journey, and whether the narrator has gone on her own journey. If she has, does it coincide with Paul's? She will remain (does she?) after the story as its only final witness:

> The sound of an approaching train woke him, and he started to his feet, remembering only his resolution, and afraid lest he should be too late. He stood watching the approaching locomotive, his teeth chattering, his lips drawn away from them in a frightened smile; once or twice he glanced nervously sidewise, as though he were being watched. When the right moment came, he jumped. As he fell, the folly of his haste occurred to him with merciless clearness, the vastness of what he had left undone. There flashed through his brain, clearer than ever before, the blue of Adriatic water, the yellow of Algerian sands.

The first sentence reminds us of the separateness of the narrator and Paul: she continues to be conscious while Paul has slept. But she then fuses herself with Paul's inner life, again using her language to explain the meaning of his sudden action. The sentence that follows, beginning "He stood watching . . ." returns to the technique of the beginning of the story, emphasizing observable behavior—it could be spoken by any other passenger waiting for a train, seeing a strange-looking young man, whose nervousness makes him stand out. In the next, much briefer sentence, the narrator states the suicidal action: "When the right moment came, he jumped." In some respects, this is as straightforward and declarative a sentence as could be used, efficient in its economy—but for that one word in the introductory clause, "right" as an adjective modifying "moment." Whose word is this? Is it Paul's thought? That he has finally found the "perfect" time to do something? Is it simply an objective statement of fact: "right" meaning the exact moment when he will be hit by the train? Is it an ironic comment by the narrator, editorializing that there can be no right moment for self-destruction? Is it possibly a harsh, almost demonic comment by the narrator, who sees nothing but ruin and waste ahead of Paul, so that this moment will be the best he will ever have to control his destiny, given the foolishness of his recent actions? Try different ways of saying the sentence—how does your narrator give meaning to the word "right"?

The narrator then reenters Paul's mind, filtering his consciousness, but in a kind of summary that is clearly marked by her own perspective on it, using words like "folly" and "merciless clearness" and "the vastness of what he had left undone," followed by the images of "the blue of Adriatic water, the yellow of Algerian sands." Are these images of things Paul actually saw or are they meant to represent the cosmopolitan dreams Paul spun for himself on Cordelia Street back in Pittsburgh? They seem to look forward to the film techniques developed later in the twentieth century, in which a character's final moments are represented through a sequence of images either drawn from his life (as in "his life flashed before his eyes") or representing the process of dying and his dream/fantasy life. Paul is almost beyond consciousness at this point, so the narrator, and her language, stands in for him just as she has throughout the story, watching him, using her own style to report him to the narratee and audience. As Paul said, in his one actual speech, his "sort of way" has made him someone who lacks intention regarding his own consciousness; he is always receptive, a passive audience, not the writer of his own life, more conscious than self-conscious (other than in this one sentence). This is followed by the concluding paragraph of the story:

> He felt something strike his chest, and that his body was being thrown swiftly through the air, on and on, immeasurably far and fast, while his limbs gently relaxed. Then, because the picture making mechanism was crushed, the disturbing visions flashed into black, and Paul dropped back into the immense design of things.

The first sentence removes Paul from the realm of the living and, equally important in narrative terms, from the realm of consciousness itself. The opening clause is a kind of unknowing, one might even say preconscious (postconscious?) recording of physical, sensory impression and experience: "something" crushes his chest—he no longer even registers that it is a train that has hit him, or that he has been the agent of this act of self-erasure. The narrator then watches Paul or, more specifically, "his body," for she, too, now reduces him in this moment to a physical phenomenon, but notice the lyric, almost poetic way she describes this shocking, violent motion: "thrown swiftly through the air, on and on, immeasurably far and fast . . ." If we were to actually witness such a scene, the mangling of the body at an incredible speed would make us turn away, but the narrator, maintaining her role as reporter not simply of event but of "temperament," gives Paul a kind of grace, even the salvation of "limbs gently relaxed," in contrast to the constant twitching which has been documented as a kind of "hysterical" symptom throughout the story. The next sentence shifts back again to the narrator's (and our) perspective on Paul. It starts by describing his brain (and possibly his eyes) as "the picture making mechanism," the word *mechanism* connoting the kind of scientific classification that views the human being as a subset of physics and technology, and then uses the language of technology to note the exact moment of death: "the disturbing visions flashed into black," which is as close as early-twentieth-century language gets to distancing brain death from anything religious, and finally ends with a more open, somewhat mystical final action: "Paul dropped back into the immense design of things."

What is this "immense design" for Paul and what is it for the narrator? Is it a realm of relief, putting Paul beyond a world which will never accept him? Is it a nihilistic "nowhere" to which we all eventually return? Is it the "immense design" of narrative, where stories live continuously as long as there is a narrator to shape Paul's brief life into a plot with meaning that will continue to emerge as long as there are audiences to listen, to witness his "case"?

Third-Person Narration, Omniscient: "Knowing" and the Performance of the Novel

The last point-of-view technique we will consider in this chapter is third-person omniscient narration. *Omniscience* literally means all-knowing:

as we have discussed earlier, there is debate over whether such narrators are indeed all-knowing or whether they have limited access to the character or characters whose consciousness they present for the reader. The narrative technique of stream of consciousness, for example, is meant to simulate how the conscious and unconscious parts of the mind blend, overlap, ricochet off each other; works by writers such as James Joyce, William Faulkner, and Virginia Woolf are foundations of this technique.

In third-person omniscient narration, there is usually what feels like an intimate relationship between the narrator and one or, at most, a small number of characters within the scene of story. Different critics describe this relationship in a number of ways. Some, building on the metaphor of M. H. Abrams, the great scholar of romantic literature, speak of the narrator as both "mirror" and "lamp," as a figure who both mirrors the appearance and consciousness of a character but also illuminates the character's interiority. One thing third-person omniscient narration can do is provide the reader with insight into the characters that the characters themselves do not have. In "Paul's Case," the narrator closes in on Paul's inner life as the story progresses; since so much of the story is centered around Paul's inability to understand or name his differentness, we might see the narrator as moving from a mirror of exteriors and appearances to a lamp illuminating him from within in language that begins to resemble his. The French theorist Gerard Genette calls this kind of narrative technique *focalization,* and such a narrator moves between external focalization and internal focalization.

An interesting question and one that provides particular challenges for group performance of prose fiction with third-person omniscient narration is whether the relationship between the narrator and the character being focalized is open or closed, that is, conscious to both or only known by the narrator. Some directors create a sense of conversation between narrator and character, suggesting that the narrator is a companion or, in some cases, a doppelgänger. Others prefer to keep the narrator as a kind of master puppeteer, in which the narrator not only describes the entire scene and provides a kind of ventriloquism for the various characters but also sees into the mind of the protagonist, although the protagonist cannot, in turn, speak back to the narrator; in this approach, the narrator becomes both a superego for the protagonist and a spokesperson for the unconscious. (The superego is the Freudian idea that each individual personality is, in a sense, moderated in part by the external values and knowledge imposed by society.)

While the most familiar kind of third-person omniscient narrator selects one central character to focalize, there are many instances in which third-person narrators choose to provide knowledge of the inner lives of multiple characters, alternating the point of view between characters from chapter to chapter or within chapters from scene to scene. Generally, the greater the number of characters a narrator chooses to focalize, the more diffuse the sense of the reader's identification with and insight into any specific character is likely to be.

In addition, omniscient narrators use a number of specific techniques to represent speech and consciousness, traditionally distinguished as direct discourse, indirect discourse, and free indirect style. Direct discourse is, as you might guess, speech presented as such, a transcript of actual conversation; an example would be something as straightforward as

"Where are you going?" Maisie asked Sir Claude,

from Henry James's novel *What Maisie Knew.* Indirect discourse removes the immediacy of the speech one step away through a stylistic filtering into narration, for example,

Maisie asked Sir Claude where he was going.

Notice that this approach still includes the substance of Maisie's question but maintains the narrator's overt voice. The third form, called free indirect style or free indirect speech (among other terms) might take the same thought and internalize it, in a sentence such as

Maisie wondered where Sir Claude might be going: what might it mean for her own future and that of her dear friend Mrs. Wix.

Here, the thought is Maisie's and includes the emotional sentiments about her governess, Mrs. Wix. The clauses that follow the colon are clearly Maisie "speaking" but still placed technically in the third person. Such an approach allows for a greater fluidity of presentation of a character's interiority in language that comes close to the character's own way of perceiving the world but maintaining the grammatical point of view of the omniscient narrator.

For our final text example in this chapter, we will look at a selection from Henry James's novel *What Maisie Knew.* The novel was written in

1897, at the beginning of the development of psychological realism as the dominant form of modern fiction, and it is often credited with pointing the way to the use of third-person omniscient narration to capture and express how the characters perceived the world around them and made sense of people and social interactions. James's novels are often filled with ambiguity and multiple possibilities, a pleasure for readers whose experience of the world is filled with nuances and gray areas, a frustration for those who prefer narration to be straightforward and clearly ordered.

What Maisie Knew provides us with some fascinating examples of the use of third-person omniscient narration and the ways in which this approach combines both reportorial description and interior focalization, offering performers opportunities for experimenting with various techniques for presentation. The plot of the novel was derived from a "germ" James discovered at a dinner party where a companion related the story of an unusual custody arrangement for a child following a divorce, in which the parents initially took turns caring for the child, but upon remarriage each tried to push the child off on the other, leaving the child all but abandoned. Summarized, the story follows the trials and tribulations of Maisie Farange, the daughter of divorcing parents, from the age of six to her early teens. Beale and Ida fairly quickly lose interest in using Maisie as a piece of property by which to exert power over each other, and the focus shifts to Maisie's stepparents, the second Mrs. Beale (Miss Overmore, Maisie's governess during the period when she lives with her father) and Ida's second husband, Sir Claude; also central to the plot is Mrs. Wix, an aging, somewhat uneducated governess who takes care of Maisie when she lives with her mother. The novel follows Maisie as she is shuttled back and forth between the two houses and as the two new marriages dissolve, with the second Mrs. Beale and Sir Claude eventually falling in love with each other and proposing to take Maisie to live with them as a family. While Maisie loves Sir Claude the most of all her "protectors," she gives him a choice: she will live with him only if he gives up Mrs. Beale, otherwise she will live with Mrs. Wix and a financially uncertain future. She does this knowing Sir Claude, as charming and affectionate as he is, will not, cannot give up Mrs. Beale, and the novel ends with Maisie and Mrs. Wix traveling by boat into an unknown but morally certain future.

While the language of the novel is decidedly of its period and characteristic of James's own diction and sentence length and construction, it remains in many respects as fresh in its topicality and in its perspective as today's tabloids chronicling the growing divorce rate and the fate of the children from such families. What makes James's accomplishment so rewarding to the reader is his use of narrative technique to fulfill the promise of the title of the novel. He establishes a third-person narrator who reports in extensive and exquisite detail the external drama surrounding the divorce and its aftermath: there are memorable scenes of Maisie and her companions throughout London and surrounding parts of England, moments of high drama and bitterly ironic comedy in drawing rooms and at exhibitions. At the same time, within the first chapter, he sets a limit on the presentation of omniscience: while his narrator will be able to observe all manner of exteriors, the only interiority he will present is that of Maisie, beginning at age six. Maisie is the object/subject of focalization within the novel: while the narrator will interpret the meanings of the actions of other characters, he never fully enters their minds. Thus, the novel is as much about the progress of Maisie's consciousness and cognition as it is about a set of childish adults.

James provides a kind of prologue to the novel, untitled and unnumbered, as if to clearly set it off from the novel itself, in which he summarizes for the reader the background leading to Maisie's own story; this is akin to the kind of exposition one often finds in the first scene of a play. James establishes the voice and attitude of his narrator in the opening sentence: "The litigation had seemed interminable and had in fact been complicated; but by the decision on the appeal the judgment of the divorce-court was confirmed as to the assignment of the child." The language is formal, legalistic in tone but also suggests a bored observer, perhaps a court reporter who has had to sit through days of arguments. Notice that the voice of the narrator winds its way to the most important element only at the end of the sentence—"the assignment of the child." At this point, the child is not named, gendered, or given an age but is part of a settlement, like furniture or real estate. The second sentence, even longer, presents the two parents, providing a moral assessment of each and making it clear that neither is to make a claim on our sympathy:

> The father, who, though bespattered from head to foot, had made good his case, was, in pursuance of this triumph, appointed to keep her: it was not so much that the mother's character had been more absolutely damaged as that the brilliancy of a lady's complexion (and this lady's, in court, was immensely remarked) might be more regarded as showing the spots.

Look carefully at how the narrator deploys these descriptions. The father is described as "bespattered from head to foot," a physical image drawn from fashion, followed by the concession that he nonetheless had "made good his case" and that, because of this "triumph," suggesting a kind of battle royal between the two, "appointed to keep her." The last phrase suggests less a desire to live with a daughter he loves than a decision handed down from above—as well as a sense of possessiveness. Thus, the narrator warns us, we are already in a world lacking in moral sense and need to be prepared for something other than a sentimental late-Victorian tale of the child as household angel, worshipped by parents.

Chapter 1 of the novel in its complete form can be found on pp. 461–63. In reading it, try to determine where the narrator is speaking entirely from his point of view and where he begins to give us more of "what Maisie knows." In the first sentence, the narrator provides us with a summary description of where things initially stand, remarking that "the new arrangement was inevitably confounding to a young intelligence," one of the first of many statements throughout the novel designed to describe the state of Maisie's consciousness. The paragraph as a whole, though, remains firmly rooted in the narrator's mind and language. In the second paragraph, we still seem to be primarily with the narrator, though here there are glimmerings of what is going on inside Maisie's head: "Even at that moment, however, she had a scared anticipation of fatigue, a guilty sense of not rising to the occasion . . ." As with "Paul's Case," this is the narrator's language but the protagonist's thoughts, sensations, and emotions.

It is in the third complete paragraph where the narrator opens up Maisie's consciousness to the audience. Notice here how the narrator, while continuing to maintain his reportorial function, allows us access to the little girl's way of knowing: "Thus from the first, Maisie not only felt it, but knew she felt it." The narrator is making an important mental distinction here between emotional sensing and intellectual awareness. Skipping to a little later in the paragraph, we have the narrator moving deeper into the language and perceptions of a six-year-old, with less interpreting and summarizing than filtering in language that more closely expresses the child's perspective:

> If the skin on Moddle's face had to Maisie the air of being unduly, almost painfully, stretched, it never presented that appearance so much as when she uttered, as she often had occasion to utter, such words. *The child wondered if they didn't make it hurt more than*

usual; but it was only after some time that she was able to attach to the picture of her father's sufferings, and more particularly to her nurse's manner about them, the meaning for which these things had waited. (Italics added.)

While much of this prose remains in the narrator's voice, we have italicized a sentence that provides an example of the narrator using what we have called free indirect style: here we get Maisie's perception and thoughts in language that could indeed be spoken by a six-year-old but phrased within the grammatical voice of the third person. Try speaking this passage. How could you signal the shift in discourse style here? Would you adopt Maisie's voice entirely in the italicized phrase? Would you maintain the narrator's? Could you combine them?

Look at the next paragraph, beginning, "She had the knowledge . . ." Going through it sentence by sentence, try to determine which sentences belong to the narrator, which to Maisie, and whether any seem to fuse the two consciousnesses (grammatically, they are all in some form of third person, of course). For the occasional moments of direct discourse (principally the offstage pass Beale makes at Moddle), do you say them *as* those characters (providing distinct characters for them, perhaps even contrasting lines of focus and bodily postures), as if Maisie is hearing them and repeating them to herself, or as the narrator reporting them?

The end of the chapter provides a moment of extreme discomfort for Maisie but high comedy for the narrator and audience. Maisie, still somewhat of an unformed vessel, only just beginning to understand how her parental arrangement will work and how she will need to learn to fit into the system (a rather large task for a six-year-old), responds to her mother's question as to whether Maisie's father sent a message:

> "He said I was to tell you, from him," she faithfully reported, "that you're a nasty horrid pig!"

Certainly much of the ironic pleasure to be had from this excruciating moment is in the way in which the mask of politeness is ripped away from the "arrangement," as Maisie serves as messenger of most ill tidings between parents. The narrator's brief intrusion of a dialogue cue, "she faithfully reported," is critical to the ironic effect—"faithfully" speaks to the innocence and goodness and honesty of Maisie and "reported" suggests that Maisie is simply an objective messenger, but what we and the narrator share is the deeply bitter subtext of the exchange. One can speculate as to Maisie's "knowingness" at this point: to what degree is she aware that repeating the phrase "nasty horrid pig" will not make her mother happy?

We suggest you work on an analysis of this chapter (or at least an extended section of it) on your own and in class. Map out the contours of the narration, describing the progress of Maisie's consciousness. What remains constant about her as a person? Work on both descriptive and scenic sections of this chapter, integrating the kinds of visualization, focus, and vocal and physical techniques that will help you embody the details of the scene, the attitudes of narrator and of Maisie, and the dramatic interaction between the three major characters, making sure to find ways to distinguish each from the other while maintaining an overall integrity of the sense of this as a narrated scene, overseen by the omniscient narrator. You may find it useful to adapt it to a mini chamber theater script and stage it. Where does the narrator stand in relation to the characters? At what points does the narrator direct descriptions with an onstage focus, watching the characters? At what points does he speak directly to the audience, taking us into his confidence? Do the narrator and Maisie ever speak to each other? Why or why not?

This discussion of James's novel can only give you the beginning of what a thorough and detailed study of the novel for the purposes of performing its point of view and consciousness entails. Should you choose to work with a novel in performance, you would of course read the entire novel from which your selection is drawn, giving the section you are performing the careful, close attention we have tried to suggest one can achieve with our example of *What Maisie Knew*.

Other Forms of Point of View: First Person Plural and Second Person

We will look in briefly at two other forms of point of view—much less common, particularly in English-language traditions of fiction—which you may nonetheless encounter in your reading and performing. The first one we will examine is first person plural point of view—texts written in the "we" voice. Brian Richardson, in *Unnatural Voices: Extreme Narration in Modern and Contemporary Fiction*, traces traditions of the "we" point of view across different national and linguistic traditions in the past two centuries; he suggests that there are a number of consistent qualities associated with this narrative perspective. One is that first person plural fiction "may represent an intimate or a vast group and its composition may—and usually does—change during the course of the fiction" (p. 38). Thus, one can imagine this point of view representing everything from a couple telling their story jointly to a story of an entire race or planet of people. With the latter, the "we" may itself be somewhat of a fiction in literal terms—it may be a single individual speaking (or trying to speak) for a larger group of people. In everyday conversation, we encounter such discourse frequently—perhaps most annoyingly in childhood memories of teachers instructing us as to how "we" were to act ("We don't speak out of turn in class," which was usually a way of saying, "I'm telling you not to talk when I'm talking!"). But there are, as Richardson convincingly demonstrates, a number of examples of fiction that set out to create a genuinely collective, multiple sense of voice using the "we," which we are distinguishing from works of fiction in which there are multiple, but singular first-person narrators, such as a number of novels by William Faulkner.

A second and intriguing characteristic Richardson notes in tracing the history of such narrative strategies is that many of these texts focus on issues of class and collectivity, as the "we" tends to presuppose a "they/ them" and may also presuppose political themes and issues—thus, novels about empire, colonization, and collective enterprises, such as utopias and dystopias, are ripe and natural opportunities to explore the "we-ness" of a point of view, both in imagining societies where voices speak together in harmony and ones where totalitarianism has replaced individual agency. Richardson's book includes a bibliography of fictional texts written in the "we" point of view should you wish to explore these in more detail.

What are the principal challenges for the performer in the first person plural point of view? For the solo performer, it is somehow embodying multiplicity in a singular voice and body—how do we transcend, interrogate, complicate our "oneness" in grappling with the "manyness" such a text suggests? In a sense, it may be like trying to sing a choral work as a soloist. How does a single voice suggest either many different ones (the challenge of dramatic literature, as well as other forms which place characters into dialogue) and how does a single voice suggest many voices speaking *as* one, without reducing the chorus to the very different occurrence of the single voice?

Perhaps not surprisingly, two of the most notable recent American novels to utilize the first person plural point of view are about the workplace, Joshua Ferris's *Then We Came to the End* and Ed Parks's *Personal Days*. The contemporary office is a place where many Americans experience both the positive and negative qualities of collectivity on a daily basis. The popularity of both the British and the American versions of the television comedy *The Office* attests to the pervasive force of workplace "performance" as central to our social and psychological lives. Work is where we spend something close to half our waking lives at least five days a week for most of our adult lives. It becomes an arena in which we both desire to bond with others in collective experiences and resist what seems like the diminishment of our individual selves by the rules, regulations, policies, and procedures. The blurring of lines between work and home promoted by digital and virtual workplaces ("telecommuting") may make the struggle to balance "I-ness" and "we-ness" even more complicated.

Let us look at just the opening paragraph of Ferris's novel, which was a finalist for the National Book Award. The title of the chapter, interestingly phrased in second person, is "You Don't Know What's in My Heart":

> We were fractious and overpaid. Our mornings lacked promise. At least those of us who smoked had something to look forward to at ten-fifteen. Most of us liked most everyone, a few of us hated specific individuals, one or two people loved everyone and everything. Those who loved everyone were unanimously reviled. We loved free bagels in the morning. They happened all too infrequently. Our benefits were astonishing in comprehensiveness and quality of care. Sometimes we questioned whether they were worth it. We thought moving to India might be better, or going back to nursing school. Doing something with the handicapped or working with our hands. No one ever acted on these impulses, despite their daily, sometimes hourly contractions. Instead we met in conference rooms to discuss the issues of the day. (p. 3)

There are sentences or phrases that seem to create dialogue between people included in the collective, either helping each other, elaborating on things just said, or disputing them, such as the categorization of people as "liking," "loving," and "hating"—clearly there is an acknowledgment that not everyone in the office is the same. If you had a group of performers with whom to work on this paragraph, would you divide the sentences and phrases up—if so, how, and what kind of characters would you assign to each? Or would you attempt something like a Greek chorus, in which performers speak in as close to unison as possible—and if so, how would you "orchestrate" this? Would you want it to sound robotic? Melodic and rhythmic? Some combination of effects, or some mixture of solo and group speech?

Similarly, try working on the passage in more detail as a solo performer. Do you find yourself taking on multiple personalities—possibly in almost cartoonish ways, to suggest different attitudes or qualities of voice and demeanor? Can you do this and still maintain the sense of multiple voices speaking simultaneously? Is there a kind of leveling of personality that the collective "we" imposes on the text's sense of voice and perspective—and hence on the performer's approach to it?

We will now move on to second person point of view. As noted earlier, in English there is typically no consistent, standard distinction between singular and plural forms of "you."

If the central challenge first person plural point of view poses for the performer is the tension between individual and collective voice and identity, then we might say that the central challenge posed by second person point of view is a metaphysical and ontological one, of the status and identity of the speaker in time and space and in relation to characters within the story and to narratees and audiences (for example, respectively, the scene of story and the scene of discourse). In simpler terms: *who* is the "you" in second person narration? Various critics have addressed this question; and what most rule out as authentically second person narration is the colloquial use of "you," as in "You know how it is when you can't get to sleep" or similar phrases. These are seen as focused on point of view and merely turns of phrase that are meant to establish a common bond between speaker and listener.

Again, Brian Richardson, in *Unnatural Voices*, provides us with some helpful distinctions, this time between what he sees as the three principal ways in which second person narration is employed in fiction:

1. Standard form: "usually in the present tense, about a single protagonist, who is referred to in the second person; the 'you' often designates the narrator and the narratee as well" (p. 20).
2. Hypothetical form: involves a "consistent use of the imperative . . . frequent employment of the future tense . . . and unambiguous distinction between narrator and narratee" (p. 29).

3. Autotelic form: the you "is at times the actual reader of the text whose story is juxtaposed and can merge with the characters in the fiction" (p. 30).

So, in the standard form, the "you" becomes a central character, story-teller, and listener, all at the same time—a kind of closed system in which the reader or listener may stand as an eavesdropper on an interior experience or, conversely, may be asked to stand with the performer as an actor in the narrative. In the standard form, the "you" extends an invitation to imagine oneself immediately in the experience of the action of the story.

The hypothetical form draws a clearer distinction between teller and listener, both within the world of the story and in the interplay of author and audience. The narratee may indeed be a character in the sense in which we are used to using that term, but not a character who embraces the "I" actively nor someone who is simply observed or whose consciousness is filtered overtly through the narrator. One writer who has used this form of second person narration most consistently and, based on critical response, most successfully is Lorrie Moore (whose work Richardson discusses). Moore's collection of short stories, *Self-Help*, includes a number of stories cast in the familiar nonfiction form of the self-help manual. Within this form, Moore varies her technique considerably; in some stories, such as "The Kid's Guide to Divorce," the "you," addressing a child living with his mother after divorce, mentions names, people, and events with a specificity that gives the feel of a realistic short story, and the effect of the "you" is to create a sense of distance and dissonance between the child, his mother, and the unnaturalness of the new living situation. Even in stories that in some ways seem to be more generalized, such as "How to Become a Writer," Moore alternates between a "you" that extends beyond the specific location of the story and a "you" that has a biographical identity in a very particular place and time. An example of the first is the following passage:

Why write? Where does writing come from? These are questions to ask yourself. They are like: Where does dust come from? Or: Why is there war? Or: If there's a God then why is my brother now a cripple?

These are questions that you keep in your wallet, like calling cards. These are questions, your creative writing teacher says, that are good to address in your journals but rarely in your fiction.

> The writing professor this fall is stressing the Power of the Imagination. Which means he doesn't want long descriptive stories about your camping trip last July. He wants you to start in a realistic context but then to alter it. Like recombinant DNA. He wants you to let your imagination sail, to let it grow big-bellied in the wind. This is a quote from Shakespeare. (pp. 122–23)

Other than the phrase "why is my brother now a cripple," this passage could be seen as the kind of universal experience college students have when they take a beginning creative writing class—from the larger questions of purpose and process to the almost stock professor who uses somewhat vacuous metaphors (recombinant DNA for the transformative process of making fiction) and the occasional motto from a great writer that passes for pedagogy. While the specific details (perhaps including the crippled brother) may vary, those who have taken this kind of class can recognize the somewhat dampening experience.

But in the very next paragraph, Moore uses the second person to rather different effect:

> Tell your roommate your great idea, your great exercise of imaginative power: a transformation of Melville to contemporary life. It will be about monomania and the fish-eat-fish world of life insurance in Rochester, New York. The first line will be "Call me Fishmeal," and it will feature a menopausal suburban husband named Richard, who because he is so depressed all the time is called Mopey Dick by his witty wife Elaine. Say to your roommate, "Mopey Dick, get it?" Your roommate looks at you, her face blank as a large Kleenex. She comes up to you, like a buddy, and puts an arm around your burdened shoulders. "Listen, Francie," she says, slow as speech therapy. "Let's go out and get a big beer." (p. 123)

While the sense of wit and even the tongue-in-cheek style (with its pleasure in the puns on "Fishmeal" and "Mopey Dick") provide consistency between the first passage we quoted and this one, perhaps pointing to a kind of authorial narrator backstage, this paragraph is much more specific—we learn the name of the "you" (Francie), and we see her in a more specific performative instance than in the first one. An interesting question here, following Richardson's taxonomy, is why choose the imperative (command) grammatical form? Imagine different ways of handling this form in performance — is it a set of instructions (for "self-help")? Dictatorial orders? Does it suggest a narrator who must guide the narratee (Francie) because she is so "at sea" (so to speak) about how to become a writer? If you were to adapt this story for group performance, would you have separate performers for the narrator and Francie? Could a single performer successfully perform both roles simultaneously? What would be different in each approach? Where is the actual audience in each case? Could you address the audience and invite or command them to become the "Francie" who is also the "you"? Think about how you would use the performance space, proximity to audience, and onstage and offstage focus to embody your perspective on the story.

We will be exploring the relationships between aesthetic form and cultural meaning in more detail in the next chapter and end our discussion here of second person point of view with a very brief story that asks us to consider how something so bound up in artistic technique might have political and rhetorical significance as well. The following story is from the collection *At the Bottom of the River*, by the Antiguan writer Jamaica Kincaid (who now resides in New York City), and is reprinted here in its entirety.

Girl

Wash the white clothes on Monday and put them on the stone heap; wash the color clothes on Tuesday and put them on the clothesline to dry; don't walk barehead in the hot sun; cook pumpkin fritters in very hot sweet oil; soak your little cloths right after you take them off; when buying cotton to make yourself a nice blouse, be sure that it doesn't have gum on it, because that way it won't hold up well after a wash; soak salt fish overnight before you cook it; is it true that you sing benna in Sunday school?; always eat your food in such a way that it won't turn someone else's stomach; on Sundays try to walk like a lady and not like the slut you are so bent on becoming; don't sing benna in Sunday school; you mustn't speak to wharf-rat boys, not even to give directions; don't eat fruits on the street—flies will follow you; *but I don't sing benna on Sundays at all and never in Sunday school*; this is how to sew on a button; this is how to make a button-hole for the button you have just sewed on; this is how to hem a dress when you see the hem coming down and so to prevent yourself from looking like the slut I know you are so bent on becoming;

this is how you iron your father's khaki shirt so that it doesn't have a crease; this is how you iron your father's khaki pants so that they don't have a crease; this is how you grow okra—far from the house, because okra tree harbors red ants; when you are growing dasheen, make sure it gets plenty of water or else it makes your throat itch when you are eating it; this is how you sweep a corner; this is how you sweep a whole house; this is how you sweep a yard; this is how you smile to someone you don't like too much; this is how you smile to someone you don't like at all; this is how you smile to someone you like completely; this is how you set a table for tea; this is how you set a table for dinner; this is how you set a table for dinner with an important guest; this is how you set a table for lunch; this is how you set a table for breakfast; this is how to behave in the presence of men who don't know you very well, and this way they won't recognize immediately the slut I have warned you against becoming; be sure to wash every day, even if it is with your own spit; don't squat down to play marbles—you are not a boy, you know; don't pick people's flowers—you might catch something; don't throw stones at blackbirds, because it might not be a blackbird at all; this is how to make a bread pudding; this is how to make doukona; this is how to make a pepper pot; this is how to make a good medicine for a cold; this is how to make a good medicine to throw away a child before it even becomes a child; this is how to catch a fish; this is how to throw back a fish you don't like, and that way something bad won't fall on you; this is how to bully a man; this is how a man bullies you; this is how to love a man, and if this doesn't work there are other ways, and if they don't work don't feel too bad about giving up; this is how to spit in the air if you feel like it; and this is how to move quick so that it doesn't fall on you; this is how to make ends meet; always squeeze bread to make sure it's fresh; *but what if the baker won't let me feel the bread?*; you mean to say that after all you are really going to be the kind of woman who the baker won't let near the bread? (pp. 3–5)

Instead of taking you through an analysis of this text, we will pose some questions and suggestions for you to work with this on your own and with other students and performers. (Be sure to look up any words you don't know, especially the references drawn from Caribbean culture!) Consider the story in terms of Richardson's typology of second person narration and decide which of the three kinds dominates. Are there other kinds of point of view in this story besides second person? How many characters are there in the story? Determine how many sentences and paragraphs there are and consider how this affects performance decisions. Consider the relationship between narrator and narratee and between author (real and/or implied) and reader (real and/or implied) and how you will communicate this through performance techniques.

No doubt, as you read and work on this story for performance, a number of questions about place, time, and culture will emerge for you. In the next chapter, we will consider such issues of location in prose fiction and in performance.

KEY TERMS

character—round versus flat

focalization

narratee

narratology

plot

point of view

scene/summary/description

scene of discourse

scene of story

story

Chapter 9

PERFORMING PROSE FICTION II: LOCATIONS AND LANGUAGE

Through the fence, between the curling flower spaces,
I could see them hitting.
—BENJAMIN, APRIL SEVENTH, 1928

When the shadow of the sash appeared on the curtains
it was between seven and eight o'clock and then I
was in time again, hearing the watch.
—QUENTIN, JUNE SECOND, 1910

Once a bitch always a bitch, what I say.
—JASON, APRIL SIXTH, 1928

The day dawned bleak and chill, a moving wall of gray light out of
the northeast which, instead of dissolving into moisture, seemed
to disintegrate into minute and venomous particles, like dust that,
when Dilsey opened the door of the cabin and emerged, needled
laterally into her flesh, precipitating not so much a moisture as a
substance partaking of the quality of thin, not quite congealed oil.
—NARRATOR, APRIL EIGHTH, 1928

Read aloud the four sentences above. What do you notice about each?
What kind of character do you infer for each? How does each sentence
suggest the way each speaker orients himself or herself toward the world
in which he or she lives? Are some more marked by a sense of place? By

a sense of time? By neither or by some combination of the two? Do any of the sentences reveal anything about the speaker's cultural location or attitudes?

These are the first sentences of each of the four major sections of William Faulkner's 1929 novel *The Sound and the Fury*, one of several novels set in the fictional Yoknapatawpha County in Mississippi. The novel is told from the points of view of the three brothers of the Compson family and ends with a fourth section told from a third person omniscient point of view by an unnamed narrator. The novel takes place mostly during Easter week of 1928, although, as the second sentence suggests, there are journeys back into the past as well. As Faulkner memorably said, and Quentin's sentence embodies, "The past is not dead, it's not even the past." Within the world of the novel, each of the male narrators represents a distinct way of understanding and living (or not) in the world—and what binds the brothers together is an obsession, sometimes positive, sometimes negative, toward their only sister, Caddy, who, by the time of the novel, has long left the family and the county, abandoning her only daughter, also named Quentin. Benjamin is described as an "idiot," a term we do not use today (as it now carries the stigma of the eugenic categories of an earlier era), but which, in the world of the novel, echoes Shakespeare's eloquent phrase from act 5 of *Macbeth*: "it is a tale/Told by an idiot, full of sound and fury,/Signifying nothing." Benjy (as he is referred to throughout the novel) is not capable of distinguishing between past and present and seems to have little concept of a future (other than a child's eagerness for holidays such as Christmas and his birthday). His sentence sets him in a kind of eternal present, in which his experience watching men play golf on the field that used to be part of his family's property coexists with his memories of days spent with his beloved sister when they were children. It would be most accurate to say that language "speaks" Benjy—he is not capable of actual speech. Faulkner does not specify the exact nature of Benjy's impairment—it has been represented as both cognitive disability (mental retardation) and as a form of autism. He is capable of great emotional response, but others (with the exception of his sister) seem only able to project their own consciousness and subjectivities on him. He lives in a world of a never-ending present in a physical space that has an immediacy to him indistinguishable from memories of the place in other times.

Quentin's sentence is the only one set outside the few days in which the primary action of the novel occurs. As you read it, notice how it unfolds syntactically and stylistically in ways that are almost the extreme opposite of Benjy's. If Benjy's field of consciousness is dominated by the present moment of the golf course, Quentin's is a kind of disembodied awareness of almost ghostly, haunted perception of light and shape—"the shadow of the sash appeared on the curtains"—less an image of a gestalt, a wholeness, and instead a kind of metonymic substitution of a part for the whole landscape of his dormitory room at Harvard. The shadow— the fading of light—brings Quentin back into a world of time "between seven and eight o'clock," a range of specificity unavailable to Benjy. In fact, Quentin is able to verify his own consciousness of time through "the watch" (which he inherited from his grandfather and which he will break before the end of his section, concordant with his suicide). He describes himself as "in time again." What would it mean to be "in time"? Perhaps more difficult, what would it mean to be "outside of time," which may be a pun on being "out of time," the time left for him as a conscious, living being coming to its conclusion? Think about how such a person might relate to his physical surroundings. How aware of space and place would he be? Try relating to whatever space you are in as you perform this sentence.

Our third speaker is Jason, the son who, despite his moral venality, is the character who is most grounded in what most readers would experience as temporal and spatial "real" worlds. For that reason, perhaps, his sentence is the shortest of the three and comments least on the specifics of either where or when he is speaking—Jason lives in a world of practicality and business, and his sentence is a kind of motto of what he views as a truth of character and, however sexist, of femininity. He does not identify who the "bitch" is (we will learn it refers to Caddy's daughter, who has robbed him of money he had in turn stolen, and by extension, it always refers to Caddy herself, who has been cast out from the family because of her sexually scandalous acts). Jason seems to care very little about the emotional or psychological meanings of place and time—he is neither surrounded by the field which encloses Benjy nor subject to the disappearing sanity time marks for Quentin. He just *is*, and his sentence places him in the world in which he judges people based on what they can do for him.

The fourth sentence takes us outside the dramatis personae of the Compson brothers to the omniscient narrator, who views and interprets this world, but from the scene of discourse. Try reading it aloud again—you may find it quite a challenge to keep the sentence whole and continuous without taking some breaths! It begins by locating narrator and narratee in both time and place—dawn and "bleak and chill." While we may not yet know exactly where we are, we have a sense of temperature and mood, followed by detailed and elaborate images of light, air, and physical phenomena (such as "particles, like dust") and then the appearance of a character, the Negro servant Dilsey, who serves as the emotional, spiritual, and ethical center of the novel. The sentence not only brings Dilsey into the world of this day (it is Easter Sunday, a day of rebirth and resurrection that has great cultural and symbolic meaning for the novel and for Dilsey in particular), but it reveals her in very corporeal terms as "needled laterally into her flesh." What would it mean to be "needled laterally"? The narrator describes the daylight as "precipitating not so much a moisture as a substance partaking of the quality of thin, not quite congealed oil." Dilsey is, in some way, equated with the natural world, associated with the same kind of physical, almost molecular way the light of the morning is described. But the "congealed oil" locates Dilsey in a particular cultural world, where she lives in poverty only a step or two above the slavery of her forebears in the American South. While this is only hinted at in this sentence, the novel is filled with the world of early-twentieth-century cultural practices and objects from the postbellum experience of Faulkner's world. There is much that can be said about Faulkner's choice to end his novel with an omniscient narrator; and while all three of the Compson brothers are allowed to tell their own versions of the family narrative (including one who apparently cannot actually speak aloud), Dilsey is not allowed her own voice, except in the direct discourse of exterior dialogue.

Some critics would argue that Dilsey is privileged by the narrator's more complex style, suggesting that she is the fullest, most rounded of the characters because she is the one chosen for such attention and focalization. Others would argue that the decision to place a mediating narrator between Dilsey and the consciousness of the audience carries with it cultural implications regarding both her gender and her race, suggesting a somewhat conflicted perspective by the narrator (and, by implication, by Faulkner himself) toward women and Negroes (the term used at the time). That these are some of his most memorable and embodied characters need not contradict the sense of a complicated cultural standpoint within the novel. It is possible to see Faulkner and his narrator as having great admiration for Dilsey while at the same time finding a kind of denial or suppression of the representation of the vernacular culture of Negroes in the South of the early twentieth century.

In the previous chapter on prose fiction we focused on techniques of point of view and how the handling of point of view expressed different ways of representing consciousness and the relationship between narrator, character, and audience (narratee). In this chapter, we will expand the discussion to two central objects of consciousness (remember our claim that consciousness is always consciousness of something, built on the central tenet of the branch of philosophy known as phenomenology). Here, we will encourage you to explore what the critic and theorist Homi K. Bhabha calls "location." Bhabha, whose perspective is postcolonial, defines location not as simply a physical place, but as an intersection of space and time and expands both of these terms to include the specifics of place and territory on the one hand and history, as well as internally experienced time, on the other. The Soviet theorist Mikhail Bakhtin used the term *chronotope* (literally "time-space") to describe this relationship, which he saw as interdependent.

We will examine how space/place/territory and time/history intersect in fictional texts and how writers use such intersections along with what theorists call vernacular culture, the culture produced by the people who live in a specific time and place (and who are typically outside the formal and academic realms of the production of "high art"). We will also look at the challenges posed for performers by such texts and such aesthetic and cultural dimensions of prose fiction. Whereas in the previous chapter we focused less on cultural, social, and political aspects of prose fiction and more on formal and structural elements, in this chapter we will consider more overtly how location—space and time (and their attendant related terms and concepts)—carries cultural significance and how performers themselves participate in dialogues with such texts through their own work. While ultimately, as Bhabha and Bakhtin both argue, we agree that space and time cannot ever really be disengaged from each other—and that they must be placed in an intersectional relationship with each other to capture their complexity—we will, for the purposes of analysis, look at each individually, acknowledging when the other needs to be considered. We will also consider ways of representing vernacular culture, specifically through the language of narration and dialogue in prose fiction, against the backdrop of the critical and cultural set of perspectives grouped under the rubric "postcolonialism." At the end of the chapter we consider the intersection of space, time, and vernacular language/culture in a single text.

Space, Place, and Territory

We are distinguishing between the terms *space, place,* and *territory* in ways that are intended to illuminate the complex relationships between consciousness, experience, and culture. In doing so, one of our goals is to help you as performers and readers to understand how different approaches may intersect with each other and not necessarily negate one another. We will start by briefly defining two terms: *phenomenology* and *postcolonialism. Phenomenology* refers to a philosophical method of study that investigates consciousness and how we as human subjects experience the world—what such philosophers call the "lived world" or the *Lebenswelt*—through consciousness. In our previous chapter, much of our exploration of kinds of narrators was informed by a very broad sense of phenomenological method, where an understanding of how narrators and characters experience the worlds they narrate or inhabit became a focus for the performer's approach. As a technical method of philosophical inquiry, there is a fairly extensive and specific set of steps and terms associated with phenomenology, but we will not detail those here. Our main point is to identify phenomenology as a way of trying to understand the world and the texts we choose to perform, as well as the act of performance. What is important to keep in mind is that its central interest in consciousness should not be equated with a completely idiosyncratic subjectivity, in which each individual's experience is wholly independent of anyone else's; indeed, one of the goals of phenomenology is to try to discover and articulate systems of intersubjectivity, shared ways of experiencing the world in consciousness. In recent decades, phenomenology has come under criticism by theorists such as Michel Foucault for what they have viewed as its disengagement from history, culture, and politics—for the very transcendental position it seeks to adopt.

Aspects of our approach in this chapter are rooted in a phenomenological outlook, but we too share some of the concerns articulated by its critics: even when looking at a literary text from a more formal or structural perspective, we cannot help but consider cultural dimensions, as well (nor would we want to). The four sentences we quoted from Faulkner's novel illustrate an attempt to describe and analyze how each character's consciousness of the world is oriented in both shared and differing ways, but they also bring cultural and historical attitudes, particularly toward women and people of color, into our analysis.

We are also bringing a cultural perspective to our analysis, most specifically, a postcolonial perspective. *Postcolonial* is a complex term, used by different scholars to mean different things in different contexts. In its broadest sense, postcolonialism is interested in dialogue with texts and events and perspectives that have emerged as a result of centuries of European domination over non-Western cultures and nations during the periods of empire and imperialism. In particular, because narrative is so central to the ways in which we make sense of individual and collective identity and because prose fiction allows writer, reader, and performer to engage in both realistic and imagined worlds, it seems a particularly fitting place in which to explore the multilayered perspectives of what we have described as phenomenological and postcolonial perspectives — indeed, to see how they intersect simultaneously when we work on texts in performance. The critical theorist R. Radhakrishnan argues, in his book *History, the Human, and the World Between,* that the groundedness of phenomenology has much to offer the more ideologically driven field of postcolonial studies, and vice versa.

So, on to our first set of terms and relations: space/place/territory. Space is the broadest of our categories, and we are using it here very specifically to refer to the physical, psychological, and, in some cases, philosophical and spiritual dimensions of phenomena. Traditional physics and geometry name three dimensions — the point, the line, and the solid; more recently, a fourth dimension, time, has been included (we will consider time in a separate section). While we begin with mathematical and scientific ways of thinking about space, we also acknowledge that most ways of experiencing space do not remain abstract for very long.

Place tends to be less abstract a concept. Tim Cresswell, in *Place: A Short Introduction,* puts it this way: "When humans invest meaning in a portion of space and then become attached to it in some way (naming it is one such way), it becomes a place" (p. 10). Cresswell then proceeds to distinguish between place and landscape, suggesting that landscapes tend to be something we as viewers are outside of — "Places are very much things to be inside of."

Can you come up with examples of areas that you have experienced as "pure" space? How can you describe your relationship to them as separate from your attachment to them, in Cresswell's terms? Does space almost immediately become place as soon as humans interact with it? Think about the language we use — "wide open spaces" to describe areas that have not yet become places for us. Have you ever experienced an area as a space that others have experienced as a place? Bruce recalls that, when he first moved to a rural part of the state of Nebraska, he initially experienced it as a kind of "space"—indeed as an absence of place, as he grew up on the edge of a large city, itself bordered by one of the Great Lakes. The lack of water, the fairly flat contours of the geography, and the comparative absence of urban markers all made him experience it as something that was *not* there. Yet, when he mentioned this to his students, many of whom had lived their entire lives fewer than fifty miles from the town in which he was living, they were able to name and describe eloquently things that made this space a place for them: everything from the songs of birds (captured in Willa Cather's novels about Nebraska, her home region) to the motion of fields of corn and wheat to more people-oriented aspects of place, such as communities of fewer than one hundred people, their schools, churches, and other ways of bonding in specific space with others.

Recall in chapter 2 the excerpt from Dickens's *Bleak House* in which the London fog is described in great detail. What parts of this description seem to you most evocative of space? At what points does Dickens clearly delineate place? Are the two ever really distinguished from each other in this selection? How does the narrator "invest" in this fog and how does he attach it in meaningful ways to his consciousness of the city? How would a fog in contemporary San Francisco or Seattle (or your own hometown) differ in detail and meaning? Try performing Dickens's description, moving through the imagined space/place. There are other texts in this book you might explore in this way: the hospital in Carol's personal narrative of her brother's death (in chapter 5) or the landscapes of poetry throughout the book or Pittsburgh and New York City in another era in "Paul's Case," by Willa Cather (chapter 8). Try performing a description of some aspect of space and place from an area very familiar to you. Can you narrate and perform the space in which you have class, shifting it in meaningful ways from space to place?

A postcolonial perspective on these matters would want to consider the historical, social, political, and cultural dimensions of place as inextricable from the ways in which we experience them and make meaning from them. Here, the third idea in our trio of concepts becomes relevant: *territory*. David Delaney, a legal scholar, has defined territory as a "bounded social space that inscribes a certain sort of meaning onto defined segments of the material world" (p. 14). Perhaps the most important words in this definition are "bounded" and "social." A territory is a special kind of space, a place that is bounded, that is, as important for what is outside of it, for what is not allowed to be considered part of it, as for what it contains. That such a space is social is also critical: it is a shared space, but shared by people whose affiliations may simply be coincidence of geography or whose affiliations may be based on categories of identity, practice, place, or history. Territory may be disputed—think of the ongoing conflicts about sections of Israel and other areas in the news; it may contain heterogeneous groups who learn to live together or who constantly fight with each other. In American culture, we often see concepts of territory played out in popular performance. Examples that come readily to mind are *West Side Story* (one of the working titles was "The Turf Is Ours," suggesting how "ownership" of city blocks becomes the stage for tragedy in that play), films and television series set in schools, such as *The Breakfast Club, Mean Girls,* and *Superbad,* in which cafeterias, classrooms, and hallways become territories, with strict borders which must be observed and transgressed only at great personal risk, within the microcosm of high school culture. Sociologists such as Erving Goffman and philosophers such as Michel Foucault have written extensively about "total institutions"—those spaces and places that enclose people completely in regimented ways, often against the will of the inhabitants—these include prisons, asylums, concentration camps, some hospitals, and, some might argue, schools, as well. Ideas about territory have become even more complex with the development of systems of virtual reality, including simulated worlds such as Second Life. Science fiction writers, such as William Gibson, who coined the term *hypertext* in his novel *Neuromancer,* and Neal Stephenson, whose novel *Snow Crash* is often viewed as representing a virtual world akin to Second Life for the first time in fiction, and Orson Scott Card, whose novel *Ender's Game* took the experience of the video game and extended it to actual strategies for conducting warfare, all offer rich texts for exploration of the limits of territory as a concept and as a set of practices and experiences.

You might, as an experiment, consider the ways in which your performance classroom functions as a territory (or set of territories). Early in a semester or quarter, there is often a fair amount of testing of the arrangement of space and place and where students fit into it. Different teachers arrange classrooms in ways that suit their pedagogical purposes, as well as the relationships they wish to establish between themselves and students. Do you notice that certain students tend to sit in specific parts of a classroom and, after the initial period of exploration, do not cross lines? Why do you think this is so, if this is the case? Have you ever tried sitting in a different part of the classroom and felt as if you were making a statement by doing so? One can often feel a change in mood, physiologically, when making such a shift. Expand this experiment to places you frequent—neighborhoods, restaurants, and other gathering places. How does changing the borders of the territory (either within a single space or in blurring or redrawing the boundaries of inside/outside) change the meaning of the territory? We often talk about "breaking the fourth wall" in theater—this is yet another use of the language of borders and territories to describe aesthetic and cultural practice.

We will now examine a specific text for the ways in which it presents space, place, and territory, and how such representation leads to a sense of what Bhabha calls location. We will consider both phenomenological and postcolonial aspects of this text's space/place/territory, the physical aspects of location, how the language suggests a kind of consciousness (what phenomenologists call "intentionality") of the space, and how the historical and cultural dimensions, read through a postcolonial lens, transform space into place and territory.

Our text is E. M. Forster's 1924 novel A Passage to India, set in India during the 1920s, one of the last decades of British rule, collectively known as the Raj (which ended in 1947). The novel, a rich, complex story of relationships between British people living in India and working for the government and native Indians, some resistant to British rule, some desiring to assimilate with it, some living in what Bhabha and others have called "hybridity," a sense of a new identity combining elements of Indian and Anglo culture. At the center of the novel is an Indian physician, Dr. Aziz, and his relations with members of a British family, headed by Mrs. Moore, an elderly, spiritual woman, whose son Ronny is a functionary in the British rule in India and who is accompanied by Ronny's fiancée, Miss Adela Quested, a restless young woman who is both fascinated and, at times, frightened by the India she encounters.

Forster divides the novel into three major sections, each named by a category of space or place which also becomes the stage for an exploration of territory, the literal and figurative boundaries that can either unite or separate people from each other: "Mosque," "Caves," "Temple." Notice that the first and third name religious spaces that are institutionalized into places and territories, aligned with the two dominant Eastern religions associated with Indian history spanning centuries before the setting of the novel—Islam and Hinduism. The middle section, "Caves," does not carry religious associations with it, but something closer to space, though that space becomes a contested place, where boundaries are blurred and where events are disputed, never fully articulated or explained—something that precedes fully historical or cultural consciousness. The caves are literal spaces and places—Forster calls them the "Marabar Caves," a substitute for the actual Barabar Caves which inspired this nominally fictional space within the world of his novel.

The excerpt from Forster's novel, on pp. 464–68, begins with the opening of part 2, "Caves." As you read it, consider the degree to which Forster and his narrator move between description of space as a kind of phenomenal area and place as a geographical, cultural, and historical location. The opening suggests the degree to which Forster, who spent time in India, wishes the reader to associate geographical reality with spiritual and cultural dimensions: "The Ganges, though flowing from the foot of Vishnu and through Siva's hair, is not an ancient stream. Geology, looking further than religion, knows of a time when neither the river nor the Himalayas that nourished it existed, and an ocean flowed over the holy places of Hindustan." You may need to look up the proper nouns in these sentences, which suggest a narrator who wants his audience to know this river in specific ways—as part of an ongoing mythic narrative (its religious dimensions), but also as a product of natural history. How does this hybrid discourse place the performer both in the lived world of the river while at the same time giving voice to the historical and cultural narratives that point toward postcolonial matters?

Continue through the chapter, identify those parts of the narration that invoke the physicality of the space and those that emphasize such cultural practices as tourism and economic development. Forster is deliberately keeping the hybrid experience of India under British control at the forefront of the reader's consciousness of the landscape. In the third paragraph, he asks the reader to identify with a touristic experience of the caves that also carries with it elements of spiritual and cognitive confusion, which makes us especially aware of the ways in which the caves may indeed provide an experience that seems transcendent, but which may actually be muddled by all the elements of identity, cultural belonging, and historical positioning we carry with us into them:

Having seen one such cave, having seen two, having seen three, four, fourteen, twenty-four, the visitor returns to Chandrapore uncertain whether he has had an interesting experience or a dull one or any experience at all. He finds it difficult to discuss the caves, or to keep them apart in his mind, for the pattern never varies, and no carving, not even a bees'-nest or a bat distinguishes one from another. Nothing, nothing attaches to them, and their reputation — for they have one — does not depend upon human speech.

Try performing this passage both as the narrator observing the traveler and as the traveler himself attempting, in the third person, to articulate this experience, whose boundary from the social world of the return to the city becomes a line which speech, as an expression of consciousness, cannot embody. Is Forster saying that the caves cannot be apprehended in consciousness? Or can consciousness exist apart from language? Forster is careful to limit this description to that of "the visitor," but who is this? Is the visitor anyone who enters the cave, no matter what their nationality, ethnicity, religious belief, historical lineage? Or is the visitor only the non-Indian, whose experience of the caves can only be temporary and touristic? As the "Caves" section is set between "Mosque" and "Temple," one might argue that Forster is asking us to see the Marabar Caves as a space that, by the time of the novel, no longer attaches itself to anything social or cultural for any spectator. He says that, after all, "they are all older than spirit." Consider the multiple meanings this sentence may have.

Try performing longer sections from this chapter. Because of the third person point of view, the performer has many different options for creating a sense of identity for the narrator. One might be to create a "super-tour guide," someone who is leading us through the caves, giving us commentary as we move through them. If so, how is this tour guide different from others? How does this tour guide relate to those to whom he is speaking? There might be a degree of irony in the very act of describing the physicality of the caves, as the narrator suggests their full meaning and power is beyond words. Another possibility would be to consider the narrator as someone taking his audience on a religious pilgrimage into the spiritual experience of a space that precedes the products of civilization (the mosques and temples, and the Christian churches that are not part of the novel). How would the narrator's tone and way of relating to the imagined space of the cave and to his audience be different if the purpose of the trip was devotion rather than sightseeing? As a class, you might try sharing the narration, passing the description from one performer to another to create a sense of communal experience of language within the cave, or in chorus, finding words, sentences, and phrases that speak from a shared intersubjectivity of the caves rather than from a purely individual, subjective perception. How would you position yourselves within the performance space? Try using movement to create the sense of a territory marked off from the ordinary, from the everyday, from the Chandrapore outside your classroom.

Another way to explore the tensions between different cultural experiences of the caves might be to expand your reach to texts that describe the actual Barabar Caves that inspired Forster's Marabar Caves, keeping in mind that they are not identical. In particular, it might be useful to find descriptions written by Indian authors, who bring a different set of experiences, cultural knowledge, and relationships regarding the caves. Forster's text, while sympathetic to the damaging effects of British oppression for Indian culture, nonetheless cannot help being written from the perspective of someone who comes to India as an outsider with a different history rather than someone who grew up in the culture and whose family has lived there for centuries. See if you can find photographs or other visual images—these might serve as a countertext, producing a postcolonial dialogue with Forster's text. How might such a dialogue between verbal and visual language create a productive set of intertexts?

Included in the excerpt from the novel is a second passage, which begins on p. 465. This passage is not as purely descriptive as the first one and places the experience of the caves in a social setting, in which the borders between inside and outside make its role as a territory more explicit. This segment presents Mrs. Moore experiencing one of the Marabar Caves in ways she had not anticipated and which cause her deep discomfort—physical, psychological, and spiritual. Notice that Forster shifts from a more observational, reportorial, or editorial perspective to the omniscient narrator who focalizes the phenomenological experience of Mrs. Moore's consciousness in that space. As with the Willa Cather and Henry James excerpts in the previous chapter, the passage can be analyzed for the shifts in point of view. When does Forster's narrator describe Mrs. Moore and her experience? When does the language take on the elements of free indirect style, fusing the third person and the first person voices? Think about what is achieved when such shifts occur, not simply in character development and revelation, but in the sense of space, place, and territory as lived and cultural experiences. Miss Quested (Adela) and Dr. Aziz also have roles to play in this excerpt;

while the drama between them takes on much greater prominence in the remainder of the novel, their initial experiences of the caves must be placed in relation to Mrs. Moore's for the enormity of the toll the visit takes on Mrs. Moore to be as full and powerful as possible. Perhaps, along with the narrator and Mrs. Moore, an equally important character in this excerpt is the cave itself; critical to the success of a performance will be how you choose to have the cave speak its ominous, profound "Boum." Is it a sound all can hear, or does it appear only within the cave of Mrs. Moore's consciousness? Consider how its prominence might throw into question the degree to which outsiders, the colonizers, actually have any real power over the country of India.

Time: Experience, History, Culture

Time, which is often matched with space in theories of physics and of myth and spirituality and with place and territory in sociology, politics, and other fields of cultural study, is typically more difficult to describe and analyze, in part because it lacks the materiality, the thingness we more easily access with space and place. At the same time, most of us carry around a deeply intuitive sense of what time means and of its complexity in human experience, even though we may not often examine it. While it is outside the scope of our discussion to present the various competing theories of time currently debated in the physical sciences, it is safe to say that we can no longer assume that time moves in a single direction; developments in quantum physics suggest many more possibilities than our standard metaphor of "time's arrow," a phrase first coined by the astrophysicist Arthur Eddington. We are not suggesting that it is not possible or even probable to see time as pointing, like an arrow, from a moment in a past toward a future moment; indeed, this is how most of us intuitively think of time and, therefore, how we often experience time consciousness in our everyday lives. Rather, we want you to consider what other possibilities might exist in trying to conceive of time.

For our purposes, more important than resolving these rather thorny questions about the physics of time is the question of how we "perform" time, both in the phenomenological sense of how we live in our days — consciously and, from a psychological sense, unconsciously — and how time is also a deeply cultural and historical experience. If you have studied intercultural communication, you are no doubt aware of different systems cultures use for measuring time, from what constitutes a week or month, to larger, more abstract notions of time, such as the Australian aboriginal idea of dreamtime as a mythic period of creation but also an ongoing present in which the members of that culture participate. Think about something as seemingly everyday as the Western system for numbering years based on assumptions about the date of the birth of Christ. The principal way of dividing historical time is identified as B.C. (before Christ) and A.D. (anno Domini, Latin for "in the year of our Lord"). We tend to assume A.D., and more often these days we see the abbreviation B.C.E., "before the Common Era" (sometimes, "before the Christian Era" or "before the current era"). Which are you more familiar with? Can you see how arbitrary this kind of division is, and how there is the presence of an implied dominant paradigm? What is "common" about the years presumed to be part of the Common Era? Do you belong to a culture or group that marks years in different ways?

It is also true, as studies in anthropology and intercultural communication indicate, that different cultures experience time in different ways—not simply in terms of how years are marked, but in how time holds meaning for various cultures and what practices and acts are considered appropriate or part of belonging to a culture. In certain Native American cultures, for example, there are oral narratives that are only appropriate to tell during winter months, such as certain trickster tales, and to tell such tales in other seasons is to violate something sacred about that time period for that culture. It is interesting to note that many cultures, particularly those that have been subjugated or are not dominant, often talk about "_____ time" (fill in the blank with the name of the culture), which often means a later time than what is posted for an event; members of that culture understand that time is looser and more fluid within their own cultural events, and the term may also be used as a somewhat ironic and self-deprecating criticism of members of that culture. "Gay time," "queer time," "crip time," and so on, all point to the same bonding idea that, among other members of the culture, there is an assumption that events will always start late, perhaps because there is an assumed mutual understanding—an intersubjectivity—about the boundaries of time. It may also be a political move, suggesting that precision and timeliness are values imposed from the dominant culture, such that stretching time limits becomes a form of resistance.

Time has been one of the great subjects for artists, from Salvador Dalí's famous painting *The Persistence of Memory*, in which clocks are depicted as melting, to musical compositions by John Cage, who experimented with silence, repetition, length, and other features of time to expand our sense of musical time as an expression of the mutability of experiential time. Writers of fiction have been equally inventive and eloquent about time: Marcel Proust, for example, whose multivolume novel *In Search of Lost Time* (or *Remembrance of Things Past*) takes as its main event the narrator's sense memory of a madeleine (a French pastry) dipped in tea, which takes him back to recollections of childhood and a narrative that spans decades in French society, in which the interplay between social time and internal, subjective time consciousness may be viewed as the work's central dialogue. James Joyce, on the other hand, focused on a single day in Dublin in his novel *Ulysses*, in which the decade-long journey of Odysseus back to Ithaca after the Trojan War is recapitulated in twenty-four hours in a series of episodes, each mirroring a major book in Homer's epic, using various narrative techniques, including some that focus particularly on time as cyclical, nonchronological, personal, political, and so forth.

The great German novelist Thomas Mann has written about the complexities of time in narrative, most particularly in his novel *The Magic Mountain*, which tells the story of a young man, Hans Castorp, who spends seven years in a tuberculosis sanitorium. It is worth quoting Mann at length, from chapter 7:

> Can one narrate time—time as such, in and of itself? Most certainly not, what a foolish undertaking that would be. The story would go: "Time passed, ran on, flowed in a mighty stream," and on and on in the same vein. No one with any common sense could call that a narrative . . . Time is the *element* of narration, just as it is the element of life—is inextricably bound up with it, as bodies are in space . . . Narrative . . . has two kinds of time: first, its own real time, which like musical time defines its movements and presentation; and second, the time of its contents, which has a perspective quality that can vary widely, from a story in which the narrative's imaginary time is almost or indeed totally coincident with its musical time, to one in which it stretches out over light-years. (pp. 531–32)

Mann comes to the conclusion that one can narrate *about* time, and that time can be the subject of the kinds of storytelling that fiction writers perform. The passage above points to simultaneous ways of thinking about time of particular relevance to the performer: what we might think of performance time, the time it takes to perform a text (its duration), and content time, the span of time covered by the events of a story. If you think back to the terms of discourse discussed in chapter 8 as rhythm of action, you can see how durational time and content time can either correspond in roughly equivalent ways (in scene) or can collapse time (in summary) or slow time down (in description). Think, too, about the ways in which writers of fiction can omit or elide time—jumping from one year to another, for example, or reorder events, in some ways defying "time's arrow," using flashbacks and, less frequently, flash-forwards, to try to imitate the various ways the self is oriented temporally in multiple directions, often at the same "time."

An area both philosophers and psychologists consider is how time and memory are bound up in each other and how memory operates, not simply in neurological terms (although there are fascinating and exciting advances in neuroscience that are likely to contribute to deeper and more sophisticated ways of understanding how somatic—or body-based—our memories are), but in terms of what it means to have a memory, to have an experience that comes from the past but exists in the present. For example, a central question philosophers, particularly phenomenologists, often ask is what is the nature of the imaginal and sensory experiences we have in memory? Are they recalled from some storehouse contained within the body and within consciousness, or are they new products, essentially being created in the act of remembering (a new "membering," if you will)?

A novelist whose work is centrally concerned with the experience of time in consciousness is the British writer Virginia Woolf. In such novels as *To the Lighthouse* and *The Waves*, she explored the experience of consciousness, particularly the lines between sanity and madness, and the ways in which the streams of consciousness could be represented through language. As with writers like Proust and Joyce, time becomes a central figure (if not a character) in her fiction. One of her most renowned novels is *Mrs. Dalloway*, in which she follows the lives of about twenty characters on a day in London in June of 1923. She focuses particularly on the inner life of her title character, Clarissa Dalloway, a well-to-do middle-aged British housewife, as she makes final preparations for a dinner party she is giving that evening. Clarissa is by turns loving and cold, vain and self-critical, superficial and empathic—in other words, she is human, like all of us. Into her room, as she is trying to do some mending, comes a former sweetheart, Peter Walsh, whom she has not seen in many years and who has returned from a stint working in India under something of a cloud.

In the following paragraphs, Clarissa and Peter remember an incident from many years earlier, a holiday in the country that at the time may have seemed trivial, but which set them each on their life courses, no longer considering each other as a possible spouse. Notice how Woolf creates a sense of intersubjectivity in her narration, so that indirect discourse, particularly free indirect style, creates a sense of unspoken but authentic dialogue between these two, as though they can read each other's minds. They share a common history, a common time from the past, while in this very present scene:

> Then, just as happens on a terrace in the moonlight, when one person begins to feel ashamed that he is already bored, and yet as the other sits silent, very quiet, sadly looking at the moon, does not like to speak, moves his foot, clears his throat, notices some iron scroll on a table leg, stirs a leaf, but says nothing—so Peter Walsh did now. For why go back like this to the past? he thought. Why make him think of it again? Why make him suffer, when she had tortured him so infernally? Why?
>
> "Do you remember the lake?" she said, in an abrupt voice, under the pressure of an emotion which caught her heart, made the muscles of her throat stiff, and contracted her lips in a spasm as she said "lake." For she was a child, throwing bread to the ducks, between her parents, and at the same time a grown woman coming to her parents who stood by the lake, holding her life in her arms which, as she neared them, grew larger and larger in her arms, until it became a whole life, a complete life, which she put down by them and said, "This is what I have made of it! This!" And what had she made of it? What, indeed? sitting there sewing this morning with Peter.
>
> She looked at Peter Walsh; her look, passing through all that time and that emotion, reached him doubtfully; settled on him tearfully; and rose and fluttered away, as a bird touches a branch and rises and flutters away. Quite simply she wiped her eyes. (pp. 42–43)

As you have no doubt noticed, very little actually happens in these three paragraphs—that is, in terms of externalized action. Two people sit in a room, one of them asks a fairly innocuous question, they exchange looks, one finds herself tearful and wipes her eyes.

Yes, but in other ways, everything imaginable that can happen within and between two people happens in this passage, as well. They make a deep emotional, some might even say spiritual connection, without having to speak aloud; they return psychically to their shared past; they reckon with the changes the years have wrought on their feelings for each other—noticing both the constancy of something "central which permeates," to borrow a phrase Woolf uses elsewhere in the novel; and they acknowledge the irreversibility of their human, mortal, physical, and social lives. In particular, the middle paragraph captures all the complexity of time's many arrows for Clarissa—she exists in the present, a woman who has intimations of her own mortality (she has been ill in recent months), she recalls with a vividness of scene and action a childhood memory of throwing bread to ducks with her parents, and then also some less determinate time in which the bread is somehow transformed into her life, metaphorically, which she "puts down" by them, taking responsibility for the choices she made that ushered her into adulthood. And all of this happens in an instant within this paragraph—language, by its linearity, sequencing it into individual phrases as it must, but the sense should be of it all happening at the same time in the reality the flood of memories creates in her mind and body.

Try performing this passage, paying special attention to issues of timing and phrasing as they capture the sense of memory and presence in Woolf's language. How many Clarissas are present in each of the sentences? When Peter describes how she had tortured him, see if you can give your audience both the young man and the middle-aged man in the same voice, body, and language. You might also try dividing the text for different voices—are they in dialogue, overlapping, in unison? Where in the body are the images located? Make sure Clarissa's memory of throwing the bread carries with it bodily memory—practice being that child, making her way to the lake, perhaps scared and thrilled at the same time by the other living creatures, and then locating that feeling in the aging woman. How are these bodily ways of knowing and acting similar to and different from each other?

We have focused on the phenomenon of time in our discussion of the excerpt from Woolf. Following Bhabha's idea of location, in which time and space are interwoven, can you now add the dimension of space and place to your performance? Think about the multiple places in which this brief encounter occurs: a sewing room in a London home, with the noise of the city from the streets below as a backdrop; a lakeside at the height of Victorian England; the same lakeside, about ten years later, peopled not by protective parents, but by competing suitors and friends. A postcolonial perspective would challenge us to complicate the sense of time and place—location—even further. This is not just any time, any day in June, nor is it just any home, but a day in June in 1923, just a few years after the end of World War I, when England and its citizens are still struggling to restore a sense of safety and comfort to their domestic lives (a subplot in the novel parallels Clarissa and a young veteran, Septimus Warren Smith, who suffers from shell shock, what today would be called posttraumatic stress disorder). It is also a very white, upper-middle-class household, and the contrast between Richard, Clarissa's dull but financially and professionally successful husband, and Peter, always scraping to get by on the fringes of what is acceptable, is an important part of what happens between these two people. History and the culture of the British class system, including Peter's own experience with colonialism in India, are part of the fabric of this very intimate interpersonal encounter between two formerly romantic partners. While historical and cultural texts of time may not be as apparent or overt, they are necessarily present and inextricable from the kinds of people Woolf creates in this novel; if you are going to perform Clarissa and Peter, it is important to locate them in both space and time, in their geographical/cultural and historical places. Where are territorial boundaries drawn between them? Do they live within "institutions," visible and invisible—what Benedict Anderson calls "imagined communities"?

We will now turn to one more fictional text in which issues of time challenge the performer, by another British novelist, this time one more contemporary: Martin Amis's *Time's Arrow*, published in 1991, when it was short-listed for the Booker Prize, arguably the most prestigious literary award given in England. Rather than providing you with background to the novel, read the following excerpt from it. As you read and when you finish, see if you can articulate your initial responses to it, including what you think it is describing, what about it you may have found confusing, and how you make sense of it.

The standard affair, nowadays, will start something like this. It starts, in effect, with a moment of *horror*.

Most typically, it starts with a late-night drive to some little restaurant. The waiter has just brought us our dough, our honorarium or whatever it is, and we're sitting there quietly snorting or drooling into our brandy balloon, and relishing a perspicacious perfecto. We become aware that people are looking at us. And we don't like it when people are looking at us . . . Then our eyes will be firmly caught and firmly held by a bent female figure hurrying in through the door and across the room toward us. Fair, dark, slim, plump, elegant, not so elegant. Then she spins round. It's a big power moment when they spin round, with the flourish of challenge, and we get to see what they look like. Speaking personally for now, it's always cause for alarm, when they spin round—whatever they look like. Because here's the weird thing about these relationships with women: you get everything on the first date. Well, every now and then it's the second date, but generally it's the first. Instant invasion. Instant invasion and lordship. An hour or two here, max, is all it takes. Oh, mercy. You can go up to a woman on a street corner and start yelling at her and ten minutes later she's back at your place doing God knows what. On more than one occasion the first physical contact, the first touch, has been a slap or a shove: the swipe of her hand across Tod's feeble leer of—what? Lust? Contempt? All that needs to happen, in between, is this moment of horror I mentioned. It activates; it legitimates. It seems to be a necessary condition.

So she'll settle at the table, flushed, exalted, imperious, resolute—anyway, thoroughly pissed off—and I'll get the ball rolling with something like,

"Don't go—please."

"Goodbye, Tod."

"Don't go."

"It's no good."

"Please."

"There's no future for us."

Which I greet, I confess, with a silent, "Yeah yeah." Tod resumes:

"Elsa," he says, or Rosemary or Juanita or Betty-Jean. "You're very special to me."

"Like hell."

"But I love you."

"I can't look you in the eye."

I have noticed in the past, of course, that most conversations would make much better sense if you ran them backward. But with this man-woman stuff, you could run them any way you liked—and still get no further forward.

"Please. You can sleep over."

"This is goodbye, Tod."

"Beth," he'll say. Or Trudy or whatever.

"It just doesn't sit well with me anymore."

"Give me one more chance."

Then they launch into this routine. It lasts from nuts to soup. Don't get them wrong: Tod has his good points. He is, it is widely allowed, "very affectionate" (I think I know what that means. But how would *they* know?) (pp. 51–52)

Try to describe your first encounter with this passage. One immediate question you are likely to have is who the narrator is. The narrator speaks from an "I," so you probably initially assume, based on the conventions of literature in which you have been schooled, that this narrator is a character within the scene of story. The narrator also speaks in the first person plural ("we"), but in contexts that typically suggest the "we" refers to the narrator and his date. But then the narrator refers to the man involved in the affair as "Tod," suggesting some kind of distance or separation of identity between "I" and "Tod," unless this is the technique of someone referring to themselves in the third person.

In addition to trying to locate the identity of the narrator and his or her relationship to the characters in the scene (Tod and Elsa—or whichever woman it is this time), another puzzle might be trying to figure out the logical sequence and connection between the events narrated in this scene. The narrator announces in the first sentence that the passage will be describing "the standard affair," from the perspective of some sort of typical twentieth-century middle-class Western male—there is nothing particularly enlightened about Tod or the narrator. But, as we follow the narrator's description of the sequence of events, which is a very familiar pattern of courtship and interaction (meetings in restaurants and bars, quarrels over character and affection, moments initiating erotic contact), there still seems to be something off about them, as the narrator himself notes when he says, "most conversations would make much better sense if you ran them backwards." (We cannot imagine a female narrator here, although we can well imagine a female performer "performing" the masculinity of this text in a kind of knowing and possibly parodic, critical tone.)

In addition to reading this section aloud as a solo performer, try turning it into a scene using three performers: the narrator, Tod, and the woman ("Elsa," for our purposes). Have the narrator set the scene: where might he be located physically in relation to the characters and to the physical places in which it occurs? Have the performers playing Tod and Elsa speak only the dialogue given in quotation marks (the direct discourse), but have them try to enact physically the actions the narrator describes. Will they perform the actions simultaneously with the narrator's spoken descriptions of them? Before the narrator describes them? After? Try all three—what different effects emerge with each timing of them? As the three performers work together, what do you notice about the relationship between time, space, action, and the dramatic arc of the beginning, middle, and end of the affair?

Now, following the narrator's own observation, reverse the whole thing chronologically. This may, at first, seem like an unusual, even absurd direction, but try it out and see what happens. Begin at the point at which we ended the excerpt (the scene goes on in the novel) and read and enact the scene in the opposite order. When you get to the exchanges of dialogue, stop and try performing them a few times, first in the order Amis gave them in the novel and then in the reverse order. For example, begin with:

> TOD: Don't go—please.
> ELSA: Goodbye, Tod.
> TOD: Don't go.
> ELSA: It's no good.
> TOD: Please.
> ELSA: There's no future for us.
> TOD: Elsa, you're very special to me.
> ELSA: Like hell.
> TOD: But I love you.
> ELSA: I can't look you in the eye.

Now try:

> ELSA: I can't look you in the eye.
> TOD: But I love you.
> ELSA: Like hell.
> TOD: Elsa, you're very special to me.

ELSA: There's no future for us.
TOD: Please.
ELSA: It's no good.
TOD: Don't go.
ELSA: Goodbye, Tod.
TOD: Don't go—please.

Are the conversations the same whichever direction they go? If you agree that they are, what do you think this says about the nature of social interaction, about the scripted, even clichéd way we learn to perform very personal and emotional exchanges? If you think there are differences in the meaning of the lines when they are sequenced in a different order, try to specify how they are different; for example, how is the exchange "There's no future for us / Elsa, you're very special to me" different from "Elsa, you're very special to me / There's no future for us"? This passage raises the questions of what we might call the recursiveness of language and the reversibility of time and action, at a kind of microcosmic level—in what direction does time's arrow actually move?

Now go back and add in the narration—you may have to rekey it in order to get the sentences in the reverse order (don't try reversing word order within sentences—Amis has not used a palindromic technique!). Again, see if the order in which actions take place and the ways in which the narrator describes these actions carry significance when performed in reverse. What seemed like the beginning of a standard affair now makes more sense as the end of the affair.

Part of the confusion, of course, lies in the narrator's acceptance of the time he observes and experiences as "normal"—that is, forward-moving. You have no reason to doubt this, based on this brief, unframed excerpt (which is one reason we chose not to introduce the selection in any way)—most people view life as moving into the future, not into the past. Thus, we assume a kind of ordinary, commonsensical orientation toward time and the causality of how one event follows another (unless we assume a completely chaotic view of the universe, down to the smallest of social interactions). The narrator appears to be reliable, observing the scene between Tod and Elsa, and even the presence of the articulated "I" does not necessarily call this into question, as we have noted in previous chapters that there are works of fiction in which the authorial or observational narrator employs the "I" from time to time.

Obviously, a reading of the complete novel would help illuminate the overall technique Amis uses with regard to time and allow us to extrapolate from it to larger cultural issues he may be raising. The novel begins with the narrator describing himself in an operating room, with doctors working to save his life, and then proceeds to follow this narrator and his companion-character, Dr. Tod Friendly, over the course of decades of the life of the latter. We eventually discover that the narrating "I" is both part of and apart from Tod—he is, one might say, the transcendental "soul" of Tod—that part of Tod that is not enmeshed in the accumulated personal history Tod has acquired over his long life, but something attached to and separate from his overall sense of being. This narrator travels spatially and temporally, historically and individually with Tod, but in reverse time, as if the narrator's consciousness of Tod's life and the events of the world are a film running in reverse.

This explains not only the somewhat comic and cynical representation of courting rituals in the passage discussed above, but also scenes that appear to be surreal or phantasmagoric—in particular, scenes describing physical and medical events that are graphic and difficult to imagine, such as doctors implanting aborted fetuses in women's wombs, surgeons packing cancerous tumors into patients. Economic transactions seem puzzling and oddly utopian—people arrive at restaurants and are given money (the "dough, our honorarium or whatever it is" the narrator mentions at the beginning of the selection quoted above) in order to get them to eat the food they will be served. While Amis cannot completely sustain this (although he pushes it quite far, including scatological scenes in reverse, which may push the reader to certain imaginative limits), at a certain point (we suspect it varies from individual to individual) the reader discovers the secret of time in this novel and then reads in a kind of double way—both with the narrator as naive observer of time's arrow in reverse and as the knowing "implied reader" who views time in a more traditional, normative way. Which of these roles is that of the "narratee"? It might be possible to suggest that we are asked by this novel to perform both roles in a knowing, just as the performer simultaneously is and is not the narrator and the character and the narrator is and is not Tod. By the end of the novel, Tod has reached infancy, indeed the moment of conception, and disappears from the scene of story—and all that is left is the narrator as soul, the narrator as a kind of progenitor of a scene of discourse.

At this point, you may be wondering, what is the purpose of Amis's temporal method? Is it simply a "neat" technique, a kind of exercise in creative writing undertaken in order to become more attuned to manipulating time in narrative? This seems to us a very reasonable and important question, one we think the novel itself goes a long way toward answering, for about two thirds of the way through, the novel takes a historical and geographical turn that we as readers might not have expected—to Auschwitz, one of the most notorious Nazi concentration camps, where Tod Friendly (the name itself, as critics have pointed out, seems phony from the start, an amalgam of the German word for "death" and the ultimate American quality of amiability) reveals himself to be Odilo Unverdorben, a doctor assisting a character based on Dr. Josef Mengele, who experimented on inmates throughout the war. The reversal of time takes on tragic and ironic dimensions at this point, as the narrator, who seems blissfully unaware of history, sees the Nazis performing restorative surgery to Jews, disabled people, twins, and the other groups on whom Mengele practiced his experiments, which usually led to the death (the extermination) of the "patients." Our narrator even sees Nazis rebuilding the Jewish ghettos in cities and finally Jews moving freely in the cities. It is as if the war has ended, but, of course, the end is actually only the prelude to the Holocaust to come.

What do you suppose Amis is trying to say about human beings, about history, and about how we experience time and agency through his thematic use of time through reverse sequencing? Certainly one thing that occurs to us is that the narrator's lack of awareness of the "real" order of time may stand in larger metaphoric relationship for the willful ignorance of history by groups of people, for the apparent disregard for the fact that actions have consequences, that an act cannot be reversed, whether it is a spat between lovers or the extermination of a class of human beings. It may also speak to how we as humans bring our faulty consciousness and ethically benighted perspectives to bear upon history and on choices—that we may deny the implications of our own causality in the world. The narrator, because he is a soul rather than an embodied, historically situated, and culturally conscious subject, stands outside actions and does not understand their moral weight—the *horror* he rather melodramatically assigns to the start (in reality, the end) of the affair. We have used the words *real* and *reality* a number of times to distinguish our own sense of time from the narrator's but it is worth considering whether there are ways in which the narrator's sense of beginnings and endings has its own truth — is the "beginning" also always an "ending" and vice versa?

In addition to working with this excerpt from the novel (and we hope you will be inspired to seek out and read the entire book), you might apply some of Amis's techniques of playing in self-conscious ways with time in various fictional texts you may be considering for performance. What significant changes in the location, in the complex sense in which Bhabha uses the term, occur when not only place is shifted or transformed but time itself becomes more plastic, less uniform in its direction?

Performing the Vernacular: Locating Language and Culture

The third concept we will discuss in this chapter is that of the vernacular. As Dohra Ahmad explains, in her introduction to the anthology *Rotten English*, a collection of vernacular literature, the term originally referred to the languages of slaves and other oppressed people from groups that had been colonized by dominant cultures, either as a minority within a geographical region or as a people whose land has been taken over by outsiders. Poetry, fiction, and other kinds of creative writing written in the language of the oppressed was often referred to as "dialect literature" and carried with it a kind of patronizing or condescending attitude toward the culture; much of it was written by people outside the group, so the sense of colonization and oppression was doubled. Ahmad sees one of the principal projects of vernacular studies as a "reclaiming and valorizing" of previously devalued "linguistic codes": it is marked by the "choice of composing in linguistic codes that are primarily spoken rather than written and also ones that have generally been perceived as having a lower status than Standard English" (p. 16). This definition, of course, assumes English as the language against which vernacular language is measured, but the idea of the vernacular can be applied to any language and culture in which there is a power imbalance between one group and another.

Ahmad goes on to clarify what she sees as particularly radical about vernacular literature. She writes of its productive "duality": "from an openly debased slave language, to a mode associated with avant-garde experimentation and literary prowess" (p. 16). So, for Ahmad, it is not simply that vernacular literature reclaims the language spoken (and sometimes written) by oppressed, often indigenous groups, but that it actually demonstrates a more sophisticated and complex understanding of stylistic and narrative techniques. As she suggests, literary writers who work in vernacular traditions are not as concerned with what we might call ethnographic transcription of languages, but with how such languages may be used for artistic, cultural, and critical ends—a high form of what linguists call "code-switching," the ability to move between different languages and, more specifically, between different dialects or variations of a single language, usually depending on context and audience, such as the movement between African Amerian Vernacular English and Standard American English, or between various forms of Mexican Spanish, Mesoamerican native languages, and Standard American English, and/ or combinations of these together, as discussed by the feminist Latina scholar and poet Gloria Anzaldúa.

One thing we need to acknowledge before we proceed further is a distinction between vernacular language and culture per se and vernacular literature that emerges both from members of the usually subjugated cultures and from individuals who stand in a hybrid relationship somewhere between the oppressed culture(s) and the typically more elite cultures in which literary art is written, published, and distributed. As you might imagine, there can be tensions between and within these various groups of people; even people who share a common culture of origin may find their lives—and power relations—moving along different trajectories, with some gaining power and others remaining in subordinate economic and political positions, the latter sometimes feeling the former have benefited unduly from the status of those who remain less powerful.

Think about this argument. To what degree does it seem to have merit? Are there ways in which the literary artist can be seen as working to empower the vernacular culture? How? Can you think of examples from either your knowledge of literature or from popular culture (music, film, television, and so forth) in which vernacular culture and language have been appropriated by outsiders? One example often cited is rap music, which has its origins in the urban culture of African Americans (and to some extent, Hispanics), but which now finds its largest audience among white middle-class American adolescent and postadolescent males and is controlled financially by recording companies led primarily by people outside rap culture. Can people outside a vernacular culture ethically participate in that culture? This question is a critical one for performers to consider. At its best, the literary artist may be seen as endeavoring to establish a dialogic relationship between cultures, but he or she must do so with deep knowledge and respect for the vernacular culture, its people and traditions, and the meaning of its language; the same is true for the performer.

We have already explored a piece of prose fiction written in vernacular language: Jamaica Kincaid's "Girl" (p. 287) in chapter 8. Here we will look at its vernacular characteristics, approaching it in more complex ways than a purely formal analysis might lead to.

One of the most distinctive aspects of the story, as we pointed out, is its use of the second person point of view—"you," with an unnamed, arguably unspecified narrative identity. We considered the possible meanings and effects of such a choice of narrative perspective: a narrator who is guiding the "girl" of the title, or who is instructing, or who is ordering. What are the differences between each of these verbs, and how do they help you make choices about characterizing the narrator and her relationship to the girl? It is also possible that the "you" is someone very specific in the life of the girl—her mother, another female relative, a member of the community (and does it matter if that community member is male or female? We think it does), a collective voice of the community, or even voices from outside the community, imposing their will on the girl.

From the first reading of this compact story it suggests vernacular culture knowledge necessary for an informed understanding. Unless you were raised in the culture from which the story emerges or among people who were raised in that culture—that of Antigua, a small island in the Caribbean—some words in the story are likely to be foreign to you; hence, you will need to look up "benna," "doukona," "pepper pot," and so on. Beyond this, though, there are cultural beliefs and practices that will require some research, as they form much of the substance of the story's actions—the everyday performances of daily life for a female in this culture. Kincaid, who left Antigua several decades ago, moves easily between the dialect of her home island and the Standard American English of New York City and the literary circles in which she travels. In her memoirs, the narrative voice she adopts is that of Standard American English, with the vernacular voice of Antigua emerging primarily in moments of reported direct discourse, spoken by her relatives and other residents of the island—she rarely depicts herself speaking in the vernacular.

The style of "Girl," then, falls into a tradition Ahmad identifies as key to vernacular literature. It is not an attempt to transcribe Antiguan indigenous speech (a combination of English, French, and African-inflected words, grammar, and syntax) but, as Ahmad suggests, the work of a literary artist who stands in a hybrid relationship between her home culture and her adopted one. Look closely at the story—can you identify linguistic patterns or features that violate what you have been taught about how English grammar "should" be spoken or written? Which ones are they? What rules do they break? Can you still understand what the narrator is saying? The discipline of linguistics distinguishes between *descriptive* and *prescriptive* grammars, the former describing how people actually use language as groups in daily life and the latter articulating rules that groups of people (usually those in power, academic or otherwise) dictate as "proper." There is considerable debate today about the roles of descriptive and prescriptive approaches to language in society and education.

Think about how Kincaid's choice to employ vernacular language in this story is key to its meaning and to how you might choose to perform it. As we've suggested, Kincaid is capable of using Standard American English (as are many who choose to communicate primarily in vernacular English in their daily lives): it is not that they do not have knowledge nor even what the linguist Noam Chomsky calls "competence" (ability to speak in the Standard version), but that they choose to "perform" (another term Chomsky uses) in the vernacular, because it may be easier, more familiar, or, most important, it most richly and complexly expresses their thoughts and feelings and best communicates these to the audience they wish to reach. So why would Kincaid choose to write in the vernacular here, particularly as her implied audience (the majority, anyway) is not Antiguan natives, but readers who might encounter this story in *The New Yorker* or in a popular anthology?

We would suggest that the vernacular voice is essential to everything the story is trying to do. To write it in Standard American English would be to have the narrator stand at a greater distance from the life and world of the girl and her community. Even if this "girl" has long since left the Antigua of her childhood, the use of the vernacular suggests how much she has internalized the voices that spoke to her and, in a sense, "spoke her" (that is, made her into the kind of female her culture demanded she be), even if she has resisted it and eventually abandoned it. If we locate the story in the present of the girl's shift from childhood to adolescence (which the present tense of the story might argue for), then the vernacular language becomes even more forceful. Questions of location we considered above—space/place/territory and time/history—become intimately tied to the vernacular language and culture we encounter in Kincaid's story. This brief story offers a variety of possibilities—try performing it as the girl of the title, mimicking the voices she hears or internalizing them against her will. Try performing it as one or more of the women of the village. Try it as someone who no longer actively participates in the culture, but who carries it within her. What emerges from each approach? How might a group of performers approach it? How might you use performance space in ways that articulate your understanding of the connection between vernacular culture and the substance of the story?

We have emphasized the differences between standard and nonstandard forms of English thus far in our discussion of the vernacular in performance. Equally powerful can be those texts and performances that represent the lives and practices of people from oppressed or subjugated groups, whether they use Standard American English or combine it with vernacular language. Without falling into what has been called a culture of victimhood, in which we emphasize what has held people back and what keeps people disempowered, it might be worth your taking time to think about the different cultural groups to which you belong that are not part of what you define as the dominant culture, and what kinds of knowledge, language, and actions you engage in with other members of these groups that help you bond or experience relatedness, give you a sense of kinship, and help you celebrate your history and resist attempts to erase or dilute the traditions of your culture. For example, African American slaves in the pre–Civil War South (and parts of the North) were not permitted to marry legally; as a substitute, a tradition was established of "jumping the broom," in which a couple jumped over a broom as a symbol of their commitment to each other. The origins of this tradition have been debated extensively; some find its origins in West African traditions (some folklore scholars trace it to European or nomadic traditions as well), some see it as established by plantation owners to keep slaves "happy." Today, of course, heterosexual couples of color are able to marry legally, but some couples include the ritual of jumping the broom as part of the ceremony, to remind them and those gathered of a shared heritage, a way of honoring countless black men and women who committed themselves authentically and fully even when the law did not acknowledge them. We have heard of same-sex couples, black and not, performing the same ritual as a sign of a solidarity with traditions of marriage exclusion shared by various people outside white heteronormativity. Thus, performances that originate in the experiences of historically oppressed groups can retain power in contemporary society.

KEY TERMS

descriptive vs. prescriptive grammars

dialogism

intersubjectivity

location

phenomenology

place

postcolonialism

space

territory

time's arrow

vernacular culture

Chapter 10

SOLO PERFORMANCE OF DRAMA I: INTRODUCING SCENE ANALYSIS

"Me to play," says Hamm, one of the two protagonists of Samuel Beckett's play *Endgame*. It is Hamm's first line of dialogue and announces both the themes of the play and Hamm's own positioning of himself in the play's set of conflicts: between Hamm and his servant/slave Clov; between Hamm and his antiquated parents, Nagg and Nell, legless and consigned to trash cans; between Hamm and an unidentified outside world, which has been variously described as a postholocaust world, a world destroyed by plague, pestilence, and war; and, on some levels, conflicts within Hamm between his different sides (commanding ruler of his small domain and highly dependent and vulnerable body, blind and, in this world, confined to a wheelchair). The title of Beckett's play, as rendered in English, also evokes scripted, fictive conflicts, most specifically the game of chess. In chess, the endgame is the stage of the game after the queen has been captured and all that is left are inevitable moves that lead to checkmate and the capture of the king, at which point the game is over.

Notice how Beckett renders Hamm's sentence in English: it is fragmentary, a curious syntactic construction—not "It is my turn to play" or the even more active "I play," but "Me to play." Thus he situates himself as a "me," an object, whom he directs "to play," almost as an observer or as a referee might call the plays of the game. Hamm's locution acknowledges the degree to which it is virtually impossible for him to use language in an unmediated way—that the very act of speaking creates a script that stands between action or feeling or thought and their expressions.

This is drama stripped down almost to its barest essentials—there is not much less one could have in a play and still recognize it as a play that follows in a tradition that, in the West, stretches back to the Greek tragedies of Aeschylus, Sophocles, and Euripides. More recent playwrights, such as Tom Stoppard and Tony Kushner, have created hybrid plays in which realism, intellectual problem play, and fantasy/surrealism sit side by side, often within the same dramatic frame or scene, to create a dramatic experience that defies easy categorization. In each case, one could argue that Hamm's declaration "Me to play" is equally a statement of purpose and being for playwright, characters, and audience. The word *play* is as central as the "me" in this economical motto.

The word *drama* is derived from the Greek word for "action," in turn derived from another Greek word meaning "to do." At the heart of virtually all conceptions of drama is the notion of action—"something taking its course." The nature of that something can vary widely—from the War of the Roses depicted in Shakespeare's historical plays to the whispering of stream of conscious mutterings of a disembodied mouth in a spotlight in Beckett's one-act play "Not I." For some critics and theorists, the closer one gets to the kind of experience of Beckett's "Not I," the farther one may get from drama as traditionally defined; for such critics, drama usually carries with it some notion of that which is external, even physical.

What is the "play" in a play? The word is both a noun and a verb, and one might argue that the verb precedes the noun in establishing its use in dramatic theory and criticism. "Play," at its simplest, refers to the kind of activity that animals, human and otherwise, engage in for entertainment and pleasure, activities that typically are engaged in for their own sake with an understanding that they are not primarily intended for material profit or change. Indeed, the lines become blurred in cases such as professional athletics, when financial rewards take precedence over the value of participating in or observing the interactions of players as they run, skate, or ride, hitting, throwing, catching, and shooting or compete against one another in shows of skill, strength, and speed. For this reason, some people prefer to participate or watch amateur players, such as weekend soccer or softball leagues, where the boundaries between play and the "real world" are more easily acknowledged.

Similarly, we have probably all had the childhood experience of being engaged in play and have it take on dimensions that blur the lines of demarcation, as when an interpersonal conflict emerges in a game of house or cops and robbers that has genuine ramifications for the players outside the sphere of the playground, or, not limited to childhood, where the pleasures of building a sand castle may speak to otherwise unstated wishes, desires, dreams, and fantasies. So, while we may begin by saying that we play to place ourselves outside the realm of work, we need to add that, as Victor Turner famously said, there is a seriousness to play—in reality, it can never be entirely bracketed from everyday responsibilities. This observation about gamesmanship brings us to another important idea in dramatic play, and that is conflict. Traditionally, conflict, the heart of drama, is represented as occurring between individuals or sometimes between individuals and forces that extend beyond the human. But conflict, that sense of opposition or tension between different forces, people, or other entities is central to virtually all notions of drama.

At this point, some clarification of terminology is appropriate. You may have noticed that, thus far in this chapter, we have used the word *drama* rather than *theater* as the focus of our exploration. Sometimes the terms are used interchangeably, but there are important and useful distinctions to be drawn between the two. Perhaps the most common distinction is that *drama*, as a term, is often used to refer to the literary text being performed, as distinguished from other kinds of texts, through conventions of the genre; drama, in the terms Aristotle set down over two thousand years ago, refers to texts that are spoken through characters who are clearly defined as "not the author." Thus, a poem by Sappho in which the speaker expresses the emotions of the author would not be seen as drama, whereas the play *Oedipus the King*, in which all the dialogue is placed in the mouth of characters who are not representing the playwright, Sophocles, would be drama. This is what Aristotle called a difference in modes. As we have suggested throughout this book, contemporary criticism complicates this distinction by suggesting that all literary texts involve some kind of mediation between author and speaker, and one could also argue that Sophocles' voice and attitudes are expressed through his characters, especially the chorus.

Nonetheless, the general distinction is worth keeping in mind. Further, most critics reserve the term *drama* to describe the category of literary texts that are presented primarily through dialogue, language represented as speech—although here too exceptions immediately leap to mind, such as the soliloquies characteristic of Shakespeare's great tragedies. Some might argue that it is in the soliloquies that the conventions of genre are combined into a hybrid of the lyric element of representation of interior mental and emotional processes and the dramatization of a character who is defined as other than the playwright. Drama tends to use external action—including the external action of speech—as a way of representing social action and individual character. As we shall see, much contemporary drama "plays" with this general statement in ways that are interesting and transformative.

Notice that here we have also modified the word *performance* with "solo," whereas it was simply inferred throughout the rest of the book; we have done this to draw attention to its somewhat unique position within the kind of course you may be enrolled in and in the changing shape of the disciplinary practices of performance studies and the performance of literature in particular. Some would argue that dramatic texts are typically written with specific performance venues in mind—usually what we might think of as "theater" (hence, the distinction between "drama" and "theater" maintained by many theorists and critics); such individuals would argue that drama finds its most immediate and authentic (a tricky word) embodiment in theatrical production, usually involving multiple performers and in the realistic modes of production that dominated much of theater of the past century, productions in which an individual performer—an "actor"—played a single role within a performance, thus underscoring the audience's "willing suspension of disbelief" and encouraging actor and audience to draw a strong imaginary identification between actor and character.

Drama provides a special case in that, throughout its history, it has generally been written with performance in mind, often with a specific theater and set of performers in mind; it therefore may have been shaped in its very composition by a hypothesized performance that in and of itself involves multiple performers (as well as certain kinds of settings, scenery, costumes, and so forth—even particular theaters). But we would argue that there are many values to exploring dramatic texts through solo performance that may yield different kinds of experiences and knowledge of the dramatic text for both performer and audience. Even further, we hope to show the ways in which many contemporary plays blur conventional distinctions between drama and other kinds of texts—both those written primarily for the page and those composed with performance in mind from the start. The conventional limits of drama have been tested and, we will suggest, expanded, and thus the solo performer may indeed make claim to drama as a legitimate textual arena from which to draw, for historical, artistic, and cultural reasons and purposes.

A History of and Rationale for Solo Performance of Drama

The history of solo performance of drama is longer and richer than might first be expected, especially if one broadens the scope of the category beyond the conventions of oral interpretation of literature. Going back to the ancient Greek tragedians, we find the origins of drama in the dithy-rambic chorus, more narrative in its nature than dramatic. Tradition marks Thespis as the first actor/playwright to step out of the chorus and speak as an individual. While much of this history can never be recovered, it is important to note that Western theater began as a choral art, sung or chanted, and then added individual speaking voices. Aeschylus is supposed to have added a second actor and Sophocles a third. Rarely did the Greek tragedians have more than three characters onstage at a time (not including the chorus); it is possible that these three actors took on multiple roles, though never within the same scene. Thus we see in the origins of the art the kind of fluidity of roles, assisted by stage-craft such as masks, that has become a hallmark of the solo performer of drama. Whether Thespis spoke in monologues or in dialogue with the chorus we will probably never know with certainty, and whether he assumed different roles in different scenes is open to debate. What is most important for our purposes is an acknowledgment that performers and audiences, as far back as we have records, participated together in conventional performance practices that allowed the performer of drama to assume more than one character within a single performance.

Throughout history, we also have had a consistent practice of the playwright as performer, both literally and figuratively. Roman play-wrights like Seneca wrote primarily for private readings, prefiguring the nineteenth-century movement for closet drama, in which the oral perfor-mance of the dramatic text was not merely a preliminary for a staged production, but an end in itself. More common throughout history has been the practice of a playwright reading the play for the production company, including actors and the director, who will then mount a staged production. Thus, theorists such as Leland H. Roloff have suggested that the solo performance of drama offers the individual an opportunity to take on the point of view of the playwright and, in doing so, to evoke a kind of creative act, one that can be markedly different from the theat-rical production resulting from the more overtly collaborative nature of the combined work of an ensemble of actors, director, and designers. Of course, as Roloff and others would hasten to add, the solo performance is itself a collaborative act between text, performer, and audience at the very least, and others might argue that the cultural context in which such performances take place is another part of the collaboration.

In the eighteenth and nineteenth centuries, with the development of the public performance movement known as elocution (known in the early twentieth century as expression, which became interpretation or oral interpretation, as it is still often called today), there was a strong interest in the solo performance of drama. Some of this was a result of cultural prejudices against theater as a social site of "immoral" behavior, and some because of a belief that acting was itself an ethically and aesthetically "excessive" endeavor — it violated codes of modesty and, in some cases, was even viewed as a violation of the religious commandment against making false idols. Echoes of these moral and aesthetic sentiments combined with financial opportunities and exigencies of the time, and well-known actors (particularly female actors) often made a handsome income on the side doing solo readings of plays during the off season. For many, it was simply a matter of survival; for others, we can assume that it offered a kind of artistic opportunity that conventions of theater may have, in general, precluded. One of the most famous of these actress-readers was Charlotte Cushman, who was regarded as the supreme American Shakespearean actress of her time, even playing Romeo to her sister's Juliet. In addition to her cross-gender performances, Cushman was renowned for her evening-long performances of full Shakespearean plays in which she would sit at a desk or table with text in front of her and read the play — although the verb *read* does not do justice to Cushman's abilities to make the play, its characters, and their language come into being. For a detailed and insightful history of the profession of solo performance, see John S. Gentile's *Cast of One*.

Another contemporary scholar who has offered a sustained and thoughtful argument for solo performance of drama is Timothy J. Gura. In his essay "The Solo Performer and Drama," Gura suggests that the solo performance of the dramatic text is best viewed as offering a kind of deep knowledge of the dynamics of a play, some of which may be richer and more focused in solo performance, although some of them may be lost. Gura argues that there can be a "spectacle fact" that the restrictions of solo performance simply cannot put forward; he draws on such physical actions as a kiss, a pie fight, and so on, as examples. It is undeniable that the more a physical act depends on simultaneous physical contact between two characters, the more likely it is that the dramatic effect will be lost or diluted by its embodiment in the solo performer, who must typically work in an aesthetic of contiguous or sequential action.

Gura nonetheless encourages solo performers of drama to consider their role as scenographers of their own individual productions, by which he means to consider the visual (and aural and interpersonal) dimensions of the aesthetics of the single body presented for an audience. He writes of the "virtual space" evoked by the solo performance of drama and argues that the imagined space of projection, while narrower than that of the traditional stage space, may in its very narrowness and "virtualness" focus performer, audience, and therefore the play in different and productive ways.

No argument beyond this need be made for the value of the solo performance of drama from a pedagogical perspective: if solo performance can offer the student performer and classroom audience insights into aspects of a play different from those provided by a silent reading or staged production, then no more justification need be provided, as the student in the classroom is our primary focus in this book. On the one hand, the saturation of our imaginations with digital media might be an argument against the efficacy of solo performance of drama: in a world of computer-generated imagery (CGI) and Grand Theft Auto IV (or whatever version we have reached by the time you read this), one might expect that a performance approach so dependent on the virtual (or even the absent) would prove difficult or unsatisfying for audiences. But could one mount the opposite argument? Not simply that this is precisely why we need such things as solo performance of drama, that is, as a corrective to lazy imaginations (a moralistic standpoint), but in response to the reality of how imaginations are evolving, that more and more young people are participating in what was a passive audience experience in the past. Cinema has become more and more what Marshall McLuhan called a hot medium in the sense of offering what many would argue are excessive amounts of stimuli and detail, but at the same time, more and more students are gaining sophisticated knowledge of the virtual through participation in such phenomena as Facebook, MySpace, and Second Life, and it might be that the virtual, rather than the "real," has become a more dominant aesthetic realm. It may be that computer-generated images do not simply fill in for what the brain used to imagine, but that the viewer's more complex knowledge of what is entailed in such technologies makes them more participatory. The creation of avatars and participation in the worlds of digital space and imagination may offer a return to the fuller engagement of imagination.

Ibsen's *Ghosts*: A Sample Analysis of a Scene

We hope that we have sufficiently interested you in the possibilities of solo performance of drama that we may now move on to analyze a scene from a play from that perspective. Our principal goals are twofold: 1) to offer you an example of what the central elements of drama as a genre are and how they may be identified and discussed in relation to a specific scene, and 2) to then consider what the performance challenges for the solo performer of this scene might be.

We have selected a scene from Henrik Ibsen's 1881 play of social realism, *Ghosts*. Social realism refers to the movement that Ibsen, along with Anton Chekhov, Maxim Gorky, and, in some of his plays, August Strindberg pioneered, in which drama and theatrical production were used to present a slice of life onstage, usually employing what has been called the "fourth wall," a perspective in which the audience is considered to be spectators overhearing and viewing, as if under a microscope, the everyday lives of people. Of course, the everyday lives are transformed as a result of an event or events in the plot that occur within the time the play covers (sometimes a single day, sometimes years). Some playwrights pushed this stagecraft and play structure to an extreme point, which was then called naturalism. Émile Zola was one such playwright (he was also a novelist and journalist); he believed that theater should only include that which can be apprehended empirically, that is, by the physical senses. Later versions of naturalism led to such phenomena as kitchen sink realism (or kitchen sink drama), in which playwrights and directors deliberately chose characters and plots that violated Aristotle's concept of tragedy as being concerned with people of heroic stature and staged their plays with working stoves, running water, and so forth.

The social realism plays of Ibsen were seen as a corrective to the melodramatic and romantic forms and flourishes of earlier nineteenth-century playwrights. They combined the goal of presenting people and life as it "really" was (that is, including settings such as living rooms, actions such as sewing and knitting, dialogues that tended toward the mundane) with an emphasis on a critique of social mores and problems. *Ghosts* is often viewed as Ibsen's rejoinder to the criticism of his earlier play, *A Doll's House*—a play that ends with its heroine, Nora Helmer, walking out on her husband, children, and house because she can no longer live with the hypocrisy entailed in being the "doll" of the title. In a sense, *Ghosts* shows us what might happen to a woman who chooses to remain, to maintain society's standards.

The play centers on another of Ibsen's memorable female characters, Mrs. Alving, the widow of Captain Alving, a prominent sea captain. At the start of the play, Mrs. Alving is in the midst of having an orphanage built from the money she has inherited from her late husband. Her son, Oswald, has returned from studies abroad. The other characters in the play are Pastor Manders, the town clergyman, with whom Mrs. Alving has had a past, complicated relationship; Engstrand, a local handyman; and Regina, who is initially depicted as the daughter of Engstrand, but who was actually fathered by Captain Alving. While the play contains some traditionally theatrical actions, such as the offstage burning down of the orphanage at the end of the second act, most of its action unfolds in a series of scenes between the various characters, in which we see them engaged in familial and social roles and with revelations of the impact of past actions on the present. Most shocking, for its time, is Mrs. Alving's revelation that Captain Alving, far from being the upstanding citizen he appeared to be, was actually a promiscuous, hypocritical, and irresponsible husband and father, who gave Mrs. Alving syphilis as a result of his philandering, a disease she unknowingly passed on to her son. Oswald and Regina fall in love, a relationship that is thwarted by Mrs. Alving's revelation of Regina's true parentage (her mother was a maid in the Alving household, and Engstrand married her for the sake of propriety and appearance).

In the final act of the play, Oswald confesses his own sexual adventures to his mother; he is wracked with guilt, as he has begun to experience the symptoms of syphilis, until his mother reveals that he has been fated from the start to suffer from this illness (although she only comes to realize this when Oswald reveals his symptoms). Tertiary syphilis then (and still today) has the potential to lead to madness, neurological deterioration, and death. The play ends with Oswald's rather sudden decline into the later stage of the disease, where he begs his mother to kill him with the drugs he has in his pocket; as the curtain falls, Mrs. Alving remains torn, unable to act, as Oswald repeats over and over his desire for his mother to "give [him] the sun."

Perhaps what proved most troubling for initial audiences—and what gives the play its continuing power and resonance today—and in addition to its treatment of sexually transmitted disease and hints of incest, is the underlying social reality the play suggests: that someone like Mrs. Alving, depicted as virtuous for having resisted her own desire to leave her husband for Pastor Manders decades earlier (and having been instructed to return to her profligate husband by the good pastor himself) is nonetheless "punished" by the illness her husband has passed on to her and which she has "innocently" passed on to her son. If we consider that the play was composed roughly around the same time that medicine was developing the germ theory of disease, the biomedical and socioethical themes of the play parallel each other in ways that must have been discomforting for its audiences: the syphilis germ does not discriminate between those who have been faithful and those who have not, and the biblical injunction that the "sins of the fathers shall be visited upon the sons" is literally and figuratively true. That Oswald has been sexually active is presented in an open and, ultimately, nonjudgmental way in the scene in which he confesses such behaviors to his mother. She, in turn, suggests that perhaps if she had shared more openness to pleasure and "the joy of life" with her husband, he might not have turned to other women.

The play regained significant interest in the 1980s when another sexually transmitted disease, HIV/AIDS, became part of the social scene; as with syphilis a century earlier, it is deadly and it invokes all kinds of moral and moralistic discourse (in this case, around the populations where it was first identified—homosexual men and intravenous drug users—and by the modes of transmission—nonprocreative sexual activity and the use of illegal substances through needles).

Let's now turn to a central scene from the play and consider what analytic tools we need to prepare it for solo performance and what technical challenges it poses for the solo performer. The scene is from the end of act 1 of the play; you will find it on p. 469. Following conventions of the era, Ibsen has begun the play with scenes that establish the setting and the characters: we have met Regina and her father in a brief dialogue that reveals her desire to remain as a servant/companion to Mrs. Alving rather than return to her father's house, where, it is implied, she would probably end up as her mother did, sexually serving sailors and other local men. We meet Pastor Manders and observe Regina suggesting to him that she might become a servant in town (and perhaps flirting with him, using feminine wiles to play on his sense of paternal protection toward a young woman). Pastor Manders notices some forbidden books among Mrs. Alving's reading fare, and she and the minister debate the value of such literature. Oswald finally arrives onstage, and we see him engage in argument with Manders about the moral significance of unmarried couples living together, as he has seen them do in his student days. Oswald exits and Mrs. Alving and Pastor Manders are once again left alone to continue their earlier discussion. But before we analyze the scene, we will introduce some fundamental terms and ideas in dramatic analysis.

Some Dramatic Theories and Terminology

Before we discuss the actual scene, it may be useful to review a few common terms we will be using (see also pp. 248–49 in chapter 8). Aristotle's foundational text in Western drama, the *Poetics*, is often hypothesized to be a schematic set of notes commenting upon tragic drama during the golden era of Sophocles and Euripides, looking back to the earlier tragedies of Aeschylus. Aristotle declared that drama (and here he spoke exclusively about tragic drama) consisted of the following elements:

1. Plot: not simply the events contained within the play, but the shape and structure through which the action is represented.
2. Character: the individuals whose actions are represented in the play. Aristotle was particularly interested in the moral aspects of character and used the same word (*ethos*) in both the *Poetics* and the *Rhetoric*, in which he looked at the structure and function of persuasive speech.
3. Idea or theme: the philosophical issues explored in the play.
4. Language or style: the specific choices of word (diction), imagery, and rhythm (Aristotle was writing about drama composed in verse).
5. Spectacle: the visual elements of stagecraft—a concept Gura addresses at some length in his consideration of the solo performer's challenges.
6. Music: tragedy, in Aristotle's time, always involved music, including chanting, so this was an essential element of drama for him and his contemporaries.

Consider which of Aristotle's elements of drama seem to you still relevant to your experiences of drama, as a silent reader, as a performer, and as an audience member. Which seem central to a full apprehension of the scene from *Ghosts*?

In addition, the influence of psychology, political science, and sociology on the analysis of drama has been significant. We will be speaking of motivation in our discussion of the two principal characters in this scene and, while it is outside our scope to review all the competing theories and concepts of motivation present in contemporary discourse, we would emphasize Freud's and Marx's contributions to popular ways of thinking about motivation. What Freud added most importantly is the idea that all human beings possess (or are possessed by) a mental state he called the unconscious, a state of unawareness not immediately available to the individual, but nonetheless a location where drives, wishes, dreams, and desires often reside most powerfully. For Freud, motivation could not be determined exclusively by what an individual was able to assert about his or her own waking consciousness. And, while there were theorists of the social who preceded Marx (such as the Enlightenment thinkers, including Locke, Rousseau, and others), it was Marx who most powerfully argued for the role of the social in the formation of the individual: that society, in all its complexity, precedes the individual and that individual drives and desires are inextricable from the social context and forces in which the individual lives. We will not get any more technical than this about Freudian and Marxist views of character, but the more you study drama, the more you may wish to pursue the impact of these thinkers on theories of character and selfhood.

Both Freud and Marx are also useful in considering another term, *subtext*, the concept that underneath what is said and done onstage there may be—consciously or not—a competing, oppositional, or hidden alternative text at work within a character or between characters. An interesting experiment in playwriting is Alice Gerstenberg's one-act play of 1913, *Overtones*, in which four actresses take on the role of two women in a social conversation—two actresses play one woman (Harriet, "a cultured woman," and Hetty, "her primitive self") and two the other (Margaret and Maggie, likewise cultured and primitive). Imagine the possibilities of solo performance of this text, or of a duet performance in which each performer takes on both sides of one character or perhaps the cultured or primitive side of both characters. Experiments such as these led to plays like Eugene O'Neill's expressionist play *Strange Interlude*, in which individual actors speak both in their social roles and in the subtexts of their actual feelings.

One other concept that is useful is derived from the great Russian director and teacher Konstantin Stanislavsky, and that is of the dramatic unit, the "beat." While there are many ways to define this term, the simplest one might be as the smallest emotional or psychological unit of a scene—a beat begins and ends when there is a shift in motivation or objective, some say when new information is provided that shifts the focus or movement of a scene. So, while Ibsen did not break down his play into units smaller than the act, it is possible for the reader and the

performer to break down any large unit of a play into its smaller, constit-
uent beats, allowing for closer analysis of motivation. (Interestingly, there
is some argument over whether Stanislavsky derived the term from the
realm of music, where a beat might be viewed as the next-smallest iden-
tifiable unit of a musical work after the measure, or whether it is actually
a misunderstanding of the English word *bit*, a small part.) After reading
the scene from *Ghosts*, are you able to break it down into its beats? Where
do you mark the shifts, and why? How might identifying the division of
the scene into beats in different ways produce different ways of understanding the scene's role in the plot, different ways of analyzing characters
as individuals, and different ways of understanding their interaction and
interpersonal relationships?

Conflict in Ghosts

This is a scene steeped in the simultaneity of past and present. As Manders
says, "The moment is well chosen. To-morrow is the tenth anniversary
of your husband's death; to-morrow the memorial to the departed will
be unveiled; to-morrow I shall speak to the whole assembly that will be
met together. But to-day I want to speak to you alone." Notice that this
speech by Manders marks the urgency of the play's setting and action —
the ancient Greeks spoke of *kairos*, the "propitious moment" at which
an event or speech might be performed. So for Pastor Manders, this is a
moment of *kairos*. Similarly, for Mrs. Alving, Oswald's return home after
many years away is a moment of *kairos*: he is here in part for the opening
of the orphanage named to honor his father's (false) memory. Thus, while
the dialogue between Mrs. Alving and Manders may seem primarily to
be driven by the playwright's need to provide a forum for debate over
social morality, there is a sense of dramatic rightness, even urgency, to
their interaction, particularly as they revise their shared history together.

    Thus, from the start of this scene between the two characters, who
may, at first glance, seem to be mouthpieces for the playwright, one
standing for all that is liberal and open (the playwright's position) and
one standing for propriety and convention at all costs, there may be
more conflict than a simple debate. In this sense, *plot* (what happens, as
shaped and articulated by the playwright's selection of which events to
present onstage, how much attention to give them, and how to guide the
audience's understanding of them) is inextricably tied to *character* (the
agents, or individual people, involved in the dialogue and the action).

For Aristotle, plot and character were the two most important elements of drama. In some sense, he suggested that they were all that was absolutely necessary for drama. Think for a moment—in what ways is this statement true? He also stated that plot contained character—that it was, in some ways, more central to drama than character. What do you suppose he might have meant by that?

Manders and Mrs. Alving have established the social or exterior motivation, the central purpose, for their meeting—a discussion of the festivities planned for the opening of the orphanage. We have also noted, in Manders's speech, a possible psychological motivation for his visit and dialogue with Mrs. Alving: to remind her of her religious and spiritual flaws, in the case of her support of Oswald's statements about "free love," and, perhaps unconsciously, to revisit their history together, which he brings up in his reminder that she came to him when she decided to leave her husband after a year of marriage. The two aspects of motivation are clearly intertwined; what makes them so interesting for the performer is trying to decide to what degree Manders is aware of what may still reside underneath this episode from long ago. Consider the various possibilities: an unrequited love of Mrs. Alving for Manders, a mutual attraction that he knew social convention would not allow to be expressed or fulfilled, an expiation of guilt for sending her back to Captain Alving, or some combination of these, or even others we have not yet discovered. One of the tenets of realistic drama is that such motivations are rarely singular and, following Freud's theory of the unconscious, may be latent rather than overt.

Now think about Mrs. Alving at the beginning of this scene. Remember that she and Manders had had a brief quarrel over her reading material before the entrance of Oswald; this, and Oswald's own debate with Manders, may have prepared her for a more direct confrontation with him in this scene: what had remained politely indirect earlier may by now have been stoked, like a pot of water on the verge of boiling over. Her responses to Manders's rather overly pious preaching about her duty begin with some of the indirection of her dialogue from earlier in the act, lines like "Have you forgotten how unspeakably unhappy I was during that year?" and "You know quite well what sort of a life my husband was living at that time—what excesses he was guilty of." These lines suggest that she is still not quite prepared to name the thing itself—his sexual demands on her and his decision to seek sexual fulfillment with other women. Some of this indirection is historically and socially determined; they are the ways a proper woman in the Victorian era in which the play is set would try to speak through implication and inference about unpleasant and indecent matters. Some of it may suggest Mrs. Alving's own unconscious repression of sexual desire, particularly the memory of sexual desire for Pastor Manders. How will you play these exchanges? With silences punctuating what is not said?

As the scene progresses, one of the challenges you may find is that for quite some time Pastor Manders dominates the dialogue with long speeches in which he mainly utters homilies about duty. It would be easy for Mrs. Alving to be lost to the audience in the visual aesthetics of the solo performer, quite possibly in a conventional staging, as well. Therefore, Mrs. Alving's shorter speeches, often a sentence or a few phrases, become crucial to maintaining the sense of a scene between two characters. Ibsen gives the performer a lot to work with, however, as Mrs. Alving's speeches, though brief, often cut through Manders's sanctimony to a deeper truth. When he scolds her for coming "very near to imperiling the reputation of others into the bargain," she responds, "Of others? Of one other, you mean?" In these few words, she upsets Manders's comfortable rhetoric of wifely duty by forcing him to confront the degree to which he had been equally self-centered in their past encounter, more worried about his priestly reputation than about helping another person. Again, Mrs. Alving's measured words suggest her greater interior complexity: "With our priest? With our intimate friend?" This balancing of roles—"priest" and "intimate friend"—suggests that she is unwilling to allow him the luxury of retreating into his social or professional role; there is a hint, just the tip of the iceberg, that there was always something more complex present in his relationship with the Alvings.

Manders continues his diatribe against Mrs. Alving for some time, characterizing her as "overmastered all [her] life by a disastrous spirit of willfulness," suggesting she sent her child away as a way of avoiding her maternal duties. She provides no apologies for such actions, nor does she try to dispute his charge of willfulness (perhaps a sign of a kind of resistance masked by passivity), but she does contradict him when he accuses her of "hav[ing] become a stranger to him," saying, "No, no, I am not that!" It is as if he has cut to a core value she holds, and she cannot allow him to continue. Manders winds down with one climactic but equally fatuous speech in which he compares her failure as a wife to her failure as a mother and calls on her to "turn over a new leaf . . . because . . . in very truth, Mrs. Alving, you are a guilty mother!" He then adds, "That is what I have thought it my duty to say to you."

While it would be easy and tempting, given Manders's inflated rhetorical style, to reduce him to a caricature, a cartoon of an evangelist caught in his own web of desires, using his platform as a way of denying his own emotions, we think this would probably be a disservice to the play. At the very least, even if, as performers and audience members, we disagree with Manders's beliefs and moral dicta, we think a performer needs to characterize Manders as stating what he consciously believes — even if one part of his character may be using speech to deflect that which he cannot bring to consciousness. The character of Manders may be hypocritical, but probably mostly so on levels of which he himself is not aware; it takes a Mrs. Alving and the tragic events that unfold to bring him to awareness. Certainly critical to maintaining a sense of Manders as a complex, rounded character will be how the solo performer chooses to perform Mrs. Alving's relationship with him in this scene. This is where the solo performer may have to be especially creative and imaginative in making choices that will be different from those of actors playing the individual characters. As we have noted, the scene we are analyzing is characterized by Manders holding forth at length in sermonic speeches, to which Mrs. Alving responds almost as though involuntarily. One way to perform them might be to interrupt Manders's speeches even more frequently than Mrs. Alving does verbally on the page: imagine what effect it might have on the sense of scene if, as solo performer, there were moments when you shifted midspeech, perhaps even midsentence, to Mrs. Alving's perspective, showing her reacting silently to Manders. Such silent interruptions would also provide the performer and the audience with a way of rethinking the subtext (that is, the intrapersonal and inter-personal dynamics beneath the dialogue). For example, such moments of silence, with Mrs. Alving reacting (with what? amusement? annoy-ance? indignation? disbelief?), could create dimensions of discomfort for Manders that spur him on to even more high-flown, impersonal levels of oratory, as in a difficult conversation when we often speak not because we really have something substantive to add but to fill those chilling silences during which the other person does not speak. The performer might even find that such "reaction shots" (to draw a metaphor from film) might provide a way to take apart Manders's speeches to reveal the different stylistic and argumentative strategies he attempts in order to convince Mrs. Alving of her past sins and his own rectitude.

Manders "winds down," so to speak, by saying, "That is what I have thought it my duty to say to you." Is this a genuine statement of what he has come to the house to say? Or is it his own realization of what has come blurting out of his mouth over the course of the past few minutes? Is it simply the kind of awkward statement one says to signal that it is now the other person's responsibility to say something—anything? Mrs. Alving, after what Ibsen notes is "a short silence" (but surely it does not feel short to either of the characters), begins her side of the debate. Notice that Ibsen provides the stage direction, "speaking slowly and with self-control," suggesting very specifically the kind of woman Mrs. Alving is and how she will move in with deliberateness and care to make her own points. Indeed, there is something very clearly of the debate tradition in her response—a kind of refutation of the argumentative house of cards Manders has built. He anticipates her, even tries to cut her off, saying, "no doubt you wish to bring forward some excuses for your behaviour," but she interrupts (presumably with the same deliberate calmness Ibsen has indicated previously), saying, "No. I only want to tell you something." There is, in these two sentences, a simplicity that helps define Mrs. Alving's character and her motivation; some might even suggest that there is a kind of gendered politics of communication, as well. Whereas Manders felt he needed to prove and persuade, Mrs. Alving simply wants to "tell"—report, testify, express something.

The dialogue that ensues in the next section of the scene has much more give-and-take and is more overtly interruptive, as Manders tries desperately, but unsuccessfully, to stop Mrs. Alving from reproving him (which she does in fairly gentle and indirect ways) and from exposing the reality of Captain Alving's "profligacy." Contrast Mrs. Alving's speeches to those of Pastor Manders in the previous section. She simply states medical and behavioral facts about her husband, revealing that the captain remained "after nineteen years of married life, just as profligate—in his desires at all events—as he was before you married us." Notice that she has retreated to indirect language here and manages, through it, to implicate Manders in the dis-ease that marked her marriage. It can hardly be accidental that she includes the phrase "before you married us," linking Manders in his pastoral role to the facade of a marriage and to her illness. While Manders tries to minimize Captain Alving's failings as "youthful indiscretions," Mrs. Alving will not let him off the hook and instead invokes another kind of masculine discourse of authority, that of the medical: "That was what the doctor who attended him called it" (that is, a "profligate life"). When Manders responds, "I do not understand what you mean," Mrs. Alving says, "It is not necessary that you should."

This is a fascinating line, with so much potential for delivery. Is Mrs. Alving being "scientific" when she says this, suggesting that his understanding or not understanding is finally immaterial to the outcome of the captain's life? She was the one who had to live the life, and Manders's understanding or lack thereof doesn't have any bearing on it; the disease is in her, as were the soul-stealing effects of the marriage whether he, as a man of God, understands it or not. Is she bitter, an indication that she knows that Manders's way of being a minister is a zone of denial, a way of turning to religious platitudes (that is, following dogma blindly, as opposed to a more searching spirituality which she—and the play— advocates)? And is it therefore not only "not necessary" but not possible that he should understand, so blocked from genuine empathy and human understanding is he by virtue of his social and historical contexts and his own individual response to the challenges and constraints posed by them? Try speaking this line as if she is mocking him, as if she is saying that he need not worry about his understanding or not understanding—his own role and importance is finally not nearly as significant or meaningful as he seems to think.

Mrs. Alving now takes center stage the way Manders did earlier in the scene. In what amounts to a kind of personal narrative, she describes for Manders her life with Captain Alving. Manders, as listener, now plays the secondary role, but he must not become absent either, as his responses, as well as his role in Mrs. Alving's early married life, may be seen as providing her with the reasons to tell the story. His responses are critical to the balance of the scene, as were hers during the section where he dominated. We would argue that she is the more central of the two characters in the play overall, but his potential for change, at least in his understanding of what has happened and how he is implicated in it (despite Mrs. Alving's line about the lack of necessity of his understanding) are part of what makes the play powerful. He is not as capable of change and growth as Mrs. Alving (that is part of what makes her the more tragic figure), but his ability to witness her history, even at this late date, and gain some understanding adds to our knowledge of who she is.

The new piece of knowledge we gain in this segment of the scene is the implied paternity of Regina, told through Mrs. Alving's memory of a distant, but still clear, exchange she heard between the captain and Regina's mother years earlier. It is only definitively established in the last lines of the act, but everyone except poor dense Manders will have figured it out by the end of Mrs. Alving's narrative of Captain

Alving's unfaithfulness in the conservatory. The other piece of information, crucial to the building of Mrs. Alving's character, is that the new orphanage is funded entirely with the captain's money; she sees the money as polluted, and she will provide for Oswald with her own fortune. This brings the characters and the audience back into the present and indicates the strength and moral reasoning of Mrs. Alving, in contrast to Pastor Manders's uninformed and defensive characterization of her as an ethical agent. Oswald enters from his walk in the rain and Regina enters to announce dinner, bringing the younger generation back onstage. While the solo performer may be tempted to end the scene before the appearance of these two characters, it may be a challenge worth taking on, as it allows the performer and the audience to make those important connections between past and present and to see and hear the "fruits" of Captain Alving's life. They exit to finalize preparations for dinner.

This leaves the older pair alone once more, with Mrs. Alving in full possession of the knowledge of paternity, Manders not yet fully enlightened. Then, from offstage, they and we hear a scuffle, some words from Regina, and a cough from Oswald, indicating the son has made a pass at his (unbeknownst to him) half sister. Mrs. Alving reacts "wildly," as Ibsen says, to this overheard exchange, and when Manders asks her what has so disturbed her, she says, "Ghosts. The couple in the conservatory—over again." This line announces the meaning of the play's title, suggesting the figurative and, one might argue, evolutionary and biological "haunting" of the present by the past, a kind of fatalistic determinism that seems inescapable. Again, the actual revelation is done indirectly, through fragmented dialogue spoken by Pastor Manders and Mrs. Alving:

MANDERS: What are you saying! Regina—Is *she*—?
MRS. ALVING: Yes. Come. Not a word!

The two exit to the dining room. Even in this final exchange, we see their characteristic positions and attitudes: Manders, the naïf, finally realizing who Regina's father is, and Mrs. Alving determined to find her way through yet another of the challenges life—and her dead, spectral husband—have thrown down to her.

In addition to making Oswald and Regina come alive as characters, despite the brevity of their appearance, this section of the scene provides another set of challenges, more technical than characterological in nature. First, and most prominent, is what to do so with the offstage encounter between Regina and Oswald. One possibility is not to embody it, physically or vocally, and simply show how Mrs. Alving and Manders react to it. Its physical absence certainly is defensible, as Ibsen places it offstage as well. But to remove it vocally from the performance, while a way out of a clumsy situation in terms of keeping the scene's location(s) clear and coherent, avoids the effect Ibsen seems to be after—that of blurring present events with past memories (the "haunting"). Unless the audience is familiar with the play, the source of Mrs. Alving's shock will be unclear. So, how can the performer indicate this "echo"?

One possibility is to perform the stage directions that locate the offstage action and dialogue, thus add narrative to what has otherwise been a dramatic performance. This is not an unreasonable choice, but it may be intrusive or jarring for an audience who has followed the scene thus far exclusively through the drama, dialogue, and gestures of the play (putting aside whatever introduction the performer may choose to preface the performance).

Another logical option, though one that will require some technical planning and disciplined execution, is to omit the stage direction and perform Regina's line "Oswald! Are you mad? Let me go!" followed by Oswald's cough and subsequent humming, then the sound of a bottle being uncorked. It will help that Regina and Oswald exit earlier in the scene, thus the performer must make their exit absolutely clear; this can be accomplished in part by establishing, briefly, lines of placement for the two that will allow the audience to understand visually that the two characters are no longer present. Also, as they leave, the performer might show Mrs. Alving and perhaps also Pastor Manders watching them exit— perhaps with very different reactions to seeing them together.

Beyond this, how can the solo performer signal that this exchange is happening offstage? Different options build on various conventions of solo performance. One is to either raise or lower the angle of the head to project on a level visibly different from those used for the onstage characters. There is no hard-and-fast rule here, but if there is some visual way to indicate a difference between the locus where Mrs. Alving and Manders are interacting and where Regina and Oswald are heard, this may help the audience understand the separation of places. Similarly, aspects of vocal delivery can help: perhaps softer volume or lower pitch for the offstage exchange, something that will signal to the audience that, although all four characters are being embodied within the singular corporeality of the solo performer, the locations of the two pairs are different.

What we wish to stress here is that, as interesting and important as these technical challenges might be (and the testing of different options can be both creative and analytically satisfying for figuring out how to maintain the integrity of the text), what needs to remain central in the solo performance is the sense of the scene as part of the larger structure of the play's plot—the beats, the rhythmic movement of dominance through speech and intellectual and emotional speechmaking by the two central characters, the position of the scene within the act of the play as the crisis, or moment of choice, to use the Aristotelian term, where Mrs. Alving, presented with the potential for an incestuous relationship between Regina and Oswald, must now decide how to proceed, and the place of the act within the even larger movement of the play as a whole. It is important to analyze and make decisions about each of the characters, as individual fictional creations, as figures the playwright has invested with complex interior existences, and as an interpersonal dyad whose actions within their specific relationship are interdependent and guided by such things as social roles, past histories, and so forth. The balancing act—and it is both challenging and, at its best, a source of pleasure for both performer and audience—is in keeping it all together.

In the next chapter on drama, we will focus more specifically on a number of technical challenges for the solo performer of drama, with examples illustrating the problems posed and the ways in which the performer's approach is intimately tied to analytic questions about the nature of the particular plays and of solo performance in general.

KEY TERMS

beat (Stanislavsky)

drama

elocution

hot versus cool media (McLuhan)

naturalism

realism

theater

Chapter 11

SOLO PERFORMANCE OF DRAMA II: ADVANCED ISSUES IN TECHNIQUE

In this chapter, we will address some specific technical challenges for the solo performer of drama and provide an example of each. Remember that the point of such discussions is not to provide prescriptions for how you as performer must present these scenes, but to encourage you to think about how you might use some established conventions and perhaps expand on them or invent new techniques. The goal should always be to engage yourself, your text, and your audience in a clear and meaningful set of relationships, not to fulfill a set of rules that in some cases may be arbitrary and may even be counterproductive to your purposes and the purposes you find in the text you are performing.

Physical Contact and Interaction

As Timothy Gura, in "The Solo Performer and Drama," suggests, one of the greatest challenges to the solo performer of drama can be significant physical movement and action (as well as interaction) called for by the text. Thus, things like a chase, a kiss, a pie in the face, to use some of his examples, may stretch the capabilities of even the most adept and practiced performers and the most imaginative audiences. In some cases, this may mean that certain dramatic texts are simply not suitable for solo performance. But, in general, we would prefer to take the position that most dramatic literature is well served by solo performance and that performers and audiences can learn much and enjoy much in observing how such physical challenges to the solo performer illuminate both the text and the act of performance itself. As Gura also suggests, solo performance, because of its focus on the individual body and voice and the narrowing of visual focus from a full stage to the intimate space of the solo performer, can intensify, in some cases isolate (in a positive sense of allowing us to see more closely), and freeze in time what might otherwise occur in the blink of an eye in a staging involving multiple performers. Thus, what is lost in simultaneity of action may be a gain in helping us contemplate the various complex elements that go into a moment, a gesture, a point of physical contact. Some performers become quite skilled at managing razor-sharp transitions between characters so that the eye is almost tricked into seeing no gap in simultaneity.

We both remember a performance given by Lilla Heston at a Northwestern University faculty performance program over twenty years ago. Heston performed the wooing scene from act 1 of Shakespeare's *Richard III*, in which the title character attempts to romance Anne, the widow of the man he has killed, whose corpse is being carried in its coffin to burial even as Richard pleads his romantic case to Anne. At one particularly intense moment, Anne defies Richard, spitting in his face. It would seem, in theory, almost impossible to imagine a solo performer succeeding in both spitting and being spit upon in sufficiently rapid succession to create the illusion of actual contact, but Heston managed it memorably. She did not literally spit on the audience (nor, we suspect, would most actresses playing Anne literally spit on their scene partner), but, using offstage focus, she performed the bodily and facial gesture. Heston took the gesture to its conclusion and then held her body in Anne's position for just a split second, metamorphosing almost immediately into Richard's crooked, hunchbacked pose. As she did so, she showed Richard wiping away the spittle, responding to it as if his lover had just given him a passionate kiss, and resumed his speech. The choice to perform this was potentially risky, as it could have been simply ludicrous or unintentionally humorous; in Heston's performance, it was breathtaking, showing us Anne's disgust and Richard's complex emotions—abjection, arousal, irony, triumph. That both individuals were contained within a single body underscored the complex ambivalence the characters feel about themselves and toward each other throughout the play.

As an example, let us look at what is usually regarded as an ordinary point of physical contact and interaction: a handshake. Such an action would seem to necessitate two separate bodies, as did the spitting in the scene from *Richard III*. The gesture itself is rife with possible textual meanings, depending on the context and content of the script. Some handshakes are perfunctory, ritual greetings that carry little weight other than as markers of the beginnings and endings of social interactions.

Sometimes the absence of a handshake can speak volumes: imagine going through a reception line at a wedding or funeral and seeing an individual shake everyone's hand—except yours! If, instead of a handshake, the person hugs you, that carries one set of meanings (greater familiarity and intimacy); if the person simply remains immobile, speaking to you with a stiff smile, using the same tone of voice used to greet others, the absence of the handshake may read subtextually as a way of communicating a distance from you. Think about how individuals initiate a handshake and how recipients react: what does the handshake mean to each, what does it mean to them as a dyad, how does such a moment affect their relationship?

Let us look at a segment of a play where a handshake is not only performed but is discussed in anticipation of its performance. The play is Bernard Pomerance's *The Elephant Man*, first produced in 1979 and revived a few years ago on Broadway (not to be confused with the feature film also called *The Elephant Man*, directed by David Lynch, which is not based on the play). It is based on the historical figure of Joseph Merrick (renamed John in the play), an Englishman who lived from 1862 to 1890 and who had what is now thought to be Proteus syndrome, a condition that results in overgrowth of bone and skin, usually accompanied by fibrous tumors. Merrick's physical appearance provoked the label "the elephant man" (and for many years, people mistakenly thought his disease was elephantiasis). For much of his life, he lived as either an outcast or a circus freak, exploited by various people. A surgeon, Sir Frederick Treves, took on his care, and Merrick subsequently traveled in social circles, acquiring both celebrity and public affection, often seen at the theater and other events with royalty and members of London's social and theatrical set. He wrote poetry and prose and, from contemporary accounts, longed for female affection and companionship.

Two scenes, which occur sequentially in the play, can be found on pages 476–79. The scenes have somewhat elaborate titles which are typically projected onto the stage in productions of the play, evoking both Victorian music hall acts and Bertoldt Brecht's notion of alienation devices to remind the audience they are watching a play, not reality per se. In the first scene, Treves prepares the celebrated actress, Mrs. (Madge) Kendal (a historically real figure), to meet Merrick. In the second scene, Mrs. Kendal and Merrick meet and converse, the scene climaxing in the handshake between the two. Notice in the first scene, "Scene IX: Most Important Are Women," Treves specifies which hand Mrs. Kendal should shake: "And when you leave, shake his hand, the left one is usable, and really quite beautiful, and say, 'I am very pleased to have made your acquaintance, Mr. Merrick.'" Mrs. Kendal then "rehearses" this act, using Treves as her stand-in for Merrick, experimenting with different emphases in her "script." In the scene that immediately follows, "Scene X: When the Illusion Ends He Must Kill Himself," Mrs. Kendal and Merrick discuss, among other things, Shakespeare's most romantic tragedy, *Romeo and Juliet*, and Merrick's assessment of the inauthenticity of Romeo's feelings for Juliet, which gives the scene its title and also echoes the illusory nature of social interaction, the ways in which social performances may mask what is felt underneath. Indeed, Mrs. Kendal, the consummate actress, is initially able, due to her experience with audiences (such as the one she drolly describes in the previous scene as not unlike Merrick's photograph—"all huge grim head and grimace and utterly unable to clap"), to mask whatever initial response of shock or disgust she may have at encountering Merrick in the flesh for the first time. But it is clear, as the scene progresses, that she is genuinely impressed by Merrick's intelligence and touched by his emotional expressiveness and his authentic determination and loyalty to his own imagined Juliet. She goes off script when Treves enters (a signal that the encounter is to end) by declaring that she plans on introducing Merrick to "the best," that is, the most prominent people in London society. She then moves to leave and speaks the line she has rehearsed with Treves before, "Mr. Merrick, it has been a very great pleasure to make your acquaintance." While Pomerance does not provide a stage direction here, it is clear from Treves's following line ("John. Your hand. She wishes to shake your hand") that she has extended her hand, which Merrick accepts, saying, "Thank you for coming," to which she responds, "But it was my pleasure."

In most situations, this would be the kind of interactive ritual behavior Erving Goffman writes about as assumed in everyday social scripts. Because of what has preceded, we (and the characters) recognize this as a signal moment for all concerned—certainly most of all for Merrick himself. Indeed, as the scene ends, with Treves telling Mrs. Kendal that Merrick has "never shook a woman's hand before," Pomerance describes Merrick: he "sobs soundlessly, uncontrollably." The moment between Mrs. Kendal and Merrick can be electric, moving an audience to the same kind of tears and chills experienced by the characters themselves.

But an interesting question, to be faced by any actress playing Mrs. Kendal in a production of the play or by any solo performer performing the scene, is *how* Mrs. Kendal executes the shaking of the hand. In the original Broadway production, Carole Shelley, who played Mrs. Kendal, made a very dramatic, visible point of extending *not* her left hand (as Treves had directed her to do), but her right hand, thus following convention and requiring Merrick to shake it with his right hand, the one disfigured by the disease. Pomerance's stage direction does not indicate this but consider the dramatic effect of this choice: it signals to the audience a shift within Mrs. Kendal that the pleasant, witty social badinage may not have— that she does not think of Merrick simply as "an audience," someone to perform for, but as another human being, an individual, someone she wishes to view as a friend, a companion. As in British (and American) society it is customary to extend the right hand in such social rituals, Mrs. Kendal has determined she will not "compensate" or treat Merrick as different by giving him her left hand. In a staged production, it is easy for the significance of this moment to be lost in the timing of the handshake (although our memory of the moment in the original production extends back almost thirty years, suggesting its potency). As a performer, you must decide: when does Mrs. Kendal decide to divert from the "left-handed" script she and Treves have constructed? Is there a moment of hesitation as she makes the decision, realizing it will require her to shake the impaired, perhaps even "monstrous" hand? Has the emotion of the moment so swept her away that she isn't even conscious that she has deviated from the script? In the production we saw, Carole Shelley clearly communicated this as a conscious decision, not as an accident.

Consider Merrick's side of the exchange: has Treves similarly prepared him for the possibility that Mrs. Kendal will offer her hand and schooled him in what he will be expected to do? Does Merrick expect her to reach for his good (left) hand? Is he confused by this gesture? How aware is he of how his hand is viewed by others? (His physician and caregiver views Merrick throughout the play simultaneously as a dignified human and as a kind of "case" or "specimen.") Think about how he feels when their hands meet and how the handshake leads to the overflow of emotions specified by Pomerance in his stage direction. These are complex questions, even for the actor who has the responsibility of playing only one of these two roles.

Now imagine what happens when the solo performer decides to perform these scenes, and this moment in particular. Of course, the solo performer cannot or at least is unlikely to use both hands to embody the handshake (that is, use the right hand as Mrs. Kendal and the left as

Merrick)—this would violate the aesthetics of the solo performer's locus. So, as with Heston's performance of Anne spitting at Richard, exact simultaneity is necessarily sacrificed. The performer must show Mrs. Kendal extending her hand and then shift into Merrick's role. Like Richard III, the performer will be suggesting a disabled posture (the script indicates that makeup or prosthetics should not be used to try to replicate historical portraits of Merrick, which is what the film did).

Timing will be crucial here, and the solo performer has considerable latitude in making choices about this moment. Does Merrick take Mrs. Kendal's hand immediately? Do we see Mrs. Kendal initially begin to extend her left hand and then shift to the right? When does the right hand change from being Mrs. Kendal's to Merrick's? This may be further complicated by the fact that, using offstage focus, the solo performer's right hand may read to the audience as a left hand, and thus the physical embodiment of Merrick's deformed right hand becomes critical to the meaning of the moment of physical contact. Finding ways of showing Mrs. Kendal's decision to use her right hand, which must be done without sacrificing the play's characterization of her as subtle, witty, sincere, not someone trying to make an overly melodramatic point of taking his right (that is, "wrong") hand, is not simply a technical problem to be solved, but a technical decision for the solo performer that is intimately tied to the scene's meaning and power. The embodiment of the hand(s) of each of these characters within the single body of the solo performer has the power to illuminate this gesture—to allow us to see it with a kind of spotlight as a symbol of the ways in which we all are both the social Mrs. Kendal, confident, practiced in social performances, and Merrick, the man who, while witty and clever in his dialogue, is also someone vulnerable, isolated, desiring human connection. The solo performer can show us an internal drama of both sides of the self in an eloquent and embodied way.

Try performing this scene, beginning by experimenting with a classmate, each of you taking on one of these roles. Then consider flipping the roles; disregard such specifics as your own sex and play both Mrs. Kendal and John Merrick. How does each of you navigate the handshake? What do you do differently? How does it feel to be Mrs. Kendal, reaching out, John Merrick, completing the gesture? How does it feel to be both at the same time? Finally, you might each try performing the scene as a solo performer, watching each other and describing how the interaction ritual, to use Goffman's term, means different things in each of your performances. What does each of you bring to the moment and how does this radiate back to choices about character and interaction in the sections of the two scenes that precede the handshake?

Shifting Dialogue

Just as one of the principal challenges for the solo performer of drama is how to translate the simultaneity of stage bodies into the singular presence and possibilities contained within one body, so there is a similar challenge in the handling of dialogue, both physically and vocally. While dialogue frequently occurs sequentially, that is, one character speaks, finishes his or her speech, and then another character begins to speak, we also know that, in everyday life, conversation is not nearly so neatly conducted—people cut each other off, overlap, speak simultaneously. Drama of the twentieth and twenty-first centuries has often reflected this reality. The famous acting couple Alfred Lunt and Lynn Fontanne, for example, were particularly noted for disregarding the aesthetic conventions of uninterrupted dialogue and overlapping with each other; while this now strikes most of us as unremarkable, at the time (the mid-twentieth century) when they applied this technique to playwrights as varied as Noël Coward and Friedrich Dürrenmatt, it was seen as quite revolutionary. Today, there are playwrights for whom such dialogic interruptions are considered stylistic markers (David Mamet is perhaps most notable in this regard) and directors, especially for film, who have made it a whole aesthetic (such as Robert Altman).

While dialogic shifts may not require as much adaptation and invention as physical contact for the solo performer, there will still be texts and scenes within texts where the question of how to manage timing, how to indicate shifts of character and voice, and how to embody the sense of interrupted and/or overlapping dialogue will be central. Certainly, some of the general conventions of solo performance, discussed in chapter 4, will assist performer and audience: the use of angles of placement, focus, and so forth, can create a visual sense of who is speaking and when. Beyond these technical conventions, the performer's ability to make vocal, postural, and physical choices to define characters will be critical, as well as less technically driven performance choices such as character attitude, motivation, and subtext.

Nonetheless, there will come times when all these resources may still be insufficient to allow the solo performer to create the sense of a scene populated by multiple characters and, perhaps even more critically, to establish the sense of pacing and interaction required by the scene. One solution, of course, is to avoid such texts, arguing that they are not well served by solo performance (the same argument raised by some kinds of physical action). But think of what might be gained by taking on such challenges—the opportunity to experience both sides of the dialogue.

Our example for this set of challenges is Caryl Churchill's recent one-act play, *Drunk Enough to Say I Love You*, first produced in London in 2006. It is a play of extraordinary economy with a running time of approximately an hour (more or less, depending on how it is played), at times quite graphic in its detail, at times allusive and suggestive. Like most of Churchill's plays, it combines a kind of psychological fierceness with cultural and political commentary, using everyday, ordinary social situations as an opportunity to provide critiques.

Drunk Enough to Say I Love You, Churchill's exploration of the relationship between England and the United States during the much-contested second Gulf War, mixes realistic and nonrealistic theatrical conventions. Churchill does this in ways clearly intended to raise the level of the audience's discomfort through a kind of allegorical setting of two men involved in an erotic/love relationship, in which one of the men has left his wife and children for the other man (the difference, or at least tension, between an erotic relationship and a love relationship is one of the play's themes). Churchill provides virtually no background for the two men; as performers and audiences, part of the challenge is either imagining a backstory for this series of encounters (the play is presented in fairly short scenes between the two men, chronicling the development and decline of the relationship) or, more likely the play's intention, resisting the impulse to fill in what is not given about these men, why they are drawn to each other, and what they have brought to the relationship. Churchill does provide identifications for the two men that are key to the play's themes and meaning. One man is named Sam, "a country," the other Guy, "a man." In her preface, Churchill explains that she originally named the man "Jack" to indicate a kind of ordinary "everyman" but found that some audiences linked it to the Union Jack (the British flag) and read the two men as standing in parallel allegorical positions for two countries; the name was changed to "Guy" for the New York production. Her intention, she states, was to keep the relationship unequal in scope and hence power: Sam, the American, is a country and represents something larger, more engulfing than an individual, corresponding to

her view (and many other people's) of the United States as a force that
dominates world politics, often to the exclusion of the needs, desires,
and wants of others. She deliberately wants her British character, "Guy,"
to be just that—a guy, an individual seduced by the force of American
political power, willing to do almost anything to gain access to it. One
of the challenges for either two actors playing these characters or for the
solo performer playing both is how, if at all, to try to embody the difference in scope between Sam (derived from Uncle Sam, no doubt) and
Guy. An alternative is to play the relationship as if it were between two
men coming to this affair from different standpoints (Sam seems to be
more confident and assured, Guy more troubled by his act of abandoning
his wife and children) and allow the dialogue to point to the more allegorical, satiric elements of Churchill's play.

What makes Churchill's play a fascinating challenge for the solo
performer, in addition to the issues of characterization, both from interpersonal psychological and politically rhetorical positions, is Churchill's
style, which eschews not only complete sentences much of the time,
as happens in ordinary speech, but, on the printed page, many of the
conventions of written English, such as capitalization, punctuation, and
so forth, making the rapid-fire dialogue even more breathless and ambiguous in its potential for delivery. It resembles, in these respects, stream
of consciousness narration as found in the prose fiction of such writers
as William Faulkner, James Joyce, Virginia Woolf, and others, but here
externalized as dialogue. How will the solo performer manage these inter-
changes? The ancient Greeks, by the way, had a term for these passages
of alternating dialogue, which often presented a kind of debate between
characters: *stichomythia*, or "stitched speech."

Let us look at an entire scene from late in the play, scene 7. It
begins with Sam alone onstage and provides him with a monologue that
describes scenes of torture, which have unfortunately become commonplace in the language and images we receive almost daily through various
media, especially on television newscasts. Churchill's inclusion of it in
this domestic setting suggests the degree to which we have become inured
to its effects, thus making us all participants—willing or not, consciously
or not—in acts of torture:

> white double cable whip, iron wreath, beating the soles of the feet,
> put object in vagina, put object in anus, put turpentine on testicles,
> pour water over face, play very loud Indonesian music, electric

shocks to the genitals, tap a dowel through the ear into the brain, throw the prisoner out of the helicopter, show the prisoner another prisoner being thrown out of the helicopter, beating obviously, rape of course, bright light, no sleep, simulate an execution, so they think up to the last second they're going to die, play tape of women and children screaming in next room and tell prisoner it's his wife and children, sometimes it is, hang up with hands tied behind back, chop off hands, pins in eyes, insecticide in hood over the head over the head, cut off breasts, pull out heart, slit throat and pull tongue through, sulphuric acid, chop off

The speech ends here as Guy enters, but before we turn to the dialogue, let us consider briefly the challenges of Sam's speech, as they will have an impact on whatever decisions you make about how to play the dialogue that follows. Western drama has had a long tradition of using language, particularly extended monologues, to create vivid, violent, and painful images, usually of offstage actions, in the minds of the audience. In the classical drama of Greece and Rome, it was considered a violation of decorum to actually show such acts onstage (no doubt in part because such actions cannot easily be represented through theatrical action, as opposed to today, where computer-generated imagery can simulate just about anything the human mind can imagine). The self-blinding of Oedipus, the hanging of Jocasta, Medea's murder of her children—all of these were described in graphic, shocking, and haunting language. What distinguishes Sam's description? Part of what makes it so horrifying, from our perspective, is its very lack of descriptive elaboration or morally evaluative language: more than anything else, it is simply a list of actions, without any indication that the enumerator of this list is aware of the appalling implications of participation in or approval of or even mere knowledge of these actions. So as a performer, you will need to decide how Sam speaks this list. Is it a rushed, un-self-reflective delivery in a kind of monotone, reinforcing critic Elaine Scarry's observation that torture tends to obliterate language and imagination for both torturer and tortured? Is it a series of possibilities that gather an increasingly gruesome power? Does he stop at points to modify what he has said (as in "tell prisoner it's his wife and children, sometimes it is")? You might imagine what the next item in the series would be had Guy not entered to interrupt this litany. Consider the range of possible contexts in which Sam might be speaking these words—as he watches television, as he dictates possible torture strategies to other Americans. Can you think of other possible contexts?

Now read the dialogue between Guy and Sam:

GUY: hello, I've
SAM: what you
GUY: but I missed you
SAM: same as before
GUY: try and
SAM: what you put me through
GUY: I'm sorry I
SAM: hurt me
GUY: yes I
SAM: take you back I need to know if
GUY: try to
SAM: total commitment or there's no
GUY: I realize
SAM: capable
GUY: can
SAM: promise
GUY: love
SAM: nightmare here
GUY: yes
SAM: not going to be happy, hope you don't
GUY: no I don't expect
SAM: so what you
GUY: can't live
SAM: no you can't, can't
GUY: no I can't
SAM: ok then
GUY: doing?
SAM: need to teach
GUY: yes
SAM: special advisers
GUY: ok
SAM: Greece
GUY: the colonels' Greece, we're right behind
SAM: Operation Phoenix
GUY: Vietnam, operational

SAM: nobody questioned survives

GUY: forty-one thousand

SAM: teaching them in Brazil exactly how much electric shock you
    can administer without killing

GUY: because sometimes you may not want

SAM: sometimes it's not politic

GUY: and sometimes it just doesn't matter

SAM: El Salvador, Uruguay, Nicaragua, Guatemala,

GUY: delivering the manuals to Panama

SAM: and the thin wire can go in the diplomatic bag to Uruguay

GUY: thin wire?

SAM: against the gum and it increases the shock

GUY: need to be accurate

SAM: precise pain

GUY: for precise effect

SAM: so practice on beggars in soundproof room

GUY: the US Office of Public Safety

SAM: fighting terror

GUY: put Mitrione in charge of

SAM: humanitarian

GUY: expert in administration of pain

SAM: always leave them some hope, he says

GUY: people who don't need our encouragement because
    they already

SAM: Afghanistan

GUY: yes the game where the men are on horses and the prisoner

SAM: instead of a goat

GUY: one layer of skin at a time, which must take

SAM: so relatively speaking, Guantanamo

GUY: need results

SAM: need exemption from rules forbidding cruel, inhuman or
    degrading

GUY: because those rules

SAM: in the present climate

GUY: hoods over their heads or sexual

SAM: because their religion makes them upset by

GUY: menstrual blood

SAM: have to laugh

GUY: but some things we'd rather other people

SAM: 747 rendering prisoners to
GUY: because there's plenty of places where that can
SAM: can't do everything ourselves
GUY: do our best
SAM: you're doing great again
GUY: back with you
SAM: no fun though
GUY: sick today, but
SAM: just stick with it and we'll be

And this is where the scene ends, in the middle of Sam's sentence, which in everyday conversation between two lovers would be a comforting, affectionate gesture of encouragement and consolation, but here it is a chilling, open-ended declaration of the ambiguity of what such behaviors as they collaboratively describe will eventually lead them to as "countries" and as "men" (that is, individuals).

Churchill's use of multiple realms of language and discourse is extraordinary. The dialogue between the two men begins as any such encounter might—the reconciliation of two people who have quarreled and who wish to make up with each other. There is in its very generic quality a kind of universal appeal to what most audience members will have experienced at some point or another—the tug and pull as two people who have hurt each other emotionally try to heal the breach, make their desire to reunite known to each other, speak emotionally of their own needs and vulnerabilities. That the two characters are men certainly "queers" the conventions of such a scripted interaction for some, but by no means all and perhaps not even the majority, of audience members; such scenes have become part of the films and television all of us see in our media-filled lives. If the performer(s) chose to distinguish the two men vocally by standard American and British accents, that would add to a sense of distinctiveness between them.

But Churchill turns around our expectations in a most chilling way with the sudden shift, halfway through the scene, to specific, detailed references to contemporary sites of torture and espionage, not only from the Middle East, but from Latin America, where the School of the Americas has notoriously run rampant in activities of torture against those whom the intelligence agencies of the United States (the CIA, for example) have deemed to be enemies of United States' interests. We realize at this point that we are not only witnessing a reconciliation between two men depicted as lovers, but a kind of seduction-by-indoctrination (or is it indoctrination-by-seduction) of British subjects (Guy as the individual) by the United States as a superpower. The mixing of these discourses—interpersonal and geopolitical, erotic and disciplinary—are what make the play so potent.

From the point of characterization and interaction, of course, performers will need to decide what to foreground in the multiple relationships depicted here. The performer(s) might play the scene in the tone of two lovers making up after a quarrel, with all the intimacy, playfulness, and private erotic promise such exchanges carry with them, allowing the politics of the scene to emerge for the audience through the literal references Churchill includes. The opposite is also a possibility: strip the performance of any hint of overt homoeroticism and play it as two political figures—Sam recruiting a recalcitrant agent back onto the team, with the opening dialogue perhaps making the audience somewhat uncomfortable or momentarily confused by the ways in which a political-professional interview shares some of the language and conversational conventions of a love scene. Of course, a third option is to somehow convey both spheres at the same time; how might one do that vocally and physically? Recall the opening monologue that precedes Guy's entrance; it may present even more possibilities, for example, is this list a kind of pornographic reverie of Sam's deepest, darkest fantasies, playing out in the inner sanctum of his own imaginative grind house?

Whether the scene is performed by two actors or by a solo performer, Churchill's style of dialogue will require decisions in terms of pacing, response, and what we might call the integrity of the line. On the page, as is apparent to the reader, the lines tend to be very short, almost telegraphic phrases, with a few exceptions; this either represents the kind of brief responses people make to let the dominant speaker know that they are following the other's train of thought ("I realize" and "yes") or interruptions to try to take the floor, add a different thought to the topic, or shift the conversation to another topic. In life, we tend to blurt out such responses, and conversational analysts might argue whether such interjections or interruptions constitute a genuine "turn," to use their language.

Drama is not, however, identical to life conversations, although it can come close to replicating it in the hands of some playwrights, and so we are not necessarily bound by what linguists may themselves record in their data. When you read the scene on the page, how did you hear the pacing and timing of the dialogue between Guy and Sam? Was it a breathless pace, as if each can barely wait for the other to finish a thought or phrase? Are there pauses anywhere, when a character takes a moment to form a thought or phrase? Does the pace vary? Consider taking the sexual relationship as the central metaphor or image to its extreme, and imagine performing the scene as having the rhythm of a sexual encounter between two people. How long does the scene remain foreplay? Is there a climax? Do both characters finish?

Answering these questions and translating these answers into performance—and, we would add, finding these answers may only actually happen in the process of working on the scene in performance—while following similar trajectories for either two actors performing the scene or a solo performer embodying both Guy and Sam will pose special, additional issues for the solo performer. Just as the question of simultaneity poses a challenge for the solo performer of the handshake in *The Elephant Man*, so the rhythm of dialogue, both in pacing (speed) and timing (phrasing, pauses, overlaps), will be a central concern for the solo performer of *Drunk Enough to Say I Love You*. The conventions of solo performance of dialogue, in which the performer adopts very distinctly angled lines of placement to indicate different characters, may or may not be as useful here as in scenes such as those from *Ghosts*, in which each of the characters tends generally to speak in complete sentences and often in lengthy speeches and where maintaining the clear placement lines helps focus the performer and the audience visually on the speaker. Unless one decides to deliver Churchill's dialogue with the kind of rich weighty pauses that mark the plays of Harold Pinter, it may be that the sudden and frequent shifting of focus will result in whiplash and may misdirect the audience from what is being said and the emotions and ideas each character invests in this scene.

From a technical standpoint, one solution is to narrow the angles even more than usual, so that the physical back-and-forth does not become distracting. Another solution would be to do away with the angular shifts entirely and place the entire scene on one line, directly center with respect to the audience's visual plane. The solo performer in this case still has a panoply of technical tools upon which to draw—voice, attitude, posture, gesture, eye levels, and so forth. As some have argued, the best solo performers of drama should be able to distinguish characters for the audience without lines of placement, although such lines can help performer and audience in many instances, and just because they may not be necessary does not obviate their usefulness.

Of course, the decision to forgo lines of placement may initially make both the performer and audience feel as if the net has been taken away from the tightrope walker: a zone of safety will have been removed. That in and of itself may have both positive and negative effects. It definitely demands absolutely clear distinctions on the part of the performer and superior concentration by the audience. If the performer chooses to use a script as part of the performance aesthetic (with or without a lectern), the script must be even more than usual a point of reference rather than a place of retreat: almost complete memorization, with all the attendant rehearsal this requires, would be called for. Making very defined and, in some respects, essential choices about how to distinguish the two men will also be crucial and, given the sometimes subtle nuances of the play, working with extremes for the sake of simplicity may not be the best course of action.

Another way of viewing the scene and the challenge of performing it as a soloist might be to focus on it as political speech, a variety of rhetoric, and to see in its dramatic form and structure not so much a conventional realistic play with the goal of creating an illusion of live interaction between two breathing characters, but rather a Platonic philosophical dialogue in which different characters exist most significantly to stand for a particular position, point of view, or attitude. Viewed in this light, Churchill's play might open itself to other approaches to performing dialogue. Building on the idea of dispensing with placement lines, the solo performer might decide to locate this play within the political and philosophical mind of a playwright imagining such an encounter (and a series of encounters, constituting the play). The dialogue itself might become an inner dialogue in which the performer imagines the ways in which political power imbalances might be translated into commonplace domestic relations. Strong distinctions between characters would be minimized as the performer uses voice and body to underscore the ways in which all of us, whatever our gender, race, nationality, or sexuality, are under the sway of the dominant ideologies the playwright attributes to the United States. This does not mean that the audience should never be able to tell when a line has been assigned to Sam and when to Guy; rather, such a performance might help an audience realize how, according to the playwright, all Sams started out as Guys and all Guys may eventually become Sams. As Leland H. Roloff has suggested, this is the kind of situation that allows us to explore our inner "multiple personality disorders" in socially sanctioned ways!

Drunk Enough to Say I Love You provides a fairly extreme example of the challenges of shifting dialogue as part of character distinctions and transitions, but it also points up how what might seem like a fairly simple technical decision (or set of decisions) always turns back onto the text and, in doing so, helps performer and audience gain greater understanding of its complexities.

Stage Directions

A country road. A tree.
Evening.

These phrases make up one of the most famous — if briefest — descriptions of setting in modern dramatic literature: they are the first words the reader encounters in Samuel Beckett's play *Waiting for Godot*, which has inspired countless productions and an equal number of essays and volumes of commentary arguing for different interpretations of the play. But Beckett's description — a place, a single feature of the landscape, and a time of day — is deliberate in its simultaneous specificity and elusiveness: what that road looks like, in what country it exists, what kind of tree it is, and what part of evening, how much light remains, the weather, are all left up to performer, director, designer, reader, and audience. Most productions of the play we have seen have chosen to keep the actual design of setting and lighting equally open-ended, and one can certainly argue that the most important place for these elements to exist is in the imagination of the performers and the audience. As solo performer, what would you do with this stage direction? You could speak it as part of an introduction for the performance. Or you could omit it completely, throwing your audience into the limbo or netherworld the play suggests. Whatever choice you make, it will need to be a conscious choice. If you decide to speak these words, do you do so as yourself, as the playwright, or as a constructed observer or narrator, or even as one of the characters from the play, and which one would that be?

Beckett was notorious for his insistence that productions of his plays follow his descriptions of setting and his directions for action, pacing, pauses, and gestures to the letter of the script, to the point of having productions that deviated from the published script closed down. He also directed productions of many of his plays, so he was clearly deeply invested in the published script as a set of directions for performance.

Legalities of production aside, we advocate something less draconian but still informed and analytic: using distinctions drawn by Beverly Whitaker Long in her article "Evaluating Performed Literature," the script can be used as a text with some elements that must be considered certainties (that is, that *Godot* must take place where and when the text specifies), some that may be considered probabilities (the country road is not located in Antarctica, but could you make an argument for Antarctica as an appropriate setting?), and some things that are possibilities (the tree is a withered weeping willow, or the tree is in full bloom in ironic contradistinction to the state of the characters, or the tree begins each act in flower but ends leafless through some stagecraft not specified by the play).

Most staged productions of plays eschew performance of stage directions, following the reasonable notion that such directions are external to the voicing of the play's text, that is, they are not part of the dialogue that dominates the aesthetic of most drama. Examples such as the role of the stage manager in Thornton Wilder's *Our Town* are the exception rather than the norm, and even that character typically does not speak stage directions that have not been marked as part of his lines. The solo performer may make different kinds of decisions, particularly in support of the more presentational approach he or she takes in presenting a dramatic text. It is unusual for a solo performer to use a fully realized setting, and, if performing a scene involving multiple characters, it is impractical and imbalanced to adopt the costume of one of the characters. Most solo performers of drama do make careful choices about what they wear, particularly for a public performance — a pastel outfit would be out of keeping for a solo performance of *Medea,* just as dark colors might work against a high-spirited comedy such as *The Importance of Being Earnest;* neutral tones invite the audience to imagine their own designs.

Similarly, performers vary in terms of their decision to read stage directions that indicate or describe in detail gestures or movements. Harkening back to Timothy Gura's comments on the difficulties of solo performance of complex, multiple-bodied actions like chase scenes, embraces, and so forth, it may be the case that the solo performer chooses to read the stage directions that specify an action crucial to the audience's understanding of an action and to the rhythm of a scene. In other cases, the solo performer can, with some invention and careful rehearsal, communicate the gesture or action; the handshake between Mrs. Kendal and John Merrick in *The Elephant Man* is an example of an instance where describing the gesture rather than enacting it would rob the moment of some of its visual power.

In addition, the playwright may not have provided a stage direction, so the performer would have to invent an action.

One thing virtually any spoken performance of a stage direction does is shift the performance, if only for an instant, from the dramatic mode to the epic mode: from pure showing to the mixture of showing and telling that is characteristic of prose and verse narrative. There is nothing inherently wrong with such a shift, as long as performer (and, by extension, audience) is aware that it is happening. The playwright Bertolt Brecht argued in favor of what he called "epic theater," in which performer, director, playwright, and audience work consciously to remove the illusion of reality that representational drama encourages and remind all that a performance was occurring. In rehearsal, and sometimes in performance, such productions involve performers in commenting on their characters, moving simultaneously between the playing of character and the observing done by performer. The teacher and scholar Paul Gray encouraged his students to take this approach of making drama narrative in presenting solo performances, suggesting that solo performance, by its very nature, shifts modes of representation and that all solo performances of multiple-character dramatic scenes were inherently narrative in nature, as they reframed the dramatic text into a single body and self.

Some playwrights are particularly known for the extensiveness of their stage directions and descriptions of the setting, to the point that reading their plays becomes a very different experience from seeing them onstage; such playwrights almost seem to be turning their plays into novels or short stories. Their motives for doing this may vary, but some want their reading audience, who may never actually see a production of the play, to gain in silent reading some of what the actors and designers would provide in performance. Perhaps the most notable of such playwrights is the early twentieth century master of social comedy and satire George Bernard Shaw. In many of Shaw's plays, the preface and the initial stage directions take up half the length of the published form of the play. The prefaces are marked by a characteristic performative voice that is consistent with Shaw's own commentaries and critical essays; in addition to being a playwright, he was a successful and prolific writer of reviews of plays and music. His prefaces offer rich opportunities for the performer.

Shaw's stage directions are equally detailed, sometimes dense, and descriptive. While the inclusion of them in a staged production of any of his plays might make for a marathon evening at the theater, the solo performer electing to do a scene from a play or a truncated version for public or classroom presentation may find including the stage directions an interesting way to give a sense of Shaw's own literary richness, underscoring what Gray views as the solo performer's perspective on dramatic texts.

Let us look briefly at a sample from one of Shaw's opening descriptions, drawn from act 1 of his 1908 play *The Doctor's Dilemma*. This is a play that, although written about a hundred years ago, remains relevant today in its critique of the tensions between medical science, social accessibility of services, and the financial and social status of doctors. The play itself follows the dilemma of a group of well-known London physicians, with a special focus on Colenso Ridgeon, a researcher and physician who, at the outset of the play, has been awarded a knighthood for work he has done in treating tuberculosis. Ridgeon must choose between treating a gifted but morally bankrupt painter, Louis Dubedat, and an aging, poverty-stricken but essentially good man, fellow physician Dr. Blenkinsop (the obstacle is the number of spots available in the research pool); Ridgeon's choice is complicated by his growing attraction to Dubedat's attractive and loving wife, Jenny. The following is printed in the text of the play before a word of dialogue is spoken:

> On the 15th June 1903, in the early forenoon, a medical student, surname Redpenny, Christian name unknown and of no importance, sits at work in a doctor's consulting room. He devils for the doctor by answering his letters, acting as his domestic laboratory assistant, and making himself indispensable generally, in return for unspecified advantages involved by intimate intercourse with a leader of his profession, and amounting to an informal apprenticeship and a temporary affiliation. Redpenny is not proud, and will do anything he asked without reservation of his personal dignity, if he is asked in a fellow-creaturely way. He is a wide-open-eyed, ready, credulous, friendly, hasty youth, with his hair and clothes in reluctant transition from the untidy boy to the tidy doctor.
>
> Redpenny is interrupted by the entrance of an old servingwoman who has never known the cares, the preoccupations, the responsibilities, jealousies, and anxieties of personal beauty. She has the complexion of a never-washed gypsy, incurable by any detergent; and she has, not a regular beard and moustaches, which could at least be trimmed and waxed into a masculine presentableness, but a whole crop of small beards and moustaches, mostly springing

from moles all over her face. She carries a duster and toddles about meddlesomely, spying out dust so diligently that whilst she is flicking off one speck she is already looking elsewhere for another. In conversation she has the same trick, hardly ever looking at the person she is addressing except when she is excited. She has only one manner, and that is the manner of an old family nurse to a child just after it has learnt to walk. She has used her ugliness to secure indulgences unattainable to Cleopatra or Fair Rosamund, and has the further great advantage over them that age increases her qualification instead of impairing it. Being an industrious, agreeable, and popular old soul, she is a walking sermon on the vanity of feminine prettiness. Just as Redpenny has no discovered Christian name, she has no discovered surname, and is known throughout the doctors' quarter between Cavendish Square and the Marylebone Road simply as Emmy.

The consulting room has two windows looking on Queen Anne Street. Between the two is a marble-topped console, with haunched gilt legs ending in sphinx claws. The huge pier-glass which surmounts it is mostly disabled from reflection by elaborate painting on its surface of palms, ferns, lilies, tulips, and sunflowers. The adjoining wall contains the fireplace, with two arm-chairs before it. As we happen to face the corner we see nothing of the other two walls. On the right of the fireplace, or rather on the right of any person facing the fireplace, is the door. On its left is the writing table at which Redpenny sits. It is an untidy table with a microscope, several test tubes, and a spirit lamp standing up through its litter of papers. There is a couch in the middle of the room, at right angles to the console, and parallel to the fireplace. A chair stands between the couch and the windowed wall. Another in the corner. Another at the other end of the windowed wall. The windows have green Venetian blinds and rep curtains; and there is a gasalier; but it is a convert to electric lighting. The wall paper and carpets are mostly green, coeval with the gasalier and the Venetian blinds. The house, in fact, was so well furnished in the middle of the XIXth century that it stands unaltered to this day and is still quite presentable.

There is so much detail and commentary in this passage that even the silent reader may feel the need to take a breath after reading it! Remember that all of this serves to set the scene and to identify the two characters who will begin the play. What you may be surprised to learn is that these two characters, to whom Shaw has devoted so much descriptive space, will appear as fairly minor figures in act 1 and then disappear from the play entirely. Similarly, the doctor's consulting room is the setting of the (fairly long) first act, but the action of the play shifts to different settings for each of the remaining acts. Many of the details Shaw has given us about the design of the room are never immediately relevant to the action of the scene, for example, the specific flowers painted on the mirror are never commented upon, the particular scientific instruments are never used. Is Shaw simply being self-indulgent in writing about Redpenny, Emmy, and the room in such detail?

Those who do not enjoy Shaw as a playwright might be inclined to answer in the affirmative. However, another way of viewing this is that Shaw wants to provide performer and audience with a full understanding of his conception of the characters and the world they inhabit, both to provide the performer with the kind of background and potential subtext for what will be spoken and to allow readers to "play" the drama in their own minds. Consider the first two lines of actual dialogue between these two characters, whose function within the scene is primarily expository, that is, to provide background information bringing the audience up to date in terms of their point of entry into the play's action. (Note the absence of apostrophe marks; this is not a typographical error but rather a stylistic habit of Shaw's, no doubt part of his campaign to simplify the English language.)

> EMMY (*entering and immediately beginning to dust the couch*):
> Theres a lady bothering me to see the doctor.
> REDPENNY (*distracted by the interruption*): Well, she cant see the
> doctor. Look here: whats the use of telling you that the doctor cant
> take any new patients, when the moment a knock comes to the
> door, in you bounce to ask whether he can see somebody?

This fairly straightforward exchange sets up the basic situation: the lady Emmy refers to will turn out to be Jennifer Dubedat, the wife seeking medical treatment for her husband. She will not appear onstage until near the end of the act, and as the various physicians arrive, ostensibly to congratulate Ridgeon on his knighthood, they each comment on the woman in the waiting room. There is a kind of comic suspense that builds to Jenny finally gaining entrance, and Emmy's first line draws our attention to this dramatic element. Similarly, the response of Redpenny, a sort of gatekeeper for Ridgeon, maintains the principal obstacle of the rising action of the play—Ridgeon's initial refusal to treat Louis Dubedat. Such an exchange is characteristic of plays throughout history: the presence of the two minor characters provides the audience with some necessary, if perfunctory, information so that the action of the play can be set in motion. Actors often find these roles thankless unless the playwright has invested the characters with interesting and distinctive qualities.

This, we would argue, is what Shaw has done here, and the opening stage directions account for it. It is clear from the word choices and the information he has given us about Redpenny and Emmy, down to the absence of a first name for one and a last name for the other, that while these characters will be onstage only for a short time and have fairly workaday functions within the drama, Emmy, like many an old servant in Shaw, ends up having more sway over her employer than the doctor would like to admit. For the performer, whether an actor in a production or a solo performer, they are real people, of whom the doctor is fond and toward whom he has a degree of admiration (in the case of Emmy) and about whom he can be evaluative and gently critical (in the case of Redpenny, the assistant who desperately wants reflected glory). They are not, in dramatic terms, "simple" servant figures. The lengthy description helps communicate this to the performer who will take the roles, so that this brief exchange of dialogue (it goes on for about a page) is already endowed with very specific character traits and occurs in a very specific kind of room.

A reasonable question for the solo performer to ask is whether it is necessary then to perform this lengthy opening description before actually taking on the roles of the characters and speaking the dialogue. "Necessary" is probably arguable in any case. Different performance intentions and contexts will guide the performer to make different decisions. If the performer intends to perform a lengthy scene, has a limited amount of time, and/or wants to foreground the dramatic interaction between characters, economy will dictate that this stage direction, as nuanced and rich as it may be, be edited or dispensed with entirely.

If, on the other hand, the performer wishes to explore the ways in which Shaw is omnipresent, as many critics have argued, using characters as mouthpieces for his social and political attitudes, then including the stage direction will underscore this quality of his writing. This is particularly true given Shaw's stylistic and attitudinal presence in his stage directions: this is more than a simple list of objects to appear onstage or physical identifications of character; the space and time he lavishes on the description of Emmy's visage, along with his ironic and, in his own way, feminist perspective on how the absence of traditional feminine beauty has liberated her from certain social expectations and allowed her a kind of subversive "masculine" power for a woman in this time and this place, is itself worthy of performance. The solo performer must decide what the occasion and its constraints and possibilities allow for. Some may be impatient to leap into the dramatic action; some may want to wander into it in a peripatetic way. No doubt silent readers of Shaw have similar preferences, some skipping the lengthy descriptions (though with considerable loss), some taking as much pleasure from them as from the dialogue. Each approach allows the performer to construct a performance that emphasizes what he or she finds most significant in the text—and that may change from performance to performance. Stage directions, whether they are as brief (but as important to the playwright) as Beckett's initial stage description for *Godot* or as discursive as Shaw's, are part of the text; how you treat them in performance is yet another choice you will face as a solo performer of drama.

Technique is particularly crucial to the solo performer of drama because it is how she or he makes a text composed almost entirely in dialogue "legible," that is, audible and visible, to an audience. The demands of the text should always determine the technical decisions a performer makes, rather than specific technical "rules" serving to confine the performer's choices. Caryl Churchill's sparseness of language and fragmentation of utterances create a performing and performative world quite different from the elaborate, detailed, and measured stage descriptions and directions of George Bernard Shaw. Yet, even within each of these individual texts, the solo performer will find many different possibilities for engaging the play and the audience through the technical tools we have discussed in this chapter: technique does not, should not, preclude creativity and individual choices.

KEY TERMS

backstory

dialogic shifts

focus

lines of placement

stage directions

stichomythia

chapter 12

PERFORMING CHRONICLES, ETHNOGRAPHIC MATERIALS, AND OTHER NONFICTIONAL GENRES

Our book has exposed you to a wide range of materials for performance drawn from multiple genres. We have shown you ways to analyze and embody the speaker and capture the world and people who figure in the texts, whether fiction or nonfiction. In chapter 5, we began our discussion of the performance of nonfiction, introducing you to personal narratives, family histories, and memoirs. This chapter expands on that discussion.

We open with the performance of chronicles (historical documents), including a fanciful one written by a young Jane Austen, and then move on to consider performances based on narratives of place and other nonfictional sources, including political and topical issues that students can bring into their performances. Students can feature their own political values and beliefs, if they so choose, or draw on political and ideological documents and manifestos written by others. News stories, Internet blogs, and letters are lightly mentioned. Students also draw on nonfiction sources that are oral and not text-based: embodied experiences and oral tellings, cultural and ethnographic materials, interviews, as sources for nonfiction performances.

To provide a richer understanding of these materials in performance, we offer a more extensive discussion of cultural and ethnographic research and writings, showing you ways in which you can use them to develop performance scripts. We have included a discussion of how to develop scripts based on interviews with people. As background, we discuss the work of early-twentieth-century anthropologists, followed by a discussion of the work of more recent scholars of performance studies who are or have been engaged in ethnographic research, examining some qualitative interviewing techniques they use. You will recall that earlier, in chapter 5, we discussed E. Patrick Johnson's oral interviews with his grandmother, setting his interview in the context of our discussion of family stories and memoirs. In this chapter, we are focused on nonfiction texts about subjects that lie in the public arena and in global society as well as local social communities. We conclude with a discussion of three recent forays into nonfiction performances and consider three more subgenres: creative nonfiction, performative writing, and mystory. We think you will find it intriguing.

Performances Based on Chronicles

Chronicles and historical accounts offer rich materials for nonfiction performances. They rest on public events, and the events they record have the advantage of having been tested by time. That they are still of interest to many people, over many years, is a good sign when you are selecting material worthy of performance. This section considers three different historical texts, each describing the execution of Mary Queen of Scots (Mary Stuart) on February 8, 1587. Mary Stuart was the cousin of Queen Elizabeth of England (hereafter, we will refer to her as Queen Elizabeth rather than Queen Elizabeth I, since at the time of the writings, there was not yet a Queen Elizabeth II). Mary Stuart was also the mother of James, who later became James VI of Scotland; after his mother's execution and on the death of Queen Elizabeth, he became James I, King of England. Mary had been wed to the dauphin of France when she was just six years old. Widowed by the death of her husband, who had become Francis II, king of France, Mary left France for Scotland and her relatives asserted her right to reign over Scotland. We will not recount the complicated history of Mary's relationship and her struggles with Elizabeth beyond asserting several facts you need to know to make sense of the following accounts. Mary was Catholic whereas Queen Elizabeth, the daughter of Henry VIII and Anne Boleyn (who was later executed), was an Anglican Protestant.

The first account we will discuss is from *History of England, Volume XII*, by J. A. Froude, a historian, published in 1870; the second is from *Mary Queen of Scots and Her Accusers*, by John Hosack, published in 1874; and the third, "Account of the Execution of Queen Mary Stuart," a report of the manner of the execution written in the sixteenth century and included in *The Tragedy of Fotheringay*, by Mrs. Maxwell Scott. For this historical material, we are particularly indebted to a course at the University of Chicago where Carol first encountered these selections.

We have deliberately provided complete passages from each text, bearing in mind both the length of the segment and the degree of drama or excitement, so that you can cut these texts or splice them together with selective cuts, resulting in a text that can be performed within the constraints of a classroom and be under five minutes in duration. Enough of the text is present so that you can understand the event and determine which elements to emphasize and how to portray Mary Stuart.

Start with the portion of J. A. Froude's account reproduced on p. 480. As you read it, think about the speaker, the event described, and the character of the condemned, Mary Queen of Scots. Just before this segment begins, Froude recounts that Mary was allowed to take six of her people with her, including her physician and Barbara Mowbray, whose child she had baptized, as she descended the staircase and entered the great hall where the scaffold, "twelve feet square and two feet and a half high," stood, covered with black cloth (p. 336). The account continues as reproduced in the appendix, and it relies on quoted passages of direct discourse to capture Mary's praying. We are thus very aware of the voice of the historian, Froude, who is carefully orchestrating the narration with the purpose of showing how Mary staged her death, making herself appear a martyr, determined to leave a mark on history and show Queen Elizabeth as her wrongful persecutor. Froude emphasizes the spectacle of the scene, Mary's costume, her self-possession and dignified words, the pitiable plight of her women, and even mentions how she tried to use her hands to shield her neck from the hard wood of the execution block. Observe all these theatrical details. Notice the discrepancy between the way Mary wishes to be perceived and the shocking description of her "withered features of a grizzled, wrinkled old woman." Can you analyze the stance of the historian in this account, identifying his political and religious affiliation? You may want to do some independent research on Froude, the Victorian British historian who pens this account nearly three hundred years after it occurred.

Think about how you might perform this passage of historical text. To do so, you will need to analyze the narrator's motives in this account and also the motives he imputes to the characters, such as Mary Stuart, her companions, and the executioner. Think about the scene of discourse and the scene of story in ways we have discussed earlier (see chapter 8). Look carefully for textual clues that assist you in understanding the beliefs, values, and prejudices of the historian, Froude. Do his sympathies lie with Queen Mary or with Queen Elizabeth? Or are you unable to judge? How does he treat the so-called facts of the account? You are at a disadvantage because you have only a portion of his history but, nonetheless, probe it for its latent and deep meanings. Does its language give you any clues? Can you draw any inferences about the times in which Froude wrote the account from the language in the text itself? Does the writing have a nineteenth-century flavor? Does the account and its language seem particularly dated to you? Could it be the work of a contemporary historian? Would your assessment of this make a difference to how you would perform the text?

How would you want to perform the account of the actual execution? Would you offer a staged reading using a lectern or might you assume the posture of a historian sitting at his desk, mulling over the account, appearing to be in the act of composing it, deliberating about certain word choices, and seemingly reflecting on the portrait of Mary Stuart emerging from the words? Obviously, you could also stage your performance in other ways, but the important thing is to be conscious of your decisions and the reasons why you make them. How would you handle your audience, the students in the classroom? Would you use fourth-wall conventions, or would you open the performance to the audience, incorporating them into it?

Consider the manner of performance you will use. You might develop a minimalist but representational rendering of part of the account. With a few simple, well-chosen props, you could set the scene in your classroom. For example, if your classroom is equipped with a portable wooden reading stand, you might prop it on the floor, using its top surface as the execution block. You could analyze the text for clues about possible costuming. If you lack access to a costume shop where you might pull some period costumes or if you believe you cannot create a plausible imitation of the costumes and setting of the times, you might decide to use the conventions of suggestion rather than representation. If you opt for the presentational mode, you might use scarves of different colors of cloth—black and crimson—manipulating the fabrics throughout the scene to serve as both the draping cloths that cover the rails and also the black of her robe and the crimson of her petticoat described in the account.

You will want to think carefully about technical matters so that your props are smoothly integrated into your performance and do not clutter or overwhelm it. For example, if you choose to use scarves, rehearse your handling of them meticulously, deciding when to move, how to move, on what lines or words. Look at the lines describing the removal of her black robe and jacket and the revelation of the crimson satin. How are you going to deliver or perform the climactic words describing her as "blood-red from head to foot"? You might protract the delivery of the descriptive adjectives, drawing out the vowel sound in the word *black* and tapping the terminal "d" sounds while lingering over the vowels, giving the audience time to register fully the visual spectacle and giving you time to express the emotional intensity of the scene, the power of the moment, along with time in which to draw out and display the crimson scarves. Practice this kind of staging in order to experience how it feels to execute it and to develop the technical mastery necessary to handle the presentational/representational aspects of the display of the garments and props in the scene.

Turn now to John Hosack's account from *Mary Queen of Scots and Her Accusers*. It opens with Mary, "suffering at the time from one of her periodical attacks of rheumatism" (p. 163), receiving the news that Shrewsbury and Kent desire an immediate audience with her. She asks her attendants to remain as witnesses while Beale reads aloud the orders for her execution. Later, her preparations for her execution are described again, with note of her dress: "the dress she had reserved for the occasion was of rich black satin, and she wore a long white veil of crape reaching to the ground" (p. 463). We are told she then "returned to her oratory," where she remained at prayer until the sheriff arrived. After bidding farewell to those who had attended her during her imprisonment, and uttering her innocence, saying she died as a woman true to Scotland and to France and yet willing to see England and Scotland united, she bids the weeping Sir Andrew Melvill farewell. With calm nobility she declines the Anglican services offered by the dean, saying she will die in the Catholic faith. Kent urges her "to leave such Popish trumperies and carry Christ in your heart" (p. 168), and she responds that she is thankful for their prayers but cannot join them, as she is of a different faith. Read carefully how Hosack concludes his account.

Look closely at both chronicles we have discussed and compare the two. Which elements are included in both accounts and which differ? Are some elements present in one, but omitted from the other? What clues help you understand why the perspectives of the two historians are so different? One depicts her as a haggard woman, fanatic in her

Catholicism, manipulative, defiant, and highly theatrical; the other shows a woman at peace with herself and resolute in her convictions.

If you are staging this passage, you will want to give close attention to the frame narrator, looking with particular attention to the first and last lines in the passage quoted in the appendix. This passage lends itself to performance: it is compact and powerful. The narrator, an extension of the historian, Hosack, makes strong choices in the details he includes and the emotional coloration he imbues them with. Most of the details are the same in the three accounts we are using, but the ways they are used are very different. Notice how Hosack describes Mary as she puts off her robe and how he interweaves Mary's direct discourse into his account, maximizing the sympathy we feel toward her. Consider, too, how he handles the other characters present.

Would you want to employ a representational mode for your performance of this passage or a presentational one? Are there advantages in forgoing costume and props here and, rather, offering a presentational mode where you tell us, or read to us, the words of the script, using outfront focus and placement, and letting us imagine the spectacle in our mind's eye and feel the emotions?

Now let us look at "Account of the Execution of Queen Mary Stuart," reprinted in *The Tragedy of Fotheringay*, by Mrs. Maxwell Scott, which you will find on p. 491. Many of the details included in the two excerpts we have already discussed are present in this account, although with important differences. However, we shall cut to the end of the selection and begin just after she has bid her maidservants not to weep, but to pray for her and not to mourn, since now they "should see an end to all their mistress's troubles" (p. 240). A paragraph later, the account resumes:

This done one of her women, having a Corpus Christi cloth lapt up the corner ways, kissing it, put it over the Queen of Scots' face and pinned it fast to the caul of her head. Then the two women departed from her, and she kneeling down upon a cushion most resolutely and without any token or fear, she spake aloud this Psalm in Latin, "In te Domine confido, non confundat in eternum," etc. Then groping for the block she laid down her head, putting her chin on the block with both her hands, which holding there still had been cut off had they been not espied. Then lying upon the block most quietly, and stretched out her arms and legs, cryed, "In manus tuas, Domine," etc., three or four times.

Then she lying very still on the block, one of the executioners holding of her slightly with one of his hands, she endured two strokes of the other executioner with an axe, she making very small noise or none at all, and not stirring any part of her from the place where she lay; and so the executioners cut off her head, saving one little gristle, which being cut asunder he lifted up her head to the view of all the assembly and bade God save the Queen. Then her dressing of lawn falling off from her head it appeared as grey as one of threescore and ten years old, and polled very short, her face in a moment being so much altered from the form she had when she was alive as few could remember her by her dead face. Her lips stirred up and down almost a quarter of an hour after her head was cut off. Then Mr. Dean said with a loud voice, "So perish all the Queen's enemies," and afterwards the Earl of Kent came to the dead body, and standing over it with a loud voice said, "Such be the end of all the Queen's and the Gospel's enemies."

Then one of the executioners pulling off her garters espied her little dog, which was crept under her clothes, which could not be gotten forth but by force. It afterwards would not depart from the dead corpse, but came and laid between her head and her shoulders which being imbrued with her blood was carried away and washed, as all things else were, that had any blood, was either burned or clean washed, and the executioners sent away with money for their fees; not having any one thing that belonged unto her. And so every man being commanded out of the hall except the Sheriff and his men she was carried by them up into a great chamber lying ready for the surgeons to embalm her.

This account uses Elizabethan language and uses some words and spellings that may be unfamiliar to you and seem dated, such as "espied," "kertell," or "chere." You will want to preserve these archaisms in your performance. The other two accounts can be performed with contemporary American speech, intonation, inflection, and pronunciation without doing any real violence to the meaning or spirit of the text, or you may have considered using a standard British stage dialect to capture more fully the sense of the period; either choice would be appropriate. However, in the account based on the Tanner Ms. 78, f. 129, in the Bodleian Library at Oxford, you will want to try to preserve the diction and deliver the speech in such a way that it honors the period in which it is written.

Assume you are performing the passage quoted above. Some of the words may be unfamiliar to you, for example *caul* and the Latin phrases. You may decide to offer an introduction in advance of your performance and explain some of the unfamiliar language. Or you might print up a program with explanatory notes. In either case, you need to understand all the words and the Latin yourself, and you need to speak these particular words with great care. If you understand what you are saying, it is likely that you can perform these passages convincingly and in a way that they are understood, even if the audience does not know the exact translation or precise meaning of all the words. In performance, ignorance shows. Be sure you do understand what you are saying.

This account also has several lengthy sentences that may pose problems for delivery. Look at the sentence describing the dog's unwillingness to part from his mistress. Practice saying the sentence, determining when to pause and deciding how you are going to subordinate one phrase or clause to another. Finally, think about the way this account concludes. Does this account appear to be more factual than the others, or more objective? Back up your answer with textual evidence—always a good strategy when you are analyzing texts and preparing your performances. This kind of spadework often leads to deeper understanding of the text and inspires rich performance choices.

Think back to our discussion in chapter 5 about narrators who faked their identities and the way invented elements occur in nonfiction. This chronicle opens with a statement saying it is "a report of the manner of execution of the Scottish Queen performed the eighth day of February anno 1586 in the great hall within the castle of Fotheringham with relation of speeches uttered and actions happening in the said execution from the delivery of the said Scottish Queen unto Mr. Thomas Andrewes, Esq., Sheriff of the county of Northampton unto the end of the same execution" (p. 170). It certainly does offer a report, but does it also reflect biases or prejudices on the part of its recorder, the narrator? Think closely about the line between fiction and nonfiction and the subtle ways it can be blurred.

These three chronicles are rightly classified as nonfiction. They treat the same historical events but they differ in the facts they select to use and in their interpretations of them. As you have seen, two of the accounts offer radically different interpretations of Mary Queen of Scots. We would not say that the historians are being deceptive or dishonest, but we would note that they are offering accounts from different perspectives, adhering to the "facts" of the event but interpreting them differently. Earlier we discussed extensively issues regarding the reliability and unreliability of narrators in fiction, in drama, and in poetry. Apply these same techniques of analysis to these historical accounts in order to grasp their meanings and decide how to perform their narrators and the historical characters they treat. You need to pay particular attention to analyzing and understanding the motives and intentions of the historians. Thucydides, the classical father of empirical history, told the history of the Peloponnesian Wars between the Athenians and the Spartans (431–404 B.C.) through a vivid narrative that sought to describe and explain the events by reference to their understanding of actual happenings in the material world and the historical personages who so importantly shaped the events. In the case of another great, classical historian, Herodotus, we have another breed of history: he appeals to man's dreams and Gyges's invisible ring in order to tell and explain the full history of the Persian Wars that ended in 479 B.C. Part of his history is drawn from his own knowledge or from sound traditions, ones he trusted, but other parts, such as his stories of Cyrus and Croesus or the conquests of Babylon, are fabulous.

Another kind of historical material that serves students well in performance is letters, both public and personal or private. The letters (and, you could also argue, the diaries) of figures such as the famous diarists Samuel Pepys and Anaïs Nin or the diaries of writers such as Virginia Woolf lend themselves to performance. Letters written about historical events can also be intriguing, for the flavor of the times they offer, but also for the light they shed on their writers.

For example, we had a student who offered a solo performance of a letter written by a soldier during the Civil War. The student turned to historical books to find a letter written from the perspective of a soldier from the South, whose cause had been defeated, addressed to his family at home and expressing his convictions of the rightness of this war. When he first performed the letter in class, the student did not tell the audience anything about the kind of material he was sharing or the perspective from which it was written. If memory serves us, he did not make any mention of the Civil War. The student audience discerned that the letter writer was describing a war, but they did not know which war. They may have thought that World War I or II, or maybe even a more recent war was the war being described. The performer showed, rather than told, the content of the letter. We don't mean that he physically showed the letter from the soldier, or a copy of it, although that would be a possibility. Rather, we are referring to the manner in which he handled his telling. He read the words to his audience, pretending to be the soldier boy who had written them and intending to speak the letter's sentiments with utter conviction. The audience during this first performance of the text was unsettled: a few sensed strong, pro-South, Confederate sentiments, but they were not certain that they were correct in this assumption. Most students thought that the performance gained power and credibility as he progressed, and they developed empathy for the letter writer but remained unsure about its actual historical context. They did not know whether the letter writer was on the winning or the losing side of the war. Although the student performer used a Southern dialect, even that clue was not sufficient for the audience to draw conclusions about which war was being described. Had the performer wanted to clarify his performance and show more about the historical author of the letter, he might have worn a Confederate cap, carried a Confederate flag, or worn a costume to suggest a soldier from the Confederacy during the Civil War. But he chose instead to reveal none of this information explicitly; he expected the audience to comprehend his character through his spoken performance of the words in the letter.

In the first performance of this letter, the student performer did not speak with much conviction, not enough for his audience to recognize that his character was a young soldier. In a reperformance, the student performer was more successful in establishing an empathic relationship with the words of his text; he made a number of clear choices about the approximate age of his character, about his Southern dialect, and he took care with the allusions in his text to actual events. In preparing for the reperformance, he looked up the references and made sure he knew exactly what his character was saying and to what events he referred. The result was that this time, the audience could imagine the soldier he was portraying in great particularity. They recognized that the war—unnamed, but alluded to—was the Civil War, and they understood the irony and tragedy that informed the young man's words—that the war he described and the cause he espoused was doomed. After the reperformance, the audience was able to infer this historical information from his performance.

Before we move away from historical chronicles as the source for nonfiction performance, we want you to look at a whimsical and "prejudiced" account of the "History of England," penned by Jane Austen, author of *Pride and Prejudice* and other classics, when she was a child. We offer this selection to show how you can perform not only serious historical texts but also comic ones poking fun at history. We think you will delight in her picture of Queen Elizabeth and relish the affection she expresses toward Mary Stuart, whom she refers to as an "amiable Woman" brought to an "untimely, unmerited, and scandalous Death" (see p. 496 in the appendix). Think about how you might perform this, capturing the whimsy of its author and highlighting its parodic intent. You may want to try to capture its humor while at the same time raising serious questions about the voice of the narrator. Think more about the ways in which this unreliable historian in nonfiction compares to some of the unreliable narrators we encountered in our earlier discussions of prose fiction. This highly prejudiced, shameless narrator exposes in disarming ways some of the assumptions we make about the proper role of a historian in nonfiction. She has no qualms about expressing her likes and dislikes of people in history. Does she have any regard for facts? Do a little research and see what you discover. Does this selection belong in the category of nonfiction?

Performances Based on Place

If you who want to focus on place, not people, look at travelogues, memoirs, and biographical or autobiographical books to provide you with material for your performances. You could perform a script based on your neighborhood, hometown, or city. You might draw on other nonfictional sources, such as atlases, almanacs, travel guides, or geography books. To give you an example of a memoir that provides excellent material for a performance on place, we will share a passage from a recent book, *Never a City So Real*, by Alex Kotlowitz, a former staff writer at the *Wall Street Journal*. Kotlowitz wrote the heartbreaking book *There Are No Children Here*, considered by the New York Public Library to be one of the most important books of the twentieth century.

Never a City So Real is about the Chicago housing projects and their inhabitants, and in it, Kotlowitz reveals his genius for place. He captures the city through its people, but he also has a special view of the city (he's from New York but lived in Chicago for more than twenty years). Read the following passage, considering it as a part of a memoir, that is, nonfiction, written to evoke a sense of place.

The world intersects at the corner of Lawrence and Kedzie Avenues, on the city's northwest side.

The names of the commercial establishments read like an intercontinental guidebook. Within a three-block stretch, there is Raul's Tire Shop and a Supermercado, there is Holy Land Baker and Jerusalem Food and Liquor, there is Jas Hind Grocery, New Seoul Optical, Thai Little Home Café, and Patricia Cowboy's Fashion. More than half the people in this neighborhood, which is known as Albany Park, were born in a foreign country. This is America's gateway, the port of entry for newcomers to this country. For small merchandisers, the biggest-selling item is phone calling cards. One establishment sells *only* calling cards. The local Volta Elementary School offers bilingual classes in Spanish, Gujarati, Arabic, Vietnamese, and Bosnian. Six clocks in the hallway are set to the times in Sarajevo, Lima, Jerusalem, New Delhi, Hanoi, and Chicago. Albany Park, one resident told me, "is the neighborhood for everybody else who doesn't have a neighborhood."

For half a century, this community of wood-framed homes, brick bungalows, and three- and four-story tenements was home to mostly Russian and Eastern European Jews. Then in the 1960s, Koreans moved in, and they became such a political force that Lawrence Avenue was given the honorary designation of Seoul Drive. Then immigrants from unraveling nations poured in, refugees from Guatemala and El Salvador, families fleeing the fragile Mexican economy, and then Laotians, Thais, Cambodians, and Filipinos fleeing the political instability of their homelands, and finally refugees from Iran, Iraq, Lebanon, and Yemen. By this time, many of Albany Park's original settlers had moved on. Temple Beth Israel first was converted into a Korean Presbyterian church and is now a Romanian Pentecostal church. Congregation Mount Sinai became, not without irony, the Beirut Restaurant. From Albany Park, it has been suggested, you can watch the world change. (pp. 140–41)

We are asking you to read and perform this passage in order to inspire you to create a script and develop a nonfiction performance based on your own hometown or neighborhood. You can either look for sources on your town or write your own account.

Analyze how Kotlowitz describes Albany Park, beginning with a catalog of street names, its places of commerce, its racial and ethnic diversity, as though he is writing "an intercontinental guidebook." Think about the voice of the narrator and the places he describes. Can you understand the rationale for what he selects to describe and what he excludes, if you can infer it? Pay attention to the way the writer handles his own voice in his narrative and the way he reveals telling bits of information about his own values, beliefs, and politics. Try developing this segment into a performance piece, perhaps using images taken from the Internet to visually immerse your audience in the place, or you might include images of street maps, street signs, or specific places of commerce while you narrate the text.

How are you going to make your verbal text compelling through your performance of it? Since this is an exercise in the performance of nonfiction, take particular care to attend to real places, the real time, and maybe even the real author as you compile your script and develop its media components.

Since much of Kotlowitz's prose also describes the people who inhabit this area, think about how you might treat them. Would you use video footage or shots of their faces? How could you gather artifacts that express the various nationalities? What are the pitfalls of this approach? What are its advantages to you as a performer?

To what extent would you try to represent Kotlowitz in your performance? He is drawing on real places and people and he is the arbiter determining what to include and what to omit. Is he important to your nonfiction performance? If you do decide you want to make him an aspect of your performance, treating him as an ethnographer of sorts, what clues to his nature do you find in the text? In the passage we quoted, he represents himself as cosmopolitan, concerned with global populations and movements, actual commercial stores in the three-block stretch, but he also colors his account by expressing a certain breed of patriotism (and perhaps, nostalgia), stressing that this neighborhood is "America's gateway, the port of entry for newcomers to this country." Notice all the details he includes that point to the bilingual instruction, the flow of peoples and immigrants, and the intercontinental flavor of the place. He mentions "Spanish, Gujarati, Arabic, Vietnamese, and Bosnian." In the next paragraph, he speaks of the history of shifting populations who have inhabited the neighborhood, starting with the Russian and Eastern European Jews and concluding with the Yemenites. How does this catalog of peoples help us to infer Kotlowitz's political leanings? Do we sense from his choice of adjectives that he feels affection for these disadvantaged, immigrant groups? Notice his word choice when he talks about "unraveling" nations, the "fragile Mexican economy," and "political instability." He finds irony in the fact that the Congregation Mount Sinai became "the Beirut Restaurant." Think of other ways in which this same neighborhood might be described. How might a city planner or someone interested in urban renewal view it? Think about the values and beliefs implicit and explicit in Kotlowitz's account and about the way you want your beliefs and values to figure in your nonfiction performance.

A nonfiction performance of this text might focus on the neighborhood and emphasize place, in which case, you, as a performer, need to make sure you can bring these particular streets and these real people to life for your audience. You can do this by relying chiefly on your powers of speaking language so that it breathes life into the words that evoke these places; or you might choose to supplement your performance with video images of the neighborhood and its people. Think about the size of your performance space and how you will project the images, if you use photos, or blowups of still lifes, or your video or digital images. Be sure to consider the size and scale of your visuals, relative to the space where you are performing. Also, consider how you control your audience's focus, so that if you have them experiencing visuals as well as live performance, their attention goes to the images or to you in a manner you have anticipated. Rehearse the performance in the actual space and bring a buddy along to be an audience member and to check on the sight lines and audibility of your performance. It is very frustrating for an audience if they cannot see the visual displays or if they cannot hear clearly.

If you have chosen to prepare your own text for the description of place, be sure to write well and rehearse your own words. You want the language to flow, be descriptive, and to be written with style.

Performance as Political Commentary

Another popular form of nonfiction performance for students is one that allows the students to compile a script and shape the events or people described in order to deliver political commentary or make a political statement. Often, these performances draw on cultural materials and employ ethnographic techniques of gathering information about the place and its inhabitants, your research subjects. For example, you might do a performance based on the genocide in Rwanda, Hurricane Katrina, the death penalty, animal rights, gun control, a snippet of life in your dormitory, or a current issue of controversy on your campus. Later in this chapter we will discuss more fully the concept of the ethnographic interview and the research methodologies associated with this kind of work.

Anna Deavere Smith is an actress who has turned her talents to offering social commentary and creating scripts, plays, and performances about cultural conflicts. Her book *Fires in the Mirror* offers a play about the emotions and vying for political positions of the participants in the Crown Heights, Brooklyn, New York, racial incident in August 1991 when a black boy was accidentally killed by a car driven in a Lubavitcher rabbi's motorcade. A yeshiva student from a Jewish rabbinical academy was killed in retaliation by a small group of black residents in the same neighborhood, and racial violence and unrest followed. Jews were pitted against blacks, and old racial struggles resurfaced in an ugly event. In another book, *Twilight: Los Angeles, 1992*, she offered another play—a work of "documentary theater"—about the Los Angeles riots that broke out in the wake of the not-guilty verdict at the end of the trial of the four Los Angeles policemen who beat Rodney King, a black motorist dragged from his car and kicked and beaten mercilessly, an incident of terrible police brutality that was captured on video camera and aired on television for the nation to see, causing a huge outburst of rage against racism in America. In these plays and in her brilliant performances Smith takes on the voices and roles of numerous people involved in the scene or its retelling. We cite her work here to give you another example of the way nonfiction can be performed. We will return to Anna Deavere Smith's work in our final chapter.

Newspaper accounts, Internet blogs, political pamphlets, speeches, and public records and documents also provide excellent sources for nonfiction performances. For example, if you wanted to compile a script on the subject of the death penalty, you will find materials both pro and con on the matter. Look for accounts by physicians on lethal injection, materials written by prisoners and people on death row, or by lawyers defending death penalty inmates. Clarence Darrow's famous plea for leniency in the infamous case of the killing of Bobby Frank by Nathan Leopold and Richard (Dickie) Loeb is an excellent text for performance.

The chilling story of the cold-blooded, premeditated murder of a boy chosen at random, the perpetrators, and their victim continues to haunt the public imagination. In 1924, two graduate students at the University of Chicago, ages eighteen and nineteen, one quite brilliant, studying ornithology, the other malevolent and cunning, set out to commit the perfect crime. But for the fact that Leopold's glasses fell out of his pocket, the two men probably would never have been apprehended and brought to justice. There are numerous books and movies about this crime, and there are also staged versions, one written by John Logan, *Never the Sinner*, that traveled to off-Broadway sites after its inception in a staged performance at Northwestern University (some of you may know John Logan's work in Hollywood: he wrote the screenplay for the movie *Gladiator*). A recent book, *For the Thrill of It*, by Simon Baatz, gives the full story and will probably stand as the definitive account of this ghastly crime. Think about how you might perform the Leopold and Loeb murder case. You might choose to address Darrow's words to members of a hypothetical jury, and stage this in a representational manner; or you could address your words out front, incorporating the real audience into your performance. In compiling your material, you could offer a performance montage, assembling materials from a number of sources, reflecting different perspectives. You might speak also in your own voice, making your perspective a part of the performance, or you could gather materials of others and use yourself merely as the performer to express the voices and words of others. You need to decide where your own voice fits into your performance, if it does. You might want to look also at other books about grisly crimes, such as Truman Capote's *In Cold Blood*, for material to develop into a text for a nonfiction performance. The Capote book represents another variant on nonfiction, the new journalism, and we will discuss it in that context later in this chapter. In the next section, we will not dwell on the actual subject matter of the nonfiction performance since your choices are vast, but concentrate on some matters of methodology involved in performances where you draw on human subjects whom you have interviewed for your material, including the ethical choices implicit in the methodology.

Ethnography

Ethnography is defined broadly as the study of and writing about culture. Performance rituals, social dramas, and other embodied cultural behavior are often the subjects of ethnographic research. Typically, responsible ethnographic fieldwork requires what Clifford Geertz, a cultural anthropologist, called "thick description." To write about anthropological research using "thick description" requires, first, the anthropologist's immersion in the lives and culture of other peoples, and second, the writing of an account of the research that offers painstakingly exact descriptions of the findings. In the late nineteenth and early twentieth centuries, much of the ethnographic fieldwork that was done was practiced on cultures different from the anthropologist's own. These people from faraway "exotic" lands were often referred to as the other.

Early pioneering cultural anthropologists who practiced ethnography include Ruth Benedict, known for her remarkable books *Patterns of Culture* and *The Chrysanthemum and the Sword*; Margaret Mead, her pupil at Barnard College, known best for two of her books, *Coming of Age in Samoa: A Psychological Study of Primitive Youth for Western Civilization* (1928) and *Growing Up in New Guinea: A Comparative Study of Primitive Education* (1930); and Franz Boas, head of the department of anthropology at Columbia University, who wrote *Anthropology and Modern Life* (1928), *General Anthropology* (1938), and *Race, Language and Culture* (1940). Both Mead and Benedict, and also Zora Neale Hurston, studied under Franz Boas. You will recall from chapter 5 that Zora Neale Hurston, in *Tell My Horse*, wrote extensively about voodoo; Hurston's trips to Jamaica and Haiti were undertaken at the prompting of Boas. Mead and Benedict formed a very close friendship (some scholars argue that they were lovers) and shared correspondence about their fieldwork under the tutelage of Boas.

These early-twentieth-century anthropologists assumed a stance in relationship to their ethnographic subjects that is characterized by disinterested participant observation of a culture different from that of the ethnographer who studied it. The ethnographers wrote about the cultural other and often immersed themselves in the cultures of their ethnographic subjects, living in their communities for many years. Many recent anthropologists take issue with their methods and have skewered these early anthropologists and their assumptions about the cultures they studied. But these quarrels are not our subject here. In the 1980s Clifford Geertz, in an article entitled "Blurred Genres," wrote of the paradigm shift that characterized his generation of anthropologists and, in particular, anthropologists interested in performance. Mead, Benedict, and their circle, including Boas, thought of culture as stable, part of a continuous tradition with coherent structures.

Recent schools of thought, taking their impetus from the ethnographic traditions of the interpretive social sciences, stress culture and performance as a process, not static: culture is dynamic; its meanings are emergent, not determinate or fixed; the researcher of its processes stands in a double relationship to the culture, standing both within and outside of it, openly acknowledging their own participant role in relationship to the account they are rendering and the culture it represents.

James Clifford wrote an excellent book, *The Predicament of Culture: Twentieth-Century Ethnography, Literature, and Art* (1988), setting forth these new ideas about culture and performance. In the discipline of performance studies, scholars such as Victor Turner, Richard Schechner, Renato Rosaldo, Marvin Carlson, and Diana Taylor have written at length on the relationship between anthropology and theater and performance studies. Richard Schechner, as a guest editor to a special issue of *The Drama Review* in 1973, devoted the issue to the relationship between anthropology and theater. All of these scholars owe a large debt to the writings of sociologist Erving Goffman, who wrote extensively about play and theatricality in everyday life. Dwight Conquergood's work, too, reflects the influence of this group of thinkers. Recent turns in this ethnographic stance have placed even more emphasis on the responsibilities of the ethnographers to the culture they study and their roles as witnesses of and participants in the cultures they depict. In recent performance studies, theory and practice, the postmodern, postcolonial world and its cultural practices and systems of knowledge have increasingly been interrogated, with more and more insistence that the relationship between the researcher and researched be rethought, or reconfigured, and made more humble in an effort to permit scholars and practitioners of performance to better understand our complex, global, and multicultural world in which ideas from Western thought have lost some of their ascendancy and other ways of knowing and thinking, derived from other parts of our world and other peoples, have come into the purview of the academy and its professions.

The time anthropologists and ethnographers from other disciplines spend in the field, doing fieldwork, varies enormously. In ethnographic fieldwork done by scholars of performance studies, the period of study can be decades, or it can be very short and very focused. You need to be mindful of the exacting discipline necessary to understand another people, and if you are adapting ethnographic techniques for the purposes of performances in your class, be sensitive to the need to respect the other that you are representing in your performance.

Dwight Conquergood, a performance scholar who studied the Hmong and the people of Laos early in his academic career, wrote an article, "Performing as a Moral Act: Ethical Dimensions of the Ethnography of Performance" (1985). Many students of ethnographic performance in our field have found this article and its description of dialogic performance most helpful. He mapped out four different stances that performers and writers of the cultural other have assumed and argued for what he called a "dialogical performance understanding" of the subject, drawing on a concept written about by the scholar Mikhail Bakhtin. Conquergood found fault with each stance for its failure to do justice to the ethnographic subject and then identified the appropriate ethical stance for responsible ethnography. His colorful titles for the four wrongheaded stances are largely self-explanatory: 1) the custodial rip-off; 2) the ethnographer's infatuation; 3) the curator's exhibitionism; and 4) the skeptic's cop-out. As the titles convey, in each instance the ethnographer's motive for research colors and distorts the findings. The dialogic stance is one where the ethnographer recognizes his or her own positionality in the research and motives for conducting the research and is more of a witness to and participant with the subjects described than a supposedly neutral, disinterested observer. He believes that many so-called disinterested, neutral observers often fail to correctly judge their motives.

The custodial rip-off occurs when the ethnographer conducts his research with a superior, possessive attitude, controlling and displaying the other while actually showing little or no respect for the other and too high a regard for himself. The ethnographer's infatuation reflects a naive, even insulting, ignorance of the subject; in the researcher's enthusiasm for and romanticism of the other, she is likely to ignore or neglect the realities of the other, the often difficult facts, and see only the features she wants to see. As a result, she waxes rhapsodic about her research subject and, while seemingly diminishing her own importance, actually practices a very distorted version of ethnography. The curator's exhibitionism occurs when the researcher fetishizes the so-called exotic element of the other, emphasizing the distance between the researcher and the other, and in so doing, exaggerates the primitive aspects of the other—their rareness and their remoteness from civilization—while seeing himself as a collector and guardian, one who safeguards these rare and special species. The skeptic's cop-out reflects the opposite instinct on the part of the researcher: rather than focusing on the exotic in the other, emphasizing differences and ignoring similarities between herself and the other, the skeptic disparages her subject, remaining aloof and outside of the group studied, incapable of engagement with or understanding of the other.

Try shifting the frame of reference here and applying these concepts and terms to your stance as a performer of the nonfictional other. Don't let the flashiness and pizzazz of the labels get in your way, but draw on your experiences, both as someone trying to observe and perform another and as an audience member of nonfiction performances. You may want to start with Carol's account of her Haiti story in chapter 5. She called it a "tourist story," in part because she was fearful that her own account of voodoo in Haiti contained too many features of an ethnographer's infatuation with the subject. Others of you may feel that she exhibited shades of the curator's exhibitionism in her tale. Was she too consumed with displaying Haiti as the subject of her narrative at the expense of actually understanding the Haitian people? Think about these questions and Conquergood's performance paradigm to see if they help you to understand your own positionality in your nonfiction performance.

By positionality we refer not only to your physical proximity and relationship to the subjects you study, but your belief and knowledge systems, your values, your project, your motives, and a host of other matters related to the way you situate (position) yourself in relationship to the subject you study. If you apply the term *positionality* to the subjects of your research, the subjects are the focus of your approach and you have an obligation to capture their indigenous meanings and experiences, taking care to acknowledge the ways in which those meanings and experiences are in opposition to dominant practices. The concept asks you to reflect on your own role and your motives in your research in a critical manner. If you find these concepts and labels helpful, push yourselves to describe and identify the performative behaviors, both in the performance and in your writing about it, that support your decision. See if you can also analyze the performances of other class members in relationship to these concepts and this terminology. Finally, think about the ethical consequences of these stances. How do they affect the fairness, justice, and concern with accuracy in representation in your performance and those of others?

For ethical reasons, Conquergood wanted to discourage performances of the cultural other that condescended to their subjects. He warned the student of ethnographic performance to respect the other, treat the other in a way you would want to be treated, and openly acknowledge your own role in the research, the reasons behind your inquiry, and your motives, as best and as fully as you can. Don't succumb to a distorted vision that treats your subject as either less than or more than it actually is in your zeal to perform seemingly "exotic" features of people unlike yourself or in your eagerness to be flashy.

In *Critical Ethnography: Methods, Ethics, and Performance*, D. Soyini Madison offers an excellent introduction to her subject. Critical ethnography is a particular kind of ethnography wherein the ethnographer assumes an engaged, activist role in their study. If you are interested in pursuing a political purpose and an ethnographic approach to your nonfiction subject, you should consult her text. She offers advice on how to position yourself in your fieldwork, writing, and performance and provides excellent interviewing tips, showing you how to frame your interview questions and, later, how to develop a script from your research. And, most important, she features a political agenda.

Madison had seen a film related to women's human rights in Ghana, West Africa, where she lived for almost three years. In response, she developed two books, the one cited above, and *Acts of Activism: Human Rights as Radical Performance*, devoted to defining critical ethnography from a performance perspective and illuminating three case studies that demonstrate how performance and scholarship can contribute to a political activist agenda for change in the real world. The file was a documentary about Ghanaian women's fears and desperation when confronted with a father's demand that his daughter undergo female circumcision (also referred to as female incision, female genital mutilation, or by its medical nomenclature, clitorectomy). The documentary film concluded with a young woman expressing the hope and security she now feels in safe asylum in America. Madison was outraged by the film and offended by its representations of Ghana and Ghanaian women. The film was completely contrary to her own experience of and knowledge about Ghana.

Madison, an African American woman, teacher, and scholar, knew firsthand of the struggles and triumphs of courageous Ghanaian women activists. She wanted to dispute the film's interpretation of the Ghanaian women's experience, especially because the film called itself a documentary, and, to her mind, it thus had an obligation to justly represent the situation. She felt she was witnessing an imperfect and profoundly prejudiced representation of Ghanaian womanhood. She knew that the maker of the ethnographic documentary meant to do good, that she was well intentioned; but she was convinced that the film gave "a gross and dangerous misrepresentation of Ghana and her people." You can read Madison's book to learn more about how she uses the approach of critical ethnography and performance to challenge the way Ghana is perceived. She writes: "Critical ethnography . . . begins with an ethical responsibility to address processes of unfairness or injustice within a particular lived domain" (p. 5). She goes on to state that the "critical ethnographer also takes us beneath surface appearances, disrupts the *status quo*, and unsettles both neutrality and taken-for-granted assumptions by bringing to light underlying and obscure operations of power and control" (p. 5). She argues for an approach that will enable the critical ethnographer to attend to and hear (with a very special kind of hearing—let us call it deep hearing) in order to learn about "the voices and experiences of subjects whose stories are otherwise restrained and out of reach" (p. 5).

If you want to use nonfiction performance to offer a critique of given institutional practices, social practices, or regimes of knowledge, you will want to give particular attention to your positionality in your account. We defined positionality earlier, but here we want to emphasize that the word *position* refers to the place, metaphorically as well as literally, you inhabit in your own performance. In considering your positionality, you need to reflect on and understand your own cultural and personal values, assumptions, knowledge base, and ethics in order to frame your representation of the culture of the other. To develop her discussion of this brand of ethnography with its understanding of positionality, Madison draws on *Postcritical Ethnography: Reinscribing Critique* by George W. Noblit, Susana Y. Flores, and Enrique G. Murillo Jr. The emphasis in this work is on the ethnographer's own position, especially as it relates to dominant structures of power, and it keenly interrogates the beliefs and ethics of the ethnographer. Similarly, in your own decision to assume a committed, activist position in relation to your nonfiction material, you will want to question your own motives, beliefs, and knowledge and make conscious decisions in light of this inquiry about how you will handle the representation of yourself in your performance. Another useful source to consult is Charlotte Davis's *Reflexive Ethnography: A Guide to Researching Selves and Others* (1999), and a richer phenomenological inquiry into the ethics of responsibility is found in the writings of Emmanuel Levinas, especially *Totality and Infinity: An Essay on Exteriority.* Madison's book discusses Levinas's ideas about the special system of responsibilities that accrue from the dynamic of the encounter with the other; he sees it as conferring a sense of obligation to serve justice that precedes any other, more specific decision or objective on the part of the ethnographer.

This brief discussion of the ethnographic approach to nonfiction performance is designed to acquaint you with some of the issues involved in this kind of performance and to encourage you to explore these matters further, both in performance and in the scholarship of cultural performance, if this is a form of performance that interests and excites you. It is yet another example of how to perform nonfiction texts.

For classroom purposes, some students might decide to test their powers of observation and imitation by choosing to perform another student on campus, perhaps a student leader, someone in a campus group, or someone in a dormitory whom the student knows or has chosen to know for the purposes of performing them. This is no easy task. You don't want to caricature the person you are rendering, and in many cases you may not be sufficiently confident of your gift of mime to actually imitate them. Your goal here is to present the other person convincingly and believably, in a manner that honors the other and is worthy of your classmates' time. Some of your classmates may recognize the person you are performing, adding a special kind of delight for some of your audience members but also raising the bar of expectations for you. Students electing to do this kind of performance should consider using ethnographic concepts and the tool of the qualitative ethnographic interview in order to learn more about the student who is the subject of their nonfiction performance.

The Ethnographic Interview

The ethnographic interview, unlike the survey interview, seeks to give full latitude to the subjects to express themselves, not in a manner that requires verification of the truth of what is said but in a manner that aspires to know the subject more completely through the subject's own voice and experience. In this kind of qualitative interview (in contrast to the interview that seeks facts and verifiable, quantitative information), the interviewer and interviewee are, as Madison says in *Critical Ethnography*, "in partnership and dialogue as they construct memory, meaning, and experience together" (p. 25). The interview offers the possibility of exploring people's longings and desires, their social milieu, their communal strivings, their political possibilities, and their personal and social history. The interviewer's voice is not absent from the interview, although it aspires to be subordinate to the voice of the interviewee. This kind of interview is supple in its form.

You will want to think about how you can phrase interview questions in such a way that they invite openness and provide an opportunity for the subject to answer the question but, at the same time, take it in any direction they want. For example, let us say that you are doing a nonfiction performance in which you want a collage of voices and the subject is the death penalty. You have decided to interview people from your dormitory, but you do not necessarily know the people whom you will interview, and you don't want them to know anything more about your views than is necessary to have them agree to be interviewed. In short, you may think you need to tell them that you are interviewing students on their ideas about the death penalty and that you are conducting the interviewing as part of an assignment for a class. You may also want to tell them that you will be drawing on their responses for a performance. Or, if you do not do this, you need to have a justification for your decision.

In interviewing students in the kind of situation described above, what kind of opening question do you plan to ask? How can you phrase it so that it is open-ended and does not close down discussion? Will you be direct and ask: "What do you think about the death penalty?" If you use this approach, will you build from the response you get, fully prepared to let the interview take you in directions shaped by your interviewee? One technique here is to pick up a phrase or an idea your interviewee expresses and repeat it, gently urging them to say more. Another technique is to make noises of affirmation as they talk, nodding and saying "yes" and waiting through their silences until they pick up their own line of response and amplify it. Or, adopting a more intrusive strategy, you could open with a statement describing the project you are doing, your reasons for posing questions about the death penalty, perhaps followed by a statement of your own position, and then ask to know more about their position. Obviously, this could lead to quite different results from your subjects, and your own role in the interview will become more important and will be something you will want to investigate. Of course, you could decide to develop a questionnaire and use the interview situation to elicit answers to a predetermined set of questions. What are the implications of this approach? What are its strengths and weaknesses in the context of this exercise—a performance of a nonfiction subject assigned for a class?

Creative Nonfiction, Performative Writing, and Mystory

In this chapter, we have examined what might be described as chronicle traditions of nonfiction, as represented by the various descriptions of the execution of Mary Stuart, self-consciously parodic narratives such as Jane Austen's juvenilia, and ethnographic approaches, which attempt to write the lives of groups of people from their perspective and within the language, terms, and values of their culture. We might see the chronicle approach as stemming from print-centered ways of conceiving of the relationship between language and reality—that the written word can "capture" fact and truth, that the parody questions such traditions, and that ethnography returns to the oral-traditional commitment to embodied experience as the source of reality.

Yet another emerging tradition, the one with which we will conclude our chapter, takes into account the changing nature and role of media, particularly electronic and digital media, in not only our daily lives in general, but in how we "know" and "speak" lives, both personal and public. Theorists such as Walter Ong and Eric Havelock have focused on the shifts between orality and literacy from the times of the ancient Greeks to the twentieth century, looking at both Western and non-Western cultures as having equally important things to contribute to knowledge (thus implicitly and explicitly criticizing what has been called a logocentric—or writing-based—bias against cultures that exist primarily in states of orality). Marshall McLuhan pioneered modern media studies, exhorting us all to recognize and contemplate the idea that "the medium is the message," a phrase you may have heard before. What does it mean to say "the medium is the message"? McLuhan also argued that all media needed to be viewed as "extensions of man" (by which he meant all humans)—that radio extends the ear, film the eye, and so forth. Think about this: which media extend the senses of taste, touch, and smell? What about other senses beyond the traditional five; some would argue for such sensory categories as kinesthesia (the sense of motion or movement), thermal sense (heat, cold, and temperature), and sense of space (proxemics) and time (chronemics) as sensory categories. Can you think of media that extend these human senses?

Within fundamentally verbal traditions, we see developments in what are considered to be nonfiction texts. One overarching category is called "creative nonfiction," a term that is still being formed and offers room for debate as to what it contains and excludes. In its broadest sense, it is nonfiction whose techniques and purpose are not simply informative or reportorial in a traditional sense, but which uses elements of literature, such as the imagery of poetry, the points of view of prose fiction, and the conflict and dialogue of drama, to produce some of the pleasures and effects of what has been traditionally called "creative writing." It can be argued that creative nonfiction has existed in some ways since the time of the classical historians; as we have noted, Greek historians such as Herodotus and nineteenth-century historians such as Thomas

Carlyle, in *The French Revolution,* employed narrative techniques associated with myth, fairy tale, romance, and the novel. More recently, fiction writer Truman Capote claimed to have invented the nonfiction novel in his crime narrative *In Cold Blood,* a book we mentioned earlier in this chapter. While claims of invention of a particular literary form are always suspect, what Capote was pointing to was his introduction of novelistic techniques such as third person narration of the interiority of the criminals at the center of the story and description of the actions of the Clutters, the Kansas farm family whose murder formed the catalyst for the book, actions neither Capote nor anyone else could have verified with absolute certainty on the day they were killed. While he based his book on extensive research, assisted by the novelist Harper Lee, he made it clear that some of what it included was an imagining of events, experiences, and thoughts that could never be verified in any documentary way. Creative nonfiction, in general, does not tend to invent wholly fictional elements, but it uses techniques drawn from fiction and other literary genres in self-conscious ways that the audience is implicitly expected to understand. Capote includes narrative of what the Clutters were thinking on the day they were killed, and any reasonable reader will understand and accept that such narration is part of a writer's interaction with "the facts," not an attempt to pass himself off as possessing extrasensory perception. Fraud enters when a writer wholly invents and presents as fact things that did not happen and which cannot be understood by his audience in the frame of the imagination.

One kind of writing that can be classified as creative nonfiction is what in recent years has been called "performative writing." It is important to distinguish between performative writing and writing for performance. Performative writing may indeed be performed, as may any of the other kinds of texts we have discussed throughout this book, but what makes it "performative" is not its availability for performance; indeed, much of what is categorized as performative writing may never be spoken aloud. Similarly, texts written for performance are not necessarily performative, in the sense in which the term is used here, though they can be.

What makes a piece of writing performative is the way in which it actually enacts something, rather than describing or stating something. J. L. Austin and, later, John Searle developed what they called "speech act theory," in which they distinguished between utterances that actually made something happen (such as a wedding vow or a trial verdict) and those that merely describe or assert a state of being (constative utterances). While later philosophers and linguists have argued that even in constative utterances there is likely to be some kind of performance, the general distinction between kinds of speech acts is useful.

Performance theorist Della Pollock has written extensively and with depth about the characteristics of performative writing. In performative writing, which she discusses in her article "Performing Writing," she sees the ability of language to be restored to what she calls "corporeal history," a location in the body that we may associate with oral traditions and some forms of ethnography (p. 74). She argues that "writing as *doing* displaces writing as *meaning*" (p. 75). What is the distinction between doing and meaning? How is it relevant to any kind of performance you might create? Are doing and meaning totally separate realms of function and action? (Pollock does not argue that they are—notice she uses the word *displace*, not *replace*.) For Pollock, all "good writing" (her evaluative term) serves a social function. Do you agree? Why or why not?

Pollock offers what she calls six "excursions into performative writing," her use of the word *excursions* itself emphasizing doing, a set of enacted performances, rather than knowledge to be codified and absorbed. Performative writing, she suggests, is typically characterized by the following qualities:

1. It is *evocative*: it uses language to bring worlds and experiences into presence, not simply stating (or imitating) existence, but making it real and multidimensional for its readers.
2. It is *metonymic*: metonymy refers to figures of speech in which either a part of an object is meant to stand for the whole or some quality associated with an object (or person, experience, or idea) stands for it. Here, Pollock uses the term to describe the ways in which performative writing is always *partial*, in actuality and in aspiration, rather than summative, attempting to be complete (p. 82).
3. It is *subjective*: Pollock distinguishes between other uses of this word and her specialized one—performative writing focuses on "performed relationships between or among subjects" (p. 86).
4. It is *nervous*: performative writing is "anxious . . . unable to settle into a clear, linear course . . . restless . . . traversing spatial and temporal borders" (pp. 90–91).
5. It is *citational*: a citation, as you know from writing research papers, is a kind of reference, often a quotation from a related, in some cases "authoritative," text, acknowledging the ways in which

all writing is indebted to and enmeshed with previous writing
(and, by implication, writing to come).

6. It is *consequential*: something new happens as a result of a piece of
performative writing having been written and/or read; not necessarily the same thing as "rhetorical," as Pollock cautions, because
rhetoric tends to adapt itself to a specific, existing audience, and
performative writing creates a new public, and the consequences
may not yet be imagined by the writer.

While these ideas are complex, can you grasp how such a view of writing
might be inherently different (and probably formally, as well) from the
kinds of writing you typically do for classroom assignments? It is less likely
to be driven by a single thesis it is trying to "prove," and its use of what
we are accustomed to calling "evidence" or "support" will be radically
different in nature — it may be employed less to prove or state than to put
the action of knowing through language (including languages other than
verbal) into motion. Go back and think about some of the selections you
have read in this textbook — do some of them seem to you to fit Pollock's
description of performative writing more than others? Which ones? In
what ways?

A specific form of performative writing developed by the theorist and
teacher Gregory Ulmer is what he has named "mystory." Ulmer argues
that writing today — both academic and nonacademic — needs to acknowledge and address the ways in which different media have reshaped what
language does and how it does it. He calls this field *teletheory* (drawn
from the root *tele-*, meaning "across," as in *telephone* and *telegraph*),
while the specific purpose and activities of writing in cultures that have
been influenced by electronic and digital media he calls *heuretics*.
Here Ulmer returns to classical traditions of rhetoric, in which "invention," the gathering of and employment of information, arguments, and
other phenomena, was designed to make something new — and that
something new was knowledge. Ulmer contrasts heuretics with hermeneutics, the study and method of interpreting texts which has been the
dominant mode of critical and scholarly discourse for many centuries.
Hermeneutics views texts (and the language out of which they are made)
as puzzles with solutions to be figured out; heuretics views the compositional process as one of making new knowledge out of existing texts,
which combine in ways that are not simply accumulative but syncretic —
mixed together until the blend is other than the sum of its parts.

Ulmer operates under the premise that all readers (and, hence, writers) begin from where they are—a particular position, experience, and perspective—rather than from a more general set of abstract ideas. In this, he aligns himself with the contemporary historiographer Hayden White, who argues for a writing of history that begins with or engages on some level that which is personal and then moves out to larger groupings of people, events, and culture. Ulmer calls the genre of writing that emerges from heuretics "mystory," a pun on "history" (the individual speaking as an "I" versus the third person chronicler of "his") and on "mystery," in which the process is itself one of following pathways that may not initially be clear, self-evident, or directed. Ulmer notes, too, that mystory as a tradition is deeply influenced by feminism's "herstory" in its acknowledgment that personal experience is not extraneous to scholarly and intellectual discourse, but central to it and to what makes it matter. As one slogan of feminism would have it, "The personal is always the political." Ulmer encourages writers to engage personal, public, and what he calls disciplinary forms of discourse in mystory texts. By disciplinary, he is most immediately referring to the ways in which academic fields of knowledge go about their work, name their subjects, define and delineate methods, and decide on what matters—but can you see ways to expand the idea of disciplinary beyond the classroom to everyday life? Professions may be seen to be disciplinary, everything from what constitutes knowledge in nuclear physics to the knowledge of clerking at a mall. Each has its own practices, its own standards for knowledge, its own ways of talking about its subject matter.

There are many ways into and through the mystory as a form of creative nonfiction and performative writing, and its theorists are quick to point out that the very nature of it tends to preclude anything like a formula or set of ironclad instructions or directions. Mystory does tend to invoke popular culture as key to our personal experiences of knowledge—everything from film to comic books to video games to souvenirs from tourist spots and so forth—and as the discourse of electronic and digital media, which saturate our daily lives on both conscious and unconscious levels. It tends to include narratives, often multiple narratives, showing intersections between personal experience and the publicly shared stories in which we engage. Because of its emphasis on teletheory, it may take forms alternative to the printed word, and it certainly tends to extend beyond the printed word alone as medium for communication and expression. Thus, a mystory composition may just as easily be composed in video (including video that combines visual images with printed text), in hypertext links on a computer screen, in a material or geographical environment (such as an art gallery, a classroom space, an outdoor park), and it may, depending on the specific way in which its author has composed it, be experienced linearly, spatially, at various possible points of entry, and so forth. What it is not is chaotic—the most satisfying mystories eventually lead us to an experience that is meaningful and not simply random, in which we discover, along with the author, that experience in its doing, in its unfolding.

Perhaps any attempt to explain or describe a mystory will ultimately leave the reader impatient to get to it, so let's. We end the chapter with a sample of a mystory, written by Michael Bowman, a scholar, artist, and teacher who (along with his frequent collaborator and coauthor Ruth Bowman) has been both a practitioner and a theorist of the mystory, particularly as it relates as a genre to other performance traditions. "Killing Dillinger: A Mystory" can be found on p. 498. As you move through it, consider how the experience of reading it feels different from the way in which you negotiate other kinds of texts. Think about how the images, the stories, the juxtaposition of personal narrative and public history, all move you into a different way of experiencing time, space, consciousness, and perspective. What kinds of disciplinary discourse does it contain, and how are they used? Could you perform Bowman's mystory? How would it live differently in embodied performance from its performance on the page? What would it mean for you, as someone other than Bowman, to "perform" it? Can you use it as a public or disciplinary text for your own mystory?

While in some respects the chronicle, the ethnography, and the mystory may seem like very different kinds of nonfiction texts—and, indeed, in important ways they are—we encourage you to consider what connects them. One might say that the different descriptions of the execution of Mary Stuart (and Bowman, incidentally, has assembled his own mystory-based group performance based on the life and legends of Mary Stuart), while they are descriptive and rhetorical in their political uses of the scene, also push toward performativity, using language not simply to re-create the final moments in a factual way (as we have seen, the facts are deployed in very different ways) or to push the reader to a political position on Mary, but rather, to use language to perform the act of executing her. Similarly, Madison's ethnography of Ghanaian women wants to find a medium in which these women's truth and reality can take voice, and it is in this intersection of the personal and the public discourse (and disciplinary discourse, in Madison's own role as a college professor and scholarly researcher) that something new is made. Bowman's weaving together of his Hoosier history shared with the infamous criminal John Dillinger ends in a disciplinary way (notes citing academic and other sources) and in a personal, unglossed dedication, "For David / 28 Sept. 54–2 Dec. 97," a reminder that nonfiction, like all literature, is situated in the relationships between our lives (the lives of us as individuals) and "ourlives," the ones we share through interaction, language, and performance.

KEY TERMS

critical ethnography

dialogical performance

ethnography

mystory

performative writing

positionality

qualitative interviewing techniques

thick description

chapter 13

CONCLUSION:
BEYOND THE CLASSROOM

Throughout this book, we have focused on the dynamics of the performance of literature in the classroom. We hope we have whetted your interest sufficiently that you will continue your study in additional classes. In addition, many of the genres and approaches we have discussed have found their way outside the pedagogical context to more public and social environments. In this chapter, we will consider a number of different performance formats and contexts you may choose to explore—they extend public performance beyond the traditional genre of drama to hybrid, blended, and "blurred genres," to use anthropologist Clifford Geertz's term.

Monologue as Play

The monologue is not new as a dramatic form: playwrights going back centuries have felt free to place a single speaking character onstage and construct the play exclusively through the voice of that character. Strindberg's play *The Stronger* offers a superior example of a one-act play that is a monologue. In the play, two women, Mrs. X and Miss Y, meet by chance at a café. Mrs. X speaks the entire time, eventually revealing that she knows that Miss Y is Mr. X's mistress. Miss Y does not speak during the entire course of the play. Onstage, the challenge for the performer playing Miss Y is to create a complex inner life for her character, sustaining the mystery and ambiguity that permeates the play, while never herself uttering a word. The play raises the question of who, really, is the stronger of the two—Mrs. X, whose speaking role would seem to give her the upper hand, or Miss Y, who does not need speech in order to exercise (sexual) power.

While the play is, strictly speaking, a monologue (it has but a single speaker), in other respects it is within the tradition of dramatic realism in that it is set in a recognizable social place and situation and places the second character onstage. Twentieth-century playwrights have followed in this tradition, notably Samuel Beckett, Harold Pinter, and Eugène Ionesco, among others. Such playwrights often expand the cast beyond a single character, but the resulting effect is often closer to monologue than to the traditionally cast play. Consider how the solo performer can illuminate this aspect of such plays.

Historical Performance and Impersonation

A variation on the monologue as drama is the historically based one-person show, in which a solo performer plays a character from history. Such plays typically are set at a particular moment in the life of the character, but use that moment as an opportunity for an autobiographical narrative of the character's life and accomplishments. One of the earliest to gain professional acclaim was William Luce's play *The Belle of Amherst,* in which the actress Julie Harris played the poet Emily Dickinson. The Dickinson character addressed the audience throughout, treating us as visitors to her hermitlike existence in her family home in Amherst, Massachusetts. Similarly, historical figures such as Clarence Darrow, Thurgood Marshall, and others have found their way to the stage—Marshall, for example, speaking in an alumni hall at Howard University, his alma mater, in the recent play by George Stevens Jr. starring Laurence Fishburne. Such plays are typically hybrids of writings by the historical figure combined with invented speech by the contemporary playwright. Maintaining the sense of consistent voice and style of the historical figure becomes one of the principal challenges for the writer, and there is usually an attempt to create some physical resemblance between performer and historical figure.

Solo and Group Performance of
Ethnographic and Historical Material

A rather different kind of play, also written for the solo performer, is one in which a single actor is physically alone onstage but plays a number of different characters in the course of the text. Some of these texts blend the historical setting of the kinds of plays described above (for example,

The Belle of Amherst and *Thurgood*) but expand the number of characters performed. Some of these plays make clear distinctions between the
characters, sometimes using simple or more elaborate stagecraft, and
the performer usually enacts a single character for a set period of time,
then shifts to a different character, not unlike a series of one-act plays,
each focusing on a different character but tied together by a common
theme, setting, or historical period. A recent example of this is Stephen
Lang's *Beyond Glory*, based on Larry Smith's nonfiction book, in which
he tells the stories and turns into monologues the experiences of winners
of the Congressional Medal of Honor, drawn from the various wars that
have been waged since the medal was established. Lang played across a
range of age and race in his performance, using voice, body, and characterization to communicate differences in character. In addition, he had
onstage a soldier's trunk, such as those found in a barracks, as a set piece
he could use as furniture and from which he could extract costume and
prop pieces to help define and distinguish characters.

One writer-performer who has made an artistic, cultural, and critical project of similar kinds of plays is Anna Deavere Smith, whom we
mentioned in chapter 12 in the context of political performances drawing
on nonfictional materials. While a professor at Stanford University, she
began working on a research project centering around language, culture,
and identity that she called *On the Road*, which led to her two best-
known plays, *Fires in the Mirror: Crown Heights, Brooklyn, and Other
Identities* and *Twilight: Los Angeles, 1992*. Smith's approach is to allow
each character to speak at length, sometimes indicating the presence of
another character and allowing for pauses that suggest an interjection or
response by a listener (almost always the interviewer, who remains literally and vocally absent in the interaction), but all the while maintaining
the integrity of the monologue. Smith does some editing and minor revi-
sion for continuity and clarification, but her principal aim is to retain the
authenticity of voice and experience of the real person whose life and
perspective is being represented.

Indeed, she extends this beyond the mere transcript of language to
recording the interviews with these individuals, not only for the purpose of
accuracy in the printed transcription but to inform her own performances
and those of future performers who choose to work with her texts. Smith
attempts to re-create as much of the actual speech of the interview subject
as possible—including all the paralinguistic elements as she can identify,
from vocalized pauses ("ums" and "ers"), misspeaking (words that are

either not the appropriate ones or a sentence begun and then retracted or begun again), to the intonational patterns, shifts in volume, rate, and the vocal qualities of the subject, whether it be a nasalized stream of speech, a vocal cry, anything that is individually defining or culturally distinctive. An example would be the rhythms characteristic of Lubavitcher Jews, for whom English may be a second language after Yiddish or who have grown up surrounded by such people so as to mark their speech patterns. Smith does this with the Asian and Caribbean characters as well.

Smith's technique has met with praise and reservations. Those praising her approach find in it an authentic commitment to and genuine success in honoring the full, documentary presence of her interview subjects. Smith has explained that this kind of approach is her attempt to get herself as deeply (or "thickly," to use anthropologist Clifford Geertz's term for ethnography) inside the speech as she can in order to know the mind and experience of the "characters." Those who take issue with Smith's approach believe that it may indeed reproduce the external contours of speech (the same way certain kinds of linguists may reproduce the external contours of speech with symbol and transcription systems), but it does not necessarily ensure a real grasp of the inner life and cultural experience of the subject; that it is a kind of mimicry that demonstrates a good technical ear but may miss the heart of what those speech patterns express. Some find a kind of sameness to Smith's performances that make their claims to authenticity more contestable. What do you think of these two views of Smith's project and philosophy? If possible, watch one of Smith's performances to develop an informed response (look online at www.ted.com/talks/anna_deavere_smith_s_american_character.html).

Both of Smith's scripts have been performed by ensembles, in which there is either a one-to-one correspondence between performer and character (as in traditional acting) or, more often, given the demands of the script and the practicalities of casting and rehearsal, one performer taking a number of roles, either corresponding to their own identities (race, gender, age, socioeconomic status) or deliberately violating realistic identification or combining the two approaches. In addition to published texts like Smith's, you may decide to embark upon your own research-based project, using ethnographic methods to gather monologues through interviews. The resulting performance may, like Smith's, be solo in form, or you may decide to cast an ensemble of performers, again either matching one performer with each character or having each performer take on a number of different voices and roles, thus using both the everyday-life performance style associated with Smith and with other performer-writers working in this genre and the Brechtian approaches to alienation and distancing that remind performer and audience of the constructed nature of all performance. Growing in popularity in recent years have been projects emerging from community-based work, often intended to serve as social and political activism and intervention. Such productions range from Richard Geer's Swamp Gravy work, in which he collected oral histories from residents of the town of Colquitt, Georgia, and put together a performance script for them to perform that represented their history and culture through narratives, to productions done by the youth theater wing of the About Face Theatre Company in Chicago, in which LGBTQ youth work together to tell their own and each other's stories within the venue of a professional theater, with the goal of expressing their lives and calling audiences to political action.

Some plays combine elements of the two variations on historical solo drama. Perhaps the most commercially successful and critically praised of these is Doug Wright's *I Am My Own Wife*. Wright's play had a successful run, first in Chicago, then on Broadway, and now it has been produced across the country; it won both the Pulitzer Prize for Drama (the first solo script to win this award) and the Tony Award for Best Play (again, the first solo script to do so). It was closely associated with its director, Moisés Kaufman, whose work with historical and documentary materials produced two notable scripts for ensembles through his company, the Tectonic Theater Project: *Gross Indecency: The Three Trials of Oscar Wilde* and *The Laramie Project*, based on interviews and time spent by members of the ensemble in Laramie, Wyoming, after the murder of gay college student Matthew Shepard, and also closely associated with the actor who performed the script in Chicago and on Broadway, Jefferson Mays (who won a Tony for his performance). *I Am My Own Wife* is subtitled "Studies for a Play About the Life of Charlotte von Mahlsdorf," suggesting the degree to which playwright (as well as director and actor) wanted reader and audience to understand the process-oriented aspects of their project. What does "studies for a play" suggest to you about the degree to which any of these artists view the play as complete or finished?

Charlotte von Mahlsdorf was an East German transvestite who survived the Nazi regime and the Soviet occupation of Berlin (particularly the purges performed by the Stasi, the secret police) through a combination of courage, collaboration, and counterespionage. The script is based on von Mahlsdorf's own autobiographical writings and interviews the

playwright conducted with him. Wright has refashioned this material into
a series of episodes, some narrative, some dramatic interactions between
characters, some a kind of lecture, informative or philosophical discussions on such topics as the phonograph, including, as Wright describes it,
"Charlotte's beloved Edison phonograph," a forerunner of record players
and more contemporary digital technology for playing music and voices.
It is important to note that Wright lists a cast of characters numbering
thirty-five. This is different from some other historical one-person dramas
in which the intention is to have the single character quote the other
individuals they encounter; Wright is asserting the reality and presence of
all of these characters, even if they are mediated through the personage
of Charlotte von Mahlsdorf. How would this distinction translate into
different performance choices?

In the material that precedes the text of the play itself, Wright indicates that, nonetheless, the actor performing the play should wear a
single, simple costume throughout the performance, one based on the
historical von Mahlsdorf's habitual dress: "a black skirt, rimmed with
peasant piping at the hem, and a black blouse with short sleeves. There
is a black kerchief on his head, and he has on sensible black walking
shoes with scuffed toes. Around his neck is a delicate string of pearls and
he wears no makeup." Wright indicates that the only exception to this
costume should occur in the beginning of act 2, where the performer
plays Alfred Kirschner, Charlotte's lover, reading a letter he has sent from
prison. After finishing the performance of the letter, the actor transforms
himself briefly into the character Doug (based on the playwright), who
comments briefly as a kind of bridge between Alfred and Charlotte, and
then transforms himself, in character and voice and in costume, back
into Charlotte (the actor will play other characters again, just not with
any change in costume).

All of this suggests an interesting and complex tension in the play's
point of view toward its subject (Charlotte von Mahlsdorf) and its own
process (the "studies," the provisional, transparent declaration of incom-
pleteness, in the subtitle). Charlotte is so vivid and dominant a presence
in the play that her visual dress can be understood to signal the ways in
which she is always "there," even when other characters speak. (It may
also be a nod to the theatrical impracticalities of making split-second
changes in outfit, particularly for characters who may only speak for a
single line or two.) But it is a decidedly different aesthetic and dramatic
experience from that of the single-character/single-performer historical

monologues we have described above. It is different also in its sense of dialogic interaction from Smith's projects, in which multiple characters speak but usually in monologues rather than in dramatically interactive scenes.

We would add that there are many other plays that use historical materials as sources for dramatic scripts. There are those written with ensemble performance in mind, such as Jessica Blank and Erik Jensen's *The Exonerated*, which tells the life stories of individuals whose death-penalty convictions have been overturned. There are others that were originally produced with a solo performer (such as Smith's) but now are regularly performed either by solo performers or by ensembles, such as Nilaja Sun's *No Child*, which uses the playwright's experience as a public school teacher to explore and critique the "No Child Left Behind" policies of the Bush administration. Sun was also the original performer, playing herself and the other characters; it has since been marketed by its licensor, Dramatists Play Service, as open to casting from one performer to as many as there are characters in the play.

One other tradition of the one-performer/multiple-character drama worth noting is one that comes from another venue of contemporary entertainment: stand-up comedy, based either on the life of the performer or on dramatic characters invented by the performer. The actress Lily Tomlin has moved comfortably between this format and more traditional acting situations. Her production *The Search for Signs of Intelligent Life in the Universe* was written by her longtime collaborator and life partner Jane Wagner, but it is clearly crafted for Tomlin's talents and performance aesthetic. Another early pioneer of this form was Eric Bogosian, who may be best known in this form for his scripted performances *Drinking in America* and *Sex, Drugs, Rock & Roll*; like others discussed, he has worked in other performance venues, but his portraits of middle-class, disaffected young men emerged from the kind of stand-up venues in which such populations increasingly became primary audiences in the 1980s and 1990s. John Leguizamo, in full-length plays performed both on and off Broadway and on cable television, populated entire communities of characters in performances drawn from his life as a Latino young man, a kind of performance of ethnicity and culture that in earlier decades came from traditions as diverse, but in some ways continuous, as the Jewish American comedians of the Catskills (the "borscht belt") and the African American stand-up tradition of family and community narrative represented first by Bill Cosby and then in more radical, critical form by people like Dick

Gregory and Richard Pryor, and today by comics like Chris Rock, Dave Chapelle, and Wanda Sykes, among many others.

Leguizamo's work is interesting on a number of levels. Not only has it succeeded in bringing Latinos to commercial theatrical venues as audiences, but it has combined autobiographical approaches to solo performance with the more dramatizing ones discussed in this chapter. While his live solo performances are typically done with minimal transformations of costume and setting, their adaptations for cable television often involve fuller costuming and suggestive settings, the mode of production allowing for more defined and detailed design choices (although equally satiric, particularly in the drag-inflected performances of women, whose characterizations take Leguizamo and his audiences on a razor-thin walk between stereotyping and sometimes loving, sometimes profane evocations of the fantastic/fantasized feminine of the Latino imagination). There is also a sense in which, viewed as a body of work, Leguizamo's series of scripts function as an autobiography of his life as a Latino man in America and as a performer who began as community trickster and has moved into more complex positions in the entertainment industry, often playing comic roles (as in his turn as a transvestite performer in *To Wong Foo*) and often playing villains or psychotics, sometimes drawing on Latino traditions, sometimes playing without reference to his ethnicity.

Writer as Character

Although we have already alluded to some instances in which playwrights have placed themselves as characters within their plays, such as Doug Wright's *I Am My Own Wife*, in which the character Doug interviews and comments on Charlotte von Mahlsdorf, there are a number of historical antecedents. One might, indirectly, see this as early as Aristophanes' ancient Greek comedy *The Frogs*, wherein Aristophanes does not place himself as a character onstage, but he is so self-referential about Athenian theater that he might as well be a character. Similarly, George Bernard Shaw, in *The Doctor's Dilemma*, makes reference to himself in the play: one character describes himself as a disciple of "Bernard Shaw," whom the character goes on to describe as the most intelligent man in society. The character also makes reference to his and Shaw's friend, James Barrie, a contemporary of Shaw's, best known as the author of *Peter Pan* (and a playwright, incidentally, whose stage directions rival Shaw's in their novelistic length and qualities). While Shaw leaves himself offstage in literal terms, the audience is made aware of the self-referential moment and, depending on their disposition, either find it amusing or intrusive. Shaw seems to intend it with some irony in the world of the play, as all the characters are open to critical scrutiny. We see this kind of self-reference in a lot of contemporary film and television, for example, the HBO series *Curb Your Enthusiasm*, and the long-running NBC hit *Seinfeld*.

Two recent plays that have placed the playwright within the world of the play as a central dramatic technique are David Henry Hwang's *Yellow Face* and Lisa Kron's *Well*.

Hwang is a Chinese American playwright, perhaps best known for his play *M. Butterfly*, based on a historical incident in which a French diplomat passed state secrets to his Chinese mistress, who is later revealed to be a man in disguise; the diplomat claimed he never knew the "woman" was a "man." Hwang gained an early success with this drama of race, culture, and sexuality. In *Yellow Face*, Hwang blurs the lines between "truth and fiction," as he said in an interview, depicting a character named DHH, who has unwittingly (in a move paralleling that of the French diplomat in *M. Butterfly*) approved the casting of a non-Asian actor in his most recent play, after having participated vocally in the protests against similar casting of the musical *Miss Saigon*. This plot is placed in juxtaposition with the travails of Hwang's own father, who was investigated for possible illegal financing of American politics by Chinese interests. Hwang mixes real-life characters, identified as such, with ones who are amalgams of reality and fiction, even one who has drolly been christened "Name Withheld on Advice of Counsel," suggesting the complex and intricate relationship between legal and dramatic realms of discourse. That Hwang names his character DHH suggests a modicum of distance he is putting between his historical, "factual" self and the dramatized self. Given that so much of the play is about questions of authenticity (much dialogue is given over to trying to establish even a shred of "authentically Asian" heritage for the disputed actor), so Hwang's own placement of himself as character in the play is equally problematic. Thus, *Yellow Face* spans lyric and dramatic modes in which the voice of the writer and the voices of dramatized characters interact, blend, question, and reflect on each other's reality. Think about what a solo performer might bring to such a play: any solo performer, other than Hwang, will stand in an equally complex set of relationships, if in different ways, to the play and its characters, from the ethnicity of the solo performer to what it might mean to play a character who is a real person (as did Anna Deavere Smith in her various scripts). Is there a difference between the play as documentary and the play as imagined or reimagined variation on events that may or may not have happened or whose meaning, detail, and nuance may remain in dispute?

Another interesting, if very different, instance of the writer as character in a dramatic text is Lisa Kron's play *Well*. Kron has worked memorably as a comedian, monologuist, and performance artist, particularly in the lesbian collective WOW Café, which was an important venue for experimental performance in the 1980s and 1990s. Kron's play builds on the juxtaposition of traditional theater and experimental formats she experienced during this period. It is about a number of things: Kron's health (hence, the title of the play), her work as an artist, and finally, perhaps most powerfully, her complex, loving, frustrating relationship with her aging mother, Ann. Kron combines fairly short, episodic scenes from her life, including other characters, real and fictional, with conversations between herself and her mother as characters. While it is hardly unusual for playwrights to base their plays on autobiographical and family narratives (O'Neill's *Long Day's Journey into Night* is one of the most famous of these thinly veiled family dramas), Kron has gone a step or two further, first by casting herself in the role of herself and second by bringing her mother onstage as a character and not one she has tried to disguise (this is similar to Hwang's technique in *Yellow Face*). Complicating matters, she does not cast her mother to play the role but has a professional actress do it, thus calling into question whether the Lisa Kron played by Lisa Kron is therefore intended to be any more factual or authentic than the Ann Kron (of course, it may be that casting a professional actress as her mother was a practical matter, as her mother is not a professional actress). Kron makes these issues more self-conscious for writer, performers, and audience by bringing the questions of character-in-life and character-onstage into the substance of the play's dialogue.

Media, Technology, and Solo Performance

Developments in media and technology have expanded the possibilities for both solo and ensemble performance, including that of dramatic texts. While it is outside the scope of this book to investigate in any detail the specific craft of using various technologies and new media in performance, it is worth considering how dramatic texts have used media in addition to or in concert with live performance to produce the kinds of conflict and interaction usually viewed as definitive of drama as a genre. Electronic and digital media have increased in sophistication, not simply in the ways they are produced, but in how they are theorized and utilized. In earlier periods, as these media were just beginning to be introduced into performance, some viewed them as heralding the end of the importance of the corporeal presence of the body as a defining characteristic of performance. It is probably safe to say that thinking about the place of electronic and digital media in live performance has become more complex than that concern might suggest. Digital media in particular has become very much a part of nearly all individuals' daily lives, so it is now more difficult to mark clearly where bodily reality and digital reproduction/transmission begin and end.

Consider online courses, which you may have taken or are at least aware of. Teachers initially were often resistant to them, believing that they would lead to a more passive approach to education or greater disconnection between teacher and students and a loss of the class as community. While this surely remains a danger (as it is in any teacher-student relationship, whatever the degree of actual physical presence), many teachers and students have reported that online education has become an opportunity rather than a poor substitute for an idealized face-to-face classroom environment. Putting aside the issue of convenience that online education may initially have been invented to address (it first flourished among populations where geographical distance made gathering physically in the same room impractical or where professional or social obligations, such as daytime jobs or family responsibilities, precluded more traditional pedagogical structures), the growth of virtual and/or real-time media environments has changed how people view "presence" and thus mediation is no longer just a kind of backup to a preferred reality. This does not mean that mediation does not change how people relate to each other, but what is important is to recognize that such changes have already begun and that they provide new ways of connecting with people.

How does this provide challenges and opportunities for the solo performance of drama? And where do we see it happening already? One recent example from professional theater is Peter Morgan's play *Frost/Nixon*, which takes as its subject the series of televised interviews conducted by British talk-show host David Frost with Richard Nixon after his resignation in disgrace following the Watergate scandal. In Michael Grandage's production of *Frost/Nixon*, the director and the designers as well as the playwright drew on the actual tapes of the interviews as well as Morgan's own fictional imaginings of interactions between the title characters and other characters, some historical, some imagined. Obviously, such a subject is in itself rife with possibilities for textualizing media as a backdrop for the dramatic interaction. One might even suggest that television, and the talk-show format in particular, would of necessity function as a kind of character within the play, as indeed it does. Morgan and Grandage used the potential of media in fascinating ways that allowed audiences and performers to experience simultaneously the complex juxtaposition of hyperpublic and hyperintimate dimensions of the talk show (the situation in which two people seem to be speaking one-on-one, yet witnessed by millions of people at the same time) and the live spectacle of sitting in a theater, watching actors on a stage. There were large monitors that served as a backdrop to the set and on which were projected passages drawn from the interviews, which had the effect of making both Frost and Nixon take on even larger than usual proportions (television can vary quite a bit in size and scope from the screen used in the theater, but the distance between stage and audience is a mediating factor in determining scope).

Frank Langella's performance as Richard Nixon, which took on the tragic dimensions of that other hero-villain, Shakespeare's Richard III, was a master class in simultaneous levels of performance, as befits an actor who has moved with apparent ease between stage, film, and television throughout a lengthy career. Langella, of necessity, had to project his performance at a level sufficient to reach the balconies of a traditional Broadway theater, while also being able to move into a mode that would not seem melodramatic or overplayed when the interview segments were transmitted to the screen. It is important to note that the interview segments were not prerecorded; rather, cameras were prepositioned to film the interview scenes live at each performance and transmitted the scenes in real time. Thus, both Langella and Michael Sheen (who played Frost) had to find ways to be present as live bodies being seen in three dimensions on the stage and at the same time succeed as two-dimensional "live" digital images. The audience similarly had the challenge of switching between two simultaneous sites of performance—to watch only the screen during these scenes would be to miss an important dimension of the play's "liveness," but it was almost impossible to avoid watching the screen, given its size and dimensions and the fascination we all share with how media transforms, heightens, and intensifies the real. A play that preceded *Frost/Nixon* by about fifty years but also played with the tension between present and past, presence and absence, "liveness" and mediation (keeping in mind that all those binary concepts may not be so distinct as we might initially have thought) is Samuel Beckett's *Krapp's Last Tape*, which premiered in 1958 as a curtain-raiser to his *Endgame* and premiered in the United States as a companion to Edward Albee's *The Zoo Story*, about which we will have a bit more to say below. The play is in many respects a monologue, in which the only character present is the titular Krapp, an old man, alone onstage but for a tape recorder. The play finds its dramatic conflict and tension in Krapp's relationship to this tape recorder and its contents, hence the title of the play, a signal that this hearing, this listening, this interaction between Krapp and the recording of his earlier voice, his younger self, is itself not a solo but a duet between two selves who are inextricably tied to each other and irretrievably riven from each other. What kind of physical, bodily, psychological, or historical presence do such recordings have for us?

Reframing/Recontextualizing

All literary texts are growing, changing things. Even in what may look like the most conservative, even curatorial performance, the very fact of a new performer or a new audience changes, sometimes subtly, sometimes enormously, the ways in which we understand and present a play.

Directors have frequently reframed or contextualized texts in order to provide new or fresh insights into them. Perhaps most famously, twentieth- and twenty-first-century directors have sought to reinvigorate productions of Shakespeare's plays by resetting them in different time periods, cultures, or nations in order to provide a contemporary audience with an entry into a play whose original setting may be enough of a barrier to intrude on their understanding or enjoyment of it. A recent revival of *Macbeth*, featuring actor Patrick Stewart, was set in an Eastern European country under what appears to be a kind of Stalinist totalitarian regime of terror and purges. The director and designer underscored this reframing/ recontextualization by projecting, at various points, newsreel footage from the period, including scenes of armies marching, corresponding to the military content of Shakespeare's play. The stage set was an institutional kitchen that at times also functioned as a bunker, dining hall, and emergency operating room, with the Weird Sisters portrayed as diabolical, murderous nurses in the opening scene. Not a word of dialogue was altered in the play, but the physical production provided a new context in which to understand this five-hundred-year-old play.

Let us consider another play and how a solo performer might recontextualize it in ways that open up a dialogue with previous ways of understanding the play. Edward Albee's one-act play *The Zoo Story* was first produced in 1959, in German on a double bill with Beckett's *Krapp's Last Tape* (consider how the presence of these two plays next to each other would change our experience as audience members). *The Zoo Story* is a stark encounter between two men, Peter and Jerry, in Central Park in New York City. Peter is a traditional man of his time, married with children, a businessman, mild mannered, a good citizen; Jerry, on the other hand, is garrulous, loud, dangerous from the start, intrusive and challenging to Peter's sense of stability and heteronormativity. By the end of the play, Jerry has goaded Peter into stabbing him with Jerry's own knife, and the play ends as Jerry dies, Peter looking on in horror.

The play is extremely powerful and, over the years, it has been produced many times, either on its own or in tandem with other one-act plays; it is published in a volume with another of Albee's one-act plays, *The American Dream*, written about the same time, but absurdist in tone and in characterization and plotting. Albee has indicated in interviews that, over the fifty years the play has been in existence, he has felt that it was "incomplete," that it needed another play or another act to precede it, to establish more about Peter as character and to prepare him and the audience for the action in which he will engage in *The Zoo Story*. Finally, in 2003, he received a commission to write this companion one act, which he called *Home Life*, and which, as its title suggests, shows Peter at home in the hour before he sets out for the walk in the park that will lead to *The Zoo Story*. The play consists of a conversation between Peter and his wife, Ann; they discuss their sex life, including Ann's perception of a lack of animal passion in Peter, leading Peter to a confession of what he has come to view as an act of date rape he performed while a college student and which has marked his sense of masculine sexuality ever since. The play ends without real resolution, with Peter deciding to go out for a walk to regain some composure and to think about what they have discussed.

In a sense, Albee has himself recontextualized and reframed his earlier play by adding *Home Life* to it. It will be interesting to see if *The Zoo Story* will continue to be produced as a separate play: there are certainly reasonable arguments in favor of and against doing so. What Albee has stated he wanted to do—and he had some ideas as far back as

when *The Zoo Story* was first produced—was to make Peter more understandable psychologically as a character and his interaction with Jerry
more psychologically motivated. Albee's most recent version, including
both of these plays as a single two-act play, has been published as *At Home
at the Zoo*. Of course, were you to experiment with *The Zoo Story* in ways
we have suggested for a public audience, you would need to seek permission from the playwright and his representatives.

After seeing a production of the new two-act play in New York, it
occurred to us that hearing Peter tell the story of his date rape allowed us
to understand Jerry's long and famous monologue about his landlady's
dog and its horrible fate in the second act; Peter's story is ambiguously
presented by Peter, who seems not to have been entirely clear, through
the haze of alcohol that in part fueled the act, whether he was aware of
the young woman's resistance to his advances. The added act also gave
Peter more of a narrative role to play, correcting what had seemed to be
an imbalance in *The Zoo Story* experienced on its own.

Possibilities for reframing or recontextualizing *The Zoo Story*
intrigued us. As Peter is the link between the two plays, we can imagine
a production that makes this even more explicit than it already is. Since
Peter's narrative of the date rape in the first act is presented as ambiguous,
haunting him through years of guilt and shame but still a source of defen-
siveness around what it means to be a man, we thought about what it
might bring to *The Zoo Story* to present it as a solo performance, retaining
the dialogue as written and the sense of two characters interacting, but
shifting the frame away from the "slice of life" realism in which we as
audience assume we are simply eavesdropping on or witnessing something
happening outside our fourth wall, and toward something more confrontational, more interactive, that retains the subjectivity Peter brings to his
narrative monologue in *Home Life*. A solo performance of *The Zoo Story*
would allow performer and audience to play with the same questions of
remembrance and recounting of experience as in *Home Life*. We suggest
a new frame for *The Zoo Story*, which might be summed up in a sentence
(one that need not actually be spoken and, for legal reasons, could not
be in a public performance): "The man said to me . . ." Everything else
that follows in the performance then becomes placed in the epic mode,
akin to the first person narrator who moves in and out of character and
dialogue. What kind of new context might there be for such a performance of the encounter by Peter? We thought of him returning, stained
with blood, to his home, coming upon his wife, taking on a role almost

like that of a messenger in a Greek tragedy (though a messenger much more implicated in the act of violence). Another possibility might be to place Peter in a police precinct or sitting on a bench speaking to a detective who has come, with Jerry's body still there on the ground, dead but a few minutes. It becomes the defensive attempt of Peter to explain why he was, from his point of view, forced to participate in a kind of assisted suicide.

These possibilities, of course, in a sense revise or rewrite the play and certainly run the risk of being viewed as excessive in moving beyond what the text strictly allows (and what a playwright may allow to be done with his script) and, for some audiences, violating the text's integrity. We acknowledge this, but at the same time, recommend that performers and audiences also consider such performances as ways of creating dialogue with plays as living things—not substituting this reframed approach as a better way of writing the text in performance, but as another way of expressing a performer's perspective on and relationship with a text. In its very violation, it may bring a respectfulness to the possibilities each reader and performer finds in such rich, never completed texts.

Intertextualizing/Intervening

Just as reframing or recontextualizing a single text can reveal previously hidden elements or can foreground different perspectives, so constructing performances that show intertextual relationships between various texts can have similarly creative results, for performers and audiences. We have already discussed the ways in which Rupert Gould's production of *Macbeth* reframed it in a Stalinist setting. One could also argue that the use of newsreel footage was an act of intertextuality, in which the design team, no doubt working with the director, used it to intervene between Shakespeare's language and the contemporary audience's knowledge of history. One could even imagine taking this interventionist use of intertexts even further and including newsreel footage from contemporary terrorist or totalitarian governments, to insist for the audience that they cannot retain a comfortable distance between themselves and the actions of a historically distant set of "barbarians."

One possible approach to using intertexts in what we have called an interventionist way—standing between a received or commonplace understanding of one text and another—is to place in performative relationship different dramatic (or other) texts. The nature of drama as dialogic in form makes such additional dialogues even more available and exciting, although, once again, such performances do require a kind of formal or structural intervention in which the play as written becomes revised to admit different voices into the stream of speeches the playwright has put before us.

One example might be to create intertextual dialogues as a way of exploring the scene from Ibsen's *Ghosts*, which was discussed in chapter 10. As we noted, the play received renewed interest at the beginning of the AIDS epidemic when sexually transmitted diseases became fatal conditions again; while the moral and philosophical issues Ibsen's play presented never went out of date, we would argue, the specific content of the play had perhaps become outmoded for some audiences. A traditional production of *Ghosts*, set in period costumes and with no additions or subtractions of dialogue, would still have force and power, and for many audiences the connections between syphilis in the nineteenth century and HIV/AIDS in our own era would be clear enough, as would the highly moralistic perspectives that lead to Oswald's death. The times in which we live serve as intertexts and interventions.

But another possibility would be to foreground more overtly the connections between Ibsen's play and ongoing debates and arguments about the morality of sexual behavior and disease, perhaps projecting images and printed texts about HIV/AIDS in the contemporary world as Ibsen's dialogue plays itself out. Another possibility would be to inter-weave relevant writings throughout the scene. When Larry Kramer, one of the founders of the Gay Men's Health Crisis (GMHC), the earliest activist group to address HIV/AIDS, particularly in New York City, began to write columns about AIDS in the early 1980s (HIV had not yet been identified), he was often criticized for being overly moralistic, calling for sexual restraint that many claimed placed him in a kind of repressive tradition that years of gay liberation had worked to overcome, perhaps symbolized most by the Stonewall Riot in 1969 and the development of a very strong sense of pride in sexual identity, often expressed by advocating an unlimited participation in sexual activities; he was viewed as a kind of Pastor Manders.

In 1985, Kramer's play *The Normal Heart* was first produced. It features, at its center, Ned Weeks, a gay journalist who becomes part of the GMHC and who is a stand-in for Kramer, down to the same kind of jeremiads for which he was well known (and for which, many would say, history has vindicated him). Ned's primary relationships within the play are with his heterosexual brother Ben, again a stand-in of sorts for Kramer's own brother; Dr. Emma Brookner, a disabled physician who is doing research on AIDS and who is the first person to articulate the call for sexual restraint; and, finally, Felix Turner, the gay man with whom Ned falls in love and who dies of AIDS at the end of the play, after Ned and he have been "married" by Emma (there was no legal marriage between same-sex couples in the United States at the time).

While some critics still took issue with Kramer's polemical style, the play was viewed by many as extremely powerful in putting the passions of these people in a tangible form and in making rhetorical points about government inaction and placing tragic conflicts within gay culture center stage. While, as with *Ghosts*, some of the play's details are outdated (sadly, but not surprisingly, including the statistics of deaths from HIV/AIDS, which were painted on the set and changed periodically to reflect rises in infection), its dramatic and ethical issues of love, political engagement, and the morality of care remain as central today as ever—something the critical response and audience response to a 2003 revival of the play off-Broadway demonstrated. How might you put the scene from *Ghosts* (or other scenes from the play), discussed in chapter 10, into intertextual relationship with *The Normal Heart*, or with other written, spoken, and visual texts from the AIDS epidemic? For this kind of interventionist performance, you may find ensemble performance offers advantages, not simply of clarity, but of embodiment of intertextual complexity; having two performers, for example, one playing Mrs. Alving and Ned, another playing Emma and Pastor Manders, may foreground the roles of authority in these plays—and the problems such voices pose. Having one performer play Ned and another performer play both Emma and Felix may help foreground Ned's own insistence on conflict in his life—how, whether it be the scientific voice of Emma or the radical voice of Felix, he is always in the role of a contrarian.

We have but scratched the surface of possibilities for taking performance from the classroom out into the larger social world—whether the purpose of doing so is to educate, entertain, move, or activate your audience. We hope you will carry this commitment to the value of developing relationships between performers, texts, and audiences with you into whatever public spheres you enter and that performance will continue to make a difference to you, as it does—and always will—to us.

KEY TERMS

community-based performance
digital media/digital culture
historical performance
impersonation
intertexualizing/intervening
monologue
reframing/recontextualizing
stand-up comedy
writer as character

APPENDIX OF PERFORMANCE TEXTS

JANE HAMILTON

Rehearsing *The Firebird*

The story of *The Firebird* was not clear to me at first. My grandmother had taken me to see the ballet long before I knew that Mr. Smedley was among the living. I knew I loved the girl-bird—she was dressed in red and gold, trailing tail feathers across the floor, endangering the other dancers. She was so many things it was confusing: In a way she was both the lover and the beloved, but she had power too, the power of the storyteller. She was the one who made the story take its course; it was she who arranged for true love to prevail. After the prince let her out of the cage she said in her bird-dance language, "Smash the egg basket and you'll get what you want." I couldn't say in words what it was about even though my grandmother whispered at me all through the performance. "Love," she said, right off the bat, and then "evil," and "fear," and at last "happiness."

So when Mr. Smedley passed out the scores of *The Firebird Suite*, by Igor Stravinsky, on the first day of All-Village Orchestra, I reached to my stand for a piece of Teaberry gum and chewed with reckless abandon. I closed my eyes and saw a red bird fluttering at the bolted wire cage. I was in sixth grade and played fifth-chair violin. Mr. Smedley was the conductor. I learned a lot from Mr. Smedley, but personal hygiene and comeliness were not among the gifts he bestowed. He looked as if he had been put on a medieval stretching rack and stretched beyond what his poor sunken frame could support. His skin was red and sore and pockmarked. His one suit was always wrinkled and too short in the sleeves. There his hands were hanging limp like dead chickens at his side; even when he brought them up, his baton between his chapped thumb and first finger, those hands were lifeless, something to throw in a pot with an onion and cook, and endure for Monday-night supper.

Mr. Smedley was never far from my mind, and after a year of observing his every move from my fifth chair I understood a fair amount, but there was one thing I never completely figured out. He quietly, but extravagantly, praised me when my mother came to pick me up. I stood holding my violin by its neck after rehearsal while he told my mother I had great talent and that if I kept practicing I would go far. He looked straight at my mother and lied with all the authority of a parish priest. I had no talent. I had never practiced except under duress. I was never going to go anywhere in the musical world beyond lip-syncing "Climb Ev'ry Mountain." We both knew how deep his lie went, and I grinned at him with some fear and a great deal of shame, and he smiled a lame smile at me and shrugged his shoulders. He seemed to be saying, "What the hell, let's humor your mother a little—I'm heading home for some of my ma's ham-bone soup, so why not live a little right now?"

In fact, he lived with his mother. It was common knowledge. Sometimes she came to the rehearsals. She sat in the back of the auditorium and watched him. She kept her worn coat on and her short black boots, as well as a clear plastic rain hat over her dingy hair. She sat watching, clutching her scuffed black handbag.

The first day of rehearsal, and every subsequent Thursday afternoon, my friend Tiffany and I ran down the street to the drugstore after lunch so that I could buy my five packs of Teaberry gum. She turned up her nose at the muted pink packs that she said smelled like toilet-bowl cleaner. "Not to me," I said, stuffing a piece into my mouth with the urgency of a heroin addict. I absolutely had to have something in my mouth for the ordeal of orchestra. I was too old to suck my thumb and too young to smoke, so as far as I could see gum was the only alternative.

We were dismissed early in the afternoon, herded onto the bus, and then taken to the high school at the far end of town. On the bus Tiffany sat like a lady, with her reeds in her mouth, and I continued my gum orgy. When we got to the high school auditorium I preopened all the packs and stacked them on the stand so that they'd be ready when I needed them. My stand partner had thick glasses and a sinus condition. We were equally nauseated by each other, so we left well enough alone. He snorted and dripped and blew, and I stuffed and chewed, cracked the wad in my own expert way, and swallowed hunk after hunk. My intestinal tract was probably more beautiful than anyone else's, all my gray food laced with indestructible pink ribbon. I blew bubbles with gum that was not designed to be blown. And I watched Mr. Smedley.

That first day Mr. Smedley handed out scores of *The Firebird* under the glare of Mother Smedley's beady eyes in the back row. Then he cleared his throat and started to talk. He was addressing 150 junior high students, each with their own noisemaker. He tapped his stand with his wand. Nothing doing. He tried to bring his arms up, in conductorly fashion, but his suit restrained him and he could only get them so far. He undid his cuff links, which released him only another two inches.

His words "Quiet, please" fell from his mouth and landed right by his dusty brown vinyl shoes. I looked into the thick lenses of my virtually blind stand partner and couldn't find his eyes. Then I put another piece of gum in my mouth and waited. Mr. Smedley tapped his stand again. It was clear that his suit was not going to bear the strain of the year. He started to pace back and forth, he bashed a music stand against the podium, and then he all out shouted and stomped his feet. He was practically in tears, and Mother Smedley just sat there watching. It was when he started waving his hands that the musicians quieted in spite of themselves. Our mouths hung open: The plucked chickens were coming to life and fluttering over Mr. Smedley's head—they were flapping and clucking, just about to fly south. When the quiet came they hung motionless in the air and then dropped to his sides as if they'd been shot dead. I knew in that moment, and after, when he wearily lifted his long arms over his stand and leaned toward the violas, that he did not want to be the conductor of the All-Village Orchestra. I noticed a sensation in my stomach that I'd never felt before, and in order to register it I took my gum out of my mouth and held the pink wad on my index finger. He was explaining in his reedy voice how to behave. Poor Mr. Smedley was so very tired. What he wanted, I realized in a flash, was to play his violin at Carnegie Hall; he might even have settled for the St. Louis Symphony, but something, maybe the holes in his socks, kept him from that dream. I made my hand like a visor at my brow and squinted out into the dark of the auditorium. His mother looked like the sort who would be only too glad to darn her boy's socks. I put my head down and imagined mother and son in their small unpainted house on the other side of the tracks, the rain dripping through the ceiling onto the Victrola they played their 78 records on. Even though Mr. Smedley wouldn't have been listening to "Tara" from *Gone With the Wind*, that's what I heard in my mind. He was not handy, couldn't change a tire or boil an egg or climb a ladder without tripping on his shoelaces. His power was in his hands after all, in the pads under his bitten nails. He was a violinist, first and foremost. When his mother was basting the rump roast he drank a shot of whiskey and played "The Orange Blossom Special." All the leaks in the roof instantly sealed themselves. "Mother," he then called into the kitchen as the strains of "Tara" resumed, "you can't darn for me anymore. I've got to make it on my own." And so she watched him walk to school the next day in his battered vinyl shoes, with each step the hole in his sock rising above the heel of the shoe to show itself. I opened my eyes and saw his still hands poised for the upbeat. I jammed the violin under my chin, my jaw quit, and then we played the opening of *The Firebird*, which is about as cheerful as the road to hell. We played the tremolo parts and sounded as we looked, like spastic electric toothbrushes.

We muddled through the entire pabulumized junior high version of the suite, the strings lost in the murk of all the tremolo, until Mary Clare Rankin from R. W. Emerson School blew everyone away with the final French horn solo. We had all year to practice, and there she was in the first read-through soaring through all the muck, the spitty air from her embouchure turning to gold in the dark hollow of her horn. Mary Clare had short black hair that was cut in a square around her face, a nose that turned up like a hog's, and blue eyes fringed by long dark lashes. She looked straight over her horn to Mr. Smedley's hands measuring time. Her horn sang above and beyond us, the notes floating out into the auditorium, away from the mire. We should have stopped, and certainly we wanted to, but we felt we had to follow the notes on the page, not to mention our conductor, and make the mad dash to the end. The violins made the sort of noise that must surely fill your ears when you are being suffocated in the dark by a strange man. With a flick of his wrists, Mr. Smedley cut us off. He looked past everyone as if we hadn't been playing at all and said, "Thank you, Mary Clare. Thank you." Then he stared up into the dangling lights. "Break," was all he said. He went down the steps to the middle of the auditorium and just sat there with his fingers in his mouth.

It occurred to me sometime during the first weeks of orchestra that if a bird has the power of love—the power to enchant, the power to destroy—what magic ought a young girl like myself, GeorgeAnne Mealy, have within her beating heart? As it stood, my life was filled with the drama of farce. My violin teacher, Mr. Kuscowski, had no patience for the likes of me, but I was what fed his hungry mouths, four of them in his kitchen waiting for their chow. He had eyes that brought to mind jumbo black olives. How did he sleep? It was surely a tight stretch for his lids over the bulge of those Grecian fruits. He made me sing scales, and since I had a range of a minor third I couldn't get to the other end of the octave. He thought I was faking, couldn't believe that any human had been created with a range as limited as mine. He thought my tap-dancing lessons were ridiculous, a waste of time, just plain idiotic. I was terrified of him but thought nothing of him from week to week, until he was actually in front of me, sawing his bow through his glassy rosin, waiting for me to wrench my arm under my violin and play.

My parents were parents. They believed in manners, cleanliness, education, virtue, and kindness. My best friend, Tiffany, was thinking about giving up her oboe and becoming a cheerleader; in other words, going over to the other side. She would have no problem; she was graceful and had light brown hair with a lot of silver in it. She wore fishnet stockings and immodest skirts. My homeroom and French teacher, Mrs. Vogel, had recently become a widow. Her husband, who had been second-chair viola in the Chicago Symphony Orchestra, had been murdered on the el train late one Saturday night on his way home from a concert. Mrs. Vogel was short and round, with sleek chestnut hair that she tied in a pony-tail and adorned with a red grosgrain ribbon. She wore silk dresses that hugged her bulging middle and highlighted her perspiration problem. There was always a damp silky sheen under both of her armpits. Her life had been laid bare and yet she was standing at the blackboard, day after day, perspiring to the amusement of eleven- and twelve-year-olds.

My father was often demanding to know what I had learned at school. How could I explain that school didn't have anything to do with numbers, places, dates, or the subjunctive? I watched the circles of sweat enlarge in the silk of Mrs. Vogel's dress as she conjugated *mourir*, and I saw into the endless dark pit of loss.

Other revelations came to me spasmodically. I had a vision in December, when the All-Village Orchestra drove way out of town to play a Christmas concert at a retirement home in the country. I was sitting behind Mr. Smedley. He was talking to the choral director, Mr. Rice. I sat perfectly still and straight, listening to his every word. He was telling Mr. Rice about his tenth summer, when his mother sent him to work on a farm. We were passing fields and barns and silos, and he kept polishing the steamy window with his glove so that he could see out.

"My uncle," Mr. Smedley explained, "treated me like his own boys, who had grown up on the farm. He expected me to drive the tractor even though my feet didn't reach the clutch." Imagine Mr. Smedley shrunk to the size of a ten-year-old. I squeezed my eyes shut and tried my best. "He made me mow the hayfield one day. I couldn't reach the clutch, and I was heading toward the end of the row. I knew I wasn't going to be able to stop the tractor. I was getting closer and closer and closer to the end, and I couldn't turn the tractor around because there just wasn't room, and I couldn't stop. I didn't know what to do, so I, ah, just put my head down on the steering wheel and cried until I crashed into a cedar tree at the fence line. The mower cut up the tree and the fence, but that tractor stopped." He took off his navy blue stocking hat and smoothed his greasy hair and then laughed into his chest. "I swore I was never going to be a farmer—that much I knew."

He went on to tell other tales of farm horror, but I was stuck with Mr. Smedley back on the tractor before the end of the row. I imagined him in his tight suit, his raw skin, tears coming down his face, his mother far away in the city. His cruel uncle would take him into the henhouse and beat him with a green willow twig. I knew then that the feelings I had were strong enough to have a name. What were they called? What was the unrelenting ache all through my chest each time I looked at Mr. Smedley's vinyl shoes?

Whatever the feeling, it seemed logical to imagine poor bereaved Mrs. Vogel running through the field to him, stooping in her blue silk parent-teacher conference dress, wiping the tears from his eyes while he murmured, "Patricia, Patricia," and then lying down next to him in the soft, freshly mowed hay, and lying there into the night, renaming all the constellations in French.

I whispered something of the sort to Tiffany, and she spit out her reeds and popped her hand to her mouth. We both put our heads down and laughed until we got to the outskirts of Aurora. That's all that happened after my vision, nothing more. But I noticed that I felt different as I watched Mr. Smedley from my fifth chair: It was both as if I were a vulture clutching my perch and staring down at him without blinking and as if I were a sponge, soaking up the water, brine and all, without even trying. I guess you could say I was watching, and even when I wasn't watching I was watching. I also kept my eye on Mary Clare way in the back, up on high. She was in a different orbit. She was out of reach, not only because she was in the eighth grade but also, of course, because of the power in her lips. I waited for the blast of horn to come down to the swamp waters of the strings. We sounded no better after four months of rehearsal; we were still wallowing around and there was nothing Mr. Smedley could do. We had sectional after sectional; he threatened, he begged, he stormed. He even resorted to bribery. Everyone loved playing *The Sound of Music* medley, but he didn't let us very often, unless we got that tremolo to be clear and together. To the best of my knowledge so far, precision and clarity were things that came to adults. Mr. Smedley might just as well have been teaching hyenas to sing the *Messiah*. He always adjourned to his seat in the middle of the auditorium to bite his nails.

In the end all we could do was wait for the relief of Mary Clare. I watched her licking her lips again and again before her entrance and then lifting her golden horn to her mouth. I watched Mr. Smedley actually close his eyes while he conducted her solo.

Occasionally, when we walked into the high school from the bus, Mr. Smedley was there to greet us. Every now and then he winked at me. I came, my green headband holding my long, curly red hair off my pale face, my long feet in sensible brown oxfords, my violet anklets, the cold purple knobs of my knees, my navy sailor dress, my imitation-crocodile violin case slapping against my side. He winked, not in a jeering, lecherous way but in a way that said its usual "I know you can't play a tune on that instrument." I always grinned breathlessly at him while I scrutinized his face: There were more wrinkles under his eyes than last week — he was so terribly weary. His hair was in grave danger of turning entirely into oil and spilling off his head onto the floor. That unidentified feeling rushed into my chest cavity and then up my throat, where it just sat. I had to chew my gum and swallow hard to push past the lump.

Every Thursday after lunch I sensed Mrs. Vogel watching me mournfully as I took my violin from my locker; she was thinking of the bullet holes in her dead husband's shattered heart and his forever stilled viola. In truth, I hadn't stopped thinking about what had hit me over the head on the bus to Aurora. It was perfectly natural for them to develop an interest in each other. I already knew what the lavender napkins would say at their wedding luncheon: "Bruce and Pat." There was so much to do before that day! They both had demanding careers, and so there wasn't a lot of time to meet, not to mention the nuisance of Mr. Smedley's mother always lurking around the corner. They would have to write letters. She would write on beige scented stationery, he on spiral notebook paper that had thin staff lines and was intended for composers. When Patricia received his letters she would rub the perforated edges against her cheek to simulate his pockmarked skin.

Who would write first? Mr. Smedley was not your typical man, knowing how to take the lead, but under the circumstances, the murder of Mrs. Vogel's husband, etc., it seemed unlikely that she, vulnerable and moody, would initiate the correspondence. Up in my room one cold January night I wrote the first letter.

Dear Patricia,

When I see you I am reminded of the grove of poplars near my uncle's farm. It was a refuge for me when I was a boy, a place of shimmering wetness. So it is hard for me not to think of you as Patricia of the Poplars —

for when I see you in the halls, when I pass by your door and look through the slim window and hear your French and wonder if you are gagging, so true is your accent, I have the indecent (yes! I admit it) but raging urge to fling open the door and come to you at your desk, kiss your chalky hand, and then put my weary head on your shoulder. There, I have said it.
With you near me I would feel just as I had in the poplars: that here was finally rest from the terrors of the world, from the violins in the All-Village Orchestra, to name one horror, in particular. I would remain there at your shoulder all through class, as you explained the *vous* and the *tu*, the formal and the familiar. And that, my dear, sweet Patricia of the Poplars, is what I would like, to go from the formal to the familiar.

He didn't even sign the first letter. We had been studying the deciduous trees in Earth Science: Poplars had leaves that fluttered nervously in the wind and soft pulpy wood that clogged sewer systems. The next day on the playground I showed the letter to Tiffany, and she grabbed my arm and took me to the corner of the building. "Oh, my God," was all she could say for the first five minutes, pulling at her cheeks so that her eyes nearly popped out. I sat her down on the cold asphalt and handed her my notebook. She looked up at me, and I began to compose the response:

Dear Bruce, if I may be so bold,

Do you think that I have not noticed your long face in my window? After you disappear I come to my door and press my head against the very glass. I imagine that I smell the rosin on your suit and the faintest hint of your aftershave, which you use so sparingly. I almost feel the door close its strong arms around me and rock me gently until the pain in my heart trickles down to my feet and does little more than aggravate my ingrown toenails. What relief you bring, to ease my every inch of sorrow simply by looking in on me. Someday, dear Bruce, you and I will meet freely, in a grove of poplars, perhaps—someday, in a heavenly sphere.

Until then, I am, Mrs. Vogel

She loved him, she really did, but she was still in mourning. It had been only two months since the shooting, and she knew that whatever her feeling, it wasn't proper to go from viola to violin in the wink of an eye. She would have to be wooed.
For the next several weeks Tiffany and I were transported. We had been sucked into a vortex of feeling and couldn't keep ourselves from writing. I found myself moved in the oddest places. Sitting at supper, I would feel a letter come up my throat and sit on my tongue. I could hardly get out the words "May I be

excused?" before the urgent message pushed from behind my teeth. I'd have to rush to my room and sit breathless while my mouth formed the words and my hand moved across the page. I was dimly aware that I was hooked into something far larger than myself. I didn't really feel as if the letters were coming from me, is about all I can say to explain the mystery of it. They spilled onto paper sometimes three, four, five times a day. I had a special notebook that I carried with me every-where, which held the up-to-date correspondence. As the weeks went on Tiffany composed less and became the wardrobe coordinator. She sketched the different outfits B. and P. were to wear on their various dates and filed them in her fashion notebook.

I hardly noticed my mother's eye on me, but I knew she was wondering. She'd say things such as, "What's the matter with you, GeorgeAnne? I've asked you to empty the dishwasher three times." Or, "GeorgeAnne, you've been staring out that window for ten minutes. What's going on in that head of yours?"

If only I could tell her that in my mind I was coming down the aisle, the maid of honor, in a lavender dress and a crown of daisies.

She came to the window and looked into my eyes; she tried to see through to me, but she came up against a black curtain, a NO ADMITTANCE sign. "GeorgeAnne!" she cried, shaking me. "I don't know what I'm going to do with you." I shrugged my shoulders and went to my room to dream of love. There was nothing I wanted to do more than crawl into bed and lie there and look at my ceiling, watching the two of them running toward each other from the opposite ends of the school baseball diamond. When they met and kissed I had to turn over. Something on the order of molasses was rushing in from the dark into my body, starting at my head and swirling down.

One February morning Mrs. Vogel was wearing a particular favorite of mine, her green dress; it was impossible not to be moved by the spectacle, and I found Mr. Smedley taking pen in hand during French class, against his better judgment:

Dear Patricia from the Grove of Poplars,

I see you are wearing your green silk today. It is the exact color of Ma's pea soup. You have your underarm sweat shields on, and you are dry, my love. I imagine your sad face in the palm of my hands, and I think of our leaky roof at home, and I want to cry. But then I remember that we arranged to meet in the alley after school and that, if it will not make you too sad, I will play you the favorite song of your dead husband on my violin. I will play "Embraceable You." I will kiss the soles of your pink feet and dally at your knees. I sometimes wonder at the mysterious ways of God, that he would have taken your dark-haired husband and then given you to me. I am so much damper than the ever handsome violist, my hair is falling out, and my joints are loose, and yet I adore you with a passion that is as dry as fire. Is it my love, I wonder, the strength of my yearning, that caused the sniper to flatten your husband on the corrugated doormat of the el train? We will not talk of these things; I will merely play. I am your true one,

Brucie

I was writing this in my notebook, writing it in Bruce's impetuous scrawl, hurrying to finish so that I could pass it on to Tiffany. I ripped out the note while Tiffany coughed, and then I folded it into the size of a large pea. It was when my hand was directly over the aisle for a fleeting second that I heard Mrs. Vogel's voice: "GeorgeAnne, *freeze.*" In retrospect it all seemed so inevitable; we should have had a getaway car or some plan for spontaneous combustion. My arm was suspended in midair with the paper fluttering in my closed fist. Tiffany had her head down on her desk. Our future was clear. I saw us from the back, our hands cuffed behind us as we walked through the iron door of the federal penitentiary.

Mrs. Vogel came to my desk and held out her hand. I squeezed the note harder.

"Give me the note."

"No," I said. I coughed. "Non, s'il vous plait."

"*Give me the note.*" Someone who has a perspiration problem owes it to herself not to get overly agitated.

"This will not make you happy," I said to her.

"I'm sure it will not," she said in plain English.

What was I to do? I looked left and right, I tried to pulverize the paper in my already tight fist. When I handed it over she just stood at my desk and read, and when she was done she stared at me and then turned to Tiffany and then back at me again. "Come out in the hall," she choked.

When she had closed the door behind her classroom she looked at both of us, standing against the lockers like we were about to be shot. She clenched her teeth and hissed into our faces, "Who is Brucie?" And then she burst into tears, something in and of itself so astonishing I forgot, for a moment, to be scared.

When neither of us answered she shrieked in a whisper, "Tell me. I demand to know who this Bruce is."

"He is, ah, Mr. Smedley. Mr. Bruce Smedley." I spoke staring straight ahead.

She looked at the paper in horror. "Mr. Smedley? Oh," she said, ripping at it, shaking her head, the tears running into her mouth, her nose dripping. "You girls go too far, too far."

As a result of this one single intercepted note she marched back to her room, screamed at the class to do all the exercises in the entire book, and then she flung open my desk, throwing out papers and books. Her infallible teacher radar led her straight to the bottom. She seized the perfectly plain blue spiral notebook.

Tiffany and I were bound and gagged and then prodded down to Mr. Flannigan's office. Mrs. Vogel slammed the notebook on his desk and then put her hands to her mouth. The remarkable thing was that even as it was happening, I was writing to her in my mind, to tell her to calm down, to acknowledge to herself that she was behaving like a lunatic.

We had to stand there in the office while Mr. Flannigan read every letter to himself. I knew them all, could say them by heart to myself as he read.

Dear Brucie,

What I would give to stroke your cheek, you darling toad you. I dream of sneaking past your mother's bedroom to the small room at the end of the hall, where I know you lay your lonesome head down on its white pillow. You, who do not hang pennants on the wall from the football teams of your youth but rather have busts of Beethoven on your night table. I have been married before and know the secrets of your chamber. I will come to you in the night and sing in your ear, and you will dream of the Des Plaines River and not know why. I have been robbed and made richer, stranger than fiction, as deep as truth.

I am your most dear,

Patricia of the Poplars

I put the Des Plaines River in there only because it was a local French name and I liked the sound of it.

Mr. Flannigan turned the page and read the response.

My Darling P of the P,

I dreamt of the river. I knocked down the door of my room in my sleep; I was like a horned moose bashing through the woods on his way to his velvet coated she-moose. How I desperately need to feel the blue silk of your dress on my hands; how I long to finger the flesh around your clavicle and beyond. I yanked off my red union suit and was determined to come to you, but Ma heard me, warmed me a cup of Ovaltine, and sent me back to my room. Know, my dearest, that I will not be stopped, that the day will come when we will share our roll-on antiperspirant in our very own white tiled bathroom. You will learn all of Ma's secrets, just how to boil the chicken gizzards in bacon grease, and then we will tousle on the sofa during the Boston Pops. I will wash my hair whenever you say, my love, my P of the P. You will wash your shields at the sink and turn to watch me splash in the tub—you will—

Mr. Flannigan's freckled skin underwent a color change as he read. His temples were pulsing, as if only now he was coming to life. There was something so unreal and horrifying about the proceedings I had the urge to laugh, but Tiffany was not in any way, or in any part of her self, amused. She stood with her head bowed and her hands clenched.

Mr. Flannigan was frowning and rubbing his fingers over his bristly chin when Mr. Smedley appeared at the clouded glass door, fresh from his third-grade violin class he taught every Monday at our school. He smiled at me before he remembered that he'd been told there was trouble. Mr. Flannigan pushed the letters to the edge of the desk, and Mr. Smedley began to read. Mrs. Vogel, Mr. Flannigan, and Tiffany looked at their laps and the walls while Mr. Smedley read. I watched *him*. I knew it couldn't be true, but all the same I had the distinct impression that he wanted to chuckle. Mrs. Vogel blew her nose and Mr. Flannigan swiveled around in his chair so that he could stare at the venetian blinds. Mr. Smedley looked up from the paper finally and then straight into my eyes for an instant. Just that long. Then he cleared his throat and shifted from side to side and said, "Ah well." He puckered his lips and swished some saliva around in his mouth. "If these girls were as good at their music as they are at writing there'd be some hope for the concert halls of America." All of a sudden there was noise and movement; it was Mrs. Vogel remonstrating with a pure kind of noise that had no actual meaning—she was like a little dog yapping and yapping at an imaginary postman. I remember the swirl of her pea green dress, and next I knew I was out in the waiting room. Tiffany went directly to the opposite wall and sat on the sofa there with her arms folded across her chest. I stood by the drinking fountain and thought that it was probably time to decide what order I would like to enter as a novitiate. It seemed like hours before we were both handed sealed envelopes and told to go home.

"I'm never going to speak to you again," Tiffany said.

I looked past her and saw her blue and gold pom-poms of the future flashing in my face. I nodded and walked the long way home.

My mother was on the phone when I came in. She reached out, and I put the envelope in her hand. I knew instinctively that this was not going to be taken lightly. My parents, pure American now with only faint traces of Anglo-Saxon blood in their veins, had always behaved as if they were first-generation immigrants, and education was the ticket to commerce. The institution of school was so sacred I had to be delirious before I could stay home sick.

I sat at the kitchen table and waited. When she hung up she sat down and began to cry. Her tears came from so many different wellsprings—they were tears of anger and disappointment, and, worst of all, humiliation and failure. Sometime during the ensuing discussion she was going to point out to me the number of new gray hairs that had sprouted since she had received the phone call from Mr. Flannigan.

She put her puffy face in her hands and then smacked her palms on the table. "GeorgeAnne Mealy!" she shouted. "How could you have done such a thing to Mrs. Vogel?"

There was no point in trying to explain that I was hoping to heal the wound and to kill two birds with one stone, so to speak. Turn two miseries into one resplendent joy. "Bruce and Pat"—it had sounded so right. I looked at the table and cried, not because I was ashamed but because of injustice the world over, and in particular in this newly remodeled kitchen that now had a garbage disposal and an ice crusher.

My father was brought into it, and the scolding went on at length. My mother cried again, and my father paddled me on the sofa with a wooden spatula. I was sent to my room, fetched for more talk, cried at, and then sent back. Mrs. Vogel's tragedy was described to me repeatedly; the letters, my parents explained, hurt her deeply, shamed her in ways a twelve-year-old could never understand. I had caused someone to suffer, to *suffer, did I understand?*

I was no better than a felon. I was suspended for two days and had to do hard labor for a month for Mr. Smedley. Tiffany had obviously been led to bad behavior by me and had done very little actual writing. She had left the fashion notebook at home by accident on the day of the inquisition, so the sketches of Pat in her surf-and-sand getup, her horseback-riding habit, her after-school negligee were not in the public domain. For punishment Tiffany had to wash the blackboards in Mrs. Vogel's room for two weeks.

During my suspension I stayed in my room and practiced *The Firebird*. I worked up calluses on my fingers. I tried to hear the story in the music, and when that didn't work I tried to tell the story with the music. I really listened to the sound of my violin. It was such a terrible noise, little better than the screech of a cat when you step on its tail and wait. I suspected, like so many things, that when I got older it would come clear; at sixteen, no doubt, I would tuck the violin under my chin and hear the melody.

When I went back to school I was welcomed with the measured warmth a leper receives at the village square. Mrs. Vogel refused to meet my eye, and not once, for the rest of the school year, did she call on me.

For my labor I stayed after All-Village Orchestra and helped to fold up the stands and chairs and put them on a cart. Mother Smedley waited in the back with her rain hat on. Mostly Mr. Smedley and I didn't speak. Occasionally, I ventured a thing or two. Coming toward him with my metal chairs clanging, I'd say, "Mary Clare is a pro." And he'd say, "Uh huh, terrific." And then we'd move away from each other, both of us filled with the same haunting strain.

Once, when he was having trouble collapsing a chair, I asked him what it meant.

"What what means?" he said, banging at the legs.

"The music. The horn solo."

He stopped and looked at me. "Uh"—he took a pass over his thin wet hair with his hand—"I think it's about resolution, and"—he looked out into the dark theater—"it's something you feel, here." He pounded with his fist on his sunken chest. "I guess I can't say it in words; I'm not very good at that sort of thing." He looked at me in a way that made me think a sparkler had been lit at my throat and then sizzled all the way down to my toes. He went back to wrestling with the chair, trying to get it to fold. Then he paused and leaned on a stand. "I leave it to you to describe it sometime, GeorgeAnne." I nodded and stared at the floor and then I walked straight over to him and kicked the chair. It smacked against itself and went flat.

I stayed and helped beyond my month's requirement. Now it was what I looked forward to each week: dragging the metal chairs back to the rack, mostly in silence, and Mr. Smedley's three words at the end, "Thank you, GeorgeAnne." Sometimes he gave me one pat on the shoulder with his long chapped hand.

I was virtually grounded for the rest of the year. When I cried at dinner one rainy night in April because I couldn't go to Tiffany's roller-skating party and I knew she'd invited me only because she knew I wouldn't be allowed to come, my mother said her usual line, "There's so much more to life than a skating party." She had used that tack with me so many times: There's more to life than Halloween, more to life than a new dress, more than shopping, Christmas, the school play. Each time I had to ask myself, What then? What more is there?

I went up to my room after dinner and undressed for bed in the dark. I stood at the dresser in my undershirt and underpants, snapping my barrette open and closed for the longest time. It came to me bit by bit, as my eyes slowly adjusted to the gauze texture of the dark, and I began to see. For Mrs. Vogel there was the kindness of her students; any absence of cruelty was a blessing. For Tiffany there was the relief of checking the attic and finding in the farthest corner her fashion statements still shredded to bits in a shoebox. There was the temporary glory of being on the top of the pyramid in a short pleated skirt. I looked out to the street light, blurred and standing alone in the drizzle, and suddenly I knew what there was for me. For GeorgeAnne Mealy there were two things: There was the lurking power of words, words to tell any dream in the world; but most of all there was the feeling in the back of my throat, at the roots of my hair, in the goose bumps on my knees, the knot in my stomach, of pity. I had finally found its name. Pity ran so deep in my blood I had to kneel on the wood floor and cry into my wastebasket.

When I quieted I put my nightie on and went to the window. I stood pressing my hot forehead against the cold glass. I looked out, trying to think what sorts of gifts there were for poor Mr. Smedley. I stared at the wet shining sidewalk, and it didn't take long to come to me after all. For Mr. Bruce Smedley there was Mary Clare's horn, bursting forth at his direction, shaking the podium with a love song. For Mr. Bruce Smedley there was maybe even me.

ROBERT OLEN BUTLER

The Ironworkers' Hayride

Sunnyvale, Cal.
July 14, 1911

Miss M. Brose
219 Hearst Ave.
San Francisco, Calif

Dear Mathilda,

Just a line to let you know I am still alive. I am not going on that hayride.
The young man that wants me to go with his sister in law. But she has a
cork leg. I am awfull tired that is the main reason.

Regards to all. Milton

So this fellow at the new ironworks in Sunnyvale where I am a cost-sheet man
and he is a furnace man, he comes over to me at the Ironman Saloon. I'm still
in my blue serge suit and collar, though the fellows in their overalls know me as
an okay guy, even if they mostly treat me like a hapless little brother. But this one
fellow, Zack, spots me as soon as he sets foot in the place. I'm sitting on a stool at
the bar counting the smoked almonds I'm eating and sort of working the numbers
out—how many I need to eat to cover the cost of the beer in front of me—and
wishing I could dare pull out a scrap of paper and do some downright figuring.
But that would undercut my standing among these fellows around me, who I'm
here trying to be part of, the sorts of fellows that used to daily snap my suspenders
and tweak my nose when we were all boys. So this fellow Zack presses past his
friends and makes straight for me and he claps me on the back, causing me to
revise my almond count from twenty back to nineteen, most of the twentieth one
attaching itself to the mirror behind the bar. "Milton, old man," he says, and he
proceeds for the fourth time in four days to urge me to take his sister-in-law on
the Ironworkers' hayride, which is now a mere two days off, even though he has
confessed about her having a cork leg.

"I am awful tired nights," I say, an excuse I have not yet tried on him, and he
perches on the stool next to me with a face crumpled in skepticism. I don't blame
him. He shovels coal, I add numbers. He knows this. I know this. "My eyes," I say.
"Tired eyes."

"It's dark," he says. "You got nothing much to look at except Minnie, and she's easy on the eyes, I'm telling you. And that other thing, you know, it wears a shoe and stocking like the good one."

I nod and begin gnawing the thin brown skin off a new almond. This is not my usual method. Minnie's brother-in-law is making me nervous.

He lowers his voice and leans near. "Look. Nobody but you knows about this leg thing. She walks real good. And she dresses up nice. The others will think you're a regular fellow.

I shoot him a sideways glance and turn the almond over, like a squirrel, to gnaw at the other side. I tote up all the sums of his remark. The others don't already think I'm a regular fellow. I'm not a regular fellow. If she can hide her cork leg, I can hide my irregular fellowness. Zack has let me in on a family secret with all the obligations and reciprocities attendant thereto. Though I have to point out that I never solicited this secret. It was Zack who took the stocking off the rubber foot, so to speak. No. Erase that. *He let the cat out of the bag.* There's a reason for saying things the way everybody else says them.

"How 'bout it," Zack says.

I calculate it all, and the almond is bare and white in my hand. It gives me the willies. I slip it into my mouth, out of sight. I chew fast, knowing I'm about to get popped on the back again. I swallow and then turn to Zack, and I say, "All right."

This much I take pains to learn from Zack. Minnie's leg is missing from well above the knee. She is twenty-two. Her favorite flower is the poppy. And the leg isn't really made of cork. It couldn't be, if you think about it, cork being too soft a wood to bear the weight of a twenty-two-year-old girl, or even half her weight. The leg is of wood—willow, in fact—and years ago they made a swell wooden leg in the county of Cork in Ireland. Thus the name.

As for the reason, Zack says she lost her leg as a child to a runaway horse and an overturned carriage. She was riding in it. This gives me an idea. "Zack," I say. "Think. If she goes out in the night in a wagon being pulled by a horse, won't she be caused to dwell on that terrible event?"

He bends near, putting his great paw of a hand on my shoulder. It weighs quite a lot. I'm having trouble keeping from sliding off the bar stool under its pressure. "Look, Milton," he says. "I haven't been dogging you about this for your sake, much as I . . . like you. It's Minnie who wants bad to go on this hayride. I'm not about to disappoint her."

He squeezes my shoulder like he's trying to juice an orange and I know I better speak up quick. "Sure. Okay," I say, and he lets me go.

"That's my blue-serge pal," he says.

I want to say to him, Why me? I heard you hesitate before the word *like* in your recent declaration. *Pleasantly tolerate* is more what it is. So why choose a fellow like that for his sister-in-law? But I dare not ask. And I think I know the answer. He wants to keep from informing his pals in overalls about his sister-in-law's handicap. Not to mention he sees me as a safe choice, the last male in his acquaintance who'd ever play the masher with his wife's kin.

So this is how I come to be standing at the front gate of the ironworks in collar and straw hat holding a bunch of orange poppies. I am not alone. A few dozen couples—the guys from the various work gangs, mostly, and their girls in lacy shirtwaists and skirts—are all gabbling and promenading around me, trying to choose hay companions on the four large, sweet-smelling wagons that wait along the street. There is no sign of Zack and his sister-in-law. Then two piercing yellow eyes appear down the road—the headlamps of an automobile—and the horses start puffing and stirring, and up roars Zack in his father-in-law's Model T, to the great interest of all the couples. The Ford is as black as the night sky. Zack's father-in-law was one of the first to buy this wonder for a mere $845, and the prices have been coming down already in these past two years, the blue-serge boys in Detroit squeezing their production-cost numbers as tight as Zack squeezing my shoulder. I step forward from the crowd, which is already returning to the matter of choosing wagons. The driver's side of the auto is before me and Zack gives me a nod and I nod back. Then, stepping into the blazing beams of the headlamps is Minnie of the cork leg.

She pauses there, aflame from the lamps of the Ford, and I feel like the flowers are wilting in my hand. She is swell-looking. She's wearing a blue sailor dress with the big collar and the wide, knotted tie hanging down the center of her chest, and her head is bare, her hair all gathered up there with a wide, dark ribbon circling the crown, and there is a radiance all around her—thanks to the Ford, but radiance nonetheless—her whole head is surrounded with a bright glow, like a saint, a martyred saint who has lost her leg to an evil duke—a partially martyred saint—and her face is very pale and delicate of nose and brow and ear and so forth—my eyes are dancing around her, not taking her in very objectively, I realize—her mouth is a sweet painted butterfly. I'm squeezing the life out of the flowers in my hand, I realize, crushing their stems in my fist. I try to ease up, settle down. And now her face turns and she looks at me as if she knows who I am already. I flinch a bit inside, wondering how Zack described me, but it can't be too bad, because he's responsible for setting all this up. She steps from the light.

I observe this first step carefully. I am a detail man. That's my job. And I see with her first step which leg is descended from the land of Erin, so to speak. Her left. She has started from her right leg—she would surely start from her good side—and her left leg then follows a tiny bit slowly, perhaps dragging just a very little, almost imperceptibly, and it's true if I weren't looking for this and if I weren't a detail man, I'd never know, but I am and I am and I do. Now under way, she seems quite natural. She has a blanket draped over one arm. Many of the girls have blankets. I noted that with envy when I first arrived. It is mid-July, and though it can get a bit chill in the valley even in July, I know these blankets are for spooning, and now Minnie is approaching me and she's been moved to bring a blanket. This is too much on my mind as she arrives before me.

"Milton?" she says.

"Are you subject to chills?" I say. Inexplicably. I do have a good, thick, gum-rubber eraser in my head always at the ready to wipe away my mistakes of judgment before they issue forth from my mouth. I am a man who arrives at the appropriate sum total before giving an answer. But on this occasion I have simply blurted forth the next, uncalculated thought in my head.

"I don't have an illness," she says.

My remark had nothing to do with her leg and I have to squeeze my lips shut hard to keep that assertion from coming out of my mouth now and just making things worse.

"Of course," I say. "Of course," I repeat instantly. And it only takes the briefest moment of silence following for me to add, "Of course."

"I'm Minnie," she says.

"Of course," I say, and the hand with the flowers shoots out as if my arm was artificial and the spring lever in the elbow had just let go.

But the flowers save the moment, I think.

"Poppies," Minnie says, her eyes widening at their sight, which is wide indeed because her eyes are already quite large as it is, large and dark as the skin of a Ford Model T, one of which is roaring off into the night, a Ford Model T, that is, Zack's, leaving me alone with this girl. "They're my favorites. How did you know?" she says. "*Did* you know?"

"The flowers?" I say. "Oh . . ." I pause. I could suggest a deep intuitive bond here. I'm capable of that. I can't possibly expect strict, detailed honesty to be the best policy on a date with a girl with a wooden leg anyway, but in this circumstance I opt for it. "I asked Zack," I say.

Minnie laughs, lifting her face and not holding it back at all, not covering her mouth with her hand, like girls usually do. She says, "He had it drummed into his head by my sister around my last birthday."

A few moments pass and I'm not aware of it exactly but I'm just sort of gawking at her. She looks at me and tilts her head a little. "Are you trying to picture Zack's head being drummed on by his wife?"

I gawk some more.

Minnie lowers her voice. "She's a suffragette, you see."

I realize that if I don't take myself in hand I'll spend the rest of the evening two steps behind this girl without speaking a word. I manage to say, "I didn't know."

"Oh yes. I want to vote too. Does that surprise you?"

"No."

"Or put you off?"

"No," I say, and I manage to sound emphatic.

"I won't harangue you in the hay," she says. "Don't worry."

"Okay."

I'm finally catching up, I think, certainly enough to realize that I'm still holding the flowers straight out. I lift them up at her and she's been sort of in another place too, it seems. "Oh. Sorry," she says, though it looks like she's talking to the flowers. She takes them and then fixes on me again. "You were swell to do this," she says.

So we get to the business of finding a place for the ride. Most of the other couples have already made their choices and are settling down in the hay. We drift down the row of wagons, Minnie moving along real natural next to me. We arrive at the last one, and I look inside and say to her low, so the others can't hear, "Do you know any of these people?"

"Not a one. And you?"

"Seen a couple of them around, don't know any of them."

"Any of Zack's pals?" she says.

"Not that I know of."

"Then this one's for us," she says and she's already trying to climb up into the wagon.

I step up behind her and my hands come out and sort of hang in the air on either side. She's not looking at me but she knows what I'm doing, even down to my hesitation. "You can just grab and shove if you like," she says.

So I put my hands, which I have to say are trembling more than a little, on each side of her waist and she is heavily corseted inside there and just thinking about her corset makes me go too weak to lift her. But I try. I help a little and somehow she's up on the wagon and I'm scrambling in after her.

She moves forward on her hands and knees pretty fast, heading for the far end of the wagon and I try to keep up, crawling past the other couples settling in. One guy that I've nodded to a few times at the Ironman I nod to again and he gives me a big wink, finally understanding I'm a regular fellow, I presume, and I have the problem of what to do with my face in return. A similar wink, as from a fellow fellow? Another nod, which, I instantly realize, might give an impression like some European king or somebody passing in a carriage? Nothing, just stay blank-faced or turn away? But would that be interpreted as a gesture of rejection or overreaching uppitiness? All this goes through me like turning the crank on the arcade mutoscope real slow, but my arms and legs are still moving in normal time and the decision is made by my indecision. I pass on with my mug fixed in what I'm sure is a mask of buffoonery. Then I look ahead and Minnie is just turning around in the spot she's found for us, and the whole batch of poppies are clenched in her teeth. She's got the stems in her mouth and the cluster of flower heads are bunched up at her cheek and she sees me seeing this and she flutters her eyebrows at me, and once again it's me and my face trying to figure out how to act in this world we're not quite suited for.

She has put the blanket on the straw to her right side and pats the straw to her left. I'm grateful for the instruction. I just set my face to the place where I've been told to go and I creep on. Meanwhile, Minnie takes the flowers from her mouth and lays them on the blanket. Happily, my mind catches up—she'd put the bouquet in her mouth to protect them as she crawled. This makes perfectly good sense. I have arrived safely, turning and falling into the hay beside Minnie, and we are side by side.

I lean on my elbows thrown back behind me and I cross my feet at the ankles. My mouth opens to say something and then snaps shut with no actual words coming to mind. Her wooden leg lies between us. The evening in hay lies before us. I figure I'm in trouble.

Not that I shouldn't be prepared simply to keep quiet. Especially considering I've been enlisted in this date by the girl's relative who happens to mostly know me from a bar and he knows how out of place I generally am and I've agreed to it only after I've said no a few times and even written to my sister in San Francisco that I was saying no in spite of she's the one who's always worried about me never looking up from the column of numbers in front of me to find a life with somebody, but here's a girl who's got a cork leg, not to say there isn't plenty of girl left in spite of that, but it's just the idea of this whole arrangement, which is: Let's choose Milton to take out this girl who other young men maybe would get uncomfortable around because Milton's hard up and he's also a safe choice because there's not really a red-blooded young man inside of him he's just got ink in his blood and ledgers in his brain and numbers on his lips. So under these circumstances why should I care if I don't say another word all night? I can just lie here in the hay and get through the whole thing and then everybody will leave me alone and let me go back to my numbers. See? That's the fate even *I* imagine for myself at the end of a hayride with a girl. Go back to my numbers. But in fact I do expect more from myself now. I want more. It was Minnie herself who brought this out in me. Minnie radiant in the Model T's headlights. Minnie who says just grab me and shove. Minnie who wants to vote. Why shouldn't she?

"Why shouldn't you vote?" I say, unexpectedly.

She looks at me. "Well, dog my cats," she says. "What a sweet thing to say, Milton."

And now, having been seized by one thing to say, the ink bottle in my head instantly spills all over the ledger—I'm not afraid to put it in these terms—I am who I am—and I figure I'm in an even worse predicament, since I've raised her expectations.

But Minnie seems happy to pick things up. Of course she deserves a vote, she tells me, and she goes on for a time about how women would have busted the trusts even quicker than Roosevelt and Taft—it was only this year—what a great year, though, it was, she says—that Standard Oil was finally dissolved and the tobacco trust was broken up, but even at that, look what's happening now, she says, the banks in New York are trying to monopolize the nation's credit. And Minnie is talking like sixty and I sort of settle back and let her words just carry me along about oil and railroads and steel and big corporations, and this should be working up my feelings for numbers and business and all, but that's not what's happening, the wagons have started up and I'm giving myself over to the stars above and the flow of Minnie's voice and her words are like music to me, like a fugue by Bach or something that you just take in and it shuts down all the unnecessary functions of your brain except the part that hears the music. I even feel like humming with her as she talks. Then Minnie finally has to nudge me a bit. I realize that her words have worked around to me, "You're going to cast your ballot in October, right Milton? For the woman's vote in California?"

"Of course," I say.

"Grand," she says. "Just grand." She stops talking and looks at me closely. I look at her closely. The moon is full and Minnie is bright white, like she's made of alabaster. "I'm sorry," she says.

"Why?" I say.

"I've harangued you in the hay," she says.

She seems sincerely regretful. Even in the moonlight I can read that in her face. I want to reach out and touch her, perhaps take her hand, though my own hands go rigid in panic at the thought of it. But I find I have words. "No," I say. "You've educated me."

Minnie sort of rolls her eyes. I think in pleasure. "You've exhorted me," I say.

Her eyes focus hard on me now. She leans a little in my direction and her voice pitches low. "Thank you for saying so, Milton."

Then a choir begins to sing.

For a moment, strangely, it all seems to be happening just in my head. But the voices coarsen and the music is not Bach. In fact the sound is all around me in the wagons. The others on the hayride are singing. *Shine on, shine on harvest moon up in the sky. I ain't had no lovin' since January, February, June, or July.*

This is true, certainly. And you can tote up all my Januarys, Februarys, and so forth through the whole year. For all my years. Even just counting the ones since I hit adolescence, that's better than a hundred months. I can work up an exact sum tomorrow if I want. Now things go a little sour in my head. I realize that, given my ineptness at the lovin' and spoonin' and all, I'll be adding this present month of July to the tally in spite of this hayride.

The voices roll into a verse. *I can't see why a boy should sigh, when by his side is the girl he loves so true.*

I look at Minnie. She's not singing along, but she's smiling into the wagon, and then she lays her head back on the hay. So do I. And of course I sigh. Shine on, shine on harvest moon.

Minnie and I lie there and listen, side by side, the moon shining over us and the stars, as well, no more talk being necessary, and it's just grand, even as the singing ironmen and their girls move on to other songs, first to "Whoop Whoop Whoop, Make a Noise Like a Hoop and Roll Away," and then "Oh You Spearmint Kiddo with the Wrigley Eyes," not really catching the mood I'm in—but that's still okay, I'm beside Minnie lovely Minnie with the leg of willow—and they do go on to sing "I'd Love to Live in Loveland with a Girl Like You," and there's a lot about turtledoves and hearts beating in tune and babbling brooks and that's more like it and I'm definitely thinking about Minnie though I'm not touching her and I'm not looking at her and she might as well be a distant memory, for all that. And so she soon will be, I realize. This is my only chance with her and we are sliding along in the night and the time is ticking by and I'm acting like she's not even there and now they're singing, *Waltz me around again, Willie, around around around. The music is dreamy, it's peaches and creamy, O don't let my feet touch the ground.*

I sit up at once. It sounds like Minnie beseeching me. Waltz me, Milton, don't let my feet touch the ground. That's what I need to do. I see myself sweeping her up and it makes no difference what her legs are made of, with me she need never touch the ground.

"Are you all right?" Minnie's voice slips in under the last chorus of the song. I look at her. She's sitting up, too. *I feel like a ship on an ocean of joy—I just want to holler out loud, "Ship ahoy!"* And she turns her head to the wagon and she opens her mouth and sings with the others, *Waltz me around again, Willie, around around around.* I can't take my eyes off her. There's straw caught in her hair and I want very much to lift my hand and take it out but I'm as paralyzed as ever. Then everyone is laughing and applauding themselves and the music is over and Minnie turns her face back to me.

And she winks.

I have, of course, no earthly idea what she means by this exactly. But I dare now to think that I'm pretty much okay for the moment. With this very progressive girl. With this girl who would bust the trusts and still has it in her to wink. The madness of speech comes upon me again. "I'm going to vote in October," I say, apropos of nothing but the chaos in my head. So I add, "Like I said before." Which needs further explanation. "For women to vote," I say, and I try to lock my jaw shut.

Miraculously, she seems to understand, even though I don't. She leans close. "You're right," she says. "That's just the way to waltz me around and around, Willie."

I'm glad my jaw is still locked because I'm about to impulsively correct her about my name. But I stay quiet long enough to get what she means. How clever she has made me out to be. Then, inspired, I wink.

She smiles and turns away. "Aren't you feeling a little bit chilled?" she says.

"No," I say. I am, in fact, feeling quite flushed.

Probably from the rapid disintegration of my brain cells. I turn to see what Minnie is seeing and several other couples are opening their blankets and disappearing under them.

"Yes," I say.

Minnie looks at me and of course I'm driven to explanations. "The valley gets chilly," I say. "It's all the orchards," I say. "I think they somehow, the fruit trees, absorb the heat perhaps, to make it chilly. There's no real statistics on that, however. It's probably just Northern California. The climate, you know." I stop myself at last. I'm breathless from this madness.

"So you're chilly?" she says.

"Yes," I say.

She reaches beside her and gently sets the flowers on the hay. She flashes open the blanket and lifts it and it settles over the two of us up to our shoulders and she says, "How's that?" and I say, "Fine."

We lie back to watch the night sky. We do that for a while, not saying anything, and we're still not touching at all, except maybe just barely along the upper arms, though that might only be my imagination.

It is true that the Santa Clara Valley is like one big orchard. After the earthquake, Sunnyvale started wooing San Francisco companies to reestablish themselves down here, offering free orchard land to build on. That's how the ironworks got started. But mostly it's fruit trees up and down and all around. Which is where the wagons end up, now that the singing is done and the giggling and low talk and spooning have begun. We head out into one of the big apricot orchards.

There is still a smell of sulfur smoke lingering in the air from the curing houses. "You remember last year?" Minnie says.

I know at once what she's thinking and I know it's because of the night sky and the acrid smell.

She says, "When we were all waiting to pass through the tail of Halley's Comet? Did you think that life on earth would come to an end?"

This happens to be a topic I know something about. When the astronomers decided that the tail was made up of deadly cyanogen gas I knew the numbers had to be in our favor, which was soon confirmed in news reports that plenty of people decided to overlook.

"Not for a moment," I say.

"Not for a moment?" Minnie asks, real soft.

I blunder ahead. "The tail looked pretty substantial across the sky," I say. "We passed through forty-eight trillion cubic miles of it and of course it was highly reflective of the sunlight. But you have to understand there was only about one molecule of poison per cubic yard, and since it takes ten thousand sextillion cyanogen molecules to weigh one pound—these were all known numbers well in

442 APPENDIX OF PERFORMANCE TEXTS

advance of the encounter—then a little figuring would have told us that the sum total of poison gas the planet earth was about to pass through weighed barely half an ounce."

Minnie's arms emerge from beneath the blanket and she cradles the back of her head in the palms of her hands. She studies the sky and then says, "I was frightened for a while."

And I understand at once how it is that even correctly gathered and accurately calculated numbers can sometimes be irrelevant. I also understand how much I adore this Minnie of the willow leg. I turn a bit onto my side, gently, without disturbing her gaze at the sky, so that I can look at her. And there is a comet of desire streaking through me, its tail thick with something much denser than Halley's poison. I am suddenly desperate to touch this girl, just lay a hand on her arm or brush at her hair with my fingertips—*something*—but I have neither the courage nor the confidence. And I am seized by a plan.

Even as Minnie goes on about her fear of the comet. "No matter what the scientists announced," she says. "Scientists are constantly saying things and taking them back."

I think of her artificial leg lying between us, hidden beneath the blanket.

"It's not a rational thing," she says.

The leg is part of Minnie, but it really isn't.

"We're not always rational creatures," she says.

So it stands to reason that a touch there would not constitute an actual offense, that is to say the flagrant act of a masher. Though it's a leg, after all, which is a powerful part of a girl indeed, it's not really a leg, it's a piece of wood, it's really as if you were with a girl who walked with a cane and you touched the cane, which is no offense at all, and yet, from my own private comet's point of view, it is her own personal sweet willow leg and it is attached to her and so it would still be a thrillingly tender connection to her while at the same time being a connection that no one in the world would know about, not even her, especially under a blanket, and even if they did know about it, it's not like touching the actual girl.

"Sometimes you have to face a difficult thing," she says.

I turn my attention to my left hand, but the hand is only too willing to dash ahead and I glance down the length of the blanket, gauging the contours, and my hand slithers along humpbacked under the cloth, like a mole making for the roses, which in this case is a place just below her artificial knee.

"You think you might die," Minnie says, "and even if that never was so, just the thinking of it is more or less the same."

I am drawing near and I fix on her profile, edged in moonlight, though as beautiful as she is, my attention is elsewhere.

Moles are blind but they have other highly refined senses and so it is with my hand, which expertly arrives on the scene and lifts and curls and descends, slowly, delicately, and Minnie sighs and says, "I didn't have it too bad, though."

Then I touch her. Or it. Or more precisely her skirt, the cloth is rippled beneath my palm, and her wooden leg is further within, a distant thing still, which is all right, I am very happy.

"Did you know that people actually took one look at the comet and died?" Minnie says. "Heart attacks, mostly."

My hand settles in. I surround Minnie's leg. I even squeeze it, ever so faintly.

"There was a woman named Ruth Jordan in Talladega, Alabama," Minnie says. "I read all this in the newspapers. She stepped onto the porch of her home and she looked and fell over dead. And there was another woman, in St. Louis, who was fine looking at the comet thinking it a cloud, but when they told her what she was seeing, she died."

I squeeze Minnie's leg again. And I realize I was actually *thinking* too much both those times, thinking about squeezing and thinking about having squeezed, and all the while I didn't actually *experience* the act, so I squeeze her leg again, trying to concentrate just on feeling it. Then I move my way up to the knee and even across it—Zack said the wooden part goes far up—and I feel my way back down again, squeezing all along.

"Some were simply driven insane," Minnie says. "Especially in Chicago, for some reason."

Squeeze, squeeze, move along, squeeze some more. I'm a bit breathless now. I'm growing dizzy. I love her willow leg.

"Perhaps that's just where the reporter was who wrote the story. But there were people on Chicago streetcars praying and weeping about the end of the world."

Now I slow down for moment. I make the squeezes long and lingering. Here, sweet knee, take this long caress.

"That's not necessarily insane, I suppose," Minnie says. "Something more like religious ecstasy, I guess. But there were suicides. One woman, afraid of the gas of the comet, inhaled the gas from her lamp."

Here, sweet thigh, just above the knee a long caress for you. And then another quick one further up, and then further down.

"Sometimes," Minnie says, "we are compelled to embrace the thing we fear the most, don't you think?"

But her face doesn't turn to me with this question. It's just as well. I wouldn't be able to say much at the moment. It's all I can do to keep my eyes from rolling back in my head in something like religious ecstasy.

"I can understand that, I suppose," Minnie says.

I am vaguely aware of a stir, and I look down the length of the blanket and I nearly gasp. Mr. Mole is racing furiously up and down there, absolutely crazed. I watch for a moment in awe. Up and down the leg. Up and down. It's my hand, I know. Frenzied with love. It's my own hand. I can stop it, if I choose. And so

I do. I concentrate on my hand and I have this bad news for it and I send out the message, and it stops, my hand. Though it's still lying on her leg. Okay. I let myself have this one last touch.

Minnie turns her face to me. "Weren't you a little afraid, even for a moment?" she says.

"Yes," I manage to say.

"That's natural," she says.

I gently move my hand off her leg and back to my side. I focus on catching my breath.

"Shall we find all the constellations?" Minnie says suddenly, lifting her face to the night.

"Yes," I say. "I know something about that."

And so we trace them out together, these patterns in the sky, and I count the stars that make them up while she talks about bears and archers and hunters with swords. And we go on to talk about this and that and we all sing some more songs after the others emerge from their blankets, and when the wagons have returned to the gates of the ironworks, I help Minnie down, grabbing her firmly at her waist, and for a moment it feels as if I am ready to waltz her around and around with her feet never touching the ground.

Though I don't. The Model T is idling nearby and Minnie and I stand before each other, about to part. She says, "Thank you, Milton. This has been grand."

"Yes," I say. And at this moment it does not occur to me whatsoever that Minnie would want to see me again. But what do I know? My judgment is trustworthy only to the bottom of a column of figures. For Minnie takes a step nearer to me, and she dips her face just a little without letting her eyes leave mine, and she says, "You come call on me, all right, Milton?"

I am once again without words, but I manage to nod my head so as to say yes yes I will I will. And then she smiles a sweet slow smile and says, "Just for future reference, Milton. It's the other leg."

WILLA CATHER

Paul's Case: A Study in Temperament

It was Paul's afternoon to appear before the faculty of the Pittsburgh High School
to account for his various misdemeanors. He had been suspended a week ago,
and his father had called at the Principal's office and confessed his perplexity
about his son. Paul entered the faculty room suave and smiling. His clothes were
a trifle outgrown, and the tan velvet on the collar of his open overcoat was frayed
and worn; but for all that there was something of the dandy about him, and he
wore an opal pin in his neatly knotted black four-in-hand, and a red carnation in
his buttonhole. This latter adornment the faculty somehow felt was not properly
significant of the contrite spirit befitting a boy under the ban of suspension.

Paul was tall for his age and very thin, with high, cramped shoulders and a
narrow chest. His eyes were remarkable for a certain hysterical brilliancy, and
he continually used them in a conscious, theatrical sort of way, peculiarly offensive in a boy. The pupils were abnormally large, as though he were addicted to
belladonna, but there was a glassy glitter about them which that drug does not
produce.

When questioned by the Principal as to why he was there, Paul stated,
politely enough, that he wanted to come back to school. This was a lie, but Paul
was quite accustomed to lying; found it, indeed, indispensable for overcoming
friction. His teachers were asked to state their respective charges against him,
which they did with such a rancour and aggrievedness as evinced that this was
not a usual case. Disorder and impertinence were among the offenses named, yet
each of his instructors felt that it was scarcely possible to put into words the real
cause of the trouble, which lay in a sort of hysterically defiant manner of the boy's;
in the contempt which they all knew he felt for them, and which he seemingly
made not the least effort to conceal. Once, when he had been making a synopsis
of a paragraph at the blackboard, his English teacher had stepped to his side and
attempted to guide his hand. Paul had started back with a shudder and thrust his
hands violently behind him. The astonished woman could scarcely have been
more hurt and embarrassed had he struck at her. The insult was so involuntary
and definitely personal as to be unforgettable. In one way and another, he had
made all his teachers, men and women alike, conscious of the same feeling of
physical aversion. In one class he habitually sat with his hand shading his eyes; in
another he always looked out of the window during the recitation; in another he
made a running commentary on the lecture, with humorous intention.

"Paul's Case: A Study in Temperament," by Willa Cather, originally appeared in Cather's short-
story collection *The Troll Garden* (New York: McClure, 1905). This reprinting is taken from the
authoritative edition republished in 1983 by the University of Nebraska Press. The British spellings of this edition have been preserved.

His teachers felt this afternoon that his whole attitude was symbolized by his shrug and his flippantly red carnation flower, and they fell upon him without mercy, his English teacher leading the pack. He stood through it smiling, his pale lips parted over his white teeth. (His lips were continually twitching, and be had a habit of raising his eyebrows that was contemptuous and irritating to the last degree.) Older boys than Paul had broken down and shed tears under that baptism of fire, but his set smile did not once desert him, and his only sign of discomfort was the nervous trembling of the fingers that toyed with the buttons of his overcoat, and an occasional jerking of the other hand that held his hat. Paul was always smiling, always glancing about him, seeming to feel that people might be watching him and trying to detect something. This conscious expression, since it was as far as possible from boyish mirthfulness, was usually attributed to insolence or "smartness."

As the inquisition proceeded, one of his instructors repeated an impertinent remark of the boy's, and the Principal asked him whether he thought that a courteous speech to have made a woman. Paul shrugged his shoulders slightly and his eyebrows twitched.

"I don't know," he replied. "I didn't mean to be polite or impolite, either. I guess it's a sort of way I have of saying things regardless."

The Principal, who was a sympathetic man, asked him whether he didn't think that a way it would be well to get rid of. Paul grinned and said he guessed so. When he was told that he could go, he bowed gracefully and went out. His bow was but a repetition of the scandalous red carnation.

His teachers were in despair, and his drawing master voiced the feeling of them all when he declared there was something about the boy which none of them understood. He added: "I don't really believe that smile of his comes altogether from insolence; there's something sort of haunted about it. The boy is not strong, for one thing. I happen to know that he was born in Colorado, only a few months before his mother died out there of a long illness. There is something wrong about the fellow."

The drawing master had come to realize that, in looking at Paul, one saw only his white teeth and the forced animation of his eyes. One warm afternoon the boy had gone to sleep at his drawing-board, and his master had noted with amazement what a white, blue-veined face it was; drawn and wrinkled like an old man's about the eyes, the lips twitching even in his sleep, and stiff with a nervous tension that drew them back from his teeth.

His teachers left the building dissatisfied and unhappy; humiliated to have felt so vindictive toward a mere boy, to have uttered this feeling in cutting terms, and to have set each other on, as it were, in the gruesome game of intemperate reproach. Some of them remembered having seen a miserable street cat set at bay by a ring of tormentors.

As for Paul, he ran down the hill whistling the "Soldiers' Chorus" from *Faust*, looking wildly behind him now and then to see whether some of his teachers were not there to writhe under his light-heartedness. As it was now late in the afternoon and Paul was on duty that evening as usher at Carnegie Hall, he decided that he would not go home to supper. When he reached the concert hall the doors were not yet open and, as it was chilly outside, he decided to go up into the picture gallery—always deserted at this hour—where there were some of Raffelli's gay studies of Paris streets and an airy blue Venetian scene or two that always exhilarated him. He was delighted to find no one in the gallery but the old guard, who sat in one corner, a newspaper on his knee, a black patch over one eye and the other closed. Paul possessed himself of the place and walked confidently up and down, whistling under his breath. After a while he sat down before a blue Rico and lost himself. When he bethought him to look at his watch, it was after seven o'clock, and he rose with a start and ran downstairs, making a face at Augustus, peering out from the cast room, and an evil gesture at the Venus of Milo as he passed her on the stairway.

When Paul reached the ushers' dressing room half a dozen boys were there already, and he began excitedly to tumble into his uniform. It was one of the few that at all approached fitting, and Paul thought it very becoming—though he knew that the tight, straight coat accentuated his narrow chest, about which he was exceedingly sensitive. He was always considerably excited while be dressed, twanging all over to the tuning of the strings and the preliminary flourishes of the horns in the music room; but to-night he seemed quite beside himself, and he teased and plagued the boys until, telling him that he was crazy, they put him down on the floor and sat on him.

Somewhat calmed by his suppression, Paul dashed out to the front of the house to seat the early comers. He was a model usher; gracious and smiling he ran up and down the aisles; nothing was too much trouble for him; he carried messages and brought programmes as though it were his greatest pleasure in life, and all the people in his section thought him a charming boy, feeling that he remembered and admired them. As the house filled, he grew more and more vivacious and animated, and the colour came to his cheeks and lips. It was very much as though this were a great reception and Paul were the host. Just as the musicians came out to take their places, his English teacher arrived with checks for the seats which a prominent manufacturer had taken for the season. She betrayed some embarrassment when she handed Paul the tickets, and a *hauteur* which subsequently made her feel very foolish. Paul was startled for a moment, and had the feeling of wanting to put her out; what business had she here among all these fine people and gay colours? He looked her over and decided that she was not appropriately dressed and must be a fool to sit downstairs in such togs. The tickets had probably been sent her out of kindness, he reflected as he put down a seat for her, and she had about as much right to sit there as he had.

When the symphony began Paul sank into one of the rear seats with a long sigh of relief, and lost himself as he had done before the Rico. It was not that symphonies, as such, meant anything in particular to Paul, but the first sigh of the instruments seemed to free some hilarious and potent spirit within him; something that struggled there like the Genius in the bottle found by the Arab fisherman. He felt a sudden zest of life; the lights danced before his eyes and the concert hall blazed into unimaginable splendour. When the soprano soloist came on, Paul forgot even the nastiness of his teacher's being there and gave himself up to the peculiar stimulus such personages always had for him. The soloist chanced to be a German woman, by no means in her first youth, and the mother of many children; but she wore an elaborate gown and a tiara, and above all she had that indefinable air of achievement, that world-shine upon her, which, in Paul's eyes, made her a veritable queen of Romance.

After a concert was over Paul was always irritable and wretched until he got to sleep, and to-night he was even more than usually restless. He had the feeling of not being able to let down, of its being impossible to give up this delicious excitement which was the only thing that could be called living at all. During the last number he withdrew and, after hastily changing his clothes in the dressing-room, slipped out to the side door where the soprano's carriage stood. Here he began pacing rapidly up and down the walk, waiting to see her come out.

Over yonder, the Schenley, in its vacant stretch, loomed big and square through the fine rain, the windows of its twelve stories glowing like those of a lighted card-board house under a Christmas tree. All the actors and singers of the better class stayed there when they were in the city, and a number of the big manufacturers of the place lived there in the winter. Paul had often hung about the hotel, watching the people go in and out, longing to enter and leave school-masters and dull care behind him forever.

At last the singer came out, accompanied by the conductor, who helped her into her carriage and closed the door with a cordial *auf wiedersehen* which set Paul to wondering whether she were not an old sweetheart of his. Paul followed the carriage over to the hotel, walking so rapidly as not to be far from the entrance when the singer alighted, and disappeared behind the swinging glass doors that were opened by a negro in a tall hat and a long coat. In the moment that the door was ajar it seemed to Paul that he, too, entered. He seemed to feel himself go after her up the steps, into the warm, lighted building, into an exotic, tropical world of shiny, glistening surfaces and basking ease. He reflected upon the myste-rious dishes that were brought into the dining-room, the green bottles in buckets of ice, as he had seen them in the supper party pictures of the Sunday World supplement. A quick gust of wind brought the rain down with sudden vehe-mence, and Paul was startled to find that he was still outside in the slush of the gravel driveway; that his boots were letting in the water and his scanty overcoat was clinging wet about him; that the lights in front of the concert hall were out and that the rain was driving in sheets between him and the orange glow of the windows above him. There it was, what be wanted—tangibly before him, like the fairy world of a Christmas pantomime—but mocking spirits stood guard at the doors, and, as the rain beat in his face, Paul wondered whether he were destined always to shiver in the black night outside, looking up at it.

He turned and walked reluctantly toward the car tracks. The end had to come sometime; his father in his night-clothes at the top of the stairs, explanations that did not explain, hastily improvised fictions that were forever tripping him up, his upstairs room and its horrible yellow wall-paper, the creaking bureau with the greasy plush collar-box, and over his painted wooden bed the pictures of George Washington and John Calvin, and the framed motto, "Feed my Lambs," which had been worked in red worsted by his mother.

Half an hour later, Paul alighted from his car and went slowly down one of the side streets off the main thoroughfare. It was a highly respectable street, where all the houses were exactly alike, and where business men of moderate means begot and reared large families of children, all of whom went to Sabbath-school and learned the shorter catechism, and were interested in arithmetic; all of whom were as exactly alike as their homes, and of a piece with the monotony in which they lived. Paul never went up Cordelia Street without a shudder of loathing. His home was next to the house of the Cumberland minister. He approached it to-night with the nerveless sense of defeat, the hopeless feeling of sinking back forever into ugliness and commonness that he had always had when he came home. The moment he turned into Cordelia Street he felt the waters close above his head. After each of these orgies of living, he experienced all the physical depression which follows a debauch; the loathing of respectable beds, of common food, of a house penetrated by kitchen odours; a shuddering repulsion for the flavourless, colourless mass of every-day existence; a morbid desire for cool things and soft lights and fresh flowers.

The nearer he approached the house, the more absolutely unequal Paul felt to the sight of it all: his ugly sleeping chamber; the cold bath-room with the grimy zinc tub, the cracked mirror, the dripping spiggots; his father, at the top of the stairs, his hairy legs sticking out from his night-shirt, his feet thrust into carpet slippers. He was so much later than usual that there would certainly be inquiries and reproaches. Paul stopped short before the door. He felt that he could not be accosted by his father to-night; that he could not toss again on that miserable bed. He would not go in. He would tell his father that he had no car fare and it was raining so hard he had gone home with one of the boys and stayed all night.

Meanwhile, he was wet and cold. He went around to the back of the house and tried one of the basement windows, found it open, raised it cautiously, and scrambled down the cellar wall to the floor. There he stood, holding his breath, terrified by the noise he had made, but the floor above him was silent, and there was no creak on the stairs. He found a soap-box, and carried it over to the soft ring of light that streamed from the furnace door, and sat down. He was horribly afraid of rats, so he did not try to sleep, but sat looking distrustfully at the dark, still terrified lest he might have awakened his father. In such reactions, after one of the experiences which made days and nights out of the dreary blanks of the calendar, when his senses were deadened, Paul's head was always singularly clear. Suppose his father had heard him getting in at the window and had come down and shot him for a burglar? Then, again, suppose his father had come down, pistol in hand, and he had cried out in time to save himself, and his father had been horrified to think how nearly he had killed him? Then, again, suppose a day should come when his father would remember that night, and wish there had been no warning cry to stay his hand? With this last supposition Paul entertained himself until daybreak.

The following Sunday was fine; the sodden November chill was broken by the last flash of autumnal summer. In the morning Paul had to go to church and Sabbath-school, as always. On seasonable Sunday afternoons the burghers of Cordelia Street always sat out on their front "stoops" and talked to their neighbours on the next stoop, or called to those across the street in neighbourly fashion. The men usually sat on gay cushions placed upon the steps that led down to the sidewalk, while the women, in their Sunday "waists," sat in rockers on the cramped porches, pretending to be greatly at their ease. The children played in the streets; there were so many of them that the place resembled the recreation grounds of a kindergarten. The men on the steps—all in their shirt sleeves, their vests unbuttoned—sat with their legs well apart, their stomachs comfortably protruding, and talked of the prices of things, or told anecdotes of the sagacity of their various chiefs and overlords. They occasionally looked over the multitude of squabbling children, listened affectionately to their high-pitched, nasal voices, smiling to see their own proclivities reproduced in their offspring, and interspersed their legends of the iron kings with remarks about their sons' progress at school, their grades in arithmetic, and the amounts they had saved in their toy banks.

On this last Sunday of November, Paul sat all the afternoon on the lowest step of his "stoop," staring into the street, while his sisters, in their rockers, were talking to the minister's daughters next door about how many shirt waists they had made in the last week, and how many waffles someone had eaten at the last church supper. When the weather was warm, and his father was in a particularly jovial frame of mind, the girls made lemonade, which was always brought out in a red-glass pitcher, ornamented with forget-me-nots in blue enamel. This the girls thought very fine, and the neighbors always joked about the suspicious colour of the pitcher.

To-day Paul's father sat on the top step, talking to a young man who shifted a restless baby from knee to knee. He happened to be the young man who was daily held up to Paul as a model, and after whom it was his father's dearest hope that he would pattern. This young man was of a ruddy complexion, with a compressed, red mouth, and faded, near-sighted eyes, over which he wore thick spectacles, with gold bows that curved about his ears. He was clerk to one of the magnates of a great steel corporation, and was looked upon in Cordelia Street as a young man with a future. There was a story that, some five years ago—he was now barely twenty-six—he had been a trifle dissipated but in order to curb his appetites and save the loss of time and strength that a sowing of wild oats might have entailed, he had taken his chief's advice, oft reiterated to his employees, and at twenty-one had married the first woman whom he could persuade to share his fortunes. She happened to be an angular school-mistress, much older than he, who also wore thick glasses, and who had now borne him four children, all near-sighted, like herself.

The young man was relating how his chief, now cruising in the Mediterranean, kept in touch with all the details of the business, arranging his office hours on his yacht just as though he were at home, and "knocking off work enough to keep two stenographers busy." His father told, in turn, the plan his corporation was considering, of putting in an electric railway plant in Cairo. Paul snapped his teeth; he had an awful apprehension that they might spoil it all before he got there. Yet he rather liked to hear these legends of the iron kings that were told and retold on Sundays and holidays; these stories of palaces in Venice, yachts on the Mediterranean, and high play at Monte Carlo appealed to his fancy, and he was interested in the triumphs of these cash boys who had become famous, though he had no mind for the cash-boy stage.

After supper was over, and he had helped to dry the dishes, Paul nervously asked his father whether he could go to George's to get some help in his geometry, and still more nervously asked for car fare. This latter request he had to repeat, as his father, on principle, did not like to hear requests for money, whether much or little. He asked Paul whether he could not go to some boy who lived nearer, and told him that he ought not to leave his school work until Sunday; but he gave him the dime. He was not a poor man, but he had a worthy ambition to come up in the world. His only reason for allowing Paul to usher was that he thought a boy ought to be earning a little.

Paul bounded upstairs, scrubbed the greasy odour of the dish-water from his hands with the ill-smelling soap he hated, and then shook over his fingers a few drops of violet water from the bottle he kept hidden in his drawer. He left the house with his geometry conspicuously under his arm, and the moment he got out of Cordelia Street and boarded a downtown car, he shook off the lethargy of two deadening days, and began to live again.

The leading juvenile of the permanent stock company which played at one of the downtown theatres was an acquaintance of Paul's, and the boy had been invited to drop in at the Sunday-night rehearsals whenever he could. For more than a year Paul had spent every available moment loitering about Charley Edwards's dressing-room. He had won a place among Edwards's following not only because the young actor, who could not afford to employ a dresser, often found him useful, but because he recognized in Paul something akin to what churchmen term "vocation."

It was at the theatre and at Carnegie Hall that Paul really lived; the rest was but a sleep and a forgetting. This was Paul's fairy tale, and it had for him all the allurement of a secret love. The moment he inhaled the gassy, painty, dusty odour behind the scenes, he breathed like a prisoner set free, and felt within him the possibility of doing or saying splendid, brilliant, poetic things. The moment the cracked orchestra beat out the overture from *Martha*, or jerked at the serenade from *Rigoletto*, all stupid and ugly things slid from him, and his senses were deliciously, yet delicately fired.

Perhaps it was because, in Paul's world, the natural nearly always wore the guise of ugliness, that a certain element of artificiality seemed to him necessary in beauty. Perhaps it was because his experience of life elsewhere was so full of Sabbath-school picnics, petty economies, wholesome advice as to how to succeed in life, and the unescapable odours of cooking, that he found this existence so alluring, these smartly-clad men and women so attractive, that he was so moved by these starry apple orchards that bloomed perennially under the lime-light.

It would be difficult to put it strongly enough how convincingly the stage entrance of that theatre was for Paul the actual portal of Romance. Certainly none of the company ever suspected it, least of all Charley Edwards. It was very like the old stories that used to float about London of fabulously rich Jews, who had subterranean halls there, with palms, and fountains, and soft lamps and richly apparelled women who never saw the disenchanting light of London day. So, in the midst of that smoke-palled city, enamored of figures and grimy toil, Paul had his secret temple, his wishing carpet, his bit of blue-and-white Mediterranean shore bathed in perpetual sunshine.

Several of Paul's teachers had a theory that his imagination had been perverted by garish fiction, but the truth was that he scarcely ever read at all. The books at home were not such as would either tempt or corrupt a youthful mind, and as for reading the novels that some of his friends urged upon him—well, he got what he wanted much more quickly from music; any sort of music, from an orchestra to a barrel organ. He needed only the spark, the indescribable thrill that made his imagination master of his senses, and he could make plots and pictures enough of his own. It was equally true that he was not stage-struck—not, at any rate, in the usual acceptation of that expression. He had no desire to become an actor, any more than he had to become a musician. He felt no necessity to do any of these things; what he wanted was to see, to be in the atmosphere, float on the wave of it, to be carried out, blue league after blue league, away from everything.

After a night behind the scenes, Paul found the schoolroom more than ever repulsive; the bare floors and naked walls; the prosy men who never wore frock coats, or violets in their button-holes; the women with their dull gowns, shrill voices, and pitiful seriousness about prepositions that govern the dative. He could not bear to have the other pupils think, for a moment, that he took these people seriously; he must convey to them that he considered it all trivial, and was there only by way of a jest, anyway. He had autographed pictures of all the members of the stock company which he showed his classmates, telling them the most incredible stories of his familiarity with these people, of his acquaintance with the soloists who came to Carnegie Hall, his suppers with them and the flowers he sent them. When these stories lost their effect, and his audience grew listless, he became desperate and would bid all the boys good-bye, announcing that he was going to travel for a while; going to Naples, to Venice, to Egypt. Then, next Monday, he would slip back, conscious and nervously smiling; his sister was ill, and he should have to defer his voyage until spring.

Matters went steadily worse with Paul at school. In the itch to let his instructors know how heartily he despised them and their homilies, and how thoroughly he was appreciated elsewhere, he mentioned once or twice that he had no time to fool with theorems; adding—with a twitch of the eyebrows and a touch of that nervous bravado which so perplexed them—that he was helping the people down at the stock company; they were old friends of his.

The upshot of the matter was, that the Principal went to Paul's father, and Paul was taken out of school and put to work. The manager at Carnegie Hall was told to get another usher in his stead; the doorkeeper at the theatre was warned not to admit him to the house; and Charley Edwards remorsefully promised the boy's father not to see him again.

The members of the stock company were vastly amused when some of Paul's stories reached them—especially the women. They were hard-working women, most of them supporting indigent husbands or brothers, and they laughed rather bitterly at having stirred the boy to such fervid and florid inventions. They agreed with the faculty and with his father that Paul's was a bad case.

The east-bound train was plowing through a January snowstorm; the dull dawn was beginning to show grey when the engine whistled a mile out of Newark. Paul started up from the seat where he had lain curled in uneasy slumber, rubbed the breath-misted window glass with his hand, and peered out. The snow was whirling in curling eddies above the white bottom lands, and the drifts lay already deep in the fields and along the fences, while here and there the long dead grass and dried weed stalks protruded black above it. Lights shone from the scattered houses, and a gang of labourers who stood beside the track waved their lanterns.

Paul had slept very little, and he felt grimy and uncomfortable. He had made the all-night journey in a day coach, partly because he was ashamed, dressed as he was, to go into a Pullman, and partly because he was afraid of being seen there by some Pittsburgh business man, who might have noticed him in Denny & Carson's office. When the whistle awoke him, he clutched quickly at his breast pocket, glancing about him with an uncertain smile. But the little, clay-bespattered Italians were still sleeping, the slatternly women across the aisle were in open-mouthed oblivion, and even the crumby, crying babies were for the nonce stilled. Paul settled back to struggle with his impatience as best he could.

When he arrived at the Jersey City station, he hurried through his breakfast, manifestly ill at ease and keeping a sharp eye about him. After he reached the Twenty-third Street station, he consulted a cabman, and had himself driven to a men's furnishings establishment that was just opening for the day. He spent upward of two hours there, buying with endless reconsidering and great care. His new street suit he put on in the fitting-room; the frock coat and dress clothes he had bundled into the cab with his linen. Then he drove to a hatter's and a shoe house. His next errand was at Tiffany's, where he selected his silver and a new scarf-pin. He would not wait to have his silver marked, he said. Lastly, he stopped at a trunk shop on Broadway, and had his purchases packed into various travelling bags.

It was a little after one o'clock when he drove up to the Waldorf, and after settling with the cabman, went into the office. He registered from Washington; said his mother and father had been abroad, and that he had come down to await the arrival of their steamer. He told his story plausibly and had no trouble, since he volunteered to pay for them in advance, in engaging his rooms; a sleeping-room, sitting-room, and bath.

Not once, but a hundred times, Paul had planned this entry into New York. He had gone over every detail of it with Charley Edwards, and in his scrapbook at home there were pages of description about New York hotels, cut from the Sunday papers. When he was shown to his sitting-room on the eighth floor, he saw at a glance that everything was as it should be; there was but one detail in his mental picture that the place did not realize, so he rang for the bell boy and sent him down for flowers. He moved about nervously until the boy returned, putting away his new linen and fingering it delightedly as he did so. When the flowers came he put them hastily into water, and then tumbled into a hot bath. Presently he came out of his white bath-room, resplendent in his new silk underwear, and playing with the tassels of his red robe. The snow was whirling so fiercely outside his windows that he could scarcely see across the street, but within the air was deliciously soft and fragrant. He put the violets and jonquils on the taboret beside the couch, and threw himself down, with a long sigh, covering himself with a Roman blanket. He was thoroughly tired; he had been in such haste, he had stood up to such a strain, covered so much ground in the last twenty-four hours, that he wanted to think how it had all come about. Lulled by the sound of the wind, the warm air, and the cool fragrance of the flowers, he sank into deep, drowsy retrospection.

It had been wonderfully simple; when they had shut him out of the theatre and concert hall, when they had taken away his bone, the whole thing was virtually determined. The rest was a mere matter of opportunity. The only thing that at all surprised him was his own courage—for he realized well enough that he had always been tormented by fear, a sort of apprehensive dread that, of late years, as the meshes of the lies he had told closed about him, had been pulling the muscles of his body tighter and tighter. Until now, he could not remember the time when he had not been dreading something. Even when he was a little boy it was always there—behind him, or before, or on either side. There had always been the shadowed corner, the dark place into which he dared not look, but from which something seemed always to be watching him—and Paul had done things that were not pretty to watch, he knew.

But now he had a curious sense of relief, as though he had at last thrown down the gauntlet to the thing in the corner.

Yet it was but a day since he had been sulking in the traces; but yesterday afternoon that he had been sent to the bank with Denny & Carson's deposit, as usual—but this time he was instructed to leave the book to be balanced. There was above two thousand dollars in checks, and nearly a thousand in the bank notes which he had taken from the book and quietly transferred to his pocket. At the bank he had made out a new deposit slip. His nerves had been steady enough to permit of his returning to the office, where he had finished his work and asked for a full day's holiday tomorrow, Saturday, giving a perfectly reasonable pretext. The bank book, he knew, would not be returned before Monday or Tuesday, and his father would be out of town for the next week. From the time he slipped the bank notes into his pocket until he boarded the night train for New York, he had not known a moment's hesitation. It was not the first time Paul had steered through treacherous waters.

How astonishingly easy it had all been; here he was, the thing done; and this time there would be no awakening, no figure at the top of the stairs. He watched the snow flakes whirling by his window until he fell asleep.

When he awoke, it was three o'clock in the afternoon. He bounded up with a start; half of one of his precious days gone already! He spent more than an hour in dressing, watching every stage of his toilet carefully in the mirror. Everything was quite perfect; he was exactly the kind of boy he had always wanted to be.

When he went downstairs, Paul took a carriage and drove up Fifth Avenue toward the Park. The snow had somewhat abated; carriages and tradesmen's wagons were hurrying soundlessly to and fro in the winter twilight; boys in woolen mufflers were shovelling off the doorsteps; the avenue stages made fine spots of colour against the white street. Here and there on the corners were stands, with whole flower gardens blooming under glass cases, against the sides of which the snow flakes stuck and melted; violets, roses, carnations, lilies of the valley— somehow vastly more lovely and alluring that they blossomed thus unnaturally in the snow. The Park itself was a wonderful stage winterpiece.

When he returned, the pause of the twilight had ceased, and the tune of the streets had changed. The snow was falling faster, lights streamed from the hotels that reared their dozen stories fearlessly up into the storm, defying the raging

Atlantic winds. A long, black stream of carriages poured down the avenue, intersected here and there by other streams, tending horizontally. There were a score of cabs about the entrance of his hotel, and his driver had to wait. Boys in livery were running in and out of the awning stretched across the sidewalk, up and down the red velvet carpet laid from the door to the street. Above, about, within it all was the rumble and roar, the hurry and toss of thousands of human beings as hot for pleasure as himself, and on every side of him towered the glaring affirmation of the omnipotence of wealth.

The boy set his teeth and drew his shoulders together in a spasm of realization; the plot of all dramas, the text of all romances, the nerve-stuff of all sensations was whirling about him like the snow flakes. He burnt like a faggot in a tempest.

When Paul went down to dinner, the music of the orchestra came floating up the elevator shaft to greet him. His head whirled as he stepped into the thronged corridor, and he sank back into one of the chairs against the wall to get his breath. The lights, the chatter, the perfumes, the bewildering medley of colour—he had, for a moment, the feeling of not being able to stand it. But only for a moment; these were his own people, he told himself. He went slowly about the corridors, through the writing rooms, smoking rooms, reception rooms, as though he were exploring the chambers of an enchanted palace, built and peopled for him alone.

When he reached the dining room he sat down at a table near a window. The flowers, the white linen, the many-coloured wine glasses, the gay toilettes of the women, the low popping of corks, the undulating repetitions of the *Blue Danube* from the orchestra, all flooded Paul's dream with bewildering radiance. When the roseate tinge of his champagne was added—that cold, precious, bubbling stuff that creamed and foamed in his glass—Paul wondered that there were honest men in the world at all. This was what all the world was fighting for, he reflected; this was what all the struggle was about. He doubted the reality of his past. Had he ever known a place called Cordelia Street, a place where fagged-looking business men got on the early car; mere rivets in a machine they seemed to Paul,—sickening men, with combings of children's hair always hanging to their coats, and the smell of cooking in their clothes. Cordelia Street—Ah! that belonged to another time and country; had he not always been thus, had he not sat here night after night, from as far back as he could remember, looking pensively over just such shimmering textures, and slowly twirling the stem of a glass like this one between his thumb and middle finger? He rather thought he had.

He was not in the least abashed or lonely. He had no especial desire to meet or to know any of these people; all he demanded was the right to look on and conjecture, to watch the pageant. The mere stage properties were all he contended for. Nor was he lonely later in the evening, in his lodge at the Metropolitan. He was now entirely rid of his nervous misgivings, of his forced aggressiveness, of the imperative desire to show himself different from his surroundings. He felt now that his surroundings explained him. Nobody questioned the purple; he had only to wear it passively. He had only to glance down at his attire to reassure himself that here it would be impossible for anyone to humiliate him.

He found it hard to leave his beautiful sitting-room to go to bed that night, and sat long watching the raging storm from his turret window. When he went to sleep it was with the lights turned on in his bedroom; partly because of his old timidity, and partly so that, if he should wake in the night, there would be no wretched moment of doubt, no horrible suspicion of yellow wall-paper, or of Washington and Calvin above his bed.

Sunday morning the city was practically snowbound. Paul breakfasted late, and in the afternoon he fell in with a wild San Francisco boy, a freshman at Yale, who said he had run down for a "little flyer" over Sunday. The young man offered to show Paul the night side of the town, and the two boys went out together after dinner, not returning to the hotel until seven o'clock the next morning. They had started out in the confiding warmth of a champagne friendship, but their parting in the elevator was singularly cool. The freshman pulled himself together to make his train, and Paul went to bed. He awoke at two o'clock in the afternoon, very thirsty and dizzy, and rang for ice-water, coffee, and the Pittsburgh papers.

On the part of the hotel management, Paul excited no suspicion. There was this to be said for him, that he wore his spoils with dignity and in no way made himself conspicuous. Even under the glow of his wine he was never boisterous, though he found the stuff like a magician's wand for wonder-building. His chief greediness lay in his ears and eyes, and his excesses were not offensive ones. His dearest pleasures were the grey winter twilights in his sitting-room; his quiet enjoyment of his flowers, his clothes, his wide divan, his cigarette, and his sense of power. He could not remember a time when he had felt so at peace with himself. The mere release from the necessity of petty lying, lying every day and every day, restored his self-respect. He had never lied for pleasure, even at school; but to be noticed and admired, to assert his difference from other Cordelia Street boys; and he felt a good deal more manly, more honest, even, now that he had no need for boastful pretensions, now that he could, as his actor friends used to say, "dress the part." It was characteristic that remorse did not occur to him. His golden days went by without a shadow, and he made each as perfect as he could.

On the eighth day after his arrival in New York, he found the whole affair exploited in the Pittsburgh papers, exploited with a wealth of detail which indicated that local news of a sensational nature was at a low ebb. The firm of Denny & Carson announced that the boy's father had refunded the full amount of the theft, and that they had no intention of prosecuting. The Cumberland minister had been interviewed, and expressed his hope of yet reclaiming the motherless lad, and his Sabbath-school teacher declared that she would spare no effort to that end. The rumour had reached Pittsburgh that the boy had been seen in a New York hotel, and his father had gone East to find him and bring him home.

Paul had just come in to dress for dinner; he sank into a chair, weak to the knees, and clasped his head in his hands. It was to be worse than jail, even; the tepid waters of Cordelia Street were to close over him finally and forever. The grey monotony stretched before him in hopeless, unrelieved years; Sabbath-school, Young People's Meeting, the yellow-papered room, the damp dish-towels; it all rushed back upon him with a sickening vividness. He had the old feeling that the orchestra had suddenly stopped, the sinking sensation that the play was over. The sweat broke out on his face, and he sprang to his feet, looked about him with his white, conscious smile, and winked at himself in the mirror. With something of the old childish belief in miracles with which he had so often gone to class, all his lessons unlearned, Paul dressed and dashed whistling down the corridor to the elevator.

He had no sooner entered the dining-room and caught the measure of the music than his remembrance was lightened by his old elastic power of claiming the moment, mounting with it, and finding it all sufficient. The glare and glitter about him, the mere scenic accessories had again, and for the last time, their old potency. He would show himself that he was game, he would finish the thing splendidly. He doubted, more than ever, the existence of Cordelia Street, and for the first time he drank his wine recklessly. Was he not, after all, one of those fortunate beings born to the purple, was he not still himself and in his own place? He drummed a nervous accompaniment to the Pagliacci music and looked about him, telling himself over and over that it had paid.

He reflected drowsily, to the swell of the music and the chill sweetness of his wine, that he might have done it more wisely. He might have caught an outbound steamer and been well out of their clutches before now. But the other side of the world had seemed too far away and too uncertain then; he could not have waited for it; his need had been too sharp. If he had to choose over again, he would do the same thing to-morrow. He looked affectionately about the dining-room, now gilded with a soft mist. Ah, it had paid indeed!

Paul was awakened next morning by a painful throbbing in his head and feet. He had thrown himself across the bed without undressing, and had slept with his shoes on. His limbs and hands were lead heavy, and his tongue and throat were parched and burnt. There came upon him one of those fateful attacks of clear-headedness that never occurred except when he was physically exhausted and his nerves hung loose. He lay still and closed his eyes and let the tide of things wash over him.

His father was in New York; "stopping at some joint or other," he told himself. The memory of successive summers on the front stoop fell upon him like a weight of black water. He had not a hundred dollars left; and he knew now, more than ever, that money was everything, the wall that stood between all he loathed and all he wanted. The thing was winding itself up; he had thought of that on his first glorious day in New York, and had even provided a way to snap the thread. It lay on his dressing-table now; he had got it out last night when he came blindly up from dinner, but the shiny metal hurt his eyes, and he disliked the looks of it.

He rose and moved about with a painful effort, succumbing now and again to attacks of nausea. It was the old depression exaggerated; all the world had become Cordelia Street. Yet somehow he was not afraid of anything, was absolutely calm; perhaps because he had looked into the dark corner at last and knew. It was bad enough, what he saw there, but somehow not so bad as his long fear of it had been. He saw everything clearly now. He had a feeling that he had made the best of it, that he had lived the sort of life he was meant to live, and for half an hour he sat staring at the revolver. But he told himself that was not the way, so he went downstairs and took a cab to the ferry.

When Paul arrived in Newark, he got off the train and took another cab, directing the driver to follow the Pennsylvania tracks out of the town. The snow lay heavy on the roadways and had drifted deep in the open fields. Only here and there the dead grass or dried weed stalks projected, singularly black, above it. Once well into the country, Paul dismissed the carriage and walked, floundering along the tracks, his mind a medley of irrelevant things. He seemed to hold in his brain an actual picture of everything he had seen that morning. He remembered every feature of both his drivers, of the toothless old woman from whom he had bought the red flowers in his coat, the agent from whom he had got his ticket, and all of his fellow-passengers on the ferry. His mind, unable to cope with vital matters near at hand, worked feverishly and deftly at sorting and grouping these images. They made for him a part of the ugliness of the world, of the ache in his head, and the bitter burning on his tongue. He stooped and put a handful of snow into his mouth as he walked, but that, too, seemed hot. When he reached a little hillside, where the tracks ran through a cut some twenty feet below him, he stopped and sat down.

The carnations in his coat were drooping with the cold, he noticed; their red glory all over. It occurred to him that all the flowers he had seen in the glass cases that first night must have gone the same way, long before this. It was only one splendid breath they had, in spite of their brave mockery at the winter outside the glass; and it was a losing game in the end, it seemed, this revolt against the homilies by which the world is run. Paul took one of the blossoms carefully from his coat and scooped a little hole in the snow, where he covered it up. Then he dozed awhile, from his weak condition, seemingly insensible to the cold.

The sound of an approaching train awoke him, and he started to his feet, remembering only his resolution, and afraid lest he should be too late. He stood watching the approaching locomotive, his teeth chattering, his lips drawn away from them in a frightened smile; once or twice he glanced nervously sidewise, as though he were being watched. When the right moment came, he jumped. As he fell, the folly of his haste occurred to him with merciless clearness, the vastness of what he had left undone. There flashed through his brain, clearer than ever before, the blue of Adriatic water, the yellow of Algerian sands.

He felt something strike his chest, and that his body was being thrown swiftly through the air, on and on, immeasurably far and fast, while his limbs were gently relaxed. Then, because the picture making mechanism was crushed, the disturbing visions flashed into black, and Paul dropped back into the immense design of things.

HENRY JAMES

from **What Maisie Knew**

The child was provided for, but the new arrangement was inevitably confounding to a young intelligence intensely aware that something had happened which must matter a good deal and looking anxiously out for the effects of so great a cause. It was to be the fate of this patient little girl to see much more than she at first understood, but also even at first to understand much more than any little girl, however patient, had perhaps ever understood before. Only a drummer-boy in a ballad or a story could have been so in the thick of the fight. She was taken into the confidence of passions on which she fixed just the stare she might have had for images bounding across the wall in the slide of a magic lantern. Her little world was phantasmagoric—strange shadows dancing on a sheet. It was as if the whole performance had been given for her—a mite of a half-scared infant in a great dim theatre. She was in short introduced to life with a liberality in which the selfishness of others found its account, and there was nothing to avert the sacrifice but the modesty of her youth.

Her first term was with her father, who spared her only in not letting her have the wild letters addressed to her by her mother: he confined himself to holding them up at her and shaking them, while he showed his teeth, and then amusing her by the way he chucked them, across the room, bang into the fire. Even at that moment, however, she had a scared anticipation of fatigue, a guilty sense of not rising to the occasion, feeling the charm of the violence with which the stiff unopened envelopes, whose big monograms—Ida bristled with monograms—she would have liked to see, were made to whizz, like dangerous missiles, through the air. The greatest effect of the great cause was her own greater importance, chiefly revealed to her in the larger freedom with which she was handled, pulled hither and thither and kissed, and the proportionately greater niceness she was obliged to show. Her features had somehow become prominent; they were so perpetually nipped by the gentlemen who came to see her father and the smoke of whose cigarettes went into her face. Some of these gentlemen made her strike matches and light their cigarettes; others, holding her on knees violently jolted, pinched the calves of her legs till she shrieked—her shriek was much admired—and reproached them with being toothpicks. The word stuck in her mind and contributed to her feeling from this time that she was deficient in something that would meet the general desire. She found out what it was; it was a congenital tendency to the production of a substance to which Moddle, her nurse, gave a short ugly name, a name painfully associated at dinner with the part of the joint that she didn't like. She had left behind her the time when she had no desires to

This selection is the first chapter of *What Maisie Knew,* by Henry James (New York: Penguin Books, 1969; originally published by Charles Scribner & Co., 1897).

461

meet, none at least save Moddle's, who, in Kensington Gardens, was always on
the bench when she came back to see if she had been playing too far. Moddle's
desire was merely that she shouldn't do that, and she met it so easily that the only
spots in that long brightness were the moments of her wondering what would
become of her if, on her rushing back, there should be no Moddle on the bench.
They still went to the Gardens, but there was a difference even there; she was
impelled perpetually to look at the legs of other children and ask her nurse if
they were toothpicks. Moddle was terribly truthful; she always said: "Oh my dear,
you'll not find such another pair as your own." It seemed to have to do with something else that Moddle often said: "You feel the strain—that's where it is; and
you'll feel it still worse, you know."

Thus from the first Maisie not only felt it, but knew she felt it. A part of it
was the consequence of her father's telling her he felt it too, and telling Moddle,
in her presence, that she must make a point of driving that home. She was
familiar, at the age of six, with the fact that everything had been changed on her
account, everything ordered to enable him to give himself up to her. She was to
remember always the words in which Moddle impressed upon her that he did so
give himself: "Your papa wishes you never to forget, you know, that he has been
dreadfully put about." If the skin on Moddle's face had to Maisie the air of being
unduly, almost painfully, stretched, it never presented that appearance so much
as when she uttered, as she often had occasion to utter, such words. The child
wondered if they didn't make it hurt more than usual; but it was only after some
time that she was able to attach to the picture of her father's sufferings, and more
particularly to her nurse's manner about them, the meaning for which these
things had waited. By the time she had grown sharper, as the gentlemen who had
criticized her calves used to say, she found in her mind a collection of images and
echoes to which meanings were attachable—images and echoes kept for her in
the childish dusk, the dim closet, the high drawers, like games she wasn't yet big
enough to play. The great strain meanwhile was that of carrying by the right end
the things her father said about her mother—things mostly indeed that Moddle,
on a glimpse of them, as if they had been complicated toys or difficult books, took
out of her hands and put away in the closet. A wonderful assortment of objects
of this kind she was to discover there later, all tumbled up too with the things,
shuffled into the same receptacle, that her mother had said about her father.

She had the knowledge that on a certain occasion which every day brought
nearer her mother would be at the door to take her away, and this would have
darkened all the days if the ingenious Moddle hadn't written on a paper in very
big easy words ever so many pleasures that she would enjoy at the other house.
These promises ranged from "a mother's fond love" to "a nice poached egg to
your tea," and took by the way the prospect of sitting up ever so late to see the lady
in question dressed, in silks and velvets and diamonds and pearls, to go out: so
that it was a real support to Maisie, at the supreme hour, to feel how, by Moddle's

direction, the paper was thrust away in her pocket and there clenched in her fist. The supreme hour was to furnish her with a vivid reminiscence, that of a strange outbreak in the drawing room on the part of Moddle, who, in reply to something her father had just said, cried aloud: "You ought to be perfectly ashamed of yourself—you ought to blush, sir, for the way you go on!" The carriage, with her mother in it, was at the door; a gentleman who was there, who was always there, laughed out very loud; her father, who had her in his arms, said to Moddle: "My dear woman, I'll settle *you* presently!"—after which he repeated, showing his teeth more than ever at Maisie while he hugged her, the words for which her nurse had taken him up. Maisie was not at the moment so fully conscious of them as of the wonder of Moddle's sudden disrespect and crimson face; but she was able to produce them in the course of five minutes when, in the carriage, her mother, all kisses, ribbons, eyes, arms, strange sounds and sweet smells, said to her: "And did your beastly papa, my precious angel, send any message to your own loving mamma?" Then it was that she found the words spoken by her beastly papa to be, after all, in her little bewildered ears, from which, at her mother's appeal, they passed, in her clear shrill voice, straight to her little innocent lips. "He said I was to tell you, from him," she faithfully reported, "that you're a nasty horrid pig!"

E. M. FORSTER

from A Passage to India

The Ganges, though flowing from the foot of Vishnu and through Siva's hair, is not an ancient stream. Geology, looking further than religion, knows of a time when neither the river nor the Himalayas that nourished it existed, and an ocean flowed over the holy places of Hindustan. The mountains rose, their debris silted up the ocean, the gods took their seats on them and contrived the river, and the India we call immemorial came into being. But India is really far older. In the days of the prehistoric ocean the southern part of the peninsula already existed, and the high places of Dravidia have been land since land began, and have seen on the one side the sinking of a continent that joined them to Africa, and on the other the upheaval of the Himalayas from a sea. They are older than anything in the world. No water has ever covered them, and the sun who has watched them for countless aeons may still discern in their outlines forms that were his before our globe was torn from his bosom. If flesh of the sun's flesh is to be touched anywhere, it is here, among the incredible antiquity of these hills.

Yet even they are altering. As Himalayan India rose, this India, the primal, has been depressed, and is slowly re-entering the curve of the earth. It may be that in aeons to come an ocean will flow here too, and cover the sun-born rocks with slime. Meanwhile the plain of the Ganges encroaches on them with something of the sea's action. They are sinking beneath the newer lands. Their main mass is untouched, but at the edge their outposts have been cut off and stand knee-deep, throat-deep, in the advancing soil. There is something unspeakable in these outposts. They are like nothing else in the world, and a glimpse of them makes the breath catch. They rise abruptly, insanely, without the proportion that is kept by the wildest hills elsewhere, they bear no relation to anything dreamt or seen. To call them "uncanny" suggests ghosts, and they are older than all spirit. Hinduism has scratched and plastered a few rocks, but the shrines are unfrequented, as if pilgrims, who generally seek the extraordinary, had here found too much of it. Some saddhus did once settle in a cave, but they were smoked out, and even Buddha, who must have passed this way down to the Bo Tree of Gya, shunned a renunciation more complete than his own, and has left no legend of struggle or victory in the Marabar.

The caves are readily described. A tunnel eight feet long, five feet high, three feet wide, leads to a circular chamber about twenty feet in diameter. This arrangement occurs again and again throughout the group of hills, and this is all, this is a Marabar Cave. Having seen one such cave, having seen two, having seen three,

---

This selection includes chapter 12 and the last half of chapter 14, both in part 2: "Caves," from E. M. Forster's *A Passage to India* (London: Edward Arnold, 1924). Reprinted by permission of The Society of Authors.

four, fourteen, twenty-four, the visitor returns to Chandrapore uncertain whether he has had an interesting experience or a dull one or any experience at all. He finds it difficult to discuss the caves, or to keep them apart in his mind, for the pattern never varies, and no carving, not even a bees'-nest or a bat distinguishes one from another. Nothing, nothing attaches to them, and their reputation—for they have one—does not depend upon human speech. It is as if the surrounding plain or the passing birds have taken upon themselves to exclaim "extraordinary," and the word has taken root in the air, and been inhaled by mankind.

They are dark caves. Even when they open towards the sun, very little light penetrates down the entrance tunnel into the circular chamber. There is little to see, and no eye to see it, until the visitor arrives for his five minutes, and strikes a match. Immediately another flame rises in the depths of the rock and moves towards the surface like an imprisoned spirit: the walls of the circular chamber have been most marvellously polished. The two flames approach and strive to unite, but cannot, because one of them breathes air, the other stone. A mirror inlaid with lovely colours divides the lovers, delicate stars of pink and grey interpose, exquisite nebulae, shadings fainter than the tail of a comet or the midday moon, all the evanescent life of the granite, only here visible. Fists and fingers thrust above the advancing soil—here at last is their skin, finer than any covering acquired by the animals, smoother than windless water, more voluptuous than love. The radiance increases, the flames touch one another, kiss, expire. The cave is dark again, like all the caves.

Only the wall of the circular chamber has been polished thus. The sides of the tunnel are left rough, they impinge as an afterthought upon the internal perfection. An entrance was necessary, so mankind made one. But elsewhere, deeper in the granite, are there certain chambers that have no entrances? Chambers never unsealed since the arrival of the gods. Local report declares that these exceed in number those that can be visited, as the dead exceed the living— four hundred of them, four thousand or million. Nothing is inside them, they were sealed up before the creation of pestilence or treasure; if mankind grew curious and excavated, nothing, nothing would be added to the sum of good or evil. One of them is rumoured within the boulder that swings on the summit of the highest of the hills; a bubble-shaped cave that has neither ceiling nor floor, and mirrors its own darkness in every direction infinitely. If the boulder falls and smashes, the cave will smash too—empty as an Easter egg. The boulder because of its hollowness sways in the wind, and even moves when a crow perches upon it: hence its name and the name of its stupendous pedestal: the Kawa Dol.

[. . .]

The first cave was tolerably convenient. They skirted the puddle of water, and then climbed up over some unattractive stones, the sun crashing on their backs. Bending their heads, they disappeared one by one into the interior of the hills. The small black hole gaped where their varied forms and colours had momentarily functioned. They were sucked in like water down a drain. Bland and bald rose the precipices; bland and glutinous the sky that connected the precipices; solid and white, a Brahminy kite flapped between the rocks with a clumsiness that seemed intentional. Before man, with his itch for the seemly, had been born, the planet must have looked thus. The kite flapped away. . . . Before birds, perhaps. . . . And then the hole belched and humanity returned.

A Marabar cave had been horrid as far as Mrs. Moore was concerned, for she had nearly fainted in it, and had some difficulty in preventing herself from saying so as soon as she got into the air again. It was natural enough: she had always suffered from faintness, and the cave had become too full, because all their retinue followed them. Crammed with villagers and servants, the circular chamber began to smell. She lost Aziz and Adela in the dark, didn't know who touched her, couldn't breathe, and some vile naked thing struck her face and settled on her mouth like a pad. She tried to regain the entrance tunnel, but an influx of villagers swept her back. She hit her head. For an instant she went mad, hitting and gasping like a fanatic. For not only did the crush and stench alarm her; there was also a terrifying echo.

Professor Godbole had never mentioned an echo; it never impressed him, perhaps. There are some exquisite echoes in India; there is the whisper round the dome at Bijapur; there are the long, solid sentences that voyage through the air at Mandu, and return unbroken to their creator. The echo in a Marabar cave is not like these, it is entirely devoid of distinction. Whatever is said, the same monotonous noise replies, and quivers up and down the walls until it is absorbed into the roof. "Boum" is the sound as far as the human alphabet can express it, or "bou-oum," or "ou-boum"—utterly dull. Hope, politeness, the blowing of a nose, the squeak of a boot, all produce "boum." Even the striking of a match starts a little worm coiling, which is too small to complete a circle but is eternally watchful. And if several people talk at once, an overlapping howling noise begins, echoes generate echoes, and the cave is stuffed with a snake composed of small snakes, which writhe independently.

After Mrs. Moore all the others poured out. She had given the signal for the reflux. Aziz and Adela both emerged smiling and she did not want him to think his treat was a failure, so smiled too. As each person emerged she looked for a villain, but none was there, and she realized that she had been among the mildest individuals, whose only desire was to honour her, and that the naked pad was a poor little baby, astride its mother's hip. Nothing evil had been in the cave, but she had not enjoyed herself; no, she had not enjoyed herself, and she decided not to visit a second one.

"Did you see the reflection of his match—rather pretty?" asked Adela.

"I forget . . ."

"But he says this isn't a good cave, the best are on the Kawa Dol."

"I don't think I shall go on to there. I dislike climbing."

"Very well, let's sit down again in the shade until breakfast's ready."

"Ah, but that'll disappoint him so; he has taken such trouble. You should go on; you don't mind."

"Perhaps I ought to," said the girl, indifferent to what she did, but desirous of being amiable.

The servants, etc., were scrambling back to the camp, pursued by grave censures from Mohammed Latif. Aziz came to help the guests over the rocks. He was at the summit of his powers, vigorous and humble, too sure of himself to resent criticism, and he was sincerely pleased when he heard they were altering his plans. "Certainly, Miss Quested, so you and I will go together, and leave Mrs. Moore here, and we will not be long, yet we will not hurry, because we know that will be her wish."

"Quite right. I'm sorry not to come too, but I'm a poor walker."

"Dear Mrs. Moore, what does anything matter so long as you are my guests? I am very glad you are *not* coming, which sounds strange, but you are treating me with true frankness, as a friend."

"Yes, I am your friend," she said, laying her hand on his sleeve, and thinking, despite her fatigue, how very charming, how very good, he was, and how deeply she desired his happiness. "So may I make another suggestion? Don't let so many people come with you this time. I think you may find it more convenient."

"Exactly, exactly," he cried, and, rushing to the other extreme, forbade all except one guide to accompany Miss Quested and him to the Kawa Dol. "Is that all right?" he enquired.

"Quite right, now enjoy yourselves, and when you come back tell me all about it." And she sank into the deck-chair.

If they reached the big pocket of caves, they would be away nearly an hour. She took out her writing-pad, and began, "Dear Stella, Dear Ralph," then stopped, and looked at the queer valley and their feeble invasion of it. Even the elephant had become a nobody. Her eye rose from it to the entrance tunnel. No, she did not wish to repeat that experience. The more she thought over it, the more disagreeable and frightening it became. She minded it much more now than at the time. The crush and the smells she could forget, but the echo began in some indescribable way to undermine her hold on life. Coming at a moment when she chanced to be fatigued, it had managed to murmur, "Pathos, piety, courage—they exist, but are identical, and so is filth. Everything exists, nothing has value." If one had spoken vileness in that place, or quoted lofty poetry, the comment would have been the same—"ou-boum." If one had spoken with the tongues of angels and pleaded for all the unhappiness and misunderstanding in the world, past, present, and to come, for all the misery men must undergo whatever their opinion and position, and however much they dodge or bluff—it would amount to the same, the serpent would descend and return to the ceiling. Devils are of the North, and poems can be written about them, but no one could romanticize the Marabar because it robbed infinity and eternity of their vastness, the only quality that accommodates them to mankind.

She tried to go on with her letter, reminding herself that she was only an elderly woman who had got up too early in the morning and journeyed too far, that the despair creeping over her was merely her despair, her personal weakness, and that even if she got a sunstroke and went mad the rest of the world would go on. But suddenly, at the edge of her mind, Religion appeared, poor little talkative Christianity, and she knew that all its divine words from "Let there be Light" to "It is finished" only amounted to "boum." Then she was terrified over an area larger than usual; the universe, never comprehensible to her intellect, offered no repose to her soul, the mood of the last two months took definite form at last, and she realized that she didn't want to write to her children, didn't want to communicate with anyone, not even with God. She sat motionless with horror, and, when old Mohammed Latif came up to her, thought he would notice a difference. For a time she thought, "I am going to be ill," to comfort herself, then she surrendered to the vision. She lost all interest, even in Aziz, and the affectionate and sincere words that she had spoken to him seemed no longer hers but the air's.

HENRIK IBSEN

from Ghosts

MRS. ALVING: My poor boy!

MANDERS: You may well say so. This is what it has brought him to! (MRS. ALVING *looks at him, but does not speak.*) He called himself the prodigal son. It's only too true, alas—only too true! (MRS. ALVING *looks steadily at him.*) And what do you say to all this?

MRS. ALVING: I say that Oswald was right in every single word he said.

MANDERS: Right? Right? To hold such principles as that?

MRS. ALVING: In my loneliness here I have come to just the same opinions as he, Mr. Manders. But I have never presumed to venture upon such topics in conversation. Now there is no need; my boy shall speak for me.

MANDERS: You deserve the deepest pity, Mrs. Alving. It is my duty to say an earnest word to you. It is no longer your business man and adviser, no longer your old friend, and your dead husband's old friend, that stands before you now. It is your priest that stands before you, just as he did once at the most critical moment of your life.

MRS. ALVING: And what is it that my priest has to say to me?

MANDERS: First of all I must stir your memory. The moment is well chosen. To-morrow is the tenth anniversary of your husband's death; to-morrow the memorial to the departed will be unveiled; to-morrow I shall speak to the whole assembly that will be met together. But to-day I want to speak to you alone.

MRS. ALVING: Very well, Mr. Manders, speak!

MANDERS: Have you forgotten that after barely a year of married life you were standing at the very edge of a precipice?—that you forsook your house and home?—that you ran away from your husband—yes, Mrs. Alving, ran away, ran away—and refused to return to him in spite of his requests and entreaties?

MRS. ALVING: Have you forgotten how unspeakably unhappy I was during that first year?

MANDERS: To crave for happiness in this world is simply to be possessed by a spirit of revolt. What right have we to happiness? No! we must do our duty, Mrs. Alving. And your duty was to cleave to the man you had chosen and to whom you were bound by a sacred bond.

This selection from act 1 of Ghosts, by Henrik Ibsen, is from *Four Great Plays by Henrik Ibsen*, translated by R. Farquharson Sharp, with an introduction and prefaces to each play by John Gassner (New York: E. P. Dutton and Co., 1958).

MRS. ALVING: You know quite well what sort of a life my husband was living at that time—what excesses he was guilty of.

MANDERS: I know only too well what rumour used to say of him; and I should be the last person to approve of his conduct as a young man, supposing that rumour spoke the truth. But it is not a wife's part to be her husband's judge. You should have considered it your bounden duty humbly to have borne the cross that a higher will had laid upon you. But, instead of that, you rebelliously cast off your cross, you deserted the man whose stumbling footsteps you should have supported, you did what was bound to imperil your good name and reputation, and came very near to imperiling the reputation of others into the bargain.

MRS. ALVING: Of others? Of one other, you mean.

MANDERS: It was the height of imprudence, your seeking refuge with me.

MRS. ALVING: With our priest? With our intimate friend?

MANDERS: All the more on that account. You should thank God that I possessed the necessary strength of mind—that I was able to turn you from your outrageous intention, and that it was vouchsafed to me to succeed in leading you back into the path of duty and back to your lawful husband.

MRS. ALVING: Yes, Mr. Manders, that certainly was your doing.

MANDERS: I was but the humble instrument of a higher power. And is it not true that my having been able to bring you again under the yoke of duty and obedience sowed the seeds of a rich blessing on all the rest of your life? Did things not turn out as I foretold to you? Did not your husband turn from straying in the wrong path, as a man should? Did he not, after that, live a life of love and good report with you all his days? Did he not become a benefactor to the neighbourhood? Did he not so raise you up to his level, so that by degrees you became his fellow-worker in all his undertakings—and a noble fellow-worker, too, I know, Mrs. Alving; that praise I will give you.—But now I come to the second serious false step in your life.

MRS. ALVING: What do you mean?

MANDERS: Just as once you forsook your duty as a wife, so, since then, you have forsaken your duty as a mother.

MRS. ALVING: Oh—!

MANDERS: You have been overmastered all your life by a disastrous spirit of wilfulness. All your impulses have led you towards what is undisciplined and lawless. You have never been willing to submit to any restraint. Anything in life that has seemed irksome to you, you have thrown aside recklessly and unscrupulously, as if it were a burden that you were free to rid yourself of if you would. It did not please you to be a wife any longer, and so you left your husband. Your duties as a mother were irksome to you, so you sent your child away among strangers.

MRS. ALVING: Yes, that is true; I did that.

MANDERS: And that is why you have become a stranger to him.

MRS. ALVING: No, no, I am not that!

MANDERS: You are; you must be. And what sort of a son is it that you have got back? Think over it seriously, Mrs. Alving. You erred grievously in your husband's case—you acknowledge as much, by erecting this memorial to him. Now you are bound to acknowledge how much you have erred in your son's case; possibly there may still be time to reclaim him from the paths of wickedness. Turn over a new leaf, and set yourself to reform what there may still be that is capable of reformation in him. Because (*with uplifted forefinger*) in very truth, Mrs. Alving, you are a guilty mother!—That is what I have thought it my duty to say to you.

(*A short silence.*)

MRS. ALVING (*speaking slowly and with self-control*): You have had your say, Mr. Manders, and to-morrow you will be making a public speech in memory of my husband. I shall not speak to-morrow. But now I wish to speak to you for a little, just as you have been speaking to me.

MANDERS: By all means; no doubt you wish to bring forward some excuses for your behaviour.

MRS. ALVING: No. I only want to tell you something.

MANDERS: Well?

MRS. ALVING: In all that you said just now about me and my husband, and about our life together after you had, as you put it, led me back into the path of duty— there was nothing that you knew at first hand. From that moment you never again set foot in our house—you, who had been our daily companion before that.

MANDERS: Remember that you and your husband moved out of town immediately afterwards.

MRS. ALVING: Yes, and you never once came out here to see us in my husband's lifetime. It was only the business in connection with the Orphanage that obliged you to come and see me.

MANDERS (*in a low and uncertain voice*): Helen—if that is a reproach, I can only beg you to consider—

MRS. ALVING: —the respect you owed to your calling?—yes. All the more as I was a wife who had tried to run away from her husband. One can never be too careful to have nothing to do with such reckless women.

MANDERS: My dear—Mrs. Alving, you are exaggerating dreadfully—

MRS. ALVING: Yes, yes,—very well. What I mean is this, that when you condemn my conduct as a wife you have nothing more to go upon than ordinary public opinion.

MANDERS: I admit it. What then?

MRS. ALVING: Well—now, Mr. Manders, now I am going to tell you the truth. I had sworn to myself that you should know it one day—you, and you only!

MANDERS: And what may the truth be?

MRS. ALVING: The truth is this, that my husband died just as great a profligate as he had been all his life.

MANDERS (*feeling for a chair*): What are you saying?

MRS. ALVING: After nineteen years of married life, just as profligate—in his desires at all events—as he was before you married us.

MANDERS: And can you talk of his youthful indiscretions—his irregularities—his excesses, if you like—as a profligate life!

MRS. ALVING: That was what the doctor who attended him called it.

MANDERS: I don't understand what you mean.

MRS. ALVING: It is not necessary you should.

MANDERS: It makes my brain reel. To think that your marriage—all the years of wedded life you spent with your husband—were nothing but a hidden abyss of misery.

MRS. ALVING: That and nothing else. Now you know.

MANDERS: This—this bewilders me. I can't understand it! I can't grasp it! How in the world was it possible—? How could such a state of things remain concealed?

MRS. ALVING: That was just what I had to fight for incessantly, day after day. When Oswald was born, I thought I saw a slight improvement. But it didn't last long. And after that I had to fight doubly hard—fight a desperate fight so that no one should know what sort of a man my child's father was. You know quite well what an attractive manner he had; it seemed as if people could believe nothing but good of him. He was one of those men whose mode of life seems to have no effect upon their reputations. But at last, Mr. Manders you must hear this too—at last something happened more abominable than everything else.

MANDERS: More abominable than what you have told me!

MRS. ALVING: I had borne with it all, though I knew only too well what he indulged in in secret, when he was out of the house. But when it came to the point of the scandal coming within our four walls.

MANDERS: Can you mean it! Here?

MRS. ALVING: Yes, here, in our own home. It was in there (*pointing to the nearer door on the right*) in the dining-room that I got the first hint of it. I had something to do in there and the door was standing ajar. I heard our maid come up from the garden with water for the flowers in the conservatory.

MANDERS: Well—?

MRS. ALVING: Shortly afterwards I heard my husband come in too. I heard him say something to her in a low voice. And, then I heard—(*with a short laugh*)—oh, it rings in my ears still, with its mixture of what was heartbreaking and what was so ridiculous—I heard my own servant whisper: "Let me go, Mr. Alving! Let me be!"

MANDERS: What unseemly levity on his part! But surely nothing more than levity, Mrs. Alving, believe me.

MRS. ALVING: I soon knew what to believe. My husband had his will of the girl— and that intimacy had consequences, Mr. Manders.

MANDERS (*as if turned to stone*): And all that in this house! In this house!

MRS. ALVING: I have suffered a good deal in this house. To keep him at home in the evening—and at night—I have had to play the part of boon companion in his secret drinking—bouts in his room up there. I have had to sit there alone with him, have had to hobnob and drink with him, have had to listen to his ribald senseless talk, have had to fight with brute force to get him to bed—

MANDERS (*trembling*): And you were able to endure all this!

MRS. ALVING: I had my little boy, and endured it for his sake. But when the crowning insult came—when my own servant—then I made up my mind that there should be an end of it. I took the upper hand in the house, absolutely— both with him and all the others. I had a weapon to use against him, you see; he didn't dare to speak. It was then that Oswald was sent away. He was about seven then, and was beginning to notice things and ask questions as children will. I could endure all that, my friend. It seemed to me that the child would be poisoned if he breathed the air of this polluted house. That was why I sent him away. And now you understand, too, why he never set foot here as long as his father was alive. No one knows what it meant to me.

MANDERS: You have indeed had a pitiable experience.

MRS. ALVING: I could never have gone through with it, if I had not had my work. Indeed, I can boast that I have worked. All the increase in the value of the property, all the improvements, all the useful arrangements that my husband got the honour and glory of—do you suppose that he troubled himself about any of them? He, who used to lie the whole day on the sofa reading old Official Lists! No, you may as well know that too. It was I that kept him up to the mark when he had his lucid intervals; it was I that had to bear the whole burden of it when he began his excesses again or took to whining about his miserable condition.

MANDERS: And this is the man you are building a memorial to!

MRS. ALVING: There you see the power of an uneasy conscience.

MANDERS: An uneasy conscience? What do you mean?

MRS. ALVING: I had always before me the fear that it was impossible that the truth should not come out and be believed. That is why the Orphanage is to exist, to silence all rumours and clear away all doubt.

MANDERS: You certainly have not fallen short of the mark in that, Mrs. Alving.

MRS. ALVING: I had another very good reason. I did not wish Oswald, my own son, to inherit a penny that belonged to his father.

MANDERS: Then it is with Mr. Alving's property—

MRS. ALVING: Yes. The sums of money that, year after year, I have given towards this Orphanage, make up the amount of property—I have reckoned it carefully— which in the old days made Lieutenant Alving a catch.

MANDERS: I understand.

MRS. ALVING: That was my purchase money. I don't wish it to pass into Oswald's hands. My son shall have everything from me, I am determined.

(OSWALD *comes in by the farther door on the right. He has left his hat and coat outside.*)

MRS. ALVING: Back again, my own dear boy?

OSWALD: Yes, what can one do outside in this everlasting rain? I hear dinner is nearly ready. That's good!

(REGINA *comes in from the dining-room, carrying a parcel.*)

REGINA: This parcel has come for you, ma'am. (*Gives it to her.*)

MRS. ALVING (*glancing at* MANDERS): The ode to be sung to-morrow, I expect.

MANDERS: Hm—I

REGINA: And dinner is ready.

MRS. ALVING: Good. We will come in a moment. I will just—(*begins to open the parcel*).

REGINA (*to* OSWALD): Will you drink white or red wine, sir?

OSWALD: Both, Miss Engstrand.

REGINA: *Bien*—very good, Mr. Alving. (*Goes into the dining-room.*)

OSWALD: I may as well help you to uncork it—. (*Follows her into the dining-room, leaving the door ajar after him.*)

MRS. ALVING: Yes, I thought so. Here is the ode, Mr. Manders.

MANDERS (*clasping his hand*): How shall I ever have the courage to-morrow to speak the address that—

MRS. ALVING: Oh, you will get through it.

MANDERS (*in a low voice, fearing to be heard in the dining-room*): Yes, we must raise no suspicions.

MRS. ALVING (*quietly but firmly*): No; and then this long dreadful comedy will be at an end. After to-morrow, I shall feel as if my dead husband had never lived in this house. There will be no one else here then but my boy and his mother.

(*From the dining-room is heard the noise of a chair falling; then* REGINA's *voice is heard in a loud whisper:* Oswald! Are you mad? Let me go!)

MRS. ALVING (*starting in horror*): Oh—!

(*She stares wildly at the half-open door.* OSWALD *is heard coughing and humming, then the sound of a bottle being uncorked.*)

MANDERS (*in an agitated manner*): What's the matter? What is it, Mrs. Alving?

MRS. ALVING (*hoarsely*): Ghosts. The couple in the conservatory—over again.

MANDERS: What are you saying! Regina—? Is *she*—?

MRS. ALVING: Yes. Come. Not a word!

(*Grips* MANDERS's *arm and walks unsteadily with him into the dining-room.*)

BERNARD POMERANCE

from The Elephant Man

"Most Important Are Women" (scene 9)

(MERRICK *asleep, head on knees.* TREVES, MRS. KENDAL *foreground.*)

TREVES: You have seen photographs of John Merrick, Mrs. Kendal. You are acquainted with his appearance.

MRS. KENDAL: He reminds me of an audience I played Cleopatra for in Brighton once. All huge grim head and grimace and utterly unable to clap.

TREVES: Well. My aim's to lead him to as normal a life as possible. His terror of us all comes from having been held at arm's length from society. I am determined that shall end. For example, he loves to meet people and converse. I am determined he shall. For example, he had never seen the inside of any normal home before. I had him to mine, and what a reward, Mrs. Kendal; his astonishment, his joy at the most ordinary things. Most critical I feel, however, are women. I will explain. They have always shown the greatest fear and loathing of him. While he adores them of course.

MRS. KENDAL: Ah. He is intelligent.

TREVES: I am convinced they are the key to retrieving him from his exclusion. Though, I must warn you, women are not quite real to him—more creatures of his imagination.

MRS. KENDAL: Then he is already like other men, Mr. Treves.

TREVES: So I thought, an actress could help. I mean, unlike most women, you won't give in, you are trained to hide your feelings and assume others.

MRS. KENDAL: You mean unlike most women I am famous for it, that is really all.

TREVES: Well. In any case. If you could enter the room and smile and wish him good morning. And when you leave, shake his hand, the left one is usable, and really quite beautiful, and say, "I am very pleased to have made your acquaintance, Mr. Merrick."

MRS. KENDAL: Shall we try it? Left hand out please. (*Suddenly radiant*) I am *very* pleased to have made your acquaintance Mr. Merrick. I am very *pleased* to have made your acquaintance Mr. Merrick. I am very pleased to have made your *acquaintance* Mr. Merrick. I *am* very pleased to have made *your* acquaintance Mr. Merrick. Yes. That one.

TREVES: By god, they are all splendid. Merrick will be so pleased. It will be the day he becomes a man like other men.

MRS. KENDAL: Speaking of that, Mr. Treves.

TREVES: Frederick, please.

MRS. KENDAL: Freddie, may I commit an indiscretion?

TREVES: Yes?

MRS. KENDAL: I could not help noticing from the photographs that—well—of the unafflicted parts—ah, how shall I put it? (*Points to photograph.*)

TREVES: Oh. I see! I quite. Understand. No, no, no, it is quite normal.

MRS. KENDAL: I thought as much.

TREVES: Medically speaking, uhm, you see the papillomatous extrusions which disfigure him, uhm, seem to correspond quite regularly to the osseous deformities, that is, excuse me, there is a link between the bone disorder and the skin growths, though for the life of me I have not discovered what it is or why it is, but in any case this—part—it would be therefore unlikely to be afflicted because well, that is, well, there's no bone in it. None at all. I mean.

MRS. KENDAL: Well. Learn a little every day don't we?

TREVES: I am horribly embarrassed.

MRS. KENDAL: Are you? Then he must be lonely indeed.

(*Fadeout.*)

"When the Illusion Ends He Must Kill Himself" (scene 10)

(MERRICK *sketching. Enter* TREVES, MRS. KENDAL.)

TREVES: He is making sketches for a model of St. Phillip's church. He wants someday to make a model, you see. John, my boy, this is Mrs. Kendal. She would very much like to make your acquaintance.

MRS. KENDAL: Good morning Mr. Merrick.

TREVES: I will see to a few matters. I will be back soon. (*Exits.*)

MERRICK: I planned so many things to say. I forget them. You are so beautiful.

MRS. KENDAL: How charming, Mr. Merrick.

MERRICK: Well. Really that was what I planned to say. That I forgot what I planned to say. I couldn't think of anything else I was so excited.

MRS. KENDAL: Real charm is always planned, don't you think?

MERRICK: Well. I do not know why I look like this, Mrs. Kendal. My mother was so beautiful. She was knocked down by an elephant in a circus while she was pregnant. Something must have happened, don't you think?

MRS. KENDAL: It may well have.

MERRICK: It may well have. But sometimes I think my head is so big because it is so full of dreams. Because it is. Do you know what happens when dreams cannot get out?

MRS. KENDAL: Why, no.

MERRICK: I don't either. Something must. (*Silence.*) Well. You are a famous actress.

MRS. KENDAL: I am not unknown.

MERRICK: You must display yourself for your living then. Like I did.

MRS. KENDAL: That is not myself, Mr. Merrick. That is an illusion. This is myself.

MERRICK: This is myself too.

MRS. KENDAL: Frederick says you like to read. So: books.

MERRICK: I am reading *Romeo and Juliet* now.

MRS. KENDAL: Ah. Juliet. What a love story. I adore love stories.

MERRICK: I like love stories best too. If I had been Romeo, guess what.

MRS. KENDAL: What?

MERRICK: I would not have held the mirror to her breath.

MRS. KENDAL: You mean the scene where Juliet appears to be dead and he holds a mirror up to her breath and sees—

MERRICK: Nothing. How does it feel when he kills himself because he just sees nothing?

MRS. KENDAL: Well. My experience as Juliet has been—particularly with an actor I will not name—that while I'm laying there dead dead dead, and he is lamenting excessively, I get to thinking that if this slab of ham does not part from the hamhock of his life toute suite, I am going to scream, pop off the tomb, and plunge a dagger into his scene-stealing heart. Romeos are very undependable.

MERRICK: Because he does not care for Juliet.

MRS. KENDAL: Not care?

MERRICK: Does he take her pulse? Does he get a doctor? Does he make sure? No. He kills himself. The illusion fools him because he does not care for her. He only cares about himself. If I had been Romeo, we would have got away.

MRS. KENDAL: But then there would be no play, Mr. Merrick.

MERRICK: If he did not love her, why should there be a play? Looking in a mirror and seeing nothing. That is not love. It was all an illusion. When the illusion ended he had to kill himself.

MRS. KENDAL: Why. That is extraordinary.

MERRICK: Before I spoke with people, I did not think of all these things because there was no one to bother to think them for. Now things just come out of my mouth which are true.

(TREVES *enters.*)

TREVES: You are famous, John. We are in the papers. Look. They have written up my report to the Pathological Society. Look—it is a kind of apotheosis for you.

MRS. KENDAL: Frederick, I feel Mr. Merrick would benefit by even more company than you provide; in fact by being acquainted with the best, and they with him. I shall make it my task if you'll permit. As you know, I am a friend of nearly everyone, and I do pretty well as I please and what pleases me is this task, I think.

TREVES: By god, Mrs. Kendal, you are splendid.

MRS. KENDAL: Mr. Merrick I must go now. I should like to return if I may. And so that we may without delay teach you about society, I would like to bring my good friend Dorothy Lady Neville. She would be most pleased if she could meet you. Let me tell her yes?

(MERRICK *nods yes.*)

Then until next time. I'm sure your church model will surprise us all. Mr. Merrick, it has been a very great pleasure to make your acquaintance.

TREVES: John. Your hand. She wishes to shake your hand.

MERRICK: Thank you for coming.

MRS. KENDAL: But it was my pleasure. Thank you. (*Exits, accompanied by* TREVES.)

TREVES: What a wonderful success. Do you know he's never shook a woman's hand before?

(As *lights fade* MERRICK *sobs soundlessly, uncontrollably.*)

JAMES ANTHONY FROUDE

from History of England from the Fall of Wolsey to the Defeat of the Spanish Armada

On the scaffold was the block, black like the rest; a square black cushion was placed behind it, and behind the cushion a black chair; on the right were two other chairs for the Earls. The axe leant against the rail, and two masked figures stood like mutes on either side at the back. The Queen of Scots as she swept in seemed as if coming to take a part in some solemn pageant. Not a muscle of her face could be seen to quiver; she ascended the scaffold with absolute composure, looked round her smiling, and sate down. Shrewsbury and Kent followed and took their places, the Sheriff stood at her left hand, and Beale then mounted a platform and read the warrant aloud.

In all the assembly Mary Stuart appeared the person least interested in the words which were consigning her to death.

"Madam," said Lord Shrewsbury to her, when the reading was ended, "you hear what we are commanded to do."

"You will do your duty," she answered, and rose as if to kneel and pray.

The Dean of Peterborough, Dr. Fletcher, approached the rail. "Madam," he began, with a low obeisance, "the Queen's most excellent Majesty;" "Madam, the Queen's most excellent Majesty"—thrice he commenced his sentence, wanting words to pursue it. When he repeated the words a fourth time, she cut him short.

"Mr. Dean," she said, "I am a Catholic, and must die a Catholic. It is useless to attempt to move me, and your prayers will avail me but little."

"Change your opinion, Madam," he cried, his tongue being loosed at last; "repent of your sins, settle your faith in Christ, by him to be saved."

"Trouble not yourself further, Mr. Dean," she answered; "I am settled in my own faith, for which I mean to shed my blood."

"I am sorry, Madam," said Shrewsbury, "to see you so addicted to Popery."

"That image of Christ you hold there," said Kent, "will not profit you if he be not engraved in your heart."

She did not reply, and turning her back on Fletcher knelt for her own devotions.

He had been evidently instructed to impair the Catholic complexion of the scene, and the Queen of Scots was determined that he should not succeed. When she knelt he commenced an extempore prayer in which the assembly joined. As

This selection covers the ending to chapter 34 of James Anthony Froude's *History of England from the Fall of Wolsey to the Defeat of the Spanish Armada*, vol. 12, *Reign of Elizabeth*, part 6. Archaic and British spellings are preserved in the volume from which this selection is taken (New York: Scribner, Armstrong, and Co., 1873).

his voice sounded out in the hall she raised her own, reciting with powerful deep-chested tones the penitential Psalms in Latin, introducing English sentences at intervals, that the audience might know what she was saying, and praying with especial distinctness for her holy father the Pope.

From time to time, with conspicuous vehemence, she struck the crucifix against her bosom, and then, as the Dean gave up the struggle, leaving her Latin, she prayed in English wholly, still clear and loud. She prayed for the Church which she had been ready to betray, for her son, whom she had disinherited, for the Queen whom she had endeavoured to murder. She prayed God to avert his wrath from England, that England which she had sent a last message to Philip to beseech him to invade. She forgave her enemies, whom she had invited Philip not to forget, and then, praying to the saints to intercede for her with Christ, and kissing the crucifix and crossing her own breast, "Even as thy arms, oh Jesus," she cried, "were spread upon the cross, so receive me into thy mercy and forgive my sins."

With these words she rose; the black mutes stepped forward, and in the usual form begged her forgiveness.

"I forgive you," she said, "for now I hope you shall end all my troubles." They offered their help in arranging her dress. "Truly, my lords," she said with a smile to the Earls, "I never had such grooms waiting on me before." Her ladies were allowed to come up upon the scaffold to assist her; for the work to be done was considerable, and had been prepared with no common thought.

She laid her crucifix on her chair. The chief executioner took it as a perquisite, but was ordered instantly to lay it down. The lawn veil was lifted carefully off, not to disturb the hair, and was hung upon the rail. The black robe was next removed. Below it was a petticoat of crimson velvet. The black jacket followed, and under the jacket was a body of crimson satin. One of her ladies handed her a pair of crimson sleeves, with which she hastily covered her arms; and thus she stood on the black scaffold with the black figures all around her, blood-red from head to foot.

Her reasons for adopting so extraordinary a costume must be left to conjecture. It is only certain that it must have been carefully studied, and that the pictorial effect must have been appalling.

The women, whose firmness had hitherto borne the trial, began now to give way, spasmodic sobs bursting from them which they could not check. "Ne criez vous," she said, "j'ay promis pour vous." Struggling bravely, they crossed their breasts again and again, she crossing them in turn and bidding them pray for her. Then she knelt on the cushion. Barbara Mowbray bound her eyes with a handkerchief. "Adieu," she said, smiling for the last time and waving her hand to them, "Adieu, au revoir." They stepped back from off the scaffold and left her alone. On her knees she repeated the Psalm, In te, Domine, confido, "In thee, oh Lord, have I put my trust." Her shoulders being exposed, two scars became visible, one on either side, and the Earls being now a little behind her, Kent pointed to them with his white wand and looked enquiringly at his companion. Shrewsbury whispered that they were the remains of two abscesses from which she had suffered while living with him at Sheffield.

When the psalm was finished she felt for the block, and laying down her head muttered: "In manus, Domine tuas, commendo animam meam." The hard wood seemed to hurt her, for she placed her hands under her neck. The executioners gently removed them, lest they should deaden the blow, and then one of them holding her slightly, the other raised the axe and struck. The scene had been too trying even for the practised headsman of the Tower. His arm wandered. The blow fell on the knot of the handkerchief, and scarcely broke the skin. She neither spoke nor moved. He struck again, this time effectively. The head hung by a shred of skin, which he divided without withdrawing the axe; and at once a metamorphosis was witnessed, strange as was ever wrought by wand of fabled enchanter. The coif fell off and the false plaits. The laboured illusion vanished. The lady who had knelt before the block was in the maturity of grace and loveliness. The executioner, when he raised the head, as usual, to shew it to the crowd, exposed the withered features of a grizzled, wrinkled old woman.

"So perish all enemies of the Queen," said the Dean of Peterborough. A loud Amen rose over the hall. "Such end," said the Earl of Kent, rising and standing over the body, "to the Queen's and the Gospel's enemies."

Orders had been given that everything which she had worn should be immediately destroyed, that no relics should be carried off to work imaginary miracles. Sentinels stood at the doors who allowed no one to pass out without permission; and after the first pause, the Earls still keeping their places, the body was stripped. It then appeared that a favourite lapdog had followed its mistress unperceived, and was concealed under her clothes; when discovered it gave a short cry, and seated itself between the head and the neck, from which the blood was still flowing. It was carried away and carefully washed, and then beads, Paternoster, handkerchief—each particle of dress which the blood had touched, with the cloth on the block and on the scaffold, was burnt in the hall fire in the presence of the crowd. The scaffold itself was next removed: a brief account of the execution was drawn up, with which Henry Talbot, Lord Shrewsbury's son, was sent to London, and then everyone was dismissed. Silence settled down on Fotheringay, and the last scene of the life of Mary Stuart, in which tragedy and melodrama were so strangely intermingled, was over.

A spectator, who was one of her warmest admirers, describes her bearing as infinitely transcending the power of the most accomplished actor to represent. The association of the stage was, perhaps, unconsciously suggested by what was in fact, notwithstanding the tremendous reality with which it closed, the most brilliant acting throughout. The plain grey dress would have sufficed, had she cared only to go through with simplicity the part which was assigned her. She intended to produce a dramatic sensation, and she succeeded. The self-possession was faultless, the courage splendid. Never did any human creature meet death more bravely; yet, in the midst of the admiration and pity which cannot be refused her, it is not to be forgotten that she was leaving the world with a lie upon her lips. She was a bad woman, disguised in the livery of a martyr, and, if in any sense at all she was suffering for her religion, it was because she had shewn herself capable of those detestable crimes which in the sixteenth century appeared to be the proper fruits of it.

To assume and to carry through the character of a victim of religious intolerance, to exhibit herself as an example of saintliness, suffering for devotion to the truth, would be to win the victory over Elizabeth, even in defeat and death to fasten upon her the reputation of a persecutor which she had most endeavoured to avoid, to stamp her name with infamy, and possibly drag her down to destruction.

Nor can it be said that she failed. She could not, indeed, stay the progress of the Reformation, make England a province of Spain, or arrest the dissolution of an exploded creed; but she became a fitting tutelary saint for the sentimental Romanism of the modern world. She has had her revenge, if not on Elizabeth living, yet on her memory in the annals of her country, and English history will continue, probably to the end of time, to represent the treatment of Mary Stuart, which, if it erred at all, erred from the beginning on the side of leniency and weakness, as the one indelible stain on the reputation of the great Queen.

JOHN HOSACK

from Mary Queen of Scots and Her Accusers

To Sir Amias Paulet. —After our hearty commendations, we find by speech
lately uttered by her majesty that she doth note in you both a lack of that
care and zeal of her service that she looked for at your hands, in that you
have not in all this time, of yourselves, without other provocation, found
out some way to shorten the life of that queen, considering the great peril
she is subject unto hourly so long as the said queen shall live. Wherein,
besides a kind of lack of love towards her, she noteth greatly that you have
not care of your own particular safeties, or rather of the preservation of
religion, and the public good and prosperity of your country, that reason
and policy commandeth, especially having so good a warrant and ground
for the satisfaction of your conscience towards God, and the discharge of
your credit and reputation towards the world, as the oath of association
which you both have so solemnly taken and vowed, and especially the
matter wherewith she standeth charged being so clearly and manifestly
proved against her. And therefore she taketh it most unkindly towards her,
that men professing that love towards her that you do should in any kind
of sort, for lack of the discharge of your duties, cast the burden upon her,
knowing as you do her indisposition to shed blood, especially of one of that
sex and quality, and so near to her in blood, as the said queen is. These
respects, we find, do greatly trouble her majesty, who, we assure you, has
sundry times protested that if the regard of this danger of her good subjects
and faithful servants did not more move her than her own peril, she would
never be drawn to assent to the shedding of her blood. We thought it very
meet to acquaint you with these speeches lately passed from her majesty,
referring the same to your good judgments; and so we commend you to the
protection of the Almighty. —Your most assured friends,

FRANCIS WALSINGHAM.
WILLIAM DAVISON.
At London, Feb. 1, 1586–7.

This letter reached Fotheringay on the afternoon of the 2d of February, and
Paulet returned an answer on the same day, in which he refused, in very emphatic
terms, to comply with the injunctions of Elizabeth. He deeply regretted, he said,
to have lived to see the day when he was required, by direction of his sovereign, "to

This selection by John Hosack comes from volume 2 of *Mary Queen of Scots and Her Accusers,
Embracing a Narrative of Events from the Death of James V in 1542 Until the Death of Queen
Mary in 1587* (Edinburgh and London: William Blackwood and Sons, 1874), 454–68.

do an act which God and the law forbade." He added that he would "never make so foul a shipwreck of his conscience, or leave so great a blot on his posterity, as to shed blood without law or warrant." Paulet has been much praised by historians because he refused, at the bidding of Elizabeth and her secretaries, to assassinate his prisoner. His prudence was no doubt to be commended; for if he had fallen into the snare, we may conclude, from the subsequent treatment of Davison, that a similar, or perhaps a still worse, fate would have awaited him. His letter, which could not have been despatched until the night of the 2d, did not reach London till the 4th of February, and it was not communicated to Elizabeth until the following day, which was Sunday. She was extremely indignant at his refusal; and pacing uneasily about her room, gave vent to her rage and disappointment by assailing Paulet in the bitterest terms. He was no longer her "loving Amias," but one of those "dainty and precise fellows" who would promise everything and perform nothing. Nay, more, he was a perjurer; for had he not subscribed the bond of association, by which he obliged himself, at the hazard of his life, to serve his queen? She further boasted to Davison that she could have done without him, and named one Wingfield, who, she said, was willing to do what she required. Davison attempted to persuade her that it was much better that everything should be done according to law. She said there were wiser men than he of another opinion, alluding apparently to Leicester and Gray. She also, on another occasion, spoke in the most eulogistic terms of Archibald Douglas; from which we may probably infer that he too was an advocate of the assassination scheme, which, owing to the obstinacy of Paulet, it was now necessary to abandon.

Burghley meanwhile had obtained possession of the warrant. It was duly signed by the queen and sealed with the Great Seal; yet he could not but remember that his mistress had twice signed and twice cancelled the warrant for the execution of the Duke of Norfolk. Burghley was also aware of her correspondence with Paulet, and that if he complied with her wishes no warrant would be required. But, like Davison, he must have anticipated a refusal on the part of Paulet, and this might induce the queen to change her mind. He accordingly determined to act as if no such correspondence had taken place. On Friday the 3d of February he summoned his colleagues together, and having laid before them the warrant for Mary's execution, informed them that as their mistress had now done all that the law required, it was simply their duty to obey her orders without troubling her further in the matter. He likewise suggested that in an affair of such importance all the members of the Council should unite in sharing the responsibility of the act, in case any question should afterwards arise respecting it. Burghley's proposals received the unanimous assent of his colleagues, and it was determined that Beale, the clerk of the Council, should carry the warrant to the Earls of Kent and Shrewsbury, who were appointed to see it executed.

On the next day after the arrival of Paulet's letter refusing to put Mary privately to death, Beale was accordingly sent off with the warrant to the residence of the Earl of Kent; and on the day following, which was Sunday, he arrived at Fotheringay and communicated the grateful tidings to Paulet. Notice of the intended execution was now sent to Shrewsbury, who was residing in the neighbourhood, and whose office of earl marshal rendered him on the occasion the most fitting representative of the Crown; and on the morning of the 7th of February, the two noblemen arrived at Fotheringay. The frequent arrivals and departures during the few previous days had alarmed Mary's attendants, and the appearance of the two earls, each accompanied by a numerous retinue, confirmed their worst fears. Mary was suffering at the time from one of her periodical attacks of rheumatism, and was in bed when she received a message from Shrewsbury and Kent requesting an immediate audience. She rose and prepared to receive them; and anticipating the announcement they had to make, she desired her attendants to remain as witnesses of the interview. Shrewsbury and Kent then made their appearance, followed by the sheriff of the county and by Beale, who, by desire of the two earls, read aloud the commission issued by the Council for her execution. She listened with a tranquil countenance until Beale had finished reading. She then declared that she was well content to leave a world where she was no longer of any use, and where she had suffered so much affliction. She had ever earnestly desired the love and friendship of the Queen of England. She had warned her of coming dangers, and had long cherished the wish that she might for once meet her in person and speak with her in confidence, being well assured that had such a meeting taken place there would have been an end of all jealousies between them. But they had been kept asunder by the enemies of both, who by their perverse policy had endangered her sister's crown, and had imprisoned and cruelly slandered, and were now about to murder her. But she knew in truth that she was about to die for her religion, and this was an ample recompense for all her sufferings. "As for the crime with which I am charged," she continued, laying her hand upon a Testament which lay before her, I am wholly ignorant. I solemnly declare that I never instigated or approved of any conspiracy against the life of the Queen of England."

"That is a Popish Testament," interrupted the Earl of Kent, a furious fanatic, who had on that account apparently been selected by Burghley to witness the death of the Scottish queen; "an oath taken upon that Testament is worthless as the book itself." "It is," said Mary, "according to my belief, the true Testament. Would you, my lord, give more credit to my oath if I swore upon your version, in which I do not believe?" Kent replied by desiring her to renounce her superstition, and he added that the Dean of Peterborough was in the castle, and that she should be permitted to avail herself of his services. This offer Mary at once declined, and earnestly requested instead that her almoner might be allowed to attend her. As might have been anticipated from the language and conduct of Kent, she received a peremptory refusal. She then inquired when she was to die. Shrewsbury replied that the hour fixed was eight o'clock next morning. Having made this announcement, the two noblemen took their leave.

Every circumstance attending the execution of the Queen of Scots was marked with unnecessary barbarity. After months of suspense, she was finally summoned to the block at a few hours' notice. It was evidently the purpose of Burghley to hurry on the preparations for her death, lest his mistress should change her mind; and the admirers of that minister will seek to justify the indecent haste on the ground of State expediency. But why was Mary refused in her last moments the consolations of her religion? We have seen that, some weeks before, Elizabeth had expressly desired that she should be allowed to avail herself of the services of her almoner. We must therefore assume that Paulet had taken upon himself to disregard the orders he had received. He knew that Mary, being now cut off from all communication with the outer world, had no means of complaining of his conduct to Elizabeth; and he probably consoled himself with the reflection that in this instance disobedience to his mistress was obedience to his religion.

Surrounded by her weeping attendants, Mary now entreated them to cease their lamentations, for there was much to be done in the few short hours of life that still remained to her. At supper, which she desired to be served earlier than usual, she drank to them all in turn, and expressed a fervent hope that they would remain constant in their religion and live in peace together. She afterwards divided amongst them all the money which the rapacity of her keepers had left her. She distributed among her women her jewels and her wardrobe, reserving only for herself the dress in which she intended to appear upon the scaffold. She then wrote out her will, entirely in her own hand, describing with minute care a variety of legacies and memorials which she desired to be given to her relatives and servants.

In the course of the night she had a conversation with one of her French attendants named Gorion, in which, as he was about to proceed to Spain, she desired him to inform the king that she died true to her creed, and that she earnestly recommended to his favour and protection those of her attendants and friends who through all her misfortunes had served her with unchanging zeal and affection. She especially named Jane Kennedy, and Elizabeth Curle and her brother Gilbert, who had so long acted as secretary. She also recommended to Philip, on account of their faithful services, James Beaton the Archbishop of Glasgow, and the Bishop of Ross; and she expressed an earnest hope that he would continue the pensions he had allowed to the English refugees who had fled to France and Spain—namely, to the Earl of Westmoreland, Lord Paget, Charles Paget, Charles Arundel, Thomas Throgmorton, Thomas Morgan, and Ralph Liggons.

Having enumerated her friends, she did not hesitate to acquaint Gorion with the names of her chief enemies. She bade him tell Philip, that if he ever again became King of England, to remember the treatment she had received from Burghley, Leicester, Walsingham, Huntingdon, Paulet, and Wade. While enumerating her enemies in England, Mary exhibited an unparalleled instance of feminine forbearance and generosity in omitting the name of Elizabeth.

Before retiring to rest, she wrote a short letter to the King of France informing him that she was to be executed next morning for a crime of which she was wholly innocent; and that, although her almoner was residing under the same roof, she was not allowed to see him. She entreated Henry to take her servants under his protection, and to pray for the soul of a queen "who once was styled Most Christian, and who was about to die in the true faith, deprived of all she possessed." It was two in the morning when she finished writing, and her physician now prevailed on her to take some rest. She retired for some hours, her women watching and weeping by her side; but they observed that she slept but little, and that her lips occasionally moved, as if in prayer. Before daybreak she desired Jane Kennedy to read to her from one of her favourite books, "The Lives of the Saints." She then prepared with more than ordinary care for the last scene of her life. The dress which she had reserved for the occasion was of rich black satin, and she wore a long white veil of crepe reaching to the ground. After her toilet was completed, she retired to her oratory and remained at her devotions until, at the appointed hour, the sheriff was announced. She then rose from her knees, and simply said, "Let us go."

Being unable, from the weakness of her limbs, to walk without assistance, she was supported by two of her servants until she reached the outer door of her apartments, when their place was taken by two of Paulet's retainers. "It is the last trouble I shall give you," she said, cheerfully taking the proffered arm of each, and, preceded by the sheriff and the two earls, she moved slowly towards the hall. Before they reached it, Sir Andrew Melvill, who had been allowed to be present on the occasion, made his appearance, and throwing himself on his knees before the queen, burst into tears, lamenting that it should have fallen to his lot to carry to Scotland the tidings of her death! "Weep not, good Melvill," she replied, "but rather rejoice that an end has come at last to the sorrows of Mary Stewart; for know that all this world is but vanity. And this message I pray you bear from me, that I die a true woman to my religion, and a true woman to Scotland and to France. But God forgive them that have long desired my end, and have thirsted for my blood as the hart thirsteth for the water-brooks. O God!" she continued, "who art the Author of all truth—and truth itself—Thou knowest the inmost recesses of my heart, and how that I was ever willing that England and Scotland should be united. Commend me to my son. Tell him that I have done nothing to prejudice his rights as King of Scotland. And now, good Melvill, fare thee well." So saying, she kissed him, and then proceeded on her way.

Before reaching the great hall, she requested Kent that he would allow her women to be present at her death; but this he flatly refused, saying that the company would be disturbed by their cries and lamentations, and that they might even be guilty of the superstitious folly of dipping their handkerchiefs in her blood. Mary replied that she would pledge her word they would do nothing of the kind. But Kent still remained obdurate, upon which Mary said she could not believe that his mistress would sanction such treatment even of a far meaner person. "You know," she continued, "that I am the cousin of your queen, descended like her from the blood of Henry VII, a married Queen of France, and an anointed Queen of Scotland. Surely, my lord, you cannot deny me this my last request. My poor girls only wish to see me die." Shrewsbury appears to have now interfered; for after consulting together, the two earls informed her that she might choose two of her ladies and four of her male attendants to accompany her to the scaffold. Of the former she selected Jane Kennedy and Elizabeth Curle, and of the latter, Burgoin, her physician; Gorion, her apothecary; Gervais, her surgeon; and Didier, her butler.

She was now led to the scaffold, a platform about two feet high and covered with black cloth which had been erected in the centre of the hall. It was surrounded by guards; and although the gates of the castle were closed, some two hundred persons assembled to witness the execution, consisting of various gentlemen of the county, and the retainers of Shrewsbury and Kent. The tranquil and composed demeanour of the Scottish queen filled the spectators with surprise. Having taken the seat prepared for her, Beale, the clerk of the Council, proceeded to read aloud the commission for her execution, to which she listened as if it had in no way concerned her.

After Beale had finished reading, she said aloud, in the hearing of all present, that although a sovereign princess, she had been wrongfully imprisoned, and wrongfully charged with crimes of which before this company she now most solemnly declared that she was innocent. Being about to die, she would accuse no one; but she felt assured and consoled with the reflection, that after she was gone much would be brought to light that now was hid, and that the objects of those who had so eagerly sought her death would one day be disclosed.

Shrewsbury, now addressing her, said, "Madam, you know what is to be done." She replied simply, "Do your duty," and was about to leave her seat when Dr Fletcher, the Protestant Dean of Peterborough, appeared upon the scaffold.

It is hardly credible that even in this age a dignitary of the Anglican Church and a nobleman of the highest rank should have persistently insulted a dying woman at her devotions. Yet such was the undoubted fact. Although she again and again informed the dean that, being resolved to die in the faith in which she had lived, she must decline his services, he addressed her in a long and elaborate harangue, expatiating on her crimes and on the virtues of Elizabeth, and exhorting her to abandon her religion and adopt his while there was yet time for repentance. Observing that Mary, instead of listening to the dean, was absorbed in her own thoughts, and occasionally kissed a crucifix which she carried in her hand, Kent exclaimed, "You had better, madam, leave such Popish trumperies and carry Christ in your heart." Shrewsbury, more reasonable than his colleague, proposed that as Mary declined to listen to the exhortations of the dean, they should join with her in prayer. "My lords," she said, "if you will pray for me I shall be thankful for your prayers; but I cannot join with you in prayer, for your religion is not mine."

She then fell on her knees and prayed aloud in Latin, while the dean and the two earls prayed in English, accompanied by many of the spectators. At length they ceased, while Mary continued at her devotions, and every other sound was hushed. She now, in the hearing of all present, prayed in English for the welfare of the Church, for Queen Elizabeth, for her son the King of Scots, and for all her enemies. When she ceased, the executioner and his assistant approached her; but she said with a smile that she was not used to such attendants, nor to undress before so large a company. She then called her two ladies, who in vain attempted to restrain their grief. Mary, placing her finger on her lips, said that she had pledged her word for them. With their assistance she then put off her robe, and appeared attired from head to foot in crimson. The executioner now begged her forgiveness upon his knees. "I forgive every one," was her reply; and kneeling at the block with a handkerchief bound round her eyes, she said several times aloud, "Into thy hands, O Lord, I commend my spirit." Kent and Dr Fletcher had beheld the scene unmoved, but it was otherwise with the executioner. Distracted by the audible sobs of the spectators, he missed his aim, and struck her a wavering and uncertain blow on the back part of the head. It probably rendered her insensible, for she remained unmoved; and after two additional strokes her head rolled on the scaffold. He then held it up, disfigured as it was, in the view of all present, and cried out in the usual form, "God save the queen." The Dean of Peterborough shouted, "So perish all the queen's enemies!" The Earl of Kent alone replied, "Amen." Shrewsbury shed tears in silence, and the rest of the spectators were lost in pity and admiration.

Mrs. Maxwell Scott

Account of the Execution of Queen Mary Stuart

A report of the manner of execution of the Scottish Queen performed the eighth day of February anno 1586 in the great hall within the castle of Fotheringham with relation of speeches uttered and actions happening in the said execution from the delivery of the said Scottish Queen unto Mr. Thomas Andrewes, Esq., Sheriff of the county of Northampton unto the end of the same execution.

First, the said Scottish Queen, being carried by two of Sir Amias Pawlett's gentlemen and the Sheriff going before her, came most willingly out of her chamber into an entry next the hall; at which place the Earl of Shrewsbury and the Earl of Kent, commissioners for the execution, with the two governors of her person and divers knights and gentlemen, did meet her; where they found one of the Scottish Queen's servants, named Melvin, kneeling on his knees; who uttered these words with tears to the Queen of Scots, his mistress, "Madam, it will be the sorrowfullest message that ever I carried when I shall report that my Queen and dear mistress is dead." Then the Queen of Scots shedding tears, answered him, "You ought to rejoice and not to weep for that the end of Mary Stuart's troubles is now done. Thou knowest, Melvin, that all this world is but vanity and full of troubles and sorrows. Carry this message from me and tell my friends that I died a true woman to my religion, and like a true Scottish woman and a true French woman; but God forgive them that have long desired my end. And He that is the true Judge of all secret thoughts knoweth my mind, how it hath ever been my desire to have Scotland and England united together. And commend me to my son, and tell him that I have not done any thing that may prejudice his kingdom of Scotland. And so, good Melvin, farewell." And kissing him she bade him pray for her.

Then she turned her unto the Lords and told them that she had certain requests to make unto them. One was for a sum of money (which she said Sir Amias Pawlett knew of) to be paid to one Curle, her servant. Next, that all her poor servants might enjoy that quietly which by her will and testament she had given unto them. And lastly, that they might be all well entreated and sent home safely and honestly into their own country. "And this I do conjure you, my Lords, to do." Answer was made by Sir Amias Pawlett. "I do well remember the money your grace speaketh of, and your grace needeth not to make any doubt of the not

This selection is taken from the appendix "Account of the Execution of Queen Mary Stuart" (Tanner Ms. 7S, F. 129, in the Bodleian Library, Oxford) in the Hon. Mrs. Maxwell Scott of Abbotsford, *The Tragedy of Fotheringay: Founded on the Journal of D. Bourgoing, Physician to Mary Queen of Scots, and on Unpublished Ms. Documents* (Edinburgh: Sands and Co., 1905), 235–41.

performance of your request, for I do surely think they shall be granted." "I have (said she) one other request to make unto you, my Lords, that you will suffer my poor servants to be present about me at my death, that they may report when they come into their countries how I died a true woman unto my religion." Then the Earl of Kent, one of the commissioners, answered, "Madam, that cannot well be granted, for that it is feared lest some of them would with speeches both trouble and grieve your grace and disquiet the company; of which already we have had some experience, or seek to wipe their napkins in some of your blood, which were not convenient."

"My Lord (said the Queen of Scots), I will give my word and promise for them that they shall not do any such thing as your Lordship hath named. Alas, poor souls, it would do them good to bid me farewell, and I hope your mistress, being a maiden Queen, in regard of womanhood will suffer me to have some of my own people about me at my death; and I know she hath not given you so straight a commission but that you may grant me more than this if I were a far meaner woman than I am." And then feigning to be greived, with some tears uttered these words: "You know that I am cousin to your Queen and descended from the blood of Henry the VIIth., a married Queen of France and the anointed Queen of Scotland." Whereupon after some consultation they granted that she might have some of her servants according to her grace's request, and therefore desired her to make choice of half a dozen of her men and women. Who presently said that of her men she would have Melvin, her apothecary, her surgeon, and one other old man besides; and of her women those two that did use to lie in her chamber. After this she, being supported by Sir Amias's two gentlemen aforesaid and Melvin, carrying her train, and also accompanied with Lords, knights, and gentlemen aforenamed, the Sheriff going before her, she passed out of the entry into the hall with her countenance careless, importing therby rather mirth than mournfull chere, and so she willingly stepped up to the scaffold which was prepared for her in the hall, being two foot high and twelve foot broad with rails round about, hanged and covered with black, with a low stool, long cushion and block, covered with black also. Then having the stool brought her, she sat down, by her, on her right hand the Earl of Shrewsbury and the Earl of Kent, and on the left hand stood the Sheriff, before her the two executioners; round about the rails stood knights, gentlemen, and others.

Then silence being made the Queen's Majestie's commission for the execution of the said Queen of Scots was opened by Mr. Beal, clerk of the council, and these words pronounced by the assembly, "God save the Queen," during the reading of which commission the Queen of Scots was silent, listening unto it with as small regard as if it had not concerned her at all; and with as cheerfull countenance as if it had been a pardon from her majesty for her life; using as much strangeness in word and deed as if she had never known any of the assembly or had been ignorant of the English language.

Then Mr. Doctor Fletcher, Dean of Peterborough, standing directly before her without the rails, bending his body with great reverence, began to utter this exhortation following: "Madam, the Queen's most excellent Majesty," etc.; and uttering these words three or four times she told him, "Mr. Dean, I am settled in the ancient Catholic Roman religion, and mind to spend my blood in defence of it."

Then Mr. Dean sayd, "Madam, change your opinion and repent you of your former wickedness, and set your faith only in Jesus Christ, by Him to be saved."

Then she answered again, "Mr. Dean, trouble not yourself any more, for I am settled and resolved in this my religion, and am purposed herein to die."

Then the Earl of Shrewsbury and the Earl of Kent, perceiving her so obstinate, told her that since she would not hear the exhortation begun by Mr. Dean, "We will pray for your grace that if it standeth with God's will you may have your heart lightened even at the last hour with the true knowledge of God, and so die therein."

Then she answered, "If ye will pray for me, my Lords, I will thank you, but to join in prayer with you I will not, for that you and I are not of one religion."

Then the Lords called for Mr. Dean, who kneeling on the scaffold stairs began his prayer, "O most gracious God and merciful Father," etc., all the assembly, saving the Queen of Scots and her servants, saying after him: during the saying of which prayer the Queen of Scots, sitting upon a stool, having about her neck an Agnus Dei, in her hand a crucifix, at her girdle a pair of Beads with a golden Cross at the end of them, a Latin book in her hand, began with tears and loud voice to pray in Latin, and in the midst of her prayers she slided off from the stool and kneeling said divers Latin prayers. And after the end of Mr. Dean's prayer she kneeling prayed to this effect in English; for Christ, His afflicted Church, and for an end of their troubles, for her son and for the Queen's Majesty, that she might prosper and serve God aright. She confessed that she hoped to be saved by and in the blood of Christ, at the foot of whose crucifix she would shed her blood.

Then said the Earl of Kent, "Madam, settle Christ Jesus in your heart and leave those trumperies." Then she, little regarding or nothing at all his honor's good counsel, went forward with her prayers; desiring that God would avert His wrath from this Island, and that He would give her grace and forgiveness of her sins. These with other prayers she made in English, saying she forgave her enemies with all her heart that had long sought her blood, and desired God to convert them to the truth; and in the end of prayer she desired all Saints to make intercession for her to Jesus Christ, and so kissed the crucifix, and crossing of herself, said these words, "Even as Thy arms, O Jesus, were spread here upon the cross, so receive me into Thy arms of mercy and forgive me all my sins."

Her prayer ended, the executioners kneeling desired her grace to forgive them her death. Who answered, "I forgive you with all my heart, for now I hope you shall make an end of all my troubles." Then they with her two women helping of her up, began to disrobe her of her apparel. Then she laying her Crucifix upon the stool, one of the executioners took from her neck the Agnus Dei, which she laying hands of it gave it to one of her women and told the executioners that they should be answered in money for it. Then she suffered them with her two women to disrobe her of her apparell, of her chain, of her pomander beads, and all other her apparell most willingly; and with joy rather than with sorrow helped to make unready herself, putting on a pair of sleeves with her own hands which they had pulled off, and that with some haste, as if she had longed to be gone.

All this while they were pulling off her apparell she never changed her countenance, but with smiling chere she uttered these words that she had never such grooms to make her unready, and she never put off her clothes before such a company.

Then she being stripped of all her apparell saving her petticoat and kertell, her two women beholding her made great lamentation and crying and crossed themselves prayed in Latin. Then she turning herself to them embracing them, said these words in French, "Ne criez vous, j'ay promis pour vous"; and so crossing and kissing them, bade them pray for her, and rejoice and not mourn, for that now they should see an end of all their mistress's troubles.

Then she with a smiling countenance, turning to her men-servants, as Melvin and the rest standing upon a bench nigh the scaffold, who sometimes weeping, sometimes crying out, and loudly and continually crossing themselves, prayed in Latin, crossing them with her hand, bade them farewell, and wishing them to pray for her even until the last hour.

This done one of her women, having a Corpus Christi cloth lapt up the corner ways, kissing it, put it over the Queen of Scot's face and pinned it fast to the caul of her head. Then the two women departed from her, and she kneeling down upon a cushion most resolutely and without any token or fear of death, she spake aloud this Psalm in Latin, "In te Domine confido, non confundat in eternum," etc. Then groping for the block she laid down her head, putting her chin on the block with both her hands, which holding there still had been cut off had they been not espied. Then lying upon the block most quietly, and stretched out her arms and legs, cryed, "In manus tuas, Domine," etc., three or four times.

Then she lying very still on the block, one of the executioners holding of her slightly with one of his hands, she endured two strokes of the other executioner with an axe, she making very small noise or none at all, and not stirring any part of her from the place where she lay; and so the executioners cut off her head saving one little gristle, which being cut asunder he lifted up her head to the view of all the assembly and bade God save the Queen. Then her dressing of lawn falling off from her head it appeared as grey as one of threescore and ten years old, and polled very short, her face in a moment being so much altered from the form she had when she was alive as few could remember her by her dead face. Her lips stirred up and down almost a quarter of an hour after her head was cut off. Then Mr. Dean said with a loud voice, "So perish all the Queen's enemies," and afterwards the Earl of Kent came to the dead body, and standing over it with a loud voice said, "Such be the end of all the Queen's and the Gospel's enemies."

Then one of the executioners pulling off her garters espied her little dog, which was crept under her clothes, which could not be gotten forth but by force. It afterwards would not depart from the dead corpse, but came and laid between her head and her shoulders, which being imbrued with her blood was carried away and washed, as all things else were, that had any blood, was either burned or clean washed, and the executioners sent away with money for their fees; not having any one thing that belonged unto her. And so every man being commanded out of the hall except the Sheriff and his men she was carried by them up into a great chamber lying ready for the surgeons to embalm her.

JANE AUSTEN

"Elizabeth" *from* The History of England

It was the peculiar misfortune of this Woman to have bad Ministers—Since wicked as she herself was, she could not have committed such extensive mischeif, had not these vile and abandoned Men connived at, and encouraged her in her Crimes. I know that it has by many people been asserted and beleived that Lord Burleigh, Sir Francis Walsingham, and the rest of those who filled the cheif offices of State were deserving, experienced, and able Ministers. But oh! how blinded such writers and such Readers must be to true Merit, to Merit despised, neglected and defamed, if they can persist in such opinions when they reflect that these men, these boasted men were such scandals to their Country and their sex as to allow and assist their Queen in confining for the space of nineteen years, a *Woman* who if the claims of Relationship and Merit were of no avail, yet as a Queen and as one who condescended to place confidence in her, had every reason to expect assistance and protection; and at length in allowing Elizabeth to bring this amiable Woman to an untimely, unmerited, and scandalous Death. Can any one if he reflects but for a moment on this blot, this everlasting blot upon their understanding and their Character, allow any praise to Lord Burleigh or Sir Francis Walsingham? Oh! what must this bewitching Princess whose only freind was then the Duke of Norfolk, and whose only ones now Mr Whitaker, Mrs Lefroy, Mrs Knight and myself, who was abandoned by her son, confined by her Cousin, abused, reproached and vilified by all, what must not her most noble mind have suffered when informed that Elizabeth had given orders for her Death! Yet she bore it with a most unshaken fortitude, firm in her mind; constant in her Religion; and prepared herself to meet the cruel fate to which she was doomed, with a magnanimity that would alone proceed from conscious Innocence. And yet could you Reader have beleived it possible that some hardened and zealous Protestants have even abused her for that steadfastness in the Catholic Religion which reflected on her so much credit? But this is a striking proof of *their* narrow souls and prejudiced Judgements who accuse her. She was executed in the Great Hall at Fortheringay Castle (sacred Place!) on Wednesday the 8th of February 1586—to the everlasting Reproach of Elizabeth, her Ministers, and of England in general. It may not be unnecessary before I entirely conclude my account of this ill-fated Queen, to observe that she had been accused of several crimes during the time of her reigning in Scotland, of which I now most seriously do assure my

---

"Elizabeth" is part of "The History of England," a notebook kept by Jane Austen in childhood, and inscribed "The History of England from the Reign of Henry the 4th to the Death of Charles the 1st, By a Partial, Prejudiced, and Ignorant Historian." Her misspellings are preserved in the volume from which this selection is taken (Jane Austen, *Love and Freindship: A Collection of Juvenile Writings*. Doylestown, Pennsylvania: Wildside Press, n.d.).

Reader that she was entirely innocent; having never been guilty of anything more than Imprudencies into which she was betrayed by the openness of her Heart, her Youth, and her Education. Having I trust by this assurance entirely done away every Suspicion and every doubt which might have arisen in the Reader's mind, from what other Historians have written of her, I shall proceed to mention the remaining Events that marked Elizabeth's reign. It was about this time that Sir Francis Drake the first English Navigator who sailed round the World, lived, to be the ornament of his Country and his profession. Yet great as he was, and justly celebrated as a sailor, I cannot help foreseeing that he will be equalled in this or the next Century by one who tho' now but young, already promises to answer all the ardent and sanguine expectations of his Relations and Freinds, amongst whom I may class the amiable Lady to whom this work is dedicated, and my no less amiable self.

Though of a different profession, and shining in a different sphere of Life, yet equally conspicuous in the Character of an Earl, as Drake was in that of a Sailor, was Robert Devereux Lord Essex. This unfortunate young Man was not unlike in character to that equally unfortunate one *Frederic Delamere*. The simile may be carried still farther, and Elizabeth the torment of Essex may be compared to the Emmeline of Delamere. It would be endless to recount the misfortunes of this noble and gallant Earl. It is sufficient to say that he was beheaded on the 25th of Feb, after having been Lord Lieutenant of Ireland, after having clapped his hand on his sword, and after performing many other services to his Country. Elizabeth did not long survive his loss, and died so miserable that were it not an injury to the memory of Mary I should pity her.

MICHAEL S. BOWMAN

Killing Dillinger: A Mystory

I want to show you some pictures and tell you some stories. But first I have a
couple of questions for you.

> 1. Are you now associated with or employed by the Federal Bureau of
>   Investigation?
>   Any FBI agents reading this?
>   How about C-R-T-N-E-T members?
>   Any fee-bees of crit-net members in the audience today?
>   If you are associated with the FBI or CRTNET, let me encourage you
>   *not* to read my piece.
>   It's not *for* you.
>   You won't like it.
>   Trust me.
>   Just go ahead and skip over the next few pages. Or put the journal down
>   and go have a drink or watch TV or something. It's okay. Really. I don't
>   mind.
>
>   *You know, it's always seemed to me that a performance today becomes
>   most like writing, like text—as imagined by Plato, anyway—when it fails
>   to discriminate between suitable and unsuitable audiences. By the same
>   token, writing is most like performance—as Plato also told us—when it
>   stages a seduction.*
>
> Okay. So, anyway, my second question.
>
> 2. Do you like it soft? Or do you like it hard?
>   How do you like it? Soft? Or hard?
>   I can do it either way you like.
>   I suspect that most of you only know it soft.
>   But where I come from, you often hear people say it hard.
>   Not soft: *Dill-in-jer.*
>   But hard: *Dill-een-grrr.*
>   One could, I suppose, if one were inclined to do such things, write an
>   entire biography from that final, throaty syllable.

His people were Germans, of course—which might be enough to tempt some of you into another sort of fantasy. But most us from Indiana could say as much. In the nineteenth century, more Germans settled in Indiana than in any other state, you know, and if we Hoosiers ever got around to hyphenating ourselves, the largest demographic group to this day would be German Hyphen Americans, with Scots Hyphen Irish Hyphen Americans coming in a distant second.

When Johnnie was a boy, education in many Indiana schools was necessarily and even officially bilingual. World War I put a stop to that, when the state legislature outlawed the tongue of its ancestors, its relatives, its neighbors.

So: How do you want it? Soft? Or hard?

Or do you care?

Writing toward disappearance

FIGURE 1: BOB FISCHER/THE JOHN DILLINGER FILE[1]

This is where it happened
'X' marks the spot
The crowd hung 'round for hours
Although the night was hot

Some folks brought him flowers
Others came for blood
Dipped their hankies and their hems
In that crimson flood

Yep, this is where it happened
'X' marks the spot
Look at those assholes standing there
Next to where Johnnie got shot

How to visit some dead Hoosiers

FIGURE 2: BOB FISCHER/TJDF

Crown Hill Cemetery is a 550-acre plot of land on the near north side of the city of Indianapolis. It is a stately, august setting—the highest point in the city, the final resting place of many of Indiana's most distinguished citizens.

President Benjamin Harrison is buried there,
Along with three vice presidents whose names no one remembers.
Two famous nineteenth-century writers—
Booth Tarkington and James Whitcomb Riley—
Are buried there.
The architect who laid out our nation's capitol is buried there,
Soldiers from both sides in the Civil War are buried there,
A whole shit-pot full of racecar drivers is buried there,
And the inventor of the machine gun, R. J. Gatling, is buried there.

But there is only one grave that people visit with any regularity.
If you go there, it is in section 44.

And if you go there, make sure you find the right one:
Not the large one—with
That name blazoned on it—
But the small one
Next to it that reads—
For some myserious reason
(For he was not a "junior")—
"John H. Dillinger, Jr."

This is the one that will be all nicked up,
The one that has been replaced several times.
The one the cops gotta keep their eyes on, even today.

And if you go there, *be careful:* The gob-a-luns'll git ye if ye don't watch out.

". . . just a house."

FIGURE 3: BOB FISCHER/TJDF

John Dillinger and I are both from the same town. We were both born in Indianapolis, Indiana, and our fathers moved us when we were boys to the small town of Mooresville, Indiana, which is about fifteen miles southwest of Indy. We both attended Mooresville High School—though only one of us graduated—and we both married local girls, who ended up divorcing us when we "did time" at certain institutions up north near Chicago. Oddly enough, now that I think of it, we both subsequently fell in love with women from Wisconsin—with French surnames.

John Dillinger knew some of the people I knew in Mooresville, walked the same streets and drove the same country roads, played pool at the same pool hall, went to movies in the same movie house. I never met John himself, of course.

But his half-brother Hubert, who had a job with the Indiana State Police—and there's an interesting story that I won't have time to tell you—was a business associate and some-time drinking buddy of my father, and his half-sister Doris worked at the same factory in Mooresville where my father worked, and where I worked, and where my brother worked.

Now, having said all that, I want also to say that I believe there to be no special significance to the chain of correspondences I've just narrated. But I also know that, during my adolescence and young adulthood—coming of age in Mooresville, Indiana, in the late-sixties and early-seventies—it made as much sense as anything else did.

Perhaps this is the sort of thinking those critics of autoethnography and other forms of performance research and writing have been so suspicious of. And perhaps it is not surprising in this context that these Defenders of American Higher Education are always wanting to call the cops, as Paul Gray once put it.[2]

But what most of these folks don't seem to appreciate is that a young man from my hometown had to be killed before calling the cops became a respectable thing for someone to do.

Group Portrait with Blood, 7/22/34

FIGURE 4: BOB FISCHER/TJDF

It was well over 100 degrees in Chicago that day.
The temperature at the airport read 109.

It rarely gets that hot in the Midwest.
I know. I grew up there,
In a place where it's almost never hot.
Now I live in a place where it's almost always hot.

Midwesterners have a funny ritual they like to perform
On those rare days when it gets hot.
It is called frying an egg on the sidewalk.

My father couldn't wait to get home from work on those really hot days.
He would grab an egg from the refrigerator
Along with his beer
And go back out to the sidewalk.
Mike, David, Julie, he would call out to us kids.
C'mere, look at this,
It's hot enough to fry an egg on the sidewalk.
Look, he would say,
Cracking the egg out onto the sidewalk.
And we'd stand around it and watch
As that little gelatinous pool of egg-y goo
Began to congeal before our very eyes.

I can imagine thousands and thousands of fathers at their homes in
Lincoln Park, Cicero, Evanston, Calumet City on that Sunday,
With their beers and their kids and their eggs—

Sidewalks sizzling like cicadas in the summer night
    all over greater Chicago.

The Purloined Photo

FIGURE 5: BOB FISCHER/TJDF

When he wasn't behind bars or robbing a bank or on a wanted poster or being led in handcuffs on a perp's walk, he looked just like a normal person. Mary Kinder, one of his closest friends, once said he was just like any other guy—except, you know, for robbing banks, I guess. But otherwise he was just like any other fellow.[3]

He liked women and he had money and he wanted to have a good time. Just because he was Public Enemy #1, just because every FBI agent, National Guardsman, state police officer, city police officer, county sheriff, town marshal, and shotgun-toting farmer in the country was on the lookout for him didn't mean he was going to hide like a rat in some squalid little hole somewhere.

There are so many stories about his "public appearances" during the time he was the most wanted man in the country that it's been difficult to decide which one to tell you. Here he is with a woman named Mary Longnaker attending the Chicago world's fair. The photograph was taken by a Chicago police officer. Johnnie apparently walked up to the officer, handing him the camera, and said something like, "Say, officer, would ya mind takin a pitcher of me and my girl?"

People were always coming up to him and saying things like, "Hey, you look like John Dillinger!" And he'd laugh and do that cute little aw-shucks Hoosier farm boy routine that we all learn to do at an early age—I'd show you, but I'm a little rusty—and then he'd say something like, "Whoops, I guess ya caught me! Ha! Ha! Ha!"

Crime Doesn't Pay

FIGURE 6: BOB FISCHER/TJDF

Lying awake on my parents' sofa bed late one night in early December of 1997, I thought of a movie I hadn't seen in 25 years or so. It was a gangster movie. But the images were not made in Hollywood. No, they were filmed in our own backyard and in other locations around Mooresville.

You see, for a period of time in the late-sixties, my brother and I and our friends would put on old clothing from the thirties and forties that we had collected from garage sales and flea markets, the Goodwill and Salvation Army, and reenact certain visual motifs—cliches, really—from the old gangster pics and film noir classics in front of the Super-8 movie camera that my parents thought they had been so clever in hiding from us.

Lying next to me that night, my brother's youngest son, Jesse, is moaning and tossing in his sleep. He was fourteen years old then, about the same age as his father when we were making our gangster movies. Jesse and most of his friends like to dress like gangsters too, I've noticed—although their clothes are new and fashionable and purchased in shopping malls.

When it had come time to go to bed that night—as it had to, even on that night—Jesse had become anxious, agitated, and so I invited him to sleep on the sofa bed with me so that he wouldn't have to do the asking. I looked at him for a moment, trying to stare the nightmare out of him, and to my surprise it seemed to work. He grew still, and his breathing became deeper, more relaxed.

I got up to have a cigarette, partly because I had got the jitters again, and partly because I wanted an excuse to go out to the backyard. I went through the routine of pulling on all those damned clothes—a little unnerved at how badly

my Midwestern living skills have deteriorated in the last decade. Then I stepped
out the back door, half expecting the film to start rolling.

> But I haven't lived here in so long
> And everything has changed so much
> And the color is all wrong
> And there is sound when there should be silence
> And I'm so fucking cold
> That I just stood there, spinning around
> Looking for what was gone
> Lost in my own backyard.

Biograph theater today

FIGURE 7: BOB FISCHER/TJDF

In seeking to release knowledge from the vagaries of memory and performance, science has given us an impoverished sense of ourselves and of truth. Perhaps what we need now is a method that begins with *pronuntiatio* and *memoria*, that begins with performed memories, and then looks for a style, an arrangement, and a logic of invention that will serve them, rather than vice-versa. After all, memory, as any computer user knows, is where it's at in the post-literate age. In the future, all our inventional options will be determined by how big and buffed our memories are.

At home on my computer, I can put a tiny little icon at the bottom of my screen that will tell me how much memory I have left.

I like that.

Sometimes, I like to sit there at my desk, just remembering and writing and watching the meter turn from green to amber to red, trying to exhaust my memory, to keep on going until I run out of memory. If I run out of memory, I have to shut down for awhile.

I like that, too.

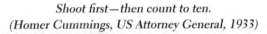

Shoot first—then count to ten.
(Homer Cummings, US Attorney General, 1933)

FIGURE 8: BOB FISCHER/TJDF

Mmmmmmmmm mmmm thinking
Moving across the world in cars
Body numbed from the neck down
Sweat eating my clothes

Moving across the world in cars
So if I had me a scientist's brain I'd say
Well our morals are genetic
Must be clear and unemotional now
Like the wiring diagram of a car
One must eliminate much
So when the bullet or voltage leaves you
Walk off see none of the thrashing
The very eyes popping like bad breakers
Believing then the moral of science or gun
Where bodies are mindless as plastic flowers you don't feed
Or give to drink
That is why I can watch the veins of highways
Squish beneath the wheels and go spinning off
And emerge living
For hours

Here's lookin' at you, kid

FIGURE 9: BOB FISCHER/TJDF

John Dillinger called me in the summer of 1968. I don't recall the exact date, but I'm certain it was in July—July of '68. He had been calling intermittently during the preceding ten years—ever since we'd moved to Mooresville in the summer of '59—but this was the first time that I was prepared to take the call.

Nineteen sixty-eight. That was a tough year.

In April of that year, my civics teacher, Mr. _____[4] had come into our classroom one afternoon, visibly upset. His eyes were red and his cheeks moist. His voice croaked as he told us what had happened in Memphis. Many of my classmates—not all of them, you understand, but most of the boys anyway—began to cheer and applaud in that obnoxious way that fifteen-year-old boys and talk show audiences do. Fists punching the air, feet stamping, subhuman grunts and growls.

He was a young man, my civics teacher, just a year or two out of college—a Kennedy man, who would always give me a hard time whenever I wore my McCarthy or Wallace buttons to class. But the look that came over his face that day in April was one I'd never seen before—the kind of look that a basically good and decent human being can get, I guess, when it is confronted with something so contemptible that it begins to mirror what it loathes. Mister Kurtz.[5]

He wanted to yell at us, I think, to call us names, maybe even hit somebody. And for just a second there it looked like he might launch into one of his impassioned lectures on "the meaning of democracy" and "the promise of American politics." But it was like he stopped believing it himself at that moment. The room got quiet as his face got redder and more twisted. *Let it out, man! Give us the money shot, baby!* But he didn't. He just gathered up his things and walked out.

Oh, he came back the next day, sort of. But he wouldn't talk to us—just turned it into a study hall. Not even McCarthy or Wallace would get a rise out of him. And in a couple of months, of course, his other hero would be dead, too. I don't know what ever happened to him, my civics teacher. He didn't come back to Mooresville in the fall of '68.

But I didn't know that then, because now it's only July of '68, and Doug Barnes and I are walking west on West Washington Street, the street we lived on, walking west and looking, walking west and looking for something, walking west and looking for something to do.

As we walked west, we heard an engine backfire from behind us as the driver of some vehicle downshifted making the turn onto West Washington Street, the street we lived on. Doug and I look back east over our shoulders in response to the noise to see a clapped out VW microbus painted up like a goddamned Easter egg with a big yellow peace sign on the side of it.

Now, growing up in Mooresville, Indiana, I'd seen all sorts of strange things—floods, fires, knife fights, gun fights, gang rapes—hell, I'd even seen goats fuck.

And Russell Soots, who lived with his wife and eight or twenty naked children in the basement of the beauty shop next door to us would sometimes get drunk enough that he'd geek a chicken for us. But I'd never seen a real, live hippie bus before.

Doug and I stop and stare as the van rattles and rolls past us, taking the *Make love not war* and *Hendrix is God* bumper stickers and the *New York license plate,* thinking to ourselves, here, surely, is one lost motherfucker.

Well, the van wheezes to a stop a few yards ahead of us. We hear the tranny grinding as the driver tries shifting gears again—the clutch in this thing is obviously shot to hell—and then the sumbitch starts backing up! Doug and I are frozen, unable to think. I tell you, a UFO could have landed there in front of us on West Washington Street and the sight would not have been any more incongruous than what we were seeing now. A few seconds of chug-a-chug-a-chug as the van backs up to the curb next to us. The engine spits once or twice, then shuts down completely.

Doug and I lean down to peer inside the van and—sure enough!—there's a couple of them longhaired hippie people we'd seen on the TV inside. The driver sticks his head out the window—I say "head," but it was just this thick, curly black bush of hair and beard with a pair of granny glasses set into it—looked just like Jerry Garcia, may he rest in peace. Next to him in the passenger seat is a skinny looking guy with even longer hair—thin-ish brown, clean shaven. Looked sorta like Todd Rundgren.

"Hey, man," says Jerry. "You live around here?" Doug and I point to our respective houses, which are only about 20 yards back east of us. "Well, man, we're looking for the John Dillinger museum. Can you give us directions?"

Doug and I look at each other, then back at Jerry. "Ain't no John Dillinger museum around here," I tell him.

Jerry looks at Todd and words are exchanged. Jerry picks up a map and points to something on it. "Well, this is Mooresville, isn't it? We're in the right town, aren't we?

"Yeah, this is Mooresville alright."

"Well, man, this is where John Dillinger's from," he tells me, as if I didn't know.

"Yeah, that's right. This is where he's from alright."

"Well, man, there's a John Dillinger museum around here somewhere."

"No they ain't." I say again, looking to Doug for support, but Doug is still too dumbstruck by what he's seeing.

"But, man, they—they had it in a book," he says, turning around as if to look for something. He and Todd exchange a few more words, then Todd crawls in the back of the van, disappearing for a few seconds. When he reappears, he has a thin paperback book clutched triumphantly in his hand. Jerry snatches it away from him and starts thumbing through it.

"Oh, right," I say, recognizing the book. "Yeah, *Trout Fishing in America*. Richard Brautigan. Page twelve or thirteen, I think." Jerry flips to the page automatically—and then he does a classic double take. Now, it's *his* turn to stop and stare.

"Man, you read this book?"

I shrug. "Sure. It's all bullshit, though."

Here's what Brautigan has to say:

Mooresville, Indiana, is the town that John Dillinger came from, and the town has a John Dillinger Museum. You can go in and look around.

Some towns are known as the peach capital of America or the cherry capital of America or the oyster capital, and there's always a festival and the photograph of a pretty girl in a bathing suit.

Mooresville, Indiana, is the John Dillinger capital of America.

Recently a man moved there with his wife, and he discovered hundreds of rats in his basement. They were huge, slow-moving child-eyed rats.

When his wife had to visit some of her relatives for a few days, the man went out and bought a .38 revolver and a lot of ammunition. Then he went down to the basement where the rats were, and he started shooting them. It didn't bother the rats at all. They acted as if it were a movie and started eating their dead companions for popcorn.

The man walked over to a rat that was busy eating a friend and placed the pistol against the rat's head. The rat did not move and continued eating away. When the hammer clicked back, the rat paused between bites and looked out of the corner of its eye. First at the pistol and then at the man. It was a kind of friendly look as if to say, "When my mother was young she sang like Deanna Durbin."

The man pulled the trigger.

He had no sense of humor.

There's always a single feature, a double feature and an eternal feature playing at the Great Theater in Mooresville, Indiana: the John Dillinger capital of America.[6]

"It's all bullshit," I tell them. I didn't figure they'd be interested in seeing the rats.

A few seconds of silence, then Jerry starts howling with laughter. "Man," he says to Todd, "do you believe this? They've got freaks in this town!" He looks at me again, laughing just as merrily as the Dancing Bear himself used to do, may he rest in peace.

"I ain't a freak," I object lamely—making sure, nonetheless, to do my best cute little aw-shucks Hoosier farm boy routine.

He just laughs and laughs, "You read *this* book, man, you're a fucking freak!" I guess he and Todd had been hitting the jokey-smoke a little hard that day. But he eventually ran out of gas and got serious again. "So, man, you're sure there's no Dillinger museum here?"

"Nope. Sorry. There's no museum." They looked so—I dunno—disappointed, you know, and they'd come all the way from New York, so I thought I'd try to cheer 'em up. "But his house is still here."

"*Really?*"

"Yeah."

"Maybe the museum's in the house?"

"No, man, it's just a house—just a regular old farm house. People live in it."

He looks at Todd and they hold a brief conference. "Okay, man, where is it? We'll check it out—maybe they'll let us look around."

Yeah, sure—I bet they will, I thought. But I started to give him directions anyway. "Just go down to the end of the street, turn right, and go about—"

"No, man. C'mon. Hop in. Show us, okay?"

Doug and I look at each other—and Doug suddenly thinks he hears his mother calling him and takes off. And me?

I got on the bus.

Image is everything

FIGURE 10: BOB FISCHER/TJDF

John Dillinger was in prison for most of his adult life, and though he is known to history as a vicious gangster, his actual "career" as a criminal was very brief— too brief, certainly, to be conflated with the story of an entire life. If it is true that

Dillinger was killed on the night of July 22, 1934, as he left the Biograph theater in Chicago, then he would have lived only thirty-one years and one month. He was in prison between the ages of twenty-one and thirty. His criminal "career" lasted a mere thirteen months, and the vast majority of writing about him focuses on that last thirteen months, when, as one observer remarked, his name became a by-word in every continent on the globe.

The other thirty years find no place in the iconography of Depression-era outlaws like Dillinger, and they are not to be found in the landscape popular-ized by Mario Puzo and Francis Ford Coppola, and currently kept before us in the seemingly inexhaustible series of cable TV programs on mobsters, mass murderers, forensic science, FBI stories, bad-boys-bad-boys-whatcha-gonna-do, and so on.

Dillinger came from a small-town, Midwestern household far away from the urban, ethnic communities that gave us our Italian, Jewish, and Irish mobsters—a household in which "family" was not at all important—nor even much of anything at all. Surrounded as a boy and a young man by an articulated poli-tics of identity—though one that hasn't come into the radarscope of any identity studies I've seen—Johnny Dillinger became an outlaw, the only political form that allowed him to reveal what Carolyn Steedman might call "the politics of envy."[7]

Or, as Johnnie himself once put it: "I'd like to have enough money to enjoy life: be clear of everything—not worry, take care of my old man and see a ball game every day."[8]

Dillinger Framed

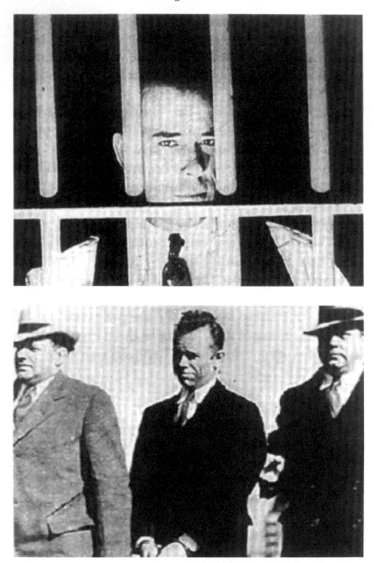

FIGURE 11: BOB FISCHER/TJDF

   I wish I had a story about me not from their eyes. Find a beginning then, the tiny picture put in mama's locket when they took her off to I guess heaven, to say it this is me remember me. Here is the place to begin in, to be in:

In April Billie and me criss-crossed the border between Indiana and Illinois. A few miles east of it a few miles west of it. Our car slipped from state to state, across little rivers, through different colors of fields. The two of us, our criss-cross like the loop-de-loop at the Chicago fair, the ridge of action rising and falling, getting narrower in radius till it ended and we drifted down to Mooresville and old folks at home.

I know what you will say that there is nothing of special interest there, of detail in this picture, I know. It is there for a beginning, for a place to be in.

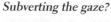

FIGURE 12: BOB FISCHER/TJDF

When Dillinger and his friends were apprehended in Tucson, Arizona, in January, 1934, it quickly developed into what we would now call a media circus. The states of Indiana, Illinois, Ohio, and Wisconsin all sent their attorneys general to Tucson to make their respective cases for extradition, and reporters and photographers from around the country were there to record every rumor and bit of gossip about the backstage wrangling to determine who would get the privilege of killing Dillinger. A bargain was eventually struck, and Indiana came away with possession of Dillinger, while Ohio had to settle for his friends, Harry Pierpont, Charlie Makley, and Russell Clark. (Illinois and Wisconsin went home empty-handed.)

During the long series of flights from Arizona to Chicago, photographers and reporters would converge on the airplane wherever it landed. The motorcade from Chicago to Crown Point, Indiana, where Dillinger was to be tried, was said to have been nearly 100 cars long, with half those cars filled with Illinois cops, Indiana cops, Indiana National Guardsmen, and vigilantes of every stripe, and the other half with reporters and other curious individuals eager to get a glimpse of the celebrity outlaw.

Meanwhile, at the "escape-proof" jail in Crown Point, Prosecuting Attorney Robert Estill had arranged for reporters, photographers, and a film crew to be present for Dillinger's arrival. Estill was preparing to make a run for the Indiana Governor's mansion, you see, and he wasn't about to miss this opportunity to have himself pictured as "The Man Who Got Dillinger."

When Dillinger arrived, everyone was surprised by his behavior. Instead of snarling and growling and kicking and screaming like Jimmy Cagney and other famous gangsters, he was friendly, outgoing, polite. And when Estill finally managed to push the crowd back and get everyone in position for the pictures that would kick off his gubernatorial campaign, Dillinger casually slipped his arm over the DA's shoulder and smiled—and Estill, no doubt acting on reflex, did likewise.

But when Dillinger escaped from Estill's "escape-proof" jail a few weeks later, with a piece of wood that had been carved into the shape of a gun, this photo began to take on a different meaning than the one Estill had intended. Estill's career was effectively finished, while Johnnie was now one of the most famous men in the world.

Is one obliged to reject one's culture before one begins to think?

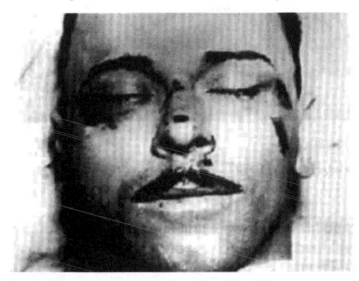

FIGURE 13: BOB FISCHER/TJDF

When I thought of him dying
Tossed several feet by bang maybe giggling
In surprise face tossed salad on contact
Pissing in his pants in pain
Face changing fast like jiffy lube o my god
My god I'm pissing myself how embarrassing

While the strangers' hands flew all over his body.

A Half-Sunday Homage to a Whole Water Benjamin
(with apologies to Richard Brautigan)⁹

FIGURE 14: BOB FISCHER/TJDF

On this funky Sunday morning in October, I've been thinking of Walter Benjamin. Ruth is out slaving away, no day off, a show to put up this week. She left here this morning before I woke up. I've been sitting here at my desk all morning like a turd in the cat box I should probably clean out before she gets home, dreaming of Walter Benjamin.

I dreamed he was working the graveyard shift at the Circle K down at the corner of Highland and State, just off campus there—and of course he was wearing one of those brown and orange smocks they have to wear and speaking without a German accent and the possessor of a different childhood from the one he'd had in Berlin. Maybe a southern Indiana childhood spent in a town like Mooresville or Bean Blossom or French Lick.

I saw him scribbling new theses on the killing of John Dillinger. I saw him working first of all with his *Denkbilder*—though he didn't call them that now because he didn't speak German anymore because that was against the law. He called them "pictures-in-my-brain." Then he started working with various items in the Circle K—empty cigarette cartons, half-pints of cheap liquor, *USA Today* (weekend edition), 55-gallon go-cups of Diet Coke, boxes of Hamburger Helper that have the little hand-man on them for the logo.

Being a shy and somewhat secretive man, he would not show his new theses to just anyone who walked in for five dollars' worth of unleaded. He showed them first to his friends, Rashmi and Vijay Parameshwar, the husband-and-wife team who were working the morning shift until they had enough to put down on their own Circle K. They looked at his theses and fainted dead away. Alone, standing over their sleeping forms, he held his theses in his hand and gave them a name. He called them, The work of art in the age of its technical reproducibility, because even though he did not speak German, he could still provide a better translation than Harry Zohn. Then he went about reviving his friends.

In a matter of months his theses were the sensation of the twentieth century, far out-stripping such shallow accomplishments as Hiroshima, Tranquility Base, or Titanic. Millions of copies of the work of art in the age of its technical reproducibility were sold in America. Paris and Berlin ordered ten thousand copies each, and they don't even have any Circle K's there.

Testimonials poured in. J. Edgar Hoover wrote, "Ten million public enemies were apprehended with the work of art in the age of its technical reproducibility."

Souvenirs

FIGURE 15: BOB FISCHER/TJDF

Dear Sis,

I thought I would write you a few lines and let you know I am still
perculating. Don't worry about me honey, for that won't help any, and
besides I am having a lot of fun. I am sending Emmett my wooden gun
and I want him to allways keep it. I see that Deputy Blunk says I had a real
forty five that's just a lot of hooey to cover up because they don't like to
admit that I locked eight deputys and a dozen trustys up with my wooden
gun before I got my hands on the two machine guns and you should have
seen their faces Ha! Ha! Ha! Pulling that off was worth ten years of my life
Ha! Ha! Dont part with my wooden gun for any price For when you feel
blue all you will have to do is look at the gun and laugh your blues away
Ha! Ha! I will be around to see all of you when the roads are better, it is
so hot around Indiana now that I would have trouble getting through so I
am sending my wife Billie. She will have a hundred dollars for you and a
hundred for Norman. I'll give you enough money for a new car the next

time I come around. I told Bud I would get him one and I want to get Dad
one. Now honey if any of you need any thing I won't forgive you if you
dont let me know. I got shot a week ago but I am all right now just a little
sore I ban one tough sweed Ha! Ha! Well honey I guess Ill close for the
time give my love to all and I hope I can see you soon.
Lots of love from Johnnie.[10]

Discourse on Method, fragments

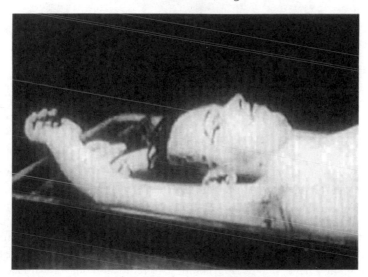

FIGURE 16: BOB FISCHER/TJDF

In any discourse on method, one can usually find a corpse. Julia Kristeva
links the detective story/murder mystery to writing in terms of "sacrifice" as the
founding moment of civilization, marking the frontier or boundary between
nature and culture. The founding violence marked in the murder of the sacri-
ficial victim, the rupture that sets the symbolic economy going, still resonates in
the irruption of the semiotic into the symbolic in the practice of textuality.[11] The
ritual performance accompanying the sacrifice, identified as the laboratory of all
art, repeats the symbolic economy itself: "The reenacting of the signifying path
taken from the symbolic unfolds the symbolic itself and—through the border that
sacrifice is about to present or has already presented on stage—opens it up to the
motility where all meaning is erased."[12] The purpose of inscribing the discourses
of mystory into the diegesis of a slide show or photo essay is to try to make appear
the trace of this frontier.

Discourse on Method, fragments (cont.)

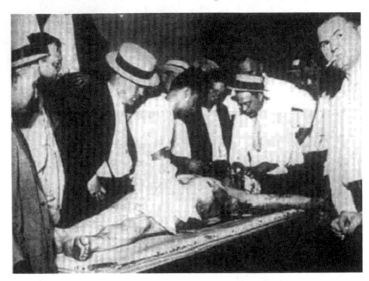

FIGURE 17: BOB FISCHER/TJDF

By way of an analogy or conceit, I would like to say that doing performance research and writing are akin to the activities of a legendary outlaw since, in both, the idiomatic (one's personal or private discourse) joins with the institutional (the recognized "grammar" of one's discipline) in order to rewrite (or, in Brecht's terms, refunction) an object of study. For the famous outlaw, this means projecting one's inimitable style or signature onto the grammar of law-breaking (e.g., robbing a bank) in order to recompose or refunction our standard attitudes toward "law and order."

Discourse on Method, fragments (cont.)

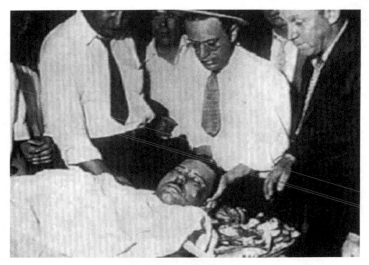

FIGURE 18: BOB FISCHER/TJDF

The illiteracy of the future will be ignorance not of reading or writing,
but of photography.
    —László Moholy-Nagy[13]

One reason for choosing a famous outlaw like John Dillinger as a model of
performance research and writing is because of the general interest in the outlaw/
trickster figure among scholars of performance and cultural studies. I agree
whole-heartedly with my friends in performance and cultural studies who have
suggested that we must, in the words of Donna Haraway, learn to speak Coyote.[14]
                    Do you want it soft? Or hard?
But I wonder sometimes whether we in performance and cultural studies are
interested in talking to a *real* Coyote.
                    Dill-in-jer. Dill-een-grrrr.

Discourse on Method, fragments (cont.)

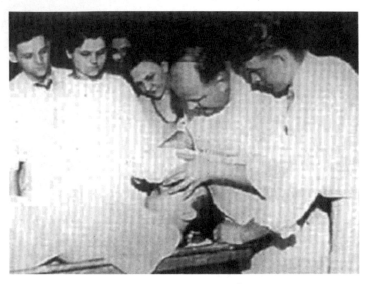

FIGURE 19: BOB FISCHER/TJDF

[. . .] social relations between the two nations are realized and lived as
a modality of immediate bodily intersubjectivity.
—Michael Jackson, "Penis Snatchers"[15]

And I wonder, too, whether we in performance and cultural studies will be
willing to stick around long enough, after we have our talks with Coyote, to see
what happens to Coyote.

Discourse on Method, fragments (concl.)

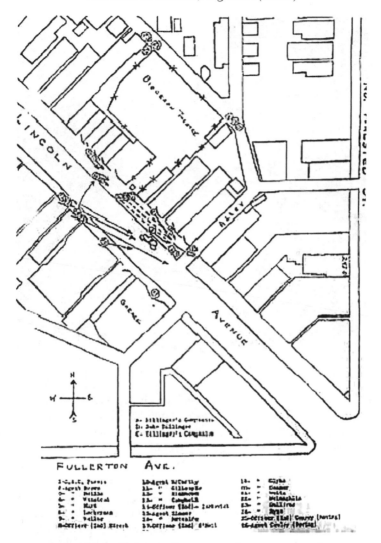

FIGURE 20: FEDERAL BUREAU OF INVESTIGATION[16]

There is no magic in effective law enforcement, no Sherlock Holmes theorizing or fictional deduction, but [. . .] before science all things must fall [. . .].

—J. Edgar Hoover, "The Adventure of Scientific Crime Control," 1937[17]

Polly + Anna

FIGURE 21: BOB FISCHER/TJDF

The Biograph theater at 2433 North Lincoln Avenue in Chicago has only one entrance, though it has several exits. Anna Sage, who is known to history as "the woman in red," emerged from this entrance at about 10:35 p.m. on July 22, 1934, after seeing a gangster movie, *Manhattan Melodrama*, starring Clark Gable, Myrna Loy, and William Powell. Walking next her as she emerged from the theater were two other people: a younger woman named Polly Hamilton Keele and Polly's companion for the evening, a man known to the two women as Jimmy Lawrence. As the handsome gangster, Blackie, played by Gable, marched defiantly to the electric chair at the end of the film, the three of them headed for the exit to beat the crowd. Others had the same idea, though, and when they came out of the theater, they were surrounded by others.

They turned left, walking southeast on Lincoln, and Polly slipped her hand through Jimmy's arm, because he liked it when she did that. As they passed by the first darkened doorway on their left, Jimmy looked incuriously at the man standing there holding an unlit cigar in his mouth. Anna had dropped back a step or so behind Polly and Jimmy, and when the man in the doorway noticed her bright orange skirt, his eyes darted quickly back to Jimmy and Polly, while his hands fumbled to strike a match to light his cigar.

As Jimmy continued to walk with Polly on his arm, he looked at the men in the car parked at the curb, and he looked at the man standing in the second doorway, and then he glanced back over his shoulder to see the men rushing up behind him from all directions pulling guns from their pockets. He gave Polly a little shove, crouched down, and took a couple of quick, waddling steps toward the alley in front of him. Several shots were fired—it is impossible now to say how many, though most accounts put the number at five—and the man who called himself Jimmy Lawrence fell face down in the alley.

A moment later, Special Agent Melvin Purvis leaned down, tossing his cigar aside, glanced quickly at the battered, bleeding face of a man he had never seen before, and asked, "What's the procedure now?" A few minutes later, the word spread among the assembled crowd that John Dillinger was dead.

Polly and Anna had disappeared.

Maybe bodies become "ours" when we recognize them as traumatic [. . .] The holes in them help us feel attached.
(Peggy Phelan)

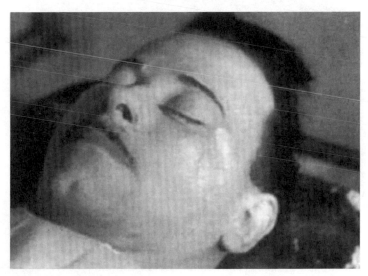

FIGURE 22: BOB FISCHER/TJDF

Jesus, I never knew that did you
The holes punched out
All filled up with bond-o
Like rust spots on a Chevrolet
Seen that at the body shop many times
Never driven a Chevy since then

The body in performance

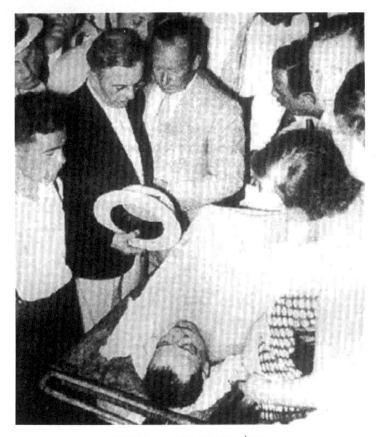

FIGURE 23: BOB FISCHER/TJDF

After shooting Johnnie
This is what happened

They'd shot him well and from the back
Made it explode under his right eye
So he wouldn't last long and couldn't run away again

Shoot first then count to ten
Minutes just to make sure
Then call the meat wagon

So many ghouls were hanging out
Ten to twenty thousand by some people's guess
That they propped him up and let 'em have a look

Twenty-five cents a head
They filed past all night long
Who says crime doesn't pay

He looked like any other fellow
One woman said
Only dead
I'll probably go through again I guess
I mean it's a moral lesson
Right?

Dillinger's Penis

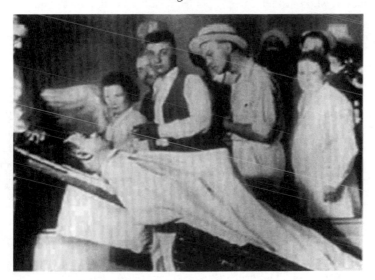

FIGURE 24: BOB FISCHER/TJDF

All narratives are about castration, right? Well, so is this one. At this point we have a crossing of the hermeneutic and the symbolic codes of our story.

Legend has it that our man was very well endowed. His penis was said to have been twenty-two or twenty-three inches long, and rumors circulated at the time that he had killed several women with it.

This photo was the first one published in the Chicago papers that next morning, and the tent-pole effect makes it appear as if the corpse has an erection—and a pretty darned big one at that. The effect is actually said to have been produced by rigor mortis in his arm—but, then, a twenty-two- or twenty-three-inch penis, fully erect, would be about as big as your arm, wouldn't it?

I've seen another version of this photo that shows several men standing around the corpse, grinning stupidly at the camera. Apparently, the police officers and reporters and doctors who were fuckin' off down at the Cook County Morgue that night had cut off about a two-foot section of broom handle and propped it up between the corpse's legs as a joke. Ha, ha, ha.

Another motif of the legend of Dillinger's penis is that it was amputated during the autopsy, preserved in formaldehyde, and sent as a trophy to J. Edgar Hoover, along with the death mask, the gun he supposedly had on him that night, and other personal effects. Unlike the gun and the death mask, however, Hoover couldn't very well keep a penis on display outside his office, and so he supposedly sent it either to the Smithsonian or the National Archives.

This macabre legend produced a hysterical sort of response from the FBI and Hoover, who must have been apoplectic at the thought that popular culture kept undermining their efforts to control the meaning of Dillinger as a small-time rat and preferred seeing him as a super-potent outlaw/trickster figure. The FBI tried to quash the rumor of Dillinger's extraordinary penis size, as well as the stories of his attractiveness to and success with women, by planting stories in the press from "confidential informants" that he was both impotent and violent with women.

Following the passage of the Freedom of Information Act, the FBI was forced to respond to the hundreds of inquiries about Dillinger's penis—and to conduct a search for it. The Bureau's internal memoranda regarding the fabled phallus have, of course, only added fuel to the fire of some conspiracy theorists, who suggest that if the Federal Government has gone to all this trouble to deny the rumor, it must be true. Now, both the National Archives and the Smithsonian have form letters to send in response to all such inquiries. The one from the Smithsonian reads:

> In response to your recent inquiry, we can assure you that anatomical specimens of John Dillinger are not, and have never been, in the collections of the Smithsonian Institution. Enclosed is a brochure describing our museums.
> Your interest in the Smithsonian Institution is appreciated.[18]

Home, sweet home

FIGURE 25: BOB FISCHER/TJDF

One of the more persistent legends about Dillinger, when I was growing up in Mooresville in the '60s, was that he was still alive.

After my encounter with Jerry and Todd, it became a matter of some importance to me to find out all I could about Dillinger. I went to the town library, which was cattycornered from our house out the back alley. The town librarian, one Bonita Marley, lived just two houses down from us, across the alley from the library. I'd known Mrs. Marley almost all my life: (1) because I'd be in her library two or three times a week checking out books, and (2) because I'd been in trouble so many times for playing in her yard.

Bonita Marley's library was one of those Carnegie things that were put up all over the country back in the early part of the century—an impressive enough edifice for a small town like Mooresville. As I recall, though, it didn't have anything like a card catalog in which one might look up a book in the normal way most of you probably grew accustomed to as children. No, Mrs. Marley arranged her library according to her own system, one that sorted the books in terms of their suitability for different audiences. The library stacks were divided neatly along gender lines, for example. If you were a male, books suitable for you would be found on the left as you entered the building, females on the right. When you were young, you'd start at the south end of the building and gradually work your way north as you got older. I suppose it was the same for the females. I don't know because I never went on the right side of the library. Mrs. Marley's toady—an anonymous, dwarfish woman—would prowl the stacks, making sure you didn't stray into an area you didn't belong.

So, late one afternoon, I casually wandered into the section for adult males—getting exactly the same sheepish, burning feeling I would get a couple years later when I walked into an adult book store for the first time—and started madly perusing the shelves looking for anything to do with Dillinger. I knelt down between the stacks to look at the bottom shelves and a shadow passed over me.

"What are you looking for, Mike?" Mrs. Marley asked—quietly, of course, but inflected in such a way that told me I was busted.

"I'm looking for books on John Dillinger," I told her. Her eyes got wide, and I think she may have been stunned momentarily, as if I'd just asked to see this month's *Playboy.* "For school," I added quickly. "I have to do a report for school."

Mrs. Marley collected herself. Her eyes closed, she swallowed hard, and her hands balled up into little fists at her sides. Then she looked at me and said, "We don't have any books like that. And even if we did, you shouldn't . . . be interested in them."

There was nothing I could do. I left the library and walked back home, upset and angry for some reason I couldn't articulate, other than to call her the same names I'd been calling her for ten years. When I got home I started slamming doors and making a ruckus in one of my usual God-I-hate-this-fucking-town teen temper tantrums. My mother, in her usual annoying way, responded by acting sweet and concerned, and so I told her what had happened.

Her reaction was not as I expected, however. Instead of telling me to calm down, instead of telling me, yes, dear, this town is filled with morons, and I'm sorry you have to live here, she got pissed off, too. She picked up the phone, dialed the library, and started reading Mrs. Marley the riot act. "Now, Bonita, I know you've got *something* over there on John Dillinger. He's the only famous person ever to come out of this godforsaken town, so you've probably got everything anybody ever wrote about him over there. Now, I'm sending Michael back over there, and you give him whatever he wants. *I'll* decide what he can read and what he can't, *not you!*"

I walked back to the library. And Mrs. Marley met me at the door. I mumbled something to her about my mother making me come, hoping to pin the rap on her, but she just crooked a finger at me and said, "Come with me."

I followed her as she began to walk north—north to the checkout desk. I followed her as she continued to walk north—*behind* the checkout desk—farther north than I'd ever been before. I followed her as she came to the north wall of the library, which had a door that led to her office, and I waited while she unlocked the door and opened it and ushered me inside.

I looked around the office, hardly believing my eyes. Inside were shelves—floor to ceiling—filled with books. As I stood there, Mrs. Marley closed the door behind us, then she moved past me to hone in on a section of shelving. She put her glasses on and scanned the shelf for a moment, then laid her hand gently on the spines of a couple of books. "Here," she said. "There isn't much. Really. But take whatever you want."

I stepped over to the shelf and looked at the three books that had Dillinger in the title. I pulled one out tentatively, looking at Mrs. Marley to make sure she wasn't going to change her mind.

"These books don't circulate," she explained. "I don't let these books out. Except in special circumstances. But go ahead, take them."

I looked at the newest one, *Dillinger: Dead or Alive?* by Jay Robert Nash. The book purported to prove that Dillinger had not been killed in Chicago in 1934; that the FBI had killed the wrong man and had covered up the mistake; and that Dillinger had taken this opportunity to make good on his oft-stated plans to leave the criminal life behind, to disappear with his loot, and to live out his life in anonymity.

Mrs. Marley sucked her tooth and shook her head as we read the dust jacket blurbs together. I looked at her and saw that her expression had changed. She was almost . . . smiling.

"Is this true?" I asked her. She made one of those sounds that a Booth Tarkington or a James Whitcomb Riley might represent as "pshaw," but which sounded to me more like "shee-it."

"No, honey—no, no!" she chuckled. "No. He's dead—long dead." Her laughter died away in a sigh, and she had an odd look in her eye. I saw it, and she saw me see it. Her eyes flew away momentarily before coming back to land on me again. Then she folded her arms across her ample bosom and became the librarian again. "Well. You've got what you wanted. Don't worry about checking them out. Keep them until you're done with your report. Now go on. I have to close up now."

"*Wait just a minute!*" I wanted to say. "You know something you're not telling me. What is it? Tell me! Tell me everything!"

I didn't know what ethnography was then. I only had my own untutored research skills to work with. I didn't know that it was okay to ask people rude questions about subjects they were uncomfortable with. So I left and let Mrs. Marley close up again.

To write history is to quote history
(Walter Benjamin)

FIGURE 26: BOB FISCHER/TJDF

Today, the spot where it happened is unmarked. There are no signs, no plaques, no tablets, nor even anything so crude as a taped-down "X" to signal to passersby that something happened here once.

It is remembered, however, in oral traditions, such as the ghost stories that tell of an apparition of a man, surrounded in bluish light, who can be seen walking into the alley, falling down, pulling himself back up, and running off down the alley, disappearing as he goes. Or the people who tell of feeling suddenly cold or chilly when they pass the spot, even on hot July days. Or of feeling suddenly anxious or afraid that someone is about to attack them from behind.

Each year on July 22, a group of enthusiasts known as the John Dillinger Died for You Society gathers at the Biograph theater to take pictures of each other in their gangster garb, to have drinks at the bar next door, to challenge each other with Dillinger trivia questions, and to tell about the latest bits of Dillinger memorabilia they've added to their collections.

Sixty-five years later, unmarked though it may be, people are still drawn to the Biograph theater for some reason. Every now and then, you can see one of them standing there, spinning around, looking for what isn't there, lost in their own gangster dreams.

For David
28 Sept. 54–2 Dec. 97

FIGURE 27: PHOTO BY FREDERICK C. STEWART

Notes

1. Bob Fischer, *The John Dillinger File*, Outlaw Archives, 1997–2000. Subsequent references to this site will be abbreviated TJDF.

2. Paul H. Gray, "Calling the Cops." Paper presented at the annual meeting of the National Communication Association. Chicago, 22 Nov. 1997.

3. I've paraphrased Ms. Kinder's remark. The original is quoted in Robert Cromie and Joseph Pinkston, *Dillinger: A Short and Violent Life* (1962; Evanston, IL: Chicago Historical Bookworks, 1990) 83.

4. I'm not being coy. I just don't remember his name.

5. No, that wasn't his name.

6. Richard Brautigan, *Trout Fishing in America* (1967; Boston: Houghton, 1989) 13.

7. Carolyn Steedman, *Landscape for a Good Woman: A Story of Two Lives* (London: Virago, 1986) 7.

8. Qtd. in William Helmer with Rick Mattix, *Public Enemies: America's Criminal Past, 1919-1940* (New York: Routledge, 1991) 199–201.

9. Cf. Brautigan, *Trout Fishing* 108.

10. Letter to Audrey (Dillinger) Hancock; qtd in John Toland, *The Dillinger Days* (New York: Random, 1963) 244–45.

11. Julia Kristeva, *Revolution in Poetic Language*, trans. Margaret Waller (New York: Columbia UP, 1984) 77.

12. Kristeva 79.

13. Qtd. in Eduardo Cadava, *Words of Light: Theses on the Photography of History* (Princeton, NJ: Princeton UP, 1997) xxx.

14. E.g. Dwight Conquergood, "Beyond the Text: Toward a Performative Cultural Politics," *The Future of Performance Studies: Visions and Revisions*, ed. Sheron J. Dailey (Annandale, VA: National Communication Association, 1998) 25–36; cf. Donna J. Haraway, *Simians, Cyborgs, and Women: The Reinvention of Nature* (New York: Routledge, 1991) 199–201.

15. Michael Jackson, *Minima Ethnographica: Intersubjectivity and the Anthropological Project* (Chicago: U of Chicago P, 1998) 50.

16. Federal Bureau of Investigation, "Dillinger, John," 1 Dec. 1998 [exerpts from file #JODIL 62-29777 in PDF format].

17. Qtd. in Richard Gid Powers, *G-MEN: The FBI in American Popular Culture* (Carbondale, IL: Southern Illinois UP, 1983) 136.

18. Qtd. in William J. Helmer, "After the Facts: Further Investigations," in G. Russell Girardin with William J. Helmer, *Dillinger: The Untold Story* (Bloomington: Indiana UP, 1994) 313.

SELECTED BIBLIOGRAPHY

Abrams, M. H. *The Mirror and the Lamp: Romantic Theory and the Critical Tradition*. New York: Oxford University Press, 1953.

Adler, Stella. *The Art of Acting*. New York: Applause, 2000.

Ahmad, Dohra, ed. *Rotten English: A Literary Anthology*. New York: Norton, 2007.

Albee, Edward. *The American Dream and the Zoo Story*. New York: Signet, 1973.

Algarín, Miguel, and Bob Holman, eds. *Aloud: Voices from the Nuyorican Poets Café*. New York: H. Holt, 1994.

Amis, Martin. *Time's Arrow*. New York: Harmony, 1991.

Anzaldúa, Gloria. *Borderlands = La Frontera*. San Francisco: Aunt Lute Books, 1999.

Aristotle. *Poetics*. Malcolm Heath, trans. New York: Penguin, 1997.

Atwood, Margaret. *Good Bones and Simple Murders*. New York: Nan A. Talese, Doubleday, 1994.

Auden, W. H. *Collected Poems*. Edward Mendelson, ed. London: Faber, 2007.

Austen, Jane. *Love and Freindship*. Foreword by Fay Weldon. London: Hesperus, 2003.

Austin, Gilbert. *Chironomia*. Mary Margaret Robb and Lester Thonssen, eds. Carbondale, Ill.: Southern Illinois University Press, 1966.

Austin, J. L. *How to Do Things with Words*. Cambridge, Mass.: Harvard University Press, 1962.

Baatz, Simon. *For the Thrill of It: Leopold, Loeb, and the Murder That Shocked Chicago*. New York: Harper, 2008.

Bacon, Wallace A. *The Art of Interpretation*, 2nd ed. New York: Holt Rinehart Winston, 1972.

Bakhtin, Mikhail M. *The Dialogic Imagination: Four Essays*. Michael Holquist, ed., Vadim Liapunov, trans. Austin: University of Texas Press, 1982.

Beckett, Samuel. *Waiting for Godot*. New York: Grove, 1954.

Bell, Madison Smartt. *Toussaint Louverture: A Biography*. New York: Pantheon Books, 2007.

Bellow, Saul. *Mr. Sammler's Planet*. New York: Viking, 1970.

Benedict, Ruth. *The Chrysanthemum and the Sword: Patterns of Japanese Culture.* Boston: Houghton Mifflin, 1946, 1989.

——. *Patterns of Culture.* Boston: Houghton Mifflin, 1934.

Bentley, Phyllis. *Some Observations on the Art of Narrative.* New York: Macmillan, 1947.

Berry, Cicely. *Voice and the Actor.* New York: Macmillan, 1973.

Berryman, John. *77 Dream Songs.* New York: Farrar, Straus and Giroux, 1964.

Bhabha, Homi K. *The Location of Culture.* London: Routledge, 1994.

——. *Nation and Narration.* London: Routledge, 1990.

Blake, William. *Songs of Innocence and Experience: Shewing the Two Contrary States of the Human Soul, 1789–1794.* New York: Oxford University Press, 1977.

Blum, Joshua, Bob Holman, and Mark Pellington. *The United States of Poetry.* New York: H. N. Abrams, 1996.

Boal, Augusto. *Theatre of the Oppressed.* Charles A. and Maria-Odilia Leal McBride, trans. New York: Urizen Books, 1979.

Boas, Franz. *Anthropology and Modern Life.* New York: Norton, 1928.

——. *Race, Language, and Culture.* New York: Macmillan, 1940.

Boas, Franz, ed. *General Anthropology.* Boston: Heath, 1938.

Booth, Wayne C. *The Rhetoric of Fiction,* rev. ed. Chicago: University of Chicago Press, 1983.

——. *The Rhetoric of Irony.* Chicago: University of Chicago Press, 1974.

Bowe, John, Marisa Bowe, and Sabin Streeter. *Gig: Americans Talk About Their Jobs.* New York: Three Rivers, 2001.

Bowman, Michael. "Killing Dillinger: A Mystory." *Text and Performance Quarterly,* vol. 20, no. 4 (October 2000): 342–74.

Brooks, Gwendolyn. *Beckonings.* Detroit: Broadside Press, 1975.

Browning, Robert. *The Poetical Works of Robert Browning,* vols. 3 and 4. Ian Jack and Rowena Fowler, eds. New York: Oxford University Press, 1988

Burke, Kenneth. *A Grammar of Motives.* New York: Prentice-Hall, 1945.

Butler, Judith. *Gender Trouble: Feminism and the Subversion of Identity.* New York: Routledge, 1990.

Butler, Robert Olen. *Had a Good Time: Stories from American Postcards.* New York: Grove/Atlantic, 2004.

Capote, Truman. *In Cold Blood: A True Account of a Multiple Murder and Its Consequences.* New York: The Modern Library, 1965.

Card, Orson Scott. *Ender's Game.* New York: Tom Doherty Associates, 1991.

Carlson, Marvin. *Performance: A Critical Introduction,* 2nd ed. New York: Routledge, 2004.

Carlyle, Thomas. *The French Revolution: A History.* New York: E. P. Dutton, 1929.

Carter, Forrest. *The Education of Little Tree: A True Story.* Albuquerque: University of New Mexico Press, 1993; originally published: New York: Delacorte Press, 1976.

Cather, Willa. *The Troll Garden.* New York: McClure, 1905.

Chatman, Seymour. *Story and Discourse: Narrative Structure in Fiction and Film.* Ithaca, N.Y.: Cornell University Press, 1990.

Chomsky, Noam. *Aspects of the Theory of Syntax.* Cambridge, Mass.: MIT Press, 1965.

Churchill, Caryl. *Drunk Enough to Say I Love You.* New York: Theatre Communications Group, 2007.

Clifford, James. *The Predicament of Culture: Twentieth-Century Ethnography, Literature, and Art.* Cambridge, Mass.: Harvard University Press, 1988.

Coleridge, Samuel Taylor. *The Poems of Samuel Taylor Coleridge.* Ernest Hartley Coleridge, ed. London: Oxford University Press, 1912.

Conquergood, Dwight. "Performing as a Moral Act: Ethical Dimensions of the Ethnography of Performance." *Literature in Performance,* vol. 5 (April 1985).

Corso, Gregory. *The Vestal Lady on Brattle, and Other Poems.* San Francisco: City Lights Books, 1955, 1969.

Couser, G. Thomas. *Vulnerable Subjects: Ethics and Life Writing.* Ithaca, N.Y.: Cornell University Press, 2004.

Cresswell, Tim. *Place: A Short Introduction.* New York: Wiley-Blackwell, 2004.

Crown, Kathleen. "'Sonic Revolutionaries': Voice and Experiment in the Spoken Word Poetry of Tracie Morris." In *We Who Love to Be Astonished: Experimental Women's Writing and Performance Poetics.* Laura Hinton and Cynthia Hogue, eds. Tuscaloosa: University of Alabama Press, 2002.

Davis, Charlotte Aull. *Reflexive Ethnography: A Guide to Researching Selves and Others.* London: Routledge, 1999.

Delaney, David. *Territory: A Short Introduction.* Oxford: Blackwell Publishing, 2005.

Delsarte, François. *The Essential Delsarte.* John W. Zorn, ed. Metuchen, N.J.: Scarecrow Press, 1968.

Diamond, Jared. *Collapse: How Societies Choose to Fail or Succeed.* New York: Viking, 2005.

Dillard, Scott. "The Art of Performing Poetry: Festivals, Slams, and Americans' Favorite Poem Project Events." *Text and Performance Quarterly,* vol. 22, no. 3 (July 2002): 217–27.

Doty, Mark. *Dog Years: A Memoir.* New York: HarperCollins, 2007.

Eleveld, Mark, ed. *The Spoken Word Revolution.* Naperville, Ill.: Sourcebooks MediaFusion, 2005.

——. *The Spoken Word Revolution Redux.* Naperville, Ill.: Sourcebooks MediaFusion, 2007.

Eliot, T. S. *The Complete Poems and Plays of T. S. Eliot.* London: Faber, 1969.

Faulkner, William. *The Sound and the Fury.* New York: Vintage, 1991.

Fausto-Sterling, Anne. *Sexing the Body: Gender Politics and the Construction of Sexuality.* New York: Basic Books, 2000.

Fenske, Mindy. *Tattoos in American Visual Culture.* New York: Palgrave Macmillan, 2007.

Ferlinghetti, Lawrence. *A Coney Island of the Mind.* New York: New Directions, 2008.

——. *Pictures of the Gone World.* San Francisco: City Lights Books, 1955.

Ferris, Joshua. *Then We Came to the End.* Boston: Little, Brown, 2007.

Fisher, Hilda B. *Improving Voice and Articulation,* 2nd ed. Boston: Houghton Mifflin, 1972.

Forster. E. M. *Aspects of the Novel.* New York: Harcourt Brace, 1927, 1956.

——. *A Passage to India.* London: Edward Arnold, 1924.

Foucault, Michel. *Discipline and Punish: The Birth of the Prison.* New York: Pantheon Books, 1978.

——. *The Order of Things: An Archaeology of the Human Sciences.* New York: Pantheon, 1971.

Frost, Robert. *The Poetry of Robert Frost.* Edward Connery Lathem, ed. New York: Holt, Reinhart, and Winston, 1969.

Froude, James Anthony. *History of England from the Fall of Wolsey to the Defeat of the Spanish Armada, Volume XII.* London: Longmans, Green, 1870.

Gates, Henry Louis. *The Signifying Monkey: A Theory of Afro-American Literary Criticism.* New York: Oxford University Press, 1988.

Geertz, Clifford. *The Interpretation of Cultures.* New York: Basic, 1973.

——. "Blurred Genres: The Refiguration of Social Thought." In *The Performance Studies Reader,* 2nd ed. Henry Bial, ed. London: Routledge, 2007.

Genette, Gerard. *Narrative Discourse.* Jane E. Lewin, trans. Ithaca, N.Y.: Cornell University Press, 1980.

Gentile, John S. *Cast of One.* Urbana, Ill.: University of Illinois Press, 1989.

Gerstenberg, Alice. *Overtones.* In *Washington Square Plays,* Edward Goodman, ed. New York: Doubleday and Page, 1916; available online at http://www.one-act-plays.com/drama/overtones.html.

Gibson, William. *Neuromancer.* Garden City, N.Y.: Doubleday, 1962.

Ginsberg, Allen. *Collected Poems 1947–1980.* New York: HarperCollins Publishers, 1955.

Goffman, Erving. *Interaction Ritual: Essays on Face-to-Face Behavior.* New York: Anchor, 1967.

——. *The Presentation of Self in Everyday Life.* New York: Anchor, 1959.

Gottschall, Jonathan, and David Sloan Wilson, eds. *The Literary Animal: Evolution and the Nature of Narrative.* Forewords by E. O. Wilson and Frederick Crews. Evanston, Ill.: Northwestern University Press, 2005.

Goyen, William. *The House of Breath*. Evanston, Ill.: Triquarterly Books/Northwestern University Press, 1999.

Grealy, Lucy. *Autobiography of a Face*. Afterword by Ann Patchett. New York: Harper Perennial, 1995, 2003.

Grealy, Suellen. "Hijacked by Grief." *The Guardian*, August 7, 2004.

Greene, Graham. *The Comedians*. New York: Viking, 1966.

Gura, Timothy J. "The Solo Performer and Drama." *The Speech Teacher*, vol. 24 (1978): 278–81.

Gura, Timothy, and Charlotte Lee. *Oral Interpretation*, 11th ed. Boston: Houghton Mifflin, 2004.

Hagen, Uta, with Haskel Frankel. *Respect for Acting*. New York: Wiley, 1973.

Hamilton, Jane. "Rehearsing *The Firebird*." *Harper's Magazine*, June 1990, pp. 62–69.

Havelock, Eric. *Preface to Plato*. Cambridge, Mass.: Belknap Press, 1963.

Herodotus. *The History*. David Greene, trans. Chicago: University of Chicago Press, 1987.

Holman, Bob, and Joshua Blumand, producer/creators. *The United States of Poetry* [videorecording]. Washington Square Films; Independent Television Service. Mark Pellington, director. Miami Lake, Fla.: KQED Video, 1996.

hooks, bell. *Ain't I a Woman*. Boston: South End Press, 1981.

Hosack, John. *Mary Queen of Scots and Her Accusers*. Edinburgh, London: W. Blackwood, 1870–1874.

Hurston, Zora Neale. *Tell My Horse: Voodoo and Life in Haiti and Jamaica*. Foreword by Ismael Reed. San Bernardino, Calif.: Borgo Press, 1990; originally published: Berkeley, Calif.: Turtle Island Foundation, 1981.

Hwang, David Henry. *Yellow Face*. New York: Theatre Communications Group, 2009.

Ibsen, Henrik. *Four Great Plays*. R. Farquharson Square, trans. New York: Bantam, 1984.

Isay, Dave, ed. *Listening Is an Act of Love: A Celebration of American Life from the StoryCorps Project*. New York: Penguin, 2007.

James, Henry. *What Maisie Knew*. New York: Penguin, 1986; originally published: London: Heinemann, 1897.

Johnson, E. Patrick. *Appropriating Blackness: Performance and the Politics of Authenticity*. Durham, N.C.: Duke University Press, 2003.

Johnson, Marilyn. *The Dead Beat: Lost Souls, Lucky Stiffs, and the Perverse Pleasures of Obituaries*. New York: HarperCollins, 2006.

Jones, Margaret B. (Margaret Seltzer). *Love and Consequences: A Memoir of Hope and Consequences*. New York: Penguin, 2008.

Kanter, Jodi. *Performing Loss: Rebuilding Community Through Theater and Writing*. Carbondale, Ill.: Southern Illinois University Press, 2007.

Kincaid, Jamaica. *At the Bottom of the River*. New York: Farrar, Straus and Giroux, 1983.

Kinzie, Mary. *A Poet's Guide to Poetry*. Chicago: University of Chicago Press, 1999.

Kotlowitz, Alex. *Never a City So Real: A Walk in Chicago*. New York: Crown Journeys, 2004.

———. *There Are No Children Here: The Story of Two Boys Growing Up in the Other America*. New York: Anchor Books, 1992.

Kramer, Larry. *The Normal Heart*. New York: Plume, 1985.

Kron, Lisa. *Well*. New York: Theatre Communications Group, 2005.

Lear, Edward. *The Complete Nonsense of Edward Lear*. New York: Dover, 1951.

Lessac, Arthur. *The Use and Training of the Human Voice*, 2nd ed. New York: DBS, 1967.

Lessing, Doris. *Alfred and Emily*. London: Fourth Estate, 2008.

Levinas, Emmanuel. *Totality and Infinity: An Essay on Exteriority*. Alphonso Lingis, trans. Pittsburgh, Pa.: Duquesne University Press, 1969.

Libera, Anne, ed. *The Second City: Almanac of Improvisation*. Evanston, Ill.: Northwestern University Press, 2004.

Linklater, Kristin. *Freeing the Natural Voice*. New York: DBS, 1976.

Lipman, Doug. *Improving Your Storytelling*. Little Rock, Ark.: August House, 1999.

Long, Beverly Whitaker. "Evaluating Performed Literature." In *Studies in Interpretation II*, Esther M. Doyle and Virginia Hastings Floyd, eds. Amsterdam: Editions Rodopi, 1977.

Long, Beverly Whitaker, and Timothy Scott Cage. "Contemporary American Ekphrastic Poetry: A Selected Bibliography." *Text and Performance Quarterly*, vol. 9, no. 4 (1989): 286–97.

Lord, Albert Bates. *Epic Singers and Oral Tradition*. Ithaca, N.Y.: Cornell University Press, 1991.

Lorde, Audre. *The Black Unicorn*. New York: W. W. Norton, 1978.

Lubbock, Percy. *The Craft of Fiction*. New York: C. Scribner's Sons, 1921.

Maclay, Joanna Hawkins. *Readers Theatre: Toward a Grammar of Practice*. New York: Random House, 1971.

Madison, D. Soyini. *Acts of Activism: Human Rights as Radical Performance*. New York: Cambridge University Press, 2010.

———. *Critical Ethnography: Methods, Ethics, and Performance*. London: Sage Publications, Inc., 2005.

———. "Performance, Personal Narratives, and Politics of Possibility." In *The Future of Performance Studies: The Next Millenium*, Sheron J. Dailey, ed. Annandale, Va.: National Communication Association, 1998.

Mann, Thomas. *The Magic Mountain*. John E. Woods, trans. New York: Vintage, 1996.

McAdams, Dan P. *The Redemptive Self: Stories Americans Live By*. New York: Oxford University Press, 2006.

McInerney, Jay. *Bright Lights, Big City*. New York: Vintage Contemporaries, 1984.

McLuhan, Marshall. *Understanding Media: The Extensions of Man*. New York: McGraw-Hill, 1964.

Mead, Margaret. *Coming of Age in Samoa: A Psychological Study of Primitive Youth for Western Civilization*. New York: W. Morrow, 1928.

———. *Growing Up in New Guinea: A Comparative Study of Primitive Education*. New York: Blue Ribbon Books, 1930.

Meisner, Sanford, and Dennis Longwell. *Sanford Meisner on Acting*. New York: Random House, 1987.

Merleau-Ponty, Maurice. *The Phenomenology of Perception*. Colin Smith, trans. New York: Humanities Press, 1962.

Moore, Lorrie. *Self-Help*. New York: Knopf, 1985.

Morgan, Peter. *Frost/Nixon*. New York: Faber and Faber, 2007.

Morris, Tracie. *Intermission*. New York: Soft Skull Press, 1998.

Mullen, Harryette. *Tall Tree Woman*. Galveston, Tex.: Energy Earth, 1981.

Nin, Anaïs. *The Diary of Anaïs Nin*. Edited and with an introduction by Gunther Stuhlmann. New York: Swallow Press, 1980.

Noblit, George W., Susana Y. Flores, and Enrique G. Murillo Jr., eds. *Postcritical Ethnography: Reinscribing Critique*. Cresskill, N.J.: Hampton Press, 2004.

Noyes, Alfred. *Collected Poems*. London: J. Murray, 1963.

Oates, Joyce Carol. *Will You Always Love Me? And Other Stories*. New York: Dutton, 1996.

Ong, Walter. *Orality and Literacy: The Technologizing of the Word*, 2nd ed. New York: Routledge, 2002.

Patchett, Ann. "The Face of Pain," *New York*, February 24, 2003.

———. *Truth and Beauty: A Friendship*. New York: HarperCollins, 2004.

Pepys, Samuel. *The Shorter Pepys*. Selected and edited by Robert Latham from *The Diary of Samuel Pepys, A New and Complete Transcription*, Robert Latham and William Matthews, eds. Berkeley: University of California Press, 1985.

Pollock, Della, ed. *Exceptional Spaces: Essays in Performance and History*. Chapel Hill: University of North Carolina Press, 1998.

———. "Performing Writing." In *The Ends of Performance*, Peggy Phelan and Jill Lane, eds. New York: New York University Press, 1998.

———. *Remembering: Oral History Performance*. New York: Palgrave Macmillan, 2005.

Pomerance, Bernard. *The Elephant Man*. New York: Grove Press, 1979.

Radhakrishnan, R. *History, the Human, and the World Between*. Durham, N.C.: Duke University Press, 2008.

Richardson, Brian. *Unnatural Voices: Extreme Narration in Modern and Contemporary Fiction.* Columbus: Ohio State University Press, 2006.

Roethke, Theodore. *Collected Poems.* New York: Doubleday, 1966.

Roloff, Leland H. *The Perception and Evocation of Literature.* Glenview, Ill.: Scott Foresman, 1973.

Rosaldo, Renato. *Culture and Truth: The Remaking of Social Analysis.* Boston: Beacon Press, 1989.

Schechner, Richard. *Between Theater and Anthropology.* Philadelphia: University of Pennsylvania Press, 1985.

——. *Performance Studies: An Introduction.* London: Routledge, 2002.

Schechner, Richard, guest editor. *The Drama Review: Special issue on Theatre and the Social Sciences,* vol. 17, no. 3 (1973).

Scott, the Hon. Mrs. Maxwell. *The Tragedy of Fotheringay: Founded on the Journal of D. Bourgoing, Physician to Mary Queen of Scots, and on Unpublished Ms. Documents.* Edinburgh: Sands and Co., 1905.

Searle, John. *Speech Acts: An Essay in the Philosophy of Language.* Cambridge: Cambridge University Press, 1969.

Shapiro, Karl, and Robert Beum. *A Prosody Handbook.* New York: Harper and Row, 1965.

Shaw, George Bernard. *The Doctor's Dilemma.* New York: Penguin, 1965.

Simon, Tom. *Poetry Under Oath: From the Testimony of William Jefferson Clinton and Monica S. Lewinsky.* New York: Workman Publishing, 1998.

Slater, Lauren. *Lying: A Metaphorical Memoir.* New York: Random House, 2000.

Smith, Anna Deavere. *Fires in the Mirror: Crown Heights, Brooklyn, and Other Identities.* Foreword by Cornel West. New York: Anchor/Doubleday, 1993.

——. *Twilight: Los Angeles, 1992.* New York: Anchor Books, 1994.

Smith, Larry. *Beyond Glory: Medal of Honor Winners in Their Own Words.* New York: Norton, 2003.

Sokal, Alan. *Beyond the Sokal Hoax: Science, Philosophy, and Culture.* New York: Oxford University Press, 2008.

The Sokal Hoax: The Sham That Shook the Academy. Edited by the editors of *Lingua Franca.* Lincoln: University of Nebraska Press, 2000.

Song, Cathy. *Secret Spaces of Childhood.* Elizabeth Goodenough, ed. Ann Arbor: University of Michigan Press, 2005.

Spolin, Viola. *Improvisation for the Theater.* Evanston, Ill.: Northwestern University Press, 1999.

Stanford Encyclopedia of Philosophy. http://plato.stanford.edu/entries/episteme-techne/.

Stanislavsky, Konstantin. *An Actor's Handbook.* Elizabeth Reynolds Hapgood, trans. New York: Theatre Arts Books, 1987.

States, Bert O. *Great Reckonings in Little Rooms: On the Phenomenology of Theater.* Berkeley: University of California Press, 1985.

Stephenson, Neal. *Snow Crash*. New York: Bantam, 1992.

Stern, Carol Simpson, and Bruce Henderson. *Performance: Texts and Contexts*. New York: Longman, 1993.

Sutton-Smith, Brian. *The Folkstories of Children*. Philadelphia: University of Pennsylvania Press, 1981.

Taylor, Diana. *The Archive and the Repertoire: Performing Cultural Memory in the Americas*. Durham, N.C.: Duke University Press, 2003.

Terkel, Studs. *Working: People Talk About What They Do All Day and How They Feel About What They Do*. New York: Pantheon, 1974.

Thao, Paja. *I Am a Shaman: A Hmong Life Story with Ethnographic Commentary*. Dwight Conquergood, ethnographer; Paja Thao, shaman. Trans. Xa Thao. Minneapolis: Southeast Asian Refugee Studies Project, Center for Urban and Regional Affairs, University of Minnesota, 1989.

Thucydides. *The Peloponnesian War*. Thomas Hobbes, trans. Chicago: University of Chicago Press, 1989.

Turner, Victor. *From Ritual to Theatre: The Human Seriousness of Play*. New York: PAJ Publications, 1982, 2001.

——. *On the Edge of the Bush: Anthropology as Experience*. Tucson: University of Arizona Press, 1985.

Ulmer, Gregory L. *Heuretics: The Logic of Invention*. Baltimore, Md.: Johns Hopkins University Press, 1994.

——. *Teletheory: Grammatology in the Age of Video*. New York: Routledge, 1989.

White, Hayden V. *The Content of the Form: Narrative Discourse and Historical Representation*. Baltimore, Md.: Johns Hopkins University Press, 1987.

Whitman, Walt. *Complete Poetry and Collected Prose*. New York: Literary Classics of the United States, 1982.

Williams, William Carlos. *Selected Poems*. Edited and with an introduction by Charles Tomlinson. New York: New Directions, 1985.

Wimsatt, W. K. *The Verbal Icon: Studies in the Meaning of Poetry*. With two preliminary essays written in collaboration with Monroe Beardsley. Lexington: University of Kentucky Press, 1954.

Woolf, Virginia. *The Diary of Virginia Woolf*, 5 vols. Anne Olivier Bell, ed. New York: Harcourt, 1977, 1985.

——. *Mrs. Dalloway*. London: Hogarth, 1925.

Wright, Doug. *I Am My Own Wife*. New York: Farrar, Straus and Giroux, 2004.

Yeats, William Butler. *The Poems of W. B. Yeats*. Richard J. Finneran, ed. New York: Macmillan, 1983.

All possible care has been taken to trace ownership and secure permission for the literary excerpts quoted in this book. The authors and the publisher would like to thank the following organizations and individuals for permission to reprint copyrighted material:

Martin Amis. *Time's Arrow* (excerpt). Copyright © 1991 by Martin Amis. Used by permission of Harmony Books, a division of Random House, Inc.

Margaret Atwood. "You Begin" from *Selected Poems II: Poems Selected and New, 1976–1986.* Copyright © 1987 by Margaret Atwood. Reprinted by permission of Houghton Mifflin Harcourt Publishing Company. All rights reserved.

W. H. Auden. "Victor" from *Collected Poems*, copyright © 1976 by Edward Mendelson, William Meredith and Monroe K. Spears, Executive of the Estate of W. H. Auden. Used by permission of Random House, Inc.

John Berryman. "Dream Song #4" from *The Dream Songs*. Reprinted by permission of Farrar, Straus and Giroux, LLC. Copyright © 1964 by John Berryman. Copyright renewed © 1992 by Kate Berryman.

John Betjeman. "Death in Leamington" from *Collected Poems*, copyright © 1979 by John Betjeman. Used by permission of John Murray Publishers.

Michael Bowman. "Killing Dillinger: A Mystory," *Text and Performance Quarterly*, copyright © National Communication Association, reprinted by permission of Taylor and Francis Ltd. (http://www.tandf.co.uk/journals) on behalf of The National Communication Association.

Gwendolyn Brooks. "A Boy Died in My Alley" from *Beckonings*. Copyright © 1975 by Gwendolyn Brooks. Reprinted by consent of Brooks Permissions.

Robert Olen Butler. "The Ironworkers' Hayride" from *Had a Good Time*. Copyright © 2004 by Robert Olen Butler. Used by permission of the author and Grove/Atlantic, Inc.

Caryl Churchill. *Drunk Enough to Say I Love You* (excerpt). Copyright © 2006 Caryl Churchill. Reprinted with permission of the publisher, Nick Hern Books (www.nickhernbooks.co.uk). Distributed in U.S. by Theatre Communications Group (www.tcg.org).